The Writer's Presence
A Pool of Readings

The Writer's Presence
A Pool of Readings

NINTH EDITION

EDITED BY

DONALD MCQUADE
University of California, Berkeley

ROBERT ATWAN
Series Editor, The Best American Essays

bedford/st.martin's
Macmillan Learning
Boston | New York

For Bedford/St. Martin's

Vice President, Editorial, Macmillan Learning Humanities: Edwin Hill
Senior Program Director for English: Leasa Burton
Program Manager: John E. Sullivan III
Marketing Manager: Joy Fisher Williams
Director of Content Development: Jane Knetzger
Senior Development Editor: Rachel Goldberg
Editorial Assistant: William Hwang
Content Project Manager: Louis C. Bruno Jr.
Senior Workflow Project Supervisor: Joe Ford
Production Supervisor: Robin Besofsky
Media Project Manager: Rand Thomas
Senior Manager of Publishing Services: Andrea Cava
Project Management: Lumina Datamatics, Inc.
Composition: Lumina Datamatics, Inc.
Director of Rights and Permissions: Hilary Newman
Photo Researcher: Kerri Wilson/Lumina Datamatics, Inc.
Permissions Editor: Angela Boehler
Senior Art Director: Anna Palchik
Text Design: Tom Carling/Books by Design, Inc.
Cover Design: John Callahan
Cover Image: Lisa Occhipinti
Printing and Binding: LSC Communications

Manufactured in the United States of America.

2 1 0 9 8 7
f   e   d   c   b   a

For information, write: Bedford/St. Martin's, 75 Arlington Street, Boston, MA 02116

ISBN 978-1-319-05660-5

Acknowledgments

Text acknowledgments and copyrights appear at the back of the book on pages 685–90, which constitute an extension of the copyright page. Art acknowledgments and copyrights appear on the same page as the art selections they cover.

Preface for Instructors

As with previous editions of *The Writer's Presence*, we began work on this ninth edition by consulting with people who know the book best—the teachers and students who use it. Their thoughtful responses and imaginative suggestions helped us develop an even more effective teaching tool. From them we discovered a great deal about the pedagogical strategies most useful to students interested in learning how to read, think, and write with more critical and imaginative intelligence. Most importantly, students wished to establish a presence in their writing that reflects their interests, values, and distinctive intellectual imagination.

We designed *The Writer's Presence* to achieve three fundamental objectives: to introduce students to a wide range of prose genres emphasizing a clear and strong presence and voice; to provide writing instructors maximum flexibility in assigning reading materials and writing models; and to support composition teachers and student writers as effectively as possible with helpful, though unobtrusive, editorial and pedagogical features. The reading materials we selected, the ways we arranged them, and the instructional resources we provided both in the book and in the comprehensive instructor's manual make this a uniquely useful collection to satisfy the interests and expectations of student writers as well as the institutional requirements of most first-year writing programs.

The Writer's Presence combines eminently readable—and teachable—writing with a simple organization and minimal editorial apparatus. Each selection showcases a writer's unique voice and provides students with accessible models designed to help them develop their own distinctive voices in the writing they produce. In arranging engaging readings both alphabetically by author and by three types of writing—personal, expository, and argumentative—this text offers instructors the freedom to explore a wide range of pedagogical options, readily adaptable to the specific abilities and needs of particular students.

ENDURING FEATURES OF *THE WRITER'S PRESENCE*

Memorable Selections with a Strong Writer's Presence

Each selection in *The Writer's Presence* displays the distinctive signature that characterizes memorable prose: the presence of a lively individual imagination. As the writers collected here attempt to explore the self, shape information into meaning, or wrestle with challenging issues, their ninety-three essays offer an array of voices, genres, and styles.

Rising stars like Roxane Gay, Yiyun Li, and Eula Biss join classic authors like Langston Hughes, Maya Angelou, and George Orwell for a grand tour of masterful writing.

Flexible Organization

Divided into three parts—personal writing, expository writing, and argumentative writing—*The Writer's Presence* offers selections that span genres, topics, and disciplines, for the greatest flexibility in the classroom. Two alternate tables of contents list the selections by rhetorical mode and by common themes, making the book easy to use for every type of course structure.

Thought-Provoking, Not Prescriptive, Apparatus

Clear, informative introductions to each part of the book discuss the conventions of personal, expository, and argumentative essays and provide examples of the rhetorical strategies common to each type of writing. "On Writing: Practical Advice from Successful Writers" offers a wealth of engaging quotations that illustrate how students can establish their own writer's presence. Instructive headnotes and stimulating discussion questions ("The Reader's Presence") frame each selection, fostering open-ended connections among the readings. We kept gloss notes to a judicious minimum—to explain obscure references, biblical and classical allusions, foreign words and phrases, and words or phrases having special or archaic meaning. Overall, we made a deliberate effort to create circumstances for reading and writing to enable students to discover and develop the integrity of their own reading and writing with the support of their instructors.

Intriguing "Writer at Work" Selections

"The Writer at Work" commentaries provide an intimate glimpse of how writers view their craft. From Virginia Woolf's take on freewriting to Rebecca Solnit's perspective on the cultural impact of essays, brief supplemental selections draw on interviews and published work to give insight into the motivations, challenges, and surprises of the writing life.

Exceptional Instructor's Manual

Penetrating and perceptive, the instructor's manual draws on decades of classroom experience and offers superlative pedagogical materials for every selection in *The Writer's Presence*. "Approaching the Essay" commentary helps position and introduce each piece, and "The Reader's Presence" explores potential answers to the critical reading

questions in the book. Finally, "Generating Writing" prompts suggest creative and stimulating ideas for student assignments.

Six Student Essay Examples

Two student essays in each part of the book, including a new annotated student essay
on climate change, model rhetorical strategies for student writers, with plenty of citation
examples.

NEW TO THIS EDITION

Twenty-Nine Timely New Selections on Issues That Matter

Powerful new selections by today's most important writers invite reading and rereading.
Journalist and National Book Award winner Ta-Nehisi Coates reflects on how race
shaped his Baltimore youth. Writer and activist Rebecca Solnit explores gender dynamics
as she observes the phenomenon of men explaining things to women. Columnist
Greg Lukianoff and social psychologist Jonathan Haidt caution that campus concerns
with "microaggressions" and "trigger warnings" do a disservice both to free speech
and to college students.

Unparalleled Diversity of Authors

The Writer's Presence boasts the most diverse collection of readings in a college reader,
representing authors from across the spectrum of ethnicities, sexual orientations, nationalities, religions, and political ideologies. The ninth edition features thirty-nine women writers and thirty-seven writers of color—more than in any previous edition. New selections
focus on immigration, racial injustice, sexual violence, transgender identity, political correctness, and gun ownership, reflecting the diversity of American college campuses today.

A Streamlined Organization

Based on user feedback, we trimmed the contents to focus only on nonfiction essays,
with more brief, teachable selections. The result is a slimmer, more portable collection.

A New "Classic" Callout in the Table of Contents

Classic selections, such as those by E. B. White, Maya Angelou, Joan Didion, and
Frederick Douglass, are called out in the table of contents, drawing attention to beloved
favorites from the past.

WE'RE ALL IN. AS ALWAYS.

Bedford/St. Martin's is as passionately committed to the discipline of English as ever, working hard to provide support and services that make it easier for you to teach your course your way.

Find **community support** at the Bedford/St. Martin's English Community (community.macmillan.com), where you can follow our *Bits* blog for new teaching ideas, download titles from our professional resource series, and review projects in the pipeline.

Choose **curriculum solutions** that offer flexible custom options, combining our carefully developed print and digital resources, acclaimed works from Macmillan's trade imprints, and your own course or program materials to provide the exact resources your students need.

Rely on **outstanding service** from your Bedford/St. Martin's sales representative and editorial team. Contact us or visit macmillanlearning.com to learn more about any of the options below.

Choose from Alternative Formats of *The Writer's Presence*

Bedford/St. Martin's offers a range of formats. Choose what works best for you and your students:

- *Paperback*   To order the paperback edition, use ISBN 978-1-319-05660-5.

- *Popular e-Book formats*   For details of our e-Book partners, visit **macmillanlearning .com/ebooks**.

Select Value Packages

Add value to your text by packaging any Bedford/St. Martin's, such as *Writer's Help 2.0* or *LaunchPad Solo for Readers and Writers*, with *The Writer's Presence* at a significant discount. Contact your sales representative for more information.

LaunchPad Solo for Readers and Writers allows students to work on what they need help with most. At home or in class, students learn at their own pace, with instruction tailored to each student's unique needs. *LaunchPad Solo for Readers and Writers* features:

- **Pre-built units that support a learning arc.** Each easy-to-assign unit is composed of a pre-test check, multimedia instruction and assessment, and a post-test that assesses what students learned about critical reading, writing process, using sources, grammar, style, and mechanics. Dedicated units also offer help for multilingual writers.

- **Diagnostics that help establish a baseline for instruction**. Assign diagnostics to identify areas of strength and improvement, and to help students plan a course of study. Use visual reports to track performance by topic, class, and student as well as improvement over time.

- **A video introduction to many topics**. Introductions offer an overview of the unit's topic, and many include a brief, accessible video to illustrate the concepts at hand.

- **Twenty-five reading selections with comprehension quizzes**. Assign a range of classic and contemporary essays, each of which includes a label indicating Lexile level, to help you scaffold instruction in critical reading.

- **Adaptive quizzing for targeted learning**. Most units include LearningCurve, game-like adaptive quizzing that focuses on areas in which each student needs the most help.

Order ISBN 978-1-319-19303-4 to package *LaunchPad Solo for Readers and Writers* with *The Writer's Presence* at a significant discount. Students who rent or buy a used book can purchase access, and instructors may request free access, at **macmillanlearning .com/readwrite**.

Writer's Help 2.0 is a powerful online writing resource that helps students find answers, whether they are searching for writing advice on their own or as part of an assignment.

- **Smart search**. Built on research with more than 1,600 student writers, the smart search in *Writer's Help* provides reliable results even when students use novice terms, such as *flow* and *unstuck*.

- **Trusted content from our best-selling handbooks**. Choose *Writer's Help 2.0, Hacker Version,* or *Writer's Help 2.0, Lunsford Version,* and ensure that students have clear advice and examples for all their writing questions.

- **Diagnostics that help establish a baseline for instruction**. Assign diagnostics to identify areas of strength and areas for improvement and to help students plan a course of study. Use visual reports to track performance by topic, class, and student, as well as improvement over time.

- **Adaptive exercises that engage students**. *Writer's Help 2.0* includes Learning-Curve, gamelike online quizzing that adapts to what students already know and helps them focus on what they need to learn.

Student access is packaged with *The Writer's Presence* at a significant discount. Order ISBN 978-1-319-19302-7 for *Writer's Help 2.0, Hacker Version,* or ISBN 978-1-319-19304-1 for *Writer's Help 2.0, Lunsford Version,* to ensure your students have easy access to online writing support. Students who rent or buy a used book can purchase access, and instructors may request free access, at **macmillanlearning.com/writershelp2**.

Instructor Resources

You have a lot to do in your course. We want to make it easy for you to find the support you need—and to get it quickly.

Resources for Teaching The Writer's Presence, Ninth Edition, is available as a PDF that can be downloaded from macmillanlearning.com. Visit the instructor resources tab for *The Writer's Presence*. In addition to suggested responses to critical reading questions and writing prompts for each selection, the instructor's manual includes a sample syllabus and a helpful section on writing informally about reading.

ACKNOWLEDGMENTS

Each revision of *The Writer's Presence* has been developed through frequent correspondence and conversations—on the phone, online, and in person—with many teachers and an appreciable number of students who have worked with *The Writer's Presence* in their classes. Since its inception, *The Writer's Presence* has been—and continues to be—a truly collaborative enterprise.

We are grateful to our colleagues across the country who took the time to tell us about what did and did not work well when they used the eighth edition: Bridgett Blaque, Truckee Meadows Community College; Rachel Bowser, Georgia Gwinnett College; Jonathan Briggs, Central New Mexico Community College; Cindy Casper, Norwalk Community College; Angie Chatman, Tunxis Community College; Michelle Chester, Towson University; Helen Duclos, Arkansas State University; John Held, Fisher College; Martha Hincks, Boston College; Stephen Mathewson, Central New Mexico Community College; Molly Maynard, Truckee Meadows Community College; Nathaniel Wallace, South Carolina State University; Abigail Wolford, College of Western Idaho.

We would especially like to acknowledge our colleagues from the Expository Writing Program at New York University who talked with us and shared their ideas as we planned the first edition of this book—Lisa Altomari, Karen Boiko, Darlene Forrest, Alfred Guy, Mary Helen Kolisnyk, Jim Marcall, Denice Martone, and Will McCormack.

We also extend our thanks to the professional staff at Macmillan for their outstanding contributions to this revision. We benefitted immeasurably from the thoughtful and imaginative assistance of our editor, Rachel Goldberg, who offered first-rate, rigorous, and supportive guidance throughout each stage of our work. Rachel was never at a loss for a thoughtful and nuanced suggestion for improving the project. Her contributions, along with the support of Edwin Hill, Vice President of the Humanities; Leasa Burton, Senior Program Director for English; and John Sullivan, Program Manager for readers, continue the exemplary tradition Joan Feinberg and Karen Henry established at the outset of this project.

We'd like to thank Lou Bruno, who coordinated every aspect of the production process with quiet skill and singular effectiveness. Arthur Johnson, our text permissions researcher, became a compelling and convincing advocate on behalf of *The Writer's Presence* in negotiating access to the most engaging nonfiction prose, selections we are delighted to include in this new edition. Diligent work by editorial assistant William Hwang and photo permissions researcher Kerri Wilson not only made this new edition of *The Writer's Presence* look and read better but also strengthened the pedagogy informing it. Many thanks to Bharathi Sriram and her colleagues from Lumina Datamatics for moving this large manuscript through the production process with unflappable good cheer and professionalism.

We continue to be grateful to Cassandra Cleghorn of Williams College; Alfred Guy of Yale University; Joanna Imm of the University of Arizona; the late Jon Roberts of St. Thomas Aquinas College; Shelley Salamensky of the University of Louisville, Los Angeles; Alix Schwartz of the University of California, Berkeley; Kate Silverstein; Darryl Stephens; and MaryJo Thomas; their helpful suggestions are still amply evident in the instructor's manual. Christine McQuade, Michael Hsu, Julian Miller, Alaska Quilici, and Ela Provost offered invaluable assistance in strengthening the research and pedagogy of the project. Special thanks to Susanne McQuade for her dedicated support and assistance as a utility infielder. As always, continued thanks are due to Gregory Atwan for his unfailing support.

We are grateful to Erskine Wilson, who artfully balances a personal commitment to writing fiction with a scholarly interest in biographical research. His informative and engaging headnotes in this new edition of *The Writer's Presence* introduce each author with insight, judgment, and responsiveness to the interests and expectations of student readers. His thoughtful contributions have strengthened the informative and pedagogical dimensions of *The Writer's Presence*.

Valerie Duff prepared the comprehensive instructor's manual accompanying this collection, *Resources for Teaching The Writer's Presence.* Dr. Duff is a poet, editor, and lecturer in English and composition at Newbury University. She also taught writing at Boston College, Boston University, and Grub Street. We are grateful to Valerie for her intelligence and imagination, and the wealth of teaching experience she brought to the project. Her work remains an invaluable pedagogical tool to assist instructors in teaching their students to read and write effectively.

The Writer's Presence grew out of our combined experiences with both the practical and theoretical issues involved in teaching writing and reading to students in first-year composition courses. But we believe a book like this (designed from top to bottom for student writers) should treat the theoretical issues we find critical only as background and not distract students from the important skills they need to learn. We invite instructors who would like to know more about the theoretical foundations of *The Writer's Presence* to explore a recent study by Nicole B. Wallack, *Crafting Presence: The American Essay and the Future of Writing Studies* (Utah State University Press, 2017). Wallack, who worked with our book in its earliest editions while at New York University, places *The Writer's Presence* in an intellectual and historical context that will foreground for instructors the full range of professional and disciplinary issues we deliberately left in the background. It is a pleasure to acknowledge Professor Wallack here.

Donald McQuade
Robert Atwan
October 2017

Contents

1. PERSONAL WRITING
Exploring Our Own Lives   23

"Every person I knew had a hellish horror of being 'called out of his name.' It was a dangerous practice to call a Negro anything that could be loosely construed as insulting because of the centuries of their having been called niggers, jigs, dinges, blackbirds, crows, boots, and spooks."

"The day of my father's funeral had also been my nineteenth birthday. As we drove him to the graveyard, the spoils of injustice, anarchy, discontent, and hatred were all around us. It seemed to me that God himself had devised, to mark my father's end, the most sustained and brutally dissonant of codas. And it seemed to me, too, that the

Thomas Chatterton Williams/ The Cheney Agency

2. EXPOSITORY WRITING
Shaping Information   283

3. ARGUMENTATIVE WRITING
Contending with Issues   505

duration—suffuses the population. Everyone knows that as the demands and expectations on couples escalated, so did divorce rates. And given the current divorce statistics (roughly 50 percent of all marriages end in divorce), all indications are that whomever you love today—your beacon of hope, the center of all your optimism—has a good chance of becoming your worst nightmare tomorrow."

Suzi Pratt/Getty Images

Alternate Tables of Contents

Selections Arranged by Theme

EDUCATION

ETHICS AND MORALITY

GENDER ROLES

HISTORY AND BIOGRAPHY

LANGUAGE AND LITERATURE

LAW, POLITICS, AND SOCIETY

THE NATURAL ENVIRONMENT

PHILOSOPHY, SPIRITUALITY, AND RELIGION

POPULAR CULTURE AND MASS MEDIA

PSYCHOLOGY AND HUMAN BEHAVIOR

RACIAL AND ETHNIC IDENTITY

SCIENCE AND TECHNOLOGY

A SENSE OF PLACE

Selections Arranged by Common Rhetorical Modes and Patterns of Development

CONSTRUCTING NARRATIVES

WRITING DESCRIPTION: PERSONS, PLACES, THINGS

USING COMPARISONS

DEFINING WORDS AND CONCEPTS

SUPPLYING INSTANCES AND EXAMPLES

CLASSIFYING IDEAS

ANALYZING AND DESCRIBING PROCESSES

ESTABLISHING CAUSES AND EFFECTS

FORMING ANALOGIES

FASHIONING ARGUMENTS: EIGHT METHODS

Arguing from Personal Experience

Short Essay Contents

A Complete Short Essay Reader (six pages or fewer)

| SHORT ESSAY CONTENTS

||||||||||||||||||||||||||||||||||||||||||||||||||||||||||||||||||||||||||||||||||||||||||||||||||||||||||||||||||||||||||||||||

The Writer's Presence
A Pool of Readings

Introduction for Students:
The Writer's Presence

PRESENCE IS A WORD—like *charisma*—that we reserve for people who create powerful and memorable impressions. Many public figures and political leaders are said to "have presence"—Martin Luther King Jr., Eleanor Roosevelt, and John F. Kennedy and his wife Jacqueline Kennedy Onassis are a few superb historical examples—as well as many athletes, dancers, and musicians. In fact, the quality of presence is found abundantly in the performing arts, where top entertainers and actors self-consciously fashion—through style, costume, and gesture—an instantly recognizable public presence. Clearly, people with presence are able to command our attention. How do they do it?

Presence is far easier to identify than it is to define. We recognize it when we see it, but how do we capture it in words? How can we begin to understand this elusive characteristic known as presence?

On one level, *presence* simply means "being present." But the word is more complex than that; it suggests much more than the mere fact of being physically present. Most dictionaries define *presence* as an ability to project a sense of self-assurance, poise, ease, or dignity. We thus speak of someone's "stage presence" or "presence of mind." But the word is also used today to suggest an impressive personality, an individual who can make his or her presence felt. As every college student knows, to be present in a classroom is not the same thing as *having a presence* there. We may be present in body but not in spirit. In that sense, presence is also a matter of individual energy and exertion, of putting something of ourselves into whatever we do.

Presence is especially important in writing, which is what this book is about. Just as we notice individual presence in sports or music or conversation, so too we discover it in good writing. If what we read seems dreary, dull, or dead, it's usually because the writer forgot to include an important ingredient: *personal presence*. That doesn't mean that your essays should be written *in* the first-person singular (this book contains many exceptional essays that don't use "I") but that your essays should be written *by* the first-person singular; in other words, your essays should reflect your personality as a writer. Interesting essays are produced by a real and distinct person, not an automaton following a set of mechanical rules and abstract principles.

PRESENCE IN WRITING

How can someone be present in writing? How can you project yourself into an essay so that it seems that you're personally there, even though all your reader sees are words on a piece of paper?

The Writer's Presence shows how talented writers establish a distinct presence in many different kinds of writing and for many different purposes and audiences. Although the book offers numerous examples, several methods for establishing presence are worth pointing out at the start. Let's examine four of the chief ways an experienced writer can be present in an essay.

1. Through Personal Experience. One of the most straightforward ways for the writer to make his or her presence felt in an essay is to include appropriate personal experiences. Of course, some assignments call for a personal essay and, in those cases, you will naturally be putting episodes from your own life at the center of your writing. But writers also find ways to build their personal experiences into essays that are informative or argumentative, or about topics other than themselves. They do this to show their close connection with a subject, to offer testimony, or to establish their personal authority on a subject. Many essays in this collection offer clear illustrations of how writers incorporate personal experience in writings on specific topics or issues.

Look, for example, at the essay by Amy Cunningham, "Why Women Smile" (page 339). This essay is primarily an explanation of a cultural phenomenon—the way women are socially conditioned to maintain a smiling attitude. However, Cunningham begins the essay not with a general observation but with a personal anecdote: "After smiling brilliantly for nearly four decades, I now find myself trying to quit." Although her essay is not "personal," her opening sentence, besides establishing her own connection with the topic, provides readers with a personal motive for her writing.

2. Through Voice. Another way a writer makes his or her presence felt is through creating a distinctive and an identifiable *voice*. Good writers want their words to be heard. They want their sentences to have rhythm, cadence, and balance. Experienced authors revise a great deal of their writing just to make sure the sentences *sound* right. They're writing for the reader's ear as well as the reader's mind. Therefore, whenever we read a piece of writing, we ought to think of it as an experience similar to listening to someone speak aloud. Doing so adds drama to writing and reading. Here is what the poet Robert Frost has to say on the subject:

> Everything written is as good as it is dramatic. . . . A dramatic necessity goes deep into the nature of the sentence. Sentences are not different enough to hold the attention

> unless they are dramatic. No ingenuity of varying structure will do. All that can save
> them is the speaking tone of voice somehow entangled in the words and fastened to
> the page for the ear of the imagination. That is all that can save poetry from singing, all
> that can save prose from itself. (Preface to *A Way Out*, in *Selected Prose of Robert Frost*)

Frost spent a good portion of his celebrated public life encouraging people to cultivate what he called "the hearing imagination." For more on voice and tone of voice, see the introduction to Part 1 (page 25).

3. Through Point of View. Another sure way for writers to establish presence is through the point of view they adopt toward a subject. Often, especially in personal essays, the writer will make clearly known his or her specific location. A good example of this can be found in Langston Hughes's recollection of a tense childhood moment during a revivalist meeting in his church, where he locates his physical presence explicitly (see "Salvation," page 120).

Point of view is not always a matter of a specific location or position. Writers are not always present in their essays as dramatic characters. In many reflective, informative, or argumentative essays, the point of view is determined more by a writer's intellectual attitude or opinions—an angle of vision—than by a precise physical perspective. As an example of how a writer establishes a personal perspective without a dominant first-person narrator, consider the following passage from John Taylor Gatto's "Against School" (page 517), an argumentative essay critiquing America's traditional school system. Although Gatto from time to time introduces his own personal background, he makes his point of view—opposition to modern education—clear to the reader without ever referring directly to himself. Note his comparison between how schools train children and how concerned parents might better handle the job:

> Now for the good news. Once you understand the logic behind modern schooling, its
> tricks and traps are fairly easy to avoid. School trains children to be employees and con-
> sumers; teach your own to be leaders and adventurers. School trains children to obey
> reflexively; teach your own to think critically and independently. Well-schooled kids have
> a low threshold for boredom; help your own to develop an inner life so that they'll never
> be bored. Urge them to take on the serious material, the *grown-up* material, in history,
> literature, philosophy, music, art, economics, theology—all the stuff schoolteachers
> know well enough to avoid. Challenge your kids with plenty of solitude so that they can
> learn to enjoy their own company, to conduct inner dialogues.

There is no first-person singular here, nor a dramatically rendered self. Yet this passage conveys a distinct point of view.

4. Through Style. Writers also establish a presence in their writing through what is usually termed *style*. By a *writing style*, critics usually mean an aggregate of verbal techniques that add up to a distinctive way of saying something. Many creative writers develop a characteristic manner of speaking that depends often on word selection, sentence structure, tone of voice, imagery, and many other elements that contribute to a distinctive and personal identity on the page. Developing a distinctive style demands more than following grammatical rules and established usage. Throughout this book, discussion questions will often target particular instances of a writer's style. For a fuller treatment of prose style, see the introduction to Part 1 (page 25).

THE SELECTIONS IN THIS BOOK

Many selections in this book, especially in Part 1, "Personal Writing: Exploring Our Own Lives," feature the first-person point of view directly. In most of these selections, the writer appears as both narrator and main character, and the writer's presence is quite observable.

But private and personal writing represent only a fraction of the different types of nonfiction that appear regularly in books, newspapers, and magazines. Many essays are written on specific topics and deal with specific issues. Most of the essays appearing in America's major periodicals, for example, are intended to be either informative or persuasive; the author wants to convey information about a particular subject (a Civil War battle, for example) or wants to express an opinion about a particular issue (such as how to deal with terrorism). Parts 2 and 3, "Expository Writing: Shaping Information" and "Argumentative Writing: Contending with Issues," illustrate writing intended to inform, argue, and persuade.

You'll notice a strong writer's presence in many of the informative and persuasive essays. This is deliberate. To write informatively or persuasively about subjects other than yourself doesn't mean that you have to disappear as a writer. Sometimes you will want to insert your own experiences and testimony into an argumentative essay; at other times, you will want to assume a distinct viewpoint concerning a piece of information; and at still other times—though you may not introduce the first-person singular—you will make your presence strongly felt in your tone of voice or simply in the way you arrange your facts and juxtapose details (see the Gatto passage on page 517). As we'll discuss further in the introduction to Part 2, at the heart of the word *information* is *form*. Writers don't passively receive facts and information in a totally finished format; they need to shape their information, to give it form. This shaping or patterning is something the writer *contributes*. A large part of the instructional purpose of this collection is to encourage you to pay more attention to the different ways writers are present in their work.

THE READER'S PRESENCE

Because almost all writing (and *all* published writing) is intended to be read, we can't dismiss the importance of the reader. Just as we find different levels of a writer's presence in a given piece of writing, so too can we detect different ways in which a reader can be present.

An author publishes a short opinion essay about gun control in a national magazine. The author herself has been the victim of a shooting, and her piece, though it includes her personal experiences, is largely made up of a concrete plan to eliminate all guns—even hunting rifles—from American life. In writing her essay, she expects a great deal of resistance to her argument. In other words, she imagines a reader who will most likely disagree with her and who needs to be won over.

Now imagine three people in a dentist's office who within the same afternoon pick up this issue of the magazine and read the essay. One of them has also been victimized by guns (her son was accidentally wounded by a hunter), and she reads the essay with great sympathy and conviction. She understands perfectly what this woman has gone through and believes in her plan completely. The next reader, a man who has never once in his life committed a crime and has no tolerance for criminals, is outraged by the essay. He was practically brought up in the woods and loves to hunt. He could never adopt a gun control plan that would in effect criminalize hunting. He's ready to fire off a letter attacking this woman's plan. The third reader also enjoys hunting and has always felt that hunting rifles should be exempt from any government regulation of firearms. But he finds the writer's plan convincing and feasible. He spends the rest of the day trying to think of counterarguments.

Obviously, these are only three of many possibilities. But you can see from this example the differences between the reader imagined by the writer and some actual readers. The one person who completely agreed with the writer was not the kind of reader the author had originally imagined or was trying to persuade; she was already persuaded. And though the other two readers were part of her intended audience, one of them could never be persuaded to her point of view, whereas the other one might.

This scenario illustrates the distinctions between *implied readers* and *actual readers*. The implied reader is the reader imagined by the writer for a particular piece of writing. In constructing arguments, for example, it is usually effective to imagine readers we are *trying* to win over to our views. Otherwise, we are simply asking people who already agree with us to agree with us—what's commonly known as "preaching to the converted" or "preaching to the choir."

In informative or critical essays, a writer also needs to consider how much the intended audience already knows about the subject. Here's a practical illustration. If you were asked to write a review of a recent film for your college newspaper, you would assume your readers had not yet seen the film (or else you might annoy them by giving away some surprises, or "spoilers"). However, if you were asked to write a critical essay about the same movie for a film course, you could assume your readers had seen the film. It's the same movie, and you have the same opinions about it, but your two essays have two different purposes, and in the process of writing them you imagine readers with two different levels of knowledge about the film.

Actual readers, of course, differ from implied readers in that they are real people—not readers intended or imagined by the writer. As you read the essays in this collection, you should be aware of at least two readers—(1) the reader you think the writer imagines for the essay and (2) the reader you are in actuality. Sometimes you will seem very close to the kind of reader the writer is imagining. In those cases, you might say that you "identify" with a particular writer, essay, or point of view. At other times, however, you will notice a great distance between the reader the author imagines and you as an actual reader. For example, you may feel excluded by the author on the basis of race, gender, class, or expected knowledge and educational level. Or you may feel you know more than the author does about a particular topic.

To help you explore your role as a reader, each selection in the book is followed by a set of questions, "The Reader's Presence." These questions are designed to orient you to the various levels of reading suggested by the selection. Some questions will ask you to identify the kind of reader you think the author imagines; other questions will prompt you to think about specific ways you may differ from the author's intended reader; still others will help you to make connections between and among the selections and authors. In general, the questions are intended to make you more deeply aware of your *presence* as a reader.

We hope you will find *The Writer's Presence* a stimulating book to read and think about. To make our presence felt as writers is as much a matter of self-empowerment as it is of faith. It requires the confidence that we can affect others, determine a course of action, or even surprise ourselves by coming up with new ideas or by acquiring new powers of articulation.

Part of the enduring pleasure of writing is precisely that element of surprise, of originality—that lifelong pleasure of discovering new resources of language, finding new means of knowing ourselves, and inventing new ways to be present in the world.

ON WRITING:
Practical Advice from

ONE OF THE MOST reassuring discoveries any student of writing can make is that there is no single way to write, no fail-proof formula to produce successful essays. The pages that follow provide an opportunity for you to study the writing process from the points of view of experienced writers—from how they search for an idea and then develop it in a first draft to how they revise and then prepare that idea for presentation in a final draft.

Like all writers, published authors speak of the problems and the pleasures of struggling to convey a clear sense of their ideas. They touch on their respect for and anxiety about mastering the skills required to write effective prose. They also describe the distinctive ways in which they compose: how they go about generating ideas for an essay, how they deal with the frustrations of procrastination and the dead ends that disrupt their progress, how they revise, and how they determine when their essays are finished and ready to be read by an audience.

The perspectives these writers present on the composing process are as varied as their backgrounds and interests. Yet the methods they follow when writing can be grouped into three general phases: **getting started, drafting**, and **revising**. Experienced writers usually start by searching for and then deciding on a subject to write about, developing their ideas about the subject, clarifying their purpose in writing, organizing their thoughts, and considering the audience they want to address. In the drafting phase, they usually carry out their detailed plan in a first draft. In the revising phase, they study what they have written and determine how they can re-envision and improve it. These designations are not a lockstep series of discrete stages that writers work through in exactly the same manner each time. They are simply patterns of activities that describe what happens when writers write.

GETTING STARTED

IN THE FIRST three phases of the writing process, a writer chooses a subject to write about if one has not been assigned, discovers a purpose for writing about the subject, generates a thesis (also called a *governing,* or *controlling, idea*), and then develops that idea in various writing exercises or in an outline to serve as the basis for producing a first draft of an essay. This is the most difficult phase of writing for most people. Because they usually face so many challenges and obstacles at this point in the writing process, most writers have more to say about this phase than any other.

Successful Writers

As every writer knows, at least intuitively, writing is not a linear but a recursive process. Writing rarely proceeds neatly from one phase to the next. Rather, the phases frequently overlap, making the process often appear messy. Yet, in tracing the movements of a writer's mind at work on an idea, we can discover and describe patterns, even though the specific circumstances and the particular moves writers make are never exactly the same every time.

Integral to each phase of the composing process is **reading**. Reading and writing function much like breathing in and breathing out. Writers read what others have written with a sense of purpose: to gather information, to understand concepts and the details that support them, to evaluate ideas, to engage in critical thinking, to assess explanations and the assumptions that inform arguments, to be entertained, to visit or envision other places and people, to challenge or inspire others, to persuade others to act, or to expand the limits of what is imagined as possible.

Reading what other writers have to say about writing should assure you that all writers—whether they are professionals, classmates, or you—grapple with many of the same basic issues as well as the same frustrations and pleasures of writing. You may also be pleasantly surprised to learn that the observations and solutions of professional writers are similar to those you may have developed in your own writing. In addition, you may find new suggestions to help you improve your writing. Recognizing what is unique and shared about the writing experience places you in the company of other writers as you develop your own voice.

■ **MARK TWAIN**

"The secret of getting ahead is getting started. The secret of getting started is breaking your complex overwhelming tasks into small manageable tasks, and then starting on the first one."

(Samuel Langhorne Clemens, 1835–1910, American author and humorist)

■ **JACK LONDON**

"You can't wait for inspiration. You have to go after it with a club."

(1876–1916, American author and journalist)

■ **MAYA ANGELOU**

"When I start a project, the first thing I do is write down, in longhand, everything I know about the subject, every thought I've ever had on it."

(1928–2014, American poet and autobiographer. See also page 34.)

■ JOHN STEINBECK

"Write freely and as rapidly as possible and throw the whole thing on paper. Never correct or rewrite until the whole thing is down. Rewriting in process is usually found to be an excuse for not going on."

(1902–1968, American novelist)

■ AKHIL SHARMA

"Writing . . . is very hard and the fact that you will find it very hard does not mean that you are stupid."

(b. 1971, Indian American author)

DEALING WITH PROCRASTINATION

The tendency to procrastinate remains one of the most common obstacles many writers face when they set out to put pen to paper or fingers on the keyboard. There is no one easy aspect of writing, other than postponing it. Many writers—whether they are professionals or students—share this trait.

■ MARGARET ATWOOD

"If I waited for perfection, I would never write a word."

(b. 1939, Canadian author and literary critic)

■ PAUL RUDNICK

"Writing is 90 percent procrastination: reading magazines, eating cereal out of the box, watching infomercials. It's a matter of doing everything you can to avoid writing, until it is about four in the morning and you reach the point where you have to write."

(b. 1957, American playwright and novelist)

■ BRIAN DOYLE

"Make a note instantly when an idea or a line or a caught remark or a memory or an epiphany hits you suddenly in the kidney. INSTANTLY. Use dollar bills and children's necks if necessary. (I once started an essay on my son Liam's neck at the beach.) Then hustle to a keyboard as fast as you can and take the note out for a stroll and see what happens. Don't think. Just start typing and see what happens. Don't control it. Don't even think 'this will be an essay.' Just start. I find that often the piece soon enough tells you what shape it wishes to take."

(1956–2017, American essayist and novelist. See also page 359.)

■ TAYARI JONES

"[To deal with writer's block] I just keep at it. I think it's a lot like using a pen that isn't working. You can make the scribbling motion and nothing happens, until suddenly it does. Who knows why. But it does. Thank the lord."

(b. 1970, African American novelist)

■ DOUGLAS ADAMS

"I love deadlines. I like the whooshing sound they make as they fly by."

(1952–2001, English author and playwright)

■ ELIZABETH HARDWICK

"I'm not sure I understand the process of writing. There is, I'm sure, something strange about imaginative concentration. The brain slowly begins to function in a different way, to make mysterious connections. Say, it is Monday, and you write a very bad draft, but if you keep trying, on Friday, words, phrases, appear almost unexpectedly. I don't know why you can't do it on Monday, or why I can't. I'm the same person, no smarter, I have nothing more at hand. . . . It's one of the things writing students don't understand. They write a first draft and are quite disappointed, or often should be disappointed. They don't understand that they have merely begun, and that they may be merely beginning even in the second or third draft."

(1916–2007, American author and literary critic)

■ MARTIN AMIS

"A lot of the time seems to be spent making coffee or trolling around, or throwing darts, or playing pinball, or picking your nose, trimming your fingernails, or staring at the ceiling. . . . Writing is waiting, for me certainly. It wouldn't bother me a bit if I didn't write one word in the morning. I'd just think, you know, not yet."

(b. 1949, English novelist)

■ MAYA ANGELOU

"One of the problems we have as writers is we don't take ourselves seriously while writing; being serious is setting aside a time and saying if it comes, good; if it doesn't come, good, I'll just sit here."

(1928–2014, American poet and autobiographer. See also page 34.)

■ ANNA QUINDLEN

"People have writer's block not because they can't write, but because they despair of writing eloquently."

(b. 1953, American author and columnist)

■ WILLIAM JAMES

"Nothing is so fatiguing as the eternal hanging on of an uncompleted task."

(1842–1910, American psychologist and philosopher)

■ ERNEST HEMINGWAY

"There is no rule on how to write. Sometimes it comes easily and perfectly: sometimes it's like drilling rock and then blasting it out with charges."

(1899–1961, American novelist and Nobel Laureate)

■ RICHARD FORD

"Writing can be complicated, exhausting, isolating, abstracting, boring, dulling, briefly exhilarating; it can be made to be grueling and demoralizing. And occasionally it can produce rewards. But it's never as hard as, say, piloting an L-1011 into O'Hare on a snowy night in January, or doing brain surgery when you have to stand up for ten hours straight, and once you start you can't just stop. If you're a writer, you can stop anywhere, any time, and no one will care or ever know. Plus, the results might be better if you do."

(b. 1944, American author)

GENERATING IDEAS

Writers rely on a seemingly limitless supply of strategies and tactics to generate a subject for an essay and to start exploring their ideas about these subjects—from deliberate reading and research to discussions with friends as well as random mental associations. For many writers, as Henry Miller (1891–1980, American novelist and painter) observes, "writing, like life itself, is a voyage of discovery."

In order to develop practiced confidence in their ability to identify an engaging subject to focus on, many writers discover their subjects in the issues and concerns in the world around them. To help keep track of their ideas, writers often rely on a journal, a daily written record of one's experiences and thoughts on particular subjects.

Many writers find that they can discover ideas about a subject by writing down everything they know about it. Often called *freewriting* or *nonstop writing*, this strategy involves pouring out words, thoughts, or feelings, without concern for grammar or punctuation or coherence. Other writers prefer to develop ideas through *brainstorming*. Unlike freewriting, which produces ideas by linking or associating one thought with another, brainstorming records thoughts as they occur, with no regard for their relation to one another. When writers brainstorm, they often leap from one thought to another without stopping to explore the connections between what may be two completely unrelated ideas.

Exercises such as freewriting and brainstorming are excellent confidence builders, especially for relatively inexperienced writers. They can help writers generate a great deal of prose in a short time and quickly see what they have to say about a subject—while resisting the urge to edit their work prematurely. Whether you write in a journal or on the back of a napkin, thinking in writing is the best way to discover the potential of a subject to engage an audience. After all, a practiced writer is usually an effective writer.

■ E. L. DOCTOROW

"Writing is an exploration. You start from nothing and learn as you go. . . . Writing is like driving at night in the fog. You can only see as far as your headlights, but you can make the whole trip that way. . . . "

(1931–2015, American novelist)

■ JOAN DIDION

"I write entirely to find out what I'm thinking, what I'm looking at, what I see and what it means. What I want and what I fear."

(b. 1934, American essayist and novelist. See also page 353.)

■ CHERYL STRAYED

"I find the most important thing for aspiring writers is for them to give themselves permission to be brave on the page, to write in the presence of fear, to go to those places that you think you can't write—really that's exactly what you need to write."

(b. 1968, American memoirist, essayist, and novelist)

- -

ENVISIONING AN AUDIENCE

Audiences loom large in the imagination of every writer. The writer's view of the reader helps determine the extent of an essay's success. The writer asks: "Who is my reader? What do I need to do to help that person to understand and appreciate what I want to say about my particular subject?" The first question addresses the knowledge, background, and predispositions of the reader toward the subject. The second points to the kinds of information or appeals to which the reader is most likely to respond.

Not all writers concern themselves with the question of audience from the outset of their work. Some writers regard audience as a matter for revision, to be considered only after they have articulated their idea and established control of their thinking in

■ FRANÇOIS MAURIAC

"Each of us is like a desert, and a literary work is like a cry from the desert, or like a pigeon let loose with a message in its claws, or like a bottle thrown into the sea. The point is: to be heard—even if by one single person."

(1885–1970, French author and Nobel laureate)

■ F. SCOTT FITZGERALD

"All good writing is swimming under water and holding your breath."

(1896–1940, American novelist)

■ ALAN LIGHTMAN

"I spend a lot of time with the first paragraph and even the first sentence because this is really the beginning of the creation of the world that I want my reader to inhabit, and I think that the first paragraph really sets the tone, the voice of the writer, and the scene, and invites the reader into the imaginary world."

(b. 1948, American professor of physics at MIT and essayist. See also page 440.)

■ JHUMPA LAHIRI

"All writing, all art is just a wild leap off a cliff because there's nothing to support you. You're creating something out of nothing."

(b. 1967, Indian American novelist and essayist. See also page 151.)

■ ERNEST HEMINGWAY

"Work every day. No matter what has happened the day or night before, get up and bite on the nail."

(1899–1961, American novelist and Nobel laureate)

■ WILLIAM FAULKNER

"Get it down. Take chances. It may be bad, but it's the only way you can do anything really good."

(1897–1962, American novelist and Nobel laureate)

■ ANDRE DUBUS III

"I think if I've learned anything over the years about writing, I've learned to follow where the writing wants to go. More times than not, I don't want to go where it wants to go at all. . . . I try to approach the act of writing in a humble state, as in I'm humbling myself to the writing and I'm opening myself up. That's why I never outline; that's more of a willful approach. I trust the writing to take me someplace that I can't foresee when I begin writing."

(b. 1959, American novelist and essayist. See also page 83.)

■ JOHN EDGAR WIDEMAN

"That sense of beginning anew, and that sense of having a direction, or at least the urge to find a direction every day means that I have set aside a kind of place in my life for words and for language to live, and that place is—reciprocates, it gives me a place to live."

(b. 1941, American novelist and essayist and professor of English at Brown University. See also page 665.)

■ JOYCE CAROL OATES

"Read, observe, listen intensely!—as if your life depended upon it."

(b. 1938, American novelist and essayist)

---

writing. Given that student writers prepare papers to satisfy course requirements, they are also mindful of the instructor's presence in their audience. Some students are intimidated by this recognition, others imagine themselves writing for a teacher with whom they feel comfortable, still others write with peers and an instructor in mind. But whether they are writing for a teacher, peers, or an audience beyond the classroom, the fact that someone will read their writing imposes a good deal of discipline on most student writers. Thinking about readers helps writers make decisions about appropriate subjects, the kinds of examples to use, the kind and level of diction to use, and the overall organization of the essay—each of which enables them to be clear and compelling in their prose.

■ DON DeLILLO

"I don't have a sense of a so-called ideal reader and certainly not of a readership, that terrific entity. I write for the page."

(b. 1936, American novelist and essayist)

■ MARIANNE MOORE

"Any writer overwhelmingly honest about pleasing himself is almost sure to please others."

(1887–1972, American poet)

■ BARBARA KINGSOLVER

"Close the door. Write with no one looking over your shoulder. Don't try to figure out what other people want to hear from you; figure out what you have to say. It's the one and only thing you have to offer."

(b. 1955, American novelist and essayist)

■ ANNIE DILLARD

"Write as if you were dying. At the same time, assume you write for an audience consisting solely of terminal patients. That is, after all, the case. What would you begin writing if you knew you would die soon? What could you say to a dying person that would not enrage by its triviality?"

(b. 1945, American essayist)

■ PICO IYER

"Writing is, in the end, that oddest of anomalies: an intimate letter to a stranger."

(b. 1957, British-born essayist and novelist of Indian origin. See also page 404.)

DRAFTING

WRITERS WORK in a strikingly wide range of different ways to produce a complete first draft. Some write to discover what they want to say. In one sense, these writers need to see what their ideas look like on paper in order to explore, develop, and revise a first draft. Other writers proceed at a much slower pace: they think carefully about what they want to say before they commit themselves to writing. These writers usually regard thinking and writing as separate, sequential intellectual activities. Still other writers create their own distinctive blend of these write/rewrite and think/write styles of drafting.

■ IAIN BANKS

"Writing is like everything else: the more you do it the better you get. Don't try to perfect as you go along, just get to the end of the damn thing. Accept imperfections. Get it finished and then you can go back."

(1954–2013, Scottish author)

■ JACQUES BARZUN

"Convince yourself that you are working in clay, not marble, on paper, not eternal bronze: Let that first sentence be as stupid as it wishes."

(1907–2012, French-born American historian of ideas and culture)

■ TOBIAS WOLFF

"For a young writer, the best thing to do is get it out. I certainly have to. I have to write at length before I can write in brief. I have to see what the terrain is before I single out that telling moment, that telling detail and cut away the others. But I have to write the others to get to that one. So you don't want to start off in a stingy way when you write. You want to be extravagant. You know you're going to rewrite anyway, so what the hell? Pump it out, see what comes. And be free in your composition. You can be an editor later. But you don't want to be an editor and a writer at the same time, when you're doing that first draft. I think that's a mistake."

(b. 1945, American memoirist, essayist, and short story writer)

■ DOROTHY ALLISON

"Sometimes, after reading the work of young authors in a workshop, I find myself asking them 'Who do you write for? Who do you write to?' Some answer me immediately—my daddy, my mama, my first lover, the preacher who scared me so badly when I was thirteen. But some just stare at me, not knowing how important the question actually is. Of course, we write for ourselves. Of course. But even making notes in a journal or commenting anonymously on some blog, we have an observer in the back of our heads—a reader, a witness. It is that witness that shapes the work—focuses it or, now and then, pushes us past what we are first willing to share. Tell me the truth, that reader/witness demands. Say what you fear. Say what you love. Tell me something no one else has ever told me. Out of that demand comes the best work—the richest most revealing narratives, what we never imagined we could share but discover in the writing."

(b. 1949, American novelist and essayist)

■ GABRIEL GARCÍA MÁRQUEZ

"When I'm writing I'm always aware that this friend is going to like this, or that another friend is going to like that paragraph or chapter, always thinking of specific people. In the end all books are written for your friends."

(1928–2014, Colombian novelist and journalist)

■ ELMORE LEONARD

"My most important piece of advice to all you would-be writers: when you write, try to leave out all the parts readers skip."

(1925–2013, American novelist and screenwriter)

■ ANNIE DILLARD

"When you write, you lay out a line of words. The line of words is a miner's pick, a woodcarver's gouge, a surgeon's probe. You wield it, and it digs a path you follow. Soon you find yourself deep in new territory. Is it a dead end or have you located the real subject? You will know tomorrow, or this time next year."

(b. 1945, American essayist)

■ MICHAEL POLLAN

"As I'm editing, I'm hearing it in my head, or sometimes I whisper it aloud to myself as I write. My ear is a very important part of how I write."

(b. 1955, American journalist, essayist, and professor of journalism at the University of California, Berkeley)

■ YAEL HEDAYA

"This is what I always tell my students. Writing is not about leaping forward like an antelope, or some other graceful creature. Writing is about moving like a crab. Sideways."

(b. 1964, Israeli novelist)

■ WALTER MOSLEY

"Your first sentence will start you out, but don't let it trip you up. The beginning is only a draft. Drafts are imperfect by definition. Your first draft is like a rich uncultivated field for the farmer: it is waiting for you to bring it into full bloom."

(b. 1952, American novelist and essayist. See also page 580.)

■ MALCOLM GLADWELL

"Good writing does not succeed or fail on the strength of its ability to persuade. It succeeds or fails on the strength of its ability to engage you, to make you think, to give you a glimpse into someone else's head."

(b. 1963, Canadian author. See also page 386.)

REVISING

WHEN WRITERS REVISE, they reexamine what they have written with an eye on strengthening their control over their ideas. In some cases, they expand or delete, substitute or reorder. In other instances, they revise to clarify or to emphasize—to reinforce or tone down particular points. More generally, they often revise either to simplify what they have written or to add a nuance. Revising provides writers with the opportunity to rethink their drafts, to help them accomplish their intentions more clearly or more fully. Revising also involves such larger concerns as determining whether the draft is logically consistent, whether its thesis or main idea is supported adequately, whether it is organized clearly enough, and whether it satisfies its audience's reasonable expectations or needs—in engaging and accessible terms. Revising enables writers to make sure their essays are as clear, precise, and effective as possible. Revising is crucial to successful writing.

■ GEORGE ORWELL

"A scrupulous writer, in every sentence that he writes, will ask himself at least four questions, thus:
(1) What am I trying to say? (2) What words will express it? (3) What image or idiom will make it clearer? (4) Is this image fresh enough to have an effect?"

(1903–1950, English novelist and essayist. See also page 195.)

■ E. M. FORSTER

"How do I know what I think until I see what I say?"

(1879–1970, English novelist and essayist)

■ NAOMI SHIHAB NYE

"If a teacher told me to revise, I thought that meant my writing was a broken-down car that needed to go to the repair shop. I felt insulted. I didn't realize the teacher was saying, 'Make it shine. It's worth it.' Now I see revision as a beautiful word of hope. It's a new vision of something. It means you don't have to be perfect the first time. What a relief!"

(b. 1952, Palestinian poet and novelist)

■ SUSAN SONTAG

"I don't write easily or rapidly. My first draft usually has only a few elements worth keeping. I have to find what those are and build from them and throw out what doesn't work, or what simply is not alive."

(1933–2004, American essayist)

■ ISAAC BASHEVIS SINGER

"The waste basket is the writer's best friend."

(1902–1991, American author and Nobel laureate)

■ VLADIMIR NABOKOV

"I have rewritten—often several times—every word I have ever published. My pencils outlast their erasers."

(1899–1977, Russian novelist)

■ ELLEN GOODMAN

"I rewrite a great deal. I'm always fiddling, always changing something. I'll write a few words—then I'll change them. I add. I subtract. I work and fiddle and keep working and fiddling, and I only stop at the deadline."

(b. 1941, American columnist)

■ E. B. WHITE

"The main thing I try to do is write as clearly as I can. Because I have the greatest respect for the reader, and if he's going to the trouble of reading what I've written—I'm a slow reader myself and I guess most people are—why, the least I can do is make it as easy as possible for him to find out what I'm trying to say, trying to get at. I rewrite a good deal to make it clear."

(1899–1985, American essayist. See also page 256.)

■ **CHRIS ABANI**

"I cut the parts I love the most."

(b. 1966, Nigerian author and poet)

■ **JOHN MCPHEE**

"[T]he aural part of writing is a big, big thing to me. I can't stand a sentence until it sounds right, and I'll go over it again and again. . . . I always read the second draft aloud, as a way of moving forward. . . . I read aloud so I can hear if it's fitting together or not. It's just as much a part of the composition as going out and buying a ream of paper."

(b. 1931, American author of narrative nonfiction)

WORKING WITH WORDS

One of the most important principles of writing well is that ideas don't generate writing as much as thinking in writing produces ideas. To write effectively doesn't mean writers are required to come up with as many words or ideas as possible about a subject. Instead, they should focus on generating the greatest impact from the ideas they have already committed to paper. Ask yourself: Do the words I've chosen express adequately the idea I'm trying to convey? Do my word choices bring the subject to life, or do they smother it with too many adjectives? Successful writers realize that there is power and elegance in simple prose and in carefully chosen diction and punctuation. Arranging and rearranging words, deciding whether an exclamation point or a semicolon best supports the writer's purpose—these basic decisions are the means by which the craft of writing is elevated to art.

■ **PICO IYER**

"Punctuation marks are the road signs placed along the highways of our communication—to control speeds, provide directions, and prevent head-on collisions."

(b. 1957, British-born essayist and novelist. See also page 404.)

■ **STEPHEN KING**

"Any word you have to hunt for in a thesaurus is the wrong word. There are no exceptions to this rule."

(b. 1947, American novelist. See also page 426.)

■ **WENDELL BERRY**

"A sentence is both the opportunity and the limit of thought—what we have to think with, and what we have to think in."

(b. 1934, American novelist and essayist)

■ **ROBERT FROST**

"All the fun is in how you say a thing."

(1874–1963, American poet)

■ **LEWIS THOMAS**

"Exclamation points are the most irritating of all. Look! they say, look at what I just said! How amazing is my thought! It is like being forced to watch someone else's small child jumping up and down crazily in the center of the living room shouting to attract attention. If a sentence really has something of importance to say, something quite remarkable, it doesn't need a mark to point it out. And if it is really, after all, a banal sentence needing more zing, the exclamation point simply emphasizes its banality!"

(1913–1993, American physician and essayist)

■ SCOTT ADAMS

"Creativity is allowing your-self to make mistakes. Art is knowing which ones to keep."

(b. 1957, American creator of the *Dilbert* comic strip and the author of several nonfiction works)

■ ELMORE LEONARD

"If it sounds like writing, I rewrite it."

(1925–2013, American novelist and screenwriter)

■ BARBARA TUCHMAN

"Nothing is more satisfying than to write a good sentence. It is no fun to write lumpishly, dully, in prose the reader must plod through like wet sand. But it is a pleasure to achieve, if one can, a clear running prose that is simple yet full of surprises. This does not just happen. It requires skill, hard work, a good ear, and continued practice."

(1912–1989, American historian)

■ MARK TWAIN

"I notice that you use plain, simple language, short words and brief sentences. That is the way to write English — it is the modern way and the best way. Stick to it; don't let fluff and flowers and verbosity creep in. When you catch an adjective, kill it. No, I don't mean utterly, but kill most of them — then the rest will be valuable. They weaken when they are close together. They give strength when they are wide apart. An adjective habit, or a wordy, diffuse, flowery habit, once fastened upon a person, is as hard to get rid of as any other vice. . . . Substitute 'damn' every time you're inclined to write 'very'; your editor will delete it and the writing will be just as it should be."

(Samuel Langhorne Clemens, 1835–1910, American author and humorist)

■ DINAW MENGESTU

"Like most writers, I take apart my sentences over and over. A bad or unpolished sentence or phrase can ruin an entire paragraph for me so I try as much as possible to work over each sentence without destroying any of its initial integrity."

(b. 1978, African novelist. See also page 181.)

■ JONATHAN SWIFT

"Proper words in proper places, make the true definition of style."

(1667–1745, Anglo-Irish satirist and essayist. See also page 630.)

■ DONALD HALL

"The paragraph [is] a mini-essay; it is also a maxi-sentence."

(b. 1928, American poet and essayist)

■ B. J. CHUTE

"Grammar is to a writer what anatomy is to a sculptor, or the scales to a musician. You may loathe it, it may bore you, but nothing will replace it, and once mastered it will support you like a rock."

(1913–1987, American novelist)

READING

ONE OF THE MOST productive exercises for any writer to practice is to read with a writer's eye. Successful writers read with focused and sustained attention to the choices writers make and to the consequences of those choices—much like how a director views a well-made film, how a musician hears a beautiful piece of music, or how a pastry chef envisions someone savoring a delicious croissant. They take pleasure and satisfaction in practicing their craft, but they also seek to learn from what they create. They notice what works and what doesn't, and they continuously ask themselves why. The same principle applies to writers: successful writers know that careful reading can produce clear and engaging prose.

■ EUDORA WELTY

"There's still a strange moment with every book when I move from the position of writer to the position of reader and I suddenly see my words with the eyes of the cold public. It gives me a terrible sense of exposure, as if I'd gotten sunburned."

(1909–2001, American novelist)

■ TONY HILLERMAN

"When I was teaching writing—and I still say it—I taught that the best way to learn to write is by reading. Reading critically, noticing paragraphs that get the job done, how your favorite writers use verbs, all the useful techniques. A scene catches you? Go back and study it. Find out how it works."

(1925–2008, American author of detective novels)

■ JOYCE CAROL OATES

"Young or beginning writers must be urged to read widely, ceaselessly, both classics and contemporaries, for without an immersion in the history of the craft, one is doomed to remain an amateur: an individual for whom enthusiasm is ninety-nine percent of the creative effort."

(b. 1938, American novelist and essayist)

■ ANNIE PROULX

"I'm basically a reader, which is the best way to learn to write. . . . You should write because you love the shape of stories and sentences and the creation of different worlds on a page. Writing comes from reading, and reading is the finest teacher of how to write. I read omnivorously—technical manuals, history, all sorts of things."

(b. 1935, American journalist and novelist)

■ TESS GALLAGHER

"When you start reading in a certain way, that's already the beginning of your writing. You're learning what you admire and you're learning to love other writers. The love of other writers is an important first step. To be a voracious, loving reader."

(b. 1943, American poet and essayist)

■ GEORGE BERNARD SHAW

"As soon as I open [a book], I occupy the book, I stomp around in it. I underline passages, scribble in the margins, leave my mark. . . . I like to be able to hear myself responding to a book, answering it, agreeing and disagreeing in a manner I recognize as peculiarly my own."

(1856–1950, Irish playwright)

■ BRIAN DOYLE

"No reading, no writing. You have got to hear lots of voices on the page to learn how to get voices onto pages. The best education for a young writer is wild wide reading. Read everything of all sorts. Get a sense of how stories can be shaped and shared. Then get your butt in the chair every day, 'lower your standards,' as the great Oregon poet William Stafford said, and type like a maniac."

(1956–2017, American essayist and novelist. See also page 359.)

■ CYNTHIA OZICK

"I read in order to write. I read out of obsession with writing. . . . I read in order to find out what I need to know."

(b. 1928, American novelist and essayist)

■ WILLIAM FAULKNER

"Read, read, read. Read everything—trash, classics, good and bad, and see how they do it. Just like a carpenter who works as an apprentice and studies the master. Read! You'll absorb it. Then write. If it is good, you'll find out. If it's not, throw it out the window."

(1897–1962, American novelist and Nobel laureate)

■ STEPHEN KING

"The real importance of reading is that it creates an ease and intimacy with the process of writing; one comes to the country of the writer with one's papers and identification pretty much in order. Constant reading will pull you into a place (a mind-set, if you like the phrase) where you can write eagerly and without self-consciousness. It also offers you a constantly growing knowledge of what has been done and what hasn't, what is trite and what is fresh, what works and what just lies there dying (or dead) on the page. The more you read, the less apt you are to make a fool of yourself with your pen or word processor. . . . '[R]ead a lot, write a lot' is the great commandment."

(b. 1947, American novelist. See also page 426.)

■ JHUMPA LAHIRI

"I love that line of Saul Bellow's: 'A writer is nothing but a reader moved to emulation.' I really do believe that."

(b. 1967, Indian American novelist and essayist. See also page 151.)

■ MASON COOLEY

"Reading gives us someplace to go when we have to stay where we are."

(1927–2002, American aphorist)

■ EDMUND BURKE

"To read without reflecting is like eating without digesting."

(1729–1797, Anglo-Irish statesman, author, orator, political theorist, and philosopher)

■ NATHANIEL HAWTHORNE

"Easy reading is damned hard writing."

(1804–1864, American novelist)

■ WALTER SAVAGE LANDOR

"What is reading but silent conversation?"

(1775–1864, English writer and poet)

WRITING IS A SKILL that develops over time and with frequent practice. Writing flourishes when someone has something important to say—and wants it to be understood by others. Developing the ability to surprise oneself—to be able to express something that one did not previously think one knew or could express—can be an enormously satisfying experience. In this sense, writing offers the opportunity to transform the world already formed by the words of others into a world of possibility—a world that writers create with the words they craft on a blank page.

PART 1

PERSONAL WRITING

Exploring Our Own Lives

How do I know what I think until I see what I say?

E. M. Forster

(1879–1970, English novelist and essayist)

WHAT IS PERSONAL WRITING?

Thanks to the Internet and the rapid rise of social media, more personal writing occurs now than ever before in history. At any moment, millions of people around the globe are telling others where they happen to be, what they are doing, who they are with, and what they are seeing and hearing. This is often accomplished quickly, in various shorthand codes, without full attention to the conventional rules of writing—grammar, spelling, and punctuation.

Whatever form or media it uses, **personal writing** is essentially writing in which someone recounts his or her own experiences. It has traditionally taken the form of diaries, journals, and—as is the focus of this part—personal essays. Such writing often (though not always) is written in the first-person singular, depends much on memory, relies heavily on narration and description, and often blends these with personal observations and reflection. In fact, of all the kinds of essays that appear in this book, the personal essay comes closest to literature. Many personal essays—such as E. B. White's "Once More to the Lake" (page 256) and George Orwell's "Shooting an Elephant" (page 195) are considered literary in the same way as are poetry, fiction, and drama. In these essays, writers pay particular attention to establishing a personal presence, turning their story into a compelling narrative, and writing literary (or artful) prose.

Though this type of writing seems commonplace now, personal essays are a relatively new form of literature. Various types of essays existed in ancient times, but critics usually consider a French writer, Michel de Montaigne (1533–1592) as the first essayist. An important part of the reason for this is that Montaigne coined the term "essay" (*essai*, in French). The word means "attempt" or "try out" and has connotations of informality and inconclusiveness. In his confessional and digressive essays, Montaigne hoped to share with readers his inner life with all its embarrassing moments, conflicting emotions, differing attitudes, and shifts of opinion. As a writer, you may decide the personal essay format best fits your writing situation if your personal story is essential to the topic at hand, if you're interested in working out something you don't quite understand about your thoughts or your experiences, or if it makes a topic that readers are unfamiliar with more immediately relatable.

STRATEGIES FOR ESTABLISHING YOUR PERSONAL PRESENCE

In writing about themselves, writers normally rely on the **first-person singular**, that ubiquitous one-letter capital "I." It may look like a simple word, but it isn't. First, though the "I" may purport to be you—the person recounting the experiences—the word can't refer to your entire character and personality, only a small portion of which may be conveyed in an essay. You don't necessarily express yourself simply by saying "I." The sentence "I went to the mall to look for a pair of jeans" does not tell us anything about you, except that you wanted to find jeans at the mall. Usually, writers need to add more personal information to make the "I" more individualized: "I went to the mall thinking that a new pair of jeans would improve my mood." Now we have more than an empty "I" that is merely an agent; we have an "I" that is becoming a character in our essay. As the essayist Scott Russell Sanders reminds us, there is a big difference between the first-person singular and the "singular first person."

As you begin writing a personal essay, don't simply assume that when you use the word "I," a reader will automatically see a one-to-one connection between that word and you. Unless you are a celebrity, the reader will only know about you from what you tell. You will need to inhabit the "I," make your presence and personality felt in the writing itself. You are not present in flesh and blood but only as the speaker of the essay. That is why your tone of voice (which we'll discuss shortly) plays such a significant role in establishing your presence as an individual.

But be warned: to avoid appearing overly self-absorbed, writers often moderate their use of "I." When every sentence begins with that pronoun — or if it appears in every sentence — then the writer will seem narcissistic and the writing monotonous. As you begin reading the essays in this section, notice how writers use (and avoid) the word "I" to give you a sense of themselves as the compelling subject of the essay.

As you begin to think of the "I" in your essay as a character, it's also useful to consider the **point of view**, the physical location from where you tell the story. For writers, the point of view is often a literal reality, an actual place or situation in which writers physically locate themselves. This occurs most frequently in autobiographical essays in which the writer is present both as the narrator and as a character. For example, in "Why I Own a Gun" (page 249), Jillian Weise devotes meticulous attention to conveying exactly where she is as she unfolds her narrative supporting her decision to be "a card-carrying member of the National Rifle Association." The essay begins, "I keep a Smith & Wesson in a drawer next to my bed."

Or consider the tremendous importance of point of view — this time in terms of perspective — to another essayist, Brent Staples. This is how Staples opens his essay:

> My first victim was a woman — white, well dressed, probably in her early twenties. I came upon her late one evening on a deserted street in Hyde Park, a relatively affluent neighborhood in an otherwise mean, impoverished section of Chicago. As I swung onto the avenue behind her, there seemed to be a discreet, uninflammatory distance between us. Not so. She cast back a worried glance. To her, the youngish black man — a broad six feet two inches with a beard and billowing hair, both hands shoved into the pockets of a bulky military jacket — seemed menacingly close. After a few more quick glimpses, she picked up her pace and was soon running in earnest. Within seconds she disappeared into a cross street. **Brent Staples**, "Just Walk on By: A Black Man Ponders His Power to Alter Public Space" (page 217)

To see why he frightens people, Staples needs to see himself in the stereotypical ways that others see him. Thus, by the middle of this opening paragraph (in the sentence beginning "To her"), he switches the point of view from his own perspective to that of the young and terrified white woman, describing his appearance as she would perceive it.

Point of view is not always a matter of a specific location or position. Writers are not always present in their essays as dramatic characters. In many reflective, informative, or argumentative essays, the point of view is determined more by a writer's intellectual attitude or opinions—an angle of vision—than by a precise physical perspective. Examples of these will be covered in the introductions to Parts 2 and 3.

Another way to give your personal essay presence is to think about the words you write as sounds, and your writing as something that has a **voice**. All words are composed of sounds, and language itself is something nearly all of us originally learned through *hearing*. Any piece of writing can be read aloud, though many readers have developed such ingrained habits of silent reading that they no longer *hear* the writing. Good writers, however, want their words to be heard. They want their sentences to have rhythm, cadence, and balance. Experienced authors revise a great deal of their writing just to make sure the sentences *sound* right. They're writing for the reader's ear as well as for the reader's mind.

In many respects, voice is the writer's "signature," what finally distinguishes the work of one writer from another. Consider how quickly we recognize voice. We've *heard* only the opening lines of a comedy routine on television, yet we instantly recognize the speaker. So, too, whenever we read a piece of writing, we ought to think of it as an experience similar to listening to someone speak aloud.

A more-specific dimension of voice is **tone**, which refers to the manner the writer adopts in addressing the reader and to the implied relationship of the writer to the reader. Tone suggests not the writer's attitude itself but the way that attitude is revealed. Our tone in writing is what we use to convey to readers a sense of our personality—do we sound formal, breezy, irreverent, satirical, matter-of-fact, flippant, bitter, nostalgic? It also demonstrates our attitude toward our subject and audience—do we seem in awe of another person, hostile about an issue, open to various points of view, surprised by another's opinion, contemptuous of our readers?

In practical terms, tone is usually a matter of diction and individual word choice. Observe how Henry Louis Gates Jr. chooses his words carefully in order to convey tone—in this case, how he felt about Sammy Davis Jr.'s versus Nat King Cole's hair.

> Sammy Davis's process I detested. It didn't look good on him. Worse still, he liked to have a fried strand dangling down the middle of his forehead, shaking it out from the crown when he sang. But Nat King Cole's hair was a thing unto itself, a beautifully sculpted work of art that he and he alone should have had the right to wear.
> **Henry Louis Gates Jr.**, "In the Kitchen" (page 96)

Note how you come to know as a reader what Gates feels about "Sammy Davis's process": he chooses to use the stronger verb "detested" instead of the more common "hated," and when speaking of Nat King Cole's hair, he sounds almost reverential, using phrases like "work of art." In addition to simply telling us what he thinks, Gates's overall tone of voice in the essay—which he establishes by means of very particular word choices (note the negative impact of "fried strand dangling")—helps us understand how he *feels* about his subject.

STRATEGIES FOR TURNING YOUR STORY INTO A COMPELLING NARRATIVE

Put simply, we **narrate** when we tell a story that recounts a sequence of events: "x happened, then y happened, and then z happened." We narrate such stories all the time in our daily conversations: "After class, I walked to the parking lot and ran into a friend I hadn't seen since high school. We decided to go to the cafeteria for coffee."

Narration also plays a large role in writing personal essays. But in writing, we need to be far more selective. We all know people who go on and on in conversation—I did this, then I went there, then I saw that, and so on. If such rambling is dull to hear in real life, it is much worse in writing, where a reader expects that a point will be reached or a story will be clear and coherent. When we write, we need not only to consider a sequence of events but also to show how events are interconnected, how one event causes or motivates another, how one thing leads to another. Suppose we revise our brief example:

> After class, I walked to the parking lot and ran into a friend I hadn't seen since high school. A lot had happened to him since then, so we decided to go to the cafeteria for coffee and to catch up.

Notice that now there's a closer connection among the sequence of events and our narrative can continue to say what exactly has happened to our friend and what we went on to talk about. But we can still do better; we can make it more interesting by including description.

In the personal narrative essay, narration and **description** usually go hand in hand. As we tell our story, we often need to describe objects, people, and places. We need to both show and tell. A personal narrative with no physical details would provide no information for readers to visualize the events you are relating. Let's further revise our example:

> After biology class, I walked through the heavy snowfall to the commuter's parking lot and literally bumped into a friend I hadn't seen since high school. Gary now sported a perfectly trimmed goatee, wore fashionable glasses, and looked like he had lost about fifty pounds. We stood in the snow and talked for a few awkward minutes. It was clear a lot had happened to him since we last saw each other, so we decided to trudge over to the cafeteria for steaming hot coffee and to catch up on our lives. I was eager to hear about his.

Note how filling in just a few details—of weather, people, movement, place—helps create a scene and allows us to picture a particular incident.

Good description demands that we observe the world around us attentively and then try to put our observations into words that will best help our readers visualize what we see. In writing, adjectives will do part of this work for us, but writers need to remember that many common adjectives are so abstract that they tell us very little. To say that something is "beautiful" or that a food is "delicious" does not get us far; these overused words merely convey the writer's impressions. Effective description is usually concrete: what exactly makes something "beautiful" or "delicious"?

When describing objects, it helps to know precise terms. There are many varieties of lettuce: were you looking at romaine or iceberg? Was the bird a cardinal or a blue jay? Is the tree you refer to a maple or an oak—and, remember, there are different kinds of maple and oak trees. Specificity can be important to descriptive writing, especially when the writer strives for precision and accuracy. Writing descriptively offers us a good opportunity to expand our vocabularies and know the world around us more intimately.

In the following example, note all of the specific details Judith Ortiz Cofer includes to describe life in her apartment building.

> The walls were thin, and voices speaking and arguing in Spanish could be heard all day. *Salsas* blasted out of radios, turned on early in the morning and left on for company. Women seemed to cook rice and beans perpetually—the strong aroma of boiling red kidney beans permeated the hallways. **Judith Ortiz Cofer**, "Silent Dancing" (page 67)

What is the significance of Cofer describing the odor in the hallways as "the strong aroma of boiling red kidney beans" rather than simply "the smell of beans"? What other details in the passage are enhanced by their specificity?

One topic people talk about most is talk, whether it's friendly gossip, what a celebrity said, or what was reported on the news. Because personal essays usually include other people—often friends, parents, and siblings—we will occasionally need to not only describe them but also refer to things they've said. The personal essay often differs from expository or argumentative writing in that quotation usually entails what someone has *said*, not something we're quoting from our reading. To report **dialogue** in writing, we use essentially two methods of quotation: direct and indirect.

A direct quotation normally appears in quotation marks and tries to capture the exact words and tone of the person speaking. Amy Chua provides excellent examples in her essay "Tough Love: Parents and Children." In a scene where Chua and her husband argue over their daughter's practicing the piano, the dialogue between them accentuates the tension between them:

> "You just don't believe in her, I accused."
> "That's ridiculous," Jed said scornfully. "Of course I do" **Amy Chua**, "Tough Love" (page 514)

An indirect quotation doesn't require quotation marks and is usually a non-verbatim report of what someone said. It does not claim to repeat someone's words exactly. Here is an example from Jamaica Kincaid. She is referring to a phone conversation with her mother:

> During a conversation over the telephone, she had once again let me know that my accomplishments—becoming a responsible and independent woman—did not amount to very much, that the life I lived was nothing more than a silly show, that she truly wished me dead. **Jamaica Kincaid**, "The Estrangement" (page 136)

Most essayists will blend direct and indirect quotation in their writing. Of course, we are seldom making an audio recording of our conversations and it is difficult to recall exact language—especially during emotional situations—from what could be many years ago. Personal essayists depend heavily on memory and try to reconstruct conversations as best they can. These are usually compressed—we don't need every line of the conversation, just the most interesting or representative parts. Here's how adding direct and indirect dialogue can contribute to our previous example.

> After biology class, I walked through the heavy snowfall to the commuter's parking lot and literally bumped into a friend I hadn't seen since high school. "Dude?" Gary seemed surprised. "What are *you* doing here?" He looked at me curiously, uncertain. He now sported a perfectly trimmed goatee, wore fashionable glasses, and looked like he had lost about fifty pounds. We stood in the snow and talked for a few awkward minutes. He mentioned that he had just driven to campus to visit a girl he met at a big party last weekend. It was clear a lot had happened to him since we last saw each other, so we decided to trudge over to the cafeteria for steaming hot coffee and to catch up on our lives. I was eager to hear about his.

Look back at our original telling of this encounter with a friend on page 28. What impact does being deliberate, adding description, and using dialogue have on our narrative? Note that as various elements were added to the first simply stated version, a personal story began to take shape, with a specific setting, a dramatic incident, a forward movement, and characters we might want to learn more about.

STRATEGIES FOR WRITING LITERARY PROSE

As mentioned earlier, the personal essay is the most literary type of essay. Unlike most other essay types, its main purpose is not explanatory, informative, or persuasive. It uses many characteristics we associate with fiction, such as narration, description, character, dialogue, and setting. It can also resemble poetry in its language and style. Although we won't cover all the literary elements here, it's worth mentioning how metaphors and similes can contribute to an effective essay, and how thinking about style and noticing verbal patterns can help your writing, too.

One challenge with personal writing is translating your personal experience into something that readers who don't know you will understand and engage with. Although common to nearly all essay forms, the use of **metaphor** allows personal essayists to communicate personal details in ways that show universal significance. Writers use metaphor when they find resemblances between different kinds of things or ideas. Similar to metaphor, a **simile** explicitly states the resemblance by adding "like" or "as." To say, "She's a rock," is to use a metaphor; to say, "She's like a rock" is to use a simile.

As you come across metaphors and similes throughout this book, you'll find they are not merely decorative but often play a significant role in the writer's expression and the essay's overall structure and design. Good writers enjoy making up original similes and metaphors and try to avoid the usual clichéd or stale ones that come to mind easily, such as calling someone's abs a "six pack," a drink "smooth as silk," a friend "smart as a whip," or an idea "crystal clear." Note the original simile the renowned American essayist Edward Hoagland uses to open his essay "On Stuttering" (page 116): "Stuttering is like trying to run with loops of rope around your feet."

As Hoagland's simile demonstrates, writers use metaphor and simile to make their writing more vivid and to offer readers a chance to visualize something in a way they may never have considered. Note that Hoagland's simile invites us to see the vocal act of stuttering.

Literary essayists will also embed metaphors and similes into their writing to reinforce an essay's dominant imagery. Many well-crafted essays depend on a network of words and images that relate to and echo each other. The writer expects the reader to connect the dots, to see and appreciate how one image at one point in the essay interacts with another. To see how this works in a piece of writing, look at Anne Fadiman's "Under Water" (page 91). At one point in this essay about a disastrous whitewater canoeing trip, the author notices a fellow student in her wilderness program "standing at a strange angle in the middle of the river." She imagines that an instructor will soon appear and "pluck him out, like a twig from a snag." An inattentive reader may easily overlook that simile, but an attentive reader will remember that her essay begins with a reference to streams in her childhood and how she liked to drop twigs into the water and watch them float downstream, and how "if they hit a snag, I freed them." The simile is an integral part of a pattern of imagery that recurs throughout the essay.

In your own writing, look for ways to use the metaphors and similes that come to you as you write. The figurative language you include can not only make an image or idea clear but also echo your larger point.

As observed in Fadiman's deliberate use of imagery, the literary essayist is always consciously crafting and shaping his or her work. This artistic presence is not always obvious. Yet, when we begin to detect in our reading certain kinds of repeated elements—a metaphor or an image, a twist on an earlier episode, a conclusion that echoes the opening—we become aware that someone is deliberately shaping experience or ideas in a special manner. We often find this type of presence in imaginative literature—especially in novels and poems—as well as in essays that possess a distinct literary flavor.

To see an example of creating a style and presence through verbal patterns, look at the opening paragraph of E. B. White's now-classic essay, "Once More to the Lake."

> One summer, along about 1904, my father rented a camp on a lake in Maine and took us all there for the month of August. We all got ringworm from some kittens

and had to rub Pond's Extract on our arms and legs night and morning, and my father rolled over in a canoe with all his clothes on; but outside of that the vacation was a success and from then on none of us ever thought there was any place in the world like that lake in Maine. We returned summer after summer—always on August 1st for one month. I have since become a salt-water man, but sometimes in summer there are days when the restlessness of the tides and the fearful cold of the sea water and the incessant wind that blows across the afternoon and into the evening make me wish for the placidity of a lake in the woods. A few weeks ago this feeling got so strong I bought myself a couple of bass hooks and a spinner and returned to the lake where we used to go, for a week's fishing and to revisit old haunts. **E. B. White**, "Once More to the Lake" (page 256)

If, in rereading this opening, you circle every use of the word *and*, you will clearly see a pattern of repetition. *And*, of course, is a very unobtrusive word, and you may not notice right away how White keeps it present throughout the passage. This repetition alone may strike you at first as of no special importance, but as you read through the essay and see how much of White's central theme depends on the idea of return and repetition (reinforced by the title's "Once More"), you will get a better sense of why the little word *and*—a word that subtly reinforces the idea of repetition itself—is so significant. Nearly all the literary essays in Part 1 will demand such attentive reading.

READING PERSONAL ESSAYS: A Checklist

To benefit the most from the readings in this part, we recommend that you read each selection, paying close attention to a number of different elements. As noted in this introduction, the personal essay requires careful reading, with special attention to both the essay's content and the writer's craft. The following checklist will serve as a convenient guide as you approach the selections in Part 1.

- Consider carefully the essay's title. In what ways does it or doesn't it reflect the author's topic? In one sentence, summarize the relationship of the title to the topic.

- Describe your immediate response to the way the essay opens, either the first sentence or the entire first paragraph. Explain what, if anything, drew you into the essay or pushed you away. To what extent did you react to content or tone of voice?

- Describe the speaker's tone of voice. What words would you use to characterize the way the person sounds to you?

- Consider how the tone of the essay reflects the writer's attitude or stance toward his or her topic. To what extent do you identify with or disagree with the writer's attitude?

- Identify the "I" of the essay. Do you get the impression that the "I" speaking is the same person as the writer? Or do you think the "I" is made up for the purposes of the essay?

- How is the essay narrated? Is the time frame in strict chronological order, or is the story told in other ways? To what extent is the time frame compressed?

- Identify the dominant tense of the essay. Is most of the telling in the past or present tense? Note changes of tense and evaluate the reasons for them.

- Try to assess how much time has elapsed between the essay's main action and its actual composition. How much of the essay depends on memory?

- Consider the writer's use of dialogue. Is the report of conversation most often direct or indirect? Do you find the dialogue realistic or artificial?

- Do you find the characters, settings, and objects described in the essay easy or difficult to visualize? Assess the writer's descriptive abilities.

- Summarize the central point of the essay. Is that point explicitly stated or was it hidden or buried?

- Describe the speaker's point of view. Is the point of view connected to the speaker's physical presence in the essay? Do we see people, places, and objects from a single point of view? To what extent does the "I" of the essay appear as a main character?

- Annotate the essay's verbal patterns. Underline repeated words or phrases. Note the use of similar images that repeatedly occur. Note any other repetitions you find.

Maya Angelou

"WHAT'S YOUR NAME, GIRL?"

MAYA ANGELOU (1928–2014) grew up in St. Louis, Missouri, and in Stamps, Arkansas, a victim of poverty, discrimination, and abuse. Angelou confronts the pain and injustice of her childhood in *I Know Why the Caged Bird Sings* (1969), from which the selection "What's Your Name, Girl?" is taken. James Baldwin, who suggested she write about her childhood, praised this book as the mark of the "beginning of a new era in the minds and hearts of all black men and women." Angelou, who received more than thirty honorary degrees, was the Reynolds Professor of American Studies at Wake Forest University. In addition to the several volumes of her autobiography, Angelou was the author of articles, short stories, and poetry. Some of her publications include *Hallelujah! The Welcome Table* (2004), a collection of essays, and several books of poetry, including *Amazing Peace: A Christmas Poem* (2005), *Mother: A Cradle to Hold Me* (2006), and *Poetry for Young People: Maya Angelou* (2007). At the request of President Bill Clinton, Angelou composed "On the Pulse of the Morning," a poem she read at his inauguration in 1993. She later served on two presidential committees and was awarded the Presidential Medal of Arts in 2000 and the Presidential Medal of Freedom in 2011. She also received three Grammy Awards, including a Grammy in

> **"When I'm writing, everything shuts down."**

2002 for her recording of *A Song Flung Up to Heaven*, the sixth book in her autobiographical series. Her most recent book was *Mom & Me & Mom* (2013), a nonfiction book delving into Angelou's relationship with her mother.

Angelou described a typical day in her life as a writer in this way: "When I'm writing, everything shuts down. I get up about five. . . . I get in my car and drive off to a hotel room: I can't write in my house, I take a hotel room and ask them to take everything off the walls so there's me, the Bible, *Roget's Thesaurus*, and some good, dry sherry and I'm at work by 6:30. I write on the bed lying down—one elbow is darker than the other, really black from leaning on it—and I write in longhand on yellow pads. Once into it, all disbelief is suspended, it's beautiful. I hate to go, but I've set for myself 12:30 as the time to leave, because after that it's an indulgence, it becomes stuff I am going to edit out anyway. . . . After dinner, I reread what I have written . . . if April is the cruellest month, then 8:00 at night is the cruellest hour because that's when I start to edit and all that pretty stuff I've written gets axed out. So if I've written ten or twelve pages in six hours, it'll end up as three or four if I'm lucky."

RECENTLY A WHITE WOMAN from Texas, who would quickly describe herself as a liberal, asked me about my hometown. When I told her that in Stamps[1] my grandmother had owned the only Negro general merchandise store since the turn of the century, she exclaimed, "Why, you were a debutante." Ridiculous and even ludicrous. But Negro girls in small Southern towns, whether poverty-stricken or just munching along on a few of life's necessities, were given as extensive and irrelevant preparations for adulthood as rich white girls shown in magazines. Admittedly the training was not the same. While white girls learned to waltz and sit gracefully with a teacup balanced on their knees, we were lagging behind, learning the mid-Victorian values with very little money to indulge them. (Come and see Edna Lomax spending the money she made picking cotton on five balls of ecru tatting thread. Her fingers are bound to snag the work and she'll have to repeat the stitches time and time again. But she knows that when she buys the thread.)

We were required to embroider and I had trunkfuls of colorful dishtowels, pillowcases, runners, and handkerchiefs to my credit. I mastered the art of crocheting and tatting, and there was a lifetime's supply of dainty doilies that would never be used in sacheted dresser drawers. It went without saying that all girls could iron and wash, but the finer touches around the home, like setting a table with real silver, baking roasts, and cooking vegetables without meat, had to be learned elsewhere. Usually at the source of those habits. During my tenth year, a white woman's kitchen became my finishing school.

Mrs. Viola Cullinan was a plump woman who lived in a three-bedroom house somewhere behind the post office. She was singularly unattractive until she smiled, and then the lines around her eyes and mouth which made her look perpetually dirty disappeared, and her face looked like the mask of an impish elf. She usually rested her smile until late afternoon when her women friends dropped in and Miss Glory, the cook, served them cold drinks on the closed-in porch.

The exactness of her house was inhuman. This glass went here and only here. That cup had its place and it was an act of impudent rebellion to place it anywhere else. At twelve o'clock the table was set. At 12:15 Mrs. Cullinan sat down to dinner (whether her husband had arrived or not). At 12:16 Miss Glory brought out the food.

It took me a week to learn the difference between a salad plate, a bread plate, and a dessert plate.

Mrs. Cullinan kept up the tradition of her wealthy parents. She was from Virginia. Miss Glory, who was a descendant of slaves that had worked for

5

---

[1] *Stamps:* A town in southwestern Arkansas. —EDS.

the Cullinans, told me her history. She had married beneath her (according to Miss Glory). Her husband's family hadn't had their money very long and what they had "didn't 'mount to much."

As ugly as she was, I thought privately, she was lucky to get a husband above or beneath her station. But Miss Glory wouldn't let me say a thing against her mistress. She was very patient with me, however, over the housework. She explained the dishware, silverware, and servants' bells.

The large round bowl in which soup was served wasn't a soup bowl, it was a tureen. There were goblets, sherbet glasses, ice-cream glasses, wine glasses, green glass coffee cups with matching saucers, and water glasses. I had a glass to drink from, and it sat with Miss Glory's on a separate shelf from the others. Soup spoons, gravy boat, butter knives, salad forks, and carving platter were additions to my vocabulary and in fact almost represented a new language. I was fascinated with the novelty, with the fluttering Mrs. Cullinan and her Alice-in-Wonderland house.

Her husband remains, in my memory, undefined. I lumped him with all the other white men that I had ever seen and tried not to see.

On our way home one evening, Miss Glory told me that Mrs. Cullinan   10 couldn't have children. She said that she was too delicate-boned. It was hard to imagine bones at all under those layers of fat. Miss Glory went on to say that the doctor had taken out all her lady organs. I reasoned that a pig's organs included the lungs, heart, and liver, so if Mrs. Cullinan was walking around without these essentials, it explained why she drank alcohol out of unmarked bottles. She was keeping herself embalmed.

When I spoke to Bailey[2] about it, he agreed that I was right, but he also informed me that Mr. Cullinan had two daughters by a colored lady and that I knew them very well. He added that the girls were the spitting image of their father. I was unable to remember what he looked like, although I had just left him a few hours before, but I thought of the Coleman girls. They were very light-skinned and certainly didn't look very much like their mother (no one ever mentioned Mr. Coleman).

My pity for Mrs. Cullinan preceded me the next morning like the Cheshire cat's smile. Those girls, who could have been her daughters, were beautiful. They didn't have to straighten their hair. Even when they were caught in the rain, their braids still hung down straight like tamed snakes. Their mouths were pouty little cupid's bows. Mrs. Cullinan didn't know what she missed. Or maybe she did. Poor Mrs. Cullinan.

For weeks after, I arrived early, left late, and tried very hard to make up for her barrenness. If she had had her own children, she wouldn't have had to ask me to run a thousand errands from her back door to the back door of her friends. Poor old Mrs. Cullinan.

2 **Bailey:** Angelou's brother. —EDS.

Then one evening Miss Glory told me to serve the ladies on the porch. After I set the tray down and turned toward the kitchen, one of the women asked, "What's your name, girl?" It was the speckled-face one. Mrs. Cullinan said, "She doesn't talk much. Her name's Margaret."

"Is she dumb?"   15

"No. As I understand it, she can talk when she wants to but she's usually quiet as a little mouse. Aren't you, Margaret?"

I smiled at her. Poor thing. No organs and couldn't even pronounce my name correctly.[3]

"She's a sweet little thing, though."

"Well, that may be, but the name's too long. I'd never bother myself. I'd call her Mary if I was you."

I fumed into the kitchen. That horrible woman would never have the   20 chance to call me Mary because if I was starving I'd never work for her. I decided I wouldn't pee on her if her heart was on fire. Giggles drifted in off the porch and into Miss Glory's pots. I wondered what they could be laughing about.

Whitefolks were so strange. Could they be talking about me? Everybody knew that they stuck together better than the Negroes did. It was possible that Mrs. Cullinan had friends in St. Louis who heard about a girl from Stamps being in court and wrote to tell her. Maybe she knew about Mr. Freeman.[4]

My lunch was in my mouth a second time and I went outside and relieved myself on the bed of four-o'clocks. Miss Glory thought I might be coming down with something and told me to go on home, that Momma would give me some herb tea, and she'd explain to her mistress.

I realized how foolish I was being before I reached the pond. Of course Mrs. Cullinan didn't know. Otherwise she wouldn't have given me the two nice dresses that Momma cut down, and she certainly wouldn't have called me a "sweet little thing." My stomach felt fine, and I didn't mention anything to Momma.

That evening I decided to write a poem on being white, fat, old, and without children. It was going to be a tragic ballad. I would have to watch her carefully to capture the essence of her loneliness and pain.

The very next day, she called me by the wrong name. Miss Glory and   25 I were washing up the lunch dishes when Mrs. Cullinan came to the doorway. "Mary?"

---

[3] ***couldn't even pronounce my name correctly:*** Angelou's first name is actually Marguerite. —EDS.

[4] **Mr. Freeman:** A friend of Angelou's mother; he was convicted of raping Angelou when she was a child. —EDS.

Miss Glory asked, "Who?"

Mrs. Cullinan, sagging a little, knew and I knew. "I want Mary to go down to Mrs. Randall's and take her some soup. She's not been feeling well for a few days."

Miss Glory's face was a wonder to see. "You mean Margaret, ma'am. Her name's Margaret."

"That's too long. She's Mary from now on. Heat that soup from last night and put it in the china tureen and, Mary, I want you to carry it carefully."

Every person I knew had a hellish horror of being "called out of his 30 name." It was a dangerous practice to call a Negro anything that could be loosely construed as insulting because of the centuries of their having been called niggers, jigs, dinges, blackbirds, crows, boots, and spooks.

Miss Glory had a fleeting second of feeling sorry for me. Then as she handed me the hot tureen she said, "Don't mind, don't pay that no mind. Sticks and stones may break your bones, but words . . . You know, I been working for her for twenty years."

She held the back door open for me. "Twenty years; I wasn't much older than you. My name used to be Hallelujah. That's what Ma named me, but my mistress give me 'Glory,' and it stuck. I likes it better too."

I was in the little path that ran behind the houses when Miss Glory shouted, "It's shorter too."

For a few seconds it was a toss-up over whether I would laugh (imagine being named Hallelujah) or cry (imagine letting some white woman rename you for her convenience). My anger saved me from either outburst. I had to quit the job, but the problem was going to be how to do it. Momma wouldn't allow me to quit for just any reason.

"She's a peach. That woman is a real peach." Mrs. Randall's maid was 35 talking as she took the soup from me, and I wondered what her name used to be and what she answered to now.

For a week I looked into Mrs. Cullinan's face as she called me Mary. She ignored my coming late and leaving early. Miss Glory was a little annoyed because I had begun to leave egg yolk on the dishes and wasn't putting much heart in polishing the silver. I hoped that she would complain to our boss, but she didn't.

Then Bailey solved my dilemma. He had me describe the contents of the cupboard and the particular plates she liked best. Her favorite piece was a casserole shaped like a fish and the green glass coffee cups. I kept his instructions in mind, so on the next day when Miss Glory was hanging out clothes and I had again been told to serve the old biddies on the porch, I dropped the empty serving tray. When I heard Mrs. Cullinan scream, "Mary!" I picked up the casserole and two of the green glass cups in readiness. As she rounded the kitchen door I let them fall on the tiled floor.

I could never absolutely describe to Bailey what happened next, because each time I got to the part where she fell on the floor and screwed up her ugly face to cry, we burst out laughing. She actually wobbled around on the floor and picked up shards of the cups and cried, "Oh, Momma. Oh, dear

Gawd. It's Momma's china from Virginia. Oh, Momma, I sorry."

Miss Glory came running in from the yard and the women from the porch crowded around. Miss Glory was almost as broken up as her mistress. "You mean to say she broke our Virginia dishes? What we gone do?"

Mrs. Cullinan cried louder. "That clumsy nigger. Clumsy little black   40 nigger."

Old speckled-face leaned down and asked, "Who did it, Viola? Was it Mary? Who did it?"

Everything was happening so fast I can't remember whether her action preceded her words, but I know that Mrs. Cullinan said, "Her name's Margaret, goddamn it, her name's Margaret!" And she threw a wedge of the broken plate at me. It could have been the hysteria which put her aim off, but the flying crockery caught Miss Glory right over her ear and she started screaming.

I left the front door wide open so all the neighbors could hear.

Mrs. Cullinan was right about one thing. My name wasn't Mary. ●

The Reader's Presence

1. At the center of this autobiographical episode is the importance of people's names in African American culture. Where does Angelou make this point clear? If she hadn't explained the problem of names directly, how might your interpretation of the episode be different? To what extent do the names of things also play an important role in the essay? What does it mean to be "called out of [one's] name" (paragraph 30)?

2. Consider Marguerite's final act carefully. What turns her sympathetic feelings for Mrs. Cullinan to anger? Why does she respond by deliberately destroying Mrs. Cullinan's china? What else could she have done? Why was that act especially appropriate? What does the china represent? How does Angelou establish our sympathy, or lack thereof, for Marguerite in the final paragraphs?

3. **CONNECTIONS:** Many coming-of-age stories involve an account not only of the child's acquisition of language but also, and perhaps more important, of the importance of social context to communication. Miss Glory's training of Marguerite as a maid involves "additions to [her] vocabulary and in fact almost represented a new language" (paragraph 8). Now consider another essay that explores the power of names and naming. How does Angelou's education compare to that of Manuel Muñoz's in "Leave Your Name at the Border" (page 187)? What is the relation between names, language, and power in each essay?

James Baldwin

NOTES OF A NATIVE SON

JAMES BALDWIN (1924–1987) grew up in New York City but moved to France in 1948 because he felt personally and artistically stifled as a gay African American man in the United States. His first novels, *Go Tell It on the Mountain* (1953) and *Giovanni's Room* (1956), and his first collection of essays, *Notes of a Native Son* (1955), were published during Baldwin's first stay abroad, where he was able to write critically about race, sexual identity, and social injustice in America. "Once I found myself on the other side of the ocean," he told an interviewer, "I could see where I came from very clearly, and I could see that I carried myself, which is my home, with me. You can never escape that. I am the grandson of a slave, and I am a writer. I must deal with both."

After nearly a decade in France, he returned to New York and became a national figure in the civil rights movement. After Baldwin's death, Henry Louis Gates Jr. eulogized him as the conscience of the nation,

> "I am the grandson of a slave, and I am a writer. I must deal with both."

for he "educated an entire generation of Americans about the civil-rights struggle and the sensibility of Afro-Americans as we faced and conquered the final barriers in our long quest for civil rights." Baldwin continued to educate through his essays, collected in *The Price of the Ticket: Collected Nonfiction* (1985).

When asked if he approached the writing of fiction and nonfiction in different ways, Baldwin responded, "Every form is different, no one is easier than another. . . . An essay is not simpler, though it may seem so. An essay is clearly an argument. The writer's point of view in an essay is always absolutely clear. The writer is trying to make the readers see something, trying to convince them of something. In a novel or a play, you're trying to show them something. The risks, in any case, are exactly the same."

The title essay of the book *Notes of a Native Son* first appeared in *Harper's* magazine in 1955. In it, Baldwin recounts the death of his father, whose funeral took place on Baldwin's nineteenth birthday—the same day a bloody race riot broke out in Harlem.

ONE

On the twenty-ninth of July, in 1943, my father died. On the same day, a few hours later, his last child was born. Over a month before this, while all our energies were concentrated in waiting for these events, there had been, in Detroit, one of the bloodiest race riots of the century. A few hours after my father's funeral, while he lay in state in the undertaker's chapel, a race riot broke out in Harlem. On the morning of the third of August, we drove my father to the graveyard through a wilderness of smashed plate glass.

The day of my father's funeral had also been my nineteenth birthday. As we drove him to the graveyard, the spoils of injustice, anarchy, discontent, and hatred were all around us. It seemed to me that God himself had devised, to mark my father's end, the most sustained and brutally dissonant of codas. And it seemed to me, too, that the violence which rose all about us as my father left the world had been devised as a corrective for the pride of his eldest son. I had declined to believe in that apocalypse which had been central to my father's vision; very well, life seemed to be saying, here is something that will certainly pass for an apocalypse until the real thing comes along. I had inclined to be contemptuous of my father for the conditions of his life, for the conditions of our lives. When his life had ended I began to wonder about that life and also, in a new way, to be apprehensive about my own.

I had not known my father very well. We had got on badly, partly because we shared, in our different fashions, the vice of stubborn pride. When he was dead I realized that I had hardly ever spoken to him. When he had been dead a long time I began to wish I had. It seems to be typical of life in America, where opportunities, real and fancied, are thicker than anywhere else on the globe, that the second generation has no time to talk to the first. No one, including my father, seems to have known exactly how old he was, but his mother had been born during slavery. He was of the first generation of free men. He, along with thousands of other Negroes, came North after 1919 and I was part of that generation which had never seen the landscape of what Negroes sometimes call the Old Country.

He had been born in New Orleans and had been quite a young man there during the time that Louis Armstrong, a boy, was running errands for the dives and honky-tonks of what was always presented to me as one of the most wicked of cities—to this day, whenever I think of New Orleans, I also helplessly think of Sodom and Gomorrah. My father never mentioned Louis Armstrong, except to forbid us to play his records; but there was a picture of him on our wall for a long time. One of my father's strong-willed female relatives had placed it there and forbade my father to take it down. He never did, but he eventually maneuvered her out of the house and when, some years later, she was in trouble and near death, he refused to do anything to help her.

He was, I think, very handsome. I gather this from photographs and   5 from my own memories of him, dressed in his Sunday best and on his way to preach a sermon somewhere, when I was little. Handsome, proud, and ingrown, "like a toenail," somebody said. But he looked to me, as I grew older, like pictures I had seen of African tribal chieftains: he really should have been naked, with warpaint on and barbaric mementos, standing among spears. He could be chilling in the pulpit and indescribably cruel in his personal life and he was certainly the most bitter man I have ever met; yet it must be said that there was something else in him, buried in him, which lent him his tremendous power and, even, a rather crushing charm. It had something to do with his blackness, I think — he was very black — with his blackness and his beauty, and with the fact that he knew that he was black but did not know that he was beautiful. He claimed to be proud of his blackness but it had also been the cause of much humiliation and it had fixed bleak boundaries to his life. He was not a young man when we were growing up and he had already suffered many kinds of ruin; in his outrageously demanding and protective way he loved his children, who were black like him and menaced, like him; and all these things sometimes showed in his face when he tried, never to my knowledge with any success, to establish contact with any of us. When he took one of his children on his knee to play, the child always became fretful and began to cry; when he tried to help one of us with our homework the absolutely unabating tension which emanated from him caused our minds and our tongues to become paralyzed, so that he, scarcely knowing why, flew into a rage and the child, not knowing why, was punished. If it ever entered his head to bring a surprise home for his children, it was, almost unfailingly, the wrong surprise and even the big watermelons he often brought home on his back in the summertime led to the most appalling scenes. I do not remember, in all those years, that one of his children was ever glad to see him come home. From what I was able to gather of his early life, it seemed that this inability to establish contact with other people had always marked him and had been one of the things which had driven him out of New Orleans. There was something in him, therefore, groping and tentative, which was never expressed and which was buried with him. One saw it most clearly when he was facing new people and hoping to impress them. But he never did, not for long. We went from church to smaller and more improbable church, he found himself in less and less demand as a minister, and by the time he died none of his friends had come to see him for a long time. He had lived and died in an intolerable bitterness of spirit and it frightened me, as we drove him to the graveyard through those unquiet, ruined streets, to see how powerful and overflowing this bitterness could be and to realize that this bitterness now was mine.

When he died I had been away from home for a little over a year. In that year I had had time to become aware of the meaning of all my father's bitter warnings, had discovered the secret of his proudly pursed lips and rigid carriage: I had discovered the weight of white people in the world. I saw that this had been for my ancestors and now would be for me an awful thing to live with and that the bitterness which had helped to kill my father could also kill me.

He had been ill a long time — in the mind, as we now realized, reliving instances of his fantastic intransigence in the new light of his affliction and endeavoring to feel a sorrow for him which never, quite, came true. We had not known that he was being eaten up by paranoia, and the discovery that his cruelty, to our bodies and our minds, had been one of the symptoms of his illness was not, then, enough to enable us to forgive him. The younger children felt, quite simply, relief that he would not be coming home anymore. My mother's observation that it was he, after all, who had kept them alive all these years meant nothing because the problems of keeping children alive are not real for children. The older children felt, with my father gone, that they could invite their friends to the house without fear that their friends would be insulted or, as had sometimes happened with me, being told that their friends were in league with the devil and intended to rob our family of everything we owned. (I didn't fail to wonder, and it made me hate him, what on earth we owned that anybody else would want.)

His illness was beyond all hope of healing before anyone realized that he was ill. He had always been so strange and had lived, like a prophet, in such unimaginably close communion with the Lord that his long silences which were punctuated by moans and hallelujahs and snatches of old songs while he sat at the living-room window never seemed odd to us. It was not until he refused to eat because, he said, his family was trying to poison him that my mother was forced to accept as a fact what had, until then, been only an unwilling suspicion. When he was committed, it was discovered that he had tuberculosis and, as it turned out, the disease of his mind allowed the disease of his body to destroy him. For the doctors could not force him to eat, either, and, though he was fed intravenously, it was clear from the beginning that there was no hope for him.

In my mind's eye I could see him, sitting at the window, locked up in his terrors; hating and fearing every living soul including his children who had betrayed him, too, by reaching toward the world which had despised him. There were nine of us. I began to wonder what it could have felt like for such a man to have had nine children whom he could barely feed. He used to make little jokes about our poverty, which never, of course, seemed very funny to us; they could not have seemed very funny to him, either, or else our all too feeble response to them would never have caused such rages. He spent great energy and achieved, to our chagrin, no small amount of success in keeping us away from the people who surrounded us, people who had all-night rent parties[1] to which we listened when we should have been sleeping, people who cursed and drank and flashed razor blades on Lenox Avenue. He could not understand why, if they had so much energy to spare, they could not use it to make their lives better. He treated almost everybody on our block with a most uncharitable asperity and neither they, nor, of course, their children were slow to reciprocate.

---

[1] **rent parties:** Part of a Harlem tradition; musicians were often hired and contributions taken to help pay the rent for needy tenants. —EDS.

The only white people who came to our house were welfare workers   10
and bill collectors. It was almost always my mother who dealt with them,
for my father's temper, which was at the mercy of his pride, was never to be
trusted. It was clear that he felt their very presence in his home to be a violation: this was conveyed by his carriage, almost ludicrously stiff, and by his
voice, harsh and vindictively polite. When I was around nine or ten I wrote
a play which was directed by a young, white schoolteacher, a woman, who
then took an interest in me, and gave me books to read and, in order to corroborate my theatrical bent, decided to take me to see what she somewhat
tactlessly referred to as "real" plays. Theater-going was forbidden in our
house, but, with the really cruel intuitiveness of a child, I suspected that the
color of this woman's skin would carry the day for me. When, at school, she
suggested taking me to the theater, I did not, as I might have done if she had
been a Negro, find a way of discouraging her, but agreed that she should
pick me up at my house one evening. I then, very cleverly, left all the rest to
my mother, who suggested to my father, as I knew she would, that it would
not be very nice to let such a kind woman make the trip for nothing. Also,
since it was a schoolteacher, I imagine that my mother countered the idea of
sin with the idea of "education," which word, even with my father, carried
a kind of bitter weight.

Before the teacher came my father took me aside to ask *why* she was
coming, what *interest* she could possibly have in our house, in a boy like
me. I said I didn't know but I, too, suggested that it had something to do
with education. And I understood that my father was waiting for me to say
something—I didn't quite know what; perhaps that I wanted his protection
against this teacher and her "education." I said none of these things and the
teacher came and we went out. It was clear, during the brief interview in our
living room, that my father was agreeing very much against his will and that
he would have refused permission if he had dared. The fact that he did not
dare caused me to despise him: I had no way of knowing that he was facing
in that living room a wholly unprecedented and frightening situation.

Later, when my father had been laid off from his job, this woman became
very important to us. She was really a very sweet and generous woman and
went to a great deal of trouble to be of help to us, particularly during one
awful winter. My mother called her by the highest name she knew: she said
she was a "Christian." My father could scarcely disagree but during the
four or five years of our relatively close association he never trusted her and
was always trying to surprise in her open, Midwestern face the genuine,
cunningly hidden, and hideous motivation. In later years, particularly when
it began to be clear that this "education" of mine was going to lead me to
perdition, he became more explicit and warned me that my white friends
in high school were not really my friends and that I would see, when I was
older, how white people would do anything to keep a Negro down. Some of
them could be nice, he admitted, but none of them were to be trusted and
most of them were not even nice. The best thing was to have as little to do

with them as possible. I did not feel this way and I was certain, in my innocence, that I never would.

But the year which preceded my father's death had made a great change in my life. I had been living in New Jersey, working in defense plants, working and living among southerners, white and black. I knew about the south, of course, and about how southerners treated Negroes and how they expected them to behave, but it had never entered my mind that anyone would look at me and expect *me* to behave that way. I learned in New Jersey that to be a Negro meant, precisely, that one was never looked at but was simply at the mercy of the reflexes the color of one's skin caused in other people. I acted in New Jersey as I had always acted, that is as though I thought a great deal of myself—I had to *act* that way—with results that were, simply, unbelievable. I had scarcely arrived before I had earned the enmity, which was extraordinarily ingenious, of all my superiors and nearly all my co-workers. In the beginning, to make matters worse, I simply did not know what was happening. I did not know what I had done, and I shortly began to wonder what *anyone* could possibly do, to bring about such unanimous, active, and unbearably vocal hostility. I knew about Jim Crow but I had never experienced it. I went to the same self-service restaurant three times and stood with all the Princeton boys before the counter, waiting for a hamburger and coffee; it was always an extraordinarily long time before anything was set before me; but it was not until the fourth visit that I learned that, in fact, nothing had ever been set before me: I had simply picked something up. Negroes were not served there, I was told, and they had been waiting for me to realize that I was always the only Negro present. Once I was told this, I determined to go there all the time. But now they were ready for me and, though some dreadful scenes were subsequently enacted in that restaurant, I never ate there again.

It was the same story all over New Jersey, in bars, bowling alleys, diners, places to live. I was always being forced to leave, silently, or with mutual imprecations. I very shortly became notorious and children giggled behind me when I passed and their elders whispered or shouted—they really believed that I was mad. And it did begin to work on my mind, of course; I began to be afraid to go anywhere and to compensate for this I went places to which I really should not have gone and where, God knows, I had no desire to be. My reputation in town naturally enhanced my reputation at work and my working day became one long series of acrobatics designed to keep me out of trouble. I cannot say that these acrobatics succeeded. It began to seem that the machinery of the organization I worked for was turning over, day and night, with but one aim: to eject me. I was fired once, and contrived, with the aid of a friend from New York, to get back on the payroll; was fired again, and bounced back again. It took a while to fire me for the third time, but the third time took. There were no loopholes anywhere. There was not even any way of getting back inside the gates.

That year in New Jersey lives in my mind as though it were the year   15
during which, having an unsuspected predilection for it, I first contracted
some dread, chronic disease, the unfailing symptom of which is a kind of
blind fever, a pounding in the skull and fire in the bowels. Once this disease
is contracted, one can never be really carefree again, for the fever, without
an instant's warning, can recur at any moment. It can wreck more important
things than race relations. There is not a Negro alive who does not have this
rage in his blood — one has the choice, merely, of living with it consciously
or surrendering to it. As for me, this fever has recurred in me, and does, and
will until the day I die.

My last night in New Jersey, a white friend from New York took me to
the nearest big town, Trenton, to go to the movies and have a few drinks. As
it turned out, he also saved me from, at the very least, a violent whipping.
Almost every detail of that night stands out very clearly in my memory. I
even remember the name of the movie we saw because its title impressed
me as being so patly ironical. It was a movie about the German occupation
of France, starring Maureen O'Hara and Charles Laughton and called *This
Land Is Mine*. I remember the name of the diner we walked into when the
movie ended: it was the "American Diner." When we walked in the count-
erman asked what we wanted and I remember answering with the casual
sharpness which had become my habit: "We want a hamburger and a cup of
coffee, what do you think we want?" I do not know why, after a year of such
rebuffs, I so completely failed to anticipate his answer, which was, of course,
"We don't serve Negroes here." This reply failed to discompose me, at least
for the moment. I made some sardonic comment about the name of the diner
and we walked out into the streets.

This was the time of what was called the "brownout," when the lights
in all American cities were very dim. When we reentered the streets something happened to me which had the force of an optical illusion, or a nightmare. The streets were very crowded and I was facing north. People were
moving in every direction but it seemed to me, in that instant, that all of
the people I could see, and many more than that, were moving toward
me, against me, and that everyone was white. I remember how their faces
gleamed. And I felt, like a physical sensation, a *click* at the nape of my
neck as though some interior string connecting my head to my body had
been cut. I began to walk. I heard my friend call after me, but I ignored
him. Heaven only knows what was going on in his mind, but he had the
good sense not to touch me — I don't know what would have happened if he
had — and to keep me in sight. I don't know what was going on in my mind,
either; I certainly had no conscious plan. I wanted to do something to crush
these white faces, which were crushing me. I walked for perhaps a block or
two until I came to an enormous, glittering, and fashionable restaurant in
which I knew not even the intercession of the Virgin would cause me to be
served. I pushed through the doors and took the first vacant seat I saw, at a
table for two, and waited.

I do not know how long I waited and I rather wonder, until today, what I could possibly have looked like. Whatever I looked like, I frightened the waitress who shortly appeared, and the moment she appeared all of my fury flowed toward her. I hated her for her white face, and for her great, astounded, frightened eyes. I felt that if she found a black man so frightening I would make her fright worthwhile.

She did not ask me what I wanted, but repeated, as though she had learned it somewhere, "We don't serve Negroes here." She did not say it with the blunt, derisive hostility to which I had grown so accustomed, but, rather, with a note of apology in her voice, and fear. This made me colder and more murderous than ever. I felt I had to do something with my hands. I wanted her to come close enough for me to get her neck between my hands.

So I pretended not to have understood her, hoping to draw her closer. And   20 she did step a very short step closer, with her pencil poised incongruously over her pad, and repeated the formula: ". . . don't serve Negroes here."

Somehow, with the repetition of that phrase, which was already ringing in my head like a thousand bells of a nightmare, I realized that she would never come any closer and that I would have to strike from a distance. There was nothing on the table but an ordinary watermug half full of water, and I picked this up and hurled it with all my strength at her. She ducked and it missed her and shattered against the mirror behind the bar. And, with that sound, my frozen blood abruptly thawed, I returned from wherever I had been, I *saw*, for the first time, the restaurant, the people with their mouths open, already, as it seemed to me, rising as one man, and I realized what I had done, and where I was, and I was frightened. I rose and began running for the door. A round, potbellied man grabbed me by the nape of the neck just as I reached the doors and began to beat me about the face. I kicked him and got loose and ran into the streets. My friend whispered, "*Run!*" and I ran.

My friend stayed outside the restaurant long enough to misdirect my pursuers and the police, who arrived, he told me, at once. I do not know what I said to him when he came to my room that night. I could not have said much. I felt, in the oddest, most awful way, that I had somehow betrayed him. I lived it over and over and over again, the way one relives an automobile accident after it has happened and one finds oneself alone and safe. I could not get over two facts, both equally difficult for the imagination to grasp, and one was that I could have been murdered. But the other was that I had been ready to commit murder. I saw nothing very clearly but I did see this: that my life, my *real* life, was in danger, and not from anything other people might do but from the hatred I carried in my own heart.

TWO

I had returned home around the second week in June—in great haste because it seemed that my father's death and my mother's confinement were both but a matter of hours. In the case of my mother, it soon became clear that she had simply made a miscalculation. This had always been her tendency and I don't believe that a single one of us arrived in the world, or has since arrived anywhere else, on time. But none of us dawdled so intolerably about the business of being born as did my baby sister. We sometimes amused ourselves, during those endless, stifling weeks, by picturing the baby sitting within in the safe, warm dark, bitterly regretting the necessity of becoming a part of our chaos and stubbornly putting it off as long as possible. I understood her perfectly and congratulated her on showing such good sense so soon. Death, however, sat as purposefully at my father's bedside as life stirred within my mother's womb and it was harder to understand why he so lingered in that long shadow. It seemed that he had bent, and for a long time, too, all of his energies toward dying. Now death was ready for him but my father held back.

All of Harlem, indeed, seemed to be infected by waiting. I had never before known it to be so violently still. Racial tensions throughout this country were exacerbated during the early years of the war, partly because the labor market brought together hundreds of thousands of ill-prepared people and partly because Negro soldiers, regardless of where they were born, received their military training in the south. What happened in defense plants and army camps had repercussions, naturally, in every Negro ghetto. The situation in Harlem had grown bad enough for clergymen, policemen, educators, politicians, and social workers to assert in one breath that there was no "crime wave" and to offer, in the very next breath, suggestions as to how to combat it. These suggestions always seemed to involve playgrounds, despite the fact that racial skirmishes were occurring in the playgrounds, too. Playground or not, crime wave or not, the Harlem police force had been augmented in March, and the unrest grew—perhaps, in fact, partly as a result of the ghetto's instinctive hatred of policemen. Perhaps the most revealing news item, out of the steady parade of reports of muggings, stabbings, shootings, assaults, gang wars, and accusations of police brutality, is the item concerning six Negro girls who set upon a white girl in the subway because, as they all too accurately put it, she was stepping on their toes. Indeed she was, all over the nation.

I had never before been so aware of policemen, on foot, on horseback,   25 on corners, everywhere, always two by two. Nor had I ever been so aware of small knots of people. They were on stoops and on corners and in doorways, and what was striking about them, I think, was that they did not seem to be talking. Never, when I passed these groups, did the usual sound of a curse or a laugh ring out and neither did there seem to be any hum of gossip. There was certainly, on the other hand, occurring between them communication extraordinarily intense. Another thing that was striking was the unexpected diversity of the people who made up these groups. Usually, for example, one would see a group of sharpies standing on the street corner, jiving the passing chicks; or a group of older men, usually, for some reason, in the vicinity of a barber shop, discussing baseball scores, or the numbers, or making rather chilling observations about women they had known. Women, in a general way, tended to be seen less often together—unless they were church women, or very young girls, or prostitutes met together for an unprofessional instant. But that summer I saw the strangest combinations: large, respectable, churchly matrons standing on the stoops or the corners with their hair tied up, together with a girl in sleazy satin whose face bore the marks of gin and the razor, or heavy-set, abrupt, no-nonsense older men, in company with the most disreputable and fanatical "race" men,[2] or these same "race" men with the sharpies, or these sharpies with the churchly women. Seventh Day Adventists and Methodists and Spiritualists seemed to be hobnobbing with Holyrollers and they were all, alike, entangled with the most flagrant disbelievers; something heavy in their stance seemed to indicate that they had all, incredibly, seen a common vision, and on each face there seemed to be the same strange, bitter shadow.

The churchly women and the matter-of-fact, no-nonsense men had children in the Army. The sleazy girls they talked to had lovers there, the sharpies and the "race" men had friends and brothers there. It would have demanded an unquestioning patriotism, happily as uncommon in this country as it is undesirable, for these people not to have been disturbed by the bitter letters they received, by the newspaper stories they read, not to have been enraged by the posters, then to be found all over New York, which described the Japanese as "yellow-bellied Japs." It was only the "race" men, to be sure, who spoke ceaselessly of being revenged—how this vengeance was to be exacted was not clear—for the indignities and dangers suffered by Negro boys in uniform; but everybody felt a directionless, hopeless bitterness, as well as that panic which can scarcely be suppressed when one knows that a human being one loves is beyond one's reach, and in danger. This helplessness and this gnawing uneasiness does something, at length, to even the toughest mind. Perhaps the best way to sum all this up is to say that the people I knew felt, mainly, a peculiar kind of relief when they knew that their boys were being shipped out of the south, to do battle overseas. It was, perhaps, like feeling that the most dangerous part of a dangerous journey had been passed and that now, even if death should come, it would come with honor and without the complicity of their countrymen. Such a death would be, in short, a fact with which one could hope to live.

It was on the twenty-eighth of July, which I believe was a Wednesday, that I visited my father for the first time during his illness and for the last time in his life. The moment I saw him I knew why I had put off this visit so long. I had told my mother that I did not want to see him because I hated him. But this was not true. It was only that I *had* hated him and I wanted to hold on to this hatred. I did not want to look on him as a ruin: it was not a ruin

---

2 *"race" men:* Baldwin seems to be thinking of self-appointed spokesmen for racial consciousness and not serious black leaders. —EDS.

|||||||||||||||||||||||||||||||||||||||||||||||||||||||||||||||||||||||||||||||||||||||||||||||||||||||||||||||||||||||||||||||||

I had hated. I imagine that one of the reasons people cling to their hates so stubbornly is because they sense, once hate is gone, that they will be forced to deal with pain.

We traveled out to him, his older sister and myself, to what seemed to be the very end of a very Long Island. It was hot and dusty and we wrangled, my aunt and I, all the way out, over the fact that I had recently begun to smoke and, as she said, to give myself airs. But I knew that she wrangled with me because she could not bear to face the fact of her brother's dying. Neither could I endure the reality of her despair, her unstated bafflement as to what had happened to her brother's life, and her own. So we wrangled and I smoked and from time to time she fell into a heavy reverie. Covertly, I watched her face, which was the face of an old woman; it had fallen in, the eyes were sunken and lightless; soon she would be dying, too.

In my childhood—it had not been so long ago—I had thought her beautiful. She had been quick-witted and quick-moving and very generous with all the children and each of her visits had been an event. At one time one of my brothers and myself had thought of running away to live with her. Now she could no longer produce out of her handbag some unexpected and yet familiar delight. She made me feel pity and revulsion and fear. It was awful to realize that she no longer caused me to feel affection. The closer we came to the hospital the more querulous she became and at the same time, naturally, grew more dependent on me. Between pity and guilt and fear I began to feel that there was another me trapped in my skull like a jack-in-the-box who might escape my control at any moment and fill the air with screaming.

She began to cry the moment we entered the room and she saw him   30
lying there, all shriveled and still, like a little black monkey. The great, gleaming apparatus which fed him and would have compelled him to be still even if he had been able to move brought to mind, not beneficence, but torture; the tubes entering his arm made me think of pictures I had seen when a child, of Gulliver, tied down by the pygmies on that island. My aunt wept and wept, there was a whistling sound in my father's throat; nothing was said; he could not speak. I wanted to take his hand, to say something. But I do not know what I could have said, even if he could have heard me. He was not really in that room with us, he had at last really embarked on his journey; and though my aunt told me that he said he was going to meet Jesus, I did not hear anything except that whistling in his throat. The doctor came back and we left, into that unbearable train again, and home. In the morning came the telegram saying that he was dead. Then the house was suddenly full of relatives, friends, hysteria, and confusion and I quickly left my mother and the children to the care of those impressive women, who, in Negro communities at least, automatically appear at times of bereavement armed with lotions, proverbs, and patience, and an ability to cook. I went downtown. By the time I returned, later the same day, my mother had been carried to the hospital and the baby had been born.

THREE

For my father's funeral I had nothing black to wear and this posed a nagging problem all day long. It was one of those problems, simple, or impossible of solution, to which the mind insanely clings in order to avoid the mind's real trouble. I spent most of that day at the downtown apartment of a girl I knew, celebrating my birthday with whisky and wondering what to wear that night. When planning a birthday celebration one naturally does not expect that it will be up against competition from a funeral and this girl had anticipated taking me out that night, for a big dinner and a night club afterwards. Sometime during the course of that long day we decided that we would go out anyway, when my father's funeral service was over. I imagine I decided it, since, as the funeral hour approached, it became clearer and clearer to me that I would not know what to do with myself when it was over. The girl, stifling her very lively concern as to the possible effects of the whisky on one of my father's chief mourners, concentrated on being conciliatory and practically helpful. She found a black shirt for me somewhere and ironed it and, dressed in the darkest pants and jacket I owned, and slightly drunk, I made my way to my father's funeral.

The chapel was full, but not packed, and very quiet. There were, mainly, my father's relatives, and his children, and here and there I saw faces I had not seen since childhood, the faces of my father's one-time friends. They were very dark and solemn now, seeming somehow to suggest that they had known all along that something like this would happen. Chief among the mourners was my aunt, who had quarreled with my father all his life; by which I do not mean to suggest that her mourning was insincere or that she had not loved him. I suppose that she was one of the few people in the world who had, and their incessant quarreling proved precisely the strength of the tie that bound them. The only other person in the world, as far as I knew, whose relationship to my father rivaled my aunt's in depth was my mother, who was not there.

It seemed to me, of course, that it was a very long funeral. But it was, if anything, a rather shorter funeral than most, nor, since there were no overwhelming, uncontrollable expressions of grief, could it be called—if I dare to use the word—successful. The minister who preached my father's funeral sermon was one of the few my father had still been seeing as he neared his end. He presented to us in his sermon a man whom none of us had ever seen—a man thoughtful, patient, and forbearing, a Christian inspiration to all who knew him, and a model for his children. And no doubt the children, in their disturbed and guilty state, were almost ready to believe this; he had been remote enough to be anything and, anyway, the shock of the incontrovertible, that it was really our father lying up there in that casket, prepared the mind for anything. His sister moaned and this grief-stricken moaning was taken as corroboration. The other faces held a dark, noncommittal thoughtfulness. This was not the man they had known, but they had scarcely expected to be confronted with *him*; this was, in a sense deeper than questions of fact, the man they had not known, and the man they had not known may have been the real one. The real man, whoever he had been, had suffered and now he was dead: this was all that was sure and all that mattered now. Every man in the chapel hoped that when his hour came he, too, would be eulogized, which is to say forgiven, and that all of his lapses, greeds, errors, and strayings from the truth would be invested with coherence and looked upon with charity. This was perhaps the last thing human beings could give each other and it was what they demanded, after all, of the Lord. Only the Lord saw the midnight tears, only He was present when one of His children, moaning and wringing hands, paced up and down the room. When one slapped one's child in anger the recoil in the heart reverberated through heaven and became part of the pain of the universe. And when the children were hungry and sullen and distrustful and one watched them, daily, growing wilder, and further away, and running headlong into danger, it was the Lord who knew what the charged heart endured as the strap was laid to the backside; the Lord alone who knew what one *would* have said if one had had, like the Lord, the gift of the living word. It was the Lord who knew of the impossibility every parent in that room faced: how to prepare the child for the day when the child would be despised and how to *create* in the child—by what means?—a stronger antidote to this poison than one had found for oneself. The avenues, side streets, bars, billiard halls, hospitals, police stations, and even the playgrounds of Harlem—not to mention the houses of correction, the jails, and the morgue—testified to the potency of the poison while remaining silent as to the efficacy of whatever antidote, irresistibly raising the question of whether or not such an antidote existed; raising, which was worse, the question of whether or not an antidote was desirable; perhaps poison should be fought with poison. With these several schisms in the mind and with more terrors in the heart than could be named, it was better not to judge the man who had gone down under an impossible burden. It was better to remember: *Thou knowest this man's fall; but thou knowest not his wrassling.*

    While the preacher talked and I watched the children—years of changing their diapers, scrubbing them, slapping them, taking them to school, and scolding them had had the perhaps inevitable result of making me love them, though I am not sure I knew this then—my mind was busily breaking out with a rash of disconnected impressions. Snatches of popular songs, indecent jokes, bits of books I had read, movie sequences, faces, voices, political issues—I thought I was going mad; all these impressions suspended, as it were, in the solution of the faint nausea produced in me by the heat and liquor. For a moment I had the impression that my alcoholic breath, inefficiently disguised with chewing gum, filled the entire chapel. Then someone began singing one of my father's favorite songs and, abruptly, I was with him, sitting on his knee, in the hot, enormous, crowded church which was the first church we attended. It was the Abyssinian Baptist Church on 138th Street. We had not gone there long. With this image, a host of others came. I had forgotten, in the rage of my growing up, how proud my father had been of me when I was little. Apparently, I had had a voice and my father had liked to show me off before the members of the church. I had forgotten what he had looked like when he was pleased but now I remembered that he had always been grinning with pleasure when my solos ended. I even remembered certain expressions on his face when he teased my mother—had he loved her? I would never know. And when had it all begun to change? For now it seemed that he had not always been cruel. I remembered being taken for a haircut and scraping my knee on the footrest of the barber's chair and I remembered my father's face as he soothed my crying and applied the stinging iodine. Then I remembered our fights, fights which had been of the worst possible kind because my technique had been silence.

I remembered the one time in all our life together when we had really   35
spoken to each other.

It was on a Sunday and it must have been shortly before I left home. We were walking, just the two of us, in our usual silence, to or from church. I was in high school and had been doing a lot of writing and I was, at about this time, the editor of the high school magazine. But I had also been a Young Minister and had been preaching from the pulpit. Lately, I had been taking fewer engagements and preached as rarely as possible. It was said in the church, quite truthfully, that I was "cooling off."

My father asked me abruptly, "You'd rather write than preach, wouldn't you?"

I was astonished at his question—because it was a real question. I answered, "Yes."

That was all we said. It was awful to remember that that was all we had *ever* said.

The casket now was opened and the mourners were being led up the   40
aisle to look for the last time on the deceased. The assumption was that the family was too overcome with grief to be allowed to make this journey alone and I watched while my aunt was led to the casket and, muffled in black, and shaking, led back to her seat. I disapproved of forcing the children to look on their dead father, considering that the shock of his death, or, more truthfully, the shock of death as a reality, was already a little more than a child could bear, but my judgment in this matter had been overruled and there they were, bewildered and frightened and very small, being led, one by one, to the casket. But there is also something very gallant about children at such moments. It has something to do with their silence and gravity and with the fact that one cannot help them. Their legs, somehow, seem *exposed*, so that it is at once incredible and terribly clear that their legs are all they have to hold them up.

I had not wanted to go to the casket myself and I certainly had not wished to be led there, but there was no way of avoiding either of these forms. One of the deacons led me up and I looked on my father's face. I cannot say that it looked like him at all. His blackness had been equivocated by powder and there was no suggestion in that casket of what his power had or could have been. He was simply an old man dead, and it was hard to believe that he had ever given anyone either joy or pain. Yet, his life filled that room. Further up the avenue his wife was holding his newborn child. Life and death so close together, and love and hatred, and right and wrong, said something to me which I did not want to hear concerning man, concerning the life of man.

After the funeral, while I was downtown desperately celebrating my birthday, a Negro soldier, in the lobby of the Hotel Braddock, got into a fight with a white policeman over a Negro girl. Negro girls, white policemen, in or out of uniform, and Negro males—in or out of uniform—were part of the furniture of the lobby of the Hotel Braddock and this was certainly not the first time such an incident had occurred. It was destined, however, to receive an unprecedented publicity, for the fight between the policeman and the soldier ended with the shooting of the soldier. Rumor, flowing immediately to the streets outside, stated that the soldier had been shot in the back, an instantaneous and revealing invention, and that the soldier had died protecting a Negro woman. The facts were somewhat different—for example, the soldier had not been shot in the back, and was not dead, and the girl seems to have been as dubious a symbol of womanhood as her white counterpart in Georgia usually is, but no one was interested in the facts. They preferred the invention because this invention expressed and corroborated their hates and fears so perfectly. It is just as well to remember that people are always doing this. Perhaps many of those legends, including Christianity, to which the world clings began their conquest of the world with just some such concerted surrender to distortion. The effect, in Harlem, of this particular legend was like the effect of a lit match in a tin of gasoline. The mob gathered before the doors of the Hotel Braddock simply began to swell and to spread in every direction, and Harlem exploded.

The mob did not cross the ghetto lines. It would have been easy, for example, to have gone over Morningside Park on the west side or to have crossed the Grand Central railroad tracks at 125th Street on the east side, to wreak havoc in white neighborhoods. The mob seems to have been mainly interested in something more potent and real than the white face, that is, in white power, and the principal damage done during the riot of the summer of 1943 was to white business establishments in Harlem. It might have been a far bloodier story, of course, if, at the hour the riot began, these establishments had still been open. From the Hotel Braddock the mob fanned out, east and west along 125th Street, and for the entire length of Lenox, Seventh, and Eighth avenues. Along each of these avenues, and along each major side street—116th, 125th, 135th, and so on—bars, stores, pawnshops, restaurants, even little luncheonettes had been smashed open and entered and looted—looted, it might be added, with more haste than efficiency. The shelves really looked as though a bomb had struck them. Cans of beans and soup and dog food, along with toilet paper, corn flakes, sardines and milk tumbled every which way, and abandoned cash registers and cases of beer leaned crazily out of the splintered windows and were strewn along the avenues. Sheets, blankets, and clothing of every description formed a kind of path, as though people had dropped them while running. I truly had not realized that Harlem *had* so many stores until I saw them all smashed open; the first time the word *wealth* ever entered my mind in relation to

Harlem was when I saw it scattered in the streets. But one's first, incongruous impression of plenty was countered immediately by an impression of
waste. None of this was doing anybody any good. It would have been better
to have left the plate glass as it had been and the goods lying in the stores.

It would have been better, but it would also have been intolerable, for
Harlem had needed something to smash. To smash something is the ghetto's
chronic need. Most of the time it is the members of the ghetto who smash
each other, and themselves. But as long as the ghetto walls are standing there
will always come a moment when these outlets do not work. That summer,
for example, it was not enough to get into a fight on Lenox Avenue, or curse
out one's cronies in the barber shops. If ever, indeed, the violence which
fills Harlem's churches, pool halls, and bars erupts outward in a more direct
fashion, Harlem and its citizens are likely to vanish in an apocalyptic flood.
That this is not likely to happen is due to a great many reasons, most hidden
and powerful among them the Negro's real relation to the white American.
This relation prohibits, simply, anything as uncomplicated and satisfactory
as pure hatred. In order really to hate white people, one has to blot so much
out of the mind—and the heart—that this hatred itself becomes an exhausting and self-destructive pose. But this does not mean, on the other hand, that
love comes easily: the white world is too powerful, too complacent, too ready
with gratuitous humiliation, and, above all, too ignorant and too innocent
for that. One is absolutely forced to make perpetual qualifications and one's
own reactions are always canceling each other out. It is this, really, which
has driven so many people mad, both white and black. One is always in the
position of having to decide between amputation and gangrene. Amputation
is swift but time may prove that the amputation was not necessary—or one
may delay the amputation too long. Gangrene is slow, but it is impossible to
be sure that one is reading one's symptoms right. The idea of going through
life as a cripple is more than one can bear, and equally unbearable is the risk
of swelling up slowly, in agony, with poison. And the trouble, finally, is that
the risks are real even if the choices do not exist.

"But as for me and my house," my father had said, "we will serve the   45
Lord." I wondered, as we drove him to his resting place, what this line had
meant for him. I had heard him preach it many times. I had preached it once
myself, proudly giving it an interpretation different from my father's. Now
the whole thing came back to me, as though my father and I were on our
way to Sunday school and I were memorizing the golden text: *And if it seem*
evil unto you to serve the Lord, choose you this day whom you will serve;
whether the gods which your fathers served that were on the other side of
the flood, or the gods of the Amorites, in whose land ye dwell: but as for me
and my house, we will serve the Lord. I suspected in these familiar lines a
meaning which had never been there for me before. All of my father's texts
and songs, which I had decided were meaningless, were arranged before me
at his death like empty bottles, waiting to hold the meaning which life would
give them for me. This was his legacy: nothing is ever escaped. That bleakly
memorable morning I hated the unbelievable streets and the Negroes and

whites who had, equally, made them that way. But I knew that it was folly, as my father would have said, this bitterness was folly. It was necessary to hold on to the things that mattered. The dead man mattered, the new life mattered; blackness and whiteness did not matter; to believe that they did was to acquiesce in one's own destruction. Hatred, which could destroy so much, never failed to destroy the man who hated and this was an immutable law.

It began to seem that one would have to hold in the mind forever two ideas which seemed to be in opposition. The first idea was acceptance, the acceptance, totally without rancor, of life as it is, and men as they are: in the light of this idea, it goes without saying that injustice is a commonplace. But this did not mean that one could be complacent, for the second idea was of equal power: that one must never, in one's own life, accept these injustices as commonplace but must fight them with all one's strength. This fight begins, however, in the heart and it now had been laid to my charge to keep my own heart free of hatred and despair. This intimation made my heart heavy and, now that my father was irrecoverable, I wished that he had been beside me so that I could have searched his face for the answers which only the future would give me now. ●

The Reader's Presence

1. Why does Baldwin open with three events: his father's death, his youngest sibling's birth, and the race riots in Detroit and Harlem? How did the death of his father serve to change Baldwin's thinking about how he would deal with racism in his life? How does Baldwin make peace with his father's memory?

2. At the end of the essay, Baldwin remembers a biblical passage his father used to quote (paragraph 45). How does Baldwin reinterpret the passage after his father's death? What does it mean in the context of being his father's son? How does it help him make sense of the race riots in Harlem?

3. **VISUAL PRESENCE:** Look carefully at the portrait of James Baldwin (page 57). In what ways is Baldwin's posture consistent with the tone of his piece? How would you characterize his body language? Use specific details from the image in developing your response.

4. **CONNECTIONS:** Examine Baldwin's description of the Harlem race riots in the third section of his essay. How does Baldwin approach the riots as a native of Harlem and as an African American? What explanations does he give for the violence? How does he use the riots to explain the relations between white and black America? Compare Baldwin's discussion of the Harlem race riots to Ta-Nehisi Coates's consideration of violence in *Between the World and Me* (page 330). Coates writes: "Not being violent enough could cost me my body. Being too violent could cost me my body. We could not get out." Explain differences you find between the ways the two writers relate to violence. Do you think those differences can be explained by the ways historical conditions have changed in the roughly sixty years that separate the worlds of Baldwin and Coates? How does Baldwin account for racial tensions in his time? How does Coates? You might also consider Baldwin's thoughts on violence in light of Steven Pinker's "Violence Vanquished" (page 591). How do you think Pinker would explain the violent riots Baldwin describes?

The Writer at Work

JAMES BALDWIN on Black English

Everett Collection/Superstock

In the following piece, Baldwin takes up a subject that is periodically scrutinized by the American mass media: Is black English a language and, if so, what kind of language is it? Whatever its current status in the eyes of the dominant society, black English is an indisputable fact of everyday life for many Americans. When Baldwin writes that blacks have "endured and transcended" American racism by means of language, he echoes William Faulkner's belief that our compulsion to talk is what will save the human race.

Since Baldwin wrote this piece in 1979, the language he so ardently defends as necessary to African American strength in the face of "brutal necessity" (that is, in defense against racism) has entered the mainstream through the spread of hip-hop culture. What might Baldwin say about white speakers of black English? Are they simply another example of the appropriation of subcultural forms by the dominant culture, a means of containing or defusing resistance? The "rules of the language are dictated by what the language must convey," Baldwin writes. Who is using black English today? For what purposes?

❝ The argument concerning the use, or the status, or the reality, of black English is rooted in American history and has absolutely nothing to do with the question the argument supposes itself to be posing. The argument has nothing to do with language itself but with the *role* of language. Language, incontestably, reveals the speaker. Language, also, far more dubiously, is meant to define the other—and, in this case, the other is refusing to be defined by a language that has never been able to recognize him.

People evolve a language in order to describe and thus control their circumstances, or in order not to be submerged by a reality that they cannot articulate. (And, if they cannot articulate it, they are submerged.) A Frenchman living in Paris speaks a subtly and crucially different language from that of the man living in Marseilles; neither sounds very much like a man living in Quebec; and they would all have great difficulty in apprehending what the man from Guadeloupe, or Martinique, is saying, to say nothing of the man from Senegal—although the "common" language of all these areas is French. But each has paid, and is paying, a different price for this "common" language, in which, as it turns out, they are not saying, and cannot be saying, the

same things: They each have very different realities to articulate, or control.

What joins all languages, and all
men, is the necessity to confront life,
in order, not inconceivably, to outwit
death: The price for this is the acceptance, and achievement, of one's tem-
poral identity. So that, for example,
though it is not taught in the schools
(and this has the potential of becoming
a political issue) the south of France
still clings to its ancient and musical
Provençal, which resists being described
as a "dialect." And much of the tension
in the Basque countries, and in Wales,
is due to the Basque and Welsh determination not to allow their languages
to be destroyed. This determination
also feeds the flames in Ireland, for
among the many indignities the Irish
have been forced to undergo at English
hands is the English contempt for their
language.

It goes without saying, then, that
language is also a political instrument,
means, and proof of power. It is the
most vivid and crucial key to identity: It reveals the private identity, and
connects one with, or divorces one from,
the larger, public, or communal identity.
There have been, and are, times, and
places, when to speak a certain language could be dangerous, even fatal.
Or, one may speak the same language,
but in such a way that one's antecedents
are revealed, or (one hopes) hidden.
This is true in France, and is absolutely
true in England: The range (and reign) of
accents on that damp little island make
England coherent for the English and
totally incomprehensible for everyone
else. To open your mouth in England is
(if I may use black English) to "put your
business in the street": You have confessed your parents, your youth, your
school, your salary, your self-esteem,
and, alas, your future.

Now, I do not know what white
Americans would sound like if there had
never been any black people in the United
States, but they would not sound the way
they sound. *Jazz*, for example, is a very
specific sexual term, as in *jazz me, baby*,
but white people purified it into the Jazz
Age. *Sock it to me*, which means, roughly,
the same thing, has been adopted by
Nathaniel Hawthorne's descendants with
no qualms or hesitations at all, along
with *let it all hang out* and *right on! Beat
to his socks*, which was once the black's
most total and despairing image of poverty, was transformed into a thing called
the Beat Generation, which phenomenon was, largely, composed of *uptight*,
middle-class white people, imitating poverty, trying to *get down*, to get *with it*,
doing their *thing*, doing their despairing
best to be *funky*, which we, the blacks,
never dreamed of doing—we *were* funky,
baby, like *funky* was going out of style.

Now, no one can eat his cake and
have it, too, and it is late in the day to
attempt to penalize black people for
having created a language that permits
the nation its only glimpse of reality, a
language without which the nation would
be even more *whipped* than it is.

I say that the present skirmish is
rooted in American history, and it is. Black
English is the creation of the black diaspora. Blacks came to the United States
chained to each other, but from different
tribes: Neither could speak the other's language. If two black people, at that bitter
hour of the world's history, had been able
to speak to each other, the institution of
chattel slavery could never have lasted as
long as it did. Subsequently, the slave was
given, under the eye, and the gun, of his
master, Congo Square, and the Bible—or
in other words, and under these conditions, the slave began the formation of the
black church, and it is within this unprecedented tabernacle that black English

began to be formed. This was not, merely, as in the European example, the adoption of a foreign tongue, but an alchemy that transformed ancient elements into a new language: *A language comes into existence by means of brutal necessity, and the rules of the language are dictated by what the language must convey.*

There was a moment, in time, and in this place, when my brother, or my mother, or my father, or my sister, had to convey to me, for example, the danger in which I was standing from the white man standing just behind me, and to convey this with a speed, and in a language, that the white man could not possibly understand, and that, indeed, he cannot understand, until today. He cannot afford to understand it. This understanding would reveal to him too much about himself, and smash that mirror before which he has been frozen for so long.

Now, if this passion, this skill, this (to quote Toni Morrison) "sheer intelligence," this incredible music, the mighty achievement of having brought a people utterly unknown to, or despised by "history"—to have brought this people to their present, troubled, troubling, and unassailable and unanswerable place—if this absolutely unprecedented journey does not indicate that black English is a language, I am curious to know what definition of language is to be trusted.

A people at the center of the Western world, and in the midst of so hostile a population, has not endured and transcended by means of what is patronizingly called a "dialect." We, the blacks, are in trouble, certainly, but we are not doomed, and we are not inarticulate because we are not compelled to defend a morality that we know to be a lie.

The brutal truth is that the bulk of white people in America never had any interest in educating black people, except as this could serve white purposes. It is not the black child's language that is in question, it is not his language that is despised: It is his experience. A child cannot be taught by anyone who despises him, and a child cannot afford to be fooled. A child cannot be taught by anyone whose demand, essentially, is that the child repudiate his experience, and all that gives him sustenance, and enter a limbo in which he will no longer be black, and in which he knows that he can never become white. Black people have lost too many black children that way.

And, after all, finally, in a country with standards so untrustworthy, a country that makes heroes of so many criminal mediocrities, a country unable to face why so many of the nonwhite are in prison, or on the needle, or standing, futureless, in the streets—it may very well be that both the child, and his elder, have concluded that they have nothing whatever to learn from the people of a country that has managed to learn so little.**"**

Raymond Carver

MY FATHER'S LIFE

Son of a laborer and a homemaker in Clatskanie, Oregon, **RAYMOND CARVER** (1938–1988) resembled the characters in the short stories for which he is widely acclaimed. Once a manual laborer, a gas station attendant, and a janitor himself, Carver acquired his vision of the working class and the desperate lives of ordinary folk through direct experience. The Pacific Northwest of Carver's writing is peopled with types such as "the waitress, the bus driver, the mechanic, the hotel keeper" — people Carver feels are "good people." First published in *Esquire* in 1984, "My Father's Life," Carver's account of his father's hardships during the Great Depression, puts a biographical spin on these "good people." Carver's short story collections, *Will You Please Be Quiet, Please?* (1976), *Cathedral* (1984), and *Where I'm Calling From* (1988), were all nominated for

> **"Writers don't need tricks or gimmicks."**

the National Book Critics Circle Award. Both *Cathedral* and *Where I'm Calling From* were also nominated for the Pulitzer Prize for fiction in 1985 and 1989, respectively. Carver's poetry is collected in *Where Water Comes Together with Other Water* (1985), recipient of the 1986 Los Angeles Times Book Prize; *Ultramarine* (1986); and *A New Path to the Waterfall* (1989).

In his essay "On Writing," Carver states, "Writers don't need tricks or gimmicks or even necessarily to be the smartest fellows on the block. At the risk of appearing foolish, a writer sometimes needs to be able to just stand and gape at this or that thing—a sunset or an old shoe—in absolute and simple amazement."

MY DAD'S NAME was Clevie Raymond Carver. His family called him Raymond and friends called him C. R. I was named Raymond Clevie Carver, Jr. I hated the "Junior" part. When I was little, my dad called me Frog, which was okay. But later, like everybody else in the family, he began calling me Junior. He went on calling me this until I was thirteen or fourteen and announced that I wouldn't answer to that name any longer. So he began calling me Doc. From then until his death, on June 17, 1967, he called me Doc, or else Son.

When he died, my mother telephoned my wife with the news. I was away from my family at the time, between lives, trying to enroll in the School of Library Science at the University of Iowa. When my wife answered the phone, my mother blurted out, "Raymond's dead!" For a moment, my wife thought my mother was telling her that I was dead. Then my mother made it clear *which* Raymond she was talking about and my wife said, "Thank God. I thought you meant *my* Raymond."

My dad walked, hitched rides, and rode in empty boxcars when he went from Arkansas to Washington State in 1934, looking for work. I don't know whether he was pursuing a dream when he went out to Washington. I doubt it. I don't think he dreamed much. I believe he was simply looking for steady work at decent pay. Steady work was meaningful work. He picked apples for a time and then landed a construction laborer's job on the Grand Coulee Dam. After he'd put aside a little money, he bought a car and drove back to Arkansas to help his folks, my grandparents, pack up for the move west. He said later that they were about to starve down there, and this wasn't meant as a figure of speech. It was during that short while in Arkansas, in a town called Leola, that my mother met my dad on the sidewalk as he came out of a tavern.

"He was drunk," she said. "I don't know why I let him talk to me. His eyes were glittery. I wish I'd had a crystal ball." They'd met once, a year or so before, at a dance. He'd had girlfriends before her, my mother told me. "Your dad always had a girlfriend, even after we married. He was my first and last. I never had another man. But I didn't miss anything."

They were married by a justice of the peace on the day they left for Washington, this big, tall country girl and a farmhand-turned-construction worker. My mother spent her wedding night with my dad and his folks, all of them camped beside the road in Arkansas.   5

In Omak, Washington, my dad and mother lived in a little place not much bigger than a cabin. My grandparents lived next door. My dad was still working on the dam, and later, with the huge turbines producing electricity and the water backed up for a hundred miles into Canada, he stood in the crowd and heard Franklin D. Roosevelt when he spoke at the construction site. "He never mentioned those guys who died building that dam," my dad said. Some of his friends had died there, men from Arkansas, Oklahoma, and Missouri.

He then took a job in a sawmill in Clatskanie, Oregon, a little town alongside the Columbia River. I was born there, and my mother has a picture of my dad standing in front of the gate to the mill, proudly holding me up to face the camera. My bonnet is on crooked and about to come untied. His hat is pushed back on his forehead, and he's wearing a big grin. Was he going in to work or just finishing his shift? It doesn't matter. In either case, he had a job and a family. These were his salad days.

In 1941 we moved to Yakima, Washington, where my dad went to work as a saw filer, a skilled trade he'd learned in Clatskanie. When war broke out, he was given a deferment because his work was considered necessary to the war effort. Finished lumber was in demand by the armed services, and he kept his saws so sharp they could shave the hair off your arm.

After my dad had moved us to Yakima, he moved his folks into the same neighborhood. By the mid-1940s the rest of my dad's family—his brother, his sister, and her husband, as well as uncles, cousins, nephews, and most of their extended family and friends—had come out from Arkansas. All because my dad came out first. The men went to work at Boise Cascade, where my dad worked, and the women packed apples in the canneries. And in just a little while, it seemed—according to my mother—everybody was better off than my dad. "Your dad couldn't keep money," my mother said. "Money burned a hole in his pocket. He was always doing for others."

The first house I clearly remember living in, at 1515 South Fifteenth   10
Street, in Yakima, had an outdoor toilet. On Halloween night, or just any night, for the hell of it, neighbor kids, kids in their early teens, would carry our toilet away and leave it next to the road. My dad would have to get somebody to help him bring it home. Or these kids would take the toilet and stand it in somebody else's backyard. Once they actually set it on fire. But ours wasn't the only house that had an outdoor toilet. When I was old enough to know what I was doing, I threw rocks at the other toilets when I'd see someone go inside. This was called bombing the toilets. After a while, though, everyone went to indoor plumbing until, suddenly, our toilet was the last outdoor one in the neighborhood. I remember the shame I felt when my third-grade teacher, Mr. Wise, drove me home from school one day. I asked him to stop at the house just before ours, claiming I lived there.

I can recall what happened one night when my dad came home late to find that my mother had locked all the doors on him from the inside. He was drunk, and we could feel the house shudder as he rattled the door. When he'd managed to force open a window, she hit him between the eyes with a colander and knocked him out. We could see him down there on the grass. For years afterward, I used to pick up this colander—it was as heavy as a rolling pin—and imagine what it would feel like to be hit in the head with something like that.

It was during this period that I remember my dad taking me into the bedroom, sitting me down on the bed, and telling me that I might have to go live with my Aunt LaVon for a while. I couldn't understand what I'd done that meant I'd have to go away from home to live. But this, too—whatever prompted it—must have blown over, more or less, anyway, because we stayed together, and I didn't have to go live with her or anyone else.

I remember my mother pouring his whiskey down the sink. Sometimes she'd pour it all out and sometimes, if she was afraid of getting caught, she'd only pour half of it out and then add water to the rest. I tasted some of his whiskey once myself. It was terrible stuff, and I don't see how anybody could drink it.

After a long time without one, we finally got a car, in 1949 or 1950, a 1938 Ford. But it threw a rod the first week we had it, and my dad had to have the motor rebuilt.

"We drove the oldest car in town," my mother said. "We could have   15
had a Cadillac for all he spent on car repairs." One time she found someone

else's tube of lipstick on the floorboard, along with a lacy handkerchief. "See this?" she said to me. "Some floozy left this in the car."

Once I saw her take a pan of warm water into the bedroom where my dad was sleeping. She took his hand from under the covers and held it in the water. I stood in the doorway and watched. I wanted to know what was going on. This would make him talk in his sleep, she told me. There were things she needed to know, things she was sure he was keeping from her.

Every year or so, when I was little, we would take the North Coast Limited across the Cascade Range from Yakima to Seattle and stay in the Vance Hotel and eat, I remember, at a place called the Dinner Bell Cafe. Once we went to Ivar's Acres of Clams and drank glasses of warm clam broth.

In 1956, the year I was to graduate from high school, my dad quit his job at the mill in Yakima and took a job in Chester, a little sawmill town in northern California. The reasons given at the time for his taking the job had to do with a higher hourly wage and the vague promise that he might, in a few years' time, succeed to the job of head filer in this new mill. But I think, in the main, that my dad had grown restless and simply wanted to try his luck elsewhere. Things had gotten a little too predictable for him in Yakima. Also, the year before, there had been the deaths, within six months of each other, of both his parents.

But just a few days after graduation, when my mother and I were packed to move to Chester, my dad penciled a letter to say he'd been sick for a while. He didn't want us to worry, he said, but he'd cut himself on a saw. Maybe he'd got a tiny sliver of steel in his blood. Anyway, something had happened and he'd had to miss work, he said. In the same mail was an unsigned post-card from somebody down there telling my mother that my dad was about to die and that he was drinking "raw whiskey."

When we arrived in Chester, my dad was living in a trailer that belonged   20 to the company. I didn't recognize him immediately. I guess for a moment I didn't want to recognize him. He was skinny and pale and looked bewildered. His pants wouldn't stay up. He didn't look like my dad. My mother began to cry. My dad put his arm around her and patted her shoulder vaguely, like he didn't know what this was all about, either. The three of us took up life together in the trailer, and we looked after him as best we could. But my dad was sick, and he couldn't get any better. I worked with him in the mill that summer and part of the fall. We'd get up in the mornings and eat eggs and toast while we listened to the radio, and then go out the door with our lunch pails. We'd pass through the gate together at eight in the morning, and I wouldn't see him again until quitting time. In November I went back to Yakima to be closer to my girlfriend, the girl I'd made up my mind I was going to marry.

He worked at the mill in Chester until the following February, when he collapsed on the job and was taken to the hospital. My mother asked if I would come down there and help. I caught a bus from Yakima to Chester, intending to drive them back to Yakima. But now, in addition to being phys-ically sick, my dad was in the midst of a nervous breakdown, though none of us knew to call it that at the time. During the entire trip back to Yakima, he didn't speak, not even when asked a direct question. ("How do you feel, Raymond?" "You okay, Dad?") He'd communicate, if he communicated at all, by moving his head or by turning his palms up as if to say he didn't know or care. The only time he said anything on the trip, and for nearly a month afterward, was when I was speeding down a gravel road in Oregon and the car muffler came loose. "You were going too fast," he said.

Back in Yakima a doctor saw to it that my dad went to a psychiatrist. My mother and dad had to go on relief, as it was called, and the county paid for the psychiatrist. The psychiatrist asked my dad, "Who is the President?" He'd had a question put to him that he could answer. "Ike," my dad said. Nevertheless, they put him on the fifth floor of Valley Memorial Hospital and began giving him electroshock treatment. I was married by then and about to start my own family. My dad was still locked up when my wife went into this same hospital, just one floor down, to have our first baby. After she had delivered, I went upstairs to give my dad the news. They let me in through a steel door and showed me where I could find him. He was sitting on a couch with a blanket over his lap. *Hey*, I thought. *What in hell is happening to my dad?* I sat down next to him and told him he was a grandfather. He waited a minute and then he said, "I feel like a grandfather." That's all he said. He didn't smile or move. He was in a big room with a lot of other people. Then I hugged him, and he began to cry.

Somehow he got out of there. But now came the years when he couldn't work and just sat around the house trying to figure what next and what he'd done wrong in his life that he'd wound up like this. My mother went from job to crummy job. Much later she referred to that time he was in the hospital, and those years just afterward, as "when Raymond was sick." The word *sick* was never the same for me again.

In 1964, through the help of a friend, he was lucky enough to be hired on at a mill in Klamath, California. He moved down there by himself to see if he could hack it. He lived not far from the mill, in a one-room cabin not much different from the place he and my mother had started out living in when they went west. He scrawled letters to my mother, and if I called she'd read them aloud to me over the phone. In the letters, he said it was touch and go. Every day that he went to work, he felt like it was the most important day of his life. But every day, he told her, made the next day that much easier. He said for her to tell me he said hello. If he couldn't sleep at night, he said, he thought about me and the good times we used to have. Finally, after a couple of months, he regained some of his confidence. He could do the work and didn't think he had to worry that he'd let anybody down ever again. When he was sure, he sent for my mother.

He'd been off from work for six years and had lost everything in that 25 time—home, car, furniture, and appliances, including the big freezer that had been my mother's pride and joy. He'd lost his good name too—Raymond Carver was someone who couldn't pay his bills—and his self-respect was gone. He'd even lost his virility. My mother told my wife, "All during that time Raymond was sick we slept together in the same bed, but we didn't have relations. He wanted to a few times, but nothing happened. I didn't miss it, but I think he wanted to, you know."

During those years I was trying to raise my own family and earn a living. But, from one thing and another, we found ourselves having to move a lot. I couldn't keep track of what was going down in my dad's life. But I did have a chance one Christmas to tell him I wanted to be a writer. I might as well have told him I wanted to become a plastic surgeon. "What are you going to write about?" he wanted to know. Then, as if to help me out, he said, "Write about stuff you know about. Write about some of those fishing trips we took." I said I would, but I knew I wouldn't. "Send me what you write," he said. I said I'd do that, but then I didn't. I wasn't writing anything about fishing, and I didn't think he'd particularly care about, or even necessarily understand, what I was writing in those days. Besides, he wasn't a reader. Not the sort, anyway, I imagined I was writing for.

Then he died. I was a long way off, in Iowa City, with things still to say to him. I didn't have the chance to tell him goodbye, or that I thought he was doing great at his new job. That I was proud of him for making a comeback.

My mother said he came in from work that night and ate a big supper. Then he sat at the table by himself and finished what was left of a bottle of whiskey, a bottle she found hidden in the bottom of the garbage under some coffee grounds a day or so later. Then he got up and went to bed, where my mother joined him a little later. But in the night she had to get up and make a bed for herself on the couch. "He was snoring so loud I couldn't sleep," she said. The next morning when she looked in on him, he was on his back with his mouth open, his cheeks caved in. *Graylooking*, she said. She knew he was dead—she didn't need a doctor to tell her that. But she called one anyway, and then she called my wife.

Among the pictures my mother kept of my dad and herself during those early days in Washington was a photograph of him standing in front of a car, holding a beer and a stringer of fish. In the photograph he is wearing his hat back on his forehead and has this awkward grin on his face. I asked her for it and she gave it to me, along with some others. I put it up on my wall, and each time we moved, I took the picture along and put it up on another wall. I looked at it carefully from time to time, trying to figure out some things about my dad, and maybe myself in the process. But I couldn't. My dad just kept moving further and further away from me and back into time. Finally, in the course of another move, I lost the photograph. It was then that I tried to recall it, and at the same time make an attempt to say something about my dad, and how I thought that in some important ways we might be alike. I wrote the poem when I was living in an apartment house in an urban area south of San Francisco, at a time when I found myself, like my dad, having trouble with alcohol. The poem was a way of trying to connect up with him.

PHOTOGRAPH OF MY FATHER IN HIS TWENTY-SECOND YEAR

October. Here in this dank, unfamiliar kitchen
I study my father's embarrassed young man's face.
Sheepish grin, he holds in one hand a string
of spiny yellow perch, in the other
a bottle of Carlsberg beer.

In jeans and flannel shirt, he leans
against the front fender of a 1934 Ford.
He would like to pose brave and hearty for his posterity,
wear his old hat cocked over his ear.
All his life my father wanted to be bold.

But the eyes give him away, and the hands
that limply offer the string of dead perch
and the bottle of beer. Father, I love you,
yet how can I say thank you, I who can't hold my liquor either
and don't even know the places to fish.

The poem is true in its particulars, except that my dad died in June and   30
not October, as the first word of the poem says. I wanted a word with more
than one syllable to it to make it linger a little. But more than that, I wanted
a month appropriate to what I felt at the time I wrote the poem—a month
of short days and failing light, smoke in the air, things perishing. June was
summer nights and days, graduations, my wedding anniversary, the birthday of one of my children. June wasn't a month your father died in.

After the service at the funeral home, after we had moved outside, a
woman I didn't know came over to me and said, "He's happier where he
is now." I stared at this woman until she moved away. I still remember the
little knob of a hat she was wearing. Then one of my dad's cousins—I didn't
know the man's name—reached out and took my hand. "We all miss him,"
he said, and I knew he wasn't saying it just to be polite.

I began to weep for the first time since receiving the news. I hadn't been
able to before. I hadn't had the time, for one thing. Now, suddenly, I couldn't
stop. I held my wife and wept while she said and did what she could do to
comfort me there in the middle of that summer afternoon.

I listened to people say consoling things to my mother, and I was glad
that my dad's family had turned up, had come to where he was. I thought I'd
remember everything that was said and done that day and maybe find a way
to tell it sometime. But I didn't. I forgot it all, or nearly. What I do remember
is that I heard our name used a lot that afternoon, my dad's name and mine.
But I knew they were talking about my dad. *Raymond*, these people kept
saying in their beautiful voices out of my childhood. *Raymond.* ▪

The Reader's Presence

1. You may have noticed that Carver begins and ends his essay with a reference to his
   and his father's name. Of what importance is this information at the opening? What
   do we learn about his relationship with his father through their names? How do
   names matter in the final paragraph?

2. Reread the essay with particular attention to the conversations between father and son. How many reported conversations can you find? What do the conversations sound like? Can you find any pattern to them? If so, describe that pattern. To what extent do these conversations help you understand Carver's relationship with his father?

3. **CONNECTIONS:** Carver includes one of his own poems in his essay (paragraph 29), as does Alice Walker in "Beauty: When the Other Dancer Is the Self" (page 232). How do these writers explore the margins between poetry and prose? What do you think a poem communicates that a passage of prose may not?

Judith Ortiz Cofer

SILENT DANCING

Born in Puerto Rico, **JUDITH ORTIZ COFER** (1952–2016) moved with her family to New Jersey in 1955. Her poetry has appeared in numerous literary magazines, and several collections of her poems have been published. Her first novel, *The Line of the Sun* (1989), was nominated for the Pulitzer Prize. "Silent Dancing" is from Cofer's 1990 essay collection, *Silent Dancing: A Partial Remembrance of a Puerto Rican Childhood*, which won a PEN/Martha Albrand special citation for nonfiction. Among her notable books are *The Latin Deli: Prose and Poetry* (1993), *An Island Like You: Stories of the Barrio* (1995), *Woman in Front of the Sun* (2000), *The Meaning of Consuelo* (2003), and *Call Me Maria* (2004). She also published a children's picture book titled *The Poet Upstairs* (2012) and a memoir, *The Cruel Country* (2015).

> "The 'infinite variety' and power of language interest me."

Reflecting on her life as a writer, Cofer has said, "The 'infinite variety' and power of language interest me. I never cease to experiment with it. As a native Puerto Rican, my first language was Spanish. It was a challenge, not only to learn English, but to master it enough to teach it and—the ultimate goal—to write poetry in it." Cofer was for many years a professor of English and creative writing at the University of Georgia.

WE HAVE A HOME MOVIE of this party. Several times my mother and I have watched it together, and I have asked questions about the silent revelers coming in and out of focus. It is grainy and of short duration, but it's a great visual aid to my memory of life at that time. And it is in color—the only complete scene in color I can recall from those years.

||||||||||||||||||||||||||||||||||||||||||||||||||||||||||||||||||||||||||||||||||||||||||||||||||||||||||||||||||||||||||||||

We lived in Puerto Rico until my brother was born in 1954. Soon after, because of economic pressures on our growing family, my father joined the United States Navy. He was assigned to duty on a ship in Brooklyn Yard—a place of cement and steel that was to be his home base in the States until his retirement more than twenty years later. He left the Island first, alone, going to New York City and tracking down his uncle who lived with his family across the Hudson River in Paterson, New Jersey. There my father found a tiny apartment in a huge tenement that had once housed Jewish families but was just being taken over and transformed by Puerto Ricans, overflowing from New York City. In 1955 he sent for us. My mother was only twenty years old, I was not quite three, and my brother was a toddler when we arrived at *El Building*, as the place had been christened by its newest residents.

My memories of life in Paterson during those first few years are all in shades of gray. Maybe I was too young to absorb vivid colors and details, or to discriminate between the slate blue of the winter sky and the darker hues of the snow-bearing clouds, but that single color washes over the whole period. The building we lived in was gray, as were the streets, filled with slush the first few months of my life there. The coat my father had bought for me was similar in color and too big; it sat heavily on my thin frame.

I do remember the way the heater pipes banged and rattled, startling all of us out of sleep until we got so used to the sound that we automatically shut it out or raised our voices above the racket. The hiss from the valve punctuated my sleep (which has always been fitful) like a nonhuman presence in the room—a dragon sleeping at the entrance of my childhood. But the pipes were also a connection to all the other lives being lived around us. Having come from a house designed for a single family back in Puerto Rico—my mother's extended-family home—it was curious to know that strangers lived under our floor and above our heads, and that the heater pipe went through everyone's apartments. (My first spanking in Paterson came as a result of playing tunes on the pipes in my room to see if there would be an answer.) My mother was as new to this concept of beehive life as I was, but she had been given strict orders by my father to keep the doors locked, the noise down, ourselves to ourselves.

It seems that Father had learned some painful lessons about prejudice   5 while searching for an apartment in Paterson. Not until years later did I hear how much resistance he had encountered with landlords who were panicking at the influx of Latinos into a neighborhood that had been Jewish for a couple of generations. It made no difference that it was the American phenomenon of ethnic turnover which was changing the urban core of Paterson, and that the human flood could not be held back with an accusing finger.

"You Cuban?" one man had asked my father, pointing at his name tag on the Navy uniform—even though my father had the fair skin and light-brown hair of his northern Spanish background, and the name Ortiz is as common in Puerto Rico as Johnson is in the United States.

"No," my father had answered, looking past the finger into his adversary's angry eyes. "I'm Puerto Rican."

"Same shit." And the door closed.

My father could have passed as European, but we couldn't. My brother and I both have our mother's black hair and olive skin, and so we lived in El Building and visited our great-uncle and his fair children on the next block. It was their private joke that they were the German branch of the family. Not many years later that area too would be mainly Puerto Rican. It was as if the heart of the city map were being gradually colored brown—*café con leche*[1] brown. Our color.

The movie opens with a sweep of the living room. It is "typical" immi-   10
grant Puerto Rican decor for the time: The sofa and chairs are square and hard-looking, upholstered in bright colors (blue and yellow in this instance), and covered with the transparent plastic that furniture salesmen then were so adept at convincing women to buy. The linoleum on the floor is light blue; if it had been subjected to spike heels (as it was in most places), there were dime-sized indentations all over it that cannot be seen in this movie. The room is full of people dressed up: dark suits for the men, red dresses for the women. When I have asked my mother why most of the women are in red that night, she has shrugged, "I don't remember. Just a coincidence." She doesn't have my obsession for assigning symbolism to everything.

The three women in red sitting on the couch are my mother, my eighteen-year-old cousin, and her brother's girlfriend. The novia is just up from the Island, which is apparent in her body language. She sits up for-mally, her dress pulled over her knees. She is a pretty girl, but her posture makes her look insecure, lost in her full-skirted dress, which she has care-fully tucked around her to make room for my gorgeous cousin, her future sister-in-law. My cousin has grown up in Paterson and is in her last year of high school. She doesn't have a trace of what Puerto Ricans call la mancha *(literally, the stain: the mark of the new immigrant—something about the posture, the voice, or the humble demeanor that makes it obvious to every-one the person has just arrived on the mainland). My cousin is wearing a tight, sequined, cocktail dress. Her brown hair has been lightened with per-oxide around the bangs, and she is holding a cigarette expertly between her fingers, bringing it up to her mouth in a sensuous arc of her arm as she talks animatedly. My mother, who has come up to sit between the two women, both only a few years younger than herself, is somewhere between the poles they represent in our culture.*

It became my father's obsession to get out of the barrio, and thus we were never permitted to form bonds with the place or with the people who lived there. Yet El Building was a comfort to my mother, who never got over yearning for *la isla*. She felt surrounded by her language: The walls were thin, and voices speaking and arguing in Spanish could be heard all day.

---

[1] **café con leche:** Coffee with cream. In Puerto Rico it is sometimes prepared with boiled milk.—COFER'S NOTE.

Salsas blasted out of radios, turned on early in the morning and left on for company. Women seemed to cook rice and beans perpetually—the strong aroma of boiling red kidney beans permeated the hallways.

Though Father preferred that we do our grocery shopping at the supermarket when he came home on weekend leaves, my mother insisted that she could cook only with products whose labels she could read. Consequently, during the week I accompanied her and my little brother to *La Bodega*—a hole-in-the-wall grocery store across the street from El Building. There we squeezed down three narrow aisles jammed with various products. Goya's and Libby's—those were the trademarks that were trusted by her *mamá*, so my mother bought many cans of Goya beans, soups, and condiments, as well as little cans of Libby's fruit juices for us. And she also bought Colgate toothpaste and Palmolive soap. (The final *e* is pronounced in both these products in Spanish, so for many years I believed that they were manufactured on the Island. I remember my surprise at first hearing a commercial on television in which Colgate rhymed with "ate.") We always lingered at La Bodega, for it was there that Mother breathed best, taking in the familiar aromas of the foods she knew from Mamá's kitchen. It was also there that she got to speak to the other women of El Building without violating outright Father's dictates against fraternizing with our neighbors.

Yet Father did his best to make our "assimilation" painless. I can still see him carrying a real Christmas tree up several flights of stairs to our apartment, leaving a trail of aromatic pine. He carried it formally, as if it were a flag in a parade. We were the only ones in El Building that I knew of who got presents on both Christmas day and *dia de Reyes*, the day when the Three Kings brought gifts to Christ and to Hispanic children.

Our supreme luxury in El Building was having our own television set. It   15 must have been a result of Father's guilty feelings over the isolation he had imposed on us, but we were among the first in the barrio to have one. My brother quickly became an avid watcher of Captain Kangaroo and Jungle Jim, while I loved all the series showing families. By the time I started first grade, I could have drawn a map of Middle America as exemplified by the lives of characters in *Father Knows Best*, *The Donna Reed Show*, *Leave It to Beaver*, *My Three Sons*, and (my favorite) *Bachelor Father*, where John Forsythe treated his adopted teenage daughter like a princess because he was rich and had a Chinese houseboy to do everything for him. In truth, compared to our neighbors in El Building, *we* were rich. My father's Navy check provided us with financial security and a standard of life that the factory workers envied. The only thing his money could not buy us was a place to live away from the barrio—his greatest wish, Mother's greatest fear.

In the home movie the men are shown next, sitting around a card table set up in one corner of the living room, playing dominoes. The clack of the ivory pieces was a familiar sound. I heard it in many houses on the Island and in many apartments in Paterson. In Leave It to Beaver, *the Cleavers played bridge in every other episode; in my childhood, the men started*

every social occasion with a hotly debated round of dominoes. The women
would sit around and watch, but they never participated in the games.

　Here and there you can see a small child. Children were always brought
to parties and, whenever they got sleepy, were put to bed in the host's bed-
room. Babysitting was a concept unrecognized by the Puerto Rican women
I knew: A responsible mother did not leave her children with any stranger.
And in a culture where children are not considered intrusive, there was no
need to leave the children at home. We went where our mother went.

　Of my preschool years I have only impressions: the sharp bite of the
wind in December as we walked with our parents toward the brightly lit
stores downtown; how I felt like a stuffed doll in my heavy coat, boots, and
mittens; how good it was to walk into the five-and-dime and sit at the counter
drinking hot chocolate. On Saturdays our whole family would walk downtown to shop at the big department stores on Broadway. Mother bought all
our clothes at Penney's and Sears, and she liked to buy her dresses at the
women's specialty shops like Lerner's and Diana's. At some point we'd go
into Woolworth's and sit at the soda fountain to eat.

　We never ran into other Latinos at these stores or when eating out,
and it became clear to me only years later that the women from El Building shopped mainly in other places—stores owned by other Puerto Ricans
or by Jewish merchants who had philosophically accepted our presence in
the city and decided to make us their good customers, if not real neighbors
and friends. These establishments were located not downtown but in the
blocks around our street, and they were referred to generically as *La Tienda,*
El Bazar, La Bodega, La Botánica. Everyone knew what was meant. These
were the stores where your face did not turn a clerk to stone, where your
money was as green as anyone else's.

　One New Year's Eve we were dressed up like child models in the Sears　20
catalogue: my brother in a miniature man's suit and bow tie, and I in black
patent-leather shoes and a frilly dress with several layers of crinoline underneath. My mother wore a bright red dress that night, I remember, and spike
heels; her long black hair hung to her waist. Father, who usually wore his
Navy uniform during his short visits home, had put on a dark civilian suit for
the occasion: We had been invited to his uncle's house for a big celebration.
Everyone was excited because my mother's brother Hernan—a bachelor
who could indulge himself with luxuries—had bought a home movie camera, which he would be trying out that night.

　Even the home movie cannot fill in the sensory details such a gathering
left imprinted in a child's brain. The thick sweetness of women's perfumes
mixing with the ever-present smells of food cooking in the kitchen: meat
and plantain *pasteles*, as well as the ubiquitous rice dish made special with
pigeon peas—*gandules*—and seasoned with precious *sofrito*[2] sent up from

---

　[2]**sofrito:** A cooked condiment. A sauce composed of a mixture of fatback, ham, tomatoes,
and many island spices and herbs. It is added to many Puerto Rican dishes for a distinctive
flavor.—COFER'S NOTE.

the Island by somebody's mother or smuggled in by a recent traveler. *Sofrito* was one of the items that women hoarded, since it was hardly ever in stock at La Bodega. It was the flavor of Puerto Rico.

The men drank Palo Viejo rum, and some of the younger ones got weepy. The first time I saw a grown man cry was at a New Year's Eve party: He had been reminded of his mother by the smells in the kitchen. But what I remember most were the boiled *pasteles*—plantain or yucca rectangles stuffed with corned beef or other meats, olives, and many other savory ingredients, all wrapped in banana leaves. Everybody had to fish one out with a fork. There was always a "trick" pastel—one without stuffing—and whoever got that one was the "New Year's Fool."

There was also the music. Long-playing albums were treated like precious china in these homes. Mexican recordings were popular, but the songs that brought tears to my mother's eyes were sung by the melancholy Daniel Santos, whose life as a drug addict was the stuff of legend. Felipe Rodríguez was a particular favorite of couples, since he sang about faithless women and brokenhearted men. There is a snatch of one lyric that has stuck in my mind like a needle on a worn groove: *De piedra ha de ser mi cama, de piedra la cabezera . . . la mujer que a mi me quiera . . . ha de quererme de veras. Ay, Ay, Ay, corazón, porque no amas.*[3] . . . I must have heard it a thousand times since the idea of a bed made of stone, and its connection to love, first troubled me with its disturbing images.

The five-minute home movie ends with people dancing in a circle—the creative filmmaker must have set it up so that all of them could file past him. It is both comical and sad to watch silent dancing. Since there is no justification for the absurd movements that music provides for some of us, people appear frantic, their faces embarrassingly intense. It's as if you were watching sex. Yet for years I've had dreams in the form of this home movie. In a recurring scene, familiar faces push themselves forward into my mind's eyes, plastering their features into distorted close-ups. And I'm asking them: "Who is *she*? Who is the old woman I don't recognize? Is she an aunt? Somebody's wife? Tell me who she is."

"See the beauty mark on her cheek as big as a hill on the lunar landscape of her face—well, that runs in the family. The women on your father's side of the family wrinkle early; it's the price they pay for that fair skin. The young girl with the green stain on her wedding dress is *La Novia*—just up from the Island. See, she lowers her eyes when she approaches the camera, as she's supposed to. Decent girls never look at you directly in the face. *Humilde*, humble, a girl should express humility in all her actions. She will make a good wife for your cousin. He should consider himself lucky to have met her only weeks after she arrived here. If he marries her quickly, she will make him a good Puerto Rican–style wife; but if he waits too long, she will be corrupted by the city—just like your cousin there."

   [3]**De piedra ha de ser . . . amas:** Lyrics from a popular romantic ballad (called a *bolero* in Puerto Rico). Freely translated: "My bed will be made of stone, of stone also my headrest (or pillow), the woman who (dares to) love me, will have to love me for real. Ay, Ay, Ay, my heart, why can't you (let me) love. . . ." —COFER'S NOTE.

"She means me. I do what I want. This is not some primitive island I live on. Do they expect me to wear a black mantilla on my head and go to mass every day? Not me. I'm an American woman, and I will do as I please. I can type faster than anyone in my senior class at Central High, and I'm going to be a secretary to a lawyer when I graduate. I can pass for an American girl anywhere—I've tried it. At least for Italian, anyway—I never speak Spanish in public. I hate these parties, but I wanted the dress. I look better than any of these *humildes* here. My life is going to be different. I have an American boyfriend. He is older and has a car. My parents don't know it, but I sneak out of the house late at night sometimes to be with him. If I marry him, even my name will be American. I hate rice and beans—that's what makes these women fat."

"Your *prima*[4] is pregnant by that man she's been sneaking around with. Would I lie to you? I'm your *Tía Política*,[5] your great-uncle's common-law wife—the one he abandoned on the Island to go marry your cousin's mother. *I* was not invited to this party, of course, but I came anyway. I came to tell you that story about your cousin that you've always wanted to hear. Do you remember the comment your mother made to a neighbor that has always haunted you? The only thing you heard was your cousin's name, and then you saw your mother pick up your doll from the couch and say: 'It was as big as this doll when they flushed it down the toilet.' This image has bothered you for years, hasn't it? You had nightmares about babies being flushed down the toilet, and you wondered why anyone would do such a horrible thing. You didn't dare ask your mother about it. She would only tell you that you had not heard her right, and yell at you for listening to adult conversations. But later, when you were old enough to know about abortions, you suspected.

"I am here to tell you that you were right. Your cousin was growing an *Americanito* in her belly when this movie was made. Soon after she put something long and pointy into her pretty self, thinking maybe she could get rid of the problem before breakfast and still make it to her first class at the high school. Well, *Niña*,[6] her screams could be heard downtown. Your aunt, her mamá, who had been a midwife on the Island, managed to pull the little thing out. Yes, they probably flushed it down the toilet. What else could they do with it—give it a Christian burial in a little white casket with blue bows and ribbons? Nobody wanted that baby—least of all the father, a teacher at her school with a house in West Paterson that he was filling with real children, and a wife who was a natural blonde.

"Girl, the scandal sent your uncle back to the bottle. And guess where your cousin ended up? Irony of ironies. She was sent to a village in Puerto Rico to live with a relative on her mother's side: a place so far away from civilization that you have to ride a mule to reach it. A real change in scenery. She found a man there—women like that cannot live without male company—but believe me, the men in Puerto Rico know how to put a saddle on a woman like her. *La Gringa*,[7] they call her. Ha, ha, ha. *La Gringa* is what she always wanted to be. . . ."

The old woman's mouth becomes a cavernous black hole I fall into. And as I fall, I can feel the reverberations of her laughter. I hear the echoes of her last

[4] **prima:** Female cousin.—COFER'S NOTE.
[5] **Tía Política:** Aunt by marriage.—COFER'S NOTE.
[6] **Niña:** Girl.—COFER'S NOTE.
[7] **La Gringa:** Derogatory epithet used here to ridicule a Puerto Rican girl who wants to look like a blonde North American.—COFER'S NOTE.

mocking words: *La Gringa, La Gringa!* And the conga line keeps moving silently past me. There is no music in my dream for the dancers.

When Odysseus visits Hades to see the spirit of his mother, he makes an   25 offering of sacrificial blood, but since all the souls crave an audience with the living, he has to listen to many of them before he can ask questions. I, too, have to hear the dead and the forgotten speak in my dream. Those who are still part of my life remain silent, going around and around in their dance. The others keep pressing their faces forward to say things about the past.

My father's uncle is last in line. He is dying of alcoholism, shrunken and shriveled like a monkey, his face a mass of wrinkles and broken arteries. As he comes closer I realize that in his features I can see my whole family. If you were to stretch that rubbery flesh, you could find my father's face, and deep within *that* face—my own. I don't want to look into those eyes ringed in purple. In a few years he will retreat into silence, and take a long, long time to die. *Move back, Tío,* I tell him. *I don't want to hear what you have to say. Give the dancers room to move. Soon it will be midnight. Who is the New Year's Fool this time?* ⬤

The Reader's Presence

1. In "Silent Dancing," Cofer explores the personal, familial, and communal transformations that resulted from moving in the 1950s to Paterson, New Jersey—to "a huge tenement that had once housed Jewish families" (paragraph 2) and to a new community that emerged from the sprawling barrio that Puerto Ricans "overflowing from New York City" (paragraph 2) called home. Reread the essay carefully, and summarize the transformations that occurred in the life of the narrator, her family, and their larger Puerto Rican community.

2. Cofer uses an account of a home movie to create a structure for her essay. What are the specific advantages and disadvantages of this strategy? How, for example, does the home movie serve as "a great visual aid" (paragraph 1) to recounting life in the barrio of Paterson, New Jersey? What effect does the fact that the home movie is in color have on what Cofer notices? on how she writes?

3. Because Cofer's essay is built around the occasion of watching a home movie, the narrator assumes the position of an observer of the scenes and people Cofer describes. What specific strategies as a writer does Cofer use to establish a presence for herself in this narrative and descriptive account of growing up?

4. **VISUAL PRESENCE:** Cofer selected a photograph of herself when she was two years old for the cover of *Silent Dancing* (see page 75). Why do you think Cofer chose this image for the cover? What message about the author does this picture convey? Cite specific details from the image in your response.

5. **CONNECTIONS:** In his attempt to aid the family's "assimilation" into American culture, Cofer's father forbids his wife and children from making friends in "El Building." Cofer and her mother were expected "to keep the doors locked, the noise down, ourselves to ourselves" (paragraph 4). As a result, Cofer at times feels alienated from her own relatives. How does her situation compare to that of the narrators in Ha Jin's "Arrival" (page 129) and Jamaica Kincaid's "The Estrangement" (page 136)?

The Writer at Work

JUDITH ORTIZ COFER on Memory and Personal Essays

The book cover is reprinted with permission from the publisher of *Silent Dancing: The Partial Remembrance of a Puerto Rican Childhood* by Judith Ortiz Cofer (© Arte Publico Press–University of Houston)

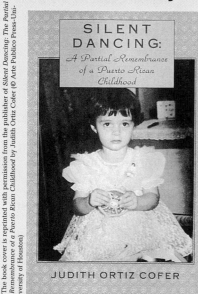

SILENT DANCING:
A Partial Remembrance of a Puerto Rican Childhood

JUDITH ORTIZ COFER

In setting out to write essays recounting her family history, Judith Ortiz Cofer found in Virginia Woolf a brilliant mentor and guide who taught her how to release the creative power of memory. In the following preface to *Silent Dancing: A Partial Remembrance of a Puerto Rican Childhood*, Cofer pays tribute to Woolf, who "understood that the very act of reclaiming her memories could provide a writer with confidence in the power of art to discover meaning and truth in ordinary events." How do Cofer's remarks in the preface (which she called "Journey to a Summer's Afternoon"), along with Woolf's "The Death of the Moth" (page 499), help illuminate the artistry of Cofer's own essay, "Silent Dancing"?

The author at the age of two, from the cover of *Silent Dancing: A Partial Remembrance of a Puerto Rican Childhood*, by Judith Ortiz Cofer. Published in 1990 by Arte Publico Press (Houston, Texas).

❝ As one gets older, childhood years are often conveniently consolidated into one perfect summer's afternoon. The events can be projected on a light blue screen; the hurtful parts can be edited out, and the moments of joy brought in sharp focus to the foreground. It is our show. But with all that on the cutting room floor, what remains to tell?

Virginia Woolf, whose vision guided my efforts as I tried to recall the faces and words of the people who are a part of my "summer's afternoon," wrote of the problem of writing truth from memory. In "A Sketch of the Past" she says, "But if I turn to my mother, how difficult it is to single her out as she really was; to imagine what she was thinking, to put a single sentence into her mouth." She accepts the fact that in writing about one's life,

one often has to rely on that combination of memory, imagination, and strong emotion that may result in "poetic truth." In preparing to write her memoirs Woolf said, "I dream, I make up pictures of a summer's afternoon."

In one of her essays from her memoir *Moments of Being*, Woolf recalls the figure of her beautiful and beloved mother who died while the author was still a child, leaving her a few precious "moments of being" from which the mature woman must piece together a childhood. And she does so not to showcase her life, extraordinary as it was, but rather out of a need most of us feel at some point to study ourselves and our lives in retrospect; to understand what people and events formed us (and, yes, what and who hurt us, too).

From "A Sketch of the Past": "Many bright colors; many distinct sounds; some human beings, caricatures; several violent moments of being, always including a circle of the scene they cut out: and all surrounded by a vast space—that is a rough visual description of childhood. This is how I shape it; and how I see myself as a child. . . ."

This passage illustrates the approach that I was seeking in writing about my family. I wanted the essays to be, not just family history, but also creative explorations of known territory. I wanted to trace back through scenes based on my "moments of being" the origins of my creative imagination. As a writer, I am, like most artists, interested in the genesis of ideas: How does a poem begin? Can the process be triggered at will? What compels some of us to examine and re-examine our lives in poems, stories, novels, memoirs?

Much of my writing begins as a meditation on past events. But memory for me is the "jumping off" point; I am not, in my poetry and my fiction writing, a slave to memory. I like to believe that the poem or story contains the "truth" of art rather than the factual, historical truth that the journalist, sociologist, scientist—most of the rest of the world—must adhere to. Art gives me that freedom. But in writing these "essays" (the Spanish word for essay, *ensayo*, suits my meaning here better—it can mean "a rehearsal," an exercise or practice), I faced the possibility that the past is mainly a creation of the imagination also, although there are facts one can research and confirm. The biographer's time-honored task can be employed on one's own life too. There are birth, marriage, and death certificates on file, there are letters and family photographs in someone's desk or attic; and there are the relatives who have assigned themselves the role of genealogist or family bard, recounting at the least instigation the entire history of your clan. One can go to these sources and come up with a *Life* in several volumes that will make your mother proud and give you the satisfaction of having "preserved" something. I am not interested in merely "canning" memories, however, and Woolf gave me the focus that I needed to justify this work. Its intention is not to chronicle my life—which in my case is still very much "in-progress," nor are there any extraordinary accomplishments to showcase; neither is it meant to be a record of public events and personal histories (in fact, since most of the characters in these essays are based on actual, living persons and real places, whenever I felt that it was necessary to protect their identities, I changed names, locations, etc.). Then, what is the purpose of calling this collection nonfiction or a memoir? Why not just call it fiction? Once again I must turn to my literary mentor for this project, Virginia Woolf, for an answer: like her, I wanted to try to connect myself to the threads of lives that have touched mine and at some point converged into the tapestry that is my memory of childhood. Virginia Woolf understood that the very act of reclaiming her memories could provide a writer with confidence in the power of art to discover meaning and truth in ordinary events. She was a time-traveler who saw the past as a real place one could return to by following the tracks left by strong emotions: "I feel that strong emotion must leave its trace; and it is only a question of discovering how we can get ourselves attached to it, so that we shall be able to live our lives through from the start."[1]

It was this winding path of memory, marked by strong emotions, that I followed in my *ensayos* of a life.**"**

[1]All quotes by Virginia Woolf are from *Moments of Being* (Harcourt Brace Jovanovich, Inc.).
—COFER'S NOTE.

Frederick Douglass

LEARNING TO READ AND WRITE

Born into slavery, **FREDERICK DOUGLASS** (1817?–1895) was taken from his mother as an infant and denied any knowledge of his father's identity. He escaped to the north at the age of twenty-one and created a new identity for himself as a free man. He educated himself and went on to become one of the most eloquent orators and persuasive writers of the nineteenth century. He was a national leader in the abolition movement and, among other activities, founded and edited the *North Star* and *Douglass' Monthly*. His public service included appointments as U.S. marshal and consul general to the Republic of Haiti. His most lasting literary accomplishment was his memoirs, which he revised several times before they were published as *The Life and Times of Frederick Douglass* (1881 and 1892). "Learning to Read and Write" is taken from these memoirs.

> Born into slavery, Frederick Douglass was taken from his mother as an infant and denied any knowledge of his father's identity.

Douglass overcame his initial reluctance to write his memoirs because, as he put it, "not only is slavery on trial, but unfortunately, the enslaved people are also on trial. It is alleged that they are, naturally, inferior; that they are so low in the scale of humanity, and so utterly stupid, that they are unconscious of their wrongs, and do not apprehend their rights." Therefore, wishing to put his talents to work "to the benefit of my afflicted people," Douglass agreed to write the story of his life.

I LIVED IN MASTER HUGH'S FAMILY about seven years. During this time, I succeeded in learning to read and write. In accomplishing this, I was compelled to resort to various stratagems. I had no regular teacher. My mistress, who had kindly commenced to instruct me, had, in compliance with the advice and direction of her husband, not only ceased to instruct, but had set her face against my being instructed by anyone else. It is due, however, to my mistress to say of her, that she did not adopt this course of treatment immediately. She at first lacked the depravity indispensable to shutting me up in mental darkness. It was at least necessary for her to have some training in the exercise of irresponsible power, to make her equal to the task of treating me as though I were a brute.

My mistress was, as I have said, a kind and tender-hearted woman; and in the simplicity of her soul she commenced, when I first went to live with her, to treat me as she supposed one human being ought to treat another. In entering upon the duties of a slaveholder, she did not seem to perceive that I sustained to her the relation of a mere chattel, and that for her to treat me as a human being was not only wrong, but dangerously so. Slavery proved as injurious to her as it did to me. When I went there, she was a pious, warm, and tender-hearted woman. There was no sorrow or suffering for which she had not a tear. She had bread for the hungry, clothes for the naked, and comfort for every mourner that came within her reach. Slavery soon proved its ability to divest her of these heavenly qualities. Under its influence, the tender heart became stone, and the lamb-like disposition gave way to one of tiger-like fierceness. The first step in her downward course was in her ceasing to instruct me. She now commenced to practice her husband's precepts. She finally became even more violent in her opposition than her husband himself. She was not satisfied with simply doing as well as he had commanded; she seemed anxious to do better. Nothing seemed to make her more angry than to see me with a newspaper. She seemed to think that here lay the danger. I have had her rush at me with a face made all up of fury, and snatch from me a newspaper, in a manner that fully revealed her apprehension. She was an apt woman; and a little experience soon demonstrated, to her satisfaction, that education and slavery were incompatible with each other.

From this time I was most narrowly watched. If I was in a separate room any considerable length of time, I was sure to be suspected of having a book, and was at once called to give an account of myself. All this, however, was too late. The first step had been taken. Mistress, in teaching me the alphabet, had given me the *inch*, and no precaution could prevent me from taking the *ell*.

The plan which I adopted, and the one by which I was most successful, was that of making friends of all the little white boys whom I met in the street. As many of these as I could, I converted into teachers. With their kindly aid, obtained at different times and in different places, I finally succeeded in learning to read. When I was sent to errands, I always took my book with me, and by doing one part of my errand quickly, I found time to get a lesson before my return. I used also to carry bread with me, enough of which was always in the house, and to which I was always welcome; for I was much better off in this regard than many of the poor white children in our neighborhood. This bread I used to bestow upon the hungry little urchins, who, in return, would give me that more valuable bread of knowledge. I am strongly tempted to give the names of two or three of those little boys, as a testimonial of the gratitude and affection I bear them; but prudence forbids—not that it would injure me, but it might embarrass them; for it is almost an unpardonable offense to teach slaves to read in this Christian country. It is enough to say of the dear little fellows, that they lived on Philpot Street, very near Durgin and Bailey's ship-yard. I used to talk this matter of slavery over with them. I would sometimes say to them, I wished I could be as free as they would be when they got to be men. "You will be free as soon as you are twenty-one, *but I am a slave for life*! Have not I as good a right to be free as you have?" These words used to trouble them; they would express for me the liveliest sympathy, and console me with the hope that something would occur by which I might be free.

I was now about twelve years old, and the thought of being *a slave for*   5
life began to bear heavily upon my heart. Just about this time, I got hold of a book entitled *The Columbian Orator*. Every opportunity I got, I used to read this book. Among much of other interesting matter, I found in it a dialogue between a master and his slave. The slave was represented as having run away from his master three times. The dialogue represented the conversation which took place between them, when the slave was retaken the third time. In this dialogue, the whole argument in behalf of slavery was brought forward by the master, all of which was disposed of by the slave. The slave was made to say some very smart as well as impressive things in reply to his master—things which had the desired though unexpected effect; for the conversation resulted in the voluntary emancipation of the slave on the part of the master.

In the same book, I met with one of Sheridan's[1] mighty speeches on and in behalf of Catholic emancipation. These were choice documents to me. I read them over and over again with unabated interest. They gave tongue to interesting thoughts of my own soul, which had frequently flashed through my mind, and died away for want of utterance. The moral which I gained from the dialogue was the power of truth over the conscience of even a slaveholder. What I got from Sheridan was a bold denunciation of slavery, and a powerful vindication of human rights. The reading of these documents enabled me to utter my thoughts, and to meet the arguments brought forward to sustain slavery; but while they relieved me of one difficulty, they brought on another even more painful than the one of which I was relieved. The more I read, the more I was led to abhor and detest my enslavers. I could regard them in no other light than a band of successful robbers, who had left their homes, and gone to Africa, and stolen us from our homes, and in a strange land reduced us to slavery. I loathed them as being the meanest as well as the most wicked of men. As I read and contemplated the subject, behold! that very discontentment which Master Hugh had predicted would follow my learning to read had

---

1 **Sheridan's:** Richard Brinsley Butler Sheridan (1751–1816), Irish dramatist and orator. —EDS.

1861 advertisement to capture a runaway slave in Maryland.

already come, to torment and sting my soul to unutterable anguish. As I writhed under it, I would at times feel that learning to read had been a curse rather than a blessing. It had given me a view of my wretched condition, without the remedy. It opened my eyes to the horrible pit, but to no ladder upon which to get out. In moments of agony, I envied my fellow-slaves for their stupidity. I have often wished myself a beast. I preferred the condition of the meanest reptile to my own. Anything, no matter what, to get rid of thinking! It was this everlasting thinking of my condition that tormented me. There was no getting rid of it. It was pressed upon me by every object within sight or hearing, animate or inanimate. The silver trump of freedom had roused my soul to eternal wakefulness. Freedom now appeared, to disappear no more forever. It was heard in every sound, and seen in every thing. It was ever present to torment me with a sense of my wretched condition. I saw nothing without seeing it, I heard nothing without hearing it, and felt nothing without feeling it. It looked from every star, it smiled in every calm, breathed in every wind, and moved in every storm.

I often found myself regretting my own existence, and wishing myself dead; and but for the hope of being free, I have no doubt but that I should have killed myself, or done something for which I should have been killed. While in this state of mind, I was eager to hear anyone speak of slavery. I was a ready listener. Every little while, I could hear something about the abolitionists. It was some time before I found what the word meant. It was always used in such connections as to make it an interesting word to me. If a slave ran away and succeeded in getting clear, or if a slave killed his master, set fire to a barn, or did anything very wrong in the mind of a slaveholder, it was spoken of as the fruit of *abolition*. Hearing the word in this connection very often, I set about learning what it meant. The dictionary afforded me little or no help. I found it was "the act of abolishing"; but then I did not know what was to be abolished. Here I was perplexed. I did not dare to ask anyone about its meaning, for I was satisfied that it was something they wanted me to know very little about. After a patient waiting, I got one of our city papers, containing an account of the number of petitions from the North, praying for the abolition of slavery in the District of Columbia, and of the slave trade between the States. From this time I understood the words *abolition* and *abolitionist*, and always drew near when that word was spoken, expecting to hear something of importance to myself and fellow-slaves. The light broke in upon me by degrees. I went one day down on the wharf of Mr. Waters; and seeing two Irishmen unloading a scow of stone, I went, unasked, and helped them. When we had finished, one of them came to me and asked me if I were a slave. I told him I was. He asked, "Are ye a slave for life?" I told him that I was. The good Irishman seemed to be deeply affected by the statement. He said to the other that it was a pity so fine a little fellow as myself should be a slave for life. He said it was a shame to hold me. They both advised me to run away to the North; that I should find friends there, and that I should be free. I pretended not to be interested in what they said, and treated them as if I did not understand them; for I feared they might be treacherous. White men have been known to encourage slaves to escape, and then, to get the reward, catch them and return them to their masters. I was afraid that these seemingly good men might use me so; but I nevertheless remembered their advice, and from that time I resolved to run away. I looked forward to a time at which it would be safe for me to escape. I was too young to think of doing so immediately; besides, I wished to learn how to write, as I might have occasion to write my own pass. I consoled myself with the hope that I should one day find a good chance. Meanwhile, I would learn to write.

The idea as to how I might learn to write was suggested to me by being in Durgin and Bailey's shipyard, and frequently seeing the ship carpenters, after hewing, and getting a piece of timber ready for use, write on the timber the name of that part of the ship for which it was intended. When a piece of timber was intended for the larboard side, it would be marked thus— "L."

When a piece was for the starboard side, it would be marked thus— "S." A piece for the larboard side forward, would be marked thus— "L.F." When a piece was for starboard side forward, it would be marked thus— "S.F." For larboard aft, it would be marked thus— "L.A." For starboard aft, it would be marked thus— "S.A." I soon learned the names of these letters, and for what they were intended when placed upon a piece of timber in the shipyard. I immediately commenced copying them, and in a short time was able to make the four letters named. After that, when I met with any boy who I knew could write, I would tell him I could write as well as he. The next word would be, "I don't believe you. Let me see you try it." I would then make the letters which I had been so fortunate as to learn, and ask him to beat that. In this way I got a good many lessons in writing, which it is quite possible I should never have gotten in any other way. During this time, my copy-book was the board fence, brick wall, and pavement; my pen and ink was a lump of chalk. With these, I learned mainly how to write. I then commenced and continued copying the Italics in *Webster's Spelling Book*, until I could make them all without looking in the book. By this time, my little Master Thomas had gone to school, and learned how to write, and had written over a number of copy-books. These had been brought home, and shown to some of our near neighbors, and then laid aside. My mistress used to go to class meeting at the Wilk Street meeting-house every Monday afternoon, and leave me to take care of the house. When left thus, I used to spend the time in writing in the spaces left in Master Thomas's copy-book, copying what he had written. I continued to do this until I could write a hand very similar to that of Master Thomas. Thus, after a long, tedious effort for years, I finally succeeded in learning how to write. ●

The Reader's Presence

1. What sort of audience does Douglass anticipate for his reminiscence? How much does he assume his readers know about the conditions of slavery?

2. What books seem to matter most to Douglass? Why? What are his motives for wanting to read and write? For Douglass, what is the relationship between literacy and freedom? How does he move from curiosity to anguish to "eternal wakefulness" in paragraph 6? What is the relationship between learning to read and learning to write?

3. **VISUAL PRESENCE:** Examine the nineteenth-century advertisement designed to capture a runaway slave (page 80). In what specific ways does the language of this advertisement reflect the slave owner's attitude toward the slave? How does this language correspond to Douglass's description of his life as a slave? Support your answer with specific examples.

4. **CONNECTIONS:** Read Azar Nafisi's excerpt from "Reading Lolita in Tehran" (page 461) and consider Nafisi's students' challenges in obtaining an education. What obstacles do the girls overcome to join Nafisi's class? How do the difficulties Douglass faced in getting an education compare with those of Nafisi's students?

Andre Dubus III

THE LAND OF NO: LOVE IN A CLASS-RIVEN AMERICA

ANDRE DUBUS III (b. 1959) is the author of several novels, most famously *House of Sand and Fog* (1999), which became the basis for a critically acclaimed film of the same name. In addition to his novels, Dubus has written a collection of short stories, *The Cage Keeper: And Other Stories* (1989) and a memoir, *Townie* (2011), describing his youth and early adulthood, as well as his relationship with his father, Andre Dubus, who was a highly regarded writer. Andre Dubus III grew up, for the most part, in rough, economically depressed mill towns in the Merrimack Valley of Massachusetts. As a youth, he was a street fighter; later, a boxer. He eventually renounced violence and began writing fiction at age twenty-two, shortly after graduating from the University of Texas at Austin, where he had earned a bachelor's degree in sociology. He has worked as a carpenter, a bartender, an office cleaner, a halfway-house counselor, and even, for six months, an assistant to a private investigator and bounty hunter. He has taught writing at Harvard University, Tufts University, Emerson College, and the University of Massachusetts Lowell, where he is currently a full-time faculty member. He also has been awarded a Guggenheim Fellowship, the National Magazine Award for fiction, and the Pushcart Prize, and he was a finalist for the Rome Prize Fellowship from the Academy of Arts and Letters.

> "Most of the time I feel stupid, insensitive, mediocre, talentless and vulnerable . . . and wrong. I've found that when that happens, it usually means I'm writing pretty well."

The range of Dubus's experiences—his journey from a difficult childhood through a variety of professions, leading eventually to a successful career as a writer, teacher, and speaker—may be responsible for giving him a unique insight into many different walks of life, insight that not only fuels his fiction but also allows for the sort of understanding that made "The Land of No: Love in Class-riven America," originally published in the *New Republic*, possible. Demonstrating a remarkable awareness of class distinctions in America, Dubus observes the chasm between rich and poor without passing judgment on the people who stand on either side. His writing process is informed by a similar humility. He has said that "[m]ost of the time I feel stupid, insensitive, mediocre, talentless and vulnerable . . . and wrong. I've found that when that happens, it usually means I'm writing pretty well." His latest book, *Dirty Love*, is a series of interconnected novellas, published in 2013.

EMILY WAS 23 YEARS OLD and had a $2 million trust fund. She also had a warm smile, spoke kindly to everyone she met, and was tall and blonde and beautiful with the erect posture of the skier and gymnast she'd once been. We lived together in Manhattan in a tiny first-floor apartment. Six shifts a week, I tended bar at a chophouse down in the garment district.

Emily (not her real name) didn't have to work, but, while she was looking for an internship at a TV studio, she found a job in a bookstore. She said she was grateful for her inherited wealth but did not earn it so would not use it. Sometimes, though, she'd dip into it to buy me things she thought I needed: a new leather jacket, hand-stitched cowboy boots, a wool sweater from Ireland. I was grateful for these things but felt undeserving. I'd never been around anyone with money before—someone who could just buy whatever she wanted whenever she wanted it.

This was in the 1980s, a decade when there were 5,000 homeless families in New York City, and what seemed like a millionaire on every block. The homeless would be huddled in the concrete corner of a subway station, or curled up under dirty blankets on a grate outside a hotel or apartment building, the smaller children tucked between a mother or father and the granite wall. I found myself giving a lot of my tips to them, more than I could afford, though in some shadowed sliver of my psyche I knew I had Emily and what was given to her: a soft, deep place to fall, something my family had never known.

It was the summer of 1970, I was eleven years old, and in our small, rented house there was no escape. They got under your clothes, under your shirt and pants and underwear, an itch you could never quite reach—between your shoulder blades, up your neck, behind your knees, and in your hair. If you took a shower and stood wet and naked in front of a window fan it helped, but only until you were dry again. Then they seemed to rise up out of your own skin: fleas, gnats, bedbugs, lice—whatever they were exactly we didn't know, only that we were besieged by them, and no matter how many times our mother called the landlord, he never sent anyone to fix the problem.

We were living in northern Massachusetts then, in an old ship-building town on the Merrimack River three miles from the Atlantic. Its downtown was an abandoned cluster of mill buildings with no glass in their windows; the sidewalks buckled and were littered with trash. Dry weeds sprouted in cracks down the center of the asphalt streets, and the only working businesses were a diner, a newsstand, and a barroom, its dim interior filled with the shadows of men and women drinking.

But it was a place of cheap rents, and it was the first town to which our young mother moved her four kids after the divorce from our father. Twenty-eight years old, she got jobs as a nurse's aide and a waitress, then earned her way through school till she was out and working in social services, helping poor families like us.

We moved often, one year three times, always for a cheaper rent. We kids spent too much time watching television, roaming the streets, getting high on stoops waiting for the school bus. Children got pregnant at 14, boys went off to reform school and later prison, my best friend to an early grave, his own knife stuck into his liver by the girlfriend he'd tormented far too long.

As predictably as leaves dropping from their branches in the fall, the landlord would be at our door asking for the rent check our mother just did not have, and we'd be moving again, loading up a U-Haul truck with what little we owned, our clothes tossed into plastic trash bags, my mother's boy-friend driving the truck while the rest of us piled into whatever Mom drove at the time—usually Japanese cars that still lived after 200,000 miles and once a '67 Cadillac that ran on only three of its eight cylinders. Our mother called it "the pig."

Some summers, we escaped all this by heading 2,000 miles south to Louisiana, where our maternal grandparents lived. We never owned a car that could make that trip so the five of us would take a bus into Boston, to a squat concrete building behind chain-link and barbed wire, its oil-spotted yard crowded with new-looking cars. Our mother would sign some papers, then we'd be climbing into a VW van, or a four-door Buick, or once a black Trans-Am with leather seats, air-conditioning, and an 8-track player with quadraphonic sound. These were repo cars, and our mother would be paid to drive them to New Orleans. It gave her enough money for gas and two rooms at a motel with a pool, then five Greyhound tickets from New Orleans to Fishville, Louisiana.

Swimming in a Holiday Inn pool somewhere south of Knoxville, I could   10
see the last of the sun glinting off our black Trans Am in the parking lot, and I knew that after we'd all cooled off there'd be enough money for burgers and Cokes, and later we'd all be lying on our hotel beds watching a color television in air-conditioned rooms. *This is what it's like to be rich,* I remem-ber thinking. *This must be it.*

One night, crossing Third Avenue for the bar on the corner, Emily and I were talking about an old friend of mine, a woman who'd gotten preg-nant in high school, dropped out, then had two more kids with the same man—someone who beat her up regularly, who had knocked out some of her teeth and put her in the hospital. After years of this, she left him, went back to school, and became a registered nurse. Emily had met her once. She liked and admired her. As we crossed Third Avenue she said, "You know the first thing I'd do if I were her?"

"What?"

"I'd get my teeth fixed."

Weeks before this, she and I had spent the night at her family's home. It was one of five they owned; her parents were away that weekend at their ranch in the Southwest. I'd never been in a house like this. It had rooms off of rooms, and in each of them were deep sofas and chairs, woven carpet over polished hard-wood floors, tasteful paintings on the walls. She asked if I was hungry, and she opened the fridge and it was stuffed with food — cold cuts and cheeses, fresh vegetables and fruit and imported condiments, milk and orange juice and European beer. Emily was the youngest of five, all of them grown and out of the house. How was it possible for a refrigerator to hold so much? Especially in a home of only two?

She was surprised at my surprise. I tried to tell her how little my mother   15 had been able to give us, how one night a friend came over with a case of beer and I just opened the fridge, and he put it on one of three empty shelves beside a jar of mustard. She looked at me as if I were exaggerating. How could I tell her how differently we'd been raised? In the circular driveway in front of her house were five Porsches her father had shipped over from England to sell here for a profit, something she told me was called the "gray market." In my family, the market was where we went for food, if there was enough money to buy some.

I did not feel sorry for myself; I felt the superior pain of the inferior, the pride of the sufferer, the shame of the poor. I could also see that my dark mood was pulling her down and that she was beginning to feel guilty for something that had little to do with her. I kept quiet and felt far away from this kind young woman who seemed to love me just the way I was, this woman I judged when she was doing no such thing to me.

But now, stepping onto the sidewalk on the other side of Third Avenue, I heard myself yelling: "You don't think she'd like to have new *teeth*? Of course she would, Emily, but she doesn't have that kind of *money*, and, if she did, it would mean no oil in the burner that month, no food in the fridge. It would mean being late with the fucking rent. But you can't even think those things because you're from the Land of Yes when the rest of us are from the Land of No. We don't even *think* we can have these things you take for granted, like new fucking *teeth*."

It wasn't the first time I'd done this to her, and it wouldn't be the last. She stood there staring at me. In her eyes was hurt and a resigned sadness, then the hard light of resentment as she turned and walked down Third Avenue, lengthening her stride, getting as far away from me as fast as she could.

Two weeks later, business at the chophouse having been slow for months, I got laid off. I spent the next month walking from one restaurant to another looking for work, but there was none. Rent was past due, and I had no money in the bank.

Maybe because of our fights over her privileged life, Emily told me she   20 would not even consider dipping into her trust fund, though she did not make enough at the bookstore to support us both. I could see she was beginning to worry.

In the fourth week, I stopped looking for bartending work and got a job cleaning apartments and offices, but I earned half what I'd made serving drinks. Any day now, the landlord would stand at our door the way he'd always stood at my mother's, his hand out for the check that would not be coming. Emily and I would have to move, but where? I saw us huddled together on a grate, or curled under blankets beneath hedges in Central Park, and I remembered one night when those bugs had gotten so bad my mother and I had slept in the pig parked out in the street. It was a humid July night, my sisters and brother miraculously asleep inside. My mother took the front, and I lay in the back. The bars had closed hours ago so we weren't worried about the drunks; we opened our windows all the way. For a long while, I stared at the ripped fabric of the ceiling. I could hear the fan in my sister's window, then the even breaths of my sleeping mother. She worked so hard and always fell asleep so fast.

Now it was dusk in Manhattan, and I was walking uptown from my new cleaning job, preparing myself to tell Emily it was time for us to start packing. But, when I walked into our tiny place, she was pulling roasted chicken from the oven, her hair pulled up and back, and she kissed me and handed me a cold European beer.

"I paid our rent."

"How?"

"How do you think?" She smiled recklessly, like she was flirting with a   25 stranger and knew she probably shouldn't but would anyway. She seemed a little drunk.

"I thought you weren't going to do that."

"We're paid up for six months." She grabbed her glass of wine and moved past me and sat on the couch. She snatched up the remote and flicked on our color television.

I couldn't deny the relief I felt. Like standing naked and wet in front of that window fan, all the itching gone. And it was clear she did not want to discuss it. I sat next to her on the couch. I sipped the beer she'd paid for. I watched whatever it was she was watching. Her hand rested in her lap, and I wanted to reach over and hold it. It was only inches away, but it may as well have been in another country, another land, one we both knew we would never be living in together. ●

The Reader's Presence

1. Dubus opens by describing Emily's affluent background and then proceeds to write about the homeless in New York. What compositional purpose and significance do you assign to beginning his essay with this dichotomy? To what extent does this beginning foreshadow the remainder of his essay?

2. Consider the interlude Dubus presents (paragraphs 4 through 10), where he recounts growing up in northern Massachusetts. What strategic purpose does this recounting of his childhood serve? Why does the narrator yell at Emily? What has she done to provoke his anger? Why does Dubus write, "I heard myself yelling" (paragraph 17)? Consider the amount of detail in the story: "a new leather jacket, hand-stitched cowboy boots, a wool sweater from Ireland" (paragraph 2). What does Dubus's invoking such detail tell us about the narrator and his identification with "the Land of No" (paragraph 17)?

3. **CONNECTIONS:** After describing his upbringing, Dubus writes, "I felt the superior pain of the inferior, the pride of the sufferer, the shame of the poor" (paragraph 16). Compare the narrator's conflicted feelings about his upbringing to those of Patti Smith in "Sticky Fingers" (page 214). How does each author deal with emotions brought on by class identity?"

The Writer at Work

ANDRE DUBUS III on the Risks of Memoir Writing

Lawrence Lucier/FilmMagic/Getty Images

Memoir writing can be a risky business. When writers publish a memoir, they often find that they have offended people from their past who may feel misrepresented, insulted, injured, and perhaps angry enough to initiate legal action. Well known as a novelist, Andre Dubus III ventured into the dangerous territory of memoir writing when he published *Townie* in 2011. The following year, he wrote an essay about the experience, appropriately called "Writing & Publishing a Memoir: What in the Hell Have I Done?" published in *River Teeth*, Volume 14 (2013). Following is a small portion of the essay (which includes how his hometown of Haverhill, Massachusetts, responded to "The Book").

❝In my hometown of Haverhill, Massachusetts, the mill town where I grew up and the setting for *Townie*, I'm told it's referred to as "The Book." . . .

Just weeks after it was published, I was to give a reading at the Haverhill Public Library. Over five hundred people showed up. The librarian introduced me, and there was enthusiastic applause, a few raucous whoops and shouts from the rear of the room. I looked out over the crowd and took them in. Many were my age, in their late forties or early fifties. Behind aging skin and hair and a few extra pounds, I recognized a face here, the eyes of another there, people I hadn't seen in over thirty years, when we'd all attended the same high school with its undercover narcs and drug dealing, its high-achieving jock kids from across the river, the leather-wearing, pony-tailed losers like me on the mill side, the kids or grandkids of immigrants from Ireland and Italy, Greece and Puerto Rico and the Dominican Republic. And there were older men and women there, too, the parents of those of us who grew up in the shadow of the Vietnam War and Watergate and Nixon flying away from the presidency in his helicopter, an echo image of what so many of our own fathers had done, though they'd driven away in Chevys or hopped a bus or just hit the road with a thumb out.

I thanked everyone for coming, then I read a few brief passages and took some questions. Mostly, though, the audience offered comments, and mostly these were words of thanks for telling our story. "Our story." I liked hearing this and was grateful for their gratitude, but I was also confused by it. I knew what they meant, that I'd written about that in-between generation we were members of; ten years younger than the Vietnam baby boomers but ten years older than Generation X, we were kids who grew up listening to early Aerosmith on eight-tracks in Z28s, drinking Haffenreffer tall boys and smoking angel dust. We grew our hair to our waists and carried pints of Southern Comfort in our Dingo boots like Janis Joplin, but the party had moved on years ago and so we were left wearing costumes, having sex too young, drinking too much, fighting in barrooms and in the street, our broke single mothers too overwhelmed to do much about it. I knew what they were thanking me for, but still, wasn't *Townie* essentially *my* story?

Years ago I read an interview with the writer Janet Burroway, in which she says that when readers go to the novel, what we're really saying to it is this: "Give me *me*." Most of us know this to be true. If the writer goes deeply enough into her characters and their stories, then they'll go deeply enough into us too, their own natures resonating with ours, like an easterly breeze moving wind chimes on a porch we'd never even known about. But with creative nonfiction/memoir, the breeze seems to be even more direct, the wind chimes closer to the front door of the house in which we live.

"Hey, don't tell me, but I know who the Murphy brothers really are. The Pecker Street gang."

The man who said that wore a dark sweater and Dickie work pants, broken capillaries blooming across his upper cheeks. He was my age, and looked pleased with himself, and I liked him right away.

"You got it," I said.

"Andre." A woman was raising her hand from the crowded center of the room. She had short gray hair and a plump, warm-looking face, her eyes lit with a street-savvy light I wouldn't want to mess with: "Now when I want people to know about my life, I just have them read your book. But what do you think of what the mayor's saying about it?"

Just days before, the Mayor of Haverhill had written on his Facebook page that I was "embellishing details" and that Haverhill had never been the tough mill town I wrote about in *Townie*. If this were a novel, his words wouldn't have bothered me at all, but this was a memoir, and when that word is printed beneath the title of a book, the contract between its writer and the reader is this:

> Dear Reader,
> Everything you read in this book happened, at least to the best of my memory, which like everyone's is seen through a deeply subjective emotional lens. Still, I have tried to be loyal to the facts as I remember them, which isn't always the truth, but it is my truth.

I was on tour when I heard about the mayor's postings. I called him and told him I was concerned, that a charge like that against a memoir could very well undermine the authority of that book. And I had not "embellished." He apologized and told me he'd only begun to read my book that morning, that he'd been reacting to published reviews and interviews which referred to 1970s Haverhill as a "depressed crime-ridden mill town."

"But Mr. Mayor, it *was*."

"Not in my neighborhood."

"Where'd you live?"

"Riverside."

"Well, I lived across from the Avenues. A much different neighborhood."

We talked a while longer. The mayor said he'd read the first hundred pages of my book, and he could see I wasn't writing so much about the town as I was about my boyhood and my family. In fact, he said, it was clear to him that I hadn't called Haverhill any of those things the newspapers were calling it, and he had to admit, there were parts of our city then, especially the bars along the river of an almost entirely boarded-up downtown, that were pretty rough.

"In fact, when I was a young lawyer, my first clients were drug dealers from near where you lived."

"Thank you."

"And my wife did remind me that I took boxing lessons to defend myself then."

"That's all I'm saying."

But the mayor, who has worked diligently to make downtown Haverhill a much more vibrant place than it was forty years ago, had every right to worry about how it was being described by the national press now. I told him I would make sure to mention things are different today. He promised to stop posting charges of embellishments on his website.

I told the woman in that library crowd that I respected the mayor, and now that he'd begun to actually read my book, he was taking back what he wrote about it.

A man standing near a window raised his hand. He looked over six feet tall and well over two hundred pounds, and he wore a black beret and a black sweater and black pants. He was my age or younger, but he was leaning on a cane. His goatee was wispy and just beginning to gray.

I called on him.

"You know your friend Cleary? Your best friend when you were kids?"

His voice was reedy and restrained, like he was trying to hold back an emotion that wasn't all good.

"Yeah? What about Cleary?"

"He was my brother."

Cleary, always clowning and stealing and drinking and getting high, the son of a hopelessly alcoholic mother and distant father, my best friend when I was thirteen, fourteen, and fifteen, stabbed to death at age twenty-five by the common-law wife he used to beat.

"Mark? Is that you?"

He nodded, and I left the podium and walked down the side aisle to Cleary's younger brother I hadn't seen in years. I hugged him and he hugged me back, and then the crowd began to clap, and I walked back to the microphone and told them just who he was.

Later, at the book-signing table, he asked me to inscribe a copy to their father. Mark told me how happy his old man was to hear that his oldest son, dead far too soon, had made it into the pages of a real book, that his son would live on now, that he wouldn't be forgotten. On the title page of the book, I wrote how much I loved and missed his son, and I wrote his son's real name and wished the father well, and signed my own.

But a week or two later, I received an email from Mark's girlfriend telling me Mark's father had read the book and that he was very, very upset. And why wouldn't he be? How could I not have thought of this earlier? I described his son as having been a wife-beater in his last days; I described how deeply alcoholic his mother had been, this woman who died of her disease not long after her oldest child had been stabbed to death; I wrote how absent he, the father, had seemed to me during those years. My God, what had I *done*?

I'd written as truly of that time as I could, that's what I'd done, but my intention never was to hurt anyone. Ever. These things rarely happen when what you write and publish is fiction.**"**

Anne Fadiman

UNDER WATER

ANNE FADIMAN (b. 1953) is an American author and teacher. Her first book, *The Spirit Catches You and You Fall Down*, an account of an epileptic Hmong child and her family living in Merced, California, won the National Book Critics Circle Award in 1997. She was the editor of the prestigious American literary quarterly the *American Scholar* for seven years, and her essays have appeared in *Harper's*, *The New Yorker*, and *The New York Times*, among many other publications. She has won national magazine awards for both reporting and essays, and in 2012, she was appointed as the inaugural Francis Writer-in-Residence at Yale University, where she teaches in the English Department and mentors students who wish to become writers and editors. Her other books include *Ex Libris: Confessions of a Common Reader* (1998) and *At Large and At Small: Familiar Essays* (2007), an essay collection from which this selection is taken.

> **"Books wrote our life story."**

In *Ex Libris*, Anne Fadiman reflected on the role of books in her life by saying that "books wrote our life story, and as they accumulated on our shelves (and on our window-sills, and underneath our sofa, and on top of our refrigerator), they became chapters in it themselves."

I WAS AN IMPATIENT CHILD who disliked obstructions: traffic jams, clogged bathtub drains, catsup bottles you had to bang. I liked to drop twigs into the stream that ran through our backyard and watch them float downstream, coaxed around rocks and branches by the distant pull of the ocean. If they hit a snag, I freed them.

When I was eighteen, rushing through life as fast as I could, I was a student on a month-long wilderness program in western Wyoming. On the third day of the course we went canoeing on the Green River, a tributary of the Colorado that begins in the glaciers of the Wind River range and flows south across the sagebrush plains. Swollen by warm-weather runoff from an unusually deep snowpack, the Green was higher and swifter that month—June of 1972—than it had been in forty years. A river at flood stage can have strange currents. There is not enough room in the channel for the water to move downstream in an orderly fashion, so it collides with itself and forms whirlpools and boils and souseholes.[1] Our instructors decided to stick to their itinerary never-theless, but they put in at a relatively easy section of the Green, one that the flood had merely upgraded, in the international system of whitewater classi-fication, from Class I to Class II. There are six levels of difficulty, and Class II was not an unreasonable challenge for novice paddlers.

The Green River did not seem dangerous to me. It seemed magnificently unobstructed. Impediments to progress—the rocks and stranded trees that under normal conditions would protrude above the surface—were mostly submerged. The river carried our aluminum canoe high and lightly, like a child on a pair of broad shoulders. We could rest our paddles on the gun-wales and let the water do our work. The sun was bright and hot. Every few minutes I dipped my bandanna in the river, draped it over my head, and let an ounce or two of melted glacier run down my neck.

I was in the bow of the third canoe. We rounded a bend and saw, fifty feet ahead, a standing wave in the wake of a large black boulder. The students in the lead canoe were attempting to avoid the boulder by backferrying, slipping crabwise across the current by angling their boat diagonally and stroking back-ward. Done right, backferrying allows paddlers to hover midstream and care-fully plan their course instead of surrendering to the water's impetuous pace. But if they lean upstream—a natural inclination, as few people choose to lean toward the difficulties that lie ahead—the current can overflow the lowered gunwale and flip the boat. And that is what happened to the lead canoe.

I wasn't worried when I saw it go over. Knowing that we might capsize   5
in the fast water, our instructors had arranged to have our gear trucked to our next campsite. The packs were safe. The water was little more than waist-deep, and the paddlers were both wearing life jackets. They would be fine. One was already scrambling onto the right-hand bank.

But where was the second paddler? Gary, a local boy from Rawlins a year or two younger than I, seemed to be hung up on something. He was standing at a strange angle in the middle of the river, just downstream from the boulder. Gary was the only student on the course who had not brought sneakers, and one of his mountaineering boots had become wedged between two rocks. The instructors would come around the bend in a moment and pluck him out, like a twig from a snag.

But they didn't come. The second canoe pulled over to the bank and ours followed. Thirty seconds passed, maybe a minute. Then we saw the standing wave bend Gary's body forward at the waist, push his face under-water, stretch his arms in front of him, and slip his orange life jacket off his shoulders. The life jacket lingered for a moment at his wrists before it floated downstream, its long white straps twisting in the current. His shirtless torso was pale and undulating, and it changed shape as hills and valleys of water flowed over him, altering the curve of the liquid lens through which we

---

[1] **boils and souseholes:** Terms from whitewater canoeing or rafting. Boils are small spots of agitated or swirling water; souseholes are formed by water flowing over submerged objects, usually rocks. —EDS.

Detail from Michelangelo's famed "Sistine Chapel" showing the figure of St. Bartholomew.

watched him. I thought: *He looks like the flayed skin of St. Bartholomew in the Sistine Chapel.*[2] As soon as I had the thought, I knew that it was dishonorable. To think about anything outside the moment, outside Gary, was a

---

[2]**Sistine Chapel:** The famed ceiling of the Sistine Chapel in Rome, one of the artistic wonders of the world, was painted by Michelangelo between 1508 and 1512. The figure of St. Bartholomew appears in one of the ceiling's many panels. —EDS.

crime of inattention. I swallowed a small, sour piece of self-knowledge: I was the sort of person who, instead of weeping or shouting or praying during a crisis, thought about something from a textbook (H. W. Janson's *History of Art*, page 93).

Once the flayed man had come, I could not stop the stream of images: Gary looked like a piece of seaweed. Gary looked like a waving hand-kerchief, Gary looked like a hula dancer. Each simile was a way to avoid thinking about what Gary *was*, a drowning boy. To remember these things is dishonorable, too, for I have long since forgotten Gary's last name and the color of his hair and the sound of his voice.

I do not remember a single word that anyone said. Somehow we got into one of the canoes, all five of us, and tried to ferry the twenty feet or so to the middle of the river. The current was so strong, and we were so incompetent, that we never even got close. Then we tried it on foot, linking arms to form a chain. The water was so cold that it stung. And it was noisy, not the roar and crash of whitewater but a groan, a terrible bass grumble, from the stones that were rolling and leaping down the riverbed. When we got close to Gary, we couldn't see him. All we could see was the reflection of the sky. A couple of times, groping blindly, one of us touched him, but he was as slippery as soap. Then our knees buckled and our elbows unlocked, and we rolled downstream, like the stones. The river's rocky load, moving invisibly beneath its smooth surface, pounded and scraped us. Eventually the current heaved us, blue-lipped and panting, onto the bank. In that other world above the water, the only sounds were the buzzing of bees and flies. Our wet sneakers kicked up red dust. The air smelled of sage and rabbit-brush and sunbaked earth.

We tried again and again, back and forth between the worlds. Wet, dry,   10
cold, hot, turbulent, still.

At first I assumed that we would save him. He would lie on the bank and the sun would warm him while we administered mouth-to-mouth resuscitation. If we couldn't get him out, we would hold him upright in the river; maybe he could still breathe. But the Green River was flowing at nearly three thousand cubic feet—about ninety tons—per second. At that rate, water can wrap a canoe around a boulder like tinfoil. Water can uproot a tree. Water can squeeze the air out of a boy's lungs, undo knots, drag off a life jacket, lever a boot so tightly into the riverbed that even if we had had ropes—the ropes that were in the packs that were in the trucks—we never could have budged him.

We kept going in, not because we had any hope of saving Gary after the first ten minutes but because we needed to save face. It would have been humiliating if the instructors had come around the bend and found us sitting in the sagebrush, a docile row of five with no hypothermia and no skinned knees. Eventually, they did come. The boats had been delayed because one of them had nearly capsized, and the instructors had made the students stop and practice backferrying until they learned not to lean upstream. Even though Gary had already drowned, the instructors did all the same things we had done, more competently but no more effectively, because they, too, would have been humiliated if they hadn't skinned their knees. Men in wetsuits, belayed with ropes, pried the body out the next morning.

Twenty-seven years have passed. My life seems too fast now, so obstructions bother me less than they once did. I am no longer in a hurry to see what is around the next bend. I find myself wanting to backferry, to hover midstream, suspended. If I could do that, I might avoid many things: harsh words, foolish decisions, moments of inattention, regrets that wash over me, like water. ◼

The Reader's Presence

1. Read Anne Fadiman's opening paragraph very carefully. What is its relevance to the rest of her short personal essay? What images in the paragraph will be repeated later? What would you consider the key word of the paragraph? In what ways does that word inform the entire essay?

2. At the moment of crisis, the author says she pictured a figure that appears in Michelangelo's famous ceiling painting in the Sistine Chapel in Rome (paragraph 7). Why does Fadiman consider her thought "dishonorable"? What do you think she means by a "crime of inattention"? How do these self-criticisms reappear in the essay's final paragraph?

3. **CONNECTIONS:** Compare and contrast Anne Fadiman's "Under Water" to George Orwell's classic essay, "Shooting an Elephant" (page 195). Both essays depend on an unfolding narrative; in what way does each writer rely on similar methods of storytelling? How do spectators play a role in the story? When she writes "we needed to save face" (paragraph 12), do you see any connections to Orwell's essay? What other similarities can you find?

The Writer at Work

ANNE FADIMAN on the Art of Editing

Chester Higgins Jr./The New York Times/Redux Pictures

Anne Fadiman has not only written numerous personal and reflective essays but also served for years as the chief editor of one of the country's finest literary quarterlies, the *American Scholar*. She recalls that experience in the introductory essay she contributed to her 2003 edition of the *Best American Essays*. As readers, we see only the final published efforts of writers (whether novelists, poets, or essayists) and it's important for student readers to understand that everything they encounter in a book like this has not only been edited professionally but re-edited and then probably edited again. In this passage from her introductory essay, Fadiman pays tribute to the importance of fastidious editing.

❝A few years ago, the author of an autobiographical essay I was planning to publish in *The American Scholar*—a very fine writer—died suddenly. The writer had no immediate relatives, so I asked his longtime editor at *The New Yorker* if he would read the edited piece, hoping he might be able to guess which of my minor changes the writer would have been likely to accept and which he would have disliked. Certainly, said the editor. Two days later, he sent the piece back to me with comments on my edits and some additional editing of his own. "My suggestions are all small sentence tweaks," he wrote. "I could hear ———'s voice in my head as I did them and I'm pretty sure they would have met with his approval—most of them, anyway." Some examples: "A man who looked unmusical" became "a man so seemingly unmusical." "They made a swift escape to their different homes" became "They scattered swiftly to their various homes." "I felt that that solidity had been fostered by his profession" became "That solidity, I felt, had been fostered by his profession." These were, indeed, only small tweaks, but their precision filled me with awe. Of *course* you couldn't look unmusical. Of *course* it was awkward to use "escape" (singular) with "homes" (plural).

Of *course* I should have caught "that that." I faxed the piece to my entire staff because editors rarely get a chance to see the work of other editors; we see only its results. This was like having a front-row seat at the Editing Olympics.

Five days later, the editor sent the piece back to us, covered with a second round of marginalia. "No doubt this is more than you bargained for," he wrote. "It's just that when the more noticeable imperfections have been taken care of, smaller ones come into view . . . I've even edited some of my own edits—e.g., on page 47, where I've changed 'dour,' which I inserted in the last go-round, to 'glowering.' This is because 'dour' is too much like 'pinched,' which I'm also suggesting."

If you're not a writer, this sort of compulsiveness may seem well nigh pathological. You may even be thinking, "What's the difference?" But if you *are* a writer, you'll realize what a gift the editor gave his old friend. Had not a word been changed, the essay would still have been excellent. Each of these "tweaks"—there were perhaps a hundred, none more earthshaking than the ones I've quoted—made it a little better, and their aggregate effect was to transform an excellent essay into a superb one.**❞**

Henry Louis Gates Jr.

IN THE KITCHEN

The critic, educator, writer, and activist **HENRY LOUIS GATES JR.** (b. 1950) is one of the more recent in a long line of African American intellectuals who are also public figures. In 1979, he became the first African American to earn a PhD from Cambridge University in its eight-hundred-year history. He has been the recipient of countless honors, including a Carnegie Foundation Fellowship, a Mellon Fellowship, a MacArthur "genius" grant for his work in literary theory, and the 1998 National Medal for the Humanities. Gates is the Alphonse Fletcher University Professor and the director of the W. E. B. Du Bois Institute for African and African American Research at Harvard University. He has been at the forefront of the movement to expand the literary canon that is studied in American schools to include the works of non-European authors. He is also known for his work as a "literary archaeologist," uncovering thousands of previously unknown stories, poems, and reviews written by African American authors between 1829 and 1940 and making those texts available to modern readers.

> **"I'm trying to recollect a lost era . . . a whole world that simply no longer exists."**

Gates has written and produced a number of documentaries aired on public television, including *African American Lives* in 2006 and *Finding Your Roots with Henry Louis Gates, Jr.* beginning in 2012, which further examines the genealogical and genetic heritage of famous Americans.

Gates's more recent books include *Black in Latin America* (2011), *Life Upon These Shores: Looking at African American History, 1513–2008* (2011), and *Encyclopedia of Africa* (2010), which he edited with Kwame Anthony Appiah.

"In the Kitchen" is taken from Gates's 1995 book *Colored People*, a memoir of his early life as part of the middle-class "colored" community of Piedmont, West Virginia. About *Colored People*, Gates says, "I'm trying to recollect a lost era, what I can call a *sepia time*, a whole world that simply no longer exists."

WE ALWAYS HAD A GAS STOVE in the kitchen, though electric cooking became fashionable in Piedmont, like using Crest toothpaste rather than Colgate, or watching Huntley and Brinkley rather than Walter Cronkite. But for us it was gas, Colgate, and good ole Walter Cronkite, come what may. We used gas partly out of loyalty to Big Mom, Mama's mama, because she was mostly blind and still loved to cook, and she could feel her way better with gas than with electric.

But the most important thing about our gas-equipped kitchen was that Mama used to do hair there. She had a "hot comb"—a fine-tooth iron instrument with a long wooden handle—and a pair of iron curlers that opened and closed like scissors: Mama would put them into the gas fire until they glowed. You could smell those prongs heating up.

I liked what that smell meant for the shape of my day. There was an intimate warmth in the women's tones as they talked with my mama while she did their hair. I knew what the women had been through to get their hair ready to be "done," because I would watch Mama do it herself. How that scorched kink could be transformed through grease and fire into a magnificent head of wavy hair was a miracle to me. Still is.

||||||||||||||||||||||||||||||||||||||||||||||||||||||||||||||||||||||||||||||||||||||||||||||||||||||||||||||||||||||||||||||||||||||||||

Mama would wash her hair over the sink, a towel wrapped round her shoulders, wearing just her half-slip and her white bra. (We had no shower until we moved down Rat Tail Road into Doc Wolverton's house, in 1954.) After she had dried it, she would grease her scalp thoroughly with blue Bergamot hair grease, which came in a short, fat jar with a picture of a beautiful colored lady on it. It's important to grease your scalp real good, my mama would explain, to keep from burning yourself.

Of course, her hair would return to its natural kink almost as soon as   5 the hot water and shampoo hit it. To me, it was another miracle how hair so "straight" would so quickly become kinky again once it even approached some water.

My mama had only a "few" clients whose heads she "did" — and did, I think, because she enjoyed it, rather than for the few dollars it brought in. They would sit on one of our red plastic kitchen chairs, the kind with the shiny metal legs, and brace themselves for the process. Mama would stroke that red-hot iron, which by this time had been in the gas fire for a half hour or more, slowly but firmly through their hair, from scalp to strand's end. It made a scorching, crinkly sound, the hot iron did, as it burned its way through the damp kink, leaving in its wake the straightest of hair strands, each of them standing up long and tall but drooping at the end, like the top of a heavy willow tree. Slowly, steadily, with deftness and grace, Mama's hands would transform a round mound of Odetta kink[1] into a darkened swamp of everglades. The Bergamot made the hair shiny; the heat of the hot iron gave it a brownish-red cast. Once all the hair was as straight as God allows kink to get, Mama would take the well-heated curling iron and twirl the straightened strands into more or less loosely wrapped curls. She claimed that she owed her strength and skill as a hairdresser to her wrists, and her little finger would poke out the way it did when she sipped tea. Mama was a southpaw, who wrote upside down and backwards to produce the cleanest, roundest letters you've ever seen.

The "kitchen" she would all but remove from sight with a pair of shears bought for this purpose. Now, the *kitchen* was the room in which we were sitting, the room where Mama did hair and washed clothes, and where each of us bathed in a galvanized tub. But the word has another meaning, and the "kitchen" I'm speaking of now is the very kinky bit of hair at the back of the head, where our neck meets the shirt collar. If there ever was one part of our African past that resisted assimilation, it was the kitchen. No matter how hot the iron, no matter how powerful the chemical, no matter how stringent the mashed-potatoes-and-lye formula of a man's "process," neither God nor woman nor Sammy Davis, Jr., could straighten the kitchen. The kitchen was permanent, irredeemable, invincible kink. Unassimilably African. No matter what you did, no matter how hard you tried, nothing could dekink a person's kitchen. So you trimmed it off as best you could.

1 **Odetta kink:** A reference to Odetta Holmes Felious Gordon, a popular African American folk singer of the 1960s who helped popularize the hairstyle known as the "afro." —EDS.

Odetta Holmes Felious Gordon.

When hair had begun to "turn," as they'd say, or return to its natural kinky glory, it was the kitchen that turned first. When the kitchen started creeping up the back of the neck, it was time to get your hair done again. The kitchen around the back, and nappy edges at the temples.

Sometimes, after dark, Mr. Charlie Carroll would come to have his hair done. Mr. Charlie Carroll was very light-complected and had a ruddy nose, the kind of nose that made me think of Edmund Gwenn playing Kris Kringle in *Miracle on 34th Street*. At the beginning, they did it after Rocky and I had gone to sleep. It was only later that we found out he had come to our house so Mama could iron his hair—not with a comb and curling iron but with our very own Proctor-Silex steam iron. For some reason, Mr. Charlie would conceal his Frederick Douglass mane[2] under a big white Stetson hat, which I never saw him take off. Except when he came to our house, late at night, to have his hair pressed.

(Later, Daddy would tell us about Mr. Charlie's most prized piece of   10
knowledge, which the man would confide only after his hair had been pressed, as a token of intimacy. "Not many people know this," he'd say in a tone of circumspection, "but George Washington was Abraham Lincoln's daddy." Nodding solemnly, he'd add the clincher: "A white man told me." Though he was in dead earnest, this became a humorous refrain around the house— "a white man told me" —used to punctuate especially preposterous assertions.)

---

[2] **Frederick Douglass mane:** Frederick Douglass (1817?–1895), an escaped slave who became a prominent African American writer, abolitionist, and orator (see page 77). —EDS.

Frederick Douglass.

My mother furtively examined my daughters' kitchens whenever we went home for a visit in the early eighties. It became a game between us. I had told her not to do it, because I didn't like the politics it suggested of "good" and "bad" hair. "Good" hair was straight. "Bad" hair was kinky. Even in the late sixties, at the height of Black Power, most people could not bring themselves to say "bad" for "good" and "good" for "bad." They still said that hair like white hair was "good," even if they encapsulated it in a disclaimer like "what we used to call 'good.'"

Maggie would be seated in her high chair, throwing food this way and that, and Mama would be cooing about how cute it all was, remembering how I used to do the same thing, and wondering whether Maggie's flinging her food with her left hand meant that she was going to be a southpaw too. When my daughter was just about covered with Franco-American SpaghettiOs, Mama would seize the opportunity and wipe her clean, dipping her head, tilted to one side, down under the back of Maggie's neck. Sometimes, if she could get away with it, she'd even rub a curl between her fingers, just to make sure that her bifocals had not deceived her. Then she'd sigh with satisfaction and relief, thankful that her prayers had been answered. No kink . . . yet. "Mama!" I'd shout, pretending to be angry. (Every once in a while, if no one was looking, I'd peek too.)

I say "yet" because most black babies are born with soft, silken hair. Then, sooner or later, it begins to "turn," as inevitably as do the seasons or the leaves turn on a tree. And if it's meant to turn, it *turns*, no matter how hard you try to stop it. People once thought baby oil would stop it. They were wrong.

Everybody I knew as a child wanted to have good hair. You could be as ugly as homemade sin dipped in misery and still be thought attractive if you had good hair. Jesus Moss was what the girls at Camp Lee, Virginia, had called Daddy's hair during World War II. I know he played that thick head of hair for all it was worth, too. Still would, if he could.

My own hair was "not a bad grade," as barbers would tell me when they   15 cut my head for the first time. It's like a doctor reporting the overall results of the first full physical that he had given you. "You're in good shape" or "Blood pressure's kind of high; better cut down on salt."

I spent much of my childhood and adolescence messing with my hair. I definitely wanted straight hair. Like Pop's.

When I was about three, I tried to stick a wad of Bazooka bubble gum to that straight hair of his. I suppose what fixed that memory for me is the spanking I got for doing so: he turned me upside down, holding me by the feet, the better to paddle my behind. Little *nigger*, he shouted, walloping away. I started to laugh about it two days later, when my behind stopped hurting.

When black people say "straight," of course, they don't usually mean "straight" literally, like, say, the hair of Peggy Lipton (the white girl on *The Mod Squad*) or Mary of Peter, Paul and Mary fame; black people call that "stringy" hair. No, "straight" just means not kinky, no matter what contours the curl might take. Because Daddy had straight hair, I would have done *anything* to have straight hair—and I used to try everything to make it straight, short of getting a process, which only riffraff were dumb enough to do.

Of the wide variety of techniques and methods I came to master in the great and challenging follicle prestidigitation, almost all had two things in common: a heavy, oil-based grease and evenly applied pressure. It's no accident that many of the biggest black companies in the fifties and sixties made hair products. Indeed, we do have a vast array of hair grease. And I have tried it all, in search of that certain silky touch, one that leaves neither the hand nor the pillow sullied by grease.

I always wondered what Frederick Douglass put on *his* hair, or Phillis   20 Wheatley.[3] Or why Wheatley has that rag on her head in the little engraving

---

[3] ***Phillis Wheatley*** (1753?–1784): An African-born slave who became America's first major black poet. —EDS.

in the frontispiece of her book. One thing is for sure: you can bet that when Wheatley went to England to see the Countess of Huntington, she did not stop by the Queen's Coiffeur on the way. So many black people still get their hair straightened that it's a wonder we don't have a national holiday for Madame C. J. Walker, who invented the process for straightening kinky hair, rather than for Dr. King. Jheri-curled or "relaxed" — it's still fried hair.

I used all the greases, from sea-blue Bergamot, to creamy vanilla Duke (in its orange-and-white jar), to the godfather of grease, the formidable Murray's. Now, Murray's was some *serious* grease. Whereas Bergamot was like oily Jell-O and Duke was viscous and sickly sweet, Murray's was light brown and *hard*. Hard as lard and twice as greasy, Daddy used to say whenever the subject of Murray's came up. Murray's came in an orange can with a screw-on top. It was so hard that some people would put a match to the can, just to soften it and make it more manageable. In the late sixties, when Afros came into style, I'd use Afro-Sheen. From Murray's to Duke to Afro-Sheen: that was my progression in black consciousness.

We started putting hot towels or washrags over our greased-down Murray's-coated heads, in order to melt the wax into the scalp and follicles. Unfortunately, the wax had a curious habit of running down your neck, ears, and forehead. Not to mention your pillowcase.

Another problem was that if you put two palmfuls of Murray's on your head, your hair turned white. Duke did the same thing. It was a challenge: if you got rid of the white stuff, you had a magnificent head of wavy hair. Murray's turned kink into waves. Lots of waves. Frozen waves. A hurricane couldn't have blown those waves around.

That was the beauty of it. Murray's was so hard that it froze your hair into the wavy style you brushed it into. It looked really good if you wore a part. A lot of guys had parts *cut* into their hair by a barber, with clippers or a straight-edge razor. Especially if you had kinky hair — in which case you'd generally wear a short razor cut, or what we called a Quo Vadis.

Being obsessed with our hair, we tried to be as innovative as possible.   25 Everyone knew about using a stocking cap, because your father or your uncle or the older guys wore them whenever something really big was about to happen, secular or sacred, a funeral or a dance, a wedding or a trip in which you confronted official white people, or when you were trying to look really sharp. When it was time to be clean, you wore a stocking cap. If the event was really a big one, you made a new cap for the occasion.

A stocking cap was made by asking your mother for one of her hose, cutting it with a pair of scissors about six inches or so from the open end, where the elastic goes to the top of the thigh. Then you'd knot the cut end, and behold — a conical-shaped hat or cap, with an elastic band that you pulled down low on your forehead and down around your neck in the back. A good stocking cap, to work well, had to fit tight and snug, like a press. And it had to fit that tightly because it *was* a press: it pressed your hair with the force of the hose's elastic. If you greased your hair down real good and left the stocking cap on long enough—*voilà*: you got a head of pressed-against-the-scalp waves. If you used Murray's, and if you wore a stocking cap to sleep, you got a *whole lot* of waves. (You also got a ring around your forehead when you woke up, but eventually that disappeared.)

And then you could enjoy your concrete 'do. Swore we were bad, too, with all that grease and those flat heads. My brother and I would brush it out a bit in the morning so it would look—ahem—"natural."

Grown men still wear stocking caps, especially older men, who generally keep their caps in their top drawer, along with their cuff links and their see-through silk socks, their Maverick tie, their silk handkerchief, and whatever else they prize most.

A Murrayed-down stocking cap was the respectable version of the process, which, by contrast, was most definitely not a cool thing to have, at least if you weren't an entertainer by trade.

Zeke and Keith and Poochie and a few other stars of the basketball team   30
all used to get a process once or twice a year. It was expensive, and to get one you had to go to Pittsburgh or D.C. or Uniontown, someplace where there were enough colored people to support a business. They'd disappear, then reappear a day or two later, strutting like peacocks, their hair burned slightly red from the chemical lye base. They'd also wear "rags" or cloths or handkerchiefs around it when they slept or played basketball. Do-rags, they were called. But the result was *straight* hair with a hint of wave. No curl. Do-it-yourselfers took their chances at home with a concoction of mashed potatoes and lye.

The most famous process, outside of what Malcolm X describes in his *Autobiography* and maybe that of Sammy Davis, Jr., was Nat King Cole's. Nat King Cole had patent-leather hair.

"That man's got the finest process money can buy." That's what Daddy said the night Cole's TV show aired on NBC, November 5, 1956. I remember the date because everyone came to our house to watch it and to celebrate one of Daddy's buddies' birthdays. Yeah, Uncle Joe chimed in, they can do shit to his hair that the average Negro can't even *think* about—secret shit.

Nat King Cole was *clean*. I've had an ongoing argument with a Nigerian friend about Nat King Cole for twenty years now. Not whether or not he could sing; any fool knows that he could sing. But whether or not he was a handkerchief-head for wearing that patent-leather process.

Sammy Davis's process I detested. It didn't look good on him. Worse still, he liked to have a fried strand dangling down the middle of his forehead, shaking it out from the crown when he sang. But Nat King Cole's hair was a thing unto itself, a beautifully sculpted work of art that he and he alone should have had the right to wear.

The only difference between a process and a stocking cap, really, was   35
taste; yet Nat King Cole—unlike, say, Michael Jackson—looked *good* in his process. His head looked like Rudolph Valentino's in the twenties, and some say it was Valentino that the process imitated. But Nat King Cole wore a

Gems/Getty Images

Nat King Cole.

process because it suited his face, his demeanor, his name, his style. He was as clean as he wanted to be.

I had forgotten all about Nat King Cole and that patent-leather look until the day in 1971 when I was sitting in an Arab restaurant on the island of Zanzibar, surrounded by men in fezzes and white caftans, trying to learn how to eat curried goat and rice with the fingers of my right hand, feeling two million miles from home, when all of a sudden the old transistor radio sitting on top of a china cupboard stopped blaring out its Swahili music to play "Fly Me to the Moon" by Nat King Cole. The restaurant's din was not affected at all, not even by half a decibel. But in my mind's eye, I saw it: the King's sleek black magnificent tiara. I managed, barely, to blink back the tears. ■

The Reader's Presence

1. At what point in the essay do you, as a reader, begin to become aware of the social or political significance of the hair-straightening process? At what point in his own development does Gates begin to ascribe a political significance to hair? How would you describe his attitude toward the "kitchen"? toward the "process"? toward the prominent black Americans whom he names in the essay?

2. How would you characterize the author's voice in this essay? Which words and phrases hark back to the language of his home and family? How does Gates integrate these words and phrases into the text? What difference, if any, does it make to you as a reader when he puts certain words, such as *kitchen* or *good*, in quotation marks, as opposed to the passages in which phrases (such as "ugly as homemade sin dipped in misery" [paragraph 14]) are not set off in the text in this way?

3. **VISUAL PRESENCE:** Compare and contrast the portraits of Odetta Holmes Felious Gordon (page 99), Frederick Douglass (page 100), and Nat King Cole (page 104). What words and phrases would you choose to describe each person's appearance? After reading Gates's essay, how does each person's hairstyle affect how you perceive him or her? Support your answer with specific evidence from the text.

4. **CONNECTIONS:** Compare and contrast Gates's essay with James Baldwin's "Notes of a Native Son" (page 40). How does each writer come to terms with a sense of his racial identity? To what specific extent are Gates's ideas about black resistance to assimilation, published in 1995, similar to and different from those of Baldwin, published in 1955? Which essay did you find more compelling to read? Explain why.

Michihiko Hachiya
FROM HIROSHIMA DIARY

On August 6, 1945, the United States dropped an atomic bomb on the Japanese city of Hiroshima and introduced a new, devastating weapon into modern war. Two days later, the U.S. military dropped another bomb, on Nagasaki, forcing the Japanese government into an unconditional surrender. For years, the Japanese survivors of the blasts suffered from unhealing burns, radiation poisoning, cancers, and a score of other illnesses. At first, the Japanese had no idea what had hit them, though

> At first, the Japanese had no idea what had hit them, though rumors of a new secret weapon circulated rapidly.

rumors of a new secret weapon circulated rapidly. Most Americans today know of the bombing mainly through repeated images of the mushroom cloud itself; rarely do they see photographs or footage of the destruction and casualties. One of the most vivid accounts of the bombing and its immediate aftermath can be found in a diary kept by a Hiroshima physician, MICHIHIKO HACHIYA (1903–1980), who, though severely injured himself, miraculously found the time to record both his professional observations of a medical nightmare and his human impressions of an utterly destroyed community. Published on the tenth anniversary of the bombing of Hiroshima, *Hiroshima Diary* (1955) gained widespread attention. The diary runs only for some two months, from the moment of the blast on the sunny morning of August 6 to the end of September, when the American occupation was well under way.

WHAT HAD HAPPENED?

August 6, 1945

Badly injured from the blast, Dr. Hachiya managed to make his way to the hospital where he served as director and which, fortunately, was quite near his house. He spent several days in bed and did not begin writing his diary until August 8. As we can see from the following passage, however, the events were still fresh in his mind.

THE HOUR WAS EARLY; the morning still, warm, and beautiful. Shimmering leaves, reflecting sunlight from a cloudless sky, made a pleasant contrast with shadows in my garden as I gazed absently through wide-flung doors opening to the south.

Clad in drawers and undershirt, I was sprawled on the living room floor exhausted because I had just spent a sleepless night on duty as an air warden in my hospital.

Suddenly, a strong flash of light startled me—and then another. So well does one recall little things that I remember vividly how a stone lantern in the garden became brilliantly lit and I debated whether this light was caused by a magnesium flare or sparks from a passing trolley.

Garden shadows disappeared. The view where a moment before all had been so bright and sunny was now dark and hazy. Through swirling dust I could barely discern a wooden column that had supported one corner of my house. It was leaning crazily and the roof sagged dangerously.

Moving instinctively, I tried to escape, but rubble and fallen timbers barred the way. By picking my way cautiously I managed to reach the *rōka*[1] and stepped down into my garden. A profound weakness overcame me, so I stopped to regain my strength. To my surprise I discovered that I was completely naked. How odd! Where were my drawers and undershirt?

What had happened?

5

1 *rōka:* A narrow outside hall. —EDS.

All over the right side of my body I was cut and bleeding. A large splinter was protruding from a mangled wound in my thigh, and something warm trickled into my mouth. My cheek was torn, I discovered as I felt it gingerly, with the lower lip laid wide open. Embedded in my neck was a sizable fragment of glass which I matter-of-factly dislodged, and with the detachment of one stunned and shocked I studied it and my blood-stained hand.

Where was my wife?

Suddenly thoroughly alarmed, I began to yell for her: "Yaeko-san! Yaeko-san! Where are you?"

Blood began to spurt. Had my carotid artery been cut? Would I bleed to   10
death? Frightened and irrational, I called out again: "It's a five-hundred-ton bomb! Yaeko-san, where are you? A five-hundred-ton bomb has fallen!"

Yaeko-san, pale and frightened, her clothes torn and blood-stained, emerged from the ruins of our house holding her elbow. Seeing her, I was reassured. My own panic assuaged, I tried to reassure her.

"We'll be all right," I exclaimed. "Only let's get out of here as fast as we can."

She nodded, and I motioned for her to follow me.

The shortest path to the street lay through the house next door so through the house we went—running, stumbling, falling, and then running again until in headlong flight we tripped over something and fell sprawling into the street. Getting to my feet, I discovered that I had tripped over a man's head.

"Excuse me! Excuse me, please!" I cried hysterically.   15

There was no answer. The man was dead. The head had belonged to a young officer whose body was crushed beneath a massive gate.

We stood in the street, uncertain and afraid, until a house across from us began to sway and then with a rending motion fell almost at our feet. Our own house began to sway, and in a minute it, too, collapsed in a cloud of dust. Other buildings caved in or toppled. Fires sprang up and whipped by a vicious wind began to spread.

It finally dawned on us that we could not stay there in the street, so we turned our steps towards the hospital. Our home was gone; we were wounded and needed treatment; and after all, it was my duty to be with my staff. This latter was an irrational thought—what good could I be to anyone, hurt as I was.

We started out, but after twenty or thirty steps I had to stop. My breath became short, my heart pounded, and my legs gave way under me. An overpowering thirst seized me and I begged Yaeko-san to find me some water. But there was no water to be found. After a little my strength somewhat returned and we were able to go on.

I was still naked, and although I did not feel the least bit of shame, I was   20
disturbed to realize that modesty had deserted me. On rounding a corner we came upon a soldier standing idly in the street. He had a towel draped across his shoulder, and I asked if he would give it to me to cover my nakedness. The soldier surrendered the towel quite willingly but said not a word. A little later I lost the towel, and Yaeko-san took off her apron and tied it around my loins.

Our progress towards the hospital was interminably slow, until finally, my legs, stiff from drying blood, refused to carry me farther. The strength, even the will, to go on deserted me, so I told my wife, who was almost as badly hurt as I, to go on alone. This she objected to, but there was no choice. She had to go ahead and try to find someone to come back for me.

Yaeko-san looked into my face for a moment, and then, without saying a word, turned away and began running towards the hospital. Once, she looked back and waved and in a moment she was swallowed up in the gloom. It was quite dark now, and with my wife gone, a feeling of dreadful loneliness overcame me.

I must have gone out of my head lying there in the road because the next thing I recall was discovering that the clot on my thigh had been dislodged and blood was again spurting from the wound. I pressed my hand to the bleeding area and after a while the bleeding stopped and I felt better.

Could I go on?

I tried. It was all a nightmare—my wounds, the darkness, the road ahead. 25 My movements were ever so slow; only my mind was running at top speed.

In time I came to an open space where the houses had been removed to make a fire lane. Through the dim light I could make out ahead of me the hazy outlines of the Communications Bureau's big concrete building, and beyond it the hospital. My spirits rose because I knew that now someone would find me; and if I should die, at least my body would be found.

I paused to rest. Gradually things around me came into focus. There were the shadowy forms of people, some of whom looked like walking ghosts. Others moved as though in pain, like scarecrows, their arms held out from their bodies with forearms and hands dangling. These people puzzled me until I suddenly realized that they had been burned and were holding their arms out to prevent the painful friction of raw surfaces rubbing together. A naked woman carrying a naked baby came into view. I averted my gaze. Perhaps they had been in the bath. But then I saw a naked man, and it occurred to me that, like myself, some strange thing had deprived them of their clothes. An old woman lay near me with an expression of suffering on her face; but she made no sound. Indeed, one thing was common to everyone I saw—complete silence. . . .

PIKADON

August 9, 1945

As the wounded poured into Dr. Hachiya's hospital, the physicians tried to make sense of the symptoms and injuries, which did not resemble those of ordinary bombings. Because many of the patients with horrible symptoms showed no obvious signs of injuries, Dr. Hachiya could only speculate about what might have occurred. He had no idea as yet what type of weapon had been used against them.

Today, Dr. Hanaoka's[2] report on the patients was more detailed. One observation particularly impressed me. Regardless of the type of injury, nearly

2 ***Dr. Hanaoka:*** Head of internal medicine. —EDS.

everybody had the same symptoms. All had a poor appetite, the majority had nausea and gaseous indigestion, and over half had vomiting.

Not a few had shown improvement since yesterday. Diarrhea, though, continued to be a problem and actually appeared to be increasing. Distinctly alarming was the appearance of blood in the stools of patients who earlier had only diarrhea. The isolation of these people was becoming increasingly difficult.

One seriously ill man complained of a sore mouth yesterday, and today,   30 numerous small hemorrhages began to appear in his mouth and under his skin. His case was the more puzzling because he came to the hospital complaining of weakness and nausea and did not appear to have been injured at all.

This morning, other patients were beginning to show small subcutaneous hemorrhages, and not a few were coughing and vomiting blood in addition to passing it in their stools. One poor woman was bleeding from her privates. Among these patients there was not one with symptoms typical of anything we knew, unless you could excuse those who developed signs of severe brain disease before they died.

People walking through the ruins of Hiroshima in the weeks following the atomic bomb blast. Photo by Bernard Hoffman.

Bernard Hoffman/Getty Images

Dr. Hanaoka believed the patients could be divided into three groups:

1. Those with nausea, vomiting, and diarrhea who were improving.
2. Those with nausea, vomiting, and diarrhea who were remaining stationary.
3. Those with nausea, vomiting, and diarrhea who were developing hemorrhage under the skin or elsewhere.

Had these patients been burned or otherwise injured, we might have tried to stretch the logic of cause and effect and assume that their bizarre symptoms were related to injury, but so many patients appeared to have received no injury whatsoever that we were obliged to postulate an insult heretofore unknown.

The only other possible cause for the weird symptoms observed was a sudden change in atmospheric pressure. I had read somewhere about bleeding that follows ascent to high altitudes and about bleeding in deep sea divers who ascend too rapidly from the depths. Having never seen such injury I could not give much credence to my thoughts.

Still, it was impossible to dismiss the thought that atmospheric pressure   35
had had something to do with the symptoms of our patients. During my student days at Okayama University, I had seen experiments conducted in a pressure chamber. Sudden, temporary deafness was one symptom everyone complained of if pressure in the chamber was abruptly altered.

Now, I could state positively that I heard nothing like an explosion when we were bombed the other morning, nor did I remember any sound during my walk to the hospital as houses collapsed around me. It was as though I walked through a gloomy, silent motion picture. Others whom I questioned had had the same experience.

Those who experienced the bombing from the outskirts of the city characterized it by the word: *pikadon*.[3]

How then could one account for my failure and the failure of others to hear an explosion except on the premise that a sudden change in atmospheric pressure had rendered those nearby temporarily deaf: Could the bleeding we were beginning to observe be explained on the same basis?

Since all books and journals had been destroyed, there was no way to corroborate my theories except by further appeal to the patients. To that end Dr. Katsube[4] was asked to discover what else he could when he made ward rounds.

It was pleasing to note my scientific curiosity was reviving, and I lost no   40
opportunity to question everyone who visited me about the bombing of Hiroshima. Their answers were vague and ambiguous, and on one point

---

[3] **pikadon:** *Pika* means a glitter, sparkle, or bright flash of light, like a flash of lightning. *Don* means a boom! or loud sound. Together, the words came to mean to the people of Hiroshima an explosion characterized by a flash and a boom. Hence: "flash-boom!" Those who remember the flash only speak of the "*pika*"; those who were far enough from the hypocenter to experience both speak of the "*pikadon*." —EDS.

[4] ***Dr. Katsube:*** Chief of surgery. —EDS.

only were they in agreement: a new weapon had been used. *What* the new weapon was became a burning question. Not only had our books been destroyed, but our newspapers, telephones, and radios as well. ●

The Reader's Presence

1. In many ways, it is fortunate that one of the diaries kept immediately after the atomic blast was written by a medical doctor. Why? How does it contribute to the diary's historical value? Could this be a disadvantage? Would you have preferred to read a patient's diary instead? Why or why not?

2. Hachiya's first entry, on August 6, was written a few days after the events it depicts. What indications do you receive from the writing that the entry was predated? Can you detect any differences from the second entry (August 9), which was apparently composed on the stated day?

3. **VISUAL PRESENCE:** Examine carefully the photograph of Hiroshima after the atomic bomb blast (page 109). What were your initial reactions to the photograph? How does the image compare with Hachiya's description of the events immediately following the attack? Support your response with specific details from the photograph and Hachiya's essay.

4. **CONNECTIONS:** Hachiya's confusion reveals itself in his writing in many ways: short paragraphs, multiple questions, and unconfirmed guesses. Throughout, his matter-of-fact language belies his panic. In what specific ways does Hachiya's characterization of the bombing of Hiroshima compare with Christopher Hitchens's account of being waterboarded ("Believe Me, It's Torture," page 531)?

Silas Hansen
WHAT REAL MEN DO

Recent discussions of gender have taught us that human identities cannot be placed into neat little boxes. Our habits and hobbies, our likes and dislikes, are not necessarily determined by our chromosomes. And yet, some pastimes can be difficult to reconcile with traditional expectations about gender. For **SILAS HANSEN**, this means recognizing that football and *Mean Girls* are not incompatible. In "What Real Men Do," Hansen reminds us that we need not limit ourselves to gendered stereotypes.

> For Silas Hansen, football and *Mean Girls* are not incompatible.

An established essayist, Hansen discovered his affinity for writing nonfiction in college. He graduated from the State University of New York at Brockport and received an MFA in creative writing from the Ohio State University. He writes frequently on gender and identity, with essays appearing in *Slate*, the *Normal School*, *Hayden's Ferry Review*, *Puerto del Sol*, and *Colorado Review*, among other publications.

Hansen is an assistant professor at Ball State University in Muncie, Indiana, where he teaches creative nonfiction. He encourages his students to think for themselves, even if that means disagreeing with their teachers: "I teach my students what I know—what the experts have said, what others have done, what has and hasn't worked so far—and then ask them to think critically about whether or not that rings true for them and their work."

A REAL MAN ISN'T AFRAID OF ANYTHING

He has heard people say this his whole life, even when he was a kid, even back when he was still trying, desperately trying, to be happy as a girl—and later, too, after he told people the truth of his gender ("Just trying to help," they would say)—so he knows it must be true: He shouldn't be afraid of *anything*.

Except that there are so many things that are actually terrifying, like outer space—sometimes he can't even look at the night sky without his heart racing because *it never ends*, it literally goes on forever, there are just stars and planets and solar systems out there, and who knows how many, and how could that *not* be terrifying?—and bats—because they carry rabies—and raccoons—for the same reason—and also the dark, because who knows what's out there? Can we ever really be sure?

But he is definitely not afraid when he's home alone at night, except when he accidentally reads something terrifying on the Internet or sees something on TV. He tells himself that the chances of falling victim to whatever he just read about online—killer bees, or a possible serial killer in southeastern Ohio, or maybe those mysterious lights over Los Angeles last week—are small, so unimaginably small, because it's not like the scary things are hacking into his computer and looking to see what he's reading and then showing up *just after he finishes the article . . .* and yet he can't help but immediately jump out of bed and go make sure all of the doors and windows are locked, just to be safe.

And he is definitely not afraid of spiders, because they're more afraid of him than he is of them. Except when he sees one walk across his ceiling right before bed, and then he tries to smack it with a broom, and he's not sure if he killed it or just made it angry and knocked it into his bed, so he has to go sleep on the couch until he can do laundry in the morning and make sure it's really, absolutely, 100% not hiding within his sheets. Or when he reads about brown recluse spiders—again, on the Internet, the starting point for all fears—and then goes outside to mow his lawn, opens the garage door, and finds spider eggs on the floor, and so he declares that the garage is dead to him now, he simply doesn't have one; if he looks out the windows on the back of his house he sees just his yard, and the alley behind it, and nothing else, especially not a building that used to be a garage where he *absolutely will not* be keeping his car this winter because *it doesn't exist.*

A REAL MAN WATCHES FOOTBALL

He spends his weekends in his living room or in bars, wearing his team's   5
jersey while he drinks beer and yells at the TV. He gets upset—so upset he yells loud enough to scare his cat off the couch—when his team's quarterback—their first real hope in years—is out for two weeks with a knee injury, and they put in the backup, a first-round draft pick who has never lived up to the hype, and he lets the Jaguars pick him off three plays in a row, and they go from 3–0 to 21–3 in just four minutes.

He sits on bar patios and friends' front porches and in his dad's friend's living room, and he talks about football. He talks about the NFL Power Rankings in Week 7, and about the NCAA's new playoff system, and about how the Cardinals/the Bengals/Clemson/Ohio State might do in the post-season this year. He holds a beer in one hand during these conversations—always a beer, or maybe some whiskey; he saves the red wine or the mixed drinks for some other time, for at home or at a different bar or around people who aren't his Football Friends—and he makes sure his voice sounds lower, lower than when he gets called "ma'am" on the phone or in the McDonald's drive-thru, and he makes sure not to talk so much with his hands when he says things like "third-down conversion" or "pass interference" or "three-and-out" and waits for the approving nod from the other guys.

When his social media feeds blow up with news of another football player accused of sexual assault, or another football player accused of domestic violence, or another coach who signs another player accused of sexual assault or domestic violence or assault and battery, or when another high school football player dies on the field or another one goes back in the game, even though he probably shouldn't, he tries not to think too much about it. He tries to tell himself that he can like the game and dislike the players, that he can like the game and dislike the culture, that the culture can change, that the players understand the risks, and they're adults. Because he likes football, that's part of it, but even more than that, he doesn't want to lose what watching football gives him: something to talk about with his father when they talk on the phone, something to talk about with other men that makes him feel like he's part of the club, like he belongs there.

A REAL MAN KNOWS HOW TO DO THINGS AROUND THE HOUSE

When he buys his first home, just after turning 28, he tells himself he'll do it all: pull up the carpets and install new flooring and strip wallpaper and paint the walls and maybe even build a raised-bed vegetable garden in the backyard, where he can grow tomatoes and cucumbers and zucchini. He buys a house that needs a lot of work—*cosmetic* work, though, nothing in terms of the structure or plumbing or electrical, at least not that he can see—because he wants to do it all. He grew up in a house where his father did these things—built decks and front porches, tore down walls and built additions—but he never helped, never learned, and now he wants to prove that he can. He wants to prove it to everyone else, of course, but he mostly wants to prove it to himself.

But then he moves in and realizes the doors don't close all the way—"probably because the house has settled," his father says on the phone—and so he goes to the hardware store and buys a circular saw and the right blade to put in it and some clamps to hold the door steady as he cuts. He takes the door to the guest bedroom/office off its hinges and carries it to the dining room, where he can rest it on the table, and he tries to keep the door from hitting the walls, from getting stuck in the doorframes along the way, but he fails. The whole time, his hands are shaking because he's never done this before, never used a tool more powerful than an electric drill to hang a coat rack or a picture frame. Once he gets the door on the table and clamps it down, he realizes his hands are shaking too much to hold the saw steady, so he grabs his laptop and watches circular saw tutorials on YouTube to try to convince himself he can do it.

Eventually, he works up the nerve to go back to the dining room, to plug in the saw, to hold it steady. He remembers to hold it with both hands, to start it before he presses the blade to wood just like they said in the videos, and somehow, holding his breath the whole time, he manages to trim off just shy of a quarter inch. 10

Later, after his heartbeat returns to normal and he confirms that he didn't cut off any fingers, he carries the door back to the guest room/office, hitting it against the walls and the doorframes along the way, and puts it back on its hinges. He tries not to think about the big gap between the top of the door and the doorframe, since he accidentally took too much off, or the cut that is far from even, or the fact that it still doesn't latch, and instead reminds himself that the door shuts, now, and *he* made that happen.

A REAL MAN DOESN'T WATCH *THOSE* TV SHOWS AND MOVIES

By *those*, of course, he means things like *Downton Abbey*, which he definitely has not seen every episode of at least four times. Instead, he watches reruns of *Sports Night* and *Friday Night Lights* and *The X-Files*, and he watched every new episode of *Mad Men* when it aired, and he *definitely* doesn't have 82 episodes of *Dr. Quinn, Medicine Woman* reruns waiting for him on his DVR right now. And when he watches movies, he sticks to *Batman* and *The X-Men* and *Saving Private Ryan*, and he absolutely does *not* watch *Love Actually* every year on Christmas Eve—which is absolutely *not* his one beloved Christmas tradition—or know a quote from *Mean Girls* for virtually all contexts, or know all of the major plot points of *Runaway Bride*, in order, nearly twenty years after it premiered.

And if he does watch these things—if he does, sometimes, after watching football all day Sunday, need to counteract it all with a few episodes of *Gilmore Girls* before bed—he thinks that he's the only one, that it's weird, that he probably shouldn't admit these things to people—until one day, when he's on his friends' porch.

They have just finished drafting their fantasy football teams, and so there they are, six men in their twenties, sitting on the porch, PBR tall boys in their hands, talking about whether it was smarter to draft Dez Bryant or Julio Jones, or Aaron Rodgers or Tom Brady, and then, somehow—he won't remember later how it happened—one of them says something about *When Harry Met Sally.*

"Oh, best movie, hands down," one of his friends says, and he says, 15 "Really?" and his friend says, "What? You don't think so? Don't tell me you prefer the Meg Ryan of *You've Got Mail,*" and then his friend proceeds to rank her movies, with *Kate and Leopold* on the very bottom, *You've Got Mail* beating it out only slightly, *City of Angels* and *Sleepless in Seattle* in the middle, and *When Harry Met Sally* on top. They all argue about this for a while—the exact placement of *You've Got Mail,* and whether or not *Kate and Leopold* even deserves to be considered, and what about *French Kiss*?

And during this whole conversation, even when he's participating, he can't stop thinking about how strange this all is, how unexpected—six men in their twenties, six guys with beards, most of them wearing flannel in August, debating the hierarchy of Meg Ryan's 1990s romantic comedy performances, so wholeheartedly embracing this side of themselves. And, for once, he stops worrying about what he's supposed to do, and he embraces that side of himself, too. ●

The Reader's Presence

1. Silas Hansen writes in the third person ("he"), but he is clearly writing about himself. Speaking in the third person can suggest distance from the subject (as opposed to using the more personal "I"). Yet deliberately repeating "he" reinforces the male identity described in the essay. How would you perceive Hansen and the story he tells had he written in the first person? Support your response by pointing to—and analyzing—specific passages from the essay and by focusing on the effects of specific words and phrases.

2. Hansen unfolds different meanings and examples of the word "terrifying." Which definitions and examples do you find most and least engaging and persuasive? Explain why. Hansen also frequently describes himself through negation: "he is definitely not afraid of spiders." In another instance, Hansen writes: "Because he likes football, that's part of it, but even more than that, he doesn't want to lose what watching football gives him" (paragraph 6). What are the effects of choosing to assert some truths about himself in this way, but not others?

3. **CONNECTIONS:** In Hansen's essay, men have a community he is eager to participate in, despite his reservations about what "real men" are supposed to do. Consider how Hansen's view of gender roles resembles and differs from Katha Pollitt's in "Why Boys Don't Play with Dolls" (page 478) and from Rebecca Solnit's in "Men Explain Things

to Me" (page 492). How would you compare Hansen, Politt's and Solnit's views of identity and self-doubt? Compare Hansen's view of gender roles with Politt's and Solnit's. What principles, according to Politt and Solnit, make it difficult for Hansen to reconcile interests that do not fit into longstanding stereotypes?

Edward Hoagland

ON STUTTERING

EDWARD HOAGLAND (b. 1932) is an essayist, a nature writer, and a novelist. In 1951, Hoagland joined the Ringling Bros. and Barnum & Bailey Circus and wrote a novel about his experience: *Cat Man* (1956) was accepted for publication before he graduated from Harvard and the book won the Houghton Mifflin Literary Fellowship Award. He has received several other honors, including two Guggenheim Fellowships, an O. Henry Award, an award from the American Academy of Arts and Letters, and a Lannan Foundation Award. Having taught at Bennington College in Vermont for almost twenty years, Hoagland retired in 2005.

> **"Most of us live like stand-up comedians on a vaudeville stage."**

Hoagland's essays cover a wide range of topics, such as personal experiences, wild animals, travels to other countries, and ecological crises. Among his many highly regarded books are *Walking the Dead Diamond River* (1973), *African Calliope* (1979), *Balancing Acts* (1992), *Tigers & Ice* (1999), and *Hoagland on Nature* (2003). His latest book, *Children Are Diamonds: An African Apocalypse*, was published in 2013.

In his memoir, *Compass Points* (2001), Hoagland writes: "Most of us live like stand-up comedians on a vaudeville stage—the way an essayist does—by our humble wits, messing up, swallowing an aspirin, knowing Hollywood won't call, thinking no one we love will die today, just another day of sunshine and rain."

STUTTERING IS LIKE TRYING to run with loops of rope around your feet. And yet you feel that you do want to run because you may get more words out that way before you trip: an impulse you resist so other people won't tell you to "calm down" and "relax." Because they themselves may stammer a little bit when jittery or embarrassed, it's hard for a real stutterer like me to convince a new acquaintance that we aren't perpetually in such a nervous state and that it's quite normal for us to be at the mercy of strangers. Strangers are usually civilized, once the rough and sometimes inadvertently hurtful process of recognizing what is wrong with us is over (that we're not laughing, hiccuping, coughing, or whatever) and in a way we plumb them for traces of schadenfreude. A stutterer knows who the good guys are in any crowded room, as well as the location of each mocking gleam, and even the St. Francis type, who will wait until he thinks nobody is looking to wipe a fleck of spittle off his face.

I've stuttered for more than sixty years, and the mysteries of the encumbrance still catch me up: being reminded every morning that it's engrained in my fiber, although I had forgotten in my dreams. Life can become a matter of measuring the importance of anything you have to say. Is it better to remain a pleasant cipher who ventures nothing in particular but chuckles immoderately at everyone else's conversation, or instead to subject your several companions to the ordeal of watching you struggle to expel opinions that are either blurred and vitiated, or made to sound too emphatic, by all the huffing and puffing, the facial contortions, tongue biting, blushing, and suffering? "Write it down," people often said to me in school; indeed I sold my first novel before I left college.

Self-confidence can reduce a stutter's dimensions (in that sense you do "outgrow" it), as will affection (received or felt), anger, sexual arousal, and various other hormonal or pheromonal states you may dip into in the shorter term. Yet it still lurks underfoot, like a trapdoor. I was determined not to be impeded and managed to serve a regular stint in the Army by telling the draft-board psychiatrist that I wanted to and was only stammering from "nervousness" with him. Later I also contrived to become a college professor, thanks to the patience of my early students. Nevertheless, through childhood and adolescence, when I was almost mute in public, I could talk without much difficulty to one or two close friends, and then to the particular girl I was necking with. In that case, an overlapping trust was then the lubricant, but if it began to evaporate as our hopes for permanence didn't pan out, I'd start regretfully, apologetically but willy-nilly, to stutter with her again. Adrenaline, when I got mad, operated in a similar fashion, though only momentarily. That is, if somebody made fun of me or treated me cavalierly and a certain threshold was crossed, a spurt of chemistry would suddenly free my mouth and—like Popeye grabbing a can of spinach—I could answer him. Poor Billy Budd[1] didn't learn this technique (and his example frightened me because of its larger implications). Yet many stutterers develop a snappish temperament, and from not just sheer frustration but the fact that being more than ready to "lose one's temper" (as Billy wasn't) actually helps. As in jujitsu, you can trap an opponent by employing his strength and cruelty against him; and bad guys aren't generally smart enough to know that if they wait me out, I'll bog down helplessly all over again.

[1] ***Poor Billy Budd:*** A reference to the main character in Herman Melville's novella *Billy Budd* (published 1924). Billy Budd's speech impediment plays a pivotal role in the plot, leading to his hanging. —EDS.

Overall, however, stuttering is not so predictable. Whether rested or exhausted, fibbing or speaking the Simon-pure truth, and when in the company of chums or people whom I don't respect, I can be fluent or tied in knots. I learned young to be an attentive listener, both because my empathy for others' worries was honed by my handicap and because it was in my best interest that they talk a lot. And yet a core in you will hemorrhage if you become a mere assenter. How many opinions can you keep to yourself before you choke on them (and turn into a stick of furniture for everybody else)? So, instead, you measure what's worth specifying. If you agree with two-thirds of what's being suggested, is it worth the labor of breathlessly elaborating upon the one-third where you differ? There were plenty of times when a subject might come up that I knew more about than the rest of the group, and it used to gall me if I had held my peace till maybe closeted afterward with a close friend. A stymieing bashfulness can also slide a stutterer into slack language because accurate words are so much harder to say than bland ones. You're tempted to be content with an approximation of what you mean in order to escape the scourge of being exact. A sort of football game is going on in your head—the tacklers live there too—and the very effort of pausing to figure out the right way to describe something will alert them to how to pull you down. Being glib and sloppy generates less blockage.

But it's important not to err in the opposite direction, on the side of ten-dentiousness, and insist on equal time only because you are a pain in the neck with a problem. You can stutter till your tongue bleeds and your chest is sore from heaving, but so what, if you haven't anything to say that's worth the humiliation? Better to function as a kind of tuning fork, vibrating to other people's anguish or apprehensiveness, as well as your own. A handicap can be cleansing. My scariest moments as a stutterer have been (1) when my daughter was learning to talk and briefly got the impression that she was supposed to do the same; (2) once when I was in the woods and a man shot in my direction and I had to make myself heard loud and fast; and (3) when anticipating weddings where I would need either to propose a toast or say "I do." Otherwise my impediment ceased to be a serious blight about the time I lost my virginity: just a sort of cleft to step around—a squint and gasp of hesitation that indicated to people I might want to be friends with or interview that I wasn't perfect either and perhaps they could trust me.

At worst, during my teens, when I was stuttering on vowels as well as consonants and spitting a few words out could seem interminable, I tried some therapies. But "Slow Speech" was as slow as the trouble itself; and repeatedly writing the first letter of the word that I was stuttering on with my finger in my pocket looked peculiar enough to attract almost as much attention. It did gradually lighten with my maturity and fatherhood, professional recognition, and the other milestones that traditionally help. Nothing "slew" it, though, until at nearly 60 I went semiblind for a couple of years, and this emergency eclipsed—completely trumped—the lesser difficulty. I felt I simply had to talk or die, and so I talked. Couldn't do it gratuitously or lots, but I talked enough to survive. The stutter somehow didn't hold water and ebbed away, until surgery restored my vision and then it returned, like other normalcies.

5

Such variations can make a stutter seem like a sort of ancillary eccentricity, or a personal Godzilla. But the ball carrier in your head is going to have his good days too—when he can swivel past the tacklers, improvising a broken-field dash so that they are out of position—or even capture their attention with an idea so intriguing that they stop and listen. Not for long, however: The message underlying a stutter is rather like mortality, after all. Real reprieves and fluency are not for you and me. We blunder along, stammering—then not so much—through minor scrapes and scares, but not unscathed. We're not Demosthenes, of course. And poor Demosthenes, if you look him up, ended about as sadly as Billy Budd. People tend to. ▇

The Reader's Presence

1. Why does Hoagland compare his stutter to a football game (paragraph 4)? Explore the metaphor fully. For example, what position does Hoagland play? Who are the tacklers who are trying to pull him down? How many touchdowns does he score in his life, according to his essay? What strategies does he develop to avoid anticipated blockers? Would you say he's winning or losing? Why?

2. In what specific ways do Hoagland's sentences and paragraphs begin and end as you might have anticipated? Can you detect written signs of his stutter? What kinds of verbal hesitations and restatements happen when someone stutters? Where—and with what effects—are there similar hesitations and restatements in Hoagland's essay? Imagine Hoagland speaking this essay. At which points do you think that he would hesitate? Rewrite a paragraph to include the imagined stuttering and compare it to the original paragraph. What changes in meaning occur in the rewritten version?

3. **CONNECTIONS:** Read David Sedaris's "Me Talk Pretty One Day" (page 210) and compare his and Hoagland's approaches to handling difficulties with speech. What strategies do they use to deal with being less than fluent? To what extent do their limitations affect their feelings about themselves? about the world around them? Who deals more effectively with not being able to communicate easily? Why?

The Writer at Work

EDWARD HOAGLAND on What an Essay Is

Oscar White/Getty Images

Known as one of the America's finest essayists, Edward Hoagland began his career writing fiction. In this passage from his introduction to *The Best American Essays 1999*, Hoagland describes how he thinks essays work and the idiosyncratic ways essayists—like himself—approach the act of writing them. Essays, he reminds us, are different from articles and documents: they don't necessarily offer objective information and they don't require their writers to be authorities about anything other than their own experiences. All good essays, he suggests, encapsulate their writer's presence. In these literary beliefs he is a direct descendant of Montaigne (1533–1592), whom many consider the inventor of the modern essay. Montaigne, too, was skeptical of authority and wrote essays that appear to follow the drifts of an interior dialogue carried on with himself. After reading Hoagland's brief but thoughtful passage, consider how it comments on his essay on stuttering.

❝Essays are how we speak to one another in print—caroming thoughts not merely in order to convey a certain packet of information, but with a special edge or bounce of personal character in a kind of public letter. You multiply yourself as a writer, gaining height as though jumping on a trampoline, if you can catch the gist of what other people have also been feeling and clarify it for them. Classic essay subjects, like the flux of friendship, "On Greed," "On Religion," "On Vanity," or solitude, lying, self-sacrifice, can be major-league yet not require Bertrand Russell to handle them. A layman who has diligently looked into something, walking in the mosses of regret after the death of a parent, for instance, may acquire an intangible authority, even without being memorably angry or funny or possessing a beguiling equanimity. *He* cares; therefore, if he has tinkered enough with his words, we do too.

An essay is not a scientific document. It can be serendipitous or domestic, satire or testimony, tongue-in-cheek or a wail of grief. Mulched perhaps in its own contradictions, it promises no sure objectivity, just the condiment of opinion on a base of observation, and sometimes such leaps of illogic or superlogic that they may work a bit like magic realism in a novel: namely, to simulate the mind's own processes in a murky and incongruous world. More than being instructive, as a magazine article is, an essay has a slant, a seasoned personality behind it that ought to weather well. Even if we think the author is telling us the earth is flat, we might want to listen to him elaborate upon the fringes of his premise because the bristle of his narrative and what he's seen intrigues us. He has a cutting edge, yet balance too. A given body of information is going to be eclipsed, but what lives in art is spirit, not factuality, and we respond to Montaigne's human touch despite four centuries of technological and social change.❞

Langston Hughes

SALVATION

One of the leading figures of the Harlem Renaissance, **LANGSTON HUGHES** (1902–1967) was a prolific writer. He started his career as a poet, but he also wrote fiction, autobiography, biography, history, and plays, and he worked at various times as a journalist. One of his most famous poems, "The Negro Speaks of Rivers," was written while he was in high school. Although Hughes traveled widely, most of his writings are concerned with the lives of urban working-class African Americans.

Hughes used the rhythms of blues and jazz to bring to his writing a distinctive expression of black culture and experience. His work continues to be popular today, especially collections of short stories such as *The Ways of White Folks* (1934), volumes of poetry such as *Montage of a Dream Deferred* (1951), and his series of vignettes on the character Jesse B. Simple, collected and published from 1950 to 1965. Hughes published two volumes of autobiography; "Salvation" is taken from the first of these, *The Big Sea* (1940).

> "I only knew the people I had grown up with, and they weren't the people whose shoes were always shined, who had been to Harvard, or who had heard of Bach. But they seemed to me good people too."

Throughout his work, Hughes refused to idealize his subject. "Certainly," he said, "I personally knew very few people anywhere who were wholly beautiful and wholly good. Besides I felt that the masses of our people had as much in their lives to put into books as did those more fortunate ones who had been born with some means and the ability to work up to a master's degree at a Northern college." Expressing the writer's truism on writing about what one knows best, he continued, "Anyway, I didn't know the upper-class Negroes well enough to write much about them. I only knew the people I had grown up with, and they weren't the people whose shoes were always shined, who had been to Harvard, or who had heard of Bach. But they seemed to me good people too."

I WAS SAVED FROM SIN when I was going on thirteen. But not really saved. It happened like this. There was a big revival at my Auntie Reed's church. Every night for weeks there had been much preaching, singing, praying, and shouting, and some very hardened sinners had been brought to Christ, and the membership of the church had grown by leaps and bounds. Then just before the revival ended, they held a special meeting for children, "to bring the young lambs to the fold." My aunt spoke of it for days ahead. That night I was escorted to the front row and placed on the mourners' bench with all the other young sinners, who had not yet been brought to Jesus.

My aunt told me that when you were saved you saw a light, and something happened to you inside! And Jesus came into your life! And God was with you from then on! She said you could see and hear and feel Jesus in your soul. I believed her. I had heard a great many old people say the same thing and it seemed to me they ought to know. So I sat there calmly in the hot, crowded church, waiting for Jesus to come to me.

The preacher preached a wonderful rhythmical sermon, all moans and shouts and lonely cries and dire pictures of hell, and then he sang a song about the ninety and nine safe in the fold, but one little lamb was left out in the cold. Then he said: "Won't you come? Won't you come to Jesus? Young lambs, won't you come?" And he held out his arms to all us young sinners there on the mourners' bench. And the little girls cried. And some of them jumped up and went to Jesus right away. But most of us just sat there.

A great many old people came and knelt around us and prayed, old women with jet-black faces and braided hair, old men with work-gnarled hands. And the church sang a song about the lower lights are burning, some poor sinners to be saved. And the whole building rocked with prayer and song.

Still I kept waiting to *see* Jesus.   5

Finally all the young people had gone to the altar and were saved, but one boy and me. He was a rounder's son named Westley. Westley and I were surrounded by sisters and deacons praying. It was very hot in the church, and getting late now. Finally Westley said to me in a whisper: "God damn! I'm tired o' sitting here. Let's get up and be saved." So he got up and was saved.

Then I was left all alone on the mourners' bench. My aunt came and knelt at my knees and cried, while prayers and song swirled all around me in the little church. The whole congregation prayed for me alone, in a mighty wail of moans and voices. And I kept waiting serenely for Jesus, waiting, waiting — but he didn't come. I wanted to see him, but nothing happened to me. Nothing! I wanted something to happen to me, but nothing happened.

I heard the songs and the minister saying: "Why don't you come? My dear child, why don't you come to Jesus? Jesus is waiting for you. He wants you. Why don't you come? Sister Reed, what is this child's name?"

"Langston," my aunt sobbed.

"Langston, why don't you come? Why don't you come and be saved? Oh,   10
Lamb of God! Why don't you come?"

Now it was really getting late. I began to be ashamed of myself, holding everything up so long. I began to wonder what God thought about Westley, who certainly hadn't seen Jesus either, but who was now sitting proudly on the platform, swinging his knickerbockered legs and grinning down at me, surrounded by deacons and old women on their knees praying. God had not struck Westley dead for taking his name in vain or for lying in the temple. So I decided that maybe to save further trouble, I'd better lie, too, and say that Jesus had come, and get up and be saved.

So I got up.

Suddenly the whole room broke into a sea of shouting, as they saw me rise. Waves of rejoicing swept the place. Women leaped in the air. My aunt threw her arms around me. The minister took me by the hand and led me to the platform.

When things quieted down, in a hushed silence, punctuated by a few ecstatic "Amens," all the new young lambs were blessed in the name of God. Then joyous singing filled the room.

That night, for the first time in my life but one — for I was a big boy   15
twelve years old — I cried. I cried, in bed alone, and couldn't stop. I buried my head under the quilts, but my aunt heard me. She woke up and told my

uncle I was crying because the Holy Ghost had come into my life, and because I had seen Jesus. But I was really crying because I couldn't bear to tell her that I had lied, that I had deceived everybody in the church, that I hadn't seen Jesus, and that now I didn't believe there was a Jesus anymore, since he didn't come to help me. ◼

The Reader's Presence

1. Pay close attention to Hughes's two opening sentences. How would you describe their tone? How do they suggest the underlying pattern of the essay? How do they introduce the idea of deception right from the start? Who is being deceived in the essay? Is it the congregation? God? Hughes's aunt? the reader?

2. Hughes's essay is full of hyperbole, much of it expressing the heightened emotion of religious conversion. What is the purpose of the exclamation points Hughes uses in paragraph 2? Who is speaking these sentences? Where are other examples of overstatement? How does Hughes incorporate lyrics from songs into his prose (see especially paragraph 3)? Why not simply quote from the songs directly? How do these stylistic decisions affect your sense of the scene? Do you feel aligned with Hughes? Why or why not?

3. **CONNECTIONS:** How does Hughes use the character of Westley? To what extent is Westley essential in the narrative? Explain why. How does Westley's role compare to secondary characters such as, for example, Clyde in Jerald Walker's "Scattered Inconveniences" (page 239) or Yafei in Ha Jin's "Arrival" (page 129)?

The Writer at Work

LANGSTON HUGHES on *How to Be a Bad Writer (in Ten Easy Lessons)*

Library of Congress, Prints & Photographs Division, Reproduction number LC-USZ62-92598 (b&w film copy neg.)

Established authors are frequently asked for tips on writing. Here Langston Hughes reverses the practice and offers young writers some memorable advice on how to write poorly. "How to Be a Bad Writer" first appeared in the *Harlem Quarterly* (Spring 1950). Some of Hughes's suggestions no longer seem applicable today, thanks in part to his own literary efforts. But which lessons do you think are still worth paying attention to?

66 1. Use all the clichés possible, such as "He had a gleam in his eye," or "Her teeth were white as pearls."

2. If you are a Negro, try very hard to write with an eye dead on the white market—use modern stereotypes of older stereotypes—big burly Negroes, criminals, low-lifers, and prostitutes.

3. Put in a lot of profanity and as many pages as possible of near-pornography and you will be so modern you pre-date Pompeii in your lonely crusade toward the best-seller lists. By all means be misunderstood, unappreciated, and ahead of your time in print and out, then you can be felt-sorry-for by your own self, if not the public.

4. Never characterize characters. Just name them and then let them go for themselves. Let all of them talk the same way. If the reader hasn't imagination enough to make something out of cardboard cut-outs, shame on him!

5. Write about China, Greece, Tibet, or the Argentine pampas—anyplace you've never seen and know nothing about. Never write about anything you know, your home town, or your home folks, or yourself.

6. Have nothing to say, but use a great many words, particularly high-sounding words, to say it.

7. If a playwright, put into your script a lot of hand-waving and spirituals, preferably the ones everybody has heard a thousand times from Marion Anderson to the Golden Gates.

8. If a poet, rhyme June with moon as often and in as many ways as possible. Also use *thee*'s and *thou*'s and *'tis* and *o'er*, and invert your sentences all the time. Never say, "The sun rose, bright and shining." But, rather, "Bright and shining rose the sun."

9. Pay no attention to spelling or grammar or the neatness of the manuscript. And in writing letters, never sign your name so anyone can read it. A rapid scrawl will better indicate how important and how busy you are.

10. Drink as much liquor as possible and always write under the influence of alcohol. When you can't afford alcohol yourself, or even if you can, drink on your friends, fans, and the general public.

If you are white, there are many more things I can advise in order to be a bad writer, but since this piece is for colored writers, there are some things I know a Negro just will not do, not even for writing's sake, so there is no use mentioning them. **99**

Margo Jefferson
FROM *NEGROLAND*

With a Pulitzer Prize in criticism (1995), a book on Michael Jackson (2006), and now a memoir, **MARGO JEFFERSON** (b. 1947) has shifted her topics significantly over the past two decades. "I wanted to experiment as a writer," she says about her decision to write a memoir.

"I'd written varieties of criticism for so long. I wanted to use those skills in a new way—to explore a culture."

Jefferson has taught nonfiction writing at Columbia, Princeton, and the New School. She has also written for a number of publications, including *Newsweek* and the *New York Times*, where she served as theater critic. In *Negroland: A Memoir* (2015), from which this essay is adapted, Jefferson turns her critical eye inward to consider her family's position among the affluent black community of Chicago in the 1950s and 1960s.

> **"I'd written varieties of criticism for so long. I wanted to use those skills in a new way—to explore a culture."**

In an interview with the *Writer* magazine, Jefferson noted, "I have always struggled with self-censorship. That has been a huge battle for me. My little drawers are filled with writing — that's true of many writers — that I gave up on, decided what's the point because it will never see the light of day or this is shameful or embarrassing. So yes, I thought it's time. If not now, when?"

Margo Jefferson.

I

ARE WE RICH?

Mother raises those plucked, deep-toned eyebrows that did such excellent expressive work for women in the 1950s. Lift the penciled arch by three to four millimeters for bemused doubt, blatant disdain, or disapproval just playful enough to lure the speaker into more error. Mother's lips form a small, cool smile that mirrors her eyebrow arch. She places a small, emphatic space between each word: *Are. We. Rich?* Then she adds, with a hint of weariness, *Why do you ask?*

I ask because I had been told that day. *Your family must be rich.* A school-mate had told me and I'd faltered, with no answer, flattered and ashamed to be. We were supposed to eschew petty snobberies at the University of Chicago Laboratory School: intellectual superiority was our task. Other fathers were doctors. Other mothers dressed well and drove stylish cars. Wondering what had stirred that question left me anxious and a little queasy.

Mother says, *We are not rich. And it's impolite to ask anyone that question. Remember that. If you're asked again, you should just say, "We're comfortable."* I take her words in and push on, because my classmate had asked a second question.

Are we upper class?   5

Mother's eyebrows settle now. She sits back in the den chair and pauses for effect. I am about to receive general instruction in the liturgies of race and class.

We're considered upper-class Negroes and upper-middle-class Americans, Mother says. *But of course most people would like to consider us Just More Negroes.*

II

Ginny asked me if we know their janitor, Mr. Johnson. She thinks he lives near us. Ginny had spoken of him so affectionately I longed to say I knew our janitor as well and that he liked me as much as Mr. Johnson seemed to like her. She had rights of intimacy with her janitor that I lacked.

It's a big neighborhood, Mother says. *Why would we know her janitor? White people think Negroes all know each other, and they always want you to know their janitor. Do they want to know our laundryman?*

That would be Wally, a smiling, big-shouldered white man who delivered   10 crisply wrapped shirts and cheerful greetings to our back door every week.

Good morning, Mrs. Jefferson, he'd say. *Morning, doctor. Hello, girls.*

Hello, Wally, we'd chime back from the breakfast table. Then one afternoon I was in the kitchen with Mother doing something minor and domestic like helping unpack groceries, when she said slowly, not looking at me. *I saw Wally at Sears today. I was looking at vacuum cleaners. And I looked up and saw him* — here she paused for a moment of Rodgers and Hammerstein[1] irony — *across a crowded room. He was turning his head away, hoping he wouldn't have to speak. Wally the laundryman was trying to cut me.* She made a small *hmmm* sound, a sound of futile disdain. *I don't even shop at Sears except for appliances.*

Langston Hughes[2] said, *Humor is laughing at what you haven't got when you ought to have it* — the right, in this case, to snub or choose to speak

---

[1] ***Rodgers and Hammerstein:*** Composer Richard Rodgers (1902–1979) and Oscar Hammerstein (1895–1960) created some of the best known musicals in American theatrical history, including *South Pacific, The Sound of Music,* and *The King and I.* —EDS.

[2] ***Langston Hughes:*** Prominent African American poet, novelist, playwright, and essayist (for more, see page 120). —EDS.

kindly to your laundryman in a store where he must shop for clothes and you shop only for appliances.

Still, Wally went on delivering laundry with cheerful deference, and we responded with cool civility. Was there no Negro laundry to do Daddy's shirts as well or better? Our milkman was a Negro. So was our janitor, our plumber, our carpenter, our upholsterer, our caterer, and our seamstress. Though I don't remember all their names, I know their affect was restful. Comfortable.

If perchance a Negro employee did his work in a sloppy or sullen way (and it did happen), Mother and Daddy had two responses. One was a period wisecrack along the lines of "Well, some of us are lazy, quiet as it's kept." *Humor is laughing at what you haven't got when you ought to have it:* in this case a spotless race reputation.   15

The second was somber and ominously layered: Some Negroes would rather work for white people. They don't resent their status in the same way.

Let's unpack that. Let's say you are a Negro cleaning woman, on your knees at this minute, scrubbing the bathtub with its extremely visible ring of body dirt, because whoever bathed last night thought, *How nice. I don't have to clean the tub because Cleo/Melba/Mrs. Jenkins comes tomorrow!* Tub done, you check behind the toilet (a washcloth has definitely fallen back there); the towels are scrunched, not hung on the racks, and you've just come from the children's bedroom where sheets will have to be untangled and almost throttled into shape before they can be sorted for the wash. Cleo/Melba/Mrs. Jenkins will do that.

Would you rather look at the people you do all that for and think, *If the future of this country is anything like its past, I will never be able to have what these white people have,* or would you rather look at them and think, *Well, if I'd had the chance to get an education like Dr. and Mrs. Jefferson did, if I hadn't had to start doing housework at fifteen to help my family out when we moved up here from Mississippi, then maybe I could be where they are.*

Whose privilege would you find more bearable?

Who are "you"? How does your sociological vita—race or ethnicity,   20 class, gender, family history—affect your answer?

Whoever you are, reader, please understand this: never did my parents, my sister, or I leave a dirty bathtub for Mrs. Blake to clean. (My sister and I called her Mrs. Blake. Mother called her Blake.) She was broad, not fat. She had very short, very straightened hair that she patted flat and put behind her ears. When it got humid in the basement, where the washer and dryer were, or in the room where she ironed clothes, short pieces of hair would defy hot comb and oil to stick up. My sister and I never made direct fun of her hair—Mother would have punished our rudeness—but we did find many occasions to mock Negro hair that blatantly defied rehabilitation. We used hot combs and oil, but more discreetly. And our hair was longer.

Mrs. B's voice was southern South Side: leisurely and nasal. Now that I've given my adult attention to the classic blues singers, I can say she had the weighted country diction of Ma Rainey and the short nasal tones of Sippie Wallace.[3] Vowels rubbed down, end-word consonants dropped or muffled.

Mother made clear that we were never to leave our beds unmade when Mrs. Blake was coming. She was not there to pick up after us. When we were old enough, we stripped our own beds each week and folded the linen before putting it in the hamper for her to remove and wash.

Mother's paternal grandmother, great-aunt, and aunt had been in service, so she was sensitive to inappropriate childish presumption.

Mrs. Blake ate her lunch (a hot lunch which Mother made from dinner   25
leftovers) in the kitchen. When her day was done, Mr. Blake and their daughters drove to our house. He sent his daughters to the front door to pick her up. They had the same initials we did. Mildred and Diane. Margo and Denise. Mother brought us to the front door to exchange hellos with them. Sometimes Mrs. Blake left carrying one or two bags of neatly folded clothes. What did Mildred and Diane think as they unfolded, studied, and fit themselves into our used ensembles and separates? ●

The Reader's Presence

1. Margo Jefferson's essay begins with the question, *"Are we rich?"* What is the significance of this question for Jefferson as a child? For her parents? What is the difference between the privilege of white families in the essay and that of Jefferson's family? See, for example, paragraph 19, where she asks, "Whose privilege would you find more bearable?" Early in the essay, she observes that when her mother speaks, "I am about to receive general instruction in the liturgies of race and class" (paragraph 6). What are the resonances or associations of the word "liturgies"? How are these "liturgies" represented in Jefferson's memories of her childhood?

2. Jefferson appears as both character and narrator within her story. In what specific ways is her dual role reflected in the structure of each memory she presents? She writes dialogue in italics. As a reader, what do you see as the advantages and disadvantages of this choice? Much of this essay gravitates around the importance of tone. How would you characterize Jefferson's voice throughout the essay? Is it consistent, or does it shift at any moments in the essay? If so, when and with what effect(s)? Comment on Jefferson's use of humor and irony. Please support your response by analyzing the effects of specific passages.

3. **CONNECTIONS:** Compare and contrast Jefferson's essay with Thomas Chatterton Williams's "Black and Blue and Blond" (page 272). Both authors focus on race by drawing on examples from memory. How do their understandings of "gradations of blackness" differ? Which author treats race and ethnicity more effectively? Support your responses with substantial analysis of passages from each essay.

---

3 *Ma Rainey* (1886–1939) and *Sippie Wallace* (1898–1986): Two of the leading African American blues singers of their day. —EDS.

Ha Jin

ARRIVAL

HA JIN (b. 1956) is an award-winning Chinese American author. Born Jin Xuefei, in the Liaoning province of northern China, he grew up in rural China and joined the People's Liberation Army of China at age fourteen, serving for several years along what was then the Sino-Soviet border. He left the army at nineteen and began his studies at Heilongjiang University in Harbin, China, when he was twenty-one. He received a bachelor's degree in English from Heilongjiang in 1981 and a master's degree in American literature at Shandong University in 1984. In 1985, he left China to work toward a PhD in English

> **Ha Jin grew up in rural China and joined the People's Liberation Army of China at age fourteen.**

at Brandeis University in Massachusetts. Although his original intention had been to return to China to teach and write, he decided to remain in the United States after the Tiananmen Square massacre in 1989. He took the pen name "Ha Jin" when he decided to write exclusively in English, and has published more than a dozen books under that name since 1990, including critically acclaimed novels as well as collections of poetry and short stories. He had only been writing in English for a dozen years when his novel *Waiting* won the National Book Award in 1999. He has also received two PEN/Faulkner Awards, the Flannery O'Connor Award for short fiction, the PEN/Hemingway Award, and the Asian American Literary Award. His most recent books include *The Boat Rocker* (2016); *A Map of Betrayal* (2014); and *Nanjing Requiem: A Novel* (2011). He teaches writing at Boston University.

Explaining how the Tiananmen Square massacre changed him, Ha Jin said, "I served in the Chinese army, and the army was called the People's Army, so we were from the people and supposed to serve the people and protect the people. I was shocked that the field armies would go into the city and really suppress civilians. Then my son arrived. That was a turning point. It was clear that he would be an American."

IN COLLEGE, English meant humiliation to me. When I was assigned to major in the language in 1977 at Heilongjiang University,[1] I knew only dozens of English words and was put in the lowest class, where I stayed

---

[1] *Heilongjiang University:* Located in Harbin, China, the university today numbers 35,000 students. —EDS.

four years. We were the first group of undergraduates admitted through the entrance exams after the Cultural Revolution,[2] after colleges had been closed for a decade. There was no hope for a late starter like me to catch up with the students in the faster English classes, so I kind of gave up and avoided working hard on my English. But in 1980, writers such as Hemingway, Faulkner, Bellow and Malamud suddenly became immensely popular in China after American literature had mostly been banned for three decades. I was fascinated by their fiction: Their literary subject matter was not confined to politics and social movements, as it was in China, and the techniques they used—such as stream of consciousness and multiple narrative points of view—were unheard of to me. I made up my mind to study American literature after college. For that, I would have to pass an advanced English test, so I began applying myself.

In 1982, I got into the graduate program in American literature at Shandong University,[3] but I was not a good student—at least, my professor didn't like me, probably because I married in my first year there when I was supposed to concentrate on my studies. There were only three graduate students in my year, and we had American professors teaching us most of the time. Back then, no doctoral degree in our field was offered in China, so the only way to continue my graduate work was to go abroad. Beatrice Spade, my American literature professor, encouraged me to apply to some U.S. universities, and in the winter of 1984, I started sending out applications.

The next spring, Brandeis University,[4] which I knew nothing about and which had been recommended to me by Professor Spade, notified me of my admission and offered me a scholarship, but I wasn't very excited. I was 28, and unable to imagine living outside of China.

Since childhood, I had lived a peripatetic life, most of the time separated from my parents, so I was quite independent. But the United States was so far away and so enigmatic that ever since I had started the application, I had been possessed by a relentless emotion, as if I was about to fall ill. The previous October, Professor Spade had introduced me to a group of top American scholars in a delegation that visited our university. They were staying at a hotel in Jinan City, and I spoke with Professor Alan Trachtenberg, the head of American studies at Yale, for a preliminary interview. I was a bundle of nerves, and when he asked if I had questions for him, I blurted out, "I don't know if I can survive in America." The question, more existential than literal, must have been tormenting me for months and just gushed out. Professor Trachtenberg's eyes flashed behind his glasses—he was surprised, but there was no way for me to clarify, to say that physically I could survive for sure, but

---

2 *Cultural Revolution:* A massive political reform movement launched by Mao Zedong in 1965 mainly to suppress counterrevolutionary activities. —EDS.

3 *Shandong University:* With some 60,000 students on a sprawling campus in Jinan, the university is one of the largest and most prestigious in China. —EDS.

4 *Brandeis University:* A noted university in Waltham, Massachusetts, just outside Boston. —EDS.

that I was more concerned about my quest for a meaningful existence, which I had no idea how to accomplish in the United States.

So, I blew my opportunity with Yale. I had my scholarship from Brandeis, though, and now I had to get permission from my university to go abroad. That meant I would have a J-1 visa that required its holder to return after graduation. To me, this was no problem, as I viewed my studies in America as no more than a sojourn. Besides, the authorities, to prevent me from defecting, would not allow my wife and child to go with me, so I would have to return anyway, the sooner, the better.

A schoolmate, Yafei, and I were allowed to leave together. He was going to MIT to study linguistics. After mid-August, we went to Beijing to go through a few days of "the training," which was more like a formality consisting of speeches given by officials and brief introductions to the United States.

One of the officials, a squat, smiling man, told us to be careful about sexual contact with foreigners and not to catch VD, but he also said, "It's understandable if you have a fling with someone when you are there, because we are not puritans."

Everything went smoothly in Beijing, except that three days before our scheduled departure, we were informed that the plane tickets were no longer available, though our school had paid for them long before. Apparently, our tickets had been given to "more important people." Desperate, Yafei contacted a distant relative who had some pull with the airport. To get the tickets, we would have to give the man some brand-name cigarettes. His wife was fond of 555's, and we decided to offer him two cartons. I didn't smoke and had no idea where to buy foreign cigarettes, which regular stores didn't carry. Yafei, always resourceful, got them without difficulty, and we split the cost, each paying 30 yuan,[5] almost half our monthly salary. We took a bus to the man's home to hand him the bribe. He met us in the doorway of his apartment and gave us the plane tickets after taking the cigarettes. Though he didn't let us in, through a narrow pane of glass on a door I caught a glimpse of his wife lying in bed smoking. On our way back to our dorm, Yafei said that the woman's father was a high-ranking official. Years later, whenever I thought of going back to China, the image of the young woman with a haggard face and bedraggled hair smoking expensive cigarettes would come to mind and make me wince.

Yafei and I boarded a plane without anyone seeing us off. I had never flown before, so the shifting and tilting cityscape of Beijing viewed from the air was exhilarating. However, the Boeing had a peculiar smell that nauseated us. It was a typical American odor, sharp and artificial, like a combination of chemicals and perfumes. Even lunch, Parmesan chicken and salad, tasted strange and gave off the same awful smell. I would find it everywhere in America, even on vegetables and fruits in supermarkets, but in a week or so I would get used to it, unable to detect it anymore.

---

[5] **yuan:** Basis of Chinese currency; in 2011, a yuan was worth approximately 16 cents. —EDS.

Professor Peter Swiggart, a middle-aged man with chestnut hair and a   10
roundish, good-natured face, was assigned by the international program at
Brandeis to be my host, so he agreed to pick me up at Logan International
Airport.

The moment I sat in the passenger seat of his car, he told me to "buckle
up." I had no clue what he was talking about. He pulled his seat belt; still,
I didn't know how to use mine, never having seen one in a car before. I
thought to myself, *This is like a ride on a plane.* That was the only connection I could make with the seat belt. Professor Swiggart helped me push the
buckle into the slot.

My graduate dormitory at Brandeis was a three-story building by the
Charles River. I had two roommates. Benny was from Israel, and Hosan from
South Korea. Hosan, a broad-framed man with a square face, was a sec-
ond-year graduate student in the chemistry department, which had a number
of Chinese students, so he spread the word among them about my arrival,
probably because I was an oddity studying literature instead of science.

The next afternoon, I strolled along the Charles. The sky was clear and
high, much higher than the sky in China, thanks to the absence of smog.
A pudgy angler was fishing with a tallboy of beer in his hand. Behind us,
Canada geese strutted and mallards waddled. A young mother and her toddler boy were tossing potato chips at the waterfowl. Soon the man caught
a bass, about a foot and a half long, wriggling like crazy. He unhooked the
fish, observed it for a few seconds. "Dammit, it's you again," he said, and, to
my amazement, dropped it back into the water.

"You don't keep your fish?" I asked him.

"Nope."   15

"You can't eat it?" I was still baffled.

"I'm fishin' jus' for fun."

It occurred to me that people here had a different view of nature. That
night, I wrote in my first letter to my best friend: "By comparison, our old
land must be overused and exhausted. Nature is extraordinarily generous
to America."

My roommate Benny was a first-year graduate student in Judaic studies.
He was a skinny man and had a German girlfriend, Bettina, who had just
arrived as a special student, doing graduate work at Brandeis for one year.
At first, I thought that they both spoke English fluently, but I soon discovered that their vocabulary wasn't that rich and that they might not know
more English than I did. Yet compared with theirs, my spoken English was
quite shabby, partly because I had learned it mainly from books. For example,
several times I introduced myself as "a freshman," assuming that the word
referred to a first-year grad student as well. I couldn't understand the news
on TV at all, and it took me two months to be able to follow TV shows. Some
Chinese students in our dorm loved watching American wrestling, believing
that the stunts, the moves, the pain were all real.

Below us, on the first floor, lived a young Indian couple, both graduate   20
students. The wife, Aparna, was tall and vivacious, specializing in social
policy and management. One evening, as we were having tea in their living
room, she asked me, "Why didn't you bring your wife and child with you?"
"They were not allowed to come with me," I said.
"Who didn't allow them?"
"The government."
"Why not sue your government?"
Stumped, I didn't know how to answer. But the question has stayed with   25
me since. It shook me, as I realized that democracy fundamentally meant
the equality between the individual and the country. Such a thought was
something few Chinese would dare to entertain.
When I left home, it was understood between my wife, Lisha, and me
that I would live abroad for four years without coming back to visit her,
because I was unlikely to be able to afford the airfare. Our 2-year-old son
had been staying with her parents, and, right before my departure, Lisha and
I went to see him; he was too young to worry about my imminent absence
from his life. Even when I said goodbye, he hardly paid me any mind. After
my arrival in Boston, I noticed that some Chinese graduate students had
their spouses with them, so I began to figure out how to bring Lisha over.
I spoke to a woman at the graduate school admissions at Brandeis, saying:
"I want my wife to join me here. I miss her terribly." She didn't respond, her
face wooden and her eyes dropped, as if I had asked for something beyond
reason. The prolonged silence made clear that no assistance would come
from her office.
Gradually, I found out that everyone who came here was entitled to have
a visa for his or her spouse, but there was another difficulty, namely money.
The U.S. Embassy in Beijing would demand that my wife show that I had
at least $4,000 in my bank account. To earn that amount, I began working
on and off campus. I started in the periodical section of the main library and
learned to operate the copiers and the microfilm and microfiche machines.
My fellow graduate student Dan Morris used to be a custodian at Waltham
Hospital, but now he was too busy with his studies to keep all the hours, so
he split the job with me. We each worked 20 hours a week in the medical
building, vacuuming floors, cleaning toilets, washing glass doors, picking up
trash from the offices and keeping the parking lot clean. We wore beepers
at work so that the doctors and nurses could page us if they needed help.
The job was undemanding, but I often got confused. For instance, a patient
once told me to keep an eye on his "burgundy station wagon" because its
lock was broken. I had no idea what kind of car a station wagon was and
had to ask several people about that. A physician who spoke English with
a Greek accent often wiggled his forefinger to summon me over when he
wanted me to change a light bulb or clean away a patch of vomit on his
office floor. I hated that gesture, which at first seemed to mean that he could
pull me around with just one finger. But gradually I became accustomed to it
as I saw that many others used it without any condescension. Despite some

twinge of discomfort, I liked the job, mainly because I could rest my mind while I worked. I had to be very careful about my time and energy. At the outset of the semester, the director of graduate studies had told me that the English department had admitted Asian PhD candidates before, but none of them had survived the intensity of the graduate work, so I had to prove that I could manage it.

For new arrivals in America, there was always the sinister attraction of money. Suddenly one could make $4 or $5 an hour, which was equal to a whole week's wages back home. If you were not careful, you could fall into the money-grubbing trap. Some Chinese students didn't continue with their graduate work because they couldn't stop making money. One fellow from Shanghai started working part time in a museum on campus but soon stopped showing up in his lab in the physics department, dropped out of graduate school within a semester, and began taking courses to learn how to sell real estate. Another in American studies, who loved teaching as a profession, could no longer write his dissertation after taking a clerical job in a bank—sometimes he put in more than 60 hours a week, the overtime even harder to resist.

One evening, as I was cleaning the front entrance of the medical building, a slender Hispanic woman carrying a baby stopped to watch me work. She was under 30, with honey-colored hair, and might have been a single mother. A moment later, she stepped closer and handed her pacifier-sucking baby to me, saying, "You like kids?" Her round eyes were glowing while a hesitant smile cracked her face.

I was perplexed but managed to say, "Sorry, I am busy now." I kept 30 spraying Windex on the glass door. After scraping the glass clean, I observed my face in the mirror inside the men's room. I looked a bit melancholy and frazzled. But how on earth, I wondered, had that woman sensed my yearning for family?

My coursework and two part-time jobs kept me so busy that I rarely ate dinner. I would cook twice a week—a potful of rice or spaghetti mixed with vegetables and chicken generally lasted me a few days. Back home, I wouldn't eat chicken or beef, because, unlike pork, they had tasted strange to me. But now I just ate whatever I could get. Fortunately, in America, food was very affordable. But my eating habit soon gave me a stomachache. I went to the infirmary, and the doctor said I had developed a digestive disorder and must eat regularly, three meals a day. That was out of the question, thanks to my hectic schedule. But my stomach problem made Lisha eager to join me here.

Despite my effort to earn money for her visa, she was not sure if she would be able to come. With the help of a doctor's letter about my illness, she had obtained a three-month leave from the school where she taught, but the Chinese authorities wouldn't let her bring our child. She was having difficulty getting a passport even for herself. For two months, she went to various offices every day to ask for permission to visit me. Sometimes she swept floors and wiped desks in those places just to earn the officials' mercy so they might issue her the papers.

During my absence, she had been raising our child alone on her teacher's salary. I missed him and often looked at the photos she mailed me. I could not afford to call home, since it cost more than $3 a minute. Worse, very few families in China had a phone back then, and if I was going to call, Lisha would have to go to an office to wait for the call. When she spoke, there would be people around, listening. Once in a while, she would send me the imprints of our child's hands and feet to give me a better sense of how much he had grown. In the Boston area, I had encountered young couples from China who had their children with them, and I could see that eventually I might be able to bring my son over, too, but the first step was to get his mother out.

However, even after Lisha got her passport, she began having second thoughts about leaving our son behind and coming alone. In her letters, she even bragged teasingly about how orderly her life had become without me around and said that, as we had planned, she could manage without seeing me for four years. I assured her that our family would be reunited in time, but she should come over first. She was worried about her lack of English, as well, and I told her that she could easily learn it once she was here. I also wrote her about American amenities: She could take a hot shower at home every day; she could do laundry in a washer and dryer, no need to hand-launder anything; and she needn't burn honeycomb briquettes to cook, as electric and gas stoves were commonplace in America. What's more, the air here was so fresh and clean that your collar didn't get black even after you wore a white shirt for days, and that you needn't wipe your shoes.

After a few more exchanges of letters, she finally decided to come once I had earned the $4,000.   35

At the end of the semester, I completed my four courses with decent grades, which convinced the department of my ability. Then, one evening, my friend Jia-yang, a first-year graduate student in the biology department, came by to ask if he could borrow $1,000 from me, saying that his wife was going to apply for a visa, and he needed enough money in his bank account. I was stupefied, as it had never crossed my mind that I could have borrowed cash from friends, perhaps because it was such a big sum. I lent Jia-yang the money, and he promised to lend me some when Lisha began her application. And, two months later, he did. Now Lisha and I wouldn't have to wait for long to be together again, for me to show her my new American life. ◼

The Reader's Presence

1. Before coming to the United States to study, Jin worried whether he could survive in America. "Arrival" is an account of his survival. What did Jin worry about mostly? For example, what do you think he means when he writes "that physically I could survive for sure, but . . . I was more concerned about my quest for a meaningful existence, which I had no idea how to accomplish in the United States" (paragraph 4)? Based on Jin's essay, do you think Jin achieves "a meaningful existence" in America? Why or why not?

2. At one point in his essay, Jin suggests that he never forgot an image associated with the bribe he was forced to make to obtain his plane ticket: "Years later, whenever I

thought of going back to China, the image of the young woman with a haggard face and bedraggled hair smoking expensive cigarettes would come to mind and make me wince" (paragraph 8). Why do you think that image affected Jin so powerfully? How is it associated with his native country?

3. **CONNECTIONS:** Compare Jin's "Arrival" with Dinaw Mengestu's "Home at Last" (page 181). What immigrant experiences do you find similar in each selection? Of what importance, for example, is the role of family for each writer?

Jamaica Kincaid
THE ESTRANGEMENT

Born in Antigua in 1949, JAMAICA KINCAID moved to the United States at age seventeen to work as an au pair in New York. Although she is known primarily for her fiction, Kincaid is by no means a stranger to nonfiction: she began her writing career as a journalist, penning articles for the *Village Voice* and *Ingenue* magazines. In 1976, she became a staff writer for the *New Yorker*, a position she kept for nine years. Her first book of fiction, a collection of unified short stories centering on the coming of age of a Caribbean girl and titled *At the Bottom of the River* (1983), won the Morton Darwen Zabel Award of the American Academy of Arts and Letters and was nominated for the PEN/Faulkner Award. Her first novel, *Annie John* (1983), was a finalist for the 1985 international Ritz Paris Hemingway Award. Her 1996 book, *The Autobiography of My Mother*, was a finalist for the PEN/Faulkner Award. Her most recent book, *See Now Then: A Novel*, was published in 2013. She teaches in both the English and the African and African American Studies departments at Harvard University.

> Born in Antigua in 1949, Jamaica Kincaid moved to the United States at seventeen to work as an au pair in New York.

THREE YEARS before my mother died, I decided not to speak to her again. And why? During a conversation over the telephone, she had once again let me know that my accomplishments—becoming a responsible and independent woman—did not amount to very much, that the life I lived was nothing more than a silly show, that she truly wished me dead. I didn't disagree. I didn't tell her that it would be just about the best thing in the world not to hear this from her.

And so, after that conversation, I never spoke to her, said a word to her of any kind, and then she died and her death was a shock to me, not because I would miss her presence and long for it, but because I could not believe that such a presence could ever be stilled.

For many years and many a time, her children, of which I was the only female, wondered what would happen to her, as we wondered what would happen to us; because she seemed to us not a mother at all but a God, not a Goddess but a God.

How to explain in this brief space what I mean? When we were children and in need of a mother's love and care, there was no better mother to provide such an ideal entity. When we were adolescents, and embracing with adolescent certainty our various incarnations, she could see through the thinness of our efforts, she could see through the emptiness of our aspirations; when we fell apart, there she was, bringing us dinner in jail or in a hospital ward, cold compresses for our temples, or just standing above us as we lay flat on our backs in bed. That sort of mother is God.

Her death was a shock, not because I would miss her, but because I could not believe such a presence could be stilled.   5

I am the oldest, by 9, 11, and 13 years, of four children. My three brothers and I share only our mother; they have the same father, I have a different one. I knew their father very well, better than they did, but I did not know my own. (When I was seven months in her womb, my mother quarreled with the man with whom she had conceived me and then ran away with the money he had been saving up to establish a little business for himself. He never forgave her.) I didn't mind not knowing my real father, because in the place I am from, Antigua, when people love you, your blood relationship to them is not necessarily the most important component. My mother's husband, the father of my brothers, loved me, and his love took on the shape of a father's love: he told me about himself when he was a boy and the things he loved to do and the ways in which his life changed for better and worse, giving me some idea about how he came to be himself, my father, the father of my brothers, the person married to my mother.

She was a very nice person, apparently; that is what everybody said about her at her funeral. There were descriptions of her good and self-less deeds, kindnesses, generosity, testaments of her love expressed in humor. We, her children, looked at one another in wonder then, for such a person as described was not at all known to us. The person we knew, our Mother, said horrible things to us more often than not.

The youngest of my three brothers died of AIDS when he was 33 years of age. In the years he spent actively dying, our mother tended to him with the greatest tenderness that was absent all the time before he was dying. Before he got sick, before he became afflicted with that disease, his mother, my mother too, quarreled with him and disparaged him. This was enabled by the fact that he did not know how to go off somewhere and make a home of any kind for himself. Yes, he had been unable to move out into the world, away from this woman, his mother, and become the sole possessor of his own destiny, with all the loss and gain that this implies.

The two remaining brothers and I buried her right next to him, and we were not sure we should have done that: for we didn't know even now, if he wanted to spend eternity lying beside her, since we were sure we would rather be dead than spend eternity lying next to her.

Is this clear? It is to me right now as I write it: I would rather be dead   10 than spend eternity with our mother! And do I really mean that when I say it? Yes, I really mean just that: after being my mother's daughter, I would rather be dead than spend eternity with her.

By the time my mother died, I was not only one of her four children, I had become the mother of two children: a girl and then a boy. This was bliss, my two children in love with me, and I with them. Nothing has gone wrong, as far as I can see, but tears have been shed over my not being completely enthusiastic about going to a final basketball game in a snowstorm, or saying something I should have kept in my mind's mouth. A particularly unforgivable act in my children's eyes is a book's dedication I made to them; it read: "With blind, instinctive, and confused love to Annie and Harold, who from time to time are furiously certain that the only thing standing between them and a perfect union with their mother is the garden, and from time to time, they are correct."[1]

I wrote this with a feeling of overbrimming love for them, my children. I was not thinking of my own mother directly, not thinking of her at all consciously at that exact time, but then again, I am always thinking of my mother; I believe every action of a certain kind that I make is completely influenced by her, completely infused with her realness, her existence in my life.

I am now middle-aged (59 years of age); I not only hope to live for a very long time after this, I will be angry in eternity if this turns out not to be the case. And so in eternity will my children want to be with me? And in eternity will I, their mother, want to be with them?

In regard to my children, eternity is right now, and I always want to be with them. In regard to my mother, my progenitor, eternity is beyond now, and is that not forever? I will not speak to her again in person, of that I am certain, but I am not sure that I will never speak to her again. For in eternity is she in me, and are even my children speaking to her? I do not know, I do not know. ■

The Reader's Presence

1. Note how frequently Kincaid uses repetition in her brief essay—for example, the repetition of the word "eternity" toward the end of the selection. How does her use of repetition throughout the essay affect your response? Select a paragraph to read aloud. How would you describe Kincaid's tone of voice? For example, how would you interpret her tone of voice in her final sentence, which is also deliberately repetitive?

---

1 Kincaid is a dedicated gardener and has written several books on gardening. —EDS.

2. When Kincaid writes that she "would rather be dead than spend eternity with our mother" (paragraph 10), what do you think she means? In what way is that remark puzzling? How do you interpret it?

3. **CONNECTIONS:** Kincaid wrote this essay for a magazine in 2009; compare it with her miniature, one-paragraph short story "Girl" below, published in 1978. Based on this essay, do you think the story is autobiographical? In what ways does the story inform the essay?

Jamaica Kincaid

GIRL

WASH THE WHITE CLOTHES on Monday and put them on the stone heap; wash the color clothes on Tuesday and put them on the clothes-line to dry; don't walk barehead in the hot sun; cook pumpkin fritters in very hot sweet oil; soak your little clothes right after you take them off; when buying cotton to make yourself a nice blouse, be sure that it doesn't have gum on it, because that way it won't hold up well after a wash; soak salt fish overnight before you cook it; is it true that you sing benna¹ in Sunday School?; always eat your food in such a way that it won't turn someone else's stomach; on Sundays try to walk like a lady and not like the slut you are so bent on becoming; don't sing benna in Sunday School; you mustn't speak to wharf-rat boys, not even to give directions; don't eat fruits on the street—flies will follow you; *but I don't sing benna on Sundays at all and never in Sunday School*; this is how to sew on a button; this is how to make a buttonhole for the button you have just sewed on; this is how to hem a dress when you see the hem coming down and so to prevent yourself from looking like the slut I know you are so bent on becoming; this is how you iron your father's khaki shirt so that it doesn't have a crease; this is how you iron your father's khaki pants so that they don't have a crease; this is how you grow okra—far from the house, because okra tree harbors red ants; when you are growing dasheen,² make sure it gets plenty of water or else it makes your throat itch when you are eating it; this is how you sweep a corner; this is how you sweep a whole house; this is how you sweep a yard; this is how you smile to someone you don't like too much; this is how you smile to someone you don't like at all; this is how you smile to someone you like completely; this is how

¹ **benna:** Popular calypso-like music. —EDS.
² **dasheen:** A starchy vegetable. —EDS.

you set a table for tea; this is how you set a table for dinner; this is how you set a table for dinner with an important guest; this is how you set a table for lunch; this is how you set a table for breakfast; this is how to behave in the presence of men who don't know you very well, and this way they won't recognize immediately the slut I have warned you against becoming; be sure to wash every day, even if it is with your own spit; don't squat down to play marbles—you are not a boy, you know; don't pick people's flowers—you might catch something; don't throw stones at blackbirds, because it might not be a blackbird at all; this is how to make a bread pudding; this is how to make doukona;[3] this is how to make pepper pot; this is how to make a good medicine for a cold; this is how to make a good medicine to throw away a child before it even becomes a child; this is how to catch a fish; this is how to throw back a fish you don't like, and that way something bad won't fall on you; this is how to bully a man; this is how a man bullies you; this is how to love a man, and if this doesn't work there are other ways, and if they don't work don't feel too bad about giving up; this is how to spit up in the air if you feel like it, and this is how to move quick so that it doesn't fall on you; this is how to make ends meet; always squeeze bread to make sure it's fresh; *but what if the baker won't let me feel the bread?*; you mean to say that after all you are really going to be the kind of woman who the baker won't let near the bread? ▩

The Reader's Presence

1. Whose voice dominates this story? To whom is the monologue addressed? What effect(s) does the speaker seek to have on the listener? Where does the speaker appear to have acquired her values? Categorize the kinds of advice you find in the story. Identify sentences in which one category of advice merges into another. How are the different kinds of advice alike, and to what extent are they contradictory?

2. The girl speaks only two lines, both of which are italicized. In each case, what prompts her to speak? What is the result? Stories generally create the expectation that at least one main character will undergo a change. What differences, if any, do you notice between the girl's first and second lines of dialogue (and the replies she elicits), differences that might suggest that such a change has taken place? If you do notice any differences, in whom do you notice them? Analyze the girl's character based not only on what she says but on what she hears (if one can assume that this monologue was not delivered all in one sitting, but is rather the distillation of years' worth of advice, as heard by the girl).

3. **CONNECTIONS:** Consider the role of gender in this story. What gender stereotypes does the main speaker perpetuate? Look not only at the stereotypes that affect women but also at those that define the roles of men. What can you infer about the males who remain behind the scenes? Read Amy Cunningham's "Why Women Smile" (page 339). What gender stereotypes influence whether—and when—women smile? To what extent do gender roles and cultural expectations determine the patterns—and consequences—of when men and women smile?

3 *doukona:* Cornmeal. —EDS.

The Writer at Work

JAMAICA KINCAID on "Girl"

New York Times Co./Getty Images

To many readers, "Girl" appears to be an odd and confusing short story. It's far shorter than most published stories and consists almost entirely of a monologue spoken by a mother to her daughter. Readers may wonder: What makes this a story? In the following passage from an interview with Jamaica Kincaid, Allan Varda asks the author some questions about this intriguing little story and discovers behind its composition a larger agenda that we might not perceive from a single reading. How do Kincaid's answers to Varda's questions help you better understand what's happening in the story? In what ways?

❝ *AV:* There is a litany of items in "Girl" from a mother to her daughter about what to do and what not to do regarding the elements of being "a nice young lady." Is this the way it was for you and other girls in Antigua?

JK: In a word, yes.

AV: Was that good or bad?

JK: I don't think it's the way I would tell my daughter, but as a mother I would tell her what I think would be best for her to be like. This mother in "Girl" was really just giving the girl an idea about the things she would need to be a self-possessed woman in the world.

AV: But you didn't take your mother's advice?

JK: No, because I had other ideas on how to be a self-possessed woman in the world. I didn't know that at the time. I only remember these things. What the mother in the story sees as aids to living in the world, the girl might see as extraordinary oppression, which is one of the things I came to see.

AV: Almost like she's Mother England.

JK: I was just going to say that. I've come to see that I've worked through the relationship of the mother and the girl to a relationship between Europe and the place that I'm from, which is to say, a relationship between the powerful and the powerless. The girl is powerless and the mother is powerful. The mother shows her how to be in the world, but at the back of her mind she thinks she never will get it. She's deeply skeptical that this child could ever grow up to be a self-possessed woman and in the end she reveals her skepticism; yet even within the skepticism is, of course, dismissal and scorn. So it's not unlike the relationship between the conquered and the conqueror.

Geeta Kothari

IF YOU ARE WHAT YOU EAT, THEN WHAT AM I?

Writer and educator **GEETA KOTHARI** (b. 1962) was born in New York City of Indian parents who emigrated from New Delhi, India. Kothari is the fiction editor of the literary journal the *Kenyon Review* and teaches at the University of Pittsburgh. She is a two-time recipient of the fellowship in literature from the Pennsylvania Council on the Arts and the editor of an anthology, *Did My Mama Like to Dance? and Other Stories about Mothers and Daughters* (1994). Her fiction and nonfiction work has appeared in a number of journals, including the *Massachusetts Review* and *Fourth Genre*. Her essay "If You Are What You Eat, Then What Am I?" was first published in the *Kenyon Review* in 1999 and was selected for the *Best American Essays 2000*.

> **Geeta Kothari is a two-time recipient of the fellowship in literature from the Pennsylvania Council on the Arts.**

Kothari clearly understands the relationship among culture, family, and food and "the tacit codes of the people you live with," as the Michael Ignatieff quotation that opens the essay underscores.

To belong is to understand the tacit codes of the people you live with.
—*MICHAEL IGNATIEFF, Blood and Belonging*

I

THE FIRST TIME my mother and I open a can of tuna, I am nine years old. We stand in the doorway of the kitchen, in semi-darkness, the can tilted toward daylight. I want to eat what the kids at school eat: bologna, hot dogs, salami—foods my parents find repugnant because they contain pork and meat by-products, crushed bone and hair glued together by chemicals and fat. Although she has never been able to tolerate the smell of fish, my mother buys the tuna, hoping to satisfy my longing for American food.

Indians, of course, do not eat such things.

The tuna smells fishy, which surprises me because I can't remember anyone's tuna sandwich actually smelling like fish. And the tuna in those sandwiches doesn't look like this, pink and shiny, like an internal organ. In fact, this looks similar to the bad foods my mother doesn't want me to eat.

She is silent, holding her face away from the can while peering into it like a half-blind bird.

"What's wrong with it?" I ask.

She has no idea. My mother does not know that the tuna everyone else's   5
mothers made for them was tuna *salad*.

"Do you think it's botulism?"

I have never seen botulism, but I have read about it, just as I have read about but never eaten steak and kidney pie.

There is so much my parents don't know. They are not like other parents, and they disappoint me and my sister. They are supposed to help us negotiate the world outside, teach us the signs, the clues to proper behavior: what to eat and how to eat it.

We have expectations, and my parents fail to meet them, especially my mother, who works full time. I don't understand what it means, to have a mother who works outside and inside the home; I notice only the ways in which she disappoints me. She doesn't show up for school plays. She doesn't make chocolate-frosted cupcakes for my class. At night, if I want her attention, I have to sit in the kitchen and talk to her while she cooks the evening meal, attentive to every third or fourth word I say.

We throw the tuna away. This time my mother is disappointed. I go to   10
school with tuna eaters. I see their sandwiches, yet cannot explain the discrepancy between them and the stinking, oily fish in my mother's hand. We do not understand so many things, my mother and I.

II

On weekends, we eat fried chicken from Woolworth's on the back steps of my father's first-floor office in Murray Hill. The back steps face a small patch of garden—hedges, a couple of skinny trees, and gravel instead of grass. We can see the back windows of the apartment my parents and I lived in until my sister was born. There, the doorman watched my mother, several months pregnant and wearing a sari, slip on the ice in front of the building.

My sister and I pretend we are in the country, where our American friends all have houses. We eat glazed doughnuts, also from Woolworth's, and french fries with catsup.

III

My mother takes a catering class and learns that Miracle Whip and mustard are healthier than mayonnaise. She learns to make egg salad with chopped celery, deviled eggs with paprika, a cream cheese spread with bits of fresh ginger and watercress, chicken liver pâté, and little brown and white checkerboard sandwiches that we have only once. She makes chicken *à la king* in puff pastry shells and eggplant parmesan. She acquires smooth wooden paddles, whose purpose is never clear, two different egg slicers, several wooden spoons, icing tubes, cookie cutters, and an electric mixer.

IV

I learn to make tuna salad by watching a friend. My sister never acquires a taste for it. Instead, she craves:

> bologna
> hot dogs
> bacon
> sausages

and a range of unidentifiable meat products forbidden by my parents. Their restrictions are not about sacred cows, as everyone around us assumes; in a pinch, we are allowed hamburgers, though lamb burgers are preferable. A "pinch" means choosing not to draw attention to ourselves as outsiders, impolite visitors who won't eat what the host serves. But bologna is still taboo.

V

Things my sister refuses to eat: butter, veal, anything with *jeera*.[1] The 15 babysitter tries to feed her butter sandwiches, threatens her with them, makes her cry in fear and disgust. My mother does not disappoint her; she does not believe in forcing us to eat, in using food as a weapon. In addition to pbj, my sister likes pasta and marinara sauce, bologna and Wonder bread (when she can get it), and fried egg sandwiches with turkey, cheese, and horseradish. Her tastes, once established, are predictable.

VI

When we visit our relatives in India, food prepared outside the house is carefully monitored. In the hot, sticky monsoons in New Delhi and Bombay, we cannot eat ice cream, salad, cold food, or any fruit that can't be peeled. Definitely no meat. People die from amoebic dysentery, unexplained fevers, strange boils on their bodies. We drink boiled water only, no ice. No sweets except for jalebi, thin fried twists of dough in dripping hot sugar syrup. If we're caught outside with nothing to drink, Fanta, Limca, Thums Up (after Coca-Cola is thrown out by Mr. Gandhi) will do. Hot tea sweetened with sugar, served with thick creamy buffalo milk, is preferable. It should be boiled, to kill the germs on the cup.

---

1 *jeera:* Cumin. —EDS.

My mother talks about "back home" as a safe place, a silk cocoon frozen in time where we are sheltered by family and friends. Back home, my sister and I do not argue about food with my parents. Home is where they know all the rules. We trust them to guide us safely through the maze of city streets for which they have no map, and we trust them to feed and take care of us, the way parents should.

Finally, though, one of us will get sick, hungry for the food we see our cousins and friends eating, too thirsty to ask for a straw, too polite to insist on properly boiled water.

At my uncle's diner in New Delhi, someone hands me a plate of aloo tikki, fried potato patties filled with mashed channa dal[2] and served with a sweet and sour chutney. The channa, mixed with hot chilies and spices, burned my tongue and throat. I reach for my Fanta, discard the paper straw, and gulp the sweet orange soda down, huge draughts that sting rather than soothe.

When I throw up later that day (or is it the next morning, when a stom-   20
achache wakes me up from deep sleep?), I cry over the frustration of being singled out, not from the pain my mother assumes I'm feeling as she holds my hair back from my face. The taste of orange lingers in my mouth, and I remember my lips touching the cold glass of the Fanta bottle.

At that moment, more than anything, I want to be like my cousins.

VII

In New York, at the first Indian restaurant in our neighborhood, my father orders with confidence, and my sister and I play with the silverware until the steaming plates of lamb biryani[3] arrive.

What is Indian food? my friends ask, their noses crinkling up.

Later, this restaurant is run out of business by the new Indo-Pak-Bangladeshi combinations up and down the street, which serve similar food. They use plastic cutlery and Styrofoam cups. They do not distinguish between North and South Indian cooking, or between Indian, Pakistani, and Bangladeshi cooking, and their customers do not care. The food is fast, cheap, and tasty. Dosa, a rice flour crepe stuffed with masala[4] potato, appears on the same trays as chicken makhani.[5]

Now my friends want to know, Do you eat curry at home?   25

One time, my mother makes lamb vindaloo[6] for guests. Like dosa, this is a South Indian dish, one that my Punjabi mother has to learn from a

---

[2] *channa dal:* A dish made of the split kernel of beans in the chickpea family. —EDS.

[3] *lamb biryani:* A dish made of lamb, spices, basmati rice, and yogurt. —EDS.

[4] *masala:* A blend of spices common to Indian food, often includes cinnamon, cardamom, cumin, caraway, and many others. —EDS.

[5] *chicken makhani:* A dish combining chicken with a butter-based tomato sauce. —EDS.

[6] *lamb vindaloo:* A spicy marinated lamb dish. —EDS.

cookbook. For us, she cooks everyday food—yellow dal, rice, chapati, bhaji. Lentils, rice, bread, and vegetables. She has never referred to anything on our table as "curry" or "curried," but I know she has made chicken curry for guests. Vindaloo, she explains, is a curry too. I understand, then, that curry is a dish created for guests, outsiders, a food for people who eat in restaurants.

VIII

I have inherited brown eyes, black hair, a long nose with a crooked bridge, and soft teeth with thin enamel. I am in my twenties, moving to a city far from my parents, before it occurs to me that jeera, the spice my sister avoids, must have an English name. I have to learn that haldi = turmeric, methi = fenugreek. What to make with fenugreek, I do not know. My grandmother used to make methi roti[7] for our breakfast, corn bread with fresh fenugreek leaves served with a lump of homemade butter. No one makes it now that she's gone, though once in a while my mother will get a craving for it and produce a facsimile ("The corn meal here is wrong") that only highlights what she's really missing: the smells and tastes of her mother's house.

I will never make my grandmother's methi roti or even my mother's unsatisfactory imitation of it. I attempt chapati:[8] it takes six hours, three phone calls home, and leaves me with an aching back. I have to write translations down: jeera = cumin. My memory is unreliable. But I have always known garam = hot.

IX

My mother learns how to make brownies and apple pie. My father makes only Indian food, except for loaves of heavy, sweet, brown bread that I eat with thin slices of American cheese and lettuce. The recipe is a secret, passed on to him by a woman at work. Years later, when he finally gives it to me, when I ask for it, I end up with three bricks of gluten that even the birds and my husband won't eat.

X

My parents send me to boarding school, outside of London. They imagine   30 that I will overcome my shyness and find a place for myself in this all-girls' school. They have never lived in England, but as former subjects of the British Empire, they find London familiar, comfortable in a way New York—my mother's home for over twenty years by now—is not. Americans still don't know what to call us; their Indians live on reservations, not in

---

[7] **roti:** A round puffy flatbread. —EDS.
[8] **chapati:** A type of roti, or flatbread. —EDS.

Manhattan. Because they understand the English, my parents believe the English understand us.

I poke at my first school lunch—thin, overworked pastry in a puddle of lumpy gravy. The lumps are chewy mushrooms, maybe, or overcooked shrimp.

"What is this?" I don't want to ask, but I can't go on eating without knowing.

"Steak and kidney pie."

The girl next to me, red-haired, freckled, watches me take a bite from my plate. She has been put in charge of me, the new girl, and I follow her around all day, a foreigner at the mercy of a reluctant and angry tour guide. She is not used to explaining what is perfectly and utterly natural.

"What, you've never had steak and kidney pie? Bloody hell."   35

My classmates scoff, then marvel, then laugh at my ignorance. After a year, I understand what is on my plate: sausage rolls, blood pudding, Spam, roast beef in a thin, greasy gravy, all the bacon and sausage I could possibly want. My parents do not expect me to starve.

The girls at school expect conformity; it has been bred into them, through years of uniforms and strict rules about proper behavior. I am thirteen and contrary, even as I yearn for acceptance. I declare myself a vegetarian and doom myself to a diet of cauliflower cheese and baked beans on toast. The administration does not question my decision; they assume it's for vague, undefined religious reasons, although my father, the doctor, tells them it's for my health. My reasons, from this distance of many years, remain murky to me.

Perhaps I am my parents' daughter after all.

XI

When she is three, sitting on my cousin's lap in Bombay, my sister reaches for his plate and puts a chili in her mouth. She wants to be like the grown-ups who dip green chilies in coarse salt and eat them like any other vegetable. She howls inconsolable animal pain for what must be hours. She doesn't have the vocabulary for the oily heat that stings her mouth and tongue, burns a trail through her small tender body. Only hot, sticky tears on my father's shoulder.

As an adult, she eats red chili paste, mango pickle, kimchee,[9] foods that   40
make my eyes water and my stomach gurgle. My tastes are milder. I order raita[10] at Indian restaurants and ask for food that won't sear the roof of my mouth and scar the insides of my cheeks. The waiters nod, and their eyes shift—a slight once-over that indicates they don't believe me. I am Indian,

---

[9] **kimchee:** A spicy Korean dish made of fermented cabbage and other vegetables. —EDS.
[10] **raita:** A yogurt-based condiment, often including cilantro, mint, and cucumber. —EDS.

aren't I? My father seems to agree with them. He tells me I'm asking for the impossible, as if he believes the recipes are immutable, written in stone during the passage from India to America.

XII

I look around my boyfriend's freezer one day and find meat: pork chops, ground beef, chicken pieces, Italian sausage. Ham in the refrigerator, next to the homemade Bolognese sauce. Tupperware filled with chili made from ground beef and pork.

He smells different from me. Foreign. Strange.

I marry him anyway.

He has inherited blue eyes that turn gray in bad weather, light brown hair, a sharp pointy nose, and excellent teeth. He learns to make chili with ground turkey and tofu, tomato sauce with red wine and portobello mushrooms, roast chicken with rosemary and slivers of garlic under the skin.

He eats steak when we are in separate cities, roast beef at his mother's   45 house, hamburgers at work. Sometimes I smell them on his skin. I hope he doesn't notice me turning my face, a cheek instead of my lips, my nose wrinkled at the unfamiliar, musky smell.

XIII

And then I realize I don't want to be a person who can find Indian food only in restaurants. One day, my parents will be gone, and I will long for the foods of my childhood, the way they long for theirs. I prepare for this day the way people on TV prepare for the end of the world. They gather canned goods they will never eat while I stockpile recipes I cannot replicate. I am frantic, disorganized, grabbing what I can, filing scribbled notes haphazardly. I regret the tastes I've forgotten, the meals I have inhaled without a thought. I worry that I've come to this realization too late.

XIV

Who told my mother about Brie? One day we were eating Velveeta, the next day Brie, Gouda, Camembert, Port Salut, Havarti with caraway, Danish fontina, string cheese made with sheep's milk. Who opened the door to these foreigners that sit on the refrigerator shelf next to last night's dal?

Back home, there is one cheese only, which comes in a tin, looks like Bakelite, and tastes best when melted.

And how do we go from Chef Boyardee to fresh pasta and homemade sauce, made with Redpack tomatoes, crushed garlic, and dried oregano? Macaroni and cheese, made with fresh cheddar and whole milk, sprinkled with bread crumbs and paprika. Fresh eggplant and ricotta ravioli, packed with marinara sauce and fresh mozzarella.

My mother will never cook beef or pork in her kitchen, and the foods she 50 knew in her childhood are unavailable. Because the only alternative to the supermarket, with its TV dinners and canned foods, is the gourmet Italian deli across the street, by default our meals become socially acceptable.

XV

If I really want to make myself sick, I worry that my husband will one day leave me for a meat-eater, for someone familiar who doesn't sniff him suspiciously for signs of alimentary infidelity.

XVI

Indians eat lentils. I understand this as absolute, a decree from an unidentifiable authority that watches and judges me.

So what does it mean that I cannot replicate my mother's dal? She and my father show me repeatedly, in their kitchen, in my kitchen. They coach me over the phone, buy me the best cookbooks, and finally write down their secrets. Things I'm supposed to know but don't. Recipes that should be, by now, engraved on my heart.

Living far from the comfort of people who require no explanation for what I do and who I am, I crave the foods we have shared. My mother convinces me that moong is the easiest dal to prepare, and yet it fails me every time: bland, watery, a sickly greenish-yellow mush. These imperfect imitations remind me only of what I'm missing.

But I have never been fond of moong dal.[11] At my mother's table it is 55 the last thing I reach for. Now I worry that this antipathy toward dal signals something deeper, that somehow I am not my parents' daughter, not Indian, and because I cannot bear the touch and smell of raw meat, though I can eat it cooked (charred, dry, and overdone), I am not American either.

I worry about a lifetime purgatory in Indian restaurants where I will complain that all the food looks and tastes the same because they've used the same masala.

XVII

About the tuna and her attempts to feed us, my mother laughs. She says, "You were never fussy. You ate everything I made and never complained."

---

11 *moong dal:* A dish made of split green lentils. —EDS.

My mother is at the stove, wearing only her blouse and petticoat, her sari carefully folded and hung in the closet. She does not believe a girl's place is in the kitchen, but she expects me to know that too much hing can ruin a meal, to know without being told, without having to ask or write it down. Hing = asafoetida.

She remembers the catering class. "Oh, that class. You know, I had to give it up when we got to lobster. I just couldn't stand the way it looked."

She says this apologetically, as if she has deprived us, as if she suspects   60
that having a mother who could feed us lobster would have changed the course of our lives.

Intellectually, she understands that only certain people regularly eat lobster, people with money or those who live in Maine, or both. In her catering class there were people without jobs for whom preparing lobster was a part of their professional training as caterers. Like us, they wouldn't be eating lobster at home. For my mother, however, lobster was just another American food, like tuna — different, strange, not natural yet somehow essential to belonging.

I learned how to prepare and eat lobster from the same girl who taught me tuna salad. I ate bacon at her house, too. And one day this girl, with her houses in the country and Martha's Vineyard, asked me how my uncle was going to pick me up from the airport in Bombay. In 1973, she was surprised to hear that he used a car, not an elephant. At home, my parents and I laughed, and though I never knew for sure if she was making fun of me, I still wanted her friendship.

My parents were afraid my sister and I would learn to despise the foods they loved, replace them with bologna and bacon and lose our taste for masala. For my mother, giving up her disgust of lobster, with its hard exterior and foreign smell, would mean renouncing some essential difference. It would mean becoming, decidedly, definitely, American — unafraid of meat in all its forms, able to consume large quantities of protein at any given meal. My willingness to toss a living being into boiling water and then get past its ugly appearance to the rich meat inside must mean to my mother that I am, somehow, someone she is not.

But I haven't eaten lobster in years. In my kitchen cupboards, there is a thirteen-pound bag of basmati rice, jars of lime pickle, mango pickle, and ghee,[12] cans of tuna and anchovies, canned soups, coconut milk, and tomatoes, rice noodles, several kinds of pasta, dried mushrooms, and unlabeled bottles of spices: haldi, jeera, hing. When my husband tries to help me cook, he cannot identify all the spices. He gets confused when I forget their English names and remarks that my expectations of him are unreasonable.

I am my parents' daughter. Like them, I expect knowledge to pass from   65
me to my husband without one word of explanation or translation. I want him to know what I know, see what I see, without having to tell him exactly what it is. I want to believe the recipes never change. ▄

---

12 **_ghee:_** Clarified butter. —EDS.

The Reader's Presence

1. Kothari worries in the essay whether she is "[her] parents' daughter" (paragraph 38). Why is this of concern? How is that concern related to the title of her essay? At the end of the essay, she says definitively: "I am my parents' daughter" (paragraph 65). How has she reached that conclusion in the process of writing the essay?

2. Consider the ways food relates to cultural identity. How does Kothari characterize American foods? In what ways does she enjoy them? In what ways does she find them distasteful? For example, how is her husband—who is never named—described in terms of his favorite foods? In what ways do husband and wife differ from each other? How does Kothari suggest that their culinary differences could affect their relationship?

3. **CONNECTIONS:** Read Kothari's essay in conjunction with Judith Ortiz Cofer's "Silent Dancing" (page 67). Although one writes about food and the other about ethnic values, discuss how each writer deals with conflict between a family's values and assimilation into a different culture. You might also consider Kothari's attention to ethnic cuisine in contrast to Eric Schlosser's description in "Why McDonald's Fries Taste So Good" (page 481) of American fast food. To what extent to you think fast-food chains help undermine cultural heritage as it is expressed in various ethnic cuisines, such as Kothari's Indian recipes? Support your points with specific references to each text.

Jhumpa Lahiri

MY TWO LIVES

JHUMPA LAHIRI (b. 1967) is perhaps best known for her debut collection of short stories, *Interpreter of Maladies* (1999), which won the Pulitzer Prize for Fiction in 2000 and has sold more than 15 million copies worldwide. Born in London, she is the daughter of Indian immigrants. Her family left the United Kingdom for the United States when she was two years old, and she has said that she considers herself American. She has received a number of prestigious literary awards, including the Pulitzer Prize (2000), the PEN/O. Henry Prize (1999), a Guggenheim Fellowship (2002), and the Asian American Literary Award (2009) for her 2008 collection of short stories, *Unaccustomed Earth*.

> Of growing up the child of Indian immigrants, Lahiri has said,
> "It was always a question of allegiance, of choice."

She is also the author of two novels: *The Lowland* (2013) and *The Namesake* (2003), which was the basis for a film of the same title in 2006. Lahiri's most recent book is *In Other Words* (2016), a memoir. Her fiction is largely autobiographical, exploring the complicated identity issues faced by first- and second-generation Indian immigrants as they attempt to make sense of their lives in America within the context of Indian cultural values. Of growing up the child of Indian immigrants, she has said, "It was always a question of allegiance, of choice. I wanted to please my parents and meet their expectations. I also wanted to meet the expectations of my American peers, and the expectations I put on myself to fit into American society."

I HAVE LIVED IN THE UNITED STATES for almost 37 years and anticipate growing old in this country. Therefore, with the exception of my first two years in London, "Indian-American" has been a constant way to describe me. Less constant is my relationship to the term. When I was growing up in Rhode Island in the 1970s I felt neither Indian nor American. Like many immigrant offspring I felt intense pressure to be two things, loyal to the old world and fluent in the new, approved of on either side of the hyphen. Looking back, I see that this was generally the case. But my perception as a young girl was that I fell short at both ends, shuttling between two dimensions that had nothing to do with one another.

At home I followed the customs of my parents, speaking Bengali and eating rice and dal with my fingers. These ordinary facts seemed part of a secret, utterly alien way of life, and I took pains to hide them from my American friends. For my parents, home was not our house in Rhode Island but Calcutta, where they were raised. I was aware that the things they lived for—the Nazrul songs they listened to on the reel-to-reel, the family they missed, the clothes my mother wore that were not available in any store in any mall—were at once as precious and as worthless as an outmoded currency.

I also entered a world my parents had little knowledge or control of: school, books, music, television, things that seeped in and became a fundamental aspect of who I am. I spoke English without an accent, comprehending the language in a way my parents still do not. And yet there was evidence that I was not entirely American. In addition to my distinguishing name and looks, I did not attend Sunday school, did not know how to ice-skate, and disappeared to India for months at a time. Many of these friends proudly called themselves Irish-American or Italian-American. But they were several generations removed from the frequently humiliating process of immigration, so that the ethnic roots they claimed had descended underground whereas mine were still tangled and green. According to my parents I was not American, nor would I ever be no matter how hard I tried. I felt doomed by their pronouncement, misunderstood and gradually defiant. In spite of the first lessons of arithmetic, one plus one did not equal two but zero, my conflicting selves always canceling each other out.

When I first started writing I was not conscious that my subject was the Indian-American experience. What drew me to my craft was the desire to force the two worlds I occupied to mingle on the page as I was not brave enough, or mature enough, to allow in life. My first book was published in 1999, and around then, on the cusp of a new century, the term "Indian-American" has become part of this country's vocabulary. I've heard it so often that these days, if asked about my background, I use the term myself, pleasantly surprised that I do not have to explain further. What a difference from my early life, when there was no such way to describe me, when the most I could do was to clumsily and ineffectually explain.

As I approach middle age, one plus one equals two, both in my work and in my daily existence. The traditions on either side of the hyphen dwell in me like siblings, still occasionally sparring, one outshining the other depending on the day. But like siblings they are intimately familiar with one another, forgiving and intertwined. When my husband and I were married five years ago in Calcutta we invited friends who had never been to India, and they came full of enthusiasm for a place I avoided talking about in my childhood, fearful of what people might say. Around non-Indian friends, I no longer feel compelled to hide the fact that I speak another language. I speak Bengali to my children, even though I lack the proficiency to teach them to read or write the language. As a child I sought perfection and so denied myself the claim to any identity. As an adult I accept that a bicultural upbringing is a rich but imperfect thing.

While I am American by virtue of the fact that I was raised in this country, I am Indian thanks to the efforts of two individuals. I feel Indian not because of the time I've spent in India or because of my genetic composition but rather because of my parents' steadfast presence in my life. They live three hours from my home; I speak to them daily and see them about once a month. Everything will change once they die. They will take certain things with them — conversations in another tongue, and perceptions about the difficulties of being foreign. Without them, the back-and-forth life my family leads, both literally and figuratively, will at last approach stillness. An anchor will drop, and a line of connection will be severed.

I have always believed that I lack the authority my parents bring to being Indian. But as long as they live they protect me from feeling like an impostor. Their passing will mark not only the loss of the people who created me but the loss of a singular way of life, a singular struggle. The immigrant's journey, no matter how ultimately rewarding, is founded on departure and deprivation, but it secures for the subsequent generation a sense of arrival and advantage. I can see a day coming when my American side, lacking the counterpoint India has until now maintained, begins to gain ascendancy and weight. It is in fiction that I will continue to interpret the term "Indian-American," calculating that shifting equation, whatever answers it may yield.

The Reader's Presence

1. Lahiri begins by asserting, "I have lived in the United States for almost 37 years and anticipate growing old in this country. Therefore, with the exception of my first two years in London, 'Indian-American' has been a constant way to describe me." Consider the significance of the syntax of her second sentence, in which "Indian-American" is placed before the personal pronoun "me." What does this suggest about how Lahiri views her divided cultural identity?

2. What role does writing play in Lahiri's sense of cultural identity? In what ways does writing allow her to attempt to come to terms with her "conflicted selves"? Through writing, Lahiri desires to "force the two worlds I occupied to mingle on the page" (paragraph 4), and yet she describes herself in plural terms ("my conflicting selves," paragraph 3). How does she rectify this conflict?

3. **CONNECTIONS:** Lahiri mentions "the traditions on either side of the hyphen" (paragraph 5) in reference to the hyphen separating her cultural descriptor, Indian-American. In what specific ways is the hyphen a metaphor for her experience with her "bicultural upbringing" (paragraph 5)? In what ways are Lahiri's experiences similar to those of Judith Ortiz Cofer, described in her essay "Silent Dancing" (page 67)?

Laila Lalami

MY LIFE AS A MUSLIM IN THE WEST'S "GRAY ZONE"

For Moroccan American writer **LAILA LALAMI**, being Muslim presents certain challenges. The September 11 attacks and the activity of terrorist groups such as ISIS have encouraged increasingly polarized attitudes toward the Islamic religion in America. In "My Life as a Muslim in the West's 'Gray Zone,'" Lalami explores some of the history behind this development and the pressures that terrorism places on Muslims, such as she and her daughter, in the Western world.

> **"I always recommend reading with a pencil in hand."**

Lalami is the author of three novels. Her third book, *The Moor's Account* (2014), received multiple awards and was a finalist for the Pulitzer Prize for fiction. Her writing has appeared in the *Los Angeles Times*, the *New York Times*, the *Guardian*, and the *Nation*, among numerous other publications. She holds a PhD in linguistics and teaches creative writing at the University of California, Riverside.

"The most reliable and most enjoyable way of improving your writing," Lalami has said, "is to read widely and deeply. I always recommend reading with a pencil in hand."

SOME MONTHS AGO, I gave a reading from my most recent novel in Scottsdale, Ariz. During the discussion that followed, a woman asked me to talk about my upbringing in Morocco. It's natural for readers to be curious about a writer they've come to hear, I told myself. I continued to tell myself this even after the conversation drifted to Islam, and then to ISIS. Eventually, another woman raised her hand and said that the only Muslims she saw when she turned on the television were extremists. "Why aren't we hearing more from people like you?" she asked me.

"You are," I said with a nervous laugh. "Right now." I wanted to tell her that there were plenty of ordinary Muslims in this country. We come in all races and ethnicities. Some of us are more visible by virtue of beards or head scarves. Others are less conspicuous, unless they give book talks and it becomes clear that they, too, identify as Muslims.

To be fair, I'm not a very good Muslim. I don't perform daily prayers anymore. I have never been on a pilgrimage to Mecca. I partake of the forbidden drink. I do give to charity whenever I can, but I imagine that this would not be enough to save me were I to have the misfortune, through an accident of birth or migration, to live in a place like Raqqa, Syria, where in the last two years, the group variously known as Daesh, ISIL or ISIS has established a caliphate: a successor to past Islamic empires. Life in Raqqa reportedly follows rules that range from the horrifying to the absurd: The heads of people who have been executed are posted on spikes in the town's main square; women must wear a *niqab*[1] and be accompanied by a male companion when they go out; smoking and swearing are not allowed; chemistry is no longer taught in schools and traffic police are not permitted to have whistles because ISIS considers them un-Islamic.

As part of its efforts to spread its message outside the territory it controls, ISIS puts out an English-language magazine, *Dabiq*, which can be found online. In February, *Dabiq* featured a 12-page article, complete with high-resolution photos and multiple footnotes, cheering the terrorist attacks of Sept. 11 and claiming that they made manifest for the world two camps: the camp of Islam under the caliphate and the camp of the West under the crusaders. The article ran under the title "The Extinction of the Grayzone." The gray zone is the space inhabited by any Muslim who has not joined the ranks of either ISIS or the crusaders. Throughout the article, these Muslims are called "the grayish," "the hypocrites" and, for variety, "the grayish hypocrites."

On Nov. 13, men who had sworn allegiance to ISIS struck the city of   5
Paris, killing 130 people at different locations mostly in the 10th and 11th arrondissements, neighborhoods that are known for their multiculturalism.

---

[1] **niqab:** Arabic; face covering worn by Muslim women. — EDS.

As soon as I heard about the attacks, I tried to reach a cousin of mine, who is studying in Paris. I couldn't. I spent the next two hours in a state of crushing fear until he posted on Facebook that he was safe. Relieved, I went back to scrolling through my feed, which is how I found out that my friend Najlae Benmbarek, a Moroccan journalist, lost her cousin. A recently married architect, Mohamed Amine Ibnolmobarak was eating dinner with his wife at the Carillon restaurant when an ISIS terrorist killed him.

It was probably not a coincidence that the Paris attacks were aimed at restaurants, a concert hall and a sports stadium, places of leisure and community, nor that the victims included Muslims. As *Dabiq* makes clear, ISIS wants to eliminate coexistence between religions and to create a response from the West that will force Muslims to choose sides: either they "apostatize and adopt" the infidel religion of the crusaders or "they perform *hijrah*[2] to the Islamic State and thereby escape persecution from the crusader governments and citizens." For ISIS to win, the gray zone must be eliminated.

Whose lives are gray? Mine, certainly. I was born in one nation (Morocco) speaking Arabic, came to my love of literature through a second language (French) and now live in a third country (America), where I write books and teach classes in yet another language (English). I have made my home in between all these cultures, all these languages, all these countries. And I have found it a glorious place to be. My friends are atheists and Muslims, Jews and Christians, believers and doubters. Each one makes my life richer.

This gray life of mine is not unique. I share it with millions of people around the world. My brother in Dallas is a practicing Muslim—he prays, he fasts, he attends mosque—but he, too, would be considered to be in the gray zone, because he despises ISIS and everything it stands for.

Most of the time, gray lives go unnoticed in America. Other times, especially when people are scared, gray lives become targets. Hate crimes against Muslims spike after every major terrorist attack. But rather than stigmatize this hate, politicians and pundits often stoke it with fiery rhetoric, further diminishing the gray zone. Every time the gray zone recedes, ISIS gains ground.

The language that ISIS uses may be new, but the message is not. When   10
President George W. Bush spoke to a joint session of Congress after the terrorist attacks of Sept. 11, he declared, "Either you are with us or you are with the terrorists." It was a decisive threat, and it worked well for him in those early, confusing days, so he returned to it. "Either you are with us," he said in 2002, "or you are with the enemy. There's no in between." This polarized thinking led to the United States invasion of Iraq, which led to the destabilization of the Middle East, which in turn led to the creation of ISIS.

Terrorist attacks affect all of us in the same way: We experience sorrow and anger at the loss of life. For Muslims, however, there is an additional layer of grief as we become subjects of suspicion. Muslims are called upon

---

[2] **hijrah:** Arabic; a journey or migration; the word has a spiritual significance, recalling the flight of Muhammad from Mecca to Medina to escape persecution in 622. — EDS.

Shepherd Fairey's "We the People" posters designed for the 2017 Women's March, as seen in Times Square.

to condemn terrorism, but no matter how often or how loud or how clear the condemnations, the calls remain. Imagine if, after every mass shooting in a school or a movie theater in the United States, young white men in this country were told that they must publicly denounce gun violence. The reason this is not the case is that we presume each young white man to be solely responsible for his actions, whereas Muslims are held collectively responsible. To be a Muslim in the West is to be constantly on trial.

The attacks in Paris have generated the same polarization as all previous attacks have. Even though most of the suspects were French and Belgian nationals who could have gained entry to the United States on their passports, Republican governors in 30 states say that they will refuse to take in any refugees from Syria without even more stringent screening. Barely two days after the attacks, Jeb Bush told CNN's Jake Tapper that the United States should focus its efforts only on helping Syrian refugees who are Christian.

Ted Cruz went a step further, offering to draft legislation that would ban Muslim Syrian refugees from the United States. When he was asked by Dana Bash of CNN what would have happened to him if his father, a Cuban refugee who was fleeing communism, had been refused entry, he implied that it was a different situation because of the special risks associated with ISIS.

As it happens, I am married to a son of Cuban refugees. Like Cruz's father, they came to this country because America was a safe haven. What would have been their fate if an American legislator said that they could not be allowed in because the Soviet Union was trying to infiltrate the United States?

The other day, my daughter said to me, "I want to be president." She   15
has been saying this a lot lately, usually the morning after a presidential
debate, when our breakfast-table conversation veers toward the elections.
My daughter is 12. She plays the violin and the guitar; she loves math and
history; she's quick-witted and sharp-tongued and above all she's very kind
to others. "I'd vote for you," I told her. And then I looked away, because I
didn't have the heart to tell her that half the people in this country—in her
country—say they would not vote for a Muslim presidential candidate.

I worry about her growing up in a place where some of the people who
are seeking the highest office in the land cannot make a simple distinction
between Islam and ISIS, between Muslim and terrorist. Ben Carson has said
he "would not advocate that we put a Muslim in charge of this nation."

Right now, my daughter still has the innocence and ambition that are the
natural attributes of the young. But what will happen when she comes of age
and starts to realize that her life, like mine, is constantly under question?
How do you explain to a child that she is not wanted in her own country? I
have not yet had the courage to do that. My daughter has never heard of the
gray zone, though she has lived in it her entire life. Perhaps this is my attempt
at keeping the world around all of us as gray as possible. It is a form of resistance, the only form of resistance I know. ▓

The Reader's Presence

1. Laila Lalami's essay gravitates around her defining—and promoting—the "gray
   zone." As you reread her essay, identify the specific characteristics of the "gray
   zone." In what specific ways does she broaden and "thicken" her description of "the
   gray zone"? Lalami concludes her essay by observing: "Perhaps this is my attempt at
   keeping the world around all of us as gray as possible. It is a form of resistance, the
   only form of resistance I know" (paragraph 17). Given how she characterizes "the
   gray zone" throughout her essay, what, exactly, does the gray zone resist?

2. Reread paragraphs 3, 10–13, and 16, where Lalami describes ISIS, the terrorist group.
   What specific connections does she draw between this group's religious message and
   the political rhetoric surrounding terrorism in the United States? What reasonable
   implications does Lalami suggest Muslims can draw about living in the United States?
   Refer to specific passages to support each point. How effective is Lalami's choice to
   frame her essay with personal narratives?

3. **CONNECTIONS:** Laila Lalami expresses concern for her daughter's future in a
   country where her life "is constantly under question" (paragraph 17). Identify and
   compare the specific points she makes here with those Edwidge Danticat emphasizes
   in "Message to My Daughters" (page 346). In what specific ways do these writers
   underscore the points made in their essays by writing about their children? You might
   also consider the specific ways in which Lalami's essay intersects with the narrative
   Pico Iyer unfolds in "The Terminal Check" (page 404) about the endemic distrust
   people with intersecting identities experience daily. How does each writer combine
   narrative with examples to create an appreciable sense of anxiety about one's security in a culture of suspicion?

Yiyun Li

TO SPEAK IS TO BLUNDER

YIYUN LI (b. 1972) writes so clearly, and with such gravity, that it is easy to believe she has never written in any language other than English. To a certain extent, this is true. Born in Beijing, Li chose to become a writer years after she arrived in the United States to study immunology. More significantly, she chose to renounce her native tongue and write in English. In "To Speak Is to Blunder," excerpted from her memoir *Dear Friend, From My Life I Write to You in Your Life* (2017), Li explores this decision and the power of words and language to influence the way we think, feel, and even dream.

> **Yiyun Li explores her decision to renounce her native Chinese and write in English.**

Li's writing has appeared in the *New Yorker*, *Best American Short Stories,* and the *Paris Review*, among other publications. She received the Frank O'Connor International Short Story Award for her first collection, *A Thousand Years of Good Prayers* (2005), and a Gold Medal California Book Award for her first novel, *Vagrants* (2009). Her prose has been translated into over twenty languages, but she has declined to have her work printed in Chinese.

Li currently teaches creative writing at the University of California, Davis. Essays, Li has said, "require that I have a voice more than I usually do in my stories. I'm trying to get used to starting a sentence with 'I'—and often still change it to 'one'—and I'm trying to get used to the idea that I have to take a center stage at times in the essays."

IN A DREAM THE OTHER NIGHT, I was back in Beijing, at the entrance of my family's apartment complex, where a public telephone, a black rotary, had once been guarded by the old women from the neighborhood association. They used to listen without hiding their disdain or curiosity while I was on the phone with friends; when I finished, they would complain about the length of the conversation before logging it in to their book and calculating the charge. In those days, I accumulated many errands before I went to use the telephone, lest my parents notice my extended absence. My allowance—which was what I could scrimp and save from my lunch money—was spent on phone calls and stamps and envelopes. Like a character in a Victorian novel, I checked our mail before my parents did and collected letters to me from friends before my parents could intercept them.

In my dream, I asked for the phone. Two women came out of a front office. I recognized them: in real life, they are both gone. No, they said; the service is no longer offered, because everyone has a cell phone these days. There was nothing extraordinary about the dream—a melancholy visit to the past in this manner is beyond one's control—but for the fact that the women spoke to me in English.

Years ago, when I started writing in English, my husband asked if I understood the implication of the decision. What he meant was not the practical concerns, though there were plenty: the nebulous hope of getting published; the lack of a career path as had been laid out in science, my first field of postgraduate study in America; the harsher immigration regulation I would face as a fiction writer. Many of my college classmates from China, as scientists, acquired their green cards under a National Interest Waiver. An artist is not of much importance to any nation's interest.

My husband, who writes computer programs, was asking about language. Did I understand what it meant to renounce my mother tongue?

Nabokov[1] once answered a question he must have been tired of being asked: "My private tragedy, which cannot, indeed should not, be anybody's concern, is that I had to abandon my natural language, my natural idiom." That something is called a tragedy, however, means it is no longer personal. One weeps out of private pain, but only when the audience swarms in and claims understanding and empathy do people call it a tragedy. One's grief belongs to oneself; one's tragedy, to others.

I often feel a tinge of guilt when I imagine Nabokov's woe. Like all intimacies, the intimacy between one and one's mother tongue can be comforting and irreplaceable, yet it can also demand more than what one is willing to give, or more than one is capable of giving. If I allow myself to be honest, my private salvation, which cannot and should not be anybody's concern, is that I disowned my native language.

In the summer and autumn of 2012, I was hospitalized in California and in New York for suicide attempts, the first time for a few days, and the second time for three weeks. During those months, my dreams often took me back to Beijing. I would be standing on top of a building—one of those gray, Soviet-style apartment complexes—or I would be lost on a bus traveling through an unfamiliar neighborhood. Waking up, I would list in my journal images that did not appear in my dreams: a swallow's nest underneath a balcony, the barbed wires at the rooftop, the garden where old people sat and exchanged gossip, the mailboxes at street corners—round, green, covered by dust, with handwritten collection times behind a square window of half-opaque plastic.

Yet I have never dreamed of Iowa City, where I first landed in America, in 1996, at the age of twenty-three. When asked about my initial impression of the place, I cannot excavate anything from memory to form a meaningful

5

---

[1] **Vladimir Nabokov** (1899–1977): Russian-born novelist of international fame who also wrote in English and became a U.S. citizen in 1945. For more on Nabokov, see Azar Nafisi, "Reading Lolita in Tehran" (page 461). — EDS.

answer. During a recent trip there from my home in California, I visited a neighborhood that I used to walk through every day. The one-story houses, which were painted in pleasantly muted colors, with gardens in the front enclosed by white picket fences, had not changed. I realized that I had never described them to others or to myself in Chinese, and when English was established as my language they had become everyday mundanities. What happened during my transition from one language to another did not become memory.

People often ask about my decision to write in English. The switch from one language to another feels natural to me, I reply, though that does not say much, just as one can hardly give a convincing explanation as to why someone's hair turns gray on one day but not on another. But this is an inane analogy, I realize, because I do not want to touch the heart of the matter. Yes, there is something unnatural, which I have refused to accept. Not the fact of writing in a second language—there are always Nabokov and Conrad[2] as references, and many of my contemporaries as well—or that I impulsively gave up a reliable career for writing. It's the absoluteness of my abandonment of Chinese, undertaken with such determination that it is a kind of suicide.

The tragedy of Nabokov's loss is that his misfortune was easily explained   10
by public history. His story—of being driven by a revolution into permanent exile—became the possession of other people. My decision to write in English has also been explained as a flight from my country's history. But unlike Nabokov, who had been a published Russian writer, I never wrote in Chinese. Still, one cannot avoid the fact that a private decision, once seen through a public prism, becomes a metaphor. Once, a poet of Eastern European origin and I—we both have lived in America for years, and we both write in English—were asked to read our work in our native languages at a gala. But I don't write in Chinese, I explained, and the organizer apologized for her misunderstanding. I offered to read Li Po or Du Fu or any of the ancient poets I had grown up memorizing, but instead it was arranged for me to read poetry by a political prisoner.

A metaphor's desire to transcend diminishes any human story; its ambition to illuminate blinds those who create metaphors. In my distrust of metaphors I feel a kinship with George Eliot:[3] "We all of us, grave or light, get our thoughts entangled in metaphors, and act fatally on the strength of them." My abandonment of my first language is personal, so deeply personal that I resist any interpretation—political or historical or ethnographical. This, I know, is what my husband was questioning years ago: was I prepared to be turned into a symbol by well-intentioned or hostile minds?

Chinese immigrants of my generation in America criticize my English for not being native enough. A compatriot, after reading my work, pointed

---

[2] ***Joseph Conrad*** (1857–1924): Polish-born writer considered one of the greatest British novelists. — EDS.

[3] ***George Eliot:*** Pen name of the prominent British novelist Mary Anne Evans (1819–1880). — EDS.

out, in an e-mail, how my language is neither lavish nor lyrical, as a real writer's language should be: you write only simple things in simple English, you should be ashamed of yourself, he wrote in a fury. A professor—an American writer—in graduate school told me that I should stop writing, as English would remain a foreign language to me. Their concerns about ownership of a language, rather than making me as impatient as Nabokov, allow me secret laughter. English is to me as random a choice as any other language. What one goes toward is less definitive than that from which one turns away.

Before I left China, I destroyed the journal that I had kept for years and most of the letters written to me, those same letters I had once watched out for, lest my mother discover them. What I could not bring myself to destroy I sealed up and brought with me to America, though I will never open them again. My letters to others I would have destroyed, too, had I had them. These records, of the days I had lived time and time over, became intolerable now that my time in China was over. But this violent desire to erase a life in a native language is only wishful thinking. One's relationship with the native language is similar to that with the past. Rarely does a story start where we wish it had, or end where we wish it would.

One crosses the border to become a new person. One finishes a manuscript and cuts off the characters. One adopts a language. These are false and forced frameworks, providing illusory freedom, as time provides illusory leniency when we, in anguish, let it pass monotonously. "To kill time," an English phrase that still chills me: time can be killed but only by frivolous matters and purposeless activities. No one thinks of suicide as a courageous endeavor to kill time.

During my second hospital stay, in New York, a group of nursing students came to play bingo one Friday night. A young woman, another patient, asked if I would join her. Bingo, I said, I've never in my life played that. She pondered for a moment, and said that she had played bingo only in the hospital. It was her eighth hospitalization when I met her; she had taken middle-school courses for a while in the hospital, when she was younger, and, once, she pointed out a small patch of fenced-in green where she and other children had been let out for exercise. Her father often visited her in the afternoon, and I would watch them sitting together playing a game, not attempting a conversation. By then, all words must have been inadequate, language doing little to help a mind survive time.

Yet language is capable of sinking a mind. One's thoughts are slavishly bound to language. I used to think that an abyss is a moment of despair becoming interminable; but any moment, even the direst, is bound to end. What's abysmal is that one's erratic language closes in on one like quicksand: "You are nothing. You must do anything you can to get rid of this nothingness." We can kill time, but language kills us.

"Patient reports feeling . . . like she is a burden to her loved ones"—much later, I read the notes from the emergency room. I did not have any recollection of the conversation. *A burden to her loved ones:* this language must have been provided to me. I would never use the phrase in my thinking or my writing. But my resistance has little to do with avoiding a platitude. To say "a burden" is to grant oneself weight in other people's lives; to call them "loved ones" is to fake one's ability to love. One does not always want to be subject to self-interrogation imposed by a cliché.

When Katherine Mansfield[4] was still a teenager, she wrote in her journal about a man next door playing "Swanee River"[5] on a cornet, for what seemed like weeks. "I wake up with the 'Swanee River,' eat it with every meal I take, and go to bed eventually with 'all de world am sad and weary' as a lullaby." I read Mansfield's notebooks and Marianne Moore's[6] letters around the same time, when I returned home from New York. In a letter, Moore described a night of fundraising at Bryn Mawr. Maidens in bathing suits and green bathing tails on a raft: "It was Really most realistic . . . way down upon the Swanee River."

I marked the entries because they reminded me of a moment I had forgotten. I was nine, and my sister thirteen. On a Saturday afternoon, I was in our apartment and she was on the balcony. My sister had joined the middle-school choir that year, and in the autumn sunshine she sang in a voice that was beginning to leave girlhood. "Way down upon the Swanee River. Far, far away. That's where my heart is turning ever; That's where the old folks stay."

The lyrics were translated into Chinese. The memory, too, should be in Chinese. But I cannot see our tiny garden with the grapevine, which our father cultivated and which was later uprooted by our wrathful mother, or the bamboo fence dotted with morning glories, or the junk that occupied half the balcony—years of accumulations piled high by our hoarder father—if I do not name these things to myself in English. I cannot see my sister, but I can hear her sing the lyrics in English. I can seek to understand my mother's vulnerability and cruelty, but language is the barrier I have chosen. "Do you know, the moment I die your father will marry someone else?" my mother used to whisper to me when I was little. "Do you know that I cannot die, because I don't want you to live under a stepmother?" Or else, taken over by inexplicable rage, she would say that I, the only person she had loved, deserved the ugliest death because I did not display enough gratitude. But I have given these moments—what's possible to be put into English—to my characters. Memories, left untranslated, can be disowned; memories untranslatable can become someone else's story.

20

Over the years, my brain has banished Chinese. I dream in English. I talk to myself in English. And memories—not only those about America but also those about China; not only those carried with me but also those archived with the wish to forget—are sorted in English. To be orphaned from my native language felt, and still feels, like a crucial decision.

---

4 **Katherine Mansfield** (1888–1923): famous New Zealand short story writer. — EDS.
5 **"Swanee River":** Popular song composed by Stephen Foster in 1851. — EDS.
6 **Marianne Moore** (1887–1972): Prominent American poet known for her innovative techniques. — EDS.

When we enter a world—a new country, a new school, a party, a family or a class reunion, an army camp, a hospital—we speak the language it requires. The wisdom to adapt is the wisdom to have two languages: the one spoken to others, and the one spoken to oneself. One learns to master the public language not much differently from the way that one acquires a second language: assess the situations, construct sentences with the right words and the correct syntax, catch a mistake if one can avoid it, or else apologize and learn the lesson after a blunder. Fluency in the public language, like fluency in a second language, can be achieved with enough practice.

Perhaps the line between the two is, and should be, fluid; it is never so for me. I often forget, when I write, that English is also used by others. English is my private language. Every word has to be pondered before it becomes a word. I have no doubt—can this be an illusion?—that the conversation I have with myself, however linguistically flawed, is the conversation that I have always wanted, in the exact way I want it to be.

In my relationship with English, in this relationship with the intrinsic distance between a nonnative speaker and an adopted language that makes people look askance, I feel invisible but not estranged. It is the position I believe I always want in life. But with every pursuit there is the danger of crossing a line, from invisibility to erasure.

There was a time when I could write well in Chinese. In school, my   25 essays were used as models; in the Army, where I spent a year of involuntary service between the ages of eighteen and nineteen, our squad leader gave me the choice between drafting a speech for her and cleaning the toilets or the pigsties—I always chose to write. Once, in high school, I entered an oratory contest. Onstage, I saw that many of the listeners were moved to tears by the poetic and insincere lies I had made up; I moved myself to tears, too. It crossed my mind that I could become a successful propaganda writer. I was disturbed by this. A young person wants to be true to herself and to the world. But it did not occur to me to ask: Can one's intelligence rely entirely on the public language; can one form a precise thought, recall an accurate memory, or even feel a genuine feeling, with only the public language?

My mother, who loves to sing, often sings the songs from her childhood and youth, many of them words of propaganda from the 1950s and 60s. But there is one song she has reminisced about all her life because she does not know how to sing it. She learned the song in kindergarten, the year Communism took over her home town; she can remember only the opening line.

There was an old woman in the hospital in New York who sat in the hallway with a pair of shiny red shoes. I feel like Dorothy,[7] she said as she showed me the shoes, which she had chosen from the donations to patients. Some days, her mind was lucid, and she would talk about the red shoes that hurt her feet but which she could not part with, or the medication that made her brain feel dead and left her body in pain. Other days, she talked to the

---

[7] **Dorothy:** Dorothy Gale is the well-known heroine in *The Wizard of Oz.* — EDS.

air, an endless conversation with the unseen. People who had abandoned her by going away or dying returned and made her weep.

I often sat next to this lonesome Dorothy. Was I eavesdropping? Perhaps, but her conversation was beyond encroachment. That one could reach a point where the border between public and private language no longer matters is frightening. Much of what one does—to avoid suffering, to seek happiness, to stay healthy—is to keep a safe space for one's private language. Those who have lost that space have only one language left. My grandmother, according to my mother and her siblings, had become a woman who talked to the unseen before she was sent to the asylum to die. There's so much to give up: hope, freedom, dignity. A private language, however, defies any confinement. Death alone can take it away.

Mansfield spoke of her habit of keeping a journal as "being garrulous. . . . I must say nothing affords me the same relief." Several times, she directly addressed the readers—her posterity—in a taunting manner, as though laughing at them for taking her dead words seriously. I would prefer to distrust her. But it would be dishonest not to acknowledge the solace of reading her words. It was in the immediate weeks after the second hospitalization. My life was on hold. There were diagnoses to grapple with, medications to take, protocols to implement, hospital staff to report to, but they were there only to eliminate an option. What to replace it with I could not see, but I knew it was not within anyone's capacity to answer that. Not having the exact language for the bleakness I felt, I devoured Mansfield's words like thirst-quenching poison. Is it possible that one can be held hostage by someone else's words? What I underlined and reread: Are they her thoughts or mine?

There is nought to do but WORK, but how can I work when this awful   30 weakness makes even the pen like a walking stick?

There is something profound & terrible in this eternal desire to establish contact.

It is astonishing how violently a big branch shakes when a silly little bird has left it. I expect the bird knows it and feels immensely arrogant.

One only wants to feel sure of another. That's all.

I realize my faults better than anyone else could realize them. I know exactly where I fail.

Have people, apart from those far away people, ever existed for me?   35 Or have they always failed me, and faded because I denied them reality? Supposing I were to die, as I sit at this table, playing with my Indian paper knife—what would be the difference. No difference at all. Then why don't I commit suicide?

When one thinks in an adopted language, one arranges and rearranges words that are neutral, indifferent even.

When one remembers in an adopted language, there is a dividing line in that remembrance. What came before could be someone else's life; it might as well be fiction.

What language, I wonder, does one use to feel? Or does one need a language to feel? In the hospital in New York, one of my doctors asked me to visit a class studying minds and brains. Two medical students interviewed me, following a script. The doctor who led the class, impatient with their tentativeness, sent them back to their seats and posed questions more pointed and unrelenting. To answer him, I had to navigate my thoughts, and I watched him and his students closely, as I was being watched. When he asked about feelings, I said it was beyond my ability to describe what might as well be indescribable.

"If you can be articulate about your thoughts, why can't you articulate your feelings?" the doctor asked.

It took me a year to figure out the answer. It is hard to feel in an adopted 40
language, yet it is impossible in my native language.

Often I think that writing is a futile effort; so is reading; so is living. Loneliness is the inability to speak with another in one's private language. That emptiness is filled with public language or romanticized connections.

After the dream of the public telephone, I remembered a moment in the Army. It was New Year's Eve, and we were ordered to watch the official celebration on CCTV. Halfway through the program, a girl on duty came and said that there was a long-distance call for me.

It was the same type of black rotary phone as we had back at the apartment complex, and my sister was on the line. It was the first long-distance call I had received in my life, and the next time would be four years later, back in Beijing, when an American professor phoned to interview me. I still remember the woman, calling from Mount Sinai Hospital in New York City, asking questions about my interests in immunology, talking about her research projects and life in America. My English was good enough to understand half of what she said, and the scratching noises in the background made me sweat for the missed half.

What did my sister and I talk about on that New Year's Eve? In abandoning my native language, I have erased myself from that memory. But erasing, I have learned, does not stop with a new language, and that, my friend, is my sorrow and my selfishness. In speaking and in writing in an adopted language, I have not stopped erasing. I have crossed the line, too, from erasing myself to erasing others. I am not the only casualty in this war against myself.

In an ideal world, I would prefer to have my mind reserved for thinking, 45
and thinking alone. I dread the moment when a thought trails off and a feeling starts, when one faces the eternal challenge of eluding the void for which one does not have words. To speak when one cannot is to blunder. I have spoken by having written—this piece or any piece—for myself and against myself. The solace is with the language I chose. The grief, to have spoken at all. ◼

The Reader's Presence

1. "To Speak Is to Blunder" Is written in the first person, but Li often writes sentences more abstractly by avoiding the use of "I." For example: "One's grief belongs to oneself." How does "one" differ from "I," and how does "one" affect the meaning of those sentences?

2. Li describes her decision to abandon Chinese as both a "salvation" and "a kind of suicide." How is suicide portrayed in Li's essay? How does she use this notion to express her thinking about the adequacy and the possibilities of language? Li draws quite heavily on the thinking of other writers, including Vladimir Nabokov, and especially on their thinking about the power of metaphors. What position do you think Li establishes about the importance of metaphor to sustain productive thinking in writing?

3. **CONNECTIONS:** "English is to me as random a choice as any other language. What one goes toward is less definitive than that from which one turns away" (paragraph 12). For Li, adopting English is a significant step away from her past in China. In "Small Man in a Big Country" (page 223), Alex Tizon describes a similar process as his family gives up their native language to become more American. Compare and contrast Li's and Tizon's views of their native and adopted languages. In what ways are their reasons for learning English similar? different? Point to specific instances in each essay to validate your points.

Barry Lopez
Six Thousand Lessons

"Diversity" has become one of the key terms of our culture and society. We hear it largely used in education and in the workforce, where it usually signifies the inclusion of different races, ethnicities, backgrounds, religions, and points of view. Yet we rarely picture diversity in its broadest sense—the diversity that makes up the entire earth, with its varied geographies, creatures, vegetation, landscapes, cultures, and its six thousand languages. In "Six Thousand Lessons," one of America's foremost essayists reflects on a life of exten-

> **"Be the untutored traveler, the eager reader, the enthusiastic listener."**

sive travel and the lessons it taught him about the overwhelming importance of differences. The insight he arrives at might be simply expressed but it remains nevertheless profound: "It is now my understanding that diversity is not, as I had once thought, a characteristic of life. It is, instead, a condition necessary for life" (paragraph 8).

The author of many books of essays, fiction, and literary nonfiction, **BARRY LOPEZ** (b. 1945) is a graduate of Notre Dame University and has made his home in Oregon since the late 1960s. His best-known literary achievement is the 1986 bestseller, *Arctic Dreams:*

||||||||||||||||||||||||||||||||||||||||||||||||||||||||||||||||||||||||||||||||||||||||||||||||||||||||||||||||||||||||||||||||

Imagination and Desire in a Northern Landscape, which received the National Book Award for Nonfiction. His most recent book is a collection of short stories, *Outside* (2014).

"If I were to offer any advice to young writers" Lopez has said, "it would be this: be discriminating and be discerning about the work you set for yourself. That done, be the untutored traveler, the eager reader, the enthusiastic listener. Put what you learn together carefully, and then write thoughtfully, with respect both for the reader and your sources."

WHEN I WAS A BOY I wanted to see the world. Bit by bit it happened. In 1948, at the age of three, I left my home in Mamaroneck, New York, just north of New York City, and flew with my mother to a different life in California's San Fernando Valley, outside Los Angeles. I spent my adolescent summers at the Grand Canyon and swam in the great Pacific. Later, when my mother married again, we moved to the Murray Hill section of Manhattan. Another sort of canyon. I traveled across Europe by bus when I was seventeen. I went to Mexico. In 1970 I moved to rural Oregon. I camped in the desert in Namibia and on the polar plateau, twenty kilometers from the South Pole. I flew to Bangkok and Belém, to Nairobi and Perth, and traveled out into the country beyond.

Over the years I ate many unfamiliar meals, overheard arguments on town and city streets conducted in Pashto, Afrikaans, Cree, Flemish, Aranda, and other tongues unknown to me. I prayed in houses of worship not my own, walked through refugee camps in Lebanon, and crossed impossible mountain passes on the Silk Road. Witness was what I was after, not achievement. From the beginning, I wanted to understand how very different each stretch of landscape, each boulevard, each cultural aspiration was. The human epistemologies embedded in the six thousand spoken ways of knowing God compare with the six thousand ways a river can plunge from high country to low, or the six thousand ways dawn might break over the Atacama, the Tanami, the Gobi, or the Sonora.

Anyone determined to see so many of the world's disparate faces might easily succumb to the heresy of believing one place is finally not so different from another somewhere, because in the moment he is weary of variety or otherwise not paying attention. I have found myself there. But each place is itself only, and nowhere repeated. Miss it and it's gone.

Of the six thousand valuable lessons that might be offered to a persistent traveler, here is one I received. Over the years, in speaking with Eskimo people—Yup'ik and Inupiat in Alaska and Inuit in Canada—I came to understand that they prefer to avoid the way we use collective nouns in the West to speak about a species. Their tendency is not to respond to a question about what it is that "caribou" do, but to say instead what an individual caribou once did in a particular set of circumstances—in that place, at that time of year, in those weather conditions, with these other animals around. It is important to understand, they say, that on another, apparently similar occasion, the same animal might do something different. All caribou, despite their resemblance to each other, are not only differentiated, one from the other, but are in the end unpredictable.

In Xian once, where Chinese archeologists had uncovered a marching army of terra-cotta horses and soldiers, and where visitors could view them in long pits in situ, I studied several hundred of each with a pair of binoculars. The face of each one, men and horses alike, was unique. Itself only. I've watched hundreds of impala bounding away from lions on the savannah of Botswanan Africa, and flocks of white corellas roosting at dusk in copses of gum trees at the edge of the Great Sandy Desert in Western Australia, and I have had no doubt in those moments that, with patience and tutoring, I would learn to distinguish one animal from another.

It is terrifying for me to consider, now, how television, a kind of cultural nerve gas, has compromised the world's six thousand epistemologies, generalizing them into the inutility of "what we all know" and "what we all believe." To consider the campaigns mounted for all to speak Mandarin or English in order "to make life easier." To consider how a stunning photograph of a phantom orchid can be made to stand today for all phantom orchids through time. To consider how traveling to Vienna can signify for some that you've more or less been to Prague. How, if you're pressed for time, one thing can justifiably take the place of another.

During these years of travel, my understanding of what diversity means has changed. I began with an intuition, that the world was, from place to place and from culture to culture, far more different than I had been led to believe. Later, I began to understand that to ignore these differences was not simply insensitive but unjust and perilous. To ignore the differences does not make things better. It creates isolation, pain, fury, despair. Finally, I came to see something profound. Long-term, healthy patterns of social organization, among all social life forms, it seemed to me, hinged on work that maintained the integrity of the community while at the same time granting autonomy to its individuals. What made a society beautiful and memorable was some combination of autonomy and deference that, together, minimized strife.

It is now my understanding that diversity is not, as I had once thought, a characteristic of life. It is, instead, a condition necessary for life. To eliminate diversity would be like eliminating carbon and expecting life to go on. This, I believe, is why even a passing acquaintance with endangered languages or endangered species or endangered cultural traditions brings with it so much anxiety, so much sadness. We know in our tissues that the fewer the differences we encounter in our travels, the more widespread the kingdom of Death has become. ●

The Reader's Presence

1. In his second paragraph, Lopez writes: "Witness was what I was after, not achievement." What do you think he means by this?

||||||||||||||||||||||||||||||||||||||||||||||||||||||||||||||||||||||||||||||||||||||||||||||||||||||||||||||||||||||||||||||||||

2. In the fourth paragraph, Lopez describes one of his "six thousand lessons." What do you think he means by this? What do you think he means when he says that Eskimo people "prefer to avoid the way we use collective nouns in the West to speak about a species." According to his report, how do the Eskimo people use such "collective nouns"? In your own words, explain the differences between the two noun usages. What does this difference signify and what lesson has Lopez learned?

3. **CONNECTIONS:** Diversity is the main topic of two other selections in this collection: David Brooks, "People Like Us" (page 324) and Walter Benn Michaels, "The Trouble with Diversity" (page 571). Compare and contrast "Six Thousand Lessons" to either one of these selections. Is Lopez using "diversity" in a different way than Brooks or Michaels. Would either writer agree or disagree with the values Lopez finds in diversity and difference?

Nancy Mairs
ON BEING A CRIPPLE

NANCY MAIRS (1943–2016) contributed poetry, short stories, articles, and essays to numerous journals. "On Being a Cripple" comes from *Plaintext*, a collection of essays published in 1986. Her books include *Remembering the Bone House: An Erotics of Place and Space* (1989); *Carnal Acts* (1990); *Ordinary Time: Cycles in Marriage, Faith, and Renewal* (1993); *Waist-High in the World: A Life Among the Nondisabled* (1997); *A Troubled Guest: Life and Death Stories* (2001); and her most recent, *A Dynamic God: Living an Unconventional Catholic Faith* (2007). From 1983 to 1985 Mairs served as assistant director of the Southwest Institute for Research on Women, and she also taught at the University of Arizona and at UCLA.

> **"I want a prose that is allusive and translucent."**

In *Voice Lessons: On Becoming a (Woman) Writer* (1994), she writes, "I want a prose that is allusive and translucent, that eases you into me and embraces you, not one that baffles you or bounces you around so that you can't even tell where I am. And so I have chosen to work, very, very carefully, with the language we share, faults and all, choosing each word for its capacity, its ambiguity, the space it provides for me to live my life within it, relating rather than opposing each word to the next, each sentence to the next, 'starting on all sides at once . . . twenty times, thirty times, over': the stuttering adventure of the essay."

To escape is nothing. Not to escape is nothing.
—LOUISE BOGAN

THE OTHER DAY I was thinking of writing an essay on being a cripple. I was thinking hard in one of the stalls of the women's room in my office building, as I was shoving my shirt into my jeans and tugging up my zipper. Preoccupied, I flushed, picked up my book bag, took my cane down from the hook, and unlatched the door. So many movements unbalanced me, and as I pulled the door open I fell over backward, landing fully clothed on the toilet seat with my legs splayed in front of me: the old beetle-on-its-back routine. Saturday afternoon, the building deserted, I was free to laugh aloud as I wriggled back to my feet, my voice bouncing off the yellowish tiles from all directions. Had anyone been there with me, I'd have been still and faint and hot with chagrin. I decided that it was high time to write the essay.

First, the matter of semantics. I am a cripple. I choose this word to name me. I choose from among several possibilities, the most common of which are "handicapped" and "disabled." I made the choice a number of years ago, without thinking, unaware of my motives for doing so. Even now, I'm not sure what those motives are, but I recognize that they are complex and not entirely flattering. People—crippled or not—wince at the word "cripple," as they do not at "handicapped" or "disabled." Perhaps I want them to wince. I want them to see me as a tough customer, one to whom the fates/gods/viruses have not been kind, but who can face the brutal truth of her existence squarely. As a cripple, I swagger.

But, to be fair to myself, a certain amount of honesty underlies my choice. "Cripple" seems to me a clean word, straightforward and precise. It has an honorable history, having made its first appearance in the Lindisfarne Gospel in the tenth century. As a lover of words, I like the accuracy with which it describes my condition: I have lost the full use of my limbs. "Disabled," by contrast, suggests any incapacity, physical or mental. And I certainly don't like "handicapped," which implies that I have deliberately been put at a disadvantage, by whom I can't imagine (my God is not a Handicapper General), in order to equalize chances in the great race of life. These words seem to me to be moving away from my condition, to be widening the gap between word and reality. Most remote is the recently coined euphemism "differently abled," which partakes of the same semantic hopefulness that transformed countries from "undeveloped" to "underdeveloped," then to "less developed," and finally to "developing" nations. People have continued to starve in those countries during the shift. Some realities do not obey the dictates of language.

Mine is one of them. Whatever you call me, I remain crippled. But I don't care what you call me, so long as it isn't "differently abled," which strikes me as pure verbal garbage designed, by its ability to describe anyone, to describe no one. I subscribe to George Orwell's[1] thesis that "the slovenliness of our language makes it easier for us to have foolish thoughts." And I refuse

---

[1] *Orwell:* From his essay "Politics and the English Language". — EDS.

to participate in the degeneration of the language to the extent that I deny that I have lost anything in the course of this calamitous disease; I refuse to pretend that the only differences between you and me are the various ordinary ones that distinguish any one person from another. But call me "disabled" or "handicapped" if you like. I have long since grown accustomed to them; and if they are vague, at least they hint at the truth. Moreover, I use them myself. Society is no readier to accept crippledness than to accept death, war, sex, sweat, or wrinkles. I would never refer to another person as a cripple. It is the word I use to name only myself.

I haven't always been crippled, a fact for which I am soundly grateful.   5
To be whole of limb is, I know from experience, infinitely more pleasant and useful than to be crippled; and if that knowledge leaves me open to bitterness at my loss, the physical soundness I once enjoyed (though I did not enjoy it half enough) is well worth the occasional stab of regret. Though never any good at sports, I was a normally active child and young adult. I climbed trees, played hopscotch, jumped rope, skated, swam, rode my bicycle, sailed. I despised team sports, spending some of the wretchedest afternoons of my life, sweaty and humiliated, behind a field-hockey stick and under a basketball hoop. I tramped alone for miles along the bridle paths that webbed the woods behind the house I grew up in. I swayed through countless dim hours in the arms of one man or another under the scattered shot of light from mirrored balls, and gyrated through countless more as Tab Hunter and Johnny Mathis gave way to the Rolling Stones, Creedence Clearwater Revival, Cream. I walked down the aisle. I pushed baby carriages, changed tires in the rain, marched for peace.

When I was twenty-eight I started to trip and drop things. What at first seemed my natural clumsiness soon became too pronounced to shrug off. I consulted a neurologist, who told me that I had a brain tumor. A battery of tests, increasingly disagreeable, revealed no tumor. About a year and a half later I developed a blurred spot in one eye. I had, at last, the episodes "disseminated in space and time" requisite for a diagnosis: multiple sclerosis. I have never been sorry for the doctor's initial misdiagnosis, however. For almost a week, until the negative results of the tests were in, I thought that I was going to die right away. Every day for the past nearly ten years, then, has been a kind of gift. I accept all gifts.

Multiple sclerosis is a chronic degenerative disease of the central nervous system, in which the myelin that sheathes the nerves is somehow eaten away and scar tissue forms in its place, interrupting the nerves' signals. During its course, which is unpredictable and uncontrollable, one may lose vision, hearing, speech, the ability to walk, control of bladder and/or bowels, strength in any or all extremities, sensitivity to touch, vibration, and/or pain, potency, coordination of movements—the list of possibilities is lengthy and, yes, horrifying. One may also lose one's sense of humor. That's the easiest to lose and the hardest to survive without.

In the past ten years, I have sustained some of these losses. Characteristic of MS are sudden attacks, called exacerbations, followed by remissions, and these I have not had. Instead, my disease has been slowly progressive. My left leg is now so weak that I walk with the aid of a brace and a cane; and for distances I use an Amigo, a variation on the electric wheelchair that looks rather like an electrified kiddie car. I no longer have much use of my left hand. Now my right side is weakening as well. I still have the blurred spot in my right eye. Overall, though, I've been lucky so far. My world has, of necessity, been circumscribed by my losses, but the terrain left me has been ample enough for me to continue many of the activities that absorb me: writing, teaching, raising children and cats and plants and snakes, reading, speaking publicly about MS and depression, even playing bridge with people patient and honorable enough to let me scatter cards every which way without sneaking a peek.

Lest I begin to sound like Pollyanna, however, let me say that I don't like having MS. I hate it. My life holds realities—harsh ones, some of them—that no right-minded human being ought to accept without grumbling. One of them is fatigue. I know of no one with MS who does not complain of bone-weariness; in a disease that presents an astonishing variety of symptoms, fatigue seems to be a common factor. I wake up in the morning feeling the way most people do at the end of a bad day, and I take it from there. As a result, I spend a lot of time *in extremis* and, impatient with limitation, I tend to ignore my fatigue until my body breaks down in some way and forces rest. Then I miss picnics, dinner parties, poetry readings, the brief visits of old friends from out of town. The offspring of a puritanical tradition of exceptional venerability, I cannot view these lapses without shame. My life often seems a series of small failures to do as I ought.

I lead, on the whole, an ordinary life, probably rather like the one I would 10 have led had I not had MS. I am lucky that my predilections were already solitary, sedentary, and bookish—unlike the world-famous French cellist I have read about, or the young woman I talked with one long afternoon who wanted only to be a jockey. I had just begun graduate school when I found out something was wrong with me, and I have remained, interminably, a graduate student. Perhaps I would not have if I'd thought I had the stamina to return to a full-time job as a technical editor; but I've enjoyed my studies.

In addition to studying, I teach writing courses. I also teach medical students how to give neurological examinations. I pick up freelance editing jobs here and there. I have raised a foster son and sent him into the world, where he has made me two grandbabies, and I am still escorting my daughter and son through adolescence. I go to Mass every Saturday. I am a superb, if messy, cook. I am also an enthusiastic laundress, capable of sorting a hamper full of clothes into five subtly differentiated piles, but a terrible housekeeper. I can do italic writing and, in an emergency, bathe an oil-soaked cat. I play a fiendish game of Scrabble. When I have the time and the money, I'd like to sit on my front steps with my husband, drinking Amaretto and smoking a cigar, as we imagine our counterparts in Leningrad and make sure that the sun gets down once more behind the sharp childish scrawl of the Tucson Mountains.

This lively plenty has its bleak complement, of course, in all the things I can no longer do. I will never run again, except in dreams, and one day I may have to write that I will never walk again. I like to go camping, but I can't follow George and the children along the trails that wander out of a campsite through the desert or into the mountains. In fact, even on the level I've learned never to check the weather or try to hold a coherent conversation: I need all my attention for my wayward feet. Of late, I have begun to catch myself wondering how people can propel themselves without canes. With only one usable hand, I have to select my clothing with care not so much for style as for ease of ingress and egress, and even so, dressing can be laborious. I can no longer do fine stitchery, pick up babies, play the piano, braid my hair. I am immobilized by acute attacks of depression, which may or may not be physiologically related to MS but are certainly its logical concomitant.

These two elements, the plenty and the privation, are never pure, nor are the delight and wretchedness that accompany them. Almost every pickle that I get into as a result of my weakness and clumsiness—and I get into plenty—is funny as well as maddening and sometimes painful. I recall one May afternoon when a friend and I were going out for a drink after finishing up at school. As we were climbing into opposite sides of my car, chatting, I tripped and fell, flat and hard, onto the asphalt parking lot, my abrupt departure interrupting him in mid-sentence. "Where'd you go?" he called as he came around the back of the car to find me hauling myself up by the door frame. "Are you all right?" Yes, I told him, I was fine, just a bit rattly, and we drove off to find a shady patio and some beer. When I got home an hour or so later, my daughter greeted me with "What have you done to yourself?" I looked down. One elbow of my white turtleneck with the green froggies, one knee of my white trousers, one white kneesock were blood-soaked. We peeled off the clothes and inspected the damage, which was nasty enough but not alarming. That part wasn't funny: The abrasions took a long time to heal, and one got a little infected. Even so, when I think of my friend talking earnestly, suddenly, to the hot thin air while I dropped from his view as though through a trap door, I find the image as silly as something from a Marx Brothers movie.

I may find it easier than other cripples to amuse myself because I live propped by the acceptance and the assistance and, sometimes, the amusement of those around me. Grocery clerks tear my checks out of my checkbook for me, and sales clerks find chairs to put into dressing rooms when I want to try on clothes. The people I work with make sure I teach at times when I am least likely to be fatigued, in places I can get to, with the materials I need. My students, with one anonymous exception (in an end-of-the-semester evaluation), have been unperturbed by my disability. Some even like it. One was immensely cheered by the information that I paint my own fingernails; she decided, she told me, that if I could go to such trouble over fine details, she could keep on writing essays. I suppose I became some sort of bright-fingered muse. She wrote good essays, too.

The most important struts in the framework of my existence, of course,   15
are my husband and children. Dismayingly few marriages survive the MS
test, and why should they? Most twenty-two- and nineteen-year-olds, like
George and me, can vow in clear conscience, after a childhood of chicken
pox and summer colds, to keep one another in sickness and in health so
long as they both shall live. Not many are equipped for catastrophe: the
dismay, the depression, the extra work, the boredom that a degenerative
disease can insinuate into a relationship. And our society, with its emphasis
on fun and its association of fun with physical performance, offers little
encouragement for a whole spouse to stay with a crippled partner. Children
experience similar stresses when faced with a crippled parent, and they
are more helpless, since parents and children can't usually get divorced.
They hate, of course, to be different from their peers, and the child whose
mother is tacking down the aisle of a school auditorium packed with proud
parents like a Cape Cod dinghy in a stiff breeze jolly well stands out in a
crowd. Deprived of legal divorce, the child can at least deny the mother's
disability, even her existence, forgetting to tell her about recitals and PTA
meetings, refusing to accompany her to stores or church or the movies,
never inviting friends to the house. Many do.

But I've been limping along for ten years now, and so far George and
the children are still at my left elbow, holding tight. Anne and Matthew vacuum floors and dust furniture and haul trash and rake up dog droppings and
button my cuffs and bake lasagna and Toll House cookies with just enough
grumbling so I know that they don't have brain fever. And far from hiding
me, they're forever dragging me by racks of fancy clothes or through teeming school corridors, or welcoming gaggles of friends while I'm wandering
through the house in Anne's filmy pink babydoll pajamas. George generally calls before he brings someone home, but he does just as many dumb
thankless chores as the children. And they all yell at me, laugh at some of
my jokes, write me funny letters when we're apart—in short, treat me as an
ordinary human being for whom they have some use. I think they like me.
Unless they're faking. . . .

Faking. There's the rub. Tugging at the fringes of my consciousness
always is the terror that people are kind to me only because I'm a cripple. My
mother almost shattered me once, with that instinct mothers have—blind, I
think, in this case, but unerring nonetheless—for striking blows along the
fault-lines of their children's hearts, by telling me, in an attack on my selfishness, "We all have to make allowances for you, of course, because of the
way you are." From the distance of a couple of years, I have to admit that I
haven't any idea just what she meant, and I'm not sure that she knew either.
She was awfully angry. But at the time, as the words thudded home, I felt
my worst fear, suddenly realized. I could bear being called selfish: I am. But
I couldn't bear the corroboration that those around me were doing in fact
what I'd always suspected them of doing, professing fondness while silently
putting up with me because of the way I am. A cripple. I've been a little
cracked ever since.

Along with this fear that people are secretly accepting shoddy goods comes a relentless pressure to please—to prove myself worth the burdens I impose, I guess, or to build a substantial account of good will against which I may write drafts in times of need. Part of the pressure arises from social expectations. In our society, anyone who deviates from the norm had better find some way to compensate. Like fat people, who are expected to be jolly, cripples must bear their lot meekly and cheerfully. A grumpy cripple isn't playing by the rules. And much of the pressure is self-generated. Early on I vowed that, if I had to have MS, by God I was going to do it well. This is a class act, ladies and gentlemen. No tears, no recriminations, no faint-heartedness.

One way and another, then, I wind up feeling like Tiny Tim,[2] peering over the edge of the table at the Christmas goose, waving my crutch, piping down God's blessing on us all. Only sometimes I don't want to play Tiny Tim; I'd rather be Caliban,[3] a most scurvy monster. Fortunately, at home no one much cares whether I'm a good cripple or a bad cripple as long as I make vichyssoise with fair regularity. One evening several years ago, Anne was reading at the dining-room table while I cooked dinner. As I opened a can of tomatoes, the can slipped in my left hand and juice spattered me and the counter with bloody spots. Fatigued and infuriated, I bellowed, "I'm so sick of being crippled!" Anne glanced at me over the top of her book. "There now," she said, "do you feel better?" "Yes," I said, "yes, I do." She went back to her reading. I felt better. That's about all the attention my scurviness ever gets.

Because I hate being crippled, I sometimes hate myself for being a crip-   20
ple. Over the years I have come to expect—even accept—attacks of violent self-loathing. Luckily, in general our society no longer connects deformity and disease directly with evil (though a charismatic once told me that I have MS because a devil is in me) and so I'm allowed to move largely at will, even among small children. But I'm not sure that this revision of attitude has been particularly helpful. Physical imperfection, even freed of moral disapprobation, still defies and violates the ideal, especially for women, whose confinement in their bodies as objects of desire is far from over. Each age, of course, has its ideal, and I doubt that ours is any better or worse than any other. Today's ideal woman, who lives on the glossy pages of dozens of magazines, seems to be between the ages of eighteen and twenty-five; her hair has body, her teeth flash white, her breath smells minty, her underarms are dry; she has a career but is still a fabulous cook, especially of meals that take less than twenty minutes to prepare; she does not ordinarily appear to have a husband or children; she is trim and deeply tanned; she jogs, swims, plays tennis, rides a bicycle, sails, but does not bowl; she travels widely, even to out-of-the-way places like Finland and Samoa, always in the company of the ideal man, who possesses a nearly identical set of characteristics.

---

2 **Tiny Tim:** Crippled boy in Charles Dickens's *A Christmas Carol.* — EDS.
3 **Caliban:** A character in William Shakespeare's play *The Tempest.* — EDS.

There are a few exceptions. Though usually white and often blonde, she may be black, Hispanic, Asian, or Native American, so long as she is unusually sleek. She may be old, provided she is selling a laxative or is Lauren Bacall. If she is selling a detergent, she may be married and have a flock of strikingly messy children. But she is never a cripple.

Like many women I know, I have always had an uneasy relationship with my body. I was not a popular child, largely, I think now, because I was peculiar: intelligent, intense, moody, shy, given to unexpected actions and inexplicable notions and emotions. But as I entered adolescence, I believed myself unpopular because I was homely; my breasts too flat, my mouth too wide, my hips too narrow, my clothing never quite right in fit or style. I was not, in fact, particularly ugly, old photographs inform me, though I was well off the ideal; but I carried this sense of self-alienation with me into adulthood, where it regenerated in response to the depredations of MS. Even with my brace I walk with a limp so pronounced that, seeing myself on the videotape of a television program on the disabled, I couldn't believe that anything but an inchworm could make progress humping along like that. My shoulders droop and my pelvis thrusts forward as I try to balance myself upright, throwing my frame into a bony S. As a result of contractures, one shoulder is higher than the other and I carry one arm bent in front of me, the fingers curled into a claw. My left arm and leg have wasted into pipe-stems, and I try always to keep them covered. When I think about how my body must look to others, especially to men, to whom I have been trained to display myself, I feel ludicrous, even loathsome.

At my age, however, I don't spend much time thinking about my appearance. The burning egocentricity of adolescence, which assures one that all the world is looking all the time, has passed, thank God, and I'm generally too caught up in what I'm doing to step back, as I used to, and watch myself as though upon a stage. I'm also too old to believe in the accuracy of self-image. I know that I'm not a hideous crone, that in fact, when I'm rested, well dressed, and well made up, I look fine. The self-loathing I feel is neither physically nor intellectually substantial. What I hate is not me but a disease.

I am not a disease.

And a disease is not — at least not singlehandedly — going to determine who I am, though at first it seemed to be going to. Adjusting to a chronic incurable illness, I have moved through a process similar to that outlined by Elisabeth Kübler-Ross in *On Death and Dying*. The major difference — and it is far more significant than most people recognize — is that I can't be sure of the outcome, as the terminally ill cancer patient can. Research studies indicate that, with proper medical care, I may achieve a "normal" life span. And in our society, with its vision of death as the ultimate evil, worse even than decrepitude, the response to such news is, "Oh well, at least you're not going to *die*." Are there worse things than dying? I think that there may be.

I think of two women I know, both with MS, both enough older than I to have served me as models. One took to her bed several years ago and has been there ever since. Although she can sit in a high-backed wheelchair, 25 because she is incontinent she refuses to go out at all, even though incontinence pants, which are readily available at any pharmacy, could protect her from embarrassment. Instead, she stays at home and insists that her husband, a small quiet man, a retired civil servant, stay there with her except for a quick weekly foray to the supermarket. The other woman, whose illness was diagnosed when she was eighteen, a nursing student engaged to a young doctor, finished her training, married her doctor, accompanied him to Germany when he was in the service, bore three sons and a daughter, now grown and gone. When she can, she travels with her husband; she plays bridge, embroiders, swims regularly; she works, like me, as a symptomatic-patient instructor of medical students in neurology. Guess which woman I hope to be.

At the beginning, I thought about having MS almost incessantly. And because of the unpredictable course of the disease, my thoughts were always terrified. Each night I'd get into bed wondering whether I'd get out again the next morning, whether I'd be able to see, to speak, to hold a pen between my fingers. Knowing that the day might come when I'd be physically incapable of killing myself, I thought perhaps I ought to do so right away, while I still had the strength. Gradually I came to understand that the Nancy who might one day lie inert under a bedsheet, arms and legs paralyzed, unable to feed or bathe herself, unable to reach out for a gun, a bottle of pills, was not the Nancy I was at present, and that I could not presume to make decisions for that future Nancy, who might well not want in the least to die. Now the only provision I've made for the future Nancy is that when the time comes—and it is likely to come in the form of pneumonia, friend to the weak and the old—I am not to be treated with machines and medications. If she is unable to communicate by then, I hope she will be satisfied with these terms.

Thinking all the time about having MS grew tiresome and intrusive, especially in the large and tragic mode in which I was accustomed to considering my plight. Months and even years went by without catastrophe (at least without one related to MS), and really I was awfully busy, what with George and children and snakes and students and poems, and I hadn't the time, let alone the inclination, to devote myself to being a disease. Too, the richer my life became, the funnier it seemed, as though there were some connection between largesse and laughter, and so my tragic stance began to waver until, even with the aid of a brace and a cane, I couldn't hold it for very long at a time.

After several years I was satisfied with my adjustment. I had suffered my grief and fury and terror, I thought, but now I was at ease with my lot. Then one summer day I set out with George and the children across the desert for a vacation in California. Part way to Yuma I became aware that my right leg felt funny. "I think I've had an exacerbation," I told George. "What shall we do?" he asked. "I think we'd better get the hell to California," I said, "because I don't know whether I'll ever make it again." So we went on to San Diego and then to Orange, up the Pacific Coast Highway to Santa Cruz, across to Yosemite, down to Sequoia and Joshua Tree, and so back over the desert to home.

It was a fine two-week trip, filled with friends and fair weather, and I wouldn't have missed it for the world, though I did in fact make it back to California two years later. Nor would there have been any point in missing it, since in MS, once the symptoms have appeared, the neurological damage has been done, and there's no way to predict or prevent that damage.

The incident spoiled my self-satisfaction, however. It renewed my grief and fury and terror, and I learned that one never finishes adjusting to MS. I don't know now why I thought one would. One does not, after all, finish adjusting to life, and MS is simply a fact of my life—not my favorite fact, of course—but as ordinary as my nose and my tropical fish and my yellow Mazda station wagon. It may at any time get worse, but no amount of worry or anticipation can prepare me for a new loss. My life is a lesson in losses. I learn one at a time.

And I had best be patient in the learning, since I'll have to do it like it or not. As any rock fan knows, you can't always get what you want. Particularly when you have MS. You can't, for example, get cured. In recent years researchers and the organizations that fund research have started to pay MS some attention even though it isn't fatal; perhaps they have begun to see that life is something other than a quantitative phenomenon, that one may be very much alive for a very long time in a life that isn't worth living. The researchers have made some progress toward understanding the mechanism of the disease: It may well be an autoimmune reaction triggered by a slow-acting virus. But they are nowhere near its prevention, control, or cure. And most of us want to be cured. Some, unable to accept incurability, grasp at one treatment after another, no matter how bizarre: megavitamin therapy, gluten-free diet, injections of cobra venom, hypothermal suits, lymphocytopharesis, hyperbaric chambers. Many treatments are probably harmless enough, but none are curative.

The absence of a cure often makes MS patients bitter toward their doctors. Doctors are, after all, the priests of modern society, the new shamans, whose business is to heal, and many an MS patient roves from one to another, searching for the "good" doctor who will make him well. Doctors too think of themselves as healers, and for this reason many have trouble dealing with MS patients, whose disease in its intransigence defeats their aims and mocks their skills. Too few doctors, it is true, treat their patients as whole human beings, but the reverse is also true. I have always tried to be gentle with my doctors, who often have more at stake in terms of ego than I do. I may be frustrated, maddened, depressed by the incurability of my disease, but I am not diminished by it, and they are. When I push myself up from my seat in the waiting room and stumble toward them, I incarnate the limitation of their powers. The least I can do is refuse to press on their tenderest spots.

This gentleness is part of the reason that I'm not sorry to be a cripple. I didn't have it before. Perhaps I'd have developed it anyway—how could I know such a thing?—and I wish I had more of it, but I'm glad of what I have. It has opened and enriched my life enormously, this sense that my frailty and need must be mirrored in others, that in searching for and shaping

30

a stable core in a life wrenched by change and loss, change and loss, I must recognize the same process, under individual conditions, in the lives around me. I do not deprecate such knowledge, however I've come by it.

All the same, if a cure were found, would I take it? In a minute. I may be a cripple, but I'm only occasionally a loony and never a saint. Anyway, in my brand of theology God doesn't give bonus points for a limp. I'd take a cure; I just don't need one. A friend who also has MS startled me once by asking, "Do you ever say to yourself, 'Why me, Lord?'" "No, Michael, I don't," I told him, "because whenever I try, the only response I can think of is 'Why not?'" If I could make a cosmic deal, who would I put in my place? What in my life would I give up in exchange for sound limbs and a thrilling rush of energy? No one. Nothing. I might as well do the job myself. Now that I'm getting the hang of it. ●

The Reader's Presence

1. Mairs's approach to her multiple sclerosis may come across as ironic, jaunty, or tough. Near the beginning of the essay she assumes that her reader is fundamentally alienated from her: "I refuse to pretend that the only differences between you and me are the various ordinary ones that distinguish any one person from another" (paragraph 4). What are those differences? How does the essay attempt to move the reader away from awkwardness or suspicion or hostility? Does it succeed? Why or why not?

2. What does the epigraph from Louise Bogan mean to you? What might it signify in relation to Mairs's essay? What is "escape," in Mairs's context? What meanings might the word *nothing* have?

3. **CONNECTIONS:** "Lest I begin to sound like Pollyanna, however, let me say that I don't like having MS. I hate it" (paragraph 9). Discuss Mairs's admission of hatred for the disease—and for herself (paragraph 20)—in relation to Alice Walker's "abuse" of her injured eye (paragraph 30) in "Beauty: When the Other Dancer Is the Self" (page 232). What is the role of self-loathing in personal growth?

The Writer at Work

NANCY MAIRS on Finding a Voice

In writing workshops and lectures, the essayist Nancy Mairs is often asked what appears to be a simple question: How did you find your voice as a writer? Yet is the question truly a simple one? In the following passage from her book "on becoming a (woman) writer," *Voice Lessons*, Mairs closely examines the question and suggests a way it might be answered.

"The question I am most often asked when I speak to students and others interested in writing is, How did you find your voice? I have some trouble with this locution because "find" always suggests to me the discovery, generally fortuitous, of some lack or loss. I have found an occasional four-leaf clover. I have found a mate. I have, more than once, found my way home. But is a voice susceptible of the same sort of revelation or retrieval? Hasn't mine simply always been there, from my earliest lallation to the "I love you" I called after my husband on his way to school several hours ago?

But of course, I remind myself, the question doesn't concern *my* voice at all but the voice of another woman (also named Nancy Mairs, confusingly enough) whose "utterances" are, except for the occasional public reading, literally inaudible: not, strictly speaking, a voice at all, but a fabrication, a device. And when I look again at the dictionary, I see that "find" can indeed also mean "devise." The voice in question, like the woman called into being to explain its existence, is an invention.

But of whom? For simplicity's sake, we assume that the voice in a work is that of the writer (in the case of nonfiction) or one invented by her (in the case of fiction). This assumption describes the relationship between writer (the woman in front of a luminous screen) and persona (whoever you hear speaking to you right now) adequately for most readers. And maybe for most writers, too. Until that earnest student in the second row waves a gnawed pencil over her head and asks, timidly as a rule because hers is the first question, "How did you find your voice?"

As though "you" were a coherent entity already existing at some original point, who had only to open her mouth and agitate her vocal chords—or, to be precise, pick up her fingers and diddle the keys—to call the world she had in mind into being. Not just a writer, an Author. But I've examined this process over and over in myself, and the direction of this authorial plot simply doesn't ring true. In the beginning, remember, was the *Word*. Not me. And the question, properly phrased, should probably be asked of my voice: How did you find (devise, invent, contrive) your Nancy?**"**

Dinaw Mengestu

HOME AT LAST

Ethiopian-born author **DINAW MENGESTU** (b. 1978) immigrated to the United States with his parents when he was just two years old. He received a BA in English from Georgetown University and an MFA in fiction writing from Columbia University. Mengestu is the author of three novels, most recently *All Our Names* (2014). His debut novel, *The Beautiful Things That Heaven Bears* (2007), was a New York Times Notable Book and was named one of the ten best novels of 2007 by Amazon.com. He has also written extensively for magazines, such as *Harper's* and *Rolling Stone*, on global issues, including the situation in Darfur. He teaches at Georgetown University, where he's the Lannan Chair of Poetics, and he was selected as a MacArthur Fellow in 2012. His second novel, *How to Read the Air*, was published in 2010. Mengestu has said that the novel, the story of an Ethiopian American, is "less about trying to figure out how you occupy these two cultural or racial boundaries and more about what

> Dinaw Mengestu's novel is about "what it's like when you are not particularly attached to either of [the] two communities" you belong to.

it's like when you are not particularly attached to either of [the] two communities." A similar sentiment marks the following essay, "Home at Last," originally published in the Winter 2008 issue of *Open City*.

AT TWENTY-ONE I moved to Brooklyn hoping that it would be the last move I would ever make—that it would, with the gradual accumulation of time, memory, and possessions, become that place I instinctively reverted back to when asked, "So, where are you from?" I was born in Ethiopia like my parents and their parents before them, but it would be a lie to say I was *from* Ethiopia, having left the country when I was only two years old following a military coup and civil war, losing in the process the language and any direct memory of the family and culture I had been born into. I simply am Ethiopian, without the necessary "from" that serves as the final assurance of our identity and origin.

Since leaving Addis Ababa in 1980, I've lived in Peoria, Illinois; in a suburb of Chicago; and then finally, before moving to Brooklyn, in Washington, D.C., the de facto[1] capital of the Ethiopian immigrant. Others, I know, have moved much more often and across much greater distances. I've only known a few people, however, that have grown up with the oddly permanent feeling of having lost and abandoned a home that you never, in fact, really knew, a feeling that has nothing to do with apartments, houses, or miles, but rather the sense that no matter how far you travel, or how long you stay still, there is no place that you can always return to, no place where you fully belong. My parents, for all that they had given up by leaving Ethiopia, at least had the certainty that they had come from some place. They knew the country's language and culture, had met outside of coffee shops along Addis's main boulevard in the early days of their relationship, and as a result, regardless of how mangled by violence Ethiopia later became, it was irrevocably and ultimately theirs. Growing up, one of my father's favorite sayings was, "Remember, you are Ethiopian," even though, of course, there was nothing for me to remember apart from the bits of nostalgia and culture my parents had imparted. What remained had less to do with the idea that I was from Ethiopia and more to do with the fact that I was not from America.

[1] **de facto:** A Latin term often used in the law; it means "in practice" or "for all intents and purposes." — EDS.

I can't say when exactly I first became aware of that feeling—that I was always going to and never from—but surely I must have felt it during those first years in Peoria, with my parents, sister, and me always sitting on the edge of whatever context we were now supposed to be a part of, whether it was the all-white Southern Baptist Church we went to every weekend, or the nearly all-white Catholic schools my sister and I attended first in Peoria and then again in Chicago at my parents' insistence. By that point my father, haunted by the death of his brother during the revolution and the ensuing loss of the country he had always assumed he would live and die in, had taken to long evening walks that he eventually let me accompany him on. Back then he had a habit of sometimes whispering his brother's name as he walked ("Shibrew," he would mutter) or whistling the tunes of Amharic[2] songs that I had never known. He always walked with both hands firmly clasped behind his back, as if his grief, transformed into something real and physical, could be grasped and secured in the palms of his hands. That was where I first learned what it meant to lose and be alone. The lesson would be reinforced over the years whenever I caught sight of my mother sitting by herself on a Sunday after-noon, staring silently out of our living room's picture window, recalling, per-haps, her father who had died after she left, or her mother, four sisters, and one brother in Ethiopia—or else recalling nothing at all because there was no one to visit her, no one to call or see. We had been stripped bare here in America, our lives confined to small towns and urban suburbs. We had sacrificed pre-cisely those things that can never be compensated for or repaid—parents, siblings, culture, a memory to a place that dates back more than half a gen-eration. It's easy to see now how even as a family we were isolated from one another—my parents tied and lost to their past; my sister and I irrevocably assimilated. For years we were strangers even among ourselves.

By the time I arrived in Brooklyn I had little interest in where I actually landed. I had just graduated college and had had enough of the fights and arguments about not being "black" enough, as well as the earlier fights in high school hallways and street corners that were fought for simply being black. Now it was enough, I wanted to believe, to simply be, to say I was in Brooklyn and Brooklyn was home. It wasn't until after I had signed the lease on my apartment that I even learned the name of the neighborhood I had moved into: Kensington, a distinctly regal name at a price that I could afford; it was perfect, in other words, for an eager and poor writer with inflated ambitions and no sense of where he belonged.

After less than a month of living in Kensington I had covered almost   5 all of the neighborhood's streets, deliberately committing their layouts and routines to memory in a first attempt at assimilation. There was an obvious and deliberate echo to my walks, a self-conscious reenactment of my father's routine that I adopted to stave off some of my own emptiness. It wasn't just that I didn't have any deep personal relationships here, it was that I had chosen this city as the place to redefine, to ground, to secure my place in the

---

[2] **Amharic:** Language spoken in North Central Ethiopia. — EDS.

world. If I could bind myself to Kensington physically, if I could memorize and mentally reproduce in accurate detail the various shades of the houses on a particular block, then I could stake my own claim to it, and in doing so, no one could tell me who I was or that I didn't belong.

On my early-morning walks to the F train I passed in succession a Latin American restaurant and grocery store, a Chinese fish market, a Halal butcher shop, followed by a series of Pakistani and Bangladeshi takeout restaurants. This cluster of restaurants on the corner of Church and McDonald, I later learned, sold five-dollar plates of lamb and chicken biryani in portions large enough to hold me over for a day, and in more financially desperate times, two days. Similarly, I learned that the butcher and fish shop delivery trucks arrived on most days just as I was making my way to the train. If I had time, I found it hard not to stand and stare at the refrigerated trucks with their calf and sheep carcasses dangling from hooks, or at the tanks of newly arrived bass and catfish flapping around in a shallow pool of water just deep enough to keep them alive.

It didn't take long for me to develop a fierce loyalty to Kensington, to think of the neighborhood and my place in it as emblematic of a grander immigrant narrative. In response to that loyalty, I promised to host a "Kensington night" for the handful of new friends that I eventually made in the city, an evening that would have been comprised of five-dollar lamb biryani followed by two-dollar Budweisers at Denny's, the neighborhood's only full-fledged bar — a defunct Irish pub complete with terribly dim lighting and wooden booths. I never hosted a Kensington night, however, no doubt in part because I had established my own private relationship to the

Ethnic diversity in Brooklyn's Kensington neighborhood.

neighborhood, one that could never be shared with others in a single evening of cheap South Asian food and beer. I knew the hours of the call of the muezzin that rang from the mosque a block away from my apartment. I heard it in my bedroom every morning, afternoon, and evening, and if I was writing when it called out, I learned that it was better to simply stop and admire it. My landlord's father, an old gray-haired Chinese immigrant who spoke no English, gradually smiled at me as I came and went, just as I learned to say hello, as politely as possible, in Mandarin every time I saw him. The men behind the counters of the Bangladeshi takeout places now knew me by sight. A few, on occasion, slipped an extra dollop of vegetables or rice into my to-go container, perhaps because they worried that I wasn't eating enough. One in particular, who was roughly my age, spoke little English, and smiled wholeheartedly whenever I came in, gave me presweetened tea and free bread, a gesture that I took to be an acknowledgment that, at least for him, I had earned my own, albeit marginal, place here.

And so instead of sitting with friends in a brightly lit fluorescent restaurant with cafeteria-style service, I found myself night after night quietly walking around the neighborhood in between sporadic fits of writing. Kensington was no more beautiful by night than by day, and perhaps this very absence of grandeur allowed me to feel more at ease wandering its streets at night. The haphazard gathering of immigrants in Kensington had turned it into a place that even someone like me, haunted and conscious of race and identity at every turn, could slip and blend into.

Inevitably on my way home I returned to the corner of Church and McDonald with its glut of identical restaurants. On warm nights, I had found it was the perfect spot to stand and admire not only what Kensington had become with the most recent wave of migration, but what any close-knit community—whether its people came here one hundred years ago from Europe or a decade ago from Africa, Asia, or the Caribbean—has provided throughout Brooklyn's history: a second home. There, on that corner, made up of five competing South Asian restaurants of roughly equal quality, dozens of Pakistani and Bangladeshi men gathered one night after another to drink chai out of paper cups. The men stood there talking for hours, huddled in factions built in part, I imagine, around restaurant loyalties. Some nights I sat in one of the restaurants and watched from a corner table with a book in hand as an artificial prop. A few of the men always stared, curious no doubt as to what I was doing there. Even though I lived in Kensington, when it came to evening gatherings like this, I was the foreigner and tourist. On other nights I ordered my own cup of tea and stood a few feet away on the edge of the sidewalk, near the subway entrance or at the bus stop, and silently stared. I had seen communal scenes like this before, especially while living in Washington, D.C., where there always seemed to be a cluster of Ethiopians, my age or older, gathered together outside coffee shops and bars all over the city, talking in Amharic with an ease and fluency that I admired and envied. They told jokes that didn't require explanation and debated arguments that were decades in the making. All of this was coupled with the familiarity and comfort of speaking in our native tongue. At any given moment, they could have told you without hesitancy where they were from. And so I had watched,

hardly understanding a word, hoping somehow that the simple act of association and observation was enough to draw me into the fold.

Here, then, was a similar scene, this one played out on a Brooklyn   10
corner with a culture and history different from the one I had been born
into, but familiar to me nonetheless. The men on that corner in Kensington,
just like the people I had known throughout my life, were immigrants in
the most complete sense of the word—their loyalties still firmly attached
to the countries they had left one, five, or twenty years earlier. If there was
one thing I admired most about them, it was that they had succeeded, at
least partly, in re-creating in Brooklyn some of what they had lost when they
left their countries of origin. Unlike the solitary and private walks my father
and I took, each of us buried deep in thoughts that had nowhere to go, this
nightly gathering of Pakistani and Bangladeshi men was a makeshift reenactment of home. Farther down the road from where they stood were the few
remaining remnants of the neighborhood's older Jewish community—one
synagogue, a kosher deli—proof, if one was ever needed, that Brooklyn is
always reinventing itself, that there is room here for us all.

While the men stood outside on the corner, their numbers gradually
increasing until they spilled out into the street as they talked loudly among
themselves, I once again played my own familiar role of quiet, jealous
observer and secret admirer. I have no idea what those men talked about, if
they discussed politics, sex, or petty complaints about work. It never mattered anyway. The substance of the conversations belonged to them, and I
couldn't have cared less. What I had wanted and found in them, what I
admired and adored about Kensington, was the assertion that we can rebuild
and remake ourselves and our communities over and over again, in no small
part because there have always been corners in Brooklyn to do so on. I stood
on that corner night after night for the most obvious of reasons—to be
reminded of a way of life that persists regardless of context; to feel, however
foolishly, that I too was attached to something. ●

The Reader's Presence

1. Why does Mengestu consciously try to make the Kensington section of Brooklyn
   home? What had been previously missing in his life? Why can't he acknowledge that
   he is *from* Ethiopia? Do you think he succeeds in making Kensington home? How do
   you interpret his final paragraph?

2. What is Mengestu's reason for not hosting the "Kensington night" he had planned
   (paragraph 7)? Why do you think—though he says he made new friends in the
   city—that no friends appear in the essay? Note how often through the course of
   the essay he is either alone or at the edge of a group of people whose language he
   doesn't understand. How do you interpret this?

3. **VISUAL PRESENCE:** Review the photograph of a storefront in Brooklyn's Kensington neighborhood (page 184). What specific details in the image suggest the ethnic
   diversity of Mengestu's neighborhood? In what specific way(s) does your neighborhood reflect a similar diversity?

4. **CONNECTIONS:** Compare Mengestu's essay to Geeta Kothari's "If You Are What You Eat, Then What Am I?" (page 142). How does each essay illuminate ethnic identity in America? What differences and similarities can you find between each author's presentation of separation and assimilation?

Manuel Muñoz

LEAVE YOUR NAME AT THE BORDER

MANUEL MUÑOZ (b. 1972) is a California native who received a BA from Harvard University and an MFA in creative writing from Cornell University. He has published two award-winning collections of short fiction, *Zig-zagger* (2003) and *The Faith Healer of Olive Avenue* (2007), and his work has been published widely in mainstream publications, such as the *New York Times*, as well as in some of the most prestigious literary magazines in the country, including *Glimmer Train* and *Boston Review*. He received a Whiting Award and his first PEN/O. Henry Award in 2009, with two more awarded in 2015 and 2017. His first novel, *What You See in the Dark*, was published in 2011. Although he currently teaches in the Creative Writing Program at the University of Arizona, Tucson, he has said that California's Central Valley and his hometown, Dinuba, "remain the foundation of [his] fiction."

> **Manuel Muñoz has said that California's Central Valley and his hometown, Dinuba, "remain the foundation of [his] fiction."**

AT THE FRESNO AIRPORT, as I made my way to the gate, I heard a name over the intercom. The way the name was pronounced by the gate agent made me want to see what she looked like. That is, I wanted to see whether she was Mexican. Around Fresno, identity politics rarely deepen into exacting terms, so to say "Mexican" means, essentially, "not white." The slivered self-identifications Chicano, Hispanic, Mexican-American and Latino are not part of everyday life in the Valley. You're either Mexican or you're not. If someone wants to know if you were born in Mexico, they'll ask. Then you're From Over There — *de allá*. And leave it at that.

The gate agent, it turned out, was Mexican. Well-coiffed, in her 30s, she wore foundation that was several shades lighter than the rest of her skin. It was the kind of makeup job I've learned to silently identify at the mall when I'm with my mother, who will say nothing about it until we're back in the car. Then she'll stretch her neck like an ostrich and point to the darkness of her own skin, wondering aloud why women try to camouflage who they are.

I watched the Mexican gate agent busy herself at the counter, professional and studied. Once again, she picked up the microphone and, with authority, announced the name of the missing customer: "Eugenio Reyes, please come to the front desk."

You can probably guess how she said it. Her Anglicized pronunciation wouldn't be unusual in a place like California's Central Valley. I didn't have a Mexican name there either: I was an instruction guide.

When people ask me where I'm from, I say Fresno because I don't expect   5
them to know little Dinuba. Fresno is a booming city of nearly 500,000 these days, with a diversity—white, Mexican, African-American, Armenian, Hmong and Middle Eastern people are all well represented—that shouldn't surprise anyone. It's in the small towns like Dinuba that surround Fresno that the awareness of cultural difference is stripped down to the interactions between the only two groups that tend to live there: whites and Mexicans. When you hear a Mexican name spoken in these towns, regardless of the speaker's background, it's no wonder that there's an "English way of pronouncing it."

I was born in 1972, part of a generation that learned both English and Spanish. Many of my cousins and siblings are bilingual, serving as translators for those in the family whose English is barely functional. Others have no way of following the Spanish banter at family gatherings. You can tell who falls into which group: Estella, Eric, Delia, Dubina, Melanie.

It's intriguing to watch "American" names begin to dominate among my nieces and nephews and second cousins, as well as with the children of my hometown friends. I am not surprised to meet 5-year-old Brandon or Kaitlyn. Hardly anyone questions the incongruity of matching these names with last names like Trujillo or Zepeda. The English-only way of life partly explains the quiet erasure of cultural difference that assimilation has attempted to accomplish. A name like Kaitlyn Zepeda doesn't completely obscure her ethnicity, but the half-step of her name, as a gesture, is almost understandable.

Spanish was and still is viewed with suspicion: always the language of the vilified illegal immigrant, it segregated schoolchildren into English-only and bilingual programs; it defined you, above all else, as part of a lower class. Learning English, though, brought its own complications with identity. It was simultaneously the language of the white population and a path toward the richer, expansive identity of "American." But it took getting out of the Valley for me to understand that "white" and "American" were two very different things.

Something as simple as saying our names "in English" was our unwittingly complicit gesture of trying to blend in. Pronouncing Mexican names correctly was never encouraged. Names like Daniel, Olivia and Marco slipped right into the mutability of the English language.

I remember a school ceremony at which the mathematics teacher, a   10
white man, announced the names of Mexican students correctly and caused some confusion, if not embarrassment. Years later we recognized that he

spoke in deference to our Spanish-speaking parents in the audience, caring teacher that he was.

These were difficult names for a non-Spanish speaker: Araceli, Nadira, Luis (a beautiful name when you glide the *u* and the *i* as you're supposed to). We had been accustomed to having our birth names altered for convenience. Concepción was Connie. Ramón was Raymond. My cousin Esperanza was Hope—but her name was pronounced "Hopie" because any Spanish speaker would automatically pronounce the *e* at the end.

Ours, then, were names that stood as barriers to a complete embrace of an American identity, simply because their pronunciations required a slip into Spanish, the otherness that assimilation was supposed to erase. What to do with names like Amado, Lucio or Élida? There are no English "equivalents," no answer when white teachers asked, "What does your name mean?" when what they really wanted to know was "What's the English one?" So what you heard was a name butchered beyond recognition, a pronunciation that pointed the finger at the Spanish language as the source of clunky sound and ugly rhythm.

My stepfather, from Ojos de Agua, Mexico, jokes when I ask him about the names of Mexicans born here. He deliberately stumbles over pronunciations, imitating our elders who have difficulty with Bradley and Madelyn. "Ashley Sánchez. ¿Tú crees?"[1] He wonders aloud what has happened to the "nombres del rancho"—traditional Mexican names that are hardly given anymore to children born in the States: Heraclio, Madaleno, Otilia, Dominga.

My stepfather's experience with the Anglicization of his name—Antonio to Tony—ties into something bigger than learning English. For him, the erasure of his name was about deference and subservience. Becoming Tony gave him a measure of access as he struggled to learn English and get more fieldwork.

This isn't to say that my stepfather welcomed the change, only that he could not put up much resistance. Not changing put him at risk of being passed over for work. English was a world of power and decisions, of smooth, uninterrupted negotiation. There was no time to search for the right word while a shop clerk waited for him to come up with the English name of the correct part needed out in the field. Clear communication meant you could go unsupervised, or that you were even able to read instructions directly off a piece of paper. Every gesture made toward convincing an employer that English was on its way to being mastered had the potential to make a season of fieldwork profitable.

It's curious that many of us growing up in Dinuba adhered to the same rules. Although as children of farm workers we worked in the fields at an early age, we'd also had the opportunity to stay in one town long enough to finish school. Most of us had learned English early and splintered off into a dual existence of English at school, Spanish at home. But instead of recognizing the need for fluency in both languages, we turned it into a peculiar kind of battle. English was for public display. Spanish was for privacy—and privacy quickly turned to shame.

15

[1] *¿Tú crees?:* Can you believe it? — EDS.

The corrosive effect of assimilation is the displacement of one culture over another, the inability to sustain more than one way of being. It isn't a code word for racial and ethnic acculturation only. It applies to needing and wanting to belong, of seeing from the outside and wondering how to get in and then, once inside, realizing there are always those still on the fringe.

When I went to college on the East Coast, I was confronted for the first time by people who said my name correctly without prompting; if they stumbled, there was a quick apology and an honest plea to help with the pronunciation. But introducing myself was painful: already shy, I avoided meeting people because I didn't want to say my name, felt burdened by my own history. I knew that my small-town upbringing and its limitations on Spanish would not have been tolerated by any of the students of color who had grown up in large cities, in places where the sheer force of their native languages made them dominant in their neighborhoods.

It didn't take long for me to assert the power of code-switching in public, the transferring of words from one language to another, regardless of who might be listening. I was learning that the English language composed new meanings when its constrictions were ignored, crossed over or crossed out. Language is all about manipulation, or not listening to the rules.

When I come back to Dinuba, I have a hard time hearing my name   20 said incorrectly, but I have an even harder time beginning a conversation with others about why the pronunciation of our names matters. Leaving a small town requires an embrace of a larger point of view, but a town like Dinuba remains forever embedded in an either/or way of life. My step-father still answers to Tony and, as the United States-born children grow older, their Anglicized names begin to signify who does and who does not "belong" — who was born here and who is *de allá*.

My name is Manuel. To this day, most people cannot say it correctly, the way it was intended to be said. But I can live with that because I love the allit-eration of my full name. It wasn't the name my mother, Esmeralda, was going to give me. At the last minute, my father named me after an uncle I would never meet. My name was to have been Ricardo. Growing up in Dinuba, I'm certain I would have become Ricky or even Richard, and the journey toward the discovery of the English language's extraordinary power in even the most ordinary of circumstances would probably have gone unlearned.

I count on a collective sense of cultural loss to once again swing the names back to our native language. The Mexican gate agent announced Eugenio Reyes, but I never got a chance to see who appeared. I pictured an older man, cowboy hat in hand, but I made the assumption on his name alone, the clash of privileges I imagined between someone *de allá* and a Mex-ican woman with a good job in the United States. Would she speak to him in Spanish? Or would she raise her voice to him as if he were hard of hearing?

But who was I to imagine this man being from anywhere, based on his name alone? At a place of arrivals and departures, it sank into me that the currency of our names is a stroke of luck: because mine was not an easy name, it forced me to consider how language would rule me if I allowed it.

Yet I discovered that only by leaving. My stepfather must live in the Valley, a place that does not allow that choice, every day. And Eugenio Reyes—I do not know if he was coming or going. ■

The Reader's Presence

1. Consider the way Muñoz structures his essay. What is his purpose in starting with a name heard over the intercom at the Fresno Airport? What does that incident trigger? In what ways does ending his essay with further reflections on that same moment reinforce his perspective about identity? In what ways does his final paragraph complicate that perspective?

2. As a reader, would you know how to pronounce the author's name correctly? Any of the other Mexican names he mentions? Why do you think Muñoz offers no guide to pronunciation that would help English-speaking readers say the names as the author thinks they should be said? What does he feel is lost when the Mexican names are Anglicized?

3. **CONNECTIONS:** Compare "Leave Your Name at the Border" to Dinaw Mengestu's "Home at Last" (page 181). What identity issues do both writers contend with? You might also compare Muñoz's essay with Maya Angelou's reflection on names in "What's Your Name, Girl?" (page 34). How does each writer struggle with the relationship of personal names to identity?

Student Essay

MILOS KOSIC
It's Not the Name That Matters

Courtesy of Milos Kosic

When he wrote "It's Not the Name That Matters," the Serbian-born Milos Kosic was a journalism student at Northwest College, a two-year college in Powell, Wyoming. Kosic received his BA in English from the City College of New York and is currently doing graduate work in Berlin, Germany.

Kosic's essay was originally written as a response to the following assignment (which we've adapted for this edition of *The Writer's Presence*):

In almost every culture, people's names are significant. What about your name? What is its significance to you, your family, and your community? In an essay of 750 to 1,000 words, consider the issues, both personal and cultural, surrounding naming. Be sure to take into consideration the essay by Manuel Muñoz, "Leave Your Name at the Border," which addresses cultural questions like what happens to non-English names in an English-centered society. Your essay should refer to Muñoz's essay while relating a personal experience and maintaining a personal point of view.

The essay opens with a concrete scene that establishes a specific place, characters, and conditions.

"Over 70,000 died," says Cody as we look at the black walls of Vietnam Veterans Memorial. It's raining so hard in Washington that even though we are under an open umbrella, our clothes are soaking wet. Our bodies shake from the cold, and our shoes squish with every step. But we are not concerned about whether we will get sick or not. Thinking about comfort here would be inappropriate.

"Did you get our shadows in it?" asks Cody, referring to our reflections in the wall.

"Yeah, I'm recording them," I answer.

"That's way cool, dude."

Aurelie and Morgan Da/AGE Fotostock

Whenever he can, Cody avoids calling me Milos. Sometimes I feel sorry for him, because no matter how hard he tries, he always mispronounces it. Either he says "s" at the end instead of "sh" or makes the "o" sound too long. I believe that every time he tries to say "Milos" (pronounced Mee'-lösh) and a different word comes out of his mouth, he curses both my name and the people who gave it to me.

Introduces the main topic of the essay: names.

There's nobody to blame. My parents are innocent. They wanted to call me Marko, naming me after the most popular hero of Serbian traditional songs. But in the hospital wing where I came into the world, it happened that all of the baby boys in the nursery had been named Marko. Confronted with the sad discovery that their name choice was not so original, my father and mother, who believed that their child had to be unique, decided to look for a backup. Milos was the ad hoc second choice.

Luckily, Serbia has many heroes and historic figures. There was bound to be a famous Serbian Milos. I was determined to discover one and looked into the history books. I found out that the guy who killed a Turkish king a long time ago was also named Milos (Miloš Obilić, to be exact). Naming someone after a great person is a tradition in Serbia. Now instead of having to tell others that I am not the namesake of anyone special, my parents can proudly say, "He is like the famous warrior."

As I grew up, I didn't show any signs of becoming a hero. One thing that was remarkable about me, though, was my inability to pronounce the sounds "sh" and "ch," which meant that pronouncing my own name was a serious problem. Thanks to my lovely cousin Lidija, my speech disability did not pass unnoticed. Every time we had a big family gathering, Lidija would dedicate herself to drawing attention to what my "talent" was.

"Come on, tell us your name. Tell us what your parents called you!" she would insist.

Gullible kid as I was, I would answer, "My name is Miloff," and all around I would hear plenty of laughter.

At some point during my teenage years, as my voice changed, I overcame my speech disability. But if in my childhood I was the only one who couldn't pronounce Milos correctly, since I've come to the U.S., I'm now the only one who can.

Extends and deepens the theme of mispronunciation.

When I came to the U.S. to attend college, I left my name at the border. Unlike Manuel Muñoz (author of "Leave Your Name at the Border"), however, I never thought that doing so was especially significant. It was something that made sense to me. Americans cannot say Serbian words and names correctly, and I sometimes mangle English with my strong Slavonic accent. If pronunciation really matters, then for the sake of saving their language, Americans should immediately escort me back to the border. I would have no right to complain. Luckily this hasn't happened. Now it's time for me to show, as Muñoz says, the ability "to sustain more than one way of being" (190).

Meets the assignment's requirement by referring to the Muñoz essay. This reference allows Kosic to express his ideas in relation to others.

You can call me Milo. You can call me Miles or Meat-loaf, I'm fine. But I wonder what kind of person you see behind that name. Do you see a stranger? A good friend? Do you mispronounce my name because you simply cannot say it right, or you don't even want to try because for you, I'm unimportant, someone who doesn't deserve your respect?

In their essay "Trading Up: Where Do Baby Names Come From?" Steven D. Levitt and Stephen J. Dubner explain that parents choose their child's name believing that the right one can predict personal success (120). But when you meet someone named Donald, do think of someone like Donald Trump or Donald Rumsfeld—or Donald Duck?

At the Vietnam Veterans Memorial, among the 59,256 names, none of them seems better than another. As Maya Lin says in "Between Art and Architecture," "a sense of quiet, a reverence always surrounds those names" (126). The carved black stone memorial wall tells us one true thing about each of the people on it. Those Benjamins and Justins, Ricardos and Samuels fought and died in the same war. Even if I can't say some of those names correctly, every single one of them is equally honorable and worthy.

"Milos!"

Cody mispronounces my name again when he calls to point out an old guy wearing a soldier's uniform, standing in front of the memorial.

"Is he security or something?" I ask.

"No," answers Cody. "He must be looking for his old pal somewhere on the wall."

> Conclusion effectively returns to the opening and summarizes the essay's main point.

We are ready to go. The old guy remains there. In the heavy rain, he will continue searching, no matter what his pal was called. It's not the name that matters. It's the person who stands behind it.

Works Cited

Lin, Maya. "Making the Memorial." *The New York Review of Books*, 2 Nov. 2000, www.nybooks.com/articles/2000/11/02/making-the-memorial/.

Manuel, Muñoz. "Leave Your Name at the Border." *The Writer's Presence*, edited by Donald McQuade and Robert Atwan, 9th ed., Bedford/St. Martin's, 2017, pp. 187–191.

Levitt, Steven D., and Stephen J. Dubner. "Trading Up: Where Do Baby Names Come From?" *Slate.com*, 12 Apr. 2005, www.slate.com/articles/business/the_dismal_science/2005/04/trading_up.html.

> Provides a bibliography of sources the writer has drawn upon.

George Orwell

SHOOTING AN ELEPHANT

GEORGE ORWELL (1903–1950) was born Eric Arthur Blair in Bengal, India, the son of a colonial administrator. He was sent to England for his education and attended Eton on a scholarship, but rather than go on to university in 1922 he returned to the East and served with the Indian Imperial Police in Burma. Orwell hated his work and the colonial system; published posthumously, the essay "Shooting an Elephant" was based on his experience in Burma and is found in *Shooting an Elephant and Other Essays* (1950). In 1927, Orwell returned to England and began a career as a professional writer. He served briefly in the Spanish Civil War until he was wounded and then settled in Hertfordshire. Best remembered for his novels *Animal Farm* (1945) and *Nineteen Eighty-Four* (1949), Orwell also wrote articles, essays, and reviews, usually with a political point in mind.

> **"Good prose is like a windowpane."**

In 1969, Irving Howe honored Orwell as "the best English essayist since Hazlitt, perhaps since Dr. Johnson. He was the greatest moral force in English letters during the last several decades: craggy, fiercely polemical, sometimes mistaken, but an utterly free man."

In his 1946 essay "Why I Write," Orwell said that from a very early age "I knew that when I grew up I should be a writer." At first he saw writing as a remedy for loneliness, but as he grew up his reasons for writing expanded: "Looking back through my work, I see it is invariably when I lacked a *political* purpose that I wrote lifeless books." In his mature work, he relied on simple, clear prose to express his political and social convictions: "Good prose," he once wrote, "is like a windowpane."

IN MOULMEIN, in Lower Burma, I was hated by large numbers of people—the only time in my life that I have been important enough for this to happen to me. I was subdivisional police officer of the town, and in an aimless, petty kind of way anti-European feeling was very bitter. No one had the guts to raise a riot, but if a European woman went through the bazaars alone somebody would probably spit betel juice over her dress. As a police officer I was an obvious target and was baited whenever it seemed safe to do so. When a nimble Burman tripped me up on the football field and the referee (another Burman) looked the other way, the crowd yelled with hideous laughter. This happened more than once. In the end the sneering yellow faces of young men that met me everywhere, the insults hooted after me when I was at a safe distance, got badly on my nerves. The young Buddhist priests were the worst of all. There were several thousands of them in the town and none of them seemed to have anything to do except stand on street corners and jeer at Europeans.

All this was perplexing and upsetting. For at that time I had already made up my mind that imperialism was an evil thing and the sooner I chucked up my job and got out of it the better. Theoretically — and secretly, of course — I was all for the Burmese and all against the oppressors, the British. As for the job I was doing, I hated it more bitterly than I can perhaps make clear. In a job like that you see the dirty work of Empire at close quarters. The wretched prisoners huddling in the stinking cages of the lockups, the grey, cowed faces of the long-term convicts, the scarred buttocks of the men who had been flogged with bamboos — all these oppressed me with an intolerable sense of guilt. But I could get nothing into perspective. I was young and ill-educated and I had had to think out my problems in the utter silence that is imposed on every Englishman in the East. I did not even know that the British Empire is dying, still less did I know that it is a great deal better than the younger empires that are going to supplant it. All I knew was that I was stuck between my hatred of the empire I served and my rage against the evil-spirited little beasts who tried to make my job impossible. With one part of my mind I thought of the British Raj[1] as an unbreakable tyranny, as something clamped down, *in saecula saeculorum*,[2] upon the will of prostrate peoples; with another part I thought that the greatest joy in the world would be to drive a bayonet into a Buddhist priest's guts. Feelings like these are the normal by-products of imperialism; ask any Anglo-Indian official, if you can catch him off duty.

One day something happened which in a roundabout way was enlightening. It was a tiny incident in itself, but it gave me a better glimpse than I had had before of the real nature of imperialism — the real motives for which despotic governments act. Early one morning the subinspector at a police station the other end of town rang me up on the phone and said that an elephant was ravaging the bazaar. Would I please come and do something about it? I did not know what I could do, but I wanted to see what was happening and I got on to a pony and started out. I took my rifle, an old .44 Winchester and much too small to kill an elephant, but I thought the noise might be useful *in terrorem*.[3] Various Burmans stopped me on the way and told me about the elephant's doings. It was not, of course, a wild elephant, but a tame one which had gone "must."[4] It had been chained up, as tame elephants always are when their attack of "must" is due, but on the previous night it had broken its chain and escaped. Its mahout,[5] the only person who could manage it when it was in that state, had set out in pursuit, but had

---

1 **Raj:** The British administration. — EDS.
2 **in saecula saeculorum:** Forever and ever (Latin). — EDS.
3 **in terrorem:** As a warning (Latin). — EDS.
4 **"must":** Sexual arousal. — EDS.
5 **mahout:** Keeper (Hindi). — EDS.

taken the wrong direction and was now twelve hours' journey away, and in the morning the elephant had suddenly reappeared in the town. The Burmese population had no weapons and were quite helpless against it. It had already destroyed somebody's bamboo hut, killed a cow, and raided some fruit stalls and devoured the stock; also it had met the municipal rubbish van and, when the driver jumped out and took to his heels, had turned the van over and inflicted violence upon it.

The Burmese subinspector and some Indian constables were waiting for me in the quarter where the elephant had been seen. It was a very poor quarter, a labyrinth of squalid bamboo huts, thatched with palm-leaf, winding all over a steep hillside. I remember that it was a cloudy, stuffy morning at the beginning of the rains. We began questioning the people as to where the elephant had gone and, as usual, failed to get any definite information. That is invariably the case in the East; a story always sounds clear enough at a distance, but the nearer you get to the scene of events the vaguer it becomes. Some of the people said that the elephant had gone in one direction, some said that he had gone in another, some professed not even to have heard of any elephant. I had almost made up my mind that the whole story was a pack of lies, when we heard yells a little distance away. There was a loud, scandalized cry of "Go away, child! Go away this instant!" and an old woman with a switch in her hand came round the corner of a hut, violently shooing away a crowd of naked children. Some more women followed, clicking their tongues and exclaiming; evidently there was something that the children ought not to have seen. I rounded the hut and saw a man's dead body sprawling in the mud. He was an Indian, a black Dravidian[6] coolie, almost naked, and he could not have been dead many minutes. The people said that the elephant had come suddenly upon him round the corner of the hut, caught him with its trunk, put its foot on his back, and ground him into the earth. This was the rainy season and the ground was soft, and his face had scored a trench a foot deep and a couple of yards long. He was lying on his belly with arms crucified and head sharply twisted to one side. His face was coated with mud, the eyes wide open, the teeth bared and grinning with an expression of unendurable agony. (Never tell me, by the way, that the dead look peaceful. Most of the corpses I have seen looked devilish.) The friction of the great beast's foot had stripped the skin from his back as neatly as one skins a rabbit. As soon as I saw the dead man I sent an orderly to a friend's house nearby to borrow an elephant rifle. I had already sent back the pony, not wanting it to go mad with fright and throw me if it smelled the elephant.

The orderly came back in a few minutes with a rifle and five cartridges,   5 and meanwhile some Burmans had arrived and told us that the elephant was in the paddy fields below, only a few hundred yards away. As I started forward practically the whole population of the quarter flocked out of the houses and followed me. They had seen the rifle and were all shouting excitedly that I was going to shoot the elephant. They had not shown much

6 **Dravidian:** A populous Indian group. — EDS.

interest in the elephant when he was merely ravaging their homes, but it was different now that he was going to be shot. It was a bit of fun to them, as it would be to an English crowd; besides, they wanted the meat. It made me vaguely uneasy. I had no intention of shooting the elephant—I had merely sent for the rifle to defend myself if necessary—and it is always unnerving to have a crowd following you. I marched down the hill, looking and feeling a fool, with the rifle over my shoulder and an ever-growing army of people jostling at my heels. At the bottom, when you got away from the huts, there was a metaled road and beyond that a miry waste of paddy fields a thousand yards across, not yet ploughed but soggy from the first rains and dotted with coarse grass. The elephant was standing eight yards from the road, his left side towards us. He took not the slightest notice of the crowd's approach. He was tearing up bunches of grass, beating them against his knees to clean them and stuffing them into his mouth.

I had halted on the road. As soon as I saw the elephant I knew with perfect certainty that I ought not to shoot him. It is a serious matter to shoot a working elephant—it is comparable to destroying a huge and costly piece of machinery—and obviously one ought not to do it if it can possibly be avoided. And at that distance, peacefully eating, the elephant looked no more dangerous than a cow. I thought then and I think now that his attack of "must" was already passing off; in which case he would merely wander harmlessly about until the mahout came back and caught him. Moreover, I did not in the least want to shoot him. I decided that I would watch him for a little while to make sure that he did not turn savage again, and then go home.

But at that moment, I glanced round at the crowd that had followed me. It was an immense crowd, two thousand at the least and growing every minute. It blocked the road for a long distance on either side. I looked at the sea of yellow faces above the garish clothes—faces all happy and excited over this bit of fun, all certain that the elephant was going to be shot. They were watching me as they would watch a conjuror about to perform a trick. They did not like me, but with the magical rifle in my hands I was momentarily worth watching. And suddenly I realized that I should have to shoot the elephant after all: The people expected it of me and I had got to do it; I could feel their two thousand wills pressing me forward, irresistibly. And it was at this moment, as I stood there with the rifle in my hands, that I first grasped the hollowness, the futility of the white man's dominion in the East. Here was I, the white man with his gun, standing in front of the unarmed native crowd—seemingly the leading actor of the piece; but in reality I was only an absurd puppet pushed to and fro by the will of those yellow faces behind. I perceived in this moment that when the white man turns tyrant it is his own freedom that he destroys. He becomes a sort of hollow, posing dummy, the conventionalized figure of a sahib. For it is the condition of his rule that he shall spend his life in trying to impress the "natives," and so in every crisis he has got to do what the "natives" expect of him. He wears a mask, and his face grows to fit it. I had got to shoot the elephant. I had committed myself to doing it when I sent for the rifle. A sahib has got to act like a sahib; he has got to appear resolute, to know his own mind and do definite things. To come all that way, rifle in hand, with two thousand people marching at my heels, and then to trail feebly away, having done nothing—no, that was impossible. The crowd would laugh at me. And my whole life, every white man's life in the East, was one long struggle not to be laughed at.

But I did not want to shoot the elephant. I watched him beating his bunch of grass against his knees, with that preoccupied grandmotherly air that elephants have. It seemed to me that it would be murder to shoot him. At that age I was not squeamish about killing animals, but I had never shot an elephant and never wanted to. (Somehow it always seems worse to kill a *large* animal.) Besides, there was the beast's owner to be considered. Alive, the elephant was worth at least a hundred pounds; dead, he would only be worth the value of his tusks, five pounds, possibly. But I had got to act quickly. I turned to some experienced-looking Burmans who had been there when we arrived, and asked them how the elephant had been behaving. They all said the same thing: He took no notice of you if you left him alone, but he might charge if you went too close to him.

It was perfectly clear to me what I ought to do. I ought to walk up to within, say, twenty-five yards of the elephant and test his behavior. If he charged, I could shoot; if he took no notice of me, it would be safe to leave him until the mahout came back. But also I knew that I was going to do no such thing. I was a poor shot with a rifle and the ground was soft mud into which one would sink at every step. If the elephant charged and I missed him, I should have about as much chance as a toad under a steamroller. But even then I was not thinking particularly of my own skin, only of the watchful yellow faces behind. For at that moment, with the crowd watching me, I was not afraid in the ordinary sense, as I would have been if I had been alone. A white man mustn't be frightened in front of "natives"; and so, in general, he isn't frightened. The sole thought in my mind was that if anything went wrong those two thousand Burmans would see me pursued, caught, trampled on, and reduced to a grinning corpse like that Indian up the hill. And if that happened it was quite probable that some of them would laugh. That would never do. There was only one alternative. I shoved the cartridges into the magazine and lay down on the road to get a better aim.

The crowd grew very still, and a deep, low, happy sigh, as of people who　10 see the theatre curtain go up at last, breathed from innumerable throats. They were going to have their bit of fun after all. The rifle was a beautiful German thing with cross-hair sights. I did not then know that in shooting an elephant one would shoot to cut an imaginary bar running from ear-hole to ear-hole. I ought, therefore, as the elephant was sideways on, to have aimed straight at his ear-hole; actually I aimed several inches in front of this, thinking the brain would be further forward.

When I pulled the trigger I did not hear the bang or feel the kick—one never does when a shot goes home—but I heard the devilish roar of glee that went up from the crowd. In that instant, in too short a time, one would have thought, even for the bullet to get there, a mysterious, terrible change had come over the elephant. He neither stirred nor fell, but every line of his body had altered. He looked suddenly stricken, shrunken, immensely old, as though the frightful impact of the bullet had paralyzed him without knocking him down. At last, after what seemed a long time—it might have been five seconds, I dare say—he sagged flabbily to his knees. His mouth slobbered. An enormous senility seemed to have settled upon him. One could have imagined him thousands of years old. I fired again into the same spot. At the second shot he did not collapse but climbed with desperate slowness to his feet and stood weakly upright, with legs sagging and head drooping. I fired a third time. That was the shot that did it for him. You could see the agony of it jolt his whole body and knock the last remnant of strength from his legs. But in falling he seemed for a moment to rise, for as his hind legs collapsed beneath him he seemed to tower upward like a huge rock toppling, his trunk reaching skywards like a tree. He trumpeted, for the first and only time. And then down he came, his belly towards me, with a crash that seemed to shake the ground even where I lay.

I got up. The Burmans were already racing past me across the mud. It was obvious that the elephant would never rise again, but he was not dead. He was breathing very rhythmically with long rattling gasps, his great mound of a side painfully rising and falling. His mouth was wide open. I could see far down into caverns of pale pink throat. I waited a long time for him to die, but his breathing did not weaken. Finally, I fired my two remaining shots into the spot where I thought his heart must be. The thick blood welled out of him like red velvet, but still he did not die. His body did not even jerk when the shots hit him, the tortured breathing continued without a pause. He was dying, very slowly and in great agony, but in some world remote from me where not even a bullet could damage him further. I felt I had got to put an end to that dreadful noise. It seemed dreadful to see the great beast lying there, powerless to move and yet powerless to die, and not even to be able to finish him. I sent back for my small rifle and poured shot after shot into his heart, and down his throat. They seemed to make no impression. The tortured gasps continued as steadily as the ticking of a clock.

In the end I could not stand it any longer and went away. I heard later that it took him half an hour to die. Burmans were bringing dahs[7] and baskets even before I left, and I was told they had stripped his body almost to the bones by the afternoon.

Afterwards, of course, there were endless discussions about the shooting of the elephant. The owner was furious, but he was only an Indian and could do nothing. Besides, legally I had done the right thing, for a mad elephant has to be killed, like a mad dog, if its owner fails to control it. Among the Europeans opinion was divided. The older men said I was right, the younger men said it was a damn shame to shoot an elephant for killing a coolie, because the elephant was worth more than any damn Coringhee coolie. And

7 **dahs:** Large knives. — EDS.

afterwards I was very glad that the coolie had been killed; it put me legally in the right and it gave me sufficient pretext for shooting the elephant. I often wondered whether any of the others grasped that I had done it solely to avoid looking a fool. ●

The Reader's Presence

1. At the end of paragraph 2, Orwell gives the perfect expression of ambivalence, the simultaneous holding of two opposed feelings or opinions: "With one part of my mind . . . with another part . . ." How would you describe Orwell's dilemma? How would you react in such a situation? Is Orwell recommending that readers see his behavior as a model of what to do in such a conflict? To what extent is Orwell responsible for the situation in which he finds himself? What does he mean when he says that his conflicted feelings "are the normal by-products of imperialism"?

2. Some literary critics doubt that Orwell really did shoot an elephant in Burma. No external historical documentation has ever been found to corroborate Orwell's account. Yet what *internal* elements in the essay—what details or features—suggest that the episode is fact and not fiction? In other words, what makes this piece seem to be an essay and not a short story?

3. **CONNECTIONS:** Orwell's essay describes a state of extreme personal self-consciousness, even vigilance, in a situation in which one's behavior feels somehow "scripted" by society. Orwell writes, "In reality I was only an absurd puppet pushed to and fro by the will of those yellow faces behind" (paragraph 7). How does Orwell's essay compare with Brent Staples's essay "*Just Walk on By: A Black Man Ponders His Power to Alter Public Space*" (page 217)? Compare especially Orwell's use of the word *fool* in his last paragraph and Staples's use of the same word in the second paragraph of the alternate version of his essay (page 222). Do you believe both authors?

The Writer at Work

GEORGE ORWELL on the Four Reasons for Writing

ullstein bild/The Image Works

George Orwell spent much time considering the art of writing. He believed it was of the utmost political importance to write clearly and accurately. In the following passage from another essay, "Why I Write," Orwell considers a more fundamental aspect of writing: the reasons behind why people write at all. You may observe that he doesn't list the reason most college students write—to respond to an assignment. Why do you think he omitted assigned writing? Can you think of other motives he doesn't take into account?

❝ Putting aside the need to earn a living, I think there are four great motives for writing, at any rate for writing prose. They exist in different degrees in every writer, and in any one writer the proportions will vary from time to time, according to the atmosphere in which he is living. They are:

1. Sheer egoism. Desire to seem clever, to be talked about, to be remembered after death, to get your own back on grown-ups who snubbed you in childhood, etc., etc. It is humbug to pretend that this is not a motive, and a strong one. Writers share this characteristic with scientists, artists, politicians, lawyers, soldiers, successful businessmen—in short, with the whole top crust of humanity. The great mass of human beings are not acutely selfish. After the age of thirty they abandon individual ambition—in many cases, indeed, they almost abandon the sense of being individuals at all—and live chiefly for others, or are simply smothered under drudgery. But there is also the minority of gifted, willful people who are determined to live their own lives to the end, and writers belong in this class. Serious writers, I should say, are on the whole more vain and self-centered than journalists, though less interested in money.

2. Aesthetic enthusiasm. Perception of beauty in the external world, or, on the other hand, in words and their right arrangement. Pleasure in the impact of one sound on another, in the firmness of good prose or the rhythm of a good story. Desire to share an experience which one feels is valuable and ought not to be missed. The aesthetic motive is very feeble in a lot of writers, but even a pamphleteer or a writer of textbooks will have pet words and phrases which appeal to him for non-utilitarian reasons; or he may feel strongly about typography, width of margins, etc. Above the level of a railway guide, no book is quite free from aesthetic considerations.

3. Historical impulse. Desire to see things as they are, to find out true facts and store them up for the use of posterity.

4. Political purpose—using the word "political" in the widest possible sense. Desire to push the world in a certain direction, to alter other people's idea of the kind of society that they should strive after. Once again, no book is genuinely free from political bias. The opinion that art should have nothing to do with politics is itself a political attitude. **❞**

Claudia Rankine

FROM *CITIZEN: AN AMERICAN LYRIC*

In her award-winning and best-selling 2014 book, *Citizen: An American Lyric*, **CLAUDIA RANKINE** explores in poetry and prose the experiences of being black in a presumably postracial society. With meticulous observations and sensitivity to the form of unconscious racial insults known as "micro aggressions," she dramatizes—as we can see in the passages below—the almost invisible ways in which racism plays a significant role in everyday life, especially among those who claim to denounce discrimination and racism.

> Claudia Rankine dramatizes the almost invisible ways in which racism plays a significant role in everyday life.

The author of several volumes of poetry, including *Don't Let Me Be Lonely* (2004), *Plot* (2001), *The End of the Alphabet* (1998), and *Nothing in Nature Is Private* (1994). Rankine—who was born in Kingston, Jamaica, in 1963—is a professor of poetry at Yale University. She writes essays and articles regularly for the *Washington Post* and the *New York Times Magazine*. In 2014, she received the prestigious Jackson Poetry Prize.

A WOMAN you do not know wants to join you for lunch. You are visiting her campus. In the café you both order the Caesar salad. This overlap is not the beginning of anything because she immediately points out that she, her father, her grandfather, and you, all attended the same college. She wanted her son to go there as well, but because of affirmative action or minority something—she is not sure what they are calling it these days and weren't they supposed to get rid of it?—her son wasn't accepted. You are not sure if you are meant to apologize for this failure of your alma mater's legacy program; instead you ask where he ended up. The prestigious school she mentions doesn't seem to assuage her irritation. This exchange, in effect, ends your lunch. The salads arrive.

* * *

You and your partner go to see the film *The House We Live In*. You ask a friend to pick up your child from school. On your way home your phone rings. Your neighbor tells you he is standing at his window watching a menacing black guy casing both your homes. The guy is walking back and forth talking to himself and seems disturbed.

You tell your neighbor that your friend, whom he has met, is babysitting. He says, no, it's not him. He's met your friend and this isn't that nice young man. Anyway, he wants you to know, he's called the police.

Your partner calls your friend and asks him if there's a guy walking back and forth in front of your home. Your friend says that if anyone were outside he would see him because he is standing outside. You hear the sirens through the speakerphone.

Your friend is speaking to your neighbor when you arrive home. The four police cars are gone. Your neighbor has apologized to your friend and is now apologizing to you. Feeling somewhat responsible for the actions of your neighbor, you clumsily tell your friend that the next time he wants to talk on the phone he should just go in the backyard. He looks at you a long minute before saying he can speak on the phone wherever he wants. Yes, of course, you say. Yes, of course.

5

* * *

In line at the drugstore it's finally your turn, and then it's not as he walks in front of you and puts his things on the counter. The cashier says, Sir, she was next. When he turns to you he is truly surprised.

Oh my God, I didn't see you.

You must be in a hurry, you offer.

No, no, no, I really didn't see you.

The Reader's Presence

1. Rankine's book *Citizen* was nominated for awards in both poetry and criticism. Based on the above passages from the book (admittedly a small sample), can you make a case as to why the book should have been considered for both awards? Which features of the passages strike you as poetic? Which critical? How might the two be fused together?

2. Take a close look at the passage "You and your partner go to see the film. . . ." Try to describe in your own words what happened. What mistake was made? How do you interpret the mistake and how does the author compound the mistake? Why do you think she uses the word "clumsily" in the last paragraph? In what ways do the other two passages resemble this one?

3. **CONNECTIONS:** Read the three Rankine passages in the context of Lukianoff and Haidt's selection on politically correct speech (see pages 542–545). In what ways is their argument relevant to Rankine's topic? How do the authors differ on the issue of micro aggressions, though Rankine does not introduce the term? What significance do micro aggressions have for Rankine that they don't for Lukianoff and Haidt?

Marjane Satrapi

MY SPEECH AT WEST POINT

Writer-illustrator and graphic novelist **MARJANE SATRAPI** (b. 1969) was born in Iran and, after a sojourn in Europe and a return to Tehran, now lives and works in France. Her graphic memoir, *Persepolis: The Story of a Childhood* (2003), recounts in comic-book form growing up in Iran from ages six to fourteen, years that saw the overthrow of the shah, the triumph of the Islamic Revolution, and the devastating effects of war with Iraq. The book was an immediate hit in France, selling more than 150,000 copies, and has been trans-lated into numerous languages. In the United States, *Persepolis* was named a New York Times Notable Book and one of *Time* maga-

> "I figured out a long time ago that, whatever I think I know, I don't know anything. Once I realized that, I really started learning."

zine's "Best Comix of the Year." Satrapi co-directed the feature film *Persepolis* which won numerous awards including an Oscar nomination for Best Animated Feature Film of 2007. A live-action adaptation of *Chicken with Plums* came out in 2011. *Persepolis 2: The Story of a Return* (2004) picks up her story with Satrapi's departure for Austria when she was fourteen and continues through her college years back in Tehran. Satrapi's most recent graphic memoirs are *Embroideries* (2005) and *Chicken with Plums* (2006). She has also written several chil-dren's books, and her commentary and comics appear in newspapers and magazines around the world, including the *New York Times* and the *New Yorker*.

Satrapi was invited to West Point to speak in 2005. After her visit, her book *Persepolis* was put on the required reading list at the academy. "My Speech at West Point" appeared on the op-ed page of the *New York Times* on May 29, 2005.

In an interview with *Believer* magazine, Satrapi talked about what she learned not only at West Point but also through traveling and listening to people from so many disparate cultures: "I figured out a long time ago that, whatever I think I know, I don't know anything. Once I realized that, I really started learning. That's a great strength: I know that I don't know. There are some people in Iran who are fundamentalist and others who are not. I have very good Israeli friends. And I have very good American friends. We come from different cultures but share points of view. It's humanism, which we're steadily losing. That's what the comics are about in a way, trying to stop that loss."

When I was invited to speak at West Point, this is how I thought it would be: I'll go to West Point...

The major will show me around without saying a word...

Then, he will shout at me...

YOU DON'T SMOKE HERE

Then, I'll eat with 4,000 cadets in the mess hall...

The meal won't be tasty... pizza... half pepperoni

half cheese

After lunch, I will speak in front of 600 people...

I AM AGAINST THE WAR IN IRAQ.

They will all shout at me again...

I will have to continue my speech...

Democracy is not a present you give to people by bombing them.

Their general will order them to hang me...

I will DIE...

BUT...

"Here we are!"

The major shows me around...

"Here they play football. You should come and watch a game sometime!"

"great..."

"Can I smoke?"

"Of course!"

I eat with 4,000 cadets in the mess hall...

The half-pepperoni, half-cheese pizza is worse than what I thought

After my speech, the cadets come to talk to me...

"What you said was so inspiring!"

"It's great to discover another point of view!"

They are lovely and intelligent and much more open-minded than I am!

I go back to Manhattan...

I know that I don't know anything

That makes my life even more complicated...

Later, in my hotel room...

"Seven American soldiers and 10 Iraqis died today in Baghdad!"

There's still things I know that I know: I'm against the war and democracy is not a present you give to people by bombing them

The Reader's Presence

1. How would you describe Satrapi's expectations of West Point as opposed to what she actually experienced on her visit? What do her expectations imply about her view of the military academy? Where may she have received these views? In what ways do they complicate her experience? What elements of Satrapi's narrative do you find humorous? Why?

2. Satrapi's personal narrative is not just told but drawn in black and white. How would you describe her artistic style? What sort of imagery does it resemble? Do you think that the way she depicts herself in the art reinforces the way she describes herself in words? Why or why not? Explain how you see the interrelation of words and images in this graphic essay.

3. **CONNECTIONS:** Consider Satrapi's graphic essay in connection with other short personal narratives that dramatize a complicated personal experience, such as Jerald Walker's "Scattered Inconveniences" (page 239) or Brent Staples's "Just Walk on By: A Black Man Ponders His Power to Alter Public Space" (page 217). How do these narratives convey complicated moments and emotions and introduce competing perspectives? Of the three selections, choose the one you believe achieves the most satisfying resolution and explain the reasons for your choice.

The Graphic Memoirist at Work

MARJANE SATRAPI on the Language of Words and Images

Fred Hayes/Getty Images

In an interview with the literary journal *Fourth Genre*, Marjane Satrapi spoke about the unique interaction of words and images in her graphic memoirs and comics in general. The interview was conducted in November 2006 by the journal's interview editor, Robert Root, and it was published in Fall 2007.

❝ Root: I'm interested in the use of illustration in the service of autobiography or memoir or other kinds of nonfiction and how that affects the "nonfictionness" of it, the truth of it. People keep referring to your books and to Art Spiegelman's *Maus* and to Alison Bechdel's *Fun Home* as "graphic novels," but it seems to me that a more accurate term would be "graphic memoirs," since they are all autobiographical on some level.

Satrapi: Yes, they *are* autobiographical, but at the same time they search for truth. . . . If you're looking for truth you have to ask it from the Fox News and the *New York Times.* As soon as you write your story, it is a story; this is not a documentary. Of course you have to make fiction, you have to cheat, you have to make some angle around there, because the story has to turn, so that is the reconstruction of what we do. For instance, I don't know, when I write something about people and I'm mean to them, of course I would not use the real names and the real figures, even not the real story. I will create this new personage around myself. Of course, they will always be related to my experiences — what I have seen and what I have heard, or whatever — but any writer will do that, even in science fiction you do that. So the use of the drawing for me is that first of all, I am a very lousy writer. I have tried actually, you know, at one time to write. If I had to write this short article or something, here I am good. But for a novel, just forget about it. I lose all my sense of humor, I lose completely all my decency, and I become completely lousy and pathetic. If I say to myself, "Now you are a serious girl and now you are going to make some serious work," there's nothing worse than wanting to make a serious work for me. So drawing gives me the possibility of this sense of saying what I want to say.

Also, there are many things that you can say through images that you cannot say with the writing. The comic is the only media in the whole world that you can use the image plus the writing plus the imagination and plus be active while reading it. When you watch a picture, a movie, you are passive. Everything is coming to you. When you are reading comics, between one frame to the other what is happening, you have to imagine it yourself. So you are active; you have to take part actually when you read the story. It is the only medium that uses the images in this way. So, for me, comics have only convenience. . . .

Root: You've mentioned before the two languages that you work with, the language of words and the language of image, and how they come together. I wish you would elaborate a little more on that. You've said that you don't write the story and then find images to illustrate the text, that they go together and bounce off of one another. How does that work?

Satrapi: I have a small page on which I know more or less what I want to write in my story. When I start, I have these small little sketches with small drawings of people, and I have short, short dialogues going together, and once in a while I write the dialogue, and once in a while I go the other way. It's like a baby growing up. You don't have first the nose come up and then one eye and then one hand or one leg — all of it grows at the same time. Another thing also: when I work, you know, I am completely in a trance. I'm so concentrated on the work that I don't look at myself working. And I work alone on my books. So since I don't watch myself, it's very difficult for me to know what I'm doing, since I don't see what I'm doing."

David Sedaris

ME TALK PRETTY ONE DAY

DAVID SEDARIS (b. 1956) was born in Johnson City, New York, and raised in Raleigh, North Carolina. He is a dramatist whose plays (one of which won an Obie Award), written in collaboration with his sister, Amy, have been produced at La Mama and Lincoln Center. Sedaris launched his career as a wry, neurotically self-disparaging humorist on National Public Radio's *Morning Edition*, when he read aloud from "The Santaland Diaries," an autobiographical piece about working as a Christmas elf at Macy's. He has since published a number of best-selling collections, including *Naked* (1997), *Holidays on Ice* (1997), *Me Talk Pretty One Day* (2000), *When You Are Engulfed in Flames* (2008), and his newest book, *Let's Explore Diabetes with Owls* (2013), which became an immediate best-seller. His collection of fables titled *Squirrel Seeks Chipmunk: A Modest Bestiary* (with illustrations by Ian Falconer) was published in 2010 and immediately hit the *New York Times* best-seller list for fiction. His essays appear regularly in the *New Yorker* and *Esquire*. In 2001, Sedaris was named Humorist of the Year by *Time* magazine and received the Thurber Prize for American Humor. *New York Magazine* dubbed Sedaris "the most brilliantly witty New Yorker since Dorothy Parker." He currently lives in England, and his most recent publication is *Theft by Finding: Diaries 1977–2002* (2017).

> "It doesn't really matter what your life was like, you can write about anything."

Sedaris, who for two years taught writing at the Art Institute of Chicago, laments that the students in his writing classes "were ashamed of their middle-class background . . . they felt like unless they grew up in poverty, they had nothing to write about." Sedaris feels that "it doesn't really matter what your life was like, you can write about anything. It's just the writing of it that is the challenge."

AT THE AGE OF FORTY-ONE, I am returning to school and have to think of myself as what my French textbook calls "a true debutant." After paying my tuition, I was issued a student ID, which allows me a discounted entry fee at movie theaters, puppet shows, and Festyland, a far-flung amusement park that advertises with billboards picturing a cartoon stegosaurus sitting in a canoe and eating what appears to be a ham sandwich.

I've moved to Paris with hopes of learning the language. My school is an easy ten-minute walk from my apartment, and on the first day of class I arrived early, watching as the returning students greeted one another in the school lobby. Vacations were recounted, and questions were raised concerning mutual friends with names like Kang and Vlatnya. Regardless of their nationalities, everyone spoke in what sounded to me like excellent French. Some accents were better than others, but the students exhibited an ease and confidence I found intimidating. As an added discomfort, they were all young, attractive, and well dressed, causing me to feel not unlike Pa Kettle trapped backstage after a fashion show.

The first day of class was nerve-racking because I knew I'd be expected to perform. That's the way they do it here—it's everybody into the language pool, sink or swim. The teacher marched in, deeply tanned from a recent vacation, and proceeded to rattle off a series of administrative announcements. I've spent quite a few summers in Normandy, and I took a monthlong French class before leaving New York. I'm not completely in the dark, yet I understood only half of what this woman was saying.

"If you have not *meimslsxp* or *lgpdmurct* by this time, then you should not be in this room. Has everyone *apzkiubjxow*? Everyone? Good, we shall begin." She spread out her lesson plan and sighed, saying, "All right, then, who knows the alphabet?"

It was startling because (a) I hadn't been asked that question in a while   5
and (b) I realized, while laughing, that I myself did *not* know the alphabet. They're the same letters, but in France they're pronounced differently. I knew the shape of the alphabet but had no idea what it actually sounded like.

"Ahh." The teacher went to the board and sketched the letter *a.* "Do we have anyone in the room whose first name commences with an *ahh*?"

Two Polish Annas raised their hands, and the teacher instructed them to present themselves by stating their names, nationalities, occupations, and a brief list of things they liked and disliked in this world. The first Anna hailed from an industrial town outside of Warsaw and had front teeth the size of tombstones. She worked as a seamstress, enjoyed quiet times with friends, and hated the mosquito.

"Oh, really," the teacher said. "How very interesting. I thought that everyone loved the mosquito, but here, in front of all the world, you claim to detest him. How is it that we've been blessed with someone as unique and original as you? Tell us, please."

The seamstress did not understand what was being said but knew that this was an occasion for shame. Her rabbity mouth huffed for breath, and she stared down at her lap as though the appropriate comeback were stitched somewhere alongside the zipper of her slacks.

The second Anna learned from the first and claimed to love sunshine   10
and detest lies. It sounded like a translation of one of those Playmate of the Month data sheets, the answers always written in the same loopy handwriting: "Turn-ons: Mom's famous five-alarm chili! Turnoffs: insecurity and guys who come on too strong!!!!"

The two Polish Annas surely had clear notions of what they loved and hated, but like the rest of us, they were limited in terms of vocabulary, and this made them appear less than sophisticated. The teacher forged on, and we learned that Carlos, the Argentine bandonion player, loved wine, music, and, in his words, "making sex with the womens of the world." Next came a beautiful young Yugoslav who identified herself as an optimist, saying that she loved everything that life had to offer.

The teacher licked her lips, revealing a hint of the saucebox we would later come to know. She crouched low for her attack, placed her hands on the young woman's desk, and leaned close, saying, "Oh yeah? And do you love your little war?"

While the optimist struggled to defend herself, I scrambled to think of an answer to what had obviously become a trick question. How often is one asked what he loves in this world? More to the point, how often is one asked and then publicly ridiculed for his answer? I recalled my mother, flushed with wine, pounding the tabletop late one night, saying, "Love? I love a good steak cooked rare. I love my cat, and I love . . ." My sisters and I leaned forward, waiting to hear our names. "Tums," our mother said. "I love Tums."

The teacher killed some time accusing the Yugoslavian girl of masterminding a program of genocide, and I jotted frantic notes in the margins of my pad. While I can honestly say that I love leafing through medical textbooks devoted to severe dermatological conditions, the hobby is beyond the reach of my French vocabulary, and acting it out would only have invited controversy.

When called upon, I delivered an effortless list of things that I detest: blood sausage, intestinal pâtés, brain pudding. I'd learned these words the hard way. Having given it some thought, I then declared my love for IBM typewriters, the French word for *bruise*, and my electric floor waxer. It was a short list, but still I managed to mispronounce *IBM* and assign the wrong gender to both the floor waxer and the typewriter. The teacher's reaction led me to believe that these mistakes were capital crimes in the country of France. 15

"Were you always this *palicmkrexis*?" she asked. "Even a *fiuscrzsa ticiwelmun* knows that a typewriter is feminine."

I absorbed as much of her abuse as I could understand, thinking — but not saying — that I find it ridiculous to assign a gender to an inanimate object incapable of disrobing and making an occasional fool of itself. Why refer to Lady Crack Pipe or Good Sir Dishrag when these things could never live up to all that their sex implied?

The teacher proceeded to belittle everyone from German Eva, who hated laziness, to Japanese Yukari, who loved paintbrushes and soap. Italian, Thai, Dutch, Korean, and Chinese — we all left class foolishly believing that the worst was over. She'd shaken us up a little, but surely that was just an act designed to weed out the deadweight. We didn't know it then, but the coming months would teach us what it was like to spend time in the presence of a wild animal, something completely unpredictable. Her temperament was not based on a series of good and bad days but, rather, good and bad moments. We soon learned to dodge chalk and protect our heads and stomachs whenever she approached us with a question. She hadn't yet punched anyone, but it seemed wise to protect ourselves against the inevitable.

Though we were forbidden to speak anything but French, the teacher would occasionally use us to practice any of her five fluent languages.

"I hate you," she said to me one afternoon. Her English was flawless.   20 "I really, really hate you." Call me sensitive, but I couldn't help but take it personally.

After being singled out as a lazy *kfdtinvfm*, I took to spending four hours a night on my homework, putting in even more time whenever we were assigned an essay. I suppose I could have gotten by with less, but I was determined to create some sort of identity for myself: David the hard worker, David the cut-up. We'd have one of those "complete this sentence" exercises, and I'd fool with the thing for hours, invariably settling on something like "A quick run around the lake? I'd love to! Just give me a moment while I strap on my wooden leg." The teacher, through word and action, conveyed the message that if this was my idea of an identity, she wanted nothing to do with it.

My fear and discomfort crept beyond the borders of the classroom and accompanied me out onto the wide boulevards. Stopping for a coffee, asking directions, depositing money in my bank account: these things were out of the question, as they involved having to speak. Before beginning school, there'd been no shutting me up, but now I was convinced that everything I said was wrong. When the phone rang, I ignored it. If someone asked me a question, I pretended to be deaf. I knew my fear was getting the best of me when I started wondering why they don't sell cuts of meat in vending machines.

My only comfort was the knowledge that I was not alone. Huddled in the hallways and making the most of our pathetic French, my fellow students and I engaged in the sort of conversation commonly overheard in refugee camps.

"Sometime me cry alone at night."

"That be common for I, also, but be more strong, you. Much work and   25 someday you talk pretty. People start love you soon. Maybe tomorrow, okay."

Unlike the French class I had taken in New York, here there was no sense of competition. When the teacher poked a shy Korean in the eyelid with a freshly sharpened pencil, we took no comfort in the fact that, unlike Hyeyoon Cho, we all knew the irregular past tense of the verb *to defeat*. In all fairness, the teacher hadn't meant to stab the girl, but neither did she spend much time apologizing, saying only, "Well, you should have been *vkkdyo* more *kdeynfulh*."

Over time it became impossible to believe that any of us would ever improve. Fall arrived and it rained every day, meaning we would now be scolded for the water dripping from our coats and umbrellas. It was mid-October when the teacher singled me out, saying, "Every day spent with you is like having a cesarean section." And it struck me that, for the first time since arriving in France, I could understand every word that someone was saying.

Understanding doesn't mean that you can suddenly speak the language. Far from it. It's a small step, nothing more, yet its rewards are intoxicating and deceptive. The teacher continued her diatribe and I settled back, bathing in the subtle beauty of each new curse and insult.

|||||||||||||||||||||||||||||||||||||||||||||||||||||||||||||||||||||||||||||||||||||||||||||||||||||||||||||||||||||||

"You exhaust me with your foolishness and reward my efforts with nothing but pain, do you understand me?"

The world opened up, and it was with great joy that I responded, "I know 30 the thing that you speak exact now. Talk me more, you, plus, please, plus." ▪

The Reader's Presence

1. How did Sedaris take his experience—auditing a beginner's language class—and turn it into a humorous essay? What were the funniest parts of the essay? An interviewer once wrote that Sedaris's signature is "deadpan" humor. What is deadpan humor? Identify—and characterize the effectiveness of—examples of it in "Me Talk Pretty One Day."

2. Which English words would you substitute for the nonsense words that represent Sedaris's difficulties understanding his teacher's French? Have a classmate tell you what he or she thinks such words as *meimslsxp* (paragraph 4), *palicmkrexis* (paragraph 16), or *kdeynfulh* (paragraph 26) might mean. Did he or she pick the same or similar words to the ones you picked? Point to the clues Sedaris includes in the essay to hint at what such words mean. How would you rewrite the passage with different clues to indicate a different possible meaning for the nonsense words?

3. **CONNECTIONS:** How surprised were you by the last line in the essay? To what extent did you expect that Sedaris would speak fluently because he understood his teacher's French perfectly? Look at some other unexpected last lines in essays that you've read in this collection, such as Patti Smith's "Sticky Fingers" (page 214) or Jamaica Kincaid's "The Estrangement" (page 136) or any two other last lines you found surprising, and identify how each author goes about setting up the surprise. When you look back, at what point in each essay might you have expected the unexpected? Be as specific as possible in your response.

Patti Smith

STICKY FINGERS

PATTI SMITH (b. 1946) is sometimes referred to as the "Godmother of Punk" and is widely recognized for her influence on the punk rock movement in 1970s New York. Although she is perhaps best known as a singer-songwriter, Smith is also a visual artist and an award-winning author. She was born in Chicago but raised in the New Jersey suburbs of Philadelphia, where she graduated from high

> "You just keep doing your work because you have to, because it's your calling."

school in 1964. Her mother was a Jehovah's Witness and the young Smith had a strict Bible education, but she ultimately rejected organized religion. After working in a factory and briefly attending Glassboro State College (now Rowan University), she moved to New York City in 1967, where she met her life long friend, Robert Mapplethorpe, and began to experiment with various creative outlets, including painting, acting, writing, and music. By 1974, she was performing her own music in various New York City venues, and in 1975 she was signed by Arista Records. In December of that year, her debut album, *Horses*, was released to critical acclaim. Often cited as one of the greatest albums in rock history, it blends a punk rock sound with spoken word poetry.

Smith went on to release ten more albums over nearly forty years, including *Radio Ethiopia* (1976), *Easter* (1978), *Dream of Life* (1988), *Peace and Noise* (1997), *Gung Ho* (2000), and *Twelve* (2007), among others. Her most recent studio recording is *Banga*, released in 2012 by Columbia Records. Smith has cited eighteenth–nineteenth-century British poet William Blake and nineteenth-century French poet Arthur Rimbaud as her influences, and she has given literary lectures on their work. In 2005, she was named a Commander of the Ordre des Arts et des Lettres by the French Ministry of Culture. In 2007, she was inducted into the Rock and Roll Hall of Fame and, in 2010, she won the National Book Award for her memoir, *Just Kids*, which documents her relationship with Robert Mapplethorpe, who went on from their experiments with art to become an acclaimed artist and photographer. Of working as a writer and an artist she has said, "[You] can't expect to be embraced by the people . . . you write poetry books that maybe, you know, fifty people read, and you just keep doing your work because you have to, because it's your calling." "Sticky Fingers" was published in the *New Yorker* in October 2011.

WHEN I WAS TEN YEARS OLD, I lived with my family in a small ranch house in rural South Jersey. I often accompanied my mother to the A&P to buy groceries. We did not have a car, so we walked, and I would help her carry the bags.

My mother had to shop very carefully, as my father was on strike. She was a waitress, and her paycheck and tips barely sustained us. One day, while she was weighing prices, a promotional display for the World Book Encyclopedia caught my eye. The volumes were cream-colored, with forest-green spines stamped in gold. Volume I was ninety-nine cents with a ten-dollar purchase.

All I could think of, as we combed the aisles for creamed corn, dry milk, cans of Spam, and shredded wheat, was the book, which I coveted with all my being. I stood at the register with my mother, holding my breath as the cashier rang up the items. It came to over eleven dollars. My mother produced a five, some singles, and a handful of change. As she was counting out the money, I somehow found the courage to ask for the encyclopedia. "Could we get one?" I said, showing her the display. "It's only ninety-nine cents."

I did not understand my mother's mounting anxiety; she did not have enough change and had to sacrifice a large can of Le Sueur peas to pay the amount. "Not now, Patricia," she said sternly. "Today is not a good day." I packed the groceries and followed her home, crestfallen.

The next Saturday, my mother gave me a dollar and sent me to the A&P   5 alone. Two quarts of milk and a loaf of bread: that's what a dollar bought in 1957. I went straight to the World Book display. There was only one first volume left, which I placed in my cart. I didn't need a cart, but took one so I could read as I went up and down the aisles. A lot of time went by, but I had little concept of time, a fact that often got me in trouble. I knew I had to leave, but I couldn't bear to part with the book. Impulsively I put it inside my shirt and zipped up my plaid windbreaker. I was a tall, skinny kid, and I'm certain every contour of the book was conspicuous.

I strolled the aisles for several more minutes, then went through the checkout, paid my dollar, swiftly bagged the three items, and headed home with my heart pounding.

Suddenly I felt a heavy tap on my shoulder and turned to find the biggest man I had ever seen. He was the store detective, and he asked me to hand it over. I just stood in silence. "We know you stole something — you will have to be searched." Horrified, I slid the heavy book out from the bottom of my shirt.

He looked at it quizzically. "This is what you stole, an encyclopedia?"

"Yes," I whispered, trembling.

"Why didn't you ask your parents?"   10

"I did," I said, "but they didn't have the money."

"Do you know it's wrong?"

"Yes."

"Do you go to church?"

"Yes, twice a week."   15

"Well, you're going to have to tell your parents what you did."

"No, please."

"Then I will do it. What's the address?"

I was silent.

"Well, I'll have to walk you home."   20

"No, please, I will tell them."

"Do you swear?"

"Yes, yes, sir."

My mother was agitated when I arrived home. "Where were you? I needed the bread for your father's sandwiches. I told you to come right home."

And suddenly everything went green, like right before a tornado. My   25 ears were ringing, I felt dizzy, and I threw up.

My mother tended to me immediately, as she always did. She had me lie on the couch and got a cold towel for my head and sat by me with her anxious expression.

"What is it, Patricia?" she asked. "Did something bad happen?"

"Yes," I whispered. "I stole something." I told her about my lust for the book, my wrongdoing, the big detective. My mother was a good mother, but she could be explosive, and I tensed, waiting for the barrage of verbal punishment, the sentencing that always seemed to outweigh the crime. But she said nothing. She told me that she would call the store and tell the detective I had confessed, and that I should sleep.

When I awoke, sometime later, the house was silent. My mother had taken my siblings to the field to play. I sat up and noticed a brown-paper bag with my name on it. I opened it and inside was the World Book Encyclopedia, Volume I. ◼

The Reader's Presence

1. From the moment Smith lays eyes on the encyclopedia, she cannot bear to be without it: "All I could think of . . . was the book, which I coveted with all my being" (paragraph 3). Why is the encyclopedia so important to Smith? The encyclopedia is sold in the supermarket alongside such staples as milk and bread. What specific reasons can you offer in defense of the assertion that books are a necessary staple of one's life? Would you offer the same rationale in defense of the need for an encyclopedia? Why or why not? Would Smith?

2. Smith describes her desire for the encyclopedia with such words as "covet" and "lust," both of which carry religious connotations. What does Smith gain—and risk—by using language bearing such connotations? What specific language would you use to convey a clear sense of your attitude toward—and relationship with—books? with an encyclopedia?

3. **CONNECTIONS:** Compare and contrast Smith's essay with Jhumpa Lahiri's "My Two Lives" (page 151). In what specific ways is Smith's desire for the encyclopedia related to the importance of writing in Lahiri's life? Prepare a detailed account of the ways in which you believe writing and reading are connected.

Brent Staples

Just Walk on By: A Black Man Ponders His Power to Alter Public Space

As he describes in *Parallel Time: Growing Up in Black and White* (1994), **BRENT STAPLES** (b. 1951) escaped a childhood of urban poverty through success in school and his determination to be a writer. Although Staples earned a PhD in psychology from the

> **"I traveled to distant neighborhoods, sat on their curbs, and sketched what I saw in words."**

University of Chicago in 1982, his love of journalism led him to leave the field of psychology and start a career that has taken him to the *New York Times*, where he has served on the editorial board since 1990. Staples contributes to several national magazines, including *Harper's*, the *New York Times Magazine*, and *Ms.*, in which "Just Walk on By" appeared in 1986.

Parallel Time received the Anisfield-Wolf Book Award, previously won by such writers as James Baldwin, Ralph Ellison, and Zora Neale Hurston. In it he remembers how in Chicago he prepared for his writing career by keeping a journal. "I wrote on buses, on the Jackson Park el — though only at the stops to keep the writing legible. I traveled to distant neighborhoods, sat on their curbs, and sketched what I saw in words. Thursdays meant free admission at the Art Institute. All day I attributed motives to people in paintings, especially people in Rembrandts. At closing time I went to a nightclub in The Loop and spied on patrons, copied their conversations and speculated about their lives. The journal was more than 'a record of my inner transactions.' It was a collection of stolen souls from which I would one day construct a book."

MY FIRST VICTIM was a woman — white, well dressed, probably in her early twenties. I came upon her late one evening on a deserted street in Hyde Park, a relatively affluent neighborhood in an otherwise mean, impoverished section of Chicago. As I swung onto the avenue behind her, there seemed to be a discreet, uninflammatory distance between us. Not so. She cast back a worried glance. To her, the youngish black man — a broad six feet two inches with a beard and billowing hair, both hands shoved into the pockets of a bulky military jacket — seemed menacingly close. After a few more quick glimpses, she picked up her pace and was soon running in earnest. Within seconds she disappeared into a cross street.

That was more than a decade ago. I was twenty-two years old, a graduate student newly arrived at the University of Chicago. It was in the echo of that terrified woman's footfalls that I first began to know the unwieldy inheritance I'd come into — the ability to alter public space in ugly ways. It was clear that she thought herself the quarry of a mugger, a rapist, or worse. Suffering a bout of insomnia, however, I was stalking sleep, not defenseless wayfarers. As a softy who is scarcely able to take a knife to a raw chicken — let alone hold it to a person's throat — I was surprised, embarrassed, and dismayed all at once. Her flight made me feel like an accomplice in tyranny. It also made it clear that I was indistinguishable from the muggers who occasionally seeped into the area from the surrounding ghetto. That first encounter, and those that followed, signified that a vast, unnerving gulf lay between nighttime pedestrians — particularly women — and me. And I soon gathered that being perceived as dangerous is a hazard in itself. I only needed to turn a corner into a dicey situation, or crowd some frightened, armed person in a foyer somewhere, or make an errant move after being pulled over by a policeman. Where fear and weapons meet — and they often do in urban America — there is always the possibility of death.

In that first year, my first away from my hometown, I was to become thoroughly familiar with the language of fear. At dark, shadowy intersections in Chicago, I could cross in front of a car stopped at a traffic light and elicit the *thunk, thunk, thunk, thunk* of the driver—black, white, male, or female—hammering down the door locks. On less traveled streets after dark, I grew accustomed to but never comfortable with people who crossed to the other side of the street rather than pass me. Then there were the standard unpleasantries with police, doormen, bouncers, cabdrivers, and others whose business is to screen out troublesome individuals *before* there is any nastiness.

I moved to New York nearly two years ago and I have remained an avid night walker. In central Manhattan, the near-constant crowd cover minimizes tense one-on-one street encounters. Elsewhere—visiting friends in Soho,[1] where sidewalks are narrow and tightly spaced buildings shut out the sky—things can get very taut indeed.

Black men have a firm place in New York mugging literature. Norman   5
Podhoretz[2] in his famed (or infamous) 1963 essay, "My Negro Problem—And Ours," recalls growing up in terror of black males; they "were tougher than we were, more ruthless," he writes—and as an adult on the Upper West Side of Manhattan, he continues, he cannot constrain his nervousness when he meets black men on certain streets. Similarly, a decade later, the essayist and novelist Edward Hoagland extols a New York where once "Negro bitterness bore down mainly on other Negroes." Where some see mere panhandlers, Hoagland sees "a mugger who is clearly screwing up his nerve to do more than just *ask* for money." But Hoagland has "the New Yorker's quick-hunch posture for broken-field maneuvering," and the bad guy swerves away.

I often witness that "hunch posture," from women after dark on the warrenlike streets of Brooklyn where I live. They seem to set their faces on neutral and, with their purse straps strung across their chests bandolier style, they forge ahead as though bracing themselves against being tackled. I understand, of course, that the danger they perceive is not a hallucination. Women are particularly vulnerable to street violence, and young black males are drastically overrepresented among the perpetrators of that violence. Yet these truths are no solace against the kind of alienation that comes of being ever the suspect, against being set apart, a fearsome entity with whom pedestrians avoid making eye contact.

It is not altogether clear to me how I reached the ripe old age of twenty-two without being conscious of the lethality nighttime pedestrians attributed to me. Perhaps it was because in Chester, Pennsylvania, the small, angry industrial town where I came of age in the 1960s, I was scarcely noticeable against a backdrop of gang warfare, street knifings, and murders. I grew up one of the good boys, had perhaps a half-dozen fistfights. In retrospect, my shyness of combat has clear sources.

Many things go into the making of a young thug. One of those things is the consummation of the male romance with the power to intimidate. An infant discovers that random flailings send the baby bottle flying out of the crib and crashing to the floor. Delighted, the joyful babe repeats those motions again and again, seeking to duplicate the feat. Just so, I recall the

---

1 **Soho:** A district of lower Manhattan known for its art galleries. — EDS.
2 **Podhoretz:** A well-known literary critic and editor of *Commentary* magazine. — EDS.

points at which some of my boyhood friends were finally seduced by the perception of themselves as tough guys. When a mark cowered and surrendered his money without resistance, myth and reality merged—and paid off. It is, after all, only manly to embrace the power to frighten and intimidate. We, as men, are not supposed to give an inch of our lane on the highway; we are to seize the fighter's edge in work and in play and even in love; we are to be valiant in the face of hostile forces.

Unfortunately, poor and powerless young men seem to take all this nonsense literally. As a boy, I saw countless tough guys locked away; I have since buried several, too. They were babies, really—a teenage cousin, a brother of twenty-two, a childhood friend in his midtwenties—all gone down in episodes of bravado played out in the streets. I came to doubt the virtues of intimidation early on. I chose, perhaps even unconsciously, to remain a shadow—timid, but a survivor.

The fearsomeness mistakenly attributed to me in public places often has   10
a perilous flavor. The most frightening of these confusions occurred in the late 1970s and early 1980s when I worked as a journalist in Chicago. One day, rushing into the office of a magazine I was writing for with a deadline story in hand, I was mistaken for a burglar. The office manager called security and, with an ad hoc posse, pursued me through the labyrinthine halls, nearly to my editor's door. I had no way of proving who I was. I could only move briskly toward the company of someone who knew me.

Another time I was on assignment for a local paper and killing time before an interview. I entered a jewelry store on the city's affluent Near North Side. The proprietor excused herself and returned with an enormous red Doberman pinscher straining at the end of a leash. She stood, the dog extended toward me, silent to my questions, her eyes bulging nearly out of her head. I took a cursory look around, nodded, and bade her good night. Relatively speaking, however, I never fared as badly as another black male journalist. He went to nearby Waukegan, Illinois, a couple of summers ago to work on a story about a murderer who was born there. Mistaking the reporter for the killer, police hauled him from his car at gunpoint and but for his press credentials would probably have tried to book him. Such episodes are not uncommon. Black men trade tales like this all the time.

In "My Negro Problem—And Ours," Podhoretz writes that the hatred he feels for blacks makes itself known to him through a variety of avenues—one being his discomfort with that "special brand of paranoid touchiness" to which he says blacks are prone. No doubt he is speaking here of black men. In time, I learned to smother the rage I felt at so often being taken for a criminal. Not to do so would surely have led to madness—via that special "paranoid touchiness" that so annoyed Podhoretz at the time he wrote the essay.

I began to take precautions to make myself less threatening. I move about with care, particularly late in the evening. I give a wide berth to nervous people on subway platforms during the wee hours, particularly when I have exchanged business clothes for jeans. If I happen to be entering a building behind some people who appear skittish, I may walk by, letting them clear the lobby before I return, so as not to seem to be following them.

I have been calm and extremely congenial on those rare occasions when I've been pulled over by the police.

And on late-evening constitutionals along streets less traveled by, I employ what has proved to be an excellent tension-reducing measure: I whistle melodies from Beethoven and Vivaldi and the more popular classical composers. Even steely New Yorkers hunching toward nighttime destinations seem to relax, and occasionally they even join in the tune. Virtually everybody seems to sense that a mugger wouldn't be warbling bright, sunny selections from Vivaldi's *Four Seasons*. It is my equivalent of the cowbell that hikers wear when they know they are in bear country. ◼

The Reader's Presence

1. Why does Staples use the word *victim* in his opening sentence? In what sense is the white woman a "victim"? How is Staples using the term? As readers, how might we interpret the opening sentence upon first reading? How does the meaning of the term change in rereading?

2. In rereading the essay, pay close attention to the way Staples handles points of view. When does he shift viewpoints or perspectives? What is his purpose in doing so? What are some of the connections Staples makes in this essay between the point of view one chooses and one's identity?

3. **CONNECTIONS:** How does Staples behave on the street? How does he deal with the woman's anxiety? How has he "altered" his own public behavior? In what ways is his behavior on the street similar to his "behavior" as a writer? Compare this version of the essay to the alternate version that follows. What are the changes and how do those changes influence the essay's effect on the reader? How do you compare Staples's strategies—in both versions—to those of Manuel Muñoz in "Leave Your Name at the Border" (page 187)?

The Writer at Work

Another Version of *Just Walk on By*

Courtesy of Brent Staples

When he published his memoir, *Parallel Time*, in 1994, Brent Staples decided to incorporate his earlier essay into the book. He also decided to revise it substantially. As you compare the two versions, note the passages Staples retained and those he chose not to carry forward into book form. Do you agree with his changes? Why in general do you think he made them? If you had been his editor, what revision strategy would you have suggested?

❝At night, I walked to the lakefront whenever the weather permitted. I was headed home from the lake when I took my first victim. It was late fall, and the wind was cutting. I was wearing my navy pea jacket, the collar turned up, my hands snug in the pockets. Dead leaves scuttled in shoals along the streets. I turned out of Blackstone Avenue and headed west on 57th Street, and there she was, a few yards ahead of me, dressed in business clothes and carrying a briefcase. She looked back at me once, then again, and picked up her pace. She looked back again and started to run. I stopped where I was and looked up at the surrounding windows. What did this look like to people peeking out through their blinds? I was out walking. But what if someone had thought they'd seen something they hadn't and called the police. I held back the urge to run. Instead, I walked south to The Midway, plunged into its darkness, and remained on The Midway until I reached the foot of my street.

I'd been a fool. I'd been walking the streets grinning good evening at people who were frightened to death of me. I did violence to them by just being. How had I missed this? I kept walking at night, but from then on I paid attention.

I became expert in the language of fear. Couples locked arms or reached for each other's hand when they saw me. Some crossed to the other side of the street. People who were carrying on conversations went mute and stared straight ahead, as though avoiding my eyes would save them. This reminded me of an old wives' tale: that rabid dogs didn't bite if you avoided their eyes. The determination to avoid my eyes made me invisible to classmates and professors whom I passed on the street.

It occurred to me for the first time that I was big. I was 6 feet 1½ inches tall, and my long hair made me look bigger. I weighed only 170 pounds. But the navy pea jacket that Brian had given me was broad at the shoulders, high at the collar, making me look bigger and more fearsome than I was.

I tried to be innocuous but didn't know how. The more I thought about how I moved, the less my body belonged to me; I became a false character riding along inside it. I began to avoid people. I turned out of my way into side streets to spare them the sense that they were being stalked. I let them clear the lobbies of buildings before I entered, so they wouldn't feel trapped. Out of nervousness I began to whistle and discovered I was good at it. My whistle was pure and sweet—and also in tune. On the street at night I whistled popular tunes from the Beatles and Vivaldi's *Four Seasons*. The tension drained from people's bodies when they heard me. A few even smiled as they passed me in the dark.

Then I changed. I don't know why, but I remember when. I was walking west on 57th Street, after dark, coming home from the lake. The man and the woman walking toward me were laughing and talking but clammed up when they saw me. The man touched the woman's elbow, guiding her toward the curb. Normally I'd have given way and begun to whistle, but not this time. This time I veered toward them and aimed myself so that they'd have to part to avoid walking into me. The man stiffened, threw back his head and assumed the stare: eyes dead ahead, mouth open. His face took on a bluish hue under the sodium vapor streetlamps. I suppressed the urge to scream into his face. Instead I glided between them, my shoulder nearly brushing his. A few steps beyond them I stopped and howled with laughter. I called this game Scatter the Pigeons.

Fifty-seventh Street was too well lit for the game to be much fun; people didn't feel quite vulnerable enough. Along The Midway were heart-stopping strips of dark sidewalk, but these were so frightening that few people traveled them. The stretch

of Blackstone between 57th and 55th provided better hunting. The block was long
and lined with young trees that blocked out
the streetlight and obscured the heads of
people coming toward you.

One night I stopped beneath the
branches and came up on the other side,
just as a couple was stepping from their
car into their town house. The woman
pulled her purse close with one hand and
reached for her husband with the other.
The two of them stood frozen as I bore
down on them. I felt a surge of power:
these people were mine; I could do with
them as I wished. If I'd been younger,
with less to lose, I'd have robbed them,
and it would have been easy. All I'd have
to do was stand silently before them

until they surrendered their money. I
thundered, "Good evening!" into their
bleached-out faces and cruised away
laughing.

I held a special contempt for people
who cowered in their cars as they waited
for the light to change at 57th and Wood-
lawn. The intersection was always deserted
at night, except for a car or two stuck at the
red. *Thunk! Thunk! Thunk!* they hammered
down the door locks when I came into
view. Once I had hustled across the street,
head down, trying to seem harmless. Now
I turned brazenly into the headlights and
laughed. Once across, I paced the sidewalk,
glaring until the light changed. They'd
made me terrifying. Now I'd show them
how terrifying I could be.❚❚

Alex Tizon

SMALL MAN IN A BIG COUNTRY

It is not uncommon for first-generation immigrants to undergo a trying process of assimilation
because of cultural and racial differences. For **ALEX TIZON** (1959–2017), these differences
came to define his early years as his family strove to become American after emigrating from
the Philippines. In "Small Man in a Big Country," he recalls how even the shape of one's
nose had a hand in his family's quest to fit in, or as he describes it, their "self-annihilation."
His memoir on the subject, *Big Little Man:
In Search of My Asian Self*, was published
in 2014.

Tizon spent much of his writing life in
journalism, and in 1997 was co-recipient of
the Pulitzer Prize for his investigative work at
the *Seattle Times*. He was assistant professor

> Alex Tizon recalls how even
> the shape of one's nose had a
> hand in his family's quest to fit
> in, or as he describes it, their
> "self-annihilation."

of journalism at the University of Oregon until his sudden death at the age of fifty-seven. For students considering careers in journalism, Tizon offers some practical advice: "The ideal state would be to work only on stories that you care about, but the reality is that most of us, particularly at the beginning, will have to do some work that we don't exactly love. And even that can be beneficial to you as a storyteller."

OUR EARLY YEARS IN AMERICA WERE marked by relentless self-annihilation, though of course we did not see it that way at the time. Everything was done in the name of love, for the cause of fitting in, making friends, making the grade, landing the job, providing for the future, being good citizens of paradise—all so necessary and proper.

First was the abandonment of our native language and our unquestioned embrace of English, even though for my parents that abandonment meant cutting themselves off from a fluency they would never have again. Possessing a language meant possessing the world expressed in its words. Dispossessing it meant nothing less than the loss of a world and the beginning of bewilderment forever. "Language is the only homeland," said poet Czeslaw Milosz. My parents left the world that created them and now would be beginners for the rest of their lives, mumblers searching for the right word, the proper phrase that approximated what they felt inside. I wonder at the eloquence that must have lived inside them that never found a way out. How much was missed on all sides.

We left behind José Rizal[1] and picked up Mark Twain. We gave up Freddie Aguilar[2] for Frank Sinatra and the Beatles, "Bayan Ko" for "The Star-Spangled Banner" and "She loves you, yeah, yeah, yeah."

My parents' adulation of all things white and Western and their open derision of all things brown or native or Asian was the engine of their self-annihilation. Was it purely coincidence that our first car, first house, first dog in America were white? That our culminating moment in America was a white Christmas? White was the apex of humanity, the farthest point on the evolutionary arc, and therefore the closest earthly representation of ultimate truth and beauty.

I grew up hearing my parents' offhanded comments about how strong   5 and capable the Americans were, how worthy of admiration, and conversely how weak and incapable and deserving of mockery their own countrymen were: "They can't do it on their own; they need help." I heard it in their breathless admiration for mestizos—persons of mixed European and Asian blood—how elegant and commanding they were, and the more European the better. To be called "mestizo" was the ultimate flattery. White spouses were prizes; mestizo babies, blessings; they represented an instant elevation, an infusion of royal blood, the promise of a more gifted life.

---

1 *José Rizal* (1861–1896): Filipino writer, activist, and national hero executed by the Spanish for helping to inspire the Philippine Revolution. — EDS.
2 *Freddie Aguilar* (b. 1953): A leading Filipino musician widely known for his patriotic version of "Bayan Ko" ("My Country"). — EDS.

Courtesy Melissa Tizon

■ ONE LATE EVENING AT THE WHITE House I was playing on floor of my parents' bedroom closet, behind a row of shirts, when the door opened. It was my father. Instead of revealing myself, I just sat there watching him in silence, cloaked by a wall of sleeves. He changed into his house clothes and stood at a small mirror appearing to massage his nose, running an index finger and thumb along the bridge, pinching and pulling it as if to make his nose narrower and longer. He stood there doing that for a short time and then left, shutting the door behind him. I thought it curious but did not think about it again until a few months later, when I saw him do it again as he absently watched television. He didn't know I was in the room.

"What are you doing, Papa?"

It startled him. "Nothing, son. Just massaging."

"Does your nose hurt?"

He looked at me, deciding what to do next, and then he seemed to relax.   10
"Halika dito, anak. Come here, son. You should do this," he said to me. He showed me how to use my fingers to pinch the bridge of my nose and then tug on it in a sustained pull, holding it in place for twenty seconds at a time and then repeating. "You should do this every day. If you do, your nose will become more tangus. Sharper. Narrower. You'll look more mestizo. Your nose is so round! And so flat! Talagang Pilipino! So Filipino!"

"What's wrong with flat?"

"Nothing is wrong with flat. Pero, sharper, is better. People will treat you better. They'll think you come from a better family. They'll think you're smarter and mas guapo, more handsome. Talaga, anak. This is true. See my nose? The other day a woman, a puti, a white, talked to me in Spanish because she thought I was from Spain. That happens to me. I massage everyday. Don't you think I look Castilian?" He turned to show his profile. "Ay anak. My son. Believe me."

I did believe him. Just as he had believed his father when the lesson was taught to him decades earlier. These were the givens: Aquiline was better than flat. Long better than wide. Light skin better than dark. Round eyes better than chinky. Blue eyes better than brown. Thin lips better than full. Blond better than black. Tall better than short. Big better than small. The formula fated us to lose. We had landed on a continent of Big Everything.

One sunny afternoon, my father and I walked to a hardware store a few blocks from our house. As we were about to go inside, three American men in overalls and T-shirts walked out, filling the doorway and inadvertently blocking our path. They were enormous, all of them well over six feet tall, with beards and beefy arms and legs. My father and I stood looking up at this wall of denim and hair. The Americans appeared ready to scoot over. "Excuse us," my father said, and we moved to the side.

One of the men said, "Thanks." Another snickered as they passed.   15

My father leaned down and whispered in my ear, "Land of the Giants." It was the name of a television show my family had started watching, a science-fiction series about a space crew marooned on a planet of gargantuan humans. The crew members were always being picked up by enormous hands and toyed with. The show's tagline: "Mini-people—Playthings in a World of Giant Tormentors." My family was captivated by the show. I think we related to the mini-people who in every episode were confronted by impossibly large humanoids.

Americans did seem to me at times like a different species, one that had evolved over generations into supreme behemoths. Kings in overalls. They were living proof of a basic law of conquest: victors ate better. The first time I sat as a guest at an American dinner table, I could scarcely believe the bounty: a whole huge potato for each of us, a separate plate of vegetables, my own steak. A separate slab of meat just for me! At home, that single slab would have fed my entire family.

The size of American bodies came to represent American capacities in everything we desired: they were smarter, stronger, richer; they lived in comfort and had the surplus to be generous. They knew the way to beauty and bounty because they were already there, filling the entryway with their meaty limbs and boulder heads and big, toothy grins like searchlights, imploring us with their booming voices to come on in. Have a seat at the table! Americans spoke a few decibels louder than we were used to.

We were small in everything. We were poor. I mean pockets-out immigrant poor. We were undernourished and scrawny, our genetics revealing not-so-distant struggles with famine and disease and war. We were inarticulate, our most deeply felt thoughts expressed in halting, heavily accented English, which might have sounded like grunts to Americans, given how frequently we heard "Excuse me?" or "Come again?" or "What?" The quizzical look on their faces as they tried to decipher the alien sounds.

My father, who was a funny, dynamic conversationalist in his own language, a man about Manila, would never be quite so funny or dynamic or   20 quick-witted or agile or confident again. He would always be a small man in America. My mother was small, too, but it was acceptable, even desirable, for women to be small. American men found my mother attractive. She never lacked attention or employment. My father was the one most demoted in the great new land. He was supposed to be the man of the family, and he did not know which levers to pull or push, and he didn't have the luxury of a lifetime, like his children, to learn them.

I'm convinced it was because of a gnawing awareness of his limitations in the land of the giants that he was a dangerous man to belittle. Gentle and gregarious in the company of friends, he was a different person in the larger world of strangers: wary, opaque, tightly coiled. My father stood all of five feet six inches and 150 pounds, every ounce of which could turn maniacal in an instant. He took offense easily and let his fists fly quickly. He was not deterred by mass. He recognized it, yes, but became blind with fury when it trespassed on him or his family. I once watched him scold a man twice his size, an auto mechanic he thought was taking advantage of him, and threaten to leap over the counter to teach him a lesson. "You kick a man in the balls and he's not so big anymore," he once told me. Actually, he told me more than once.

My mother corroborated the stories of my father challenging other men over perceived slights, losing as many fights as he won and getting downright clobbered on a few occasions, once landing in the hospital for a week. My mother was present at some of those fights; she was the cause of at least one, in which an unfortunate young man ogled her and ended up laid out on the sidewalk.

I got another glimpse of his inner maniac once at a park in New Jersey when I was about twelve. A big red-haired kid on a bike spit on me and rode away laughing and making faces. My father followed him all the way back to where his family was picnicking and confronted the three men in the group, all Americans, one of whom was presumably the kid's father. They all appeared startled. I heard only part of the conversation that followed. "We could take care of it right now, right here," my father told the men in a low, threatening voice, his fists clenched into hard knots. He stood leaning forward, unblinking. The men averted their gaze and kept silent. On the walk back to our spot, my father said, "Tell me if that boy comes near you again." I was speechless. His mettle astonished me. But it was something more than bravery on display that day. His fury was outsized, reckless, as if something larger was at stake, and of course now I know there was.

Unlike my father, I worked hard to get along with strangers. We moved so much in those early years that I got used to strangers as companions as we passed from place to place. I learned American English, trained out whatever accent I had inherited, picked up colloquial mannerisms. I kept a confident front, not in a loudmouthed way but in a reserved, alert manner, and I got more sure-footed in my interactions as I got better at English. If I had to guess, I'd say my classmates would have described me as a little shy but smart and likable. I brooded in private. How could someone be ashamed and capable at the same time? I was fated to have a secret life.

So I worked on becoming an American, to be in some ways more   25
American than my American friends. But I learned, eventually, that I could
never reach the ideal of the beloved. And when the realization came, it
seemed to land all at once, blunt force trauma, and I felt embarrassed to
have been a believer.

It's one of the beautiful lies of the American Dream: that you can become
anything, do anything, accomplish anything, if you want it badly enough
and are willing to work for it. Limits are inventions of the timid mind. You've
got to believe. All things are possible through properly channeled effort:
work, work, work; harder, faster, more! Unleash your potential! Nothing is
beyond your reach! Just do it! I believed it all, drank the elixir to the last
drop and licked my lips for residue. I put in the time, learned to read and
write and speak more capably than my friends and neighbors, followed the
rules, did my homework, memorized the tics and slangs and idiosyncrasies
of winners and heroes, but I could never be quite as American as they. The
lie is a lie only if you fail, and I most certainly did.

When I ask myself now when this shame inside me began, I see that I
inherited the beginnings of it from my father, and he from his father, going
back in my imagination as far as the arrival of the Spanish ships almost five
hundred years ago. An ancient inherited shame. It accompanied us across
the ocean. We carried it into a country that told us: not reaching the summit
was no one's fault but your own. ■

The Reader's Presence

1. Alex Tizon states he worked to be "in some ways more American than my American
   friends" (paragraph 25). What specific reasons does he offer to support his judgment that he considers his efforts a failure? Consider the meaning of Tizon's phrase
   "self-annihilation" when formulating your answer. How does Tizon use this phrase
   to help organize his essay? What is the significance of Tizon's quoting the poet
   Czeslaw Milosz's line: "Language is the only homeland"?

2. Tizon structures much of his essay around accounts of his father. Consider why the
   author chooses to include so many examples of his father's struggling to fit in, but so
   few relating to his own experiences. What effect does his father's erratic and sometimes violent behavior have on Tizon and his view of the American ideal? Please point
   to specific words and phrases to support your response.

3. **CONNECTIONS:** In "Boxed In" (page 671), Wendy Willis observes, "I live in a cloak
   of whiteness" (paragraph 15). Compare and contrast the attitudes toward whiteness
   expressed by Tizon and Willis. In what ways does whiteness influence the identities
   of both authors? Do you think their situations are comparable? Explain why or why
   not. How might Tizon's father perceive the problem Willis describes, and why? Additionally, consider whether Tizon's concept of "self-annihilation" would apply to Willis
   and her Native American ancestors.

Maria Venegas

THE DEVIL'S SPINE

What does a four-year-old remember? She can remember her name, for one thing. But can she remember a fake name that will be needed if she wants to join her parents across the border? When asked her name by an official, will she get it right? In "The Devil's Spine," a young writer remembers her four-year-old self and the tension of a long bus ride through the treacherous Sierra Madre mountains as she struggles to memorize the identity she must use when arriving at the Arizona border.

MARIA VENEGAS immigrated at the age of four from the state of Zacatecas, Mexico. The author of essays and stories, she grew up in Chicago and attended the University of Illinois. She received her MFA from Hunter College in New York City, where she currently lives. Her first book, a memoir about her outlaw father, *Bulletproof Vest*, appeared in 2014 to wide critical acclaim. On writing the memoir, she has said in an interview: "[T]here is that old saying: Write what scares you. I never thought I'd be writing about my past—especially not my father. To write about the past is to relive it, and even though that was extremely painful, it was also cathartic."

> **"Write what scares you."**

YOU HAVE BEEN SENT FOR and now you must memorize a name. A new name. A borrowed name. Nine thousand feet above sea level, the options are laid out before you: Get the name right and you see your parents again; get the name wrong and you never see them again. It's that simple. The bus you are traveling on snakes through the clouds, around the Devil's Spine, as it makes its way along the Sierra Madre Occidental[1] mountain range.

"What is your name?" A face emerges from the clouds and asks you. It's a familiar face, a face that is so much like your mother's face, though her face has faded in your memory, the way plastic flowers tied to a cross and left on the side of the road fade in the sun.

"Maria de Jesus Venegas Robles," you respond. This is the one thing you do know—your name. But it's the wrong answer. The bus jerks to the left and the force slams your body against the window.

---

[1] **Sierra Madre Occidental:** Part of the Sierra Madre mountain system in Mexico, it runs through Mexico until it nears the U.S. border with Arizona. —EDS.

Dario Lopez-Mills/AP Images

Geography of the Devil's Spine.

"When the men in green uniforms ask what your name is, you have to say Maricela Salazar, or you will never see your parents again. Do you understand?"

But you're only four years old, and you must look so yellow, so pale, for you are handed a grapefruit wedge and instructed to suck on it. You put it in your mouth, and the bittersweet juice runs down your chin and neck as you repeat the name, over and over, like a prayer, like a wish. It's only a name. But it's the one thing that might rescue you from the void into which you slipped the day your parents vanished. The day they dropped you off at your grandmother's house and never returned. After that, you asked anyone who came by her house if they had seen them. If your grandmother took you to the corner store, the plaza, the bakery, the mercado, you asked anyone who greeted her if they had seen them. They all gave you the same tight-lipped smile, or a pat on the head. Some handed you a piece of hard candy, a chicle, or an ice cream cone—anything to get your mind off of them—because everyone knew that your parents had gone to the other side.

"What is your name?" The bus swerves right, and the sun comes at you, a giant ball of fire smacking the window and diffusing.

"Maria de Jesus Venegas Robles," you respond, as ten thousand rays of light flood the bus, blinding you. Once again, the options are laid before you. Time is running out, and if you give the men in uniforms the wrong answer, well . . .

Focus on the dust particles that are free-falling through the sunlight and settling on your boney knee as you whisper the name like a chant. Mari-cela Sala-zar. Concentrate on the citrus scent that is lingering in the air. Ma-ri-ce-la Sa-la-zar. It's the smell of something green or orange, a respite from

5

the nausea that is already creeping in. An ice cube dissolving on the tongue. *¿Qué se pela por la panza?*[2] It's a riddle, but what is it? It's only a name. A borrowed name. But it's a name you must slip into and wear like a second skin, for on the other side of that name, your parents are alive and waiting.

Though you believed them to be gone for good, ever since the day that your grandmother took you back to your house. When you arrived, you watched as she turned the skeleton key in the heavy wooden door and pushed it open. It hit against the adobe wall with a crashing blow. Everything was in place. La Virgen de Guadalupe still hung on the wall behind the couch. In the kitchen, all the dishes were in the cupboard, the pile of chopped wood sat in the corner, and the scent of the wood-burning oven still lingered in the air. In their bedroom, the bed was made and the shutters were closed. Her floral printed dresses hung in the wardrobe next to his cowboy shirts, but they weren't there. They had seemingly slid through the cracks in the limestone floor and vanished. Never again did you ask about them.

The road curves right and the shadow of the mountain falls upon you as   10 you recite the name. Maricela Salazar. It's been two years since they disappeared. Two years is not such a long time, though it's long enough. The road veers left and again you are swimming in the sun light, while in the valley below, among the thorns and boulders, are rusted out cars and trucks that plunged into their dusty grave years ago. Inside, their passengers are still strapped in, still waiting to be rescued. But there is no escape from the Devil's Spine. He who plunges into its valley stays there forever and ever. Amen.

The bus emerges from the clouds and you are struggling to memorize the name, even as the memories of everything that came before this journey are evaporating. Try and grab two handfuls of the images that are already fading: the bougainvillea in your grandmother's courtyard, the sweet sting of a honey taco, the scent of the wood-burning oven, running barefoot through the cornfields, the flight of the blackbirds at sunset, the marching sound of an approaching rainstorm, and the scent of wet earth that lingers once the storm has passed. One day you will open your clutched fists to find you have nothing—no memory of the things that came before this passage—not even a bit of red dirt under your fingernails to remind you.

"What is your name?" a man in a green uniform asks when you reach the border.

"Maricela Salazar." ●

The Reader's Presence

1. Note that the essay is written in the second-person singular: "You have been sent for and now you must memorize a name." The essay, however, is an autobiographical account of the author at the age of four. Why do you think Venegas chose to write in the second person instead of simply saying: "I have been sent for and now I must

---

[2] *¿Qué se pela por la panza?* The ending of a popular Chicano riddle: "I have a riddle that you peel through its stomach." Answer: the navel orange. The riddle seems to pop into Venegas's head because of "the citrus scent" she smells, and it reminds us that she's only a child when these events took place. — EDS.

memorize a name." What advantages do you think she gains by expressing her child-hood experiences in the second person?

2. The essay—as indicated by its title—pays close attention to the Mexican landscape as seen from the bus. What role does the landscape play in establishing a mood for the essay? How would you describe the mood? In what ways does the landscape affect the young girl's perceptions?

3. **CONNECTIONS:** Names and identity play a large role in many personal essays. Look at the importance of names in Maya Angelou's classic, "What's Your Name, Girl?" (page 34). Although they may seem like two very different experiences, what connections can you find between Angelou's essay and "The Devil's Spine?"

Alice Walker

BEAUTY: WHEN THE OTHER DANCER IS THE SELF

ALICE WALKER (b. 1944) was awarded the Pulitzer Prize and the American Book Award for her second novel, *The Color Purple* (1982), which was made into a popular film. This novel helped establish Walker's reputation as one of America's most important contemporary writers. In both her fiction and her nonfiction, she shares her compassion for the black women of America whose lives have long been largely excluded from or distorted in literary representation. Walker is also the author of other novels, short stories, several volumes of poetry, a children's biography of Langston Hughes, essays, and criticism. Her books of poetry and prose include *By the Light of My Father's Smile* (1998), *The Way Forward Is with a Broken Heart* (2000), and *Now Is the Time to Open Your Heart* (2004). Her most recent work includes a collection of essays and ruminations, *We Are the Ones We Have Been Waiting For* (2006); an illustrated poem for children, *Why War Is Never a Good Idea* (2007); *The World Will Follow Joy: Turning Madness into Flowers* (2013); and *The Cushion in the Road: Meditation and Wandering as the Whole World Awakens to Being in Harm's Way* (2013). "Beauty: When the Other Dancer Is the Self" comes from her 1983 collection, *In Search of Our Mothers' Gardens*.

> "You have to go to the bottom of the well with creativity. You have to give it everything you've got, but at the same time you have to leave that last drop for the creative spirit or for the earth itself."

When asked by an interviewer about her writing habits, Walker replied, "I think it was Hemingway who said that each day that you write, you don't try to write to the absolute end of what you feel and think. You leave a little, you know, so that the next day you have something else to go on. And I would take it a little further—the thing is being able to create out of fullness, and that in order to create out of fullness, you have to let it well up. . . . In creation you must always leave something. You have to go to the bottom of the well with creativity. You have to give it everything you've got, but at the same time you have to leave that last drop for the creative spirit or for the earth itself."

IT IS A BRIGHT SUMMER DAY in 1947. My father, a fat, funny man with beautiful eyes and a subversive wit, is trying to decide which of his eight children he will take with him to the county fair. My mother, of course, will not go. She is knocked out from getting most of us ready: I hold my neck stiff against the pressure of her knuckles as she hastily completes the braiding and the beribboning of my hair.

My father is the driver for the rich old white lady up the road. Her name is Miss Mey. She owns all the land for miles around, as well as the house in which we live. All I remember about her is that she once offered to pay my mother thirty-five cents for cleaning her house, raking up piles of her magnolia leaves, and washing her family's clothes, and that my mother—she of no money, eight children, and a chronic earache—refused it. But I do not think of this in 1947. I am two-and-a-half years old. I want to go everywhere my daddy goes. I am excited at the prospect of riding in a car. Someone has told me fairs are fun. That there is room in the car for only three of us doesn't faze me at all. Whirling happily in my starchy frock, showing off my biscuit-polished patent-leather shoes and lavender socks, tossing my head in a way that makes my ribbons bounce, I stand, hands on hips, before my father. "Take me, Daddy," I say with assurance; "I'm the prettiest!"

Later, it does not surprise me to find myself in Miss Mey's shiny black car, sharing the back seat with the other lucky ones. Does not surprise me that I thoroughly enjoy the fair. At home that night I tell the unlucky ones all I can remember about the merry-go-round, the man who eats live chickens, and the teddy bears, until they say: that's enough, baby Alice. Shut up now, and go to sleep.

It is Easter Sunday, 1950. I am dressed in a green, flocked, scalloped-hem dress (handmade by my adoring sister, Ruth) that has its own smooth satin petticoat and tiny hot-pink roses tucked into each scallop. My shoes, new T-strap patent leather, again highly biscuit-polished. I am six years old and have learned one of the longest Easter speeches to be heard that day, totally unlike the speech I said when I was two: "Easter lilies / pure and white / blossom in / the morning light." When I rise to give my speech I do so on a great wave of love and pride and expectation. People in the church stop rustling their new crinolines. They seem to hold their breath. I can tell they admire my dress, but it is my spirit, bordering on sassiness (womanishness), they secretly applaud.

"That girl's a little *mess*," they whisper to each other, pleased.

5

Naturally I say my speech without stammer or pause, unlike those who stutter, stammer, or, worst of all, forget. This is before the word "beautiful" exists in people's vocabulary, but "Oh, isn't she the *cutest* thing!" frequently floats my way. "And got so much sense!" they gratefully add . . . for which thoughtful addition I thank them to this day.

It was great fun being cute. But then, one day, it ended.

I am eight years old and a tomboy. I have a cowboy hat, cowboy boots, checkered shirt and pants, all red. My playmates are my brothers, two and four years older than I. Their colors are black and green, the only difference in the way we are dressed. On Saturday nights we all go to the picture show, even my mother; Westerns are her favorite kind of movie. Back home, "on the ranch," we pretend we are Tom Mix, Hopalong Cassidy, Lash LaRue (we've even named one of our dogs Lash LaRue); we chase each other for hours rustling cattle, being outlaws, delivering damsels from distress. Then my parents decide to buy my brothers guns. These are not "real" guns. They shoot BBs, copper pellets my brothers say will kill birds. Because I am a girl, I do not get a gun. Instantly I am relegated to the position of Indian. Now there appears a great distance between us. They shoot and shoot at everything with their new guns. I try to keep up with my bow and arrows.

One day while I am standing on top of our makeshift "garage" — pieces of tin nailed across some poles — holding my bow and arrow and looking out toward the fields, I feel an incredible blow in my right eye. I look down just in time to see my brother lower his gun.

Both brothers rush to my side. My eye stings, and I cover it with my 10 hand. "If you tell," they say, "we will get a whipping. You don't want that to happen, do you?" I do not. "Here is a piece of wire," says the older brother, picking it up from the roof; "say you stepped on one end of it and the other flew up and hit you." The pain is beginning to start. "Yes," I say. "Yes, I will say that is what happened." If I do not say this is what happened, I know my brothers will find ways to make me wish I had. But now I will say anything that gets me to my mother.

Confronted by our parents we stick to the lie agreed upon. They place me on a bench on the porch and I close my left eye while they examine the right. There is a tree growing from underneath the porch that climbs past the railing to the roof. It is the last thing my right eye sees. I watch as its trunk, its branches, and then its leaves are blotted out by the rising blood.

I am in shock. First there is intense fever, which my father tries to break using lily leaves bound around my head. Then there are chills: my mother tries to get me to eat soup. Eventually, I do not know how, my parents learn what has happened. A week after the "accident" they take me to see a doctor. "Why did you wait so long to come?" he asks, looking into my eye and shaking his head. "Eyes are sympathetic," he says. "If one is blind, the other will likely become blind too."

This comment of the doctor's terrifies me. But it is really how I look that bothers me most. Where the BB pellet struck there is a glob of whitish scar tissue, a hideous cataract, on my eye. Now when I stare at people—a favorite pastime, up to now—they will stare back. Not at the "cute" little girl, but at her scar. For six years I do not stare at anyone, because I do not raise my head.

Years later, in the throes of a mid-life crisis, I ask my mother and sister whether I changed after the "accident." "No," they say, puzzled. "What do you mean?"

What do I mean?   15

I am eight, and, for the first time, doing poorly in school, where I have been something of a whiz since I was four. We have just moved to the place where the "accident" occurred. We do not know any of the people around us because this is a different county. The only time I see the friends I knew is when we go back to our old church. The new school is the former state penitentiary. It is a large stone building, cold and drafty, crammed to over-flowing with boisterous, ill-disciplined children. On the third floor there is a huge circular imprint of some partition that has been torn out.

"What used to be here?" I ask a sullen girl next to me on our way past it to lunch.

"The electric chair," says she.

At night I have nightmares about the electric chair, and about all the people reputedly "fried" in it. I am afraid of the school, where all the students seem to be budding criminals.

"What's the matter with your eye?" they ask, critically.   20

When I don't answer (I cannot decide whether it was an "accident" or not), they shove me, insist on a fight.

My brother, the one who created the story about the wire, comes to my rescue. But then brags so much about "protecting" me, I become sick.

After months of torture at the school, my parents decide to send me back to our old community, to my old school. I live with my grandparents and the teacher they board. But there is no room for Phoebe, my cat. By the time my grandparents decide there *is* room, and I ask for my cat, she cannot be found. Miss Yarborough, the boarding teacher, takes me under her wing, and begins to teach me to play the piano. But soon she marries an African—a "prince," she says—and is whisked away to his continent.

At my old school there is at least one teacher who loves me. She is the teacher who "knew me before I was born" and bought my first baby clothes. It is she who makes life bearable. It is her presence that finally helps me turn on the one child at the school who continually calls me "one-eyed bitch." One day I simply grab him by his coat and beat him until I am satisfied. It is my teacher who tells me my mother is ill.

My mother is lying in bed in the middle of the day, something I have   25
never seen. She is in too much pain to speak. She has an abscess in her ear. I stand looking down on her, knowing that if she dies, I cannot live. She is being treated with warm oils and hot bricks held against her cheek. Finally

a doctor comes. But I must go back to my grandparents' house. The weeks pass but I am hardly aware of it. All I know is that my mother might die, my father is not so jolly, my brothers still have their guns, and I am the one sent away from home.

"You did not change," they say.

Did I imagine the anguish of never looking up?

I am twelve. When relatives come to visit I hide in my room. My cousin Brenda, just my age, whose father works in the post office and whose mother is a nurse, comes to find me. "Hello," she says. And then she asks, looking at my recent school picture, which I did not want taken, and on which the "glob," as I think of it, is clearly visible, "You still can't see out of that eye?"

"No," I say, and flop back on the bed over my book.

That night, as I do almost every night, I abuse my eye. I rant and rave   30
at it, in front of the mirror. I plead with it to clear up before morning. I tell it I hate and despise it. I do not pray for sight. I pray for beauty.

"You did not change," they say.

I am fourteen and baby-sitting for my brother Bill, who lives in Boston. He is my favorite brother and there is a strong bond between us. Understanding my feelings of shame and ugliness he and his wife take me to a local hospital, where the "glob" is removed by a doctor named O. Henry. There is still a small bluish crater where the scar tissue was, but the ugly white stuff is gone. Almost immediately I become a different person from the girl who does not raise her head. Or so I think. Now that I've raised my head I win the boyfriend of my dreams. Now that I've raised my head I have plenty of friends. Now that I've raised my head classwork comes from my lips as faultlessly as Easter speeches did, and I leave high school as valedictorian, most popular student, and *queen*, hardly believing my luck. Ironically, the girl who was voted most beautiful in our class (and was) was later shot twice through the chest by a male companion, using a "real" gun, while she was pregnant. But that's another story in itself. Or is it?

"You did not change," they say.

It is now thirty years since the "accident." A beautiful journalist comes to visit and to interview me. She is going to write a cover story for her magazine that focuses on my latest book. "Decide how you want to look on the cover," she says. "Glamorous, or whatever."

Never mind "glamorous," it is the "whatever" that I hear. Suddenly all I   35
can think of is whether I will get enough sleep the night before the photography session: If I don't, my eye will be tired and wander, as blind eyes will.

At night in bed with my lover I think up reasons why I should not appear on the cover of a magazine. "My meanest critics will say I've sold out," I say. "My family will now realize I write scandalous books."

"But what's the real reason you don't want to do this?" he asks.

"Because in all probability," I say in a rush, "my eye won't be straight."

"It will be straight enough," he says. Then, "Besides, I thought you'd made your peace with that."

And I suddenly remember that I have.   45

I remember:

I am talking to my brother Jimmy, asking if he remembers anything unusual about the day I was shot. He does not know I consider that day the last time my father, with his sweet home remedy of cool lily leaves, chose me, and that I suffered and raged inside because of this. "Well," he says, "all I remember is standing by the side of the highway with Daddy, trying to flag down a car. A white man stopped, but when Daddy said he needed somebody to take his little girl to the doctor, he drove off."

I remember:

I am in the desert for the first time. I fall totally in love with it. I am so over-whelmed by its beauty, I confront for the first time, consciously, the meaning of the doctor's words years ago: "Eyes are sympathetic. If one is blind, the other will likely become blind too." I realize I have dashed about the world madly, looking at this, looking at that, storing up images against the fading of the light. *But I might have missed seeing the desert!* The shock of that possibility — and gratitude for over twenty-five years of sight — sends me literally to my knees. Poem after poem comes — which is perhaps how poets pray.

ON SIGHT

I am so thankful I have seen
The Desert
And the creatures in the desert
And the desert Itself.

The desert has its own moon
Which I have seen
With my own eye.
There is no flag on it.

Trees of the desert have arms
All of which are always up
That is because the moon is up
The sun is up
Also the sky
The Stars
Clouds
None with flags.

If there were flags, I doubt
the trees would point.
Would you?

But mostly, I remember this: 45

I am twenty-seven, and my baby daughter is almost three. Since her birth I have worried about her discovery that her mother's eyes are different from other people's. Will she be embarrassed? I think. What will she say? Every day she watches a television program called *Big Blue Marble*. It begins with a picture of the earth as it appears from the moon. It is bluish, a little battered-looking, but full of light, with whitish clouds swirling around it. Every time I see it I weep with love, as if it is a picture of Grandma's house. One day when I am putting Rebecca down for her nap, she suddenly focuses on my eye. Something inside me cringes, gets ready to try to protect myself. All children are cruel about physical differences, I know from experience, and that they don't always mean to be is another matter. I assume Rebecca will be the same.

But no-o-o-o. She studies my face intently as we stand, her inside and me outside her crib. She even holds my face maternally between her dimpled little hands. Then, looking every bit as serious and lawyerlike as her father, she says, as if it may just possibly have slipped my attention: "Mommy, there's a *world* in your eye." (As in, "Don't be alarmed, or do anything crazy.") And then, gently, but with great interest: "Mommy, where did you *get* that world in your eye?"

For the most part, the pain left then. (So what, if my brothers grew up to buy even more powerful pellet guns for their sons and to carry real guns themselves. So what, if a young "Morehouse[1] man" once nearly fell off the steps of Trevor Arnett Library because he thought my eyes were blue.) Crying and laughing I ran to the bathroom, while Rebecca mumbled and sang herself to sleep. Yes indeed, I realized, looking into the mirror. There *was* a world in my eye. And I saw that it was possible to love it: that in fact, for all it had taught me of shame and anger and inner vision, I *did* love it. Even to see it drifting out of orbit in boredom, or rolling up out of fatigue, not to mention floating back at attention in excitement (bearing witness, a friend has called it), deeply suitable to my personality, and even characteristic of me.

That night I dream I am dancing to Stevie Wonder's song "Always" (the name of the song is really "As," but I hear it as "Always"). As I dance, whirling and joyous, happier than I've ever been in my life, another bright-faced dancer joins me. We dance and kiss each other and hold each other through the night. The other dancer has obviously come through all right, as I have done. She is beautiful, whole, and free. And she is also me. ■

The Reader's Presence

1. In her opening paragraph, Walker refers to her father's "beautiful eyes." How does that phrase take on more significance in rereading? Can you find other words, phrases, or images that do the same? For example, why might Walker have mentioned the pain of having her hair combed?

2. Note that Walker uses the present tense throughout the essay. Why might this be unusual, given her subject? What effect does it have for both writer and reader? Try rewriting the opening paragraph in the past tense. What difference do you think it makes?

3. **CONNECTIONS:** What is the meaning of Walker's occasional italicized comments? What do they have in common? Whose comments are they? To whom do they seem addressed? What time frame do they seem to be in? What purpose do you think they serve? How do they compare to those of Judith Ortiz Cofer in "Silent Dancing" (page 67)?

---

1 *Morehouse:* Morehouse College, a black men's college in Atlanta, Georgia. — EDS.

Jerald Walker

SCATTERED INCONVENIENCES

JERALD WALKER (b. 1964) was born and raised on Chicago's South Side. He attended the Iowa Writers' Workshop and later earned a PhD in interdisciplinary studies from the University of Iowa. The winner of a James A. Michener Fellowship, he has published works in numerous periodicals such as the *Iowa Review*, the *Chronicle of Higher Education*, *Mother Jones*, *Harvard Review*, and *Creative Nonfiction*, and his essays have been selected for both *The Best American Essays* and *The Best African American Essays*. He was the chair of the Writing, Literature, and Publishing faculty at Emerson College in Boston. His memoir, *Street Shadows: A Memoir of Race, Rebellion, and Redemption* (2010), received the 2011 L. L. Winship/PEN New England Award and was followed by a second memoir, *The World in Flames: A Black Boyhood in a White Supremacist Doomsday Cult* (2016). "Scattered Inconveniences" appeared in the *North American Review* in 2006.

> Jerald Walker was born and raised on Chicago's South Side.

HE BARRELED up on our left, momentarily matched our speed, then surged forward and waved a cowboy hat out the window, a bull rider in a brown Chevy. Somehow I knew he would swerve into our lane and slow down, and as he did the sound of his horn came to us over the rumble of our truck's engine. We were in a seventeen-foot Ryder that held everything we owned, junk, pretty much, with ten feet to spare. Those were, we believed, the final days of poverty. After not being able to find a teaching job for three years since completing her doctorate in art history, my wife had landed a rare tenure-track position at a state college in New England, twelve hundred miles east of Iowa City where we'd spent ten years living with tornadoes, academics, and hippies. I was going to be a stay-at-home dad, watching our fifteen-month-old during the day and writing at night. It was the perfect scenario, one we'd dreamt of for so long. All I had to do now was prevent the man in the Chevy from killing us.

I gripped the steering wheel tighter, checked the rearview mirrors in case a sudden maneuver was necessary. There were no vehicles within twenty yards, besides our reckless escort, just ten feet away.

"This guy's drunk or something," Brenda said.

I shook my head. "I *told* you we shouldn't drive in the middle of the night."

"It's only eight."

5

I checked the clock on the dashboard. "8:10."

"Well, you could just *slow down*," she said, "and let him go."

"Or," I responded, "I could crush him."

"And injure your son in the process?"

I glanced to my right. Adrian slept between us in his child seat, oblivious   10
that we were being menaced by a fool, and that his daddy, in certain situations,
particularly those that involved motor vehicles and testosterone, was a fool,
too. I tugged at his harness, and confirmed that it was secure, then gunned the
engine and lurched the truck forward. Brenda punched my arm. I lifted my foot
off the accelerator and watched the speedometer topple from 70 to 55, where
I leveled off. For a few seconds there was a gentlemanly distance between
us and the Chevy, and then it slowed, too, until it was again ten feet from our
bumper. This time I held my ground. I could feel Brenda tensing. I lowered
my window and gave him the finger, Adrian stirring as wind tore into the cab.
Brenda called me an ass, though not audibly. We'd been together long enough
that the actual use of words, at times like those, was unnecessary.

The Chevy suddenly braked and I had to as well to avoid a collision.
My heart was racing now. I tried hard to believe that we weren't dealing
with something more ominous than a souse. We were in Indiana, a state I
vaguely remembered hearing was a breeding ground for racists; perhaps
the random sight of a black family had proved too irresistible, a cat straying
into an angry dog's view.

But I had heard similar things about Iowa, only later to experience no
problems. "No problems" is not to say "nothing," though, for there were what
a black intellectual referred to as "scattered inconveniences" —women crossing the street or removing their purses from grocery carts at my approach,
security guards following me in department stores. Once, while I was working
out in the university's gym, two young men, looking my way and laughing,
began mimicking the walk of a gorilla. Silly, all of it, confirmation that the bigotry my parents faced no longer exists, that its sledgehammer impact has been
reduced, for the most part, to pebbles pitched from a naughty child's hand.
I tell myself to find victory in encounters such as these. And I usually do. But
sometimes I can't because of one simple truth: I am a racist.

Like a recovering alcoholic, I recognize that to define myself by my disease is in some way to help guard against relapse, that there is daily salvation in this constant reminder of who and what I am. My quest to be rid of
all traces of this scourge has not been easy, though I have made good progress, considering I was born during the sixties in a segregated Chicago. The
communities I grew up in were dangerous and poor, and it was the common
opinion of nearly everyone I knew that, when all was said and done, whites
were to blame. Whites discriminated against us. Whites denied us decent
housing. Whites caused us to have high unemployment and failed schools.
Crack had come from whites, and so too had AIDS. Whites, in some vague
and yet indisputable way, made the winos drink and gangbangers kill. I
came to believe, at a very early age, that in order to succeed I would have to

beat the system through the mastery of some criminal enterprise, or join it in the form of a Sambo, a sell-out, an Oreo, an Uncle Tom. In other words, I'd have to be my brother Clyde.

Clyde, who said things like, "Whites aren't an obstacle to success," and "Only *you* can stop *you.*"

We didn't like Clyde.

We watched him with disgust as he became a teenager and continued to speak without slang or profanity. He wore straight-legs and loafers instead of bell-bottoms and four-inch stacks, his only concession to soulful style an afro, which *could* have been bigger. He held a job during high school and still earned straight A's. After graduation he studied computers when his friends aspired to be postal clerks or pimps.

Our father threw him out. He was twenty-one. My twin brother and I, at fourteen, just on the threshold of a decade of lawlessness, had come home one night drunk. Clyde beat us sober with a pool stick. Outside of a few times at church, it was many years before we saw him socially again. I didn't know where he spent his exile. I was not surprised, though, when he resurfaced in the eighties in a Ford AeroStar with a Ronald Reagan sticker on his bumper. He'd rejected liberal black ideology his whole life, and so his emergence as a staunch conservative made perfect sense, as much sense as me, twenty years later, being tempted to crush a white man on I-80.

The Chevy switched lanes again, this time to the right. The driver was shouting at us through his opened window. I ignored him. He blew his horn.

Brenda asked, "What do you think he wants?"

"Our lives," I said.

He blew his horn again.

"I'm going to open my window and see what he wants."

"Do *not* do that!"

She opened her window. I couldn't make out what he was saying, and Brenda was practically hanging out the window to hear him. I leaned towards them while trying to keep the truck steady. Brenda suddenly whirled to face me. Her eyes were wide. "Stop the truck!" she demanded.

"Why?"

"The back door is open! The washer's about to fall out!"

We were towing our car behind us; the perilousness of the situation was instantly clear.

I put on my right signal and began to work my way to the shoulder. The man tooted his horn and gave me a thumbs-up, then rode off into the night. Adrian was crying and I wondered for how long. His pacifier had fallen. Brenda rooted it from his seat and slipped it between his lips. He puffed on it fiendishly, like it was long-denied nicotine.

We'd come to a stop. Our hazards were flashing. Cars and trucks rocked us gently as they hurled themselves east, towards the Promised Land. Before I opened my door, Brenda and I exchanged a quick glance. I did not have to actually say I was sorry. She did not have to actually say she forgave me. ■

The Reader's Presence

1. Why does Walker title his essay "Scattered Inconveniences"? Where in the essay do we find the phrase used? Who said it and in what context does it appear? What meaning does it take on with respect to racism? Do you think the incident Walker describes is an example of a scattered inconvenience in the same sense that the phrase appears in the essay? Why or why not?

2. In paragraph 12, Walker admits to being "a racist." In what sense is he one? Is his racism shown in the essay? If so, how? If not, why does he introduce the subject? Consider Walker's brother Clyde, who plays a fairly large part in this brief essay. What does Clyde's presence have to do with Walker's main point in the essay?

3. **CONNECTIONS:** Consider Walker's essay along with Brent Staples's "Just Walk on By: A Black Man Ponders His Power to Alter Public Space" (page 217). How would you differentiate the racial factors in each essay? How does Staples's essay conform to Walker's advice on how to tell a good story?

The Writer at Work

Jerald Walker on Telling a Good Story

Brenda Molife

As a creative writing instructor, Jerald Walker wants his students to concentrate more on story *telling* and less on the lesson or point they want to make. Nevertheless, invited by the editors to discuss his own essay and what it means to him as a reader (and not as a writer), Walker discovers that it contains a moral or point he did not set out to make. His brief explanation makes us aware that writing to a large extent is an act of discovery. But that discovery could only happen in the process of constructing the story.

❝One thing I constantly urge my creative writing students to do is to lay off the metaphors. Go easy on morals, lessons, and "points" — it's the reader's job to worry about those. Your job is simply to try to tell a good story. That was what I tried to do in "Scattered Inconveniences." However, much to my delight (I was tempted to say "surprise," but I've come to expect surprises in the act of writing, so now I'm merely delighted when they occur), I later discovered it to be highly metaphorical. As a *reader* of this essay, I could make a case that the man in the Chevy represents the sin of American racism — slavery, discrimination, and other forms of bigotry that may at any moment barrel forth to make terribly disruptive appearances in our lives. When it cannot appear itself, which these days is more often the case than not, for an exceedingly long and reckless life has left it frail and feeble, it sends an able representative, known as paranoia. I have experienced a great deal of paranoia in the black community. On Chicago's South Side, where I was raised, there always seemed to be the suspicion, if not the outright prediction, that the blatant racism practiced in previous generations would make a triumphant comeback—indeed, in the minds of some people it never left. The paranoia created by racism, it seems to me, is often worse than racism itself, in the way that not knowing something is often worse than knowing. The phrase, "*Please*, Doc, just give it to me straight!" comes to mind.

But as my wife, son, and I traveled in our truck through Indiana, I could not have it given to me straight. I did not know the intentions of the man in the Chevy. And so, regrettably, I assumed the worst. Here my actions were metaphorical, too, for what better way to express how so many racial conflicts could be averted if we simply learned to give each other the benefit of the doubt. For me, that is sometimes easier said than done, but it is what I—what we all—must constantly aspire to if complete racial reconciliation will ever be achieved. Which leads me to another metaphor, as embodied in Adrian, my toddler, sleeping so peacefully until I lost my cool; he is, of course, the future. As a result of fear and mistrust, the future is placed in jeopardy. Perhaps that is ultimately the lesson of "Scattered Inconveniences"; maybe that is its moral or "point." I will leave that for each reader to decide, because, as the *writer*, I did not set out with any of these in mind. I was simply trying to tell a good story. **🟍🟍**

LAUREN CARTER
Isn't Watermelon Delicious?

Lauren Carter graduated from Bridgewater State University in Massachusetts with a degree in English. While at Bridgewater, Carter served as editor in chief of the literary magazine *The Bridge*, where her essay "Isn't Watermelon Delicious?" first appeared. After graduating, she began to write for a newspaper full time and currently works as a freelance writer for several publications. Her topics include music and race, and she encourages fellow student writers not to "look at writing as drudgery [but to] view it as an opportunity to express yourself."

Carter wrote the following essay as a response to an assignment in an undergraduate African American literature course taught at Bridgewater State University by Jerald Walker, the author of the preceding selection. Professor Walker, who teaches in the Writing, Literature, and Publishing department at Emerson College, generously supplied us with the actual assignment.

Assignment: Malon Riggs's documentary *Black Is . . . Black Ain't . . .* ends with the following quotation: "If you have received no clear cut impression of what The Negro in America is like, then you are in the same place with me. There is no The Negro here" (Zora Neale Hurston). Hurston's point, it seems to me, is that Negroes (or coloreds or blacks or Afro-Americans or African Americans) come in such varieties that they are impossible to define as a homogeneous group. Much of this variety can be said to be the result of blues/jazz idiom, how blacks are constantly improvising new identities in an effort to adapt to changing conditions and needs. Likewise, African American fiction writers are constantly improvising on the theme of "blackness" in order to produce works that attempt to offer at least partial definitions of what it means to be African American. In your essay, work your way through the literature read in this class and discuss how each author adds to our understanding of what it means to be black.

As you read Carter's response to the assignment, observe how she blends her personal experiences of being a young black woman with a number of relevant literary works she read for Professor Walker's course. Her essay is prompted by a friend's comment about behavior corresponding to race. Where else does Carter encounter this idea? What questions does she raise about how people understand race?

<table>
<tr><td>Opens effectively with a vivid description of a specific setting.</td><td>It was just another Thursday night at Axis. White lights were flashing, music was pumping, and I was mildly buzzed. My best friend Stacey and I were making our way around the edges of the crowded dance floor, looking for a table where we could plop down and briefly escape the frenzy of the hot, crowded club. Then my favorite song came on. I don't remember what song it was; it was a long time ago and I usually had a new favorite song every other week. But at the time, the song that started playing was my favorite one, and I was ecstatic. As soon as I heard the bass line I guzzled what was left of my drink, broke out into some kind of over-enthusiastic dance move, and shouted "Let's go!"</td></tr>
</table>

Stacey looked over at me and laughed.

"God, Lauren," she said, "sometimes you're so white, and sometimes you're soooo black."

Introduces her central topic through dialogue.

It was an interesting idea. That I could be one or the other, at different times. I wondered when I was which one. So I asked her.

She started to answer, but the music was too loud, and I couldn't really make out what she was saying. I leaned in closer and asked her to repeat what she said, but she waved the idea away, saying we should go dance.

Yes, we should dance, I thought. My favorite song was on and we were attempting to have a conversation meant for a quiet café, not a loud, crowded club.

We never did have that conversation, and I never did get the answer I was looking for. What, exactly, I did that was so white. And what, exactly, I did that was so black. But the idea stuck with me. That a behavior related to a skin tone. That my behavior related to two different ones.

It wasn't a totally new idea. My black cousin Shea had told me for years that I acted "so white." I thought I was just acting like me, but apparently, with my Bart Simpson t-shirt, my "proper" speech, and my affinity for Vanilla Ice, I was masquerading as a white girl in a black girl's body. I didn't know those characteristics belonged exclusively to white people. I thought they belonged to people who liked the occasional Simpsons t-shirt, spoke the way they had learned to speak, and enjoyed listening to extremely cheesy, albeit catchy, quasi-rap music.

Or at least that's how I feel now. But then, I felt inferior — way behind in the race for true blackness. I would never catch up to her. I'd never know all the latest black sayings, never listen to all the latest black music, never wear all the latest black clothing. I'd never be as black as she was. Or so I thought.

But that's before I met the Ex-Colored Man.[1] In his auto-biography, he switched from white to black and back again, though his skin color never changed. When he discovered his blackness as a child, he still looked like a white person. But internally, he realized there was black blood running through his veins, or rather blue blood with black ancestry in it, and he withdrew. He wasn't what he thought he'd been. He couldn't stop thinking about his new blackness. Really, though, nothing had changed. Externally, at least.

So it kind of surprised me when, at the end of his story, he chose to become white again. This, after feeling morti-fied and ashamed that in a country like America, with all its talk of democracy and freedom, the black race could be persecuted so harshly. While I could attempt to analyze and judge his decision to forsake his blackness in order to better his condition, decide whether he had succumbed to the race

[Margin note:] Fulfills writing assignment by introducing course readings that she clearly connects to her personal experience.

[1] ***Ex-Colored Man:*** Referenced in Works Cited (page 249). —EDS.

game or merely decided to stop playing, the validity of his decision isn't as important as the fact that it could be made. That he could become white again, simply by deciding to be. It was a miraculous transformation. Which got me to thinking, if you can miraculously transform from black to white, or vice versa, then how real is either category?

My sister transforms all the time, depending on who's looking at her. She's black in terms of ancestry. Partially, anyway. Our mother's Italian, her father's black. And though her hair came out extremely nappy, her skin is light. Whiter than some "white" people's skin, in fact. Now that she chemically straightens her hair, most people don't know she's black unless she tells them. She can pass. Not among black people, of course, myself included. We can all see it in her features. But to the untrained eye, amongst the world at large, she can generally be perceived as white. So which is she? Is she what her ancestry dictates, or what other people's perception decides?

Poses a question that goes to the heart of her essay.

It's a ridiculous question, I know. But only as ridiculous as the fallacy it's based on. When you lump a group of people together based solely on the color of their skin, of course ridiculous questions like these come up. It'd be the same if you lumped them together based on eye color, height, or any other arbitrary characteristic over which they have no control.

Funny, that we would choose to separate and define people based on factors beyond their control. Well, maybe not funny. But certainly ingenious. And an excellent way to subordinate one group in order to elevate another. Because isn't it true that all of these external factors, in actuality, say nothing about a person's character, that the only real measure of a person is in their actions, not any physical characteristic? Isn't it true that anyone who has survived and succeeded in any facet of life did so almost exclusively because of their intellect, their intelligence, their will to persevere, not because of the pigment in their skin or the fullness of their features?

When Frederick Douglass found ways to teach himself to read, it wasn't because of his melanin content. It was because of his desire to learn, his ingenuity, his intelligence.

After six months of torture by his brutal master Covey, Douglass made the bold and beautiful statement: "You

References more of her reading by providing summaries that also support her contention about character and determination.

have seen how a man was made a slave; now you shall see how a slave was made a man."

And when he did make that journey from slavery to manhood, it wasn't because of the coil of his hair, it was because of the color of his character. When Gabriel Prosser[2] decided to lead a revolt in pursuit of freedom, it wasn't because of the size of his muscles, it was because of the size of his spirit. When blacks survived slavery, it wasn't because of the width of their noses or how many calluses they did or didn't have on their hands. It was because of the survival strategies they'd developed over time, none of which had anything to do with appearance.

The folktales and spirituals that emerged out of that era weren't developed because of the shape of someone's kneecaps; they were developed because of a will to overcome seemingly insurmountable obstacles. And when Bigger Thomas, the main character in Richard Wright's famous novel, *Native Son*, became the agent of his own demise, it wasn't, contrary to his own beliefs, because of the darkness of his skin; it was because of the darkness of his mind, and all of the things he believed he would never, and so never did, achieve.

Maybe life would be simpler if skin color really was an indicator of character, external factors determined internal worth, and similar complexions could unite us all. Then all the dark-skinned peoples of America could heed Marcus Garvey's[3] message and return home to Africa. We could take a giant plane to Uganda, and when it landed we could step down off it with open arms and scream, "Hello black people, I'm finally home!!" But in reality, that probably wouldn't work. Those Ugandans would only point out what I've come to realize over the past semester: that the significance of skin color is that it is the color of one's skin, and not much more. That it does not necessarily imply a common set of values, a standard behavior, a singular way of life.

And why should it? Aren't there a number of ways that human beings can define themselves as individuals? What about gender? Profession? Religious beliefs? Hobbies?

Uses a series of questions to reinforce her main point.

2 **Gabriel Prosser** (1776–1800): A blacksmith who was executed for planning a slave rebellion near Richmond, Virginia, in 1800. — EDS.
3 **Marcus Garvey** (1887–1940): A Jamaican journalist known for his Black Nationalism movement. — EDS.

Personality? Sexual orientation? Values? What about your attitude towards yourself, towards others, towards life? Isn't it true that race is just one ingredient in a large and complicated recipe? Why must it be the main ingredient and define all the other areas of life? I know that my life is about much more than being black, and, for that matter, being black is about much more than my skin color.

Which leads to the question: What is my blackness about? When am I really black? When I start celebrating Kwanzaa? When I fill my wardrobe with Roc-A-Wear and Phat Farm? When I stop playing Elton John? Is that what blackness is? A holiday? A piece of clothing? A song?

Funny, I never thought of being black that way. I never considered that a Dashiki would give me blackness, and I never thought that a lack of one would take it away. I always thought of black as a state of mind; a way of looking at the world. Perseverance in the face of any and all obstacles. Winning when everyone says you're bound to lose. I never looked at the color of my skin as evidence of a drum, or a slice of watermelon. I never thought I had to do, have, or say anything at all to be black. I just thought I was.

Responds to cousin's remark introduced in paragraph 8.

I never told her so, but when Shea said I was acting "so white," she was wrong. Whites don't have a monopoly on listening to Vanilla Ice, and even if they could have one, I doubt they'd want it. I was acting like me. I don't need to walk the streets with a sandwich board proclaiming what I am. I don't need to act out my blackness, just like I don't need to act out my eye color; it's simply an intrinsic part of who I am.

True, the color of my skin implies an ancestry that the color of my eyes does not, and I'm aware of that ancestry; I draw from it daily. But I don't need to wear Lugz and use slang to prove it. Maya Angelou wrote "I am the dream and the hope of the slave," and I haven't forgotten about those hopes and dreams. I understand the debt that I owe to my ancestors, and I pay it back every day, in my own way, that has nothing to do with what jeans I wear, and has everything to do with how I live my life. The size of my nose is not my inheritance. The will to survive is.

Stacey's statement in that nightclub was probably my first—or at least my most memorable—experience with double consciousness as civil rights activist W. E. B. DuBois described it, of being conscious not only of how you see yourself, but how others see you; I'd never thought of myself solely in terms of white and black, but I realized the extent to which other people could. For a long time after that night I wondered where the line between black and white was, and in what moments I crossed it. I don't wonder about that line anymore. Blackness no longer boils down to a t-shirt, or a desire to dance. It's just not that simple. Blackness is the legacy left by the people that came before me, and it's the legacy I'll leave behind me when I'm gone.

Concludes by returning to her friend's comment in opening scene and effectively introduces the concept of "double consciousness" she learned from her reading.

Works Cited

Angelou, Maya. "Still I Rise." *The Complete Collected Poems of Maya Angelou.* Random House, 1994.

Bontemps, Arna. *Black Thunder.* Beacon Press, 1992.

Douglass, Frederick. *Narrative of the Life of Frederick Douglass, an American Slave.* Barnes & Noble Classics, 2003.

DuBois, W. E. B. *The Souls of Black Folk.* Bedford/St. Martin's, 1997.

Johnson, James Weldon. *The Autobiography of an Ex-Colored Man.* Vintage Books, 1989.

Wright, Richard. *Native Son.* Harper Perennial Classics, 2003.

Jillian Weise

Why I Own a Gun

For **JILLIAN WEISE** (b. 1981), who plugs her computerized prosthetic leg into the wall at night to charge, the right to bear arms isn't so much an expression of freedom as it is a matter of survival. "Fight or flight" usually implies choice—but what if you cannot run? What if your attacker is larger, faster, and stronger? Originally published in *Tin House*, "Why I Own a Gun" describes some of the more complicated reasons behind gun ownership.

Poet, essayist, and playwright, Weise
has authored two collections of poetry, *The
Amputee's Guide to Sex* (2007) and *The Book
of Goodbyes* (2013), named a best book of
2013 by *Publishers Weekly* and NPR. She

> **"If you want to write the Great
> American Novel, write it."**

published her first novel, *The Colony*, in 2010. Her work has appeared in journals, anthologies,
and magazines, including *A Public Space* and *The New York Times*.

Weise urges writers to pursue their dreams, regardless of any disability. "To any writer
with a disability," she says, "write whatever you want. The movie theater is full but there's no
movie. If you want to write the screenplay, write it. If you want to write the Great American
Novel, write it."

I KEEP A SMITH & WESSON in a drawer next to my bed. It's a
.38 Special with a button that turns on a laser. There is no safety. Each
night, I set the alarm, lock the bedroom door, charge my phone, and plug my
prosthetic leg into the wall. Then I open the drawer and take out the revolver.
I keep my index finger along the barrel. If I ever need to use this gun, I will
be scared. But I will know how to hold it. I have planned the order of my
actions should someone break into my home: call 911 and tell them, "There
is an intruder and I have a gun." Aim the laser at the bedroom door. I have
been around guns all my life, but it was not until graduate school that I felt
the need to connect with them. Everyone is supposed to like graduate school
because the school gives you money, or the government loans you money,
and all you have to do is show up, take the exams, and write something.
I asked if I could specialize in disability studies (in truth, I just wanted to find
a woman with a disability who had written something) and the director said:
"There is no disability studies. And if there is, you will find it in theory." This
was both a damning and a poetic statement. In one sentence, the director
eliminated an entire field. In the next, he confined disability to the mind, to
theory, as if to say it's not real.

After that conversation I wanted to go as far away as possible, some
place the director would never go, and do something against his values and
theories. Target World was a fifteen-minute drive in light traffic down the
highway, located in a shopping plaza next to Harry's Corner Flooring. The
building was white concrete with a green roof. Inside I watched the mandatory video on gun safety: keep your finger off the trigger; load and unload
your gun in the range; wear ear and eye protection; be considerate of fellow customers. I rented a revolver and bought the bullets, the target, and a
half hour of time. In the gun range, there was no room for emotion or stray
thoughts. Everything became still.

Target practice is like yoga. It has accoutrements similar to the mat and
the yoga pants. Remington makes an excellent set of noise-canceling pink
earmuffs. I've been saving for a holster from Can Can Concealment. Target

Jillian Weise.

practice requires you to place your body in a specific position, such as the Isosceles, the Weaver, or the Tactical stance. Target practice is about breath. I favor the method of breathing that involves a pause. I can't hold my breath to shoot; that doesn't work for me. Instead I take a pause in the middle of exhaling to shoot the revolver. Target practice is clarifying. I walk out of the range with a sense of empowerment and confidence.

Each month I receive *America's First Freedom*. I am a card-carrying member of the National Rifle Association. It feels socially dangerous to admit this. Often I go to dinner with writers and academics who rage against gun ownership. These are smart people whose opinions I respect. They have thought deeply about the subject. They discuss studies that show how guns increase homicides, suicides, and massacres. They talk about Virginia Tech and Sandy Hook and Columbine. They tend to agree: people who own guns are misinformed or wrong or ignorant. So I dare not speak up. I wonder about the self-defense options for people like me. I am four foot six and I weigh one hundred pounds and I walk with a computerized limb. I'm not going to outrun anybody. Actually, I don't even know how to run. The best I can do is a combination of a walk and a skip. I doubt I could fight back in any meaningful way. Listening to these conversations, I feel as if the Voices of Reason are telling me: "Can't run? Can't fight back? Guess you'll have to die in that situation. We've made up our minds."

In graduate school I kept at target practice but I did not purchase a gun. Then I was out on the road for a book tour and, one night, late, a man knocked on the door of my hotel room.

5

I called the front desk. Nobody answered. The man jiggled the doorknob. I called the police. It was a small town and there had been a fatal traffic accident nearby. The police were busy. I thought about calling random numbers in the phone book. I thought about calling for pizza and being rescued by the delivery person. I thought about calling my mom. I thought about the self-protection available to me: a coat hanger, a hair dryer, and a lamp. Thirty minutes passed. The man came back and banged on the door some more. Why had he picked my door? Had he seen me earlier in the day? Did he think of me as an easy target? An hour later the police arrived. I packed my things and loaded them into my car. I was going to a bigger town, a nicer hotel with inside corridors.

"Sorry. I was scared," I said to the police.

"You were right to be scared," one of them said. He pointed his flashlight to the window of my hotel room. The man had ejaculated on it.

When I got home, I asked my dad to buy me a gun.   10

The Oscar Pistorius[1] trial is on CNN. When the case first broke, I said to my guy: "I believe him. He didn't have his legs on and he was scared. He shot through the bathroom door."

"Before you shoot," my guy said, "check to make sure I'm beside you in the bed."

The news features a reconstructed crime scene, examples of prosthetic limbs, bullet trajectories, and an endless number of specialists. But where are the disabled specialists? Where is someone to explain the perpetual fear that comes with being disabled? The news is more interested in the gender of the victim and the race of the judge. For reasons that I do not understand, disability remains hard to talk about and largely avoided by the media. Disabled narratives are either (a) he's amazing or (b) isn't it so sad? or (c) a little of both. Maybe Pistorius killed in cold blood. But his guilt or innocence is the least fascinating part of the case to me. What fascinates me is that the act of violence neutralized his disability. Pistorius used to be amazing. Now he's just another man who shot his girlfriend.

Here is my problem with guns: Not enough women use them.

Each day three women are murdered by men. I believe that when a   15
woman receives her driver's license from the DMV, she should also receive a lightweight, easy-to-use revolver. I cannot recommend my .38, because it's too much recoil for a sixteen-year-old woman. A .22 or .32 single action would suffice. The gun will come with a grip identifier, so that when the woman grips the gun, it will shoot. When anybody else grips the gun, it will not shoot. If we can put fingerprint scanners on locks, then we can figure this out. The DMV will administer written and practical tests, for women only, on driving a car and shooting a gun. The US government will waive the fee

---

[1] *Oscar Pistorius* (b. 1986): A South African sprinting champion who wears prosthetic legs and was convicted of murdering his girlfriend. Pistorius won fame in the Paralympic Games for athletes with disabilities and went on to compete in the Olympic Games. In 2013, Pistorius shot his girlfriend, Reeva Steenkamp, in their home in the middle of the night, saying he believed she was an intruder. He is currently serving a six-year sentence. — EDS.

for women to receive concealed-carry permits. Women will decide whether to conceal the gun or wear it prominently. Women will be exempt from all Gun-Free Zones.

When a woman kills in self-defense, she will receive a thirty-second ad during the Super Bowl. If surveillance footage is available, it will be shown. If not, the woman will describe in graphic detail how she killed her attacker. I come to this idea out of frustration with the that's-just-the-way-things-work mentality. Things are not working. Our approaches to ending violence against women have failed. Restraining orders have failed. Threats of prison time have failed. Preventative legislation, such as Title IX, has obviously failed. As women, we should not have to accept that some men want to rape and kill us. If a man tries to violate one of us, we should shoot for the heart. And publicize the hell out of it. Spread the word: Women are armed and dangerous.

I know about the negative consequences of gun ownership. Here I am, seven years old, watching my dad leave for work. He has a briefcase in one hand and a shotgun in the other. Mom drives me to school, through Houston traffic, and after school a guy named Michael picks me up. He is Dad's assistant. Sometimes I can convince Michael to take us to Whataburger. Once we are at my dad's pharmacy, I am stuck behind the bulletproof glass in the back office. When business is slow, I can sometimes get permission to play in the hallway next to the pharmacy.

Dad uses an instrument that looks like a butter knife to slide pills across a plastic tray. The pills collect in the ditch of the tray and Dad funnels them into a bottle. He might count five or ten pills at once and they go into the ditch. He never talks while he is counting. Another five pills go into the ditch. His father was a pharmacist and his father before him. He always knew he would be a pharmacist, but he tells me, "You can be anything you want. But don't be a pharmacist."

The insurance companies will not let Dad's regulars choose his pharmacy anymore. They are trying to run him out of business. When I grow up, there won't be any independent pharmacies left. They will all be replaced by chain stores. One of the regulars walks in and wants to know how I'm doing. Instead of asking me, the regular asks my dad: "How's she doing? How was the surgery?"

I do not think it is any of her business, so I stay hidden behind the counter 20 in the back office. I was born with birth defects, so I am always being fixed. The regular leaves and I can stop hiding. I walk the aisles in the back office where we keep the prescription drugs. I inspect the labels. The words on the labels are long and impossible to read.

One day after school, I am bored of playing with the calculator. Sometimes I order decorations from the Oriental Trading Company. The catalog shows every kind of decoration you could want: Easter eggs to place on the counter, American flags for the store windows. There are toys to buy in a gross. A gross is 144 toys. When I grow up, I am going to keep this catalog at home and order a gross of toys each month.

I ask if I can play in the hallway and Dad says yes. The pharmacy has two entrances. One is to the outside parking lot. The other is to the hallway. Both entrances are glass doors. The pharmacy is like a fishbowl with another fishbowl inside it. First the windows to the world, and second the bulletproof glass where Dad and I stay: The rest of the building is owned by a friendly doctor. His office is way down the hall, the last door, after ten doors.

The hall is the perfect place for bouncing a ball. I am out there, playing with the ball, waiting for Mom to get off work, to pick me up and take me home, where we will eat chips and salsa and watch *Oprah*. I think a lot of time has passed, so I head back to the pharmacy. I am just inside the first fishbowl when I look back and see a man approaching the door. I do not recognize him, but he probably knows about my surgeries. I want to avoid him. He opens the door to the pharmacy. I walk in front of him; I can hear his footsteps behind me. He follows me toward the back, the second fishbowl. The bulletproof glass door is open.

Then I hear my dad's voice:

"Get back here now." The tone of his voice is different. He says *now*   25
extra loud as if I have spent too much time in the hall.

I step in and my dad slams the door behind me. The sound of the door scares me. The man tries the handle. It's locked. It locks automatically. Then he just stands there, inches from us, staring at us. He is wearing a jacket and jeans. He could be anybody.

My dad breaks the silence, "Can I help you?"

"I'm looking for matches," the man says,

"We don't have matches." Dad's voice is stern. "Try the cafe across the street."

The man leaves. We watch him get in the passenger side of a car that is   30
parked backwards. It speeds out of the lot.

Dad says, "We just about got robbed."

Years before we almost get robbed, before Dad installs the bulletproof glass, and before I'm born, a man comes in with a .44 revolver.

"I want your Dilaudid,"[2] the man says.

Dad's shotgun is in the back office on its perch above the door. "That's the problem with having a gun," Dad tells me. "Once you realize you're getting robbed, you don't have access to it." He has been robbed many times. How many? I ask, but he forgets. More than a dozen times. Once again his gun is too far away. So he is on his knees in front of the locked cabinet where he keeps the narcotics.

"I want your Dilaudid," the man says again. His gun hand is shaking.   35

"I don't have any Dilaudid," Dad says.

Dad has told his employees what to do in case of a robbery: Don't initiate conversation. Don't be obvious, but look at the person. Take note of things he can't change, like the color of his eyes, the condition of his teeth, the

---

2 **Dilaudid:** an addictive opioid pain medication available only by prescription. — Eds.

shape of his mouth. All these details will help at the lineup. On this day, Dad is there alone.

The man cocks the hammer of the revolver and puts it to Dad's temple. "Mister," he says, "you better have some Dilaudid."

Dad puts the key in the lock and opens the cabinet. He hopes to get to the lineup. He knows this man's face. "Look for yourself," he says.

The man gives him a pillowcase and says, "Put everything in it."   40

Given all this, I never intended to own a gun. Guns were for my dad, for men, for protecting property. I don't know what happened in graduate school. I was being asked to pass as nondisabled and to study nondisabled writers and to accept it. Initially, I went to the shooting range to breach what was expected of me. I didn't take it seriously. I don't know if anyone takes a woman my size, the size of an adolescent, carrying a gun, seriously. The few times I have disclosed my gun ownership, I am bombarded with assumptions about why I must own a gun. I must be a Republican. I must be dense. I must not have thought through the consequences. I must be kidding. I must be reclaiming power that was denied me in my childhood. I must be ignorant of the statistics. I must be unrealistic. Somebody's going to shoot me with my gun. Somebody's going to use it against me. Why can't I carry pepper spray and a whistle? Why can't I leave it to the police?

Recently, I've been dealing with a stalker. He shows up places near my work. One time he recounted to me the kind of sandwich I'd eaten in a restaurant. I had not known he was in the restaurant. He stands by my car and stares at it. I park in a handicapped space. Due to state law, a photo of my face is on the handicapped tag that hangs from my rearview mirror. He could find my car and stare at my face in any lot. Here is a statistic I would rather not know: Disabled women are four times as likely to be sexually assaulted than nondisabled women. The Office of Access and Equity says not to worry because "nothing has happened." I have an uneasy feeling, as if I am waiting for something to happen.

I already own a gun but it has been for my home. If I'm up late and hear a noise, I put the gun on the coffee table. I don't need a permit to keep a gun on my coffee table. I do, however, need a permit to holster a gun or put it in the glove compartment of my car. So I sign up for training to get my permit to carry. I could be fired for carrying a gun to work even if I have a permit. When I'm not at work, I intend to carry.

The training takes place nights at a gun shop called Allen Arms. There are only three of us, including the instructor. All three of us are disabled.

"Why are you here?" the instructor asks.   45

I say that I want to protect myself. The other student says he's back home from three tours and he just wants to get his permit.

"No," the instructor says. "That's not it."

The veteran and I look at each other, I'm thinking: *I wish I didn't have to be here. I wish I were a man. I wish I could run away.*

"You're here to learn how to shoot another person. That's it," the instructor says. ▪

The Reader's Presence

1. "I wonder about the self-defense options for people like me" (paragraph 5). Weise frames her essay with discussions of gender and disability. Why are these important factors to consider in the larger debate about gun ownership? What specific compositional strategies does Weise use to create an animating intellectual presence for herself as she advocates for gun ownership? Weise ends her essay with the sentence: "'You're here to learn how to shoot another person. That's it.' the instructor says." In what specific ways did this ending surprise you? Review Weise's essay. What do you notice about how she prepares her readers for this surprise?

2. Weise recounts various stories about her experience involving guns. She opens with an account of her nightly routine involving a ".38 Special with a button that turns on a laser" (paragraph 1). How would you characterize Weise's sentences during these moments? What do they have in common in terms of their structure and diction? Later, she narrates a story about her father, who went to work with "a briefcase in one hand and a shotgun in the other." Choose another anecdote Weise unfolds and explain why you think she writes so effectively. Why does she include such stories? How does she interpret them with respect to her own experiences as an adult? What assumptions lead her to the conclusion that the benefits of owning a gun outweigh the potential consequences?

3. **CONNECTIONS:** Compare and contrast the depiction and the consequences of disability in Weise's essay to Nancy Mairs's "On Being a Cripple" (page 170). How are these authors' views shaped by their experiences with disability? What are the similarities and differences in the ways both essayists approach disability with respect to gender?

E. B. White

ONCE MORE TO THE LAKE

ELWYN BROOKS WHITE (1899–1985) started contributing to the *New Yorker* soon after the magazine began publication in 1925, and in the "Talk of the Town" and other columns helped establish the magazine's reputation for precise and brilliant prose. Collections of his contributions can be found in *Every Day Is Saturday* (1934), *Quo Vadimus?* (1939), and *The Wild Flag* (1946). He also wrote essays for *Harper's* on a regular basis; these essays include "Once More to the Lake"

> "I have always felt that the first duty of a writer was to ascend—to make flights, carrying others along if he could manage it."

and are collected in *One Man's Meat* (1941). In his comments on this work, the critic Jonathan Yardley observed that White is "one of the few writers of this or any century who has succeeded in transforming the ephemera of journalism into something that demands to be called literature."

Capable of brilliant satire, White could also be sad and serious, as in his compilation of forty years of writing, *Essays* (1977). Among his numerous awards and honors, White received the American Academy of Arts and Letters Gold Medal (1960), a Presidential Medal of Freedom (1963), and a National Medal for Literature (1971). He made a lasting contribution to children's literature with *Stuart Little* (1945), *Charlotte's Web* (1952), and *The Trumpet of the Swan* (1970).

White has written, "I have always felt that the first duty of a writer was to ascend—to make flights, carrying others along if he could manage it." According to White, the writer needs not only courage but also hope and faith to accomplish this goal: "Writing itself is an act of faith, nothing else. And it must be the writer, above all others, who keeps it alive—choked with laughter, or with pain."

ONE SUMMER, along about 1904, my father rented a camp on a lake in Maine and took us all there for the month of August. We all got ringworm from some kittens and had to rub Pond's Extract on our arms and legs night and morning, and my father rolled over in a canoe with all his clothes on; but outside of that the vacation was a success and from then on none of us ever thought there was any place in the world like that lake in Maine. We returned summer after summer—always on August 1st for one month. I have since become a salt-water man, but sometimes in summer there are days when the restlessness of the tides and the fearful cold of the sea water and the incessant wind that blows across the afternoon and into the evening make me wish for the placidity of a lake in the woods. A few weeks ago this feeling got so strong I bought myself a couple of bass hooks and a spinner and returned to the lake where we used to go, for a week's fishing and to revisit old haunts.

I took along my son, who had never had any fresh water up his nose and who had seen lily pads only from train windows. On the journey over to the lake I began to wonder what it would be like. I wondered how time would have marred this unique, this holy spot—the coves and streams, the hills that the sun set behind, the camps and the paths behind the camps. I was sure that the tarred road would have found it out and I wondered in what other ways it would be desolated. It is strange how much you can remember about places like that once you allow your mind to return into the grooves that lead back. You remember one thing, and that suddenly reminds you of another thing. I guess I remembered clearest of all the early mornings, when the lake was cool and motionless, remembered how the bedroom smelled of the lumber it was made of and the wet woods whose scent entered through the screen. The partitions in the camp were thin and did not extend clear to the top of the rooms, and as I was always the first up I would dress softly so as not to wake the others, and sneak out into the sweet outdoors and start out in the canoe, keeping close along the shore in the long shadows of the pines. I remembered being very careful never to rub my paddle against the gunwale for fear of disturbing the stillness of the cathedral.

The lake had never been what you would call a wild lake. There were cottages sprinkled about the shores, and it was in farming country although the shores of the lake were quite heavily wooded. Some of the cottages were owned by nearby farmers, and you would live at the shore and eat your meals at the farmhouse. That's what our family did. But although it wasn't wild, it was a fairly large and undisturbed lake and there were places in it which, to a child at least, seemed infinitely remote and primeval.

I was right about the tar: It led to within half a mile of the shore. But when I got back there, with my boy, and we settled into a camp near a farmhouse and into the kind of summertime I had known, I could tell that it was going to be pretty much the same as it had been before—I knew it, lying in bed the first morning, smelling the bedroom, and hearing the boy sneak quietly out and go off along the shore in a boat. I began to sustain the illusion that he was I, and therefore, by simple transposition, that I was my father. This sensation persisted, kept cropping up all the time we were there. It was not an entirely new feeling, but in this setting it grew much stronger. I seemed to be living a dual existence. I would be in the middle of some simple act, I would be picking up a bait box or laying down a table fork, or I would be saying something, and suddenly it would be not I but my father who was saying the words or making the gesture. It gave me a creepy sensation.

We went fishing the first morning. I felt the same damp moss covering   5
the worms in the bait can, and saw the dragonfly alight on the tip of my rod as it hovered a few inches from the surface of the water. It was the arrival of this fly that convinced me beyond any doubt that everything was as it always had been, that the years were a mirage and there had been no years. The small waves were the same, chucking the rowboat under the chin as we fished at anchor, and the boat was the same boat, the same color green and the ribs broken in the same places, and under the floor-boards the same fresh-water leavings and debris—the dead hellgrammite, the wisps of moss, the rusty discarded fishhook, the dried blood from yesterday's catch. We stared silently at the tips of our rods, at the dragonflies that came and went. I lowered the tip of mine into the water, tentatively, pensively dislodging the fly, which darted two feet away, poised, darted two feet back, and came to rest again a little farther up the rod. There had been no years between the ducking of this dragonfly and the other one—the one that was part of memory. I looked at the boy, who was silently watching his fly, and it was my hands that held his rod, my eyes watching. I felt dizzy and didn't know which rod I was at the end of.

We caught two bass, hauling them in briskly as though they were mackerel, pulling them over the side of the boat in a businesslike manner without any landing net, and stunning them with a blow on the back of the head. When we got back for a swim before lunch, the lake was exactly where we had left it, the same number of inches from the dock, and there was only the merest suggestion of a breeze. This seemed an utterly enchanted sea, this lake you could leave to its own devices for a few hours and come back to, and find that it had not stirred, this constant and trustworthy body of water. In the shallows, the dark, water-soaked sticks and twigs, smooth and old, were undulating in clusters on the bottom against the clean ribbed sand, and the track of the mussel was plain. A school of minnows swam by, each minnow with its small individual shadow, doubling the attendance, so clear and sharp in the sunlight. Some of the other campers were in swimming, along the shore, one of them with a cake of soap, and the water felt thin and clear and unsubstantial. Over the years there had been this person with the cake of soap, this cultist, and here he was. There had been no years.

Up to the farmhouse to dinner through the teeming, dusty field, the road under our sneakers was only a two-track road. The middle track was missing, the one with the marks of the hooves and splotches of dried, flaky manure. There had always been three tracks to choose from in choosing which track to walk in; now the choice was narrowed down to two. For a moment I missed terribly the middle alternative. But the way led past the tennis court, and something about the way it lay there in the sun reassured me; the tape had loosened along the backline, the alleys were green with plantains and other weeds, and the net (installed in June and removed in September) sagged in the dry noon, and the whole place steamed with midday heat and hunger and emptiness. There was a choice of pie for dessert, and one was blueberry and one was apple, and the waitresses were the same country girls, there having been no passage of time, only the illusion of it as in a dropped curtain—the waitresses were still fifteen; their hair had been washed, that was the only difference—they had been to the movies and seen the pretty girls with the clean hair.

Summertime, oh summertime, pattern of life indelible, the fade-proof lake, the woods unshatterable, the pasture with the sweetfern and the juniper forever and ever, summer without end; this was the background, and the life along the shore was the design, the cottages with their innocent and tranquil design, their tiny docks with the flagpole and the American flag floating against the white clouds in the blue sky, the little paths over the roots of the trees leading from camp to camp and the paths leading back to the outhouses and the can of lime for sprinkling, and at the souvenir counters at the store the miniature birch-bark canoes and the post cards that showed things looking a little better than they looked. This was the American family at play, escaping the city heat, wondering whether the newcomers in the camp at the head of the cove were "common" or "nice," wondering whether it was true that the people who drove up for Sunday dinner at the farmhouse were turned away because there wasn't enough chicken.

It seemed to me, as I kept remembering all this, that those times and those summers had been infinitely precious and worth saving. There had been jollity and peace and goodness. The arriving (at the beginning of August) had been so big a business in itself, at the railway station the farm wagon drawn up, the first smell of the pine-laden air, the first glimpse of the smiling farmer, and the great importance of the trunks and your father's enormous authority in such matters, and the feel of the wagon under you for the long ten-mile haul, and at the top of the last long hill catching the first view of the lake after eleven months of not seeing this cherished body of water. The shouts and cries of the other campers when they saw you, and the trunks to be unpacked, to give up their rich burden. (Arriving was less exciting nowadays, when you sneaked up in your car and parked it under a tree near the camp and took out the bags and in five minutes it was all over, no fuss, no loud wonderful fuss about trunks).

Peace and goodness and jollity. The only thing that was wrong now, really, was the sound of the place, an unfamiliar nervous sound of the outboard motors. This was the note that jarred, the one thing that would sometimes break the illusion and set the years moving. In those other summertimes all motors were inboard; and when they were at a little distance, the noise they made was a sedative, an ingredient of summer sleep. They were one-cylinder and two-cylinder engines, and some were make-and-break and some were jump-spark, but they all made a sleepy sound across the lake. The one-lungers throbbed and fluttered, and the twin-cylinder ones purred and purred, and that was a quiet sound too. But now the campers all had outboards. In the daytime, in the hot mornings, these motors made a petulant, irritable sound; at night, in the still evening when the afterglow lit the water, they whined about one's ears like mosquitoes. My boy loved our rented outboard, and his great desire was to achieve singlehanded mastery over it, and authority, and he soon learned the trick of choking it a little (but not too much), and the adjustment of the needle valve. Watching him I would remember the things you could do with the old one-cylinder engines with the heavy flywheel, how you could have it eating out of your hand if you got really close to it spiritually. Motor boats in those days didn't have clutches, and you would make a landing by shutting off the motor at the proper time and coasting in with a dead rudder. But there was a way of reversing them, if you learned the trick, by cutting the switch and putting it on again exactly on the final dying revolution of the flywheel, so that it would kick back against compression and begin reversing. Approaching a dock in a strong following breeze, it was difficult to slow up sufficiently by the ordinary coasting method, and if a boy felt he had complete mastery over his motor, he was tempted to keep it running beyond its time and then reverse it a few feet from the dock. It took a cool nerve, because if you threw the switch a twentieth of a second too soon you could catch the flywheel when it still had speed enough to go up past center, and the boat would leap ahead, charging bull-fashion at the dock.

We had a good week at the camp. The bass were biting well and the sun shone endlessly, day after day. We would be tired at night and lie down in the accumulated heat of the little bedrooms after the long hot day and the breeze would stir almost imperceptibly outside and the smell of the swamp drift in through the rusty screens. Sleep would come easily and in the morning the red squirrel would be on the roof, tapping out his gay routine. I kept remembering everything, lying in bed in the mornings—the small steamboat that had a long rounded stern like the lip of a Ubangi, and how quietly she ran on the moonlight sails, when the older boys played their mandolins and the girls sang and we ate doughnuts dipped in sugar, and how sweet the music was on the water in the shining night, and what it had felt like to think about girls then. After breakfast we would go up to the store and the things were in the same place—the minnows in a bottle, the plugs and spinners disarranged and pawed over by the youngsters from the boys' camp, the Fig Newtons and the Beeman's gum. Outside, the road was tarred and cars stood in front of the store. Inside, all was just as it had always been, except there was more Coca-Cola and not so much Moxie and root beer and birch beer and sarsaparilla. We would walk out with a bottle of pop apiece and sometimes the pop would backfire up our noses and hurt. We explored the streams, quietly, where the turtles slid off the sunny logs and dug their way into the soft bottom; and we lay on the town wharf and fed worms to the tame bass. Everywhere we went I had trouble making out which was I, the one walking at my side, the one walking in my pants.

One afternoon while we were there at that lake a thunderstorm came up. It was like the revival of an old melodrama that I had seen long ago with childish awe. The second-act climax of the drama of the electrical disturbance over a lake in America had not changed in any important respect. This was the big scene, still the big scene. The whole thing was so familiar, the first feeling of oppression and heat and a general air around camp of not wanting to go very far away. In midafternoon (it was all the same) a curious darkening of the sky, and a lull in everything that had made life tick; and then the way the boats suddenly swung the other way at their moorings with the coming of a breeze out of the new quarter, and the premonitory rumble. Then the kettle drum, then the snare, then the bass drum and cymbals, then crackling light against the dark, and the gods grinning and licking their chops in the hills. Afterward the calm, the rain steadily rustling in the calm lake, the return of light and hope and spirits, and the campers running out in joy and relief to go swimming in the rain, their bright cries perpetuating the deathless joke about how they were getting simply drenched, and the children screaming with delight at the new sensation of bathing in the rain, and the joke about getting drenched linking the generations in a strong indestructible chain. And the comedian who waded in carrying an umbrella.

When the others went swimming my son said he was going in too. He pulled his dripping trunks from the line where they had hung all through the shower, and wrung them out. Languidly, and with no thought of going in, I watched him, his hard little body, skinny and bare, saw him wince slightly as he pulled up around his vitals the small, soggy, icy garment. As he buckled the swollen belt suddenly my groin felt the chill of death. ◼

The Reader's Presence

1. In paragraph 2, White begins to reflect on the way his memory works. How does he follow the process of remembering throughout the essay? Are his memories of the lake safely stored in the past? If not, why not?

2. Go through the essay and identify words and images having to do with the sensory details of seeing, hearing, touching, and so on. How do these details contribute to the overall effect of the essay? How do they anticipate White's final paragraph?

3. **VISUAL PRESENCE:** Examine the photograph of E. B. White below. Which specific aspects of this portrait capture your attention? Explain why. How are White's writing style and subject matter reflected in this picture? Cite specific details from the image as you develop your response.

4. **CONNECTIONS:** In paragraph 4, White refers to a "creepy sensation." What is the basis of that sensation? Why is it "creepy"? What is the "dual existence" White feels he is living? How does the essay build the story of White's relationships with both his father and his son? Compare this account of intergenerational intimacy to Raymond Carver's essay "My Father's Life" (page 60).

The Writer at Work

E. B. WHITE on the Essayist

New York Times Co./Getty Images

For several generations, E. B. White has remained America's best-known essayist, his works widely available and widely anthologized. Yet in the foreword to his 1977 collected essays, when he addresses the role of the essayist, he sounds wholly modest not only about his career but also about his chosen genre: in the world of literature, he writes, the essayist is a "second-class citizen." Why do you think White thinks of himself that way, and how might that self-deprecation be reconciled with the claims of his final two paragraphs? Do you think White's description of himself as an essayist matches the actual essayist we encounter in "Once More to the Lake"? Also, do you think White's persistent use of the male pronoun is merely for grammatical convenience (the essay was written in 1977) or reflects a gender bias on his part?

"The essayist is a self-liberated man, sustained by the childish belief that everything he thinks about, everything that happens to him, is of general interest.

He is a fellow who thoroughly enjoys his work, just as people who take bird walks enjoy theirs. Each new excursion of the essayist, each new "attempt," differs from the last and takes him into new country. This delights him. Only a person who is congenitally self-centered has the effrontery and the stamina to write essays.

There are as many kinds of essays as there are human attitudes or poses, as many essay flavors as there are Howard Johnson ice creams. The essayist arises in the morning and, if he has work to do, selects his garb from an unusually extensive wardrobe: he can pull on any sort of shirt, be any sort of person, according to his mood or his subject matter—philosopher, scold, jester, raconteur, confidant, pundit, devil's advocate, enthusiast. I like the essay, have always liked it, and even as a child was at work, attempting to inflict my young thoughts and experiences on others by putting them on paper. I early broke into print in the pages of *St. Nicholas.*[1] I tend still to fall back on the essay form (or lack of form) when an idea strikes me, but I am not fooled about the place of the essay in twentieth-century American letters—it stands a short distance down the line. The essayist, unlike the novelist, the poet, and the playwright, must be content in his self-imposed role of second-class citizen. A writer who has his sights trained on the Nobel Prize or other earthly triumphs had best write a novel, a poem, or a play, and leave the essayist to ramble about, content with living a free life and enjoying the satisfactions of a somewhat undisciplined existence. (Dr. Johnson[2] called the essay "an irregular, undigested piece"; this happy practitioner has no wish to quarrel with the good doctor's characterization.)

There is one thing the essayist cannot do, though—he cannot indulge himself in deceit or in concealment, for he will be found out in no time. Desmond MacCarthy, in his introductory remarks to the 1928 E. P. Dutton & Company edition of Montaigne, observes that Montaigne "had the gift of natural candor. . . ." It is the basic ingredient. And even the essayist's escape from discipline is only a partial escape: the essay, although a relaxed form, imposes its own disciplines, raises its own problems, and these disciplines and problems soon become apparent and (we all hope) act as a deterrent to anyone wielding a pen merely because he entertains random thoughts or is in a happy or wandering mood.

I think some people find the essay the last resort of the egoist, a much too self-conscious and self-serving form for their tastes; they feel that it is presumptuous of a writer to assume that his little excursions or his small observations will interest the reader. There is some justice in their complaint. I have always been aware that I am by nature self-absorbed and egoistical; to write of myself to the extent I have done indicates a too great attention to my own life, not enough to the lives of others. I have worn many shirts, and not all of them have been a good fit. But when I am discouraged or downcast I need only fling open the door of my closet, and there, hidden behind everything else, hangs the mantle of Michel de Montaigne, smelling slightly of camphor.**"**

---

[1] **St. Nicholas:** A prominent magazine for children, founded in 1873. — Eds.
[2] **Dr. [Samuel] Johnson** (1709–1784): One of the most important and influential essayists and critics of the eighteenth century. — Eds.

Elie Wiesel

EIGHT SIMPLE, SHORT WORDS

ELIE WIESEL (1928–2016) was a Romanian-born Jewish American writer, teacher, and human-rights activist. Born in Sighet, Transylvania (a historical region of Romania), he was fifteen years old when he was sent with his family to the Nazi concentration camp at Auschwitz. His older sisters survived the experience. His mother and younger sister did not. Elie and his father were transferred to another camp, Buchenwald, where his father died shortly before the camp was liberated in April 1945. After the war, Wiesel studied in Paris, became a journalist, and decided to write a book about his experiences in the death camps. The result was his internationally acclaimed memoir, *Night (La Nuit)*, originally published in French in 1958 and since translated into more than thirty languages. Wiesel immigrated to the United States in 1955 and became an American citizen in 1963. Appointed chairman of the President's Commission on the Holo-

> Elie Wiesel established The Elie Wiesel Foundation for Humanity, dedicated to fighting intolerance, indifference, and injustice.

caust in 1978 by President Jimmy Carter, Wiesel went on to found the United States Holocaust Memorial Council in 1980. He published more than fifty books of fiction and nonfiction and received numerous awards for his literary and human-rights activities, including the Presidential Medal of Freedom, the U.S. Congressional Gold Medal, the National Humanities Medal, the Medal of Liberty, and the rank of Grand-Croix in the French Legion of Honor. In 1986, Wiesel won the Nobel Peace Prize. Soon after, with his wife Marion, he established The Elie Wiesel Foundation for Humanity, dedicated to fighting intolerance, indifference, and injustice. From 1976 until his death at age 87, he was the Andrew W. Mellon Professor in the Humanities at Boston University.

In May 1944, the police began rounding up Jews in Wiesel's hometown of Sighet, in what is now Romania, for transport in overcrowded cattle cars to the concentration camps at Auschwitz Birkenau. As the harrowing episode begins, the train has pulled out of the station at Sighet on what would be a four-day journey to the notorious camp. [EDS.]

LYING DOWN was not an option, nor could we all sit down. We decided to take turns sitting. There was little air. The lucky ones found themselves near a window; they could watch the blooming countryside flit by. After two days of travel, thirst became intolerable, as did the heat.

Freed of normal constraints, some of the young let go of their inhibitions and, under cover of darkness, caressed one another, without any thought of others, alone in the world. The others pretended not to notice.

There was still some food left. But we never ate enough to satisfy our hunger. Our principle was to economize, to save for tomorrow. Tomorrow could be worse yet.

The train stopped in Kaschau, a small town on the Czechoslovakian 5 border. We realized then that we were not staying in Hungary. Our eyes opened. Too late.

The door of the car slid aside. A German officer stepped in accompanied by a Hungarian lieutenant, acting as his interpreter.

"From this moment on, you are under the authority of the German Army. Anyone who still owns gold, silver, or watches must hand them over now. Anyone who will be found to have kept any of these will be shot on the spot. Secondly, anyone who is ill should report to the hospital car. That's all."

The Hungarian lieutenant went around with a basket and retrieved the last possessions from those who chose not to go on tasting the bitterness of fear.

"There are eighty of you in the car," the German officer added. "If anyone goes missing, you will all be shot, like dogs."

The two disappeared. The doors clanked shut. We had fallen into the 10 trap, up to our necks. The doors were nailed, the way back irrevocably cut off. The world had become a hermetically sealed cattle car.

There was a woman among us, a certain Mrs. Schächter. She was in her fifties and her ten-year-old son was with her, crouched in a corner. Her husband and two older sons had been deported with the first transport, by mistake. The separation had totally shattered her.

I knew her well. A quiet, tense woman with piercing eyes, she had been a frequent guest in our house. Her husband was a pious man who spent most of his days and nights in the house of study. It was she who supported the family.

Mrs. Schächter had lost her mind. On the first day of the journey, she had already begun to moan. She kept asking why she had been separated from her family. Later, her sobs and screams became hysterical.

On the third night, as we were sleeping, some of us sitting, huddled against each other, some of us standing, a piercing cry broke the silence:

"Fire! I see a fire! I see a fire!" 15

There was a moment of panic. Who had screamed? It was Mrs. Schächter. Standing in the middle of the car, in the faint light filtering through the windows, she looked like a withered tree in a field of wheat. She was howling, pointing through the window:

"Look! Look at this fire! This terrible fire! Have mercy on me!"

Some pressed against the bars to see. There was nothing. Only the darkness of night.

It took us a long time to recover from this harsh awakening. We were still trembling, and with every screech of the wheels, we felt the abyss opening beneath us. Unable to still our anguish, we tried to reassure each other:

"She is mad, poor woman . . ."   20

Someone had placed a damp rag on her forehead. But she nevertheless continued to scream:

"Fire! I see a fire!"

Her little boy was crying, clinging to her skirt, trying to hold her hand:

"It's nothing, Mother! There's nothing there . . . Please sit down . . ." He pained me even more than did his mother's cries.

Some of the women tried to calm her: 25

"You'll see, you'll find your husband and sons again . . . In a few days . . ."

She continued to scream and sob fitfully.

"Jews, listen to me," she cried. "I see a fire! I see flames, huge flames!"

It was as though she were possessed by some evil spirit.

We tried to reason with her, more to calm ourselves, to catch our breath,   30
than to soothe her:

"She is hallucinating because she is thirsty, poor woman . . . That's why she speaks of flames devouring her . . ."

But it was all in vain. Our terror could no longer be contained. Our nerves had reached a breaking point. Our very skin was aching. It was as though madness had infected all of us. We gave up. A few young men forced her to sit down, then bound and gagged her.

Silence fell again. The small boy sat next to his mother, crying. I started to breathe normally again as I listened to the rhythmic pounding of the wheels on the tracks as the train raced through the night. We could begin to doze again, to rest, to dream . . .

And so an hour or two passed. Another scream jolted us. The woman had broken free of her bonds and was shouting louder than before:

"Look at the fire! Look at the flames! Flames everywhere . . ."   35

Once again, the young men bound and gagged her. When they actually struck her, people shouted their approval:

"Keep her quiet! Make that madwoman shut up. She's not the only one here . . ."

She received several blows to the head, blows that could have been lethal. Her son was clinging desperately to her, not uttering a word. He was no longer crying.

The night seemed endless. By daybreak, Mrs. Schächter had settled down. Crouching in her corner, her blank gaze fixed on some faraway place, she no longer saw us.

She remained like that all day, mute, absent, alone in the midst of us.   40
Toward evening she began to shout again:

"The fire, over there!"

She was pointing somewhere in the distance, always the same place. No one felt like beating her anymore. The heat, the thirst, the stench, the lack of air, were suffocating us. Yet all that was nothing compared to her screams, which tore us apart. A few more days and all of us would have started to scream.

But we were pulling into a station. Someone near a window read to us: "Auschwitz."

Nobody had ever heard that name.   45

The train did not move again. The afternoon went by slowly. Then the doors of the wagon slid open. Two men were given permission to fetch water.

When they came back, they told us that they had learned, in exchange for a gold watch, that this was the final destination. We were to leave the train here. There was a labor camp on the site. The conditions were good. Families would not be separated. Only the young would work in the factories. The old and the sick would find work in the fields.

Confidence soared. Suddenly we felt free of the previous nights' terror. We gave thanks to God.

Mrs. Schächter remained huddled in her corner, mute, untouched by the optimism around her. Her little one was stroking her hand.

Dusk began to fill the wagon. We ate what was left of our food. At ten   50
o'clock in the evening, we were all trying to find a position for a quick nap and soon we were dozing. Suddenly:

"Look at the fire! Look at the flames! Over there!"

With a start, we awoke and rushed to the window yet again. We had believed her, if only for an instant. But there was nothing outside but darkness. We returned to our places, shame in our souls but fear gnawing at us nevertheless. As she went on howling, she was struck again. Only with great difficulty did we succeed in quieting her down.

The man in charge of our wagon called out to a German officer strolling down the platform, asking him to have the sick woman moved to a hospital car.

"Patience," the German replied, "patience. She'll be taken there soon."

Around eleven o'clock, the train began to move again. We pressed   55
against the windows. The convoy was rolling slowly. A quarter of an hour later, it began to slow down even more. Through the windows, we saw barbed wire; we understood that this was the camp.

We had forgotten Mrs. Schächter's existence. Suddenly there was a terrible scream:

"Jews, look! Look at the fire! Look at the flames!"

And as the train stopped, this time we saw flames rising from a tall chimney into a black sky.

Mrs. Schächter had fallen silent on her own. Mute again, indifferent, absent, she had returned to her corner.

We stared at the flames in the darkness. A wretched stench floated in   60
the air. Abruptly, our doors opened. Strange-looking creatures, dressed in striped jackets and black pants, jumped into the wagon. Holding flashlights and sticks, they began to strike at us left and right, shouting:

"Everybody out! Leave everything inside. Hurry up!"

We jumped out. I glanced at Mrs. Schächter. Her little boy was still holding her hand.

In front of us, those flames. In the air, the smell of burning flesh. It must have been around midnight. We had arrived. In Birkenau.

The fifteen-year-old Elie would never see his mother and seven-year-old sister, Tzipora, again. His father was ordered to the crematorium after many months of forced labor. The camp was liberated on April 11, 1945. [EDS.]

The beloved objects that we had carried with us from place to place were now left behind in the wagon and, with them, finally, our illusions.

Every few yards, there stood an SS man, his machine gun trained on us.   65
Hand in hand we followed the throng.

An SS came toward us wielding a club. He commanded:

"Men to the left! Women to the right!"

Eight words spoken quietly, indifferently, without emotion. Eight simple, short words. Yet that was the moment when I left my mother. There was no time to think, and I already felt my father's hand press against mine: we were alone. In a fraction of a second I could see my mother, my sisters, move to the right. Tzipora was holding Mother's hand. I saw them walking farther and farther away; Mother was stroking my sister's blond hair, as if to protect her. And I walked on with my father, with the men. I didn't know that this was the moment in time and the place where I was leaving my mother and Tzipora forever. I kept walking, my father holding my hand.

Behind me, an old man fell to the ground. Nearby, an SS man replaced his revolver in its holster.

My hand tightened its grip on my father. All I could think of was not to   70
lose him. Not to remain alone.

The SS officers gave the order.

"Form ranks of fives!"

There was a tumult. It was imperative to stay together.

"Hey, kid, how old are you?"

The man interrogating me was an inmate. I could not see his face, but   75
his voice was weary and warm.

"Fifteen."

"No. You're eighteen."

"But I'm not," I said. "I'm fifteen."

"Fool. Listen to what *I* say."

Then he asked my father, who answered: 80

"I'm fifty."

"No." The man now sounded angry. "Not fifty. You're forty. Do you hear? Eighteen and forty."

He disappeared into the darkness. Another inmate appeared, unleashing a stream of invectives:

"Sons of bitches, why have you come here? Tell me, why?"

Someone dared to reply: 85

"What do you think? That we came here of our own free will? That we asked to come here?"

The other seemed ready to kill him:

"Shut up, you moron, or I'll tear you to pieces! You should have hanged yourselves rather than come here. Didn't you know what was in store for you here in Auschwitz? You didn't know? In 1944?"

True. We didn't know. Nobody had told us. He couldn't believe his ears. His tone became even harsher:

"Over there. Do you see the chimney over there? Do you see it? And 90 the flames, do you see them?" (Yes, we saw the flames.) "Over there, that's where they will take you. Over there will be your grave. You still don't understand? You sons of bitches. Don't you understand anything? You will be burned! Burned to a cinder! Turned into ashes!"

His anger changed into fury. We stood stunned, petrified. Could this be just a nightmare? An unimaginable nightmare?

I heard whispers around me:

"We must do something. We can't let them kill us like that, like cattle in the slaughterhouse. We must revolt."

There were, among us, a few tough young men. They actually had knives and were urging us to attack the armed guards. One of them was muttering:

"Let the world learn about the existence of Auschwitz. Let everybody 95 find out about it while they still have a chance to escape . . ."

But the older men begged their sons not to be foolish:

"We mustn't give up hope, even now as the sword hangs over our heads. So taught our sages . . ."

The wind of revolt died down. We continued to walk until we came to a crossroads. Standing in the middle of it was, though I didn't know it then, Dr. Mengele,[1] the notorious Dr. Mengele. He looked like the typical SS officer: a cruel, though not unintelligent, face, complete with monocle. He was holding a conductor's baton and was surrounded by officers. The baton was moving constantly, sometimes to the right, sometimes to the left.

In no time, I stood before him.

"Your age?" he asked, perhaps trying to sound paternal. 100

"I'm eighteen." My voice was trembling.

"In good health?"

"Yes."

"Your profession?"

Tell him that I was a student? 105

"Farmer," I heard myself saying.

This conversation lasted no more than a few seconds. It seemed like an eternity.

The baton pointed to the left. I took half a step forward. I first wanted to see where they would send my father. Were he to have gone to the right, I would have run after him.

[1] **Dr. Mengele** (1911–1979): The infamous concentration camp physician who inspected prisoners to select those fit for labor and those who would be exterminated. He was also responsible for performing medical experiments on prisoners. — EDS.

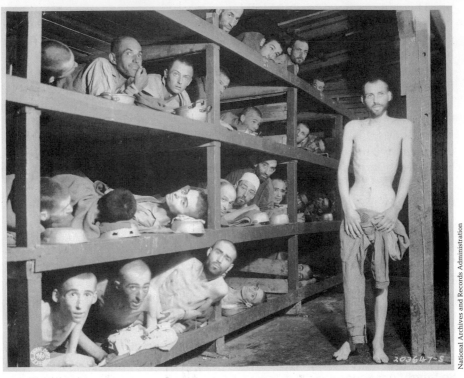

National Archives and Records Administration

Buchenwald, 1945. Wiesel is on the second row from the bottom, seventh from the left.

The baton, once more, moved to the left. A weight lifted from my heart.

We did not know, as yet, which was the better side, right or left, which 110 road led to prison and which to the crematoria. Still, I was happy, I was near my father. Our procession continued slowly to move forward.

Another inmate came over to us:

"Satisfied?"

"Yes," someone answered.

"Poor devils, you are heading for the crematorium."

He seemed to be telling the truth. Not far from us, flames, huge flames, 115 were rising from a ditch. Something was being burned there. A truck drew close and unloaded its hold: small children. Babies! Yes, I did see this, with my own eyes . . . children thrown into the flames. (Is it any wonder that ever since then, sleep tends to elude me?)

So that was where we were going. A little farther on, there was another, larger pit for adults.

I pinched myself: Was I still alive? Was I awake? How was it possible that men, women, and children were being burned and that the world kept silent? No. All this could not be real. A nightmare perhaps . . . Soon I would wake up with a start, my heart pounding, and find that I was back in the room of my childhood, with my books . . .

My father's voice tore me from my daydreams:

"What a shame, a shame that you did not go with your mother . . . I saw many children your age go with their mothers . . ."

His voice was terribly sad. I understood that he did not wish to see what 120 they would do to me. He did not wish to see his only son go up in flames.

My forehead was covered with cold sweat. Still, I told him that I could not believe that human beings were being burned in our times; the world would never tolerate such crimes . . .

"The world? The world is not interested in us. Today, everything is possible, even the crematoria . . ." His voice broke.

"Father," I said. "If that is true, then I don't want to wait. I'll run into the electrified barbed wire. That would be easier than a slow death in the flames."

He didn't answer. He was weeping. His body was shaking. Everybody around us was weeping. Someone began to recite Kaddish, the prayer for the dead. I don't know whether, during the history of the Jewish people, men have ever before recited Kaddish for themselves.

"*Yisgadal, veyiskadash, shmey raba* . . . May His name be celebrated 125 and sanctified . . ." whispered my father.

For the first time, I felt anger rising within me. Why should I sanctify His name? The Almighty, the eternal and terrible Master of the Universe, chose to be silent. What was there to thank Him for?

We continued our march. We were coming closer and closer to the pit, from which an infernal heat was rising. Twenty more steps. If I was going to kill myself, this was the time. Our column had only some fifteen steps to go. I bit my lips so that my father would not hear my teeth chattering. Ten more steps. Eight. Seven. We were walking slowly, as one follows a hearse, our own funeral procession. Only four more steps. Three. There it was now, very close to us, the pit and its flames. I gathered all that remained of my strength in order to break rank and throw myself onto the barbed wire. Deep down, I was saying good-bye to my father, to the whole universe, and, against my will, I found myself whispering the words: "*Yisgadal, veyiskadash, shmey raba* . . ." May His name be celebrated and sanctified . . ." My heart was about to burst. There I was face-to-face with the Angel of Death[2] . . .

No. Two steps from the pit, we were ordered to turn left and herded into barracks.

I squeezed my father's hand. He said:

Do you remember Mrs. Schächter, in the train?   130

Never shall I forget that night, the first night in camp, that turned my life into one long night seven times sealed.

Never shall I forget that smoke.

Never shall I forget the small faces of the children whose bodies I saw transformed into smoke under a silent sky.

---

[2] ***Angel of Death:*** A name by which Dr. Mengele was known. It isn't clear, however, if Wiesel wants to make this connection. — Eds.

Never shall I forget those flames that consumed my faith forever.

Never shall I forget the nocturnal silence that deprived me for all eter-   135
nity of the desire to live.

Never shall I forget those moments that murdered my God and my soul
and turned my dreams to ashes.

Never shall I forget those things, even were I condemned to live as long
as God Himself.

Never. ■

The Reader's Presence

1. Why do you think the inmates abuse the newly arrived prisoners? How would you describe their tone? Why do they order father and son to lie about their ages? Why do they lead the father and son to believe they are headed for the crematorium?

2. Besides offering a historical account of how Jews were herded into concentration camps, Wiesel also describes his harrowing religious experience. What impact did this experience have on his religious beliefs? What is Wiesel's purpose in the almost prayer-like litany that appears at the conclusion of the selection?

3. **VISUAL PRESENCE:** Examine carefully the photograph taken at the Buchenwald concentration camp just after the end of World War II (page 270). What were your initial reactions to this image? What specific features of this photograph capture the tone and atmosphere of Wiesel's text? Support your response with details from the image.

4. **CONNECTIONS:** How do people respond in writing when they have encountered horrific events? Compare Wiesel's recollection of his childhood internment at Auschwitz to Michihiko Hachiya's account of the bombing of Hiroshima ("Hiroshima Diary," page 105). Wiesel published his memoir of his nightmarish experiences in 1958 (originally in French), more than a decade after the events occurred. Hachiya began writing his diary a few days after the event. How do these different time frames account for the different ways in which each author makes his presence felt in his writing?

Thomas Chatterton Williams
BLACK AND BLUE AND BLOND

THOMAS CHATTERTON WILLIAMS tackles questions of racial identity without hesitation. His essays have appeared in many publications, including the *Washington Post*, the *New York Times*, and the *American Scholar*. His first book, *Losing My Cool: Love, Literature, and a Black Man's Escape from the Crowd* (2009), recounts his experiences growing up in and later escaping from the hip-hop street culture embraced by his peers.

For Williams, writing requires "patience, stamina and plenty of fuel." In his case, reading is the fuel: "I tried to fortify myself with the best nonfiction and fiction I could lay my hands on. . . They were catalysts for the creative act." Williams sees reading both as a source of practical knowledge about writing and as a pastime to be enjoyed.

> **For Williams, writing requires "patience, stamina and plenty of fuel."**

In "Black and Blue and Blond," Williams looks to the future as he considers where his biracial daughter—with her pale skin and blue eyes—fits in the larger picture of racial ancestry and cultural identity.

In 1517, Fray Bartolome de las Casas, feeling great pity for the Indians who grew worn and lean in the drudging infernos of the Antillean gold mines, proposed to Emperor Charles V that Negroes be brought to the isles of the Caribbean, so that they might grow worn and lean in the drudging infernos of the Antillean gold mines. To that odd variant on the species philanthropist we owe an infinitude of things. . . ."
—*JORGE LUIS BORGES*, "The Cruel Redeemer Lazarus Morell"

"But any fool can see that the white people are not really white, and that black people are not black."
—*ALBERT MURRAY*, The Omni-Americans

"Our white is so white you can paint a chunka coal and you'd have to crack it open with a sledge hammer to prove it wasn't white clear through."
—*RALPH ELLISON*, Invisible Man

THERE IS A MILLENNIA-OLD PHILOSOPHICAL experiment that has perplexed minds as fine and diverse as those of Socrates, Plutarch, and John Locke. It's called Theseus's Paradox (or the Ship of Theseus), and the premise is this: The mythical founding-king of Athens kept a thirty-oar ship docked in the Athenian harbor. The vessel was preserved in a sea-worthy state through the continual replacement of old timber planks with new ones, piecemeal, until the question inevitably arose: After all of the original planks have been replaced by new and different planks, is it still, in fact, the *same* ship?

For some time now, a recurring vision has put me in mind of Theseus and those shuffling pieces of wood. Only, it's people I see and not boats: a lineage of people distending over time. At the end of the line, there is a teenage boy with fair skin and blond hair and probably light eyes, seated at a café table somewhere in Europe. It is fifty or sixty years into the future. And this boy, gathered with his friends, is glibly remarking—in the dispassionate tone of one of my old white Catholic-school classmates claiming to have Cherokee or Iroquois blood—that as improbable as it would seem to look at him, apparently he had black ancestors once upon a time in America.

He says it all so matter-of-factly, with no visceral aspect to the telling. I imagine his friends' vague surprise, perhaps a raised eyebrow or two or perhaps not even that—and if I want to torture myself, I can detect an ironic smirk or giggle. Then, to my horror, I see the conversation grow not ugly or embittered or anything like that but simply pass on, giving way to other lesser matters, plans for the weekend or questions about the menu perhaps. And then it's over. Just like that, in one casual exchange, I see a history, a struggle, a whole vibrant and populated world collapse without a trace. I see an entirely different ship.

I met my wife in a bar off of the place de la Bataille de Stalingrad, in Paris. That was almost five years ago. At the time, I was at the end of my twenties and in the middle of one of the only legitimate bachelor phases I've enjoyed as an adult. Otherwise, there had been a series of more or less monogamous relationships of varying lengths: a frivolous year surfing couches with a Gujarati girl from Toronto; a poignant stint in Buenos Aires with an elegant black girl from Virginia; eight perfect then imperfect and seemingly inexorable years with a Nigerian-Italian chef from uptown Manhattan (with an interlude of six intensely felt months in college with my French TA, an exchange student from Nancy); and four turbulent teenage years with my first love, someone LL Cool J could easily describe as an around-the-way girl, from Plainfield, New Jersey. But on that clear January night, in a warm bar overlooking the frigid canal, there was no one else, and I was accountable solely to myself.

    Valentine came with a mutual friend, sat down catty-corner to me and—who knows how these things actually work—something in her bearing triggered a powerful response. I found her insouciant pout and mane of curls flowing over the old fur coat she was bundled in exotic. We hardly spoke, but before I left, I gave her my e-mail address on the chance she found herself in New York, where I was living at the time. Two months later, while there on a reporting assignment, Valentine wrote me, and we met a few days later for a drink. That was when I discovered that she was funny and not really insouciant at all, just shy about her English. It turned out we had a lot in common. I saw her a second time a month later in New York and then again on a work trip to Paris two months after that. Summer had just begun, and we fell in love extremely fast. When it was time to go home, she asked me to change my itinerary and join her in Corsica for a week. I did, and when it was really time to leave, she promised to visit me that August in New York. A few days after she landed, I proposed on a rooftop in Brooklyn, overlooking the Empire State Building and the orange Manhattan sky.

    In retrospect, it had been a very long time by then since I'd thought of   5 myself as having any kind of *type*. It wasn't a conscious decision; it was simply the more I'd studied at large universities, the more I'd traveled and lived in big cities, the more women I'd encountered at home and away—which is just to say the more I'd ventured from my own backyard and projected myself into the world—the more I found myself unwilling to preemptively cordon off any of it. And yet—however naïve this could seem now—I had somehow always also taken for granted that, when the time came to have them, my children would, like me, be black.

A year ago to the day that i write this, valentine's water broke after a late dinner. In a daze of elation, we did what we'd planned for weeks and woke our brother-in-law, who gamely drove us from our apartment in the northern ninth arrondissement to the *maternité*, all the way on Paris's southern edge. At two in the morning, we had the streets practically to ourselves, and the route he took—down the hill from our apartment, beneath the greened copper and gold of the opera house and through the splendor of the Louvre's courtyard, with its pyramids of glass and meticulous gardens, over the River Seine, with Notre Dame rising in the distance on one side and the Palais Royal and the Eiffel Tower shimmering on the other, and down the wide, leafy Boulevards Saint-Germain and Raspail, into Montparnasse, through that neon intersection of cafes from the pages of *A Moveable Feast*[1]—was unspeakably gorgeous. I am not permanently awake to Paris's beauty or even its strangeness, but that night, watching the city flit by my window, it did strike me that such a place—both glorious and fundamentally not mine—would be my daughter's hometown.

Another twenty-four hours elapsed before Marlow arrived. When Valentine finally went into labor, even I was delirious with fatigue and not so much standing by her side as levitating there, sustained by raw emotion alone and thinking incoherently at best. On the fourth or fifth push, I caught a snippet of the doctor's rapid-fire French: "something, something, something, *téte dorée* . . ." It took a minute before my sluggish mind registered and sorted the sounds; and then it hit me that she was *looking* at my daughter's head and reporting back that it was *blond*. The rest is the usual blur. I caught sight of a tray of placenta, heard a brand-new scream, and nearly fainted. The nurses whisked away my daughter, the doctor saw to my wife, and I was left to wander the empty corridor until I found the men's room, where I shut myself and wept, like all the other newborns on the floor—a saline cascade of joy and exhaustion, terror and awe mingling together and flooding out of me in unremitting sobs. When, finally, I'd washed my face and returned to meet my beautiful, healthy child, she squinted open a pair of inky-blue irises that I knew even then would lighten considerably but never turn brown. For this precious little being grasping for milk and breath, I felt the first throb of what has been every minute since then the sincerest love I know. An hour or so after that, when Valentine and the baby were back in their room for the night, I fell into a taxi, my own eyes absentmindedly retracing that awfully pretty route. For the first time I can remember, I thought of Theseus's ship.

I realize now that this vision of the boy from the future I've had in my head for the past year traces itself much further back into the past. It must necessarily stretch back at least to 1971, in San Diego, where my father, who was—hav-

---

[1] **A Moveable Feast:** Ernest Hemingway's 1964 memoir of Paris in the 1920s. — EDS.

ing been born in 1937 in Jim Crow Texas—the *grandson* of a woman wed to a man born before the Emancipation Proclamation, met my mother, the native-Californian product of European immigrants from places as diverse as Austria-Hungary, Germany, England, and France. This unlikely courtship came all of four years after the *Loving v. Virginia* verdict repealed antimiscegenation laws throughout the country. In ways that are perhaps still impossible for me to fully appreciate, their romance amounted to a radical political act, though now, some four decades on, it seems a lot less like any form of defiance than like what all successful marriages fundamentally must be: the obvious and undeniable joining of two people who love and understand each other enormously.

But that's not the beginning, either. This trajectory I now find myself on no more starts in San Diego than in Paris. Not since it is extremely safe to assume that my father, with his freckles, with his mother's Irish maiden name, and with his skin a shade of brown between polished teak and red clay, did not arrive from African shores alone. As James Baldwin, perspicacious as ever, noted of his travels around precisely the kind of segregated Southern towns my father would instantly recognize as home, the line between "whites" and "coloreds" in America has always been traversed and logically imprecise: "the prohibition . . . of the social mingling [revealing] the extent of the sexual amalgamation." There were (and still are): "Girls the color of honey, men nearly the color of chalk, hair like silk, hair like cotton, hair like wire, eyes blue, gray, green, hazel, black, like the gypsy's, brown like the Arab's, narrow nostrils, thin, wide lips, thin lips, every conceivable variation struck along incredible gamuts. . . ." Indeed, to be black (or *white)* for any significant amount of time in America is fundamentally to occupy a position on the mongrel spectrum—strict binaries have always failed spectacularly to contain this elementary truth.

And yet in spite of that, I've spent the past year trying to think my way   10 through the wholly absurd question of what it means for a person to be or not to be black. It's an existential Rubik's Cube I thought I'd solved and put away in childhood. My parents were never less than adamant on the point that both my older brother and I are black. And the in many ways simpler New Jersey world we grew up in—him in the seventies and eighties, me in the eighties and nineties—tended to receive us that way without significant protest, especially when it came to other blacks. This is probably because, on a certain level, *every* black American knows what, again, Baldwin knew: "Whatever he or anyone else may wish to believe . . . his ancestors are both white and black." Still, in the realm of lived experience, race is nothing if not an improvisational feat, and it would be in terribly bad faith to pretend there is not some fine, unspoken, and impossible-to-spell-out balance to all of this. And so I cannot help but wonder if indeed a threshold—the full consequences of which I may or may not even see in my own lifetime—has been crossed. (It's not a wholly academic exercise, either, since my father was an only child and in the past year my brother married and had a daughter with a woman from West Siberia.)

"Aw, son," pappy chuckled warmly when he cradled marlow in his arms the first time, "she's just a *palomino*!" There was—indeed, there still is—something so comforting to me in his brand of assurance. It's certainly true that in his day and in his fading Texas lexicon, black people could be utterly unflappable when presented with all kinds of improbable melanges, employing a near infinitude of esoteric terms (not infrequently drawn from the world of horse breeding, which can sound jarring to the contemporary ear) to describe them. I myself had to whip out my iPhone and Google palomino ("a pale golden or tan-colored horse with a white mane and tail, originally bred in the southwestern US"), but I'd also grown up with other vocabulary, like "high-yellow" and "mulatto," and in my father's house if nowhere else, those now-anachronistic and loaded terms "quadroon" and "octoroon."

What bizarre words these are. But what a perfectly simple reality they labor to conceal and contain. When you get all the way down to it, what all these elaborate, nebulous descriptors really signify is nothing more complicated than that, in the not-so-distant past, if she did not willfully break from her family and try her luck at passing for white (in the fashion of, say, the Creole author of *Kafka Was the Rage*, Anatole Broyard), Marlow, blue eyes and all, would have been disenfranchised and subjugated like all the rest of us—the wisdom, discipline, and brilliant style of American blackness would have been her birthright, as well. And so there was for a long time something that could be understood as a more or less genuinely unified experience—not without its terrible hardships but conversely rife with profound satisfactions—which had nothing, or very close to nothing, to do with genetics. Indeed, even though the absurdity of race is always most pellucid at the margins, my daughter's case wouldn't even have been considered marginal in the former slave states where theories about hypo-descent were most strictly observed and a person with as undetectable an amount as one thirty-second "black blood" could be "legally" designated "colored." Which is only to say, despite all of the horrifically cruel implications of so-called one-drop laws, until relatively quite recently there was a space reserved for someone like Marlow fully within the idea of what used to be called the American Negro.

But it is not hard to notice that impulse toward unquestioning inclusiveness (as a fully justifiable and admirable reaction to *exclusiveness*) is going in an increasing number of precincts wherever it is terms like Negro go to retire. The reason has less to do with black people suddenly forgetting their paradoxical origins than with the idea of whiteness continually growing, however reluctantly, less exclusive. With greater than a third of the American population now reporting at least one family member of a different race and with, since the year 2000, the option to select any combination of races on the census form, the very idea of black Americans as a fundamentally mulatto population is fraying at the seams.

Perhaps, then, mine is the last American generation for which the logic—and illogic—of racial classifications could so easily contradict, or just gloss over, the physical protestations and nuances of the body and face. Which is one of the reasons it did initially take me by such surprise to find so many recessive traits flourishing in my daughter. I was being forced to confront a truth I had, if not forgotten, certainly lost sight of for some time: My daughter does not, as so many well-meaning strangers and friends tend to put it, just "get those big blue eyes" from her mother. But despite the length and narrowness of my own nose and the beige hue of my skin, I've always only been able to see in the mirror a black man meeting my gaze. One word I have never connected or been tempted to connect with myself is *biracial*. The same goes for its updated variant, *multiracial*. Growing up where and as I did, before the turn of the last century, it simply would not have occurred to me to refer to myself by either of those designations.

The first time I lived in France, some twelve years ago to teach English in a   15
depressed and depressing industrial town along the northern border with Belgium, I often went to kebab shops late at night in which I would sometimes be greeted in Arabic. Once the young Algerian behind the counter simply demanded of me, *"Parle arabe! Parle arabe!"* and all I could do was stare at him blankly. "But why did your parents not teach you to speak Arabic!" he implored me, first in a French I hardly followed and then in an exasperated and broken English.
     "Because I'm American," I finally replied.
     "Yes, but even in America," he pressed on, "why did they not teach you *your* language?"
     "Because I'm not an Arab," I laughed uncomprehendingly, and for several beats he just looked at me.
     "But your origins, what are your *origins*?"
     "Black," I shrugged, and I can still see the look of supreme disbelief   20
unspool on that man's face. "But *you* are not black," he nearly screamed. *"Michael Jordan* is black!"
     It was an astonishingly discomfiting experience, this failure of my identity to register and, once registered, to be accepted, but one I gradually grew used to and now, after half a decade living in France, for better or worse have come to scarcely notice at all. Though it isn't just Arabs who mistake me for one of their own. Whites outside of the States are just as often oblivious to gradations of blackness. On my first trip to Paris as a student in a summer study-abroad program, some classmates and I bought ice cream behind Notre Dame. When we sat at a table on the river, a white American tourist who'd overheard us speaking confessed he was homesick and asked if he could join us. He was very friendly and younger than we were, and I can no longer recall the details of what he'd said, but very quickly he recounted an extremely off-color joke about blacks. When no one laughed and one of my friends explained his error to him, he blushed deeply, and said by way of excuse that he'd simply assumed I was Italian.
     What these encounters and many others showed me in my early adulthood is something I should have known already but failed to fully grasp:

Like the adage about politics, *all* race is local. This makes perfect sense, of course, given the basic biological reality that there is no such thing, on any measurable scientific level, as distinct races of the species *homo sapiens.* Rather, we all make, according to our own geographical and cultural orientations, inferences about people based on the loose interplay of physical traits, language, custom, and nationality, all of which necessarily lack any fixed or universal meaning (to be sure, this is not just a black thing—for most of American history it was widely held that northern and southern Europeans constituted entirely separate races). It is this fungible aspect of personal identity that bestows such a liberating (and at turns oppressive) quality to travel. In the case of coming to France in particular, this very failure to be seen and *interpreted* as one would be back home was, of course, a major selling point in the previous century for a not insignificant number of American blacks, primarily G.I.'s and artists but other types, too, who found an incredible degree of freedom from racialized stigma in Paris. For many of these expatriates, it was not that the color of their skin went unnoticed; it didn't. It is instead that it carried a crucially different set of meanings and lacked others still. France long functioned as a haven for American black people—and has never been confused as such for African and Caribbean blacks—precisely because, unlike in the US, we've been understood here first and foremost as American and not as black.

In one of the more exceptional meditations on James Baldwin and his European years, "Black Body: Rereading James Baldwin's 'Stranger in the Village,'" the Nigerian-American novelist Teju Cole in the *New Yorker* retraces a 1951 trip the writer made to Leukerbad, Switzerland, a far-flung, then all-white locale in which that very same sense of dignity that Baldwin had discovered in Paris was not always extended to him. Specifically, Cole returns again and again to his essay's true theme, which is an exploration of the various yokes, both visible and unseen, that act upon black-looking "bodies" and therefore an awful lot of black psyches:

> Leukerbad gave Baldwin a way to think about white supremacy from its first principles. It was as though he found it in its simplest form there. The men who suggested that he learn to ski so that they might mock him, the villagers who accused him behind his back of being a firewood thief, the ones who wished to touch his hair and suggested that he grow it out and make himself a winter coat, and the children who "having been taught that the devil is a black man, scream in genuine anguish" as he approached: Baldwin saw these as prototypes (preserved like coelacanths) of attitudes that had evolved into the more intimate, intricate, familiar, and obscene American forms of white supremacy that he already knew so well.

Even as he rejects what he interprets as Baldwin's "self-abnegation" in the face of European high culture— "What he loves does not love him in return . . . This is where I part ways with Baldwin"—and as he evinces a seemingly fuller appreciation of the limitlessness of his own intellectual, artistic, and frankly human birthrights— "I am not an interloper when I look at a Rembrandt portrait"—Cole also repeatedly encases the entirety of the existential

Thomas Chatterton Williams/The Cheney Agency

Thomas Chatterton Williams and his daughter.

experience of blackness in the physical stigmas of an obviously black body. "To be black," he writes, "is to bear the brunt of selective enforcement of the law, and to inhabit a psychic unsteadiness in which there is no guarantee of personal safety. You are a black body first, before you are a kid walking down the street or a Harvard professor who has misplaced his keys."

My father would certainly recognize this feeling of restricted being-in-the-world, and it is what he vigilantly reared me to brace myself for, though it has hardly ever been more than vicariously mine. To my knowledge, I've never been followed in a store, people don't cross the street when I approach, and the sole instance I've ever been pulled over in a car, I was absolutely speeding. But then again there was that time, years ago in Munich, when I was inexplicably not allowed inside that same nightclub my Irish-American friend was made to feel more than welcome to enter. By orders of magnitude, I can grasp what it would mean to endure such slights daily and the doubt and sensitivity they would engender. And so although there has been some ambiguity attached to my own nonwhite body, what I am most certain about in all of this — and perhaps this is a source of paradoxical anxiety for me — is that there will not be any with regard to my daughter's. She will not be turned away from that door or others just like it. And so as she grows and looks at me and smiles, all the while remaining innocent of all of this, I am left with some questions and they are urgent ones: What, exactly, remains of the American Negro in my daughter? Is it nothing but an expression playing around the eyes; the slightest hint of lemon in the epidermis? Is it possible to have black consciousness in a body that does not in any way look *black*?

On this point, not only Cole but also the preponderance of contemporary commentators on the subject, who cloak so much of the messiness and contradiction of lived experience in neat critical-race jargon and theories of the constructed body, do not have answers for me. I find myself looking instead to the unorthodox, self-styled Negro thinkers of the twentieth century and today, whose insights into American life in so many ways remain prescient and unrivaled. I'm thinking specifically of Albert Murray, though I'm also thinking of Ralph Ellison and Stanley Crouch. I find myself returning over and over again, in particular, to Murray's masterpiece, the ingenious and criminally neglected 1970 collection of essays and flat-out good sense, *The Omni-Americans,* and also to Crouch's wonderful commentary on it in his own collection, *Always in Pursuit.* One of Murray's signature issues, which even today too often goes de-emphasized or unsaid, is the simple fact that race—though not racism—is at its core a form of "social science fiction," and that identity, above all, is a matter of culture. For Murray, crucially, what we are really talking about is not even race at all but *ethnicity.* To be black, then, could never be merely a matter of possessing one kind of body versus another (as any Dravidian or Melanesian[2] would know). What Murray understood is "exactly what Ellison had made clear before him," writes Crouch. "Polemical reductions, if believed and acted upon, were capable of draining away all of the human complexities and the cultural facts of American life, which were far different from the patters and policies of prejudice." In other words, it would be insane to let one's own sense of self and history be determined by a nightclub bouncer or a beat cop.

Nonetheless, it's difficult to shake the sense that I have arrived at a certain bind, in many ways similar to the one familiar to secular Jews. The purpose of all these generations of struggle, I know, has always been the freedom to choose—and yet it is precisely this coveted autonomy that threatens now to annihilate the very identity that won it in the first place.

From time to time, feelings something like panic creep in. On the one hand, there is the acute and very specific panic of wondering if I have indeed permanently altered the culture or "race" or ethnicity or, yes, the very *physiognomy* of an entire line of people, like a freight train slowly but irrevocably switching tracks. On the other, there is the subtler, lower-decibel, gnawing panic, which manifests as a plain awareness of the unearned advantage. It is impossible not to feel that. At a time when, despite all of the tremendous societal progress, blackness—certainly not always but especially at that vexed intersection with poverty or the cultural signifiers of such—is still subject to all manner of violation and disrespect; at a time when blacks continue to be stopped, frisked, stalked, harassed, choked-out, and drilled with bullets in broad daylight and left in the street—what does it mean to have escaped a fate? Put baldly, what is proximity to whiteness worth and what does color cost? *And the reverse?*

[2] **Dravidian or Melanesian:** referring to the wide variety of blackness, from South Indians to Pacific Islanders. — EDS.

These are questions I don't yet know how to answer. What I do know is that I used to not just tolerate but submit to and even on some deep level *need* our society's dangerous assumptions about race, even as I suspected them to be irredeemably flawed. It is so much easier to sink deeper into a lukewarm bath than to stand up and walk away. But for my daughter's sake if not my own, I can't afford to linger any longer. Now if I find liberation in moments of doubt, it comes with the one movement I always end up having to make, indeed the only movement I can make—away from the abstract, general, and hypothetical and back into the jagged grain of the here and now, into the specificity of my love for my father, mother, brother, wife, and daughter, and into my sheer delight in their existence as distinct and irreplaceable people, not bodies or avatars or sites of racial characteristics and traits. With them, I am left with myself as the same, as a man and a human being who is free to choose and who has made choices and is ultimately fulfilled.

Yet I know that is also not enough. If the point is for everyone to build ships, set sail, and be free, if we are collectively ever going to solve this infinitely trickier paradox of racism in the absence of races, we are, all of us—black, white, and everything in between—going to have to do considerably more than contemplate façades. An entirely new framework must be built. This one's rotten to the core. ◼

The Reader's Presence

1. Thomas Chatterton Williams begins his essay by unfolding the image of a ship rebuilt plank by plank: "After all the original planks have been replaced by new and different planks, is it still, in fact, the same ship?" (paragraph 1). He concludes his essay by noting that our framework for race is "rotten to the core" (paragraph 29). What are the effects of choosing to frame his essay with this metaphor? What questions about race and ethnicity does he expect readers to resolve? Have you resolved them? Explain why or why not.

2. In paragraph 9, Williams observes: "the line between 'whites' and 'coloreds' in America has always been traversed and logically imprecise." Identify the specific strategies he uses to challenge and validate this assertion. Describe how race is portrayed in these quotations, and consider how they relate to the author's own experiences. How might the birth of Williams's daughter have influenced his need to view race with clear eyes and fresh language? To what extent does he make a convincing case that "like the adage about politics, *all* race is local" (paragraph 22)? What term(s) does Williams prefer to use instead of race? Summarize the points he makes to validate his assertion.

3. **CONNECTIONS:** Read Williams's essay alongside Kwame Anthony Appiah's "Race in the Modern World" (see page 291). Both authors write about race but in substantially different terms. How do their views of race differ? To what extent does Appiah's notion of a post racial society resolve the questions posed by Williams? Which essay do you find more engaging and convincing?

PART 2

EXPOSITORY WRITING
Shaping Information

66

Read, observe, listen intensely!—as if your life depended on it.

Joyce Carol Oates

(b. 1938, American novelist and essayist)

99

WHAT IS EXPOSITORY WRITING?

One of the most important reasons to write, especially in college and within a chosen profession, is to impart and share information. Although **exposition** has a wide range of meanings, in composition, it normally refers to discourse that provides readers with an informative report on a topic. This part, "Expository Writing: Shaping Information," will introduce you to many examples of informative writing by outstanding authors noted for their ability to explain concepts and research clearly and compellingly. These authors excel in practicing the art of exposition; that is, as writers, they know how to set out and arrange material so that it is both educational and enjoyable. Some, but not all, of the authors in this part are experts in their respective fields. Many well-known writers are *experts* in a different way—they don't know everything there is to know about economics, medicine, or psychology, for example, but they do know how to find out pertinent information in a wide variety of fields and present it engagingly. This introduction aims to provide you with strategies for becoming an expert in the same way.

Some expository writing simply lays out information that the writer knows or has researched. For example, a history assignment may call for a paper detailing the rise of the women's suffrage movement in the early twentieth century. Such a report could be based mainly on a student's reading and research, and it could focus on the various stages of the movement that led to the passage in 1920 of the Nineteenth Amendment giving women the right to vote. This kind of writing isn't a product only of classroom assignments; many print and online sources convey information in this manner.

But exposition usually involves more than a straightforward summary of the subject. When you do your own expository writing, you'll likely need to aim for a higher level of personal and intellectual engagement that can take the form of **explanation**, **analysis**, and **interpretation**. Imagine that a history assignment asks a student not only to detail the stages of the women's suffrage movement but also to *explain why* the movement succeeded in achieving its goal. A student, then, would still need to know the movement's stages but would also need to consider and select the various elements of the movement that resulted in a radical change in public opinion, including the mass demonstrations of 1916–1918 that supported the suffrage cause across the nation and set the groundwork for congressional legislation.

Information is always more than a list or an assemblage of facts and data on a subject. The facts need to be arranged in some way; the writer needs to organize information so that the presentation is clear, consistent, coherent, and convincing. After all, at the heart of the word *information* is "form." In this introduction, we'll take those three main purposes of expository writing—to explain, to analyze, and to interpret—and offer strategies you might use in your own writing.

In setting out to write an expository essay, you should explore how each of the following strategies can best help you approach your topic and establish your main points. For example, to return to our women's suffrage assignment,

|||||||||||||||||||||||||||||||||||||||||||||||||||||||||||||||||||||||||||||||||||||||||||||||||||||||||||||||||||||||||||||||

would your information be best presented by showing the causes that led to the movement, by classifying the various types of demonstrations, or by comparing the right-to-vote issue with earlier or later civil rights movements? As you can see, considering the topic with the various strategies in mind also helps you anticipate the general structural pattern of your essay. The strategies will provide you with both a way to start your paper and a way to organize the information you've gathered.

STRATEGIES FOR SHARING INFORMATION

Expository writing often involves telling a story, reporting or summarizing a sequence of events, constructing a historical chronology, recounting a biography or an autobiography, or detailing how something is done. In these instances, authors use **narrative** to draw in an audience and keep them engaged.

In the following example, note Danielle Ofri's careful narration about a trip to the morgue, and consider why this trip unfolds step-by-step. How would this passage affect the reader differently if she had simply written, "We took the elevator down to the morgue"?

> We stared at our sneakers as the elevator lurched downward. It creaked past several floors and landed with a jolt. Out we spilled, gingerly, onto the raw concrete floor. Our first stop was the morgue. **Danielle Ofri**, "SAT" (page 471)

When it is important for you to slow down and include careful details, a strong and vivid **description** can make a subject easier for the reader to follow. Effective descriptions might involve creating a picture in word or image, making information more clear, or reporting objective details to visualize a setting.

Charles Bowden brings the scene of a fiesta to life with lively verbs and images of the various groups at the party rather than simply writing, "Everyone was enjoying the fiesta." How does describing this fiesta in great detail convey important information not only about the events but also about the people attending the party?

> Over in Naco, Sonora, the final night of a fiesta is in full roar. Men drinking beer move by on horseback, groups of girls in high heels prance past. Nearby, folks play bingo, and in the band shell a group does a sound check for the big dance. **Charles Bowden**, "Our Wall" (page 317)

Expository writing often requires writers to discuss concepts and ideas with which readers might be unfamiliar. In these cases, writers use **examples** to back up claims and to clarify an idea by illustrating it, making an abstract concept more concrete, representing a larger concept or event by a single incident or image, or providing a "for instance."

Note how David Brooks uses phrases like "in fact" and "for example" to signal that he's about to provide an example that illustrates his larger point. He understands that specific evidence will be more convincing to his reader. How would this passage affect the reader differently if he had written,

"Sometimes segregated neighborhoods happen over time"? Would you be convinced without a clear example?

> In fact, evidence suggests that some neighborhoods become more segregated over time. New suburbs in Arizona and Nevada, for example, start out reasonably well integrated. **David Brooks**, "People Like Us" (page 324)

When you'd like to support a point, to make your writing more engaging with a particularly well-said statement or to include a clear explanation of a difficult concept, you can use **expert testimony** by quoting or summarizing another writer on the subject. We include more coverage of this strategy in the introduction to the argument section, but it's important to note here that writers of expository prose often draw on quotations from credible sources. It's difficult to convince readers you're an expert without demonstrating that you're familiar with the work of other experts.

In the following example, note that although it might have been as easy for James McBride to make a point about speech-song in his own words, he chose to quote Samuel A. Floyd—using his full name—and to spend time presenting Floyd's credentials. Why do you think McBride made those decisions as a writer? What impact does reading the details of Floyd's professional identity have on you as reader?

> "Speech-song has been part of black culture for a long, long time," says Samuel A. Floyd, director of the Center for Black Music Research at Columbia College in Chicago. **James McBride**, "Hip-Hop Planet" (page 451)

Even for words, we think we know the meaning of, writers often choose to build the foundation of their discussion by providing a **definition**. You might decide to do this in your own writing to clarify key terms, reflect on the significance or origins of a word, enlarge or restrict a term's meaning, eliminate confusion or ambiguity, or challenge conventional meanings and euphemisms.

In the following example, note how Lars Eighner reports his research into the meaning of the word *Dumpster*—a word we probably take for granted, but which he's invested in helping us to slow down and consider. How does knowing the origin of the word *Dumpster* help you understand how Eighner thinks about Dumpsters and prepare you for the rest of his essay?

> Long before I began Dumpster diving I was impressed with Dumpsters, enough so that I wrote the Merriam-Webster research service to discover what I could about the word "Dumpster." I learned from them that "Dumpster" is a proprietary word belonging to the Dempster Dumpster company. **Lars Eighner**, "On Dumpster Diving" (page 371)

STRATEGIES FOR ANALYZING INFORMATION

When writers are working with a complicated idea or illuminating the details of a seemingly simple concept, they might use **classification** to analyze a subject by dividing it into several key parts, organizing material into categories or types, making distinctions, constructing outlines, arranging ideas in the most appropriate order, or viewing an issue from various sides.

Because we may think we know plenty about smiling, Amy Cunningham wants the reader to consider the subject in more deliberate, categorical detail, and she draws on the research of Paul Ekman to help us do so. If she had not listed the different types of smiles classified by Ekman, would you be prepared to think about smiling as a complicated subject?

> Psychologist Paul Ekman, the head of the University of California's Human Interaction Lab in San Francisco, has identified 18 distinct types of smiles, including those that show misery, compliance, fear, and contempt. **Amy Cunningham**, "Why Women Smile" (page 339)

Sometimes the best way to analyze a subject is to **compare and contrast** it with something that highlights meaningful similarities or differences. Writers use this strategy to organize material through point-by-point resemblances or disparities, to form analogies, or to express a preference for one thing or position over another.

In the following example, note how Katha Pollitt opens her essay on children and gender stereotypes by pointing out how boys and girls differ in their preferences for toys. She then continues her essay by building on her initial contrast between girls and boys. She bases not only her first sentence but her entire essay on the strategy of comparing and contrasting.

> "It's twenty-eight years since the founding of NOW, and boys still like trucks and girls still like dolls." **Katha Pollitt**, "Why Boys Don't Play with Dolls?" (page 478)

STRATEGIES FOR INTERPRETING INFORMATION

Many research-paper assignments ask students not only to present information on a topic but also to respond to and interpret that information. We interpret when our analysis and explanation lead us to draw **independent conclusions** about a subject. Interpretation is often implicit in the writer's approach and need not be stated directly by such assertions as "I think," "I conclude," "I believe," or "in my opinion," which would become repetitive.

Observe how best-selling author Malcolm Gladwell, who compares the face-to-face demonstrations of the 1960s civil rights movement to today's social-media activism, rejects some of the claims made by the proponents of social media by explaining what might have happened had Martin Luther King Jr. had Facebook at his disposal:

> Enthusiasts for social media would no doubt have us believe that King's task in Birmingham would have been made infinitely easier had he been able to communicate with his followers through Facebook, and contented himself with tweets from a Birmingham jail. But networks are messy: think of the ceaseless pattern of correction and revision, amendment and debate, that characterizes Wikipedia. If Martin Luther King, Jr., had tried to do a wiki-boycott in Montgomery, he would have been steamrollered by the white power structure. And of what use would a digital communication tool be in a town where ninety-eight percent of the black community could be reached every Sunday morning at church? The things that King needed in Birmingham—discipline and strategy—were things that online social media cannot provide. **Malcolm Gladwell**, "Small Change: Why the Revolution Will Not Be Tweeted" (page 386)

Another way a writer might interpret information is to identify **cause and effect**. The writer can explain the cause of an event or a trend; examine how one thing influences another; explain the consequences of an action or idea; or assign credit, blame, or responsibility.

In the following example, note how Eric Schlosser uses this passage to answer the promise his title makes clear: he sets out to tell you "Why McDonald's Fries Taste So Good," and he does so with details that sound almost scientific. Why might he be interested in explaining cause and effect in this specific way, as opposed to stating more generally that McDonald's fries are cooked in beef fat?

> For decades McDonald's cooked its French fries in a mixture of about 7 percent cotton-seed oil and 93 percent beef tallow. The mixture gave the fries their unique flavor—and more saturated beef fat per ounce than a McDonald's hamburger. **Eric Schlosser**, "Why McDonald's Fries Taste So Good" (page 481)

All the strategies described can operate at all compositional levels. They can, for example, help shape a single sentence, an individual paragraph, or even the entire composition. Much effective expository writing, however, consists of a mixture of strategies. Many authors combine those that seem most appropriate for a particular point they are making. As you read the essays in this part, watch for authors' combining strategies and think about how you might use combined strategies in your own writing.

READING EXPOSITORY ESSAYS: A Checklist

To benefit the most from the readings in this part, we recommend that you read each selection, paying close attention to a number of different elements. To help you gain experience as an attentive reader of informative writing, the following checklist will serve as a convenient guide.

✔ Evaluate what opinions, if any, you've already formed about the essay's topic, and whether those opinions interfere with your ability to fairly consider the author's approach and attitude.

✔ Identify the central points of the essay. Think about (or write) how you might summarize those main points in fifty words or less.

✔ Identify and describe the author's purpose in writing the essay and identify where you find evidence of this purpose in the text itself.

✔ Keep track of any words you haven't encountered before—either by circling them or by writing them down elsewhere. Look up the meaning of the words and note the definition for future reference.

✔ Look for evidence to determine the author's intended audience and decide whether you belong to that audience. In what ways, if any, does the writing exclude you?

✔ Try to articulate your emotional reaction to the essay. Are you intrigued, surprised, shocked, confused, annoyed, or disgusted by any of the author's ideas or assumptions? How might you summarize why the essay makes you feel the way you do?

✔ Annotate the essay with an eye on emphasizing key points or memorable passages and add marginal comments and questions that track your engagement with the selection.

✔ What do you notice about the author's style of writing? Try noting patterns of language or images, the repetition of key terms and metaphors, and the overall tone of the writing.

✔ Identify any inconsistencies in the selection. Does the author make contradictory statements or present unconvincing evidence?

✔ Consider whether you've relied completely on the author's information. Try to independently check facts and verify sources for information you consider essential to the author's central concept and point of view.

Kwame Anthony Appiah

RACE IN THE MODERN WORLD

For over two centuries, race matters have remained a driving force in communities and conflicts around the globe. In "Race in the Modern World," philosopher **KWAME ANTHONY APPIAH** (b. 1954) challenges us to think about the possibilities of a postracial society, one in which we forge bonds based on common interests and responsibilities, rather than on false notions of shared biology or character. "Why, after all," he writes, "should we tie our fates to groups whose existence seems always to involve misunderstandings about the facts of human difference?"

> **Philosopher Kwame Anthony Appiah challenges us to think about the possibilities of a postracial society, one in which we forge bonds based on common interests and responsibilities, rather than on false notions of shared biology or character.**

Born in London and raised in Ghana, Appiah was named by *Forbes Magazine* as one of the world's seven most powerful thinkers in 2009. He has written extensively on morality, race, and religion, with special interest in African and African American culture. An accomplished scholar and lecturer, Appiah has taught at several universities, including Yale, Harvard, and Princeton, and currently holds the appointment of Professor of Philosophy and Law at New York University. In 2012, he was one of nine individuals presented the National Humanities Medal by Barack Obama. He has authored more than twenty books, including three murder mysteries.

IN 1900, in his "Address to the Nations of the World" at the first Pan-African Conference, in London, W. E. B. Du Bois[1] proclaimed that the "problem of the twentieth century" was "the problem of the color-line, the question as to how far differences of race—which show themselves chiefly in the color of the skin and the texture of the hair—will hereafter be made the basis of denying to over half the world the right of sharing to their utmost ability the opportunities and privileges of modern civilization."

---

[1] *W. E. B. Du Bois (1868–1963):* An American sociologist, historian, civil rights activist, Pan-Africanist, author, writer, and editor. Du Bois was the first African American to earn a doctorate and was a co-founder of the National Association for the Advancement of Colored People (NAACP) in 1909. Perhaps his best-known work today is the now classic 1903 collection of essays *The Souls of Black Folk.* —EDS.

W. E. B. Du Bois testifying before the Senate in support of the United Nations charter in 1945.

Du Bois had in mind not just race relations in the United States but also the role race played in the European colonial schemes that were then still reshaping Africa and Asia. The final British conquest of Kumasi, Ashanti's capital (and the town in Ghana where I grew up), had occurred just a week before the London conference began. The British did not defeat the Sokoto caliphate in northern Nigeria until 1903. Morocco did not become a French protectorate until 1912, Egypt did not become a British one until 1914, and Ethiopia did not lose its independence until 1936. Notions of race played a crucial role in all these events, and following the Congress of Berlin in 1878, during which the great powers began to devise a world order for the modern era, the status of the subject peoples in the Belgian, British, French, German, Spanish, and Portuguese colonies of Africa — as well as in independent South Africa — was defined explicitly in racial terms.

Du Bois was the beneficiary of the best education that North Atlantic civilization had to offer: he had studied at Fisk, one of the United States' finest black colleges; at Harvard; and at the University of Berlin. The year before his address, he had published *The Philadelphia Negro*, the first detailed sociological study of an American community. And like practically everybody else in his era, he had absorbed the notion, spread by a wide range of European and American intellectuals over the course of the nineteenth century, that race — the division of the world into distinct groups, identifiable by the new biological sciences — was central to social, cultural, and political life.

Even though he accepted the concept of race, however, Du Bois was a passionate critic of racism. He included anti-Semitism under that rubric, and after a visit to Nazi Germany in 1936, he wrote frankly in *The Pittsburgh Courier*, a leading black newspaper, that the Nazis' "campaign of race prejudice . . . surpasses in vindictive cruelty and public insult anything I have ever seen; and I have seen much." The European homeland had not been in his mind when he gave his speech on the color line, but the Holocaust certainly fit his thesis—as would many of the century's genocides, from the German campaign against the Hereros in Namibia in 1904 to the Hutu massacre of the Tutsis in Rwanda in 1994. Race might not necessarily have been *the* problem of the century—there were other contenders for the title—but its centrality would be hard to deny.

Violence and murder were not, of course, the only problems that Du   5
Bois associated with the color line. Civic and economic inequality between races—whether produced by government policy, private discrimination, or complex interactions between the two—were pervasive when he spoke and remained so long after the conference was forgotten.

All around the world, people know about the civil rights movement in the United States and the antiapartheid struggle in South Africa, but similar campaigns have been waged over the years in Australia, New Zealand, and most of the countries of the Americas, seeking justice for native peoples, or the descendants of African slaves, or East Asian or South Asian indentured laborers. As non-Europeans, including many former imperial citizens, have immigrated to Europe in increasing numbers in recent decades, questions of racial inequality there have come to the fore, too—in civic rights, education, employment, housing, and income. For Du Bois, Chinese, Japanese, and Koreans were on the same side of the color line as he was. But Japanese brutality toward Chinese and Koreans up through World War II was often racially motivated, as are the attitudes of many Chinese toward Africans and African Americans today. Racial discrimination and insult are a global phenomenon.

Of course, ethnoracial inequality is not the only social inequality that matters. In 2013, the nearly 20 million white people below the poverty line in the United States made up slightly more than 40 percent of the country's poor. Nor is racial prejudice the only significant motive for discrimination: ask Christians in Indonesia or Pakistan, Muslims in Europe, or LGBT people in Uganda. Ask women everywhere. But more than a century after his London address, Du Bois would find that when it comes to racial inequality, even as much has changed, much remains the same.

US AND THEM

Du Bois speech was an invitation to a global politics of race, one in which people of African descent could join with other people of color to end white supremacy, both in their various homelands and in the global system at large. That politics would ultimately shape the process of decolonization in

Africa and the Caribbean and inform the creation of what became the African Union. It was a politics that led Du Bois himself to become, by the end of his life, a citizen of a newly independent Ghana, led by Kwame Nkrumah.

But Du Bois was not simply an activist; he was even more a scholar and an intellectual, and his thinking reflected much of his age's obsession with race as a concept. In the decades preceding Du Bois' speech, thinkers throughout the academy — in classics, history, artistic and literary criticism, philology, and philosophy, as well as all the new life sciences and social sciences — had become convinced that biologists could identify, using scientific criteria, a small number of primary human races. Most would have begun the list with the black, white, and yellow races, and many would have included a Semitic race (including Jews and Arabs), an American Indian race, and more. People would have often spoken of various subgroups within these categories as races, too. Thus, the English poet Matthew Arnold considered the Anglo-Saxon and Celtic races to be the main components of the population of the United Kingdom; the French historian Hippolyte Taine thought the Gauls were the race at the core of French history and identity; and the U.S. politician John C. Calhoun discussed conflicts not only between whites and blacks but also between Anglo-Canadians and "the French race of Lower Canada."

People thought race was important not just because it allowed one to   10
define human groups scientifically but also because they believed that racial groups shared inherited moral and psychological tendencies that helped explain their different histories and cultures. Of course, there were always skeptics. Charles Darwin, for example, believed that his evolutionary theory demonstrated that human beings were a single stock, with local varieties produced by differences in environment, through a process that was bound to result in groups with blurred edges. But many late nineteenth-century European and American thinkers believed deeply in the biological reality of race and thought that the natural affinity among the members of each group made races the appropriate units for social and political organization.

Essentialism — the idea that human groups have core properties in common that explain not just their shared superficial appearances but also the deep tendencies of their moral and cultural lives — was not new. In fact, it is nearly universal, because the inclination to suppose that people who look alike have deep properties in common is built into human cognition, appearing early in life without much prompting. The psychologist Susan Gelman, for example, argues that "our essentializing bias is not directly taught," although it is shaped by language and cultural cues. It can be found as far back as Herodotus' *Histories* or the Hebrew Bible, which portrayed Ethiopians, Persians, and scores of other peoples as fundamentally other. "We" have always seen "our own" as more than superficially different from "them."

What was new in the nineteenth century was the combination of two logically unrelated propositions: that races were biological and so could be identified through the scientific study of the shared properties of the bodies of their members and that they were also political, having a central place in the lives of states. In the eighteenth century, the historian David Hume had written of "national character"; by the nineteenth century, using the new scientific language, Arnold was arguing that the "Germanic genius" of his own "Saxon" race had "steadiness as its main basis, with commonness and humdrum for its defect, fidelity to nature for its excellence."

If nationalism was the view that natural social groups should come together to form states, then the ideal form of nationalism would bring together people of a single race. The eighteenth-century French American writer J. Hector St. John de Crèvecoeur's[2] notion that in the New World, all races could be "melted into a new race of man"—so that it was the nation that made the race, not the race the nation—belonged to an older way of thinking, which racial science eclipsed.

THE OTHER DISMAL SCIENCE

In the decade after Du Bois' address, however, a second stage of modern argumentation about human groups emerged, one that placed a much greater emphasis on culture. Many things contributed to this change, but a driving force was the development of the new social science of anthropology, whose German-born leader in the United States, Franz Boas, argued vigorously (and with copious evidence from studies in the field) that the key to understanding the significant differences between peoples lay not in biology—or, at least, not in biology alone—but in culture. Indeed, this tradition of thought, which Du Bois himself soon took up vigorously, argued not only that culture was the central issue but also that the races that mattered for social life were not, in fact, biological at all.

In the United States, for example, the belief that anyone with one black   15 grandparent or, in some states, even one black great-grandparent was also black meant that a person could be socially black but have skin that was white, hair that was straight, and eyes that were blue. As Walter White, the midcentury leader of the National Association for the Advancement of Colored People, whose name was one of his many ironic inheritances, wrote in his autobiography, "I am a Negro. My skin is white, my eyes are blue, my hair is blond. The traits of my race are nowhere visible upon me."

Strict adherence to thinking of race as biological yielded anomalies in the colonial context as well. Treating all Africans in Nigeria as "Negroes," say, would combine together people with very different biological traits. If there were interesting traits of national character, they belonged not to races but to ethnic groups. And the people of one ethnic group—Arabs from Morocco to Oman, Jews in the Diaspora[3]—could come in a wide range of colors and hair types.

In the second phase of discussion, therefore, both of the distinctive claims of the first phase came under attack. Natural scientists denied that

---

[2] *J. Hector St. John de Crèvecoeur:* See his *Letters from an American Farmer*, 1782. —EDS.
[3] *Diaspora:* Greek term for "scattering" or "dispersion"; the term is often used historically to refer to a mass dispersion of a population from its original land or region, usually as a result of oppression. In this case, it refers to the dispersion of Jews around the world outside of Israel. —EDS.

the races observed in social life were natural biological groupings, and social scientists proposed that the human units of moral and political significance were those based on shared culture rather than shared biology. It helped that Darwin's point had been strengthened by the development of Mendelian[4] population genetics, which showed that the differences found between the geographic populations of the human species were statistical differences in gene frequencies rather than differences in some putative racial essence.

In the aftermath of the Holocaust, moreover, it seemed particularly important to reject the central ideas of Nazi racial "science," and so, in 1950, in the first of a series of statements on race, UNESCO (whose founding director was the leading biologist Sir Julian Huxley) declared that:

> Race was still taken seriously, but it was regarded as an outgrowth of sociocultural groups that had been created by historical processes in which the biological differences between human beings mattered only when human beings decided that they did. Biological traits such as skin color, facial shape, and hair color and texture could define racial boundaries if people chose to use them for that purpose. But there was no scientific reason for doing so. As the UNESCO statement said in its final paragraph, Racial prejudice and discrimination in the world today arise from historical and social phenomena and falsely claim the sanction of science.

CONSTRUCTION WORK

In the 1960s, a third stage of discussion began, with the rise of "genetic geography." Natural scientists such as the geneticist Luigi Luca Cavalli-Sforza argued that the concept of race had no place in human biology, and social scientists increasingly considered the social groups previously called "races" to be social constructions. Since the word "race" risked misleading people on this point, they began to speak more often of "ethnic" or "ethnoracial" groups, in order to stress the point that they were not aiming to use a biological system of classification. 20

In recent years, some philosophers and biologists have sought to reintroduce the concept of race as biological using the techniques of cladistics, a method of classification that combines genetics with broader genealogical criteria in order to identify groups of people with shared biological heritages. But this work does not undermine the basic claim that the boundaries of the social groups called "races" have been drawn based on social, rather than biological, criteria; regardless, biology does not generate its own political or moral significance. Socially constructed groups can differ statistically in biological characteristics from one another (as rural whites in the United States differ in some health measures from urban whites), but that is not a reason to suppose that these differences are caused by different group biologies. And even if statistical

---

4 **Mendelian:** Refers to Gregor Mendel, Austrian scientist known as the founder of modern genetics. —EDS.

differences between groups exist, that does not necessarily provide a rationale for treating individuals within those groups differently. So, as Du Bois was one of the first to argue, when questions arise about the salience of race in political life, it is usually not a good idea to bring biology into the discussion.

It was plausible to think that racial inequality would be easier to eliminate once it was recognized to be a product of sociology and politics rather than biology. But it turns out that all sorts of status differences between ethnoracial groups can persist long after governments stop trying to impose them. Recognizing that institutions and social processes are at work rather than innate qualities of the populations in question has not made it any less difficult to solve the problems.

IMAGINED COMMUNITIES

One might have hoped to see signs that racial thinking and racial hostility were vanishing—hoped, that is, that the color line would not continue to be a major problem in the twenty-first century, as it was in the twentieth. But a belief in essential differences between "us" and "them" persists widely, and many continue to think of such differences as natural and inherited. And of course, differences between groups defined by common descent can be the basis of social identity, whether or not they are believed to be based in biology. As a result, ethnoracial categories continue to be politically significant, and racial identities still shape many people's political affiliations.

Once groups have been mobilized along ethnoracial lines, inequalities between them, whatever their causes, provide bases for further mobilization. Many people now know that we are all, in fact, one species, and think that biological differences along racial lines are either illusory or meaningless. But that has not made such perceived differences irrelevant.

Around the world, people have sought and won affirmative action for their ethnoracial groups. In the United States, in part because of affirmative action, public opinion polls consistently show wide divergences on many questions along racial lines. On American university campuses, where the claim that "race is a social construct" echoes like a mantra, black, white, and Asian identities continue to shape social experience. And many people around the world simply find the concept of socially constructed races hard to accept, because it seems so alien to their psychological instincts and life experiences.

Race also continues to play a central role in international politics, in part because the politics of racial solidarity that Du Bois helped inaugurate, in co-founding the tradition of pan-Africanism, has been so successful. African Americans are particularly interested in U.S. foreign policy in Africa, and Africans take note of racial unrest in the United States: as far away as Port Harcourt, Nigeria, people protested against the killing of Michael Brown, the unarmed black teenager shot to death by a police officer last year [2014] in Missouri. Meanwhile, many black Americans have special access to Ghanaian passports, Rastafarianism in the Caribbean celebrates Africa as the home of black people, and heritage tourism from North and South America and the Caribbean to West Africa has boomed.

Pan-Africanism is not the only movement in which a group defined by a common ancestry displays transnational solidarity. Jews around the world show an interest in Israeli politics. People in China follow the fate of the Chinese diaspora, the world's largest. Japanese follow goings-on in São Paulo, Brazil, which is home to more than 600,000 people of Japanese descent—as well as to a million people of Arab descent, who themselves follow events in the Middle East. And Russian President Vladimir Putin has put his supposed concern for ethnic Russians in neighboring countries at the center of his foreign policy.

Identities rooted in the reality or the fantasy of shared ancestry, in short, remain central in politics, both within and between nations. In this new century, as in the last, the color line and its cousins are still going strong.

WOULDN'T IT BE NICE?

The pan-Africanism that Du Bois helped invent created, as it was meant to, a new kind of transnational solidarity. That solidarity was put to good use in the process of decolonization, and it was one of the forces that helped bring an end to Jim Crow in the United States and apartheid in South Africa. So racial solidarity has been used not just for pernicious purposes but for righteous ones as well. A world without race consciousness, or without ethnoracial identity more broadly, would lack such positive mobilizations, as well as the negative ones. It was in this spirit, I think, that Du Bois wrote, back in 1897, that it was "the duty of the Americans of Negro descent, as a body, to maintain their race identity until . . . the ideal of human brotherhood has become a practical possibility."

But at this point, the price of trying to move beyond ethnoracial identities   30 is worth paying, not only for moral reasons but also for the sake of intellectual hygiene. It would allow us to live and work together more harmoniously and productively, in offices, neighborhoods, towns, states, and nations. Why, after all, should we tie our fates to groups whose existence seems always to involve misunderstandings about the facts of human difference? Why rely on imaginary natural commonalities rather than build cohesion through intentional communities? Wouldn't it be better to organize our solidarities around citizenship and the shared commitments that bind political society?

Still, given the psychological difficulty of avoiding essentialism and the evident continuing power of ethnoracial identities, it would take a massive and focused effort of education, in schools and in public culture, to move into a postracial world. The dream of a world beyond race, unfortunately, is likely to be long deferred. ▪

The Reader's Presence

1. Identify and characterize what Appiah perceives to be the value—and the limitations—of race as a concept. What are the advantages/disadvantages of Appiah's having structured his essay around the history of race, rather than focusing on what it means in the present? What specific role does W. E. B. Du Bois play in this structure? Appiah questions whether society would be better off forming communities that aren't based on the things that have divided us in the past. What is the difference between "imagined" and "intentional" communities? How might existing ethnic and racial groups fit into what Appiah calls a postracial world?

2. Summarize—and then characterize—Appiah's attitude toward discussions of race on American university campuses. What, for example, are his response(s) to the idea of "shared ancestry" (paragraph 28)? According to Appiah, what role does race play in international politics? Point to specific examples to support your response. What do you understand regarding the negatives of focusing on racial issues? What, finally, are Appiah's recommendations about focusing on racial issues in identity? Summarize and then explain why you agree or disagree with his conclusion.

3. **CONNECTIONS:** In "People Like Us" (page 324), David Brooks writes, "People want to be around others who are roughly like themselves. That's called community" (paragraph 14). To what extent do you think Appiah would agree with this assertion? How does the Brooks' "dream of diversity" describes compare to the "dream of a world beyond race" in Appiah's essay?

Michael Bérubé

ANALYZE, DON'T SUMMARIZE

MICHAEL BÉRUBÉ, born in New York City in 1961, is Edwin Erle Sparks Professor of Literature and director of the Institute for the Arts and Humanities at Pennsylvania State University, where he teaches literature and cultural studies or, as he calls it, "dangeral studies" for the controversy such studies engender. "I would be selling students short if my classes did not reflect some of my beliefs about literary theory, or feminism, or postmodernism, or multiculturalism, since I have spent my entire adult life studying such things," he told a reporter in 2006. Known for sparring with conservative critics of academia, Bérubé has become a noted advocate of "liberal" liberal education, a defender of the humanities, and

> Michael Bérubé has become a noted advocate of "liberal" liberal education, a defender of the humanities, and "the professor the right loves to hate."

"the professor the right loves to hate." His books include *Marginal Forces/Cultural Centers: Tolson, Pynchon, and the Politics of the Canon* (1992); *Public Access: Literary Theory and American Cultural Politics* (1994); and *The Employment of English: Theory, Jobs, and the Future of Literary Studies* (1998). His 1996 book dealing with his son born with Down syndrome, *Life as We Know It: A Father, a Family, and an Exceptional Child* (1996), was a New York Times Notable Book of the Year. His most recent works are *The Secret Life of Stories: From Don Quixote to Harry Potter, How Understanding Intellectual Disability Transforms the Way We Read* (2016), *Rhetorical Occasions: Essays on Humans and the Humanities* (2006), and *The Left at War (Cultural Front)* (2009). He has written articles for many publications, including *Harper's*, the *New Yorker*, *Dissent*, the *New York Times Magazine*, the *Village Voice*, the *Washington Post*, and the *Nation*, as well as numerous scholarly journals such as the *Chronicle of Higher Education*, where his essay "Analyze, Don't Summarize" appeared in 2004.

THE FIRST TIME a student asked me about my "grading system," I was nonplused—and a bit intimidated. It was an innocent question, but I heard it as a challenge: I was a 25-year-old graduate student teaching my first section in an English-literature class at the University of Virginia, and I really didn't know *what* my grading system was. Nor did I feel comfortable saying, "Well, it's like Justice Stewart's[1] definition of pornography, really—I simply know an A paper when I see one."

I fumbled my way through a reply, but I was unsettled enough by the exchange to seek the advice of the professor in charge of the course (and roughly a dozen teaching assistants). He went on a sublime rant that I've never forgotten, though I'm sure I've embellished it over the years. "These students come in here," he fumed, "with the idea that *you* have to explain yourself. 'You gave me a B-plus,' they say. 'What did you take points off for?' I tell them, 'Your paper was not born with an A. Your paper was born with a "nothing," and I made up my mind about it as I read it. That's what the marginalia are—they're the record of my responses to your arguments.'"

Today I've incorporated versions of that rant into my own teaching handouts: I try to explain the differences among superior, mediocre, and failing papers, and I tell students that my skills as a reader have been honed by my many experiences with professional editors, who attend carefully to paragraph transitions, dangling modifiers, and inaccurate citations. But I've never been able to give my students a visceral idea of what goes through my head as I read their work—until now.

Like many sports fans, I've grown a bit tired of ESPN's 25th-anniversary hyper-self-awareness of itself as a sports medium. While it's great to see the network poke fun at its early years, when its anchors wore dorky sport coats

---

1 *Justice Stewart:* United States Supreme Court Justice Potter Stewart (1915–1985), who stated in a 1964 ruling that while it may be hard to describe hard-core pornography, "I know it when I see it." —EDS.

and weren't always sure when they were on the air, it's really quite tedious to be reminded of how sports-television hype helped hype TV sports.

The show *Around the Horn* has come to epitomize the general decline   5
to me. Another half-hour program with which it's paired, *Pardon the Interruption*, gives us two volatile, opinionated sportscasters disagreeing with each other in rapid-fire fashion, with but a handful of seconds devoted to each topic. *Around the Horn* takes that format and makes a game show of it, offering us sportswriters competing for whose commentary will "win" by the end of the show.

I still play an organized sport—ice hockey—and as an amateur (and aged) player, I have to say that sports talk shows like this make me wonder whether some people don't see sports as simply an opportunity for endless metacommentary . . . and, of course, as gainful employment for an entire entourage of chattering parasites. In all that noise, I think, where are the games themselves?

Imagine my surprise, then, when I watched *Around the Horn* one afternoon and realized that here, at last, was my grading system in practice.

The idea behind *Around the Horn* is simple. There are a host and four contestants, each of whom speaks briefly on a series of up-to-the-moment sports topics. Points are awarded for smart—or merely plausible—remarks, and points are deducted for obviously foolish or factually inaccurate ones. There's a mute button involved, too, and players get eliminated as the show progresses (but those aspects of the game, so far as I can tell, have no counterpart in the world of paper-grading). And—of course, for this is the point of all such sports metacommentary—the viewers at home get to disagree with and complain about the commentary, as well as the officiating.

My standard undergraduate survey-course guides for paper-writing tell students things like this: "Assume a hypothetical readership composed of people who have already read the book. That means you shouldn't say, 'In class, we discussed the importance of the clam chowder in Chapter Five.' But more important, it means *you don't have to summarize the novel.* We're your readers, and we've read the book. However, we haven't read it in quite the way *you're* reading it. We haven't focused on the same scenes and passages you're bringing to our attention, and we haven't yet seen how your argument might make sense of the book for us."

But not all of my students see the point. Every semester I'm approached   10
by some who don't quite understand why they're being asked to make an *argument* out of literary criticism. Why shouldn't they simply record their impressions of the works before them? When I tell them that an observation is not a thesis, and that their thesis isn't sufficiently specific or useful if they can't imagine anyone plausibly disagreeing with it, they ask me why they can't simply explain *what happens in the novel.*

But in what world, exactly, would such an enterprise count as analysis? Not in any world I know—not even in the ephemeral pop-culture world of sports metacommentary. Can you imagine someone showing up on *Around the Horn* and saying to host Tony Reali, "Well, Tony, let me point out that last night, the Red Sox swept the Tigers and crept to within three games of the Yankees."

"And?"

"And nothing. I'm just pointing out that the Sox won, 3–1, on a four-hitter by Schilling, while the Yanks blew another late-inning lead."

No one does that, because no one in the sports world confuses summaries with analyses.

I also tell students that an essay of 2,000 words doesn't give them all that much space to get going.   15

"You've only got a few pages to make that argument of yours. You don't need a grand introductory paragraph that begins, 'Mark Twain is one of Earth's greatest writers.' It's far better to start by giving us some idea of what you'll be arguing and why. If you like, you can even begin by pointing us to a particularly important passage that will serve as the springboard for your larger discussion: 'Not long after the second scaffold scene in *The Scarlet Letter*, when Arthur Dimmesdale joins hands with Hester Prynne and her daughter Pearl, Nathaniel Hawthorne asks us to reconsider the meaning of the scarlet A on Hester's breast.'"

On *Around the Horn*, commentators have to make their points in 15 seconds, which, as people who know me can testify, just happens to be roughly the amount of time it takes me to utter 2,000 words. So here, too, the analogy holds up.

Seriously, the sports-talk analogy is useful simply as a handy way of distinguishing between summary and analysis—and, more important, as an illustration of what happens in my grading process when a student paper cites textual evidence so compelling and unusual that it makes me go back and reread the passage in question (good!), suggests that a novel's conclusion fails to resolve the questions and tensions raised by the rest of the narrative (interesting!—possibly good, depending on the novel we're talking about), or makes claims that are directly contradicted by the literary text itself (bad! the mute button for you!).

So in a sense, I do "take off" points as I go—but then I add them back on as well, sentence by sentence, paragraph by paragraph, as I weigh the claims my students advance and the means by which they advance them.

The rules for literary analysis are the same rules in play for any kind of   20 analysis: mastery of the material. Cogency of supporting evidence. Ability to imagine and rebut salient counterarguments. Extra points for wit and style, points off for mind-numbing clichés, and permanent suspension for borrowing someone else's argument without proper attribution.

And yet, every year, I'm left with a handful of students who tell me that if *that's* what I want, I should simply assign topics to each student. "Not a chance," I reply. "Most of the mental labor of your paper takes place when you try to figure out just what you want to argue and why." As books like Thomas McLaughlin's *Street Smarts and Critical Theory* and Gerald Graff's *Clueless in Academe* have argued (with wit and style), students seem to understand this principle perfectly well when it comes to music, sports, and popular culture. It's our job to show them how it might apply to the study of literature.

My students, too, are often suspicious of what they regard as an idiosyncratic and a subjective enterprise that varies from English professor to English professor. But I can tell them there's really nothing mysterious about its mechanics. In fact, if they want to watch it in action, they can tune in to ESPN any weekday afternoon, 5 p.m. Eastern. ▪

The Reader's Presence

1. Bérubé creates an analogy between grading student essays and watching sports commentary on ESPN. Outline the points of similarity between an instructor's responding to student writing and a television commentator's comments about sports. Which aspects of this analogy do you find most—and least—convincing? What aspects of this analogy, if any, has Bérubé omitted? Summarize the distinctions Bérubé draws between "analysis" and "summary." What is the significance of Bérubé's point that "an observation is not a thesis" (paragraph 10)?

2. In paragraph 21, Bérubé notes, "As books like Thomas McLaughlin's *Street Smarts and Critical Theory* and Gerald Graff's *Clueless in Academe* have argued (with wit and style), students seem to understand this principle perfectly well when it comes to music, sports, and popular culture." Explain the extent to which you agree—or disagree—with Bérubé's assertion here. What evidence can you point to in support of—or to argue against—the spirit and substance of Bérubé's claim?

3. As you reread Bérubé's essay, what specific words and phrases do you think most accurately and effectively characterize his tone toward grading student essays? toward television commentators on sports? What do you notice about Bérubé's choice of adjectives and verbs? What are his attitudes toward what he calls "marginalia" (paragraph 2)? What do you understand him to mean when he talks about "sports as simply an opportunity for endless metacommentary" (paragraph 6)? Comment on the effectiveness of Bérubé's use of "entourage" in the phrase "an entire entourage of chattering parasites" (paragraph 6). Examine carefully Bérubé's "rules for literary analysis" in paragraph 20. Apply these criteria to the strengths and weaknesses of his essay. Which of these rules does his essay most—and least—effectively illustrate? Be as specific as possible in your response.

4. **CONNECTIONS:** In his essay "Everything You Need to Know about Writing Successfully—in Ten Minutes" Stephen King observes: "If you haven't marked up your manuscript a lot, you did a lazy job" (page 426). Compare and contrast King's and Bérubé's rules of writing. To what extent do their rules overlap despite the distinct genres in which they write? Based on their rules, which writer practices his craft more effectively? Explain why, and provide detailed analyses of each writer's prose.

Eula Biss

SENTIMENTAL MEDICINE

Eula Biss (b. 1977) writes essays like poetry, summoning vivid images as easily as facts. Her work draws heavily on personal experience and metaphor to untangle such subjects as race in America and public health. She began researching vaccination while pregnant with her son, drafting a personal essay that would eventually become her latest book, *On Immunity: An Inoculation* (2014). First published in *Harper's* in 2013, "Sentimental Medicine" tells a story ranging from dubious medical treatments to vampirism, as Biss examines fears surrounding the practice of vaccination through the lens of her experiences as a mother.

The author of an award-winning collection, *Notes from No Man's Land: American Essays* (2009), Biss has published widely,

> **Biss tends "to think of personal narrative as a perfectly viable space for intellectual exploration."**

including in *Harper's,* the *New York Times Magazine*, and the *Believer*. She currently teaches nonfiction writing at Northwestern University in Evanston, Illinois. On writing, Biss offers some advice she often shares with her students: "try not to bore yourself."

MY SON IS VACCINATED, but there is one immunization on the standard schedule he did not receive. This was meant to be his very first shot, the hepatitis B[1] vaccine administered to most infants immediately after birth. I was aware, before I became pregnant, of some fears around vaccination. But I was not prepared for the labyrinthine network of anxieties I would discover during my pregnancy, the proliferation of hypotheses, the minutiae of additives, the diversity of ideologies. Vaccines contain preservatives, adjuvants, and residues from their manufacture. They were developed from aborted fetuses, were tested in Nazi concentration camps, and are not vegan. And vaccines are metaphors, if popular literature on vaccination is to be read as literature, for capitalist corruption, cultural decadence, and environmental pollution.

The reach of this subject had exceeded the limits of my late-night research by the time my baby was due, so I visited the pediatrician I had chosen to be my son's doctor. I already knew that some people would consider

---

[1] **Hepatitis B:** A viral infection attacking the liver and causing both acute and chronic disease. —EDS.

a medical professional a dubious source of intelligence on vaccination. The money pharmaceutical companies are pouring into research, they would say, has made the information available to doctors dirty. But not all doctors are informed by research, as I would discover, and there is more than one route to unclean thinking.

When I asked the pediatrician what the purpose of the hep B vaccine was, he answered, "That's a very good question," in a tone I understood to mean this was a question he relished answering. Hep B was a vaccine for the inner city, he told me—it was designed to protect the babies of drug addicts and prostitutes. It was not something, he assured me, that people like me needed to worry about.

All that this doctor knew of me then was what he could see. He assumed, correctly, that I did not live in the inner city. It did not occur to me to clarify that although I live in the outer city of Chicago, my neighborhood looks a lot like what some people mean when they use the euphemism "inner city." In retrospect, I am ashamed by how little of his racial code I registered. Relieved to be told that this vaccine was not for people like me, I failed to consider what exactly that meant.

The belief that public-health measures are not intended for people like us   5
is widely held by people like me. Public health, we assume, is for people with less—less education, less healthy habits, less access to quality health care, less time and money. I've heard mothers of my class suggest, for instance, that the standard childhood vaccination schedule groups together multiple shots because poor mothers can't visit the doctor frequently enough to get the twenty-six recommended shots separately. (No matter that many mothers, myself included, might find so many visits daunting.) *That*, we seem to be saying of the standard schedule, *is for people like them.*

When the last nationwide smallpox epidemic began in 1898, some people believed that whites were not susceptible to the disease. It was called "nigger itch" or, where it was associated with immigrants, "Italian itch" or "Mexican bump." When smallpox broke out in New York City, police officers were sent to help enforce the vaccination of Italian and Irish immigrants in the tenements. And when smallpox arrived in Middlesboro, Kentucky, everyone in the black section of town who resisted immunization was vaccinated at gunpoint. These campaigns did limit the spread of the disease, but most of the risk of vaccination, which at that time could lead to infection with other diseases, was absorbed by the most vulnerable. The poor were forced into the service of the privileged.

Debates over vaccination, then as now, were often cast as debates over the integrity of science, though they could just as easily be understood as conversations about power. The working-class people who resisted England's 1853 provision of free, mandatory vaccination were concerned, in part, for their own liberty. Faced with fines, imprisonment, and the seizure of their property if they did not vaccinate their infants, they sometimes compared their predicament to slavery. In her history of that antivaccination movement,

Nadja Durbach returns often to the idea that the resisters saw their bodies "not as potentially contagious and thus dangerous to the social body, but as highly vulnerable to contamination and violation." Their bodies were, of course, both vulnerable and contagious. But in a time and place where the bodies of the poor were seen as a source of disease, as dangerous to others, it fell to the poor to articulate that they were also vulnerable.

If it was meaningful then for the poor to assert that they were not purely dangerous, I suspect it might be just as meaningful now for the rest of us to accept that we are not purely vulnerable. The middle class may be "threatened," but we are still, just by virtue of having bodies, dangerous. Even the little bodies of children, which nearly all the thinking common to our time encourages us to imagine as absolutely vulnerable, are dangerous in their ability to spread disease. Think of the unvaccinated boy in San Diego, for instance, who returned from a trip to Switzerland with a case of measles that infected his two siblings, five schoolmates, and four children in his doctor's waiting room. Three of these children were infants too young to be vaccinated, and one of them had to be hospitalized.

Unvaccinated children, according to a 2004 analysis of CDC[2] data, are more likely than undervaccinated children to be white and to live in households with an income of $75,000 or more—like my child. Their mothers are more likely to be, like me, married and college-educated. Undervaccinated children, meaning children who have received some but not all of their recommended immunizations, are more likely to be black, to have younger, unmarried mothers, and to live in poverty.

"Vaccination works," my father, a doctor, tells me, "by enlisting a majority in the protection of a minority." He means the minority of the population that is particularly vulnerable to a disease. The elderly, in the case of influenza. Newborns, in the case of pertussis. Pregnant women, in the case of rubella. When relatively wealthy white women choose to vaccinate our children, we may also be participating in the protection of poor black children whose single mothers have not, as a result of circumstance rather than choice, fully vaccinated them. This is a radical inversion of the historical approach to vaccination, which was once just another form of bodily servitude extracted from the poor for the benefit of the privileged. There is some truth now to the idea that public health is not strictly for people like me, but it is through us—literally through our bodies—that public health is maintained.   10

Vaccination is sometimes implicated in all the crimes of modern medicine. But vaccination was a precursor to modern medicine, not the product of it. Its roots are in folk medicine, and its first practitioners were farmers. Milkmaids in eighteenth-century England had faces unblemished by smallpox, as anyone could see. Common wisdom held that if a milkmaid milked a cow blistered with cowpox and developed some blisters on her hands, she would not contract smallpox even while nursing victims of an epidemic.

---

2 **CDC:** Centers for Disease Control and Prevention, the nation's health protection agency. —EDS.

During an outbreak in 1774, a farmer who had himself already been infected with cowpox used a darning needle to force pus from a cow's udder into the arms of his wife and two toddler boys. The farmer's neighbors were horrified. His wife's arm became red and swollen, and she fell ill before recovering from the infection, but the boys had mild reactions. They were exposed to smallpox many times over the course of their long lives, occasionally for the purpose of demonstrating their immunity, without ever contracting the disease.

Twenty years later, the country doctor Edward Jenner scraped pus from a blister on the hand of a milkmaid into an incision on the arm of an eight-year-old boy. The boy did not contract smallpox, and Jenner continued his experiment on dozens of other people, including his own infant son. Jenner had the evidence to suggest that vaccination worked, but he did not know why it worked. His innovation was based entirely on observation, not on theory. This was a century before the first virus would be identified, a century before germ theory would be validated, more than a century before penicillin would be extracted from a fungus, and long before the cause of smallpox would be understood.

The essential mechanism underlying vaccination was not new even in Jenner's time. At that point variolation, the practice of deliberately infecting a person with a minor strain of smallpox in order to prevent infection with a more deadly strain, was still somewhat novel in England but had been practiced in China and India for hundreds of years. (In China, it was said to have been "bestowed by a Taoist[3] immortal.") Variolation would later be brought to America from Africa by a slave. It was then introduced to England by an ambassador's wife, her own face scarred by smallpox, who inoculated her children after observing the practice in Turkey. Voltaire,[4] himself a survivor of a serious case of smallpox, implored the French to adopt variolation from the English.

When Voltaire wrote his letter "On Inoculation" in 1735, the primary meaning of the English word "inoculate" was still "to set a bud or scion," as apple trees are cultivated by grafting a stem from one tree onto the roots of another. There were many methods of inoculation, including the snuffing of powdered scabs and the sewing of an infected thread through the webbing between the thumb and forefinger, but in England it was often accomplished by making a slit or flap in the skin into which infectious material was placed, like the slit in the bark of a tree that receives the young stem grafted onto it. When "inoculate" was first used to describe variolation, it was a metaphor for grafting a disease, which would bear its own fruit, onto the rootstock of the body.

15

---

3 ***Taoist:*** Someone who practices Taoism, also known as Daoism, a religious or philosophical tradition of Chinese origin emphasizing living in harmony with the Tao (literally "Way")—living life kindly, compassionately, gracefully, and modestly. —EDS.

4 ***Voltaire:*** Pen name of François-Marie Arouet (1694–1778), a French writer, historian, and philosopher famous for his wit and advocacy of freedom of religion, speech, and separation of church and state. —EDS.

From somewhere deep in my childhood I can remember my father explaining with enthusiasm the principle behind the Doppler effect[5] as an ambulance sped past our car. My father marveled at the world far more often than he talked about the body, but blood types were a subject on which he spoke with some passion. People with the blood type O negative, he explained, can receive in transfusion only blood that is O negative, but people with O-negative blood can give blood to people with any other type. That's why a person with type O negative is known as a "universal donor." My father then revealed that his blood type was O negative, that he himself was a universal donor. He gave blood, he told me, as often as he could because his type was always in demand. I suspect my father knew that my blood, too, is type O negative.

I understood the idea of the universal donor more as an ethic than as a medical concept long before I knew my own blood type. But I did not yet think of that ethic as an ingenious filtering of my father's Catholic background through his medical training. I was not raised in the Church and I never took communion, so I was not reminded of Jesus offering of his blood that we all might live. But I believed, even then, that we owe each other our bodies.

The very first decision I made for my son, a decision enacted within moments of his body coming free of mine, was the donation of his umbilical-cord blood to a public bank. I myself had donated blood only once, and I wanted my son to start his life with a credit to the bank, not a debt. And this was before I, the universal donor, would become the recipient of two pints of blood in a transfusion shortly after my son's birth. Blood of the most precious type, drawn from a public bank.

If we imagine the action of a vaccine not just in terms of how it affects a single body but also in terms of how it affects the collective body of a community, it is fair to think of vaccination as a kind of banking of immunity. Contributions to this bank are donations to those who cannot or will not be protected by their own immunity. This is the principle of "herd immunity," and it is through herd immunity that mass vaccination becomes far more effective than individual vaccination.

Any given vaccine can fail to produce immunity in an individual, and   20 some vaccines, like the influenza vaccine, often fail to produce immunity. But when enough people are given even a relatively ineffective vaccine, viruses have trouble moving from host to host and cease to spread, sparing both the unvaccinated and those in whom vaccination has not produced immunity. This is why the chances of contracting measles can be higher for a vaccinated person living in a largely unvaccinated community than for an unvaccinated person living in a largely vaccinated community.

---

5 **Doppler effect:** The change in frequency or wavelength of a sound wave for an observer who is moving relative to the wave source. For example, the change of pitch heard when a vehicle sounding a siren or horn approaches, passes, and recedes. Named after the Austrian physicist Christian Doppler, who described the phenomena in 1842. —EDS.

The boundaries between our bodies begin to dissolve here. Blood and organs move between us, exiting one body and entering another, and so, too, with immunity, which is a common trust as much as it is a private account. Those of us who draw on collective immunity owe our health to our neighbors.

My father has a scar on his left arm from his smallpox vaccination half a century ago. That vaccine was responsible for the worldwide eradication of smallpox in 1980, but it remains far more dangerous than any vaccine currently on our childhood immunization schedule. The risk of death after vaccination for smallpox is, according to one estimate, about one in a million. The risk of hospitalization is about one in a hundred thousand, and the risk of serious complications is about one in a thousand.

Thirty years after routine vaccination for smallpox ended in this country, the federal government asked researchers at the University of Iowa to test the remaining stores of the vaccine for efficacy. This was in the long moment after 9/11 when every potential terrorist attack was anticipated, including the use of smallpox as a biological weapon. The smallpox vaccine proved effective even after having been stored for decades and diluted to increase the supply. But the results of the vaccine trial, says Patricia Winokur, director of the school's Vaccine Research and Education Unit, were "unacceptable by today's standards." A third of the people who received the vaccine suffered fevers or rashes and were sick, in some cases, for several days. Everyone recovered, even those who developed serious inflammations of the heart, but it was clear that the degree of risk was not what we have come to expect from immunization.

The smallpox vaccine contains far more immunizing proteins —more of the active ingredient, so to speak— than any of the vaccines we use today. In that sense, the vaccine our parents received presented a greater challenge to the immune system in one dose than do the twenty-six immunizations for fourteen diseases we now give our children over the course of two years. Still, the proliferation of childhood vaccines has become, for some of us, symbolic of American excess. *Too much, too soon,* one of the slogans of vaccine activism, could easily be a critique of just about any aspect of our modern lives.

When asked by his colleagues to address the question of whether too many 25 vaccines are given too early in life, the University of Pennsylvania pediatrics professor Paul Offit set out to quantify the capabilities of the infant immune system, which was already known to be quite impressive. Infants, after all, are exposed to an onslaught of bacteria the moment they leave the womb, even before they exit the birth canal. Any infant who does not live in a bubble is likely to find the everyday work of fighting off infections more taxing than processing weakened antigens from multiple immunizations.

Offit is the director of the Vaccine Education Center at the Children's Hospital of Philadelphia and head of its Division of Infectious Diseases. He is also, if you believe the Internet, a "Devil's servant" known as "Dr. Proffit." He earned this distinction by co-inventing a vaccine that made him several million

|||||||||||||||||||||||||||||||||||||||||||||||||||||||||||||||||||||||||||||||||||||||||||||||||||||||||||||||||||||||||||||||||||||||||||||||||

dollars. The idea that the success of his vaccine, which took twenty-five years to develop, should invalidate his expertise in immunology is somewhat baffling to Offit. But he understands the other source of his infamy. In response to the question of how many vaccines is too many, Offit determined that a child could theoretically handle a total of 100,000 vaccines or up to 10,000 vaccinations at once. He came to regret this number, though he does not believe it to be inaccurate. "The 100,000 number makes me sound like a madman," he told *Wired*. "Because that's the image: 100,000 shots sticking out of you. It's an awful image."

In a 2009 article for *Mothering* magazine, Jennifer Margulis expresses outrage that newborn infants are routinely vaccinated for hep B and wonders why she was encouraged to vaccinate her daughter "against a sexually transmitted disease she had no chance of catching." Hep B is transmitted through bodily fluids, so the most common way that newborns contract hep B is from their mothers. Babies born to women who are infected with hep B—and mothers can carry the virus without knowing it—will very likely be infected if they are not vaccinated within twelve hours of birth. Like human papillomavirus and a number of other viruses, hep B is a carcinogen. Newborns infected with it are at a high risk of developing long-term problems like liver cancer, but people of all ages can carry the disease without symptoms. Before the vaccine for hep B was introduced, the disease infected 200,000 people a year, and about a million Americans were chronically infected.

One of the mysteries of hep B immunization is that vaccinating only "high-risk" groups, which was the original public-health strategy, did not bring down rates of infection. When the vaccine was introduced in 1981, it was recommended for prisoners, health-care workers, gay men, and IV-drug users. But rates of hep B infection remained unchanged until 1991, when the vaccine was recommended for all newborns. Only mass vaccination brought down the rates of infection, and since 1991 vaccination has virtually eliminated the disease in children.

Risk, in the case of hep B, turns out to be a rather complicated assessment. There is risk in having sex with just one partner, getting a tattoo, or traveling to Asia. In many cases, the source of infection is never known. I decided before my son's birth that I did not want him vaccinated for hep B, but it did not occur to me until months later that although I did not belong to any risk groups at the moment he was born, by the time I put him to my breast I had received a blood transfusion and my status had changed.

"Everyone who is born holds dual citizenship, in the kingdom of the well and in the kingdom of the sick," Susan Sontag[6] wrote in her introduction to *Illness as Metaphor*. "Although we all prefer to use only the good passport, sooner or later each of us is obliged, at least for a spell, to identify ourselves as citizens of that other place." Sontag wrote these words while being treated for

30

---

6 **Susan Sontag** *(1933–2004):* noted American writer and intellectual; her *Illness as Metaphor* appeared in 1978. —EDS.

cancer. She wrote, as she later explained, to "calm the imagination." Those of us who have lived most of our lives in the kingdom of the well may find our imaginations already placid. Not all of us think of health as a transient state from which we may be exiled without warning. Some prefer to assume health as an identity. *I am healthy*, we say, meaning that we eat certain foods and avoid others, that we exercise and do not smoke. Health, it is implied, is the reward for living the way we live, and lifestyle is its own variety of immunity.

An 1881 handbill entitled *The Vaccination Vampire* warns of the "universal pollution" delivered by the vaccinator to the "pure babe." The macabre sexuality of the vampire dramatized the fear that there was something sexual in the act of vaccination, an anxiety that was only reinforced when sexually transmitted diseases were spread through arm-to-arm vaccination. Until the advent of the hollow needle, vaccination often left a wound that would scar — "the mark of the beast," some feared. In one 1882 sermon, vaccination was akin to an injection of sin, an "abominable mixture of corruption, the lees of human vice, and dregs of venial appetites, that in after life may foam upon the spirit, and develop hell within, and overwhelm the soul."

While vaccination now rarely leaves a mark, our fears that we will be permanently marked have remained. We fear that vaccination will invite autism or any one of the diseases of immune dysfunction now plaguing industrialized countries — diabetes, asthma, allergies. We fear that the hep B vaccine will cause multiple sclerosis, or that the diphtheria-pertussis-tetanus vaccine will cause sudden infant death syndrome. We fear that the formaldehyde in some vaccines will cause cancer, or that the aluminum in others will damage our brains.

It was the "poison of adders, the blood, entrails and excretions of rats, bats, toads and sucking whelps," that were imagined into the vaccines of the nineteenth century. This was the kind of organic matter, the filth, believed to be responsible for most disease at that time. Vaccination was dangerous then. Not because it would cause a child to grow the horns of a cow, but because it could spread diseases like syphilis when pus from one person was used to vaccinate another. Even when vaccination no longer involved an exchange of bodily fluids, bacterial infection remained a problem. In 1901, a contaminated batch of smallpox vaccine caused a tetanus outbreak that killed nine children in Camden, New Jersey. And in 1916, a typhoid vaccine carrying staph bacteria killed four children in Columbia, South Carolina.

Now our vaccines are, if all is well, sterile. Some contain preservatives to prevent the growth of bacteria. So now it is, in the antivaccine activist Jenny McCarthy's words, "the frickin' mercury, the ether, the aluminum, the antifreeze" that we fear in our vaccines. These substances are mostly, like the pollutants that threaten our environment today, inorganic. They are not of the body, or so we think. Although there is no ether or antifreeze in any vaccines, many do contain traces of the formaldehyde used to inactivate viruses. This can be alarming to those of us who associate formaldehyde with dead frogs in glass jars, but the chemical is produced by our bodies and is essential to our metabolism. The amount of formaldehyde already circulating in our systems is considerably greater than the amount we might receive through vaccination.

As for mercury, the ethylmercury preservative used in many vaccines 35 until the late 1990s, thimerosal, is now only in some flu vaccines. Ethylmercury is cleared more easily by the body than the methylmercury often found in breast milk, and a child will almost certainly get more mercury exposure from her immediate environment than from vaccination. This is true too of aluminum, an adjuvant used in some vaccines to intensify the immune response. Aluminum is in lot of things, including fruits and cereals as well as, again, breast milk. Our breast milk, it turns out, is as polluted as our environment. It contains paint thinners, dry-cleaning fluids, flame retardants, pesticides, and rocket fuel. "Most of these chemicals are found in microscopic amounts," the journalist Florence Williams notes, "but if human milk were sold at the local Piggly Wiggly, some stock would exceed federal food-safety levels for DDT residues and PCBs."[7]

When my son was six months old, at the peak of the H1N1[8] flu pandemic, another mother told me that she did not believe in herd immunity. It had not yet occurred to me then that herd immunity was subject to belief, though there is clearly something of the occult in the idea of an invisible cloak of protection cast over an entire population. Herd immunity, an observable phenomenon, is implausible only if we think of our bodies as inherently disconnected from other bodies. Which, of course, we do.

One of the unfortunate features of the term "herd immunity" is that it invites association with the term "herd mentality," a stampede toward stupidity. The herd, we assume, is foolish. Those of us who eschew the herd mentality tend to prefer a frontier mentality in which we imagine our bodies as isolated homesteads. The health of the homestead next to ours does not affect us, this thinking suggests, so long as ours is well tended.

If we were to recast the herd as a hive, perhaps the concept of shared immunity might be more appealing. Honeybees are industrious environmental do-gooders who also happen to be hopelessly interdependent. The health of any individual bee, as we know from the recent epidemic of colony collapse disorder, depends on the health of the hive.

The idea that our lives are dependent on our hive might not be very heartening. There are many well-documented instances of crowds making bad decisions—lynching is the first example that comes to mind for me. But the journalist James Surowiecki argues in *The Wisdom of Crowds* that large groups routinely solve complex problems whose solutions evade individuals. Groups of people, if they are sufficiently diverse and free to disagree, can provide us with thinking superior to that of any one expert. Groups can locate

---

[7] ***DDT . . . and PCBs:*** Chemicals banned more than 30 years ago. Yet despite cleanup efforts, our air, water, land, and bodies remain exposed to these health threats. —EDS.

[8] ***H1N1 flu pandemic:*** Also known as "swine flu," a widespread influenza. —EDS.

lost submarines, predict terrorist attacks, and reveal the cause of a new disease. Science, Surowiecki reminds us, is "a profoundly collective enterprise." It's a product of the herd.

But "herd immunity" suggests we are only so many cattle, waiting, perhaps, to be sent to slaughter. We may feel, when herded toward vaccination, that we are assuming the dumb submission of animals who look on passively as they are daily robbed of their babies' milk. It is no wonder some mothers resist a metaphoric milking.

The Circassian[9] women," wrote Voltaire, "have, from time immemorial, communicated the smallpox to their children when not above six months old by making an incision in the arm, and by putting into this incision a pustule, taken carefully from the body of another child." It was women who inoculated their children, and Voltaire mourned the fact that the "lady of some French ambassador" had not brought the technique from Constantinople to Paris. "What prompted the Circassians to introduce this custom, which seems so strange to others," Voltaire wrote, "is a motive common to all: maternal love and self-interest."

Medical care was still mainly the domain of women then, though the tradition of the female healer was already threatened. Midwives and wise women, guilty of crimes that included providing contraception and easing the pains of labor, were persecuted in the witch hunts that spread across Europe from the fifteenth to the eighteenth century. While women were being killed for their suspicious ability to heal the sick, physicians in European universities studied Plato and Aristotle but learned very little about the body. They did not experiment, did not practice science as we know it, and had little empirical data to support their treatments, which were often superstitious in nature. Women healers were also susceptible to superstition, but as far back as the early Middle Ages midwives were using ergot to speed contractions and belladonna to prevent miscarriage. St. Hildegard of Bingen catalogued the healing properties of 213 medicinal plants, and female lay healers were using recipes for painkillers and anti-inflammatories at a time when physicians were still writing scripture on the jaws of their patients to heal toothaches.

Benjamin Rush, one of the fathers of American medicine, bled his patients to, as the writers Barbara Ehrenreich and Deirdre English put it, "Transylvanian excesses." In the late eighteenth and early nineteenth centuries, patients were bled until they fainted, dosed with mercury, and blistered with mustard plasters. While women were excluded from formal medical education, male physicians competed, sometimes aggressively, with their informal practice in the home. But the art of healing, as doctors were to discover, is rather difficult to commodify. It was the pressures of the marketplace, Ehrenreich and English suggest in *For Her Own Good*, that led to the

9 **Circassian:** From a region in the North Caucasus and along the northeast shore of the Black Sea. —EDS.

practice of "heroic" medicine, which relied heavily on dangerous therapies like bleeding. The purpose of heroic medicine was not so much to heal the patient as to produce some measurable—and, ideally, dramatic—effect for which the patient could be billed. Rush, for one, was accused at the time of killing more patients than he cured.

As doctors began to replace midwives in the nineteenth century, child-birth moved into hospitals, and the maternal death rate rose. We now know that childbed fever, as puerperal sepsis was called, was spread by doctors who did not wash their hands between exams. But it was blamed on tight petticoats, fretting, and bad morals. In the twentieth century, poorly under-stood illnesses like schizophrenia would be blamed on bad mothers, as would marginalized behaviors such as homosexuality. Autism, according to a prevailing theory in the 1950s, was caused by insensitive "refrigerator mothers."

Even a moderately informed woman squinting at the rough outlines   45 of a terribly compressed history of medicine can discern that quite a bit of what has passed for science in the past two hundred years, particu-larly where women are concerned, has not been the result of scientific inquiry so much as it has been the refuse of science repurposed to support existing ideologies. In this tradition, Andrew Wakefield's now retracted 1998 *Lancet* study of twelve children with both developmental disorders and intestinal problems advanced a hypothesis that was already in the air—the children were referred to Wakefield by antivaccine activists, and the study was funded by a lawyer preparing a lawsuit built around many of the same children. Wakefield speculated, on the basis of evi-dence later revealed to be falsified, that the measles-mumps-rubella vaccine might be linked to a behavioral syndrome. While the publicity around Wakefield's paper precipitated a dramatic drop in vaccination against measles, the paper itself concluded, "We did not prove an asso-ciation between measles, mumps, and rubella vaccine and the syndrome described," and the primary finding of the study was that more research was needed. Those who went on to use Wakefield's inconclusive work to support the notion that vaccines cause autism are guilty not of igno-rance or science denial but of using weak science as it has always been used—to lend credibility to an idea that we want to believe for other reasons.

Believing that vaccination causes devastating diseases allows us to tell ourselves a story we already know—what heals may harm, and the sum of science is not always progress. "Women know very well that knowledge from the natural sciences has been used in the interests of our domination and not our liberation," the science historian Donna Haraway writes. And this understanding, she observes, can render us less vulnerable to the seductive claims of absolute truth that are sometimes made in the name of science. But it can also invite us to undervalue the place and importance of scientific knowledge. We need science, Haraway warns. And where it is not built on social domination, science can be liberating.

It is difficult to read any historical account of smallpox without encountering the word "filth." In the nineteenth century, smallpox was widely considered a disease of "filth," which meant that it was understood to be a disease of the poor. According to filth theory, any number of contagious diseases were caused by bad air that had been made foul by excrement or rot. The sanitary conditions of the urban poor threatened the middle classes, who shuttled their windows against the air blowing off the slums at night. Filth, it was thought, was responsible not just for disease but also for immorality.

Filth theory would eventually be replaced by germ theory as an understanding of the nature of contagion, but it wasn't entirely wrong or useless. Raw sewage running in the streets can certainly spread diseases—though smallpox isn't one of them—and the sanitation efforts inspired by filth theory greatly improved public health. The reversal of the Chicago River, for instance, so that sewage was not delivered directly to Lake Michigan, the city's drinking-water supply, had some obvious benefits for the citizens of Chicago.

Now, the mothers I meet on the beaches of Lake Michigan do not worry much over filth. Some of us are familiar with the hygiene hypothesis, the notion that a child's immune system needs to encounter germs to develop properly, and most of us believe that dirt is good for our kids. But the idea that toxins, rather than filth or germs, are the root cause of most maladies is a popular theory of disease among people like me. The toxins that distress us range from pesticide residue to high-fructose corn syrup. Particularly suspect substances include the bisphenol A lining our tin cans, the phthalates in our shampoos, and the chlorinated Tris in our couches and pillows.

The definition of "toxin" can be somewhat surprising if you have   50 grown accustomed to hearing it in the context of flame retardants and parabens. Though "toxin" is now often used to refer to manmade chemicals, the more precise meaning of the term is reserved for biologically produced poisons. The pertussis toxin, for example, is responsible for damage to the lungs that can cause whooping cough to linger for months after the bacteria that produced it have been killed by antibiotics. The diphtheria toxin is potent enough to cause massive organ failure, and tetanus bacteria produce a deadly neurotoxin. All of which we now protect against with vaccination.

Though "toxoid" is the term for a toxin that has been rendered no longer toxic, the existence of a class of vaccines called toxoids probably does not help quell widespread concerns that vaccination is a source of toxicity. The consumer advocate Barbara Loe Fisher routinely stokes these fears, referring to vaccines as "biological agents of unknown toxicity" and calling for the development of "nontoxic" preservatives and for more studies on the "toxicity of all other vaccine additives" and their potential "cumulative toxic effects."

In this context, fear of toxicity strikes me as an old anxiety with a new name. Where the word "filth" once suggested, with its moralistic air, the evils of the flesh, the word "toxic" now condemns the chemical evils of our industrial world. This is not to say that concerns over environmental pollution are unjustified—like filth theory, toxicity theory is anchored in legitimate dangers.

The way we now think about toxicity bears some resemblance to the way we once thought about filth. Both theories imagine urban environments as inherently unhealthy. And both allow their subscribers to maintain a sense of control over their own health by pursuing personal purity. For the filth theorist, this meant a retreat into the home, where heavy curtains and shutters might seal out the smell of the poor and their problems. Our version of this shuttering is now achieved through the purchase of purified water, air purifiers, and food marketed with the promise of purity.

Purity is the seemingly innocent concept behind a number of the most sinister social actions of the past century. A passion for bodily purity drove the eugenics movement and led to the sterilization of women and men who were deaf, blind, disabled, or just poor. Concerns for bodily purity were behind miscegenation laws that persisted more than a century after the abolition of slavery, and behind the sodomy laws that were only recently declared unconstitutional. Quite a bit of human solidarity, it seems, has been sacrificed to preserve some kind of imagined purity.

If we do not yet know exactly what the presence of a vast range of chem- 55 icals in umbilical-cord blood and breast milk might mean for the future of our children's health, we do at least know that we are no cleaner, even at birth, than our environment at large. We have more microorganisms in our guts than we have cells in our bodies—we are crawling with bacteria and we are full of chemicals. We are, in other words, continuous with everything here on earth. Including—and especially—each other.

The Reader's Presence

1. Summarize the list of reasons for and against vaccinating children. Which side of this issue do you think offers the most convincing case? Explain why. Throughout the essay, Eula Biss returns to her perspective as a mother. What specifically do her personal stories contribute to understanding and appreciating the concept of—and the issues surrounding—vaccination that a purely scientific account would not? What role do children play in debates about the nature of vaccines and their impact on children's health?

2. The word *inoculation* introduces itself to medicine as a metaphor for grafting diseases onto our own bodies. Herds, hives, vampires—why are metaphors so prevalent in Biss's descriptions of health and illness, and how do they influence the way we think about vaccines? Describe a possible metaphor for vaccination that does not have negative implications.

3. **CONNECTIONS:** In "Sentimental Medicine," Biss utilizes examples involving children—and more specifically, children's bodies. Compare and contrast the role of children in Biss's essay with Danielle Ofri's "SAT (page 471)." How do children influence their views on preventative medicine? What similarities can be drawn between Biss's explanations of vaccination and Ofri's treating a patient by tutoring him? What role does knowledge play in both essays?

Charles Bowden

OUR WALL

CHARLES BOWDEN (1945–2014) is probably best known for writing about the Mexican-American border. A contributing editor for *GQ* and *Mother Jones*, he also wrote for national publications such as *Harper's*, the *New York Times Book Review*, and *Esquire*. His many books of nonfiction include (to name just a few) *Murder City: Ciudad Juárez and the Global Economy's New Killing Fields* (2010), *Dreamland: The Way Out of Juárez* (2010), *Some of the Dead Are Still Breathing* (2009), *A Shadow in the City: Confessions of an Undercover Drug Warrior* (2005), and *Down by the River: Drugs, Money, Murder, and Family* (2004). He was a Lannan Writing

> **Advocating immigration reform and criticizing U.S. border policy, Bowden likened American foreign policy toward Mexico to "making war on the poor."**

Residency Fellow in Marfa, Texas, in 2001, and his 2006 collaboration with photographer Michael Berman, *Inferno*, received the Border Regional Library Association's Southwest Book Award. A strong advocate for immigration reform and a sharp critic of U.S. border policy, Bowden called NAFTA "a machine producing poor people" and likened U.S. foreign policy (regarding Mexico) to "making war on the poor."

IN THE SPRING OF 1929, a man named Patrick Murphy left a bar in Bisbee, Arizona, to bomb the Mexican border town of Naco, a bunny hop of about ten miles (16 kilometers). He stuffed dynamite, scrap iron, nails, and bolts into suitcases and dropped the weapons off the side of his crop duster as part of a deal with Mexican rebels battling for control of Naco, Sonora. When his flight ended, it turned out he'd hit the wrong Naco, managing to destroy property mainly on the U.S. side, including a garage and a local mining company. Some say he was drunk, some say he was sober, but everyone agrees he was one of the first people to bomb the United States from the air.

Borders everywhere attract violence, violence prompts fences, and eventually fences can mutate into walls. Then everyone pays attention because a wall turns a legal distinction into a visual slap in the face. We seem to love walls, but are embarrassed by them because they say something unpleasant about the neighbors—and us. They flow from two sources: fear and the desire for control. Just as our houses have doors and locks, so do borders call forth garrisons, customs officials, and, now and then, big walls. They give us divided feelings because we do not like to admit we need them.

Now as the United States debates fortifying its border with Mexico, walls have a new vogue. At various spots along the dusty, 1,952-mile (3,141 kilometers) boundary, fences, walls, and vehicle barriers have been constructed since the 1990s to slow the surge in illegal immigration. In San Diego, nine miles (14 kilometers) of a double-layered fence have been erected. In Arizona, the state most overrun with illegal crossings, 65 miles (105 kilometers) of barriers have been constructed already. Depending on the direction of the ongoing immigration debate, there may soon be hundreds more miles of walls.

The 800 or so residents of Naco, Arizona, where Patrick Murphy is part of the local lore, have been living in the shadow of a 14-foot-high (four meters) steel wall for the past decade. National Guard units are helping to extend the 4.6-mile (7.4 kilometers) barrier 25 miles (40 kilometers) deeper into the desert. The Border Patrol station is the biggest building in the tiny town; the copper roof glistens under the blistering sun. In 2005, a pioneering bit of guerrilla theater took place here when the Minutemen, a citizen group devoted to securing the border, staked out 20 miles (32 kilometers) of the line and patrolled it. Today about 8,000 people live in Naco, Sonora, on the Mexican side of the metal wall that slashes the two communities.

Only a dirt parking lot separates the Gay 90s bar from the Naco wall.   5
Inside, the patrons are largely bilingual and have family ties on both sides of the line. Janet Warner, one of the bartenders, has lived here for years and is one of those fortunate souls who has found her place in the sun. But thanks to the racks of stadium lights along the wall, she has lost her nights, and laments the erasure of the brilliant stars that once hung over her life. She notes that sometimes Mexicans jump the new steel wall, come in for a beer, then jump back into Mexico. The bar began in the late 1920s as a casino and with the end of Prohibition added alcohol. The gambling continued until 1961, when a new county sheriff decided to clean up things. On the back wall are photographs of Ronald and Nancy Reagan when they'd stop by on their way to a nearby Mexican ranch.

The bar is one of only a handful of businesses left. The commercial street leading to the border is lined with defunct establishments, all dead because the U.S. government sealed the entry to Mexico after 9/11 and rerouted it to the east. Leonel Urcadez, 54, a handsome man who has owned the bar for decades, has mixed feelings about the wall. "You get used to it," he says. "When they first built it, it was not a bad idea—cars were crossing illegally from Mexico and the Border Patrol would chase them. But it's so ugly."

The two Nacos came into being in 1897 around a border crossing that connected copper mines in both nations. By 1901 a railroad linked the mines. A big miners' strike in 1906, one cherished by Mexicans as foreshadowing the revolution in 1910, saw troops from both nations facing each other down at the line. The town of Naco on the Mexican side changed hands many times during the actual revolution—at first the prize was revenue from the customs house. Later, when Arizona voted itself dry in 1915, the income came from the saloons. Almost every old house in Naco, Arizona, has holes from the gun battles. The Naco Hotel, with its three-foot (one meter) mud walls, advertised its bulletproof rooms.

Diane Cook & Len Jenshel

Border Field State Park, California. This stretch of upended railway track that looks like a work of contemporary art marks the western extent of the U.S.-Mexico border.

The boundary between Mexico and the United States has always been zealously insisted upon by both countries. But initially Mexicans moved north at will. The U.S. patrols of the border that began in 1904 were mainly to keep out illegal Asian immigrants. Almost 900,000 Mexicans legally entered the United States to flee the violence of the revolution. Low population in both nations and the need for labor in the American Southwest made this migration a nonevent for decades. The flow of illegal immigrants exploded after the passage of the North American Free Trade Agreement in the early 1990s, a pact that was supposed to end illegal immigration but wound up dislocating millions of Mexican peasant farmers and many small-industrial workers.

The result: Naco was overrun by immigrants on their way north. At night, dozens, sometimes hundreds, of immigrants would crowd into motel rooms and storage rental sheds along the highway. The local desert was stomped into a powder of dust. Naco residents found their homes broken into by desperate migrants. Then came the wall in 1996, and the flow of people spread into the high desert outside the town.

|||||||||||||||||||||||||||||||||||||||||||||||||||||||||||||||||||||||||||||||||||||||||||||||||||||||||||||||||||||||||||||||||||||||||

The Border Patrol credits the wall, along with better surveillance technol- 10
ogy, with cutting the number of illegal immigrants captured near Naco's
33-mile (53 kilometers) border by half in the past year.[1] Before this new height-
ening of enforcement, the number caught each week, hiding in arroyos thick
with mesquite and yucca, often exceeded the town's population. At the moment,
the area is relatively quiet as "coyotes,"[2] or people smugglers, pause to feel out
the new reality, and the National Guard has been sent in to assist the Border
Patrol. At the nearby abandoned U.S. Army camp, the roofs are collapsing and
the adobe bricks dribble mud onto the floor. Scattered about are Mexican water
bottles—illegals still hole up here after climbing the wall.

Residents register a hodgepodge of feelings about the wall. Even those
who have let passing illegal immigrants use their phones or given them a
ride say the exodus has to stop. And even those sick of finding trash in their
yards understand why the immigrants keep coming.

"Sometimes I feel sorry for the Mexicans," says Bryan Tomlinson, 45, a
custodial engineer for the Bisbee school district. His brother Don chimes in,
"But the wall's a good thing."

A border wall seems to violate a deep sense of identity most Americans
cherish. We see ourselves as a nation of immigrants with our own goddess,
the Statue of Liberty, a symbol so potent that dissident Chinese students fabricated a version of it in 1989 in Tiananmen Square as the visual representation
of their yearning for freedom.

Walls are curious statements of human needs. Sometimes they are built
to keep restive populations from fleeing. The Berlin Wall was designed to
keep citizens from escaping from communist East Germany. But most walls
are for keeping people out. They all work for a while, until human appetites
or sheer numbers overwhelm them. The Great Wall of China, built mostly
after the mid-14th century, kept northern tribes at bay until the Manchu
conquered China in the 17th century. Hadrian's Wall, standing about 15 feet
(5 meters) high, 9 feet (3 meters) wide, and 73 miles (117 kilometers) long,
kept the crazed tribes of what is now Scotland from running amok in Roman
Britain—from A.D. 122 until it was overrun in 367. Then you have the
Maginot Line, a series of connected forts built by France after World War I to
keep the German army from invading. It was a success, except for one flaw:
The troops of the Third Reich simply went around its northwestern end and
invaded France through the Netherlands and Belgium. Now tourists visit its
labyrinth of tunnels and underground barracks.

In 1859 a rancher named Thomas Austin released 24 rabbits in Australia 15
because, he noted, "the introduction of a few rabbits could do little harm
and might provide a touch of home, in addition to a spot of hunting." By
that simple act, he launched one of the most extensive barriers ever erected
by human beings: the rabbit fences of Australia, which eventually reached
2,023 miles (3,256 kilometers). Within 35 years, the rabbits had overrun the

---

[1] This essay was published in May 2007. —EDS.
[2] *coyotes:* Smugglers paid to take people illegally across the U.S-Mexico border. —EDS.

continent, a place lacking sufficient and dedicated rabbit predators. For a century and a half, the Australian government has tried various solutions: imported fleas, poisons, trappers. Nothing has dented the new immigrants. The fences themselves failed almost instantly—rabbits expanded faster than the barriers could be built, careless people left gates open, holes appeared, and, of course, the rabbits simply dug under them.

In Naco all the walls of the world are present in one compact bundle. You have Hadrian's Wall or the Great Wall of China because the barrier is intended to keep people out. You have the Maginot Line because a 15-minute walk takes you to the end of the existing steel wall. You have the rabbit fences of Australia because people still come north illegally, as do the drugs.

Perhaps the closest thing to the wall going up on the U.S.-Mexico border is the separation wall being built by Israel in the West Bank. Like the new American wall, it is designed to control the movement of people, but it faces the problem of all walls—rockets can go over it, tunnels can go under it. It offends people, it comforts people, it fails to deliver security. And it keeps expanding.

Rodolfo Santos Esquer puts out *El Mirador*, a weekly newspaper in Naco, Sonora, and he finds the wall hateful. He stands in his cramped office—a space he shares with a small shop peddling underwear—and says, "It looks like the Berlin Wall. It is horrible. It is ugly. You feel more racism now. It is a racist wall. If people get close to the wall, the Border Patrol calls the Mexican police, and they go and question people."

And then he lightens up because he is a sunny man, and he says it actually hasn't changed his life or the lives of most people in town. Except that the coyotes now drive to the end of the wall before crossing. And as the wall grows in length, the coyotes raise their rates. Santos figures half the town is living off migrants going north—either feeding them and housing them or guiding them into the U.S. Passage to Phoenix, about 200 miles (320 kilometers) away, is now $1,500 and rising. He notes that after the wall went up in 1996, the migration mushroomed. He wonders if there is a connection, if the wall magically beckons migrants. Besides, he says, people just climb over it with ropes.

Santos fires up his computer and shows an image he snapped in the 20 cemetery of a nearby town. There, there, he points as he enlarges a section of the photo. Slowly a skull-shaped blur floats into view against the black of the night—a ghost, he believes. The border is haunted by ghosts—the hundreds who die each year from heat and cold, the ones killed in car wrecks as the packed vans of migrants flee the Border Patrol, and the increasing violence erupting between smugglers and the agents of Homeland Security. Whenever heat is applied to one part of the border, the migration simply moves to another part. The walls in southern California drove immigrants into the Arizona desert and, in some cases, to their deaths. We think of walls as statements of foreign policy, and we forget the intricate lives of the people we wall in and out.

Emanuel Castillo Erúnez, 23, takes crime and car wreck photos for *El Mirador*. He went north illegally when he was 17, walked a few days, then was picked up and returned to Mexico. He sits on a bench in the plaza, shielded by a New York Yankees cap, and sums up the local feeling about the wall simply: "Some are fine with it, some are not." He thinks of going north again, but then he thinks of getting caught again. And so he waits.

There is a small-town languor about Naco, Sonora, and the wall becomes unnoticeable in this calm. The Minutemen and National Guard terrify people. At the Hospedaje Santa María, four people wait for a chance to go over the wall and illegally enter the wealth of the United States. It is a run-down, two-story building, one of many boarding houses for migrants in Naco. Salvador Rivera, a solid man in his early 30s, has been here about a year. He worked in Washington State, but, when his mother fell ill, he returned home to Nayarit, Mexico, and is now having trouble getting past the increased security. He left behind an American girlfriend he can no longer reach.

"For so many years, we Mexicans have gone to the U.S. to work. I don't understand why they put up a wall to turn us away. It's not like we're robbing anybody over there, and they don't pay us very much."

But talk of the wall almost has to be prompted. Except for those engaged in smuggling drugs or people, border crossers in Naco, Sonora, continue to enter through the main gate, as they always have. They visit relatives on the other side, as they always have. What has changed is this physical statement, a big wall lined with bright lights, that says, yes, we are two nations.

Jesús Gastelum Ramírez lives next door to the wall, makes neon signs,   25 and looks like Willie Nelson. He watches people climb the wall and he understands a reality forgotten by most U.S. lawmakers—that simply to go through the wire instantly raises a person's income tenfold. Gastelum knows many of his neighbors smuggle people, and he understands.

Until recently, a volleyball team from the Mexican Naco and a team from the U.S. Naco used to meet once a year at the point where the wall ends on the west side of town, put up a net on the line, bring kegs of beer, and play a volleyball game. People from both Nacos would stream out to the site and watch. And then the wall would no longer exist for a spell. But it always confronts the eye.

Dan Duley, 50, operates heavy equipment and is a native of the Naco area. He was living in Germany after serving in the Air Force when the Berlin Wall came down, and he thought that was a fine thing. But here he figures something has to be done. "We need help," he says. "We're being invaded. They've taken away our jobs, our security. I'm just a blue-collar man living in a small town. And I just wish the government cared about a man who was blue."

But then, as in many conversations on the border, the rhetoric calms down. Duley, along with many other Naco residents, believes the real solution has to be economic, that jobs must be created in Mexico. There is an iron law on this border: The closer one gets to the line, the more rational the talk becomes because everyone has personal ties to people on the other side. Everyone realizes the wall is a police solution to an economic problem. The Mexicans will go over it, under it, or try to tear holes in it. Or, as is often the case, enter legally with temporary visiting papers and then melt into American communities. Of the millions of illegal immigrants living in the United States, few would have come if there wasn't a job waiting for them.

Over in Naco, Sonora, the final night of a fiesta is in full roar. Men drinking beer move by on horseback, groups of girls in high heels prance past. Nearby, folks play bingo, and in the band shell a group does a sound check for the big dance. Looming over the whole party is a giant statue of Father Hidalgo with his bald head and wild eyes. He launched the Mexican Wars of Independence in 1810. Two blocks away, the steel wall glows under a battery of lights.

In the Gay 90s bar in Naco, Arizona, a *quinceañera*, the 15th-birthday 30 celebration that introduces a young girl to the world, is firing up. There are 200 people in the saloon's back room, half from Mexico and half from the U.S. The boys wear rented tuxedo vests, the girls are dressed like goddesses. One man walks in with a baby in a black polka-dot dress with pink trim.

The birthday girl, Alyssa, stands with her family for an official portrait.

Walls come and go, but *quinceañeras* are forever, I say to the man with the baby. He nods his head and smiles.

The steel barrier is maybe a hundred feet (30 meters) away. Outside in the darkness, Mexicans are moving north, and Border Patrol agents are hunting them down. Tomorrow, work will continue on the construction of the wall as it slowly creeps east and west from the town. Tourists already come to look at it.

I have no doubt someday archaeologists will do excavations here and write learned treatises about the Great Wall of the United States. Perhaps one of them will be the descendant of a Mexican stealing north at this moment in the midnight hour. ●

The Reader's Presence

1. From his first paragraph to his last, Bowden refers to the two towns of Naco, one in the United States and the other directly across the border in Mexico. What is the significance of these two towns? How do they play a key role in the way Bowden structures and develops his essay?

2. Bowden's essay is about barriers currently being built on the Mexican-American border. What, then, is his purpose in mentioning various walls and fences in world history, as he does in paragraphs 14–15? What is the relevance of the walls and fences to his main topic?

3. **VISUAL PRESENCE:** Examine carefully the photograph of Border Field State Park in California (page 319). To what extent does this image match your expectation for what a wall looks like? In what ways is it similar to or different from the walls that Bowden describes in his essay? Cite specific examples in your answer.

4. **CONNECTIONS:** Compare "Our Wall" to the following selection, David Brooks's "People Like Us." Who do the words *our* and *us* stand for in each essay? Do you think David Brooks's perspective on human behavior applies to the people Bowden speaks with in both Naco, Arizona, and Naco, Sonora? Why or why not?

David Brooks

People Like Us

DAVID BROOKS (b. 1961) was born in Toronto and grew up in New York City and in a suburb of Philadelphia. A journalist, columnist, and self-described "comic sociologist," Brooks has authored two books of cultural commentary, *Bobos in Paradise: The New Upper Class and How They Got There* (2001) and *On Paradise Drive: How We Live Now (and Always Have) in the Future Tense* (2004), and he edited the anthology *Backward and Upward: The New Conservative Writing* (1995). After graduating from the University of Chicago, Brooks worked as a reporter for the *Wall Street Journal*. Since that time, he has served as a senior editor at the *Weekly Standard* and as a contributing editor at the *Atlantic* and *Newsweek*, where the managing editor praised his "dead-on eye for the foibles of the Beltway—and his strong sense of how what happens in the capital's conservative circles affects the rest of the country." Brooks presents commentary on National Public Radio and on *PBS Newshour*. In 2003, he joined the *New York Times* as an op-ed columnist. He teaches occasionally as a visiting professor at Yale and Duke Universities.

In a PBS interview in 2000, Brooks argued that people tend to gravitate to like-minded, like-cultured people—a "congealing pot" of people just like themselves: "Now if you look at the *New York Times* wedding page, it's this great clash of résumés. . . . Harvard marries Yale. Princeton marries Stanford. Magna cum laude marries magna cum laude. You never get a magna cum laude marrying a summa cum laude because the tensions would be too great in that wedding." "People Like Us" first appeared in the *Atlantic* in 2003. Brooks's latest book is *The Road to Character* (2015).

> In a PBS interview in 2000, David Brooks argued that people tend to gravitate to like-minded, like-cultured people—a "congealing pot" of people just like themselves.

MAYBE IT'S TIME to admit the obvious. We don't really care about diversity all that much in America, even though we talk about it a great deal. Maybe somewhere in this country there is a truly diverse neighborhood in which a black Pentecostal minister lives next to a white anti-globalization activist, who lives next to an Asian short-order cook, who lives next to a professional golfer, who lives next to a postmodern-literature professor and a cardiovascular surgeon. But I have never been to or heard of that neighborhood. Instead, what I have seen all around the country is people making strenuous efforts to group themselves with people who are basically like themselves.

Human beings are capable of drawing amazingly subtle social distinctions and then shaping their lives around them. In the Washington, D.C., area Democratic lawyers tend to live in suburban Maryland, and Republican lawyers tend to live in suburban Virginia. If you asked a Democratic lawyer to move from her $750,000 house in Bethesda, Maryland, to a $750,000 house in Great Falls, Virginia, she'd look at you as if you had just asked her to buy a pickup truck with a gun rack and to shove chewing tobacco in her kid's mouth. In Manhattan the owner of a $3 million SoHo loft would feel out of place moving into a $3 million Fifth Avenue apartment. A West Hollywood interior decorator would feel dislocated if you asked him to move to Orange County. In Georgia a barista from Athens would probably not fit in serving coffee in Americus.

It is a common complaint that every place is starting to look the same. But in the information age, the late writer James Chapin once told me, every place becomes more like itself. People are less often tied down to factories and mills, and they can search for places to live on the basis of cultural affinity. Once they find a town in which people share their values, they flock there, and reinforce whatever was distinctive about the town in the first place. Once Boulder, Colorado, became known as congenial to politically progressive mountain bikers, half the politically progressive mountain bikers in the country (it seems) moved there; they made the place so culturally pure that it has become practically a parody of itself.

But people love it. Make no mistake—we are increasing our happiness by segmenting off so rigorously. We are finding places where we are comfortable and where we feel we can flourish. But the choices we make toward that end lead to the very opposite of diversity. The United States might be a diverse nation when considered as a whole, but block by block and institution by institution it is a relatively homogeneous nation.

When we use the word "diversity" today we usually mean racial integra- 5 tion. But even here our good intentions seem to have run into the brick wall of human nature. Over the past generation reformers have tried heroically, and in many cases successfully, to end housing discrimination. But recent patterns aren't encouraging: according to an analysis of the 2000 census data, the 1990s saw only a slight increase in the racial integration of neighborhoods in the United States. The number of middle-class and upper-middle-class African-American families is rising, but for whatever reasons—racism, psychological comfort—these families tend to congregate in predominantly black neighborhoods.

In fact, evidence suggests that some neighborhoods become more segregated over time. New suburbs in Arizona and Nevada, for example, start out reasonably well integrated. These neighborhoods don't yet have reputations, so people choose their houses for other, mostly economic reasons. But as neighborhoods age, they develop personalities (that's where the Asians live, and that's where the Hispanics live), and segmentation occurs. It could be that in a few years the new suburbs in the Southwest will be nearly as segregated as the established ones in the Northeast and the Midwest.

Even though race and ethnicity run deep in American society, we should in theory be able to find areas that are at least culturally diverse. But here, too, people show few signs of being truly interested in building diverse communities. If you run a retail company and you're thinking of opening new stores, you can choose among dozens of consulting firms that are quite effective at locating your potential customers. They can do this because people with similar tastes and preferences tend to congregate by ZIP code.

The most famous of these precision marketing firms is Claritas, which breaks down the U.S. population into sixty-two psycho-demographic clusters, based on such factors as how much money people make, what they like to read and watch, and what products they have bought in the past. For example, the "suburban sprawl" cluster is composed of young families making about $41,000 a year and living in fast-growing places such as Burnsville, Minnesota, and Bensalem, Pennsylvania. These people are almost twice as

Silicon Valley, California. As David Brooks writes, "[W]hat I have seen all around the country is people making strenuous efforts to group themselves with people who are basically like themselves." (paragraph 1)

Bob Sacha/Getty Images

likely as other Americans to have three-way calling. They are two and a half times as likely to buy Light n' Lively Kid Yogurt. Members of the "towns & gowns" cluster are recent college graduates in places such as Berkeley, California, and Gainesville, Florida. They are big consumers of DoveBars and *Saturday Night Live*. They tend to drive small foreign cars and to read *Rolling Stone* and *Scientific American*.

Looking through the market research, one can sometimes be amazed by how efficiently people cluster—and by how predictable we all are. If you wanted to sell imported wine, obviously you would have to find places where rich people live. But did you know that the sixteen counties with the greatest proportion of imported-wine drinkers are all in the same three metropolitan areas (New York, San Francisco, and Washington, D.C.)? If you tried to open a motor-home dealership in Montgomery County, Pennsylvania, you'd probably go broke, because people in this ring of the Philadelphia suburbs think RVs are kind of uncool. But if you traveled just a short way north, to Monroe County, Pennsylvania, you would find yourself in the fifth motor-home-friendliest county in America.

Geography is not the only way we find ourselves divided from people unlike   10
us. Some of us watch Fox News, while others listen to NPR. Some like David Letterman, and others—typically in less urban neighborhoods—like Jay Leno. Some go to charismatic churches; some go to mainstream churches. Americans tend more and more often to marry people with education levels similar to their own, and to befriend people with backgrounds similar to their own.

My favorite illustration of this latter pattern comes from the first, non-controversial chapter of *The Bell Curve*. Think of your twelve closest friends, Richard J. Herrnstein and Charles Murray write. If you had chosen them randomly from the American population, the odds that half of your twelve closest friends would be college graduates would be six in a thousand. The odds that half of the twelve would have advanced degrees would be less than one in a million. Have any of your twelve closest friends graduated from Harvard, Stanford, Yale, Princeton, Caltech, MIT, Duke, Dartmouth, Cornell, Columbia, Chicago, or Brown? If you chose your friends randomly from the American population, the odds against your having four or more friends from those schools would be more than a billion to one.

Many of us live in absurdly unlikely groupings, because we have organized our lives that way.

It's striking that the institutions that talk the most about diversity often practice it the least. For example, no group of people sings the diversity anthem more frequently and fervently than administrators at just such elite universities. But elite universities are amazingly undiverse in their values, politics, and mores. Professors in particular are drawn from a rather narrow segment of the population. If faculties reflected the general population, 32 percent of professors would be registered Democrats and 31 percent would be registered Republicans. Forty percent would be evangelical Christians. But a recent study of several universities by the conservative Center for the

Study of Popular Culture and the American Enterprise Institute found that roughly 90 percent of those professors in the arts and sciences who had registered with a political party had registered Democratic. Fifty-seven professors at Brown were found on the voter-registration rolls. Of those, fifty-four were Democrats. Of the forty-two professors in the English, history, sociology, and political-science departments, all were Democrats. The results at Harvard, Penn State, Maryland, and the University of California at Santa Barbara were similar to the results at Brown.

What we are looking at here is human nature. People want to be around others who are roughly like themselves. That's called community. It probably would be psychologically difficult for most Brown professors to share an office with someone who was pro-life, a member of the National Rifle Association, or an evangelical Christian. It's likely that hiring committees would subtly—even unconsciously—screen out any such people they encountered. Republicans and evangelical Christians have sensed that they are not welcome at places like Brown, so they don't even consider working there. In fact, any registered Republican who contemplates a career in academia these days is both a hero and a fool. So, in a semi-self-selective pattern, brainy people with generally liberal social mores flow to academia, and brainy people with generally conservative mores flow elsewhere.

The dream of diversity is like the dream of equality. Both are based on ideals we celebrate even as we undermine them daily. (How many times have you seen someone renounce a high-paying job or pull his child from an elite college on the grounds that these things are bad for equality?) On the one hand, the situation is appalling. It is appalling that Americans know so little about one another. It is appalling that many of us are so narrow-minded that we can't tolerate a few people with ideas significantly different from our own. It's appalling that evangelical Christians are practically absent from entire professions, such as academia, the media, and filmmaking. It's appalling that people should be content to cut themselves off from everyone unlike themselves.

The segmentation of society means that often we don't even have arguments across the political divide. Within their little validating communities, liberals and conservatives circulate half-truths about the supposed awfulness of the other side. These distortions are believed because it feels good to believe them.

On the other hand, there are limits to how diverse any community can or should be. I've come to think that it is not useful to try to hammer diversity into every neighborhood and institution in the United States. Sure, Augusta National should probably admit women, and university sociology departments should probably hire a conservative or two. It would be nice if all neighborhoods had a good mixture of ethnicities. But human nature being what it is, most places and institutions are going to remain culturally homogeneous.

It's probably better to think about diverse lives, not diverse institutions. Human beings, if they are to live well, will have to move through a series of institutions and environments, which may be individually homogeneous but, taken together, will offer diverse experiences. It might also be a good idea to make national service a rite of passage for young people in this country: it would take them out of their narrow neighborhood segment and thrust them in with people unlike themselves. Finally, it's probably important for adults to get out of their own familiar circles. If you live in a coastal, socially liberal neighborhood, maybe you should take out a subscription to *The Door*, the evangelical humor magazine; or maybe you should visit Branson, Missouri. Maybe you should stop in at a megachurch. Sure, it would be superficial familiarity, but it beats the iron curtains that now separate the nation's various cultural zones.

Look around at your daily life. Are you really in touch with the broad diversity of American life? Do you care? ▪

The Reader's Presence

1. Brooks begins his argument by "admit[ting] the obvious": Americans don't care about diversity, they just like to talk as if they do. What was your initial reaction to Brooks's so-called admission? What is the effect of admitting something that many of his readers will instinctually reject? How is your opinion affected by his evidence? How well has he supported this assertion by the end of the essay?

2. Brooks claims that it is human nature for people to group together with those who have similar ideals and backgrounds. What might be the advantages of such grouping? What might be lost if Americans were truly integrated? What is lost by segregating by religion, politics, race, class, profession, and sexuality?

3. **VISUAL PRESENCE:** After examining the aerial photograph of an American residential neighborhood on page 326, describe specifically how this neighborhood is similar to or different from the neighborhood(s) you have lived in. How does the physical layout and appearance of this neighborhood reinforce Brooks's ideas about diversity in America?

4. **CONNECTIONS:** Compare Brooks's observations about how we prefer to be around "people who are basically like [our]selves" (paragraph 1) to E. B. White's classic essay "Once More to the Lake" (page 256). In what ways can Brooks's point play a role in evaluating White's essay, which was written decades earlier? In what ways does White's lake community support Brooks's perspective on diversity? For a more direct comparison of ideas, compare Brooks's essay with Walter Benn Michaels's "The Trouble with Diversity" (page 571). After reading each selection closely, list the points Brooks and Michaels agree on and those they don't. What major differences do you see between the conclusions each writer reaches?

Ta-Nehisi Coates

FROM *BETWEEN THE WORLD AND ME*

When it appeared in the fall of 2015, **TA-NEHISI COATES'** *Between the World and Me* proved to be an immediate publishing sensation. A winner of the National Book Award and a finalist for a Pulitzer Prize, the slim, eloquent book also earned for its author a prestigious MacArthur Fellowship (popularly known as a "genius grant"). A quotation from Toni Morrison took up the entire back cover, proclaiming that Coates was today's James Baldwin and that his book was "required reading." (For more on James Baldwin, see page 40.)

Born in Baltimore in 1975, Coates attended Howard University but left to start a journalism career. After stints at the *Washington City Paper, Philadelphia Weekly,* the *Village Voice,* and *Time* magazine, he wound up blogging for the *Atlantic* in 2008. In that year, he also published a memoir, *The Beautiful Struggle: A Father, Two Sons, and an Unlikely Road to Manhood.* For his recent magazine articles on such issues as reparations and mass incarceration, Coates has received several prominent awards in journalism. A serious student of popular culture, Coates in 2016 wrote a new series of comic books based on Marvel's 1966 *Black Panther* character. He currently lives with his family in Paris, France.

> In *Between the World and Me*, Coates speaks to his fifteen-year-old son about the West Baltimore he grew up in and survived.

One of Coates's literary models for *Between the World and Me* is Baldwin's 1963 classic, *The Fire Next Time,* a long essay in the form of a letter to his nephew. Coates addresses his long essay to his son. Besides Baldwin, Coates also pays homage to the influential African American writer Richard Wright, whose 1935 poem "Between the World and Me" wrenchingly describes the scene of a lynching. In the following passage from *Between the World and Me*, Coates speaks to his fifteen-year-old son about the West Baltimore he grew up in and survived.

In a review for the *New Republic*, Bijan Stephen writes that in *Between the World and Me* "Ta-Nehisi Coates interrogates the effects of a life lived under the gun, aware of the ever-present violence that is systematically and relentlessly perpetrated against black people in America."

TO BE BLACK IN THE BALTIMORE of my youth was to be naked before the elements of the world, before all the guns, fists, knives, crack, rape, and disease. The nakedness is not an error, nor pathology. The nakedness is the correct and intended result of policy, the predictable upshot of people forced for centuries to live under fear. The law did not protect us. And now, in your time, the law has become an excuse for stopping and frisking you, which is to say, for furthering the assault on your body. But a society that protects some people through a safety net of schools, government-backed home loans, and ancestral wealth but can only protect you with the club of criminal justice has either failed at enforcing its good intentions or has succeeded at something much darker. However you call it, the result was our infirmity before the criminal forces of the world. It does not matter if the agent of those forces is white or black — what matters is our condition, what matters is the system that makes your body breakable.

The revelation of these forces, a series of great changes, has unfolded over the course of my life. The changes are still unfolding and will likely continue until I die. I was eleven years old, standing out in the parking lot in front of the 7-Eleven, watching a crew of older boys standing near the street. They yelled and gestured at . . . who? . . . another boy, young, like me, who stood there, almost smiling, gamely throwing up his hands. He had already learned the lesson he would teach me that day: that his body was in constant jeopardy. Who knows what brought him to that knowledge? The projects, a drunken stepfather, an older brother concussed by police, a cousin pinned in the city jail. That he was outnumbered did not matter because the whole world had outnumbered him long ago, and what do numbers matter? This was a war for the possession of his body and that would be the war of his whole life.

I stood there for some seconds, marveling at the older boys' beautiful sense of fashion. They all wore ski jackets, the kind which, in my day, mothers put on layaway in September, then piled up overtime hours so as to have the thing wrapped and ready for Christmas. I focused in on a light-skinned boy with a long head and small eyes. He was scowling at another boy, who was standing close to me. It was just before three in the afternoon. I was in sixth grade. School had just let out, and it was not yet the fighting weather of early spring. What was the exact problem here? Who could know?

The boy with the small eyes reached into his ski jacket and pulled out a gun. I recall it in the slowest motion, as though in a dream. There the boy stood, with the gun brandished, which he slowly untucked, tucked, then untucked once more, and in his small eyes I saw a surging rage that could, in an instant, erase my body. That was 1986. That year I felt myself to be drowning in the news reports of murder. I was aware that these murders very often did not land upon the intended targets but fell upon great-aunts, PTA mothers, overtime uncles, and joyful children — fell upon them random and relentless, like great sheets of rain. I knew this in theory but could not understand it as fact until the boy with the small eyes stood across from me holding my entire body in his small hands. The boy did not shoot. His friends pulled him back. He did not need to shoot. He had affirmed my place in the order of things. He had let it be known how easily I could be selected. I took the subway home that day, processing the episode all alone. I did not tell my parents. I did not tell my teachers, and if I told my friends I would have done so with all the excitement needed to obscure the fear that came over me in that moment.

III

I remember being amazed that death could so easily rise up from the   5
nothing of a boyish afternoon, billow up like fog. I knew that West Baltimore,
where I lived; that the north side of Philadelphia, where my cousins lived; that
the South Side of Chicago, where friends of my father lived, comprised a world
apart. Somewhere out there beyond the firmament, past the asteroid belt,
there were other worlds where children did not regularly fear for their bodies. I knew this because there was a large television resting in my living
room. In the evenings I would sit before this television bearing witness to the
dispatches from this other world. There were little white boys with complete
collections of football cards, and their only want was a popular girlfriend and
their only worry was poison oak. That other world was suburban and endless,
organized around pot roasts, blueberry pies, fireworks, ice cream sundaes,
immaculate bathrooms, and small toy trucks that were loosed in wooded
backyards with streams and glens. Comparing these dispatches with the facts
of my native world, I came to understand that my country was a galaxy, and
this galaxy stretched from the pandemonium of West Baltimore to the happy
hunting grounds of *Mr. Belvedere.*[1] I obsessed over the distance between that
other sector of space and my own. I knew that my portion of the American
galaxy, where bodies were enslaved by a tenacious gravity, was black and
that the other, liberated portion was not. I knew that some inscrutable energy
preserved the breach. I felt, but did not yet understand, the relation between
that other world and me. And I felt in this a cosmic injustice, a profound
cruelty, which infused an abiding, irrepressible desire to unshackle my body
and achieve the velocity of escape.

Do you ever feel that same need? Your life is so very different from my
own. The grandness of the world, the real world, the whole world, is a known
thing for you. And you have no need of dispatches because you have seen
so much of the American galaxy and its inhabitants—their homes, their
hobbies—up close. I don't know what it means to grow up with a black president, social networks, omnipresent media, and black women everywhere in
their natural hair. What I know is that when they loosed the killer of Michael
Brown,[2] you said, "I've got to go." And that cut me because, for all our differing worlds, at your age my feeling was exactly the same. And I recall that
even then I had not yet begun to imagine the perils that tangle us. You still
believe the injustice was Michael Brown. You have not yet grappled with your
own myths and narratives and discovered the plunder everywhere around us.

Before I could discover, before I could escape, I had to survive, and this
could only mean a clash with the streets, by which I mean not just physical
blocks, nor simply the people packed into them, but the array of lethal puzzles

---

[1] *Mr. Belvedere:* Based loosely on a 1940s film character, this family sitcom ran from 1985
to 1990 and is set in the suburban Pittsburgh home of the Owens family, where a dapper English
housekeeper keeps everything running smoothly. —EDS.

[2] *Michael Brown:* On August 9, 2014, Michael Brown, an eighteen-year-old unarmed black
man, was fatally shot by a white Ferguson, Missouri, police officer, after Brown reportedly robbed
a convenience store. The controversial circumstances of the shooting resulted in national protests
and civic unrest. —EDS.

and strange perils that seem to rise up from the asphalt itself. The streets transform every ordinary day into a series of trick questions, and every incorrect answer risks a beat-down, a shooting, or a pregnancy. No one survives unscathed. And yet the heat that springs from the constant danger, from a lifestyle of near-death experience, is thrilling. This is what the rappers mean when they pronounce themselves addicted to "the streets" or in love with "the game." I imagine they feel something akin to parachutists, rock climbers, BASE jumpers,[3] and others who choose to live on the edge. Of course we chose nothing. And I have never believed the brothers who claim to "run," much less "own," the city. We did not design the streets. We do not fund them. We do not preserve them. But I was there, nevertheless, charged like all the others with the protection of my body.

The crews, the young men who'd transmuted their fear into rage, were the greatest danger. The crews walked the blocks of their neighborhood, loud and rude, because it was only through their loud rudeness that they might feel any sense of security and power. They would break your jaw, stomp your face, and shoot you down to feel that power, to revel in the might of their own bodies. And their wild reveling, their astonishing acts made their names ring out. Reps were made, atrocities recounted. And so in my Baltimore it was known that when Cherry Hill rolled through you rolled the other way, that North and Pulaski was not an intersection but a hurricane, leaving only splinters and shards in its wake. In that fashion, the security of these neighborhoods flowed downward and became the security of the bodies living there. You steered clear of Jo-Jo, for instance, because he was cousin to Keon, the don of Murphy Homes. In other cities, indeed in other Baltimores, the neighborhoods had other handles and the boys went by other names, but their mission did not change: prove the inviolability of their block, of their bodies, through their power to crack knees, ribs, and arms. This practice was so common that today you can approach any black person raised in the cities of that era and they can tell you which crew ran which hood in their city, and they can tell you the names of all the captains and all their cousins and offer an anthology of all their exploits.

To survive the neighborhoods and shield my body, I learned another language consisting of a basic complement of head nods and handshakes. I memorized a list of prohibited blocks. I learned the smell and feel of fighting weather. And I learned that "Shorty, can I see your bike?" was never a sincere question, and "Yo, you was messing with my cousin" was neither an earnest accusation nor a misunderstanding of the facts. These were the summonses that you answered with your left foot forward, your right foot back, your hands guarding your face, one slightly lower than the other, cocked like a hammer. Or they were answered by breaking out, ducking through alleys, cutting through backyards, then bounding through the door past your kid brother into your bedroom, pulling the tool out of your lambskin or from under

---

[3] ***BASE jumpers:*** Those who jump from a fixed structure or cliff with a parachute or wingsuit. "BASE" is an acronym for four kinds of fixed objects from which jumpers leap: a building, an antenna, a span, or the earth (usually a cliff). —Eds.

your mattress or out of your Adidas shoebox, then calling up your own cousins (who really aren't) and returning to that same block, on that same day, and to that same crew, hollering out, "Yeah, nigger, what's up now?" I recall learning these laws clearer than I recall learning my colors and shapes, because these laws were essential to the security of my body.

I think of this as a great difference between us. You have some acquain-   10
tance with the old rules, but they are not as essential to you as they were to me. I am sure that you have had to deal with the occasional roughneck on the subway or in the park, but when I was about your age, each day, fully one-third of my brain was concerned with who I was walking to school with, our precise number, the manner of our walk, the number of times I smiled, who or what I smiled at, who offered a pound and who did not—all of which is to say that I practiced the culture of the streets, a culture concerned chiefly with securing the body. I do not long for those days. I have no desire to make you "tough" or "street," perhaps because any "toughness" I garnered came reluctantly. I think I was always, somehow, aware of the price. I think I somehow knew that that third of my brain should have been concerned with more beautiful things. I think I felt that something out there, some force, nameless and vast, had robbed me of . . . what? Time? Experience? I think you know something of what that third could have done, and I think that is why you may feel the need for escape even more than I did. You have seen all the wonderful life up above the tree-line, yet you understand that there is no real distance between you and Trayvon Martin[4], and thus Trayvon Martin must terrify you in a way that he could never terrify me. You have seen so much more of all that is lost when they destroy your body.

The streets were not my only problem. If the streets shackled my right leg, the schools shackled my left. Fail to comprehend the streets and you gave up your body now. But fail to comprehend the schools and you gave up your body later. I suffered at the hands of both, but I resent the schools more. There was nothing sanctified about the laws of the streets—the laws were amoral and practical. You rolled with a posse to the party as sure as you wore boots in the snow, or raised an umbrella in the rain. These were rules aimed at something obvious—the great danger that haunted every visit to Shake & Bake,[5] every bus ride downtown. But the laws of the schools were aimed at something distant and vague. What did it mean to, as our elders told us, "grow up and be somebody"? And what precisely did this have to do with an education rendered as rote discipline? To be educated in my Baltimore mostly meant always packing an extra number 2 pencil and working quietly. Educated children walked in single file on the right side of the hallway, raised their hands to use

---

4 **Trayvon Martin:** A seventeen-year-old black man fatally shot on February 26, 2012, in Sanford, Florida, by George Zimmerman, a neighborhood watch volunteer, after purchasing items at a convenience store. Zimmerman reported Martin to the Sanford Police as a suspect in recent robberies. The police told Zimmerman to remain in his car until they arrived, but he followed Martin on foot, and, after an altercation, Zimmerman fatally shot Martin in the chest. After national media focused on the case, Zimmerman was eventually charged and tried. A jury acquitted him of second-degree murder and manslaughter in July 2013. —Eds.

5 **Shake & Bake:** A restaurant chain. —Eds.

the lavatory, and carried the lavatory pass when en route. Educated children never offered excuses—certainly not childhood itself. The world had no time for the childhoods of black boys and girls. How could the schools? Algebra, Biology, and English were not subjects so much as opportunities to better discipline the body, to practice writing between the lines, copying the directions legibly, memorizing theorems extracted from the world they were created to represent. All of it felt so distant to me. I remember sitting in my seventh-grade French class and not having any idea why I was there. I did not know any French people, and nothing around me suggested I ever would. France was a rock rotating in another galaxy, around another sun, in another sky that I would never cross. Why, precisely, was I sitting in this classroom?

The question was never answered. I was a curious boy, but the schools were not concerned with curiosity. They were concerned with compliance. I loved a few of my teachers. But I cannot say that I truly believed any of them. Some years after I'd left school, after I'd dropped out of college, I heard a few lines from Nas that struck me:

> *Ecstasy, coke, you say it's love, it is poison*
> *Schools where I learn they should be burned, it is poison*

That was exactly how I felt back then. I sensed the schools were hiding something, drugging us with false morality so that we would not see, so that we did not ask: Why—for us and only us—is the other side of free will and free spirits an assault upon our bodies? This is not a hyperbolic concern. When our elders presented school to us, they did not present it as a place of high learning but as a means of escape from death and penal warehousing. Fully 60 percent of all young black men who drop out of high school will go to jail. This should disgrace the country. But it does not, and while I couldn't crunch the numbers or plumb the history back then, I sensed that the fear that marked West Baltimore could not be explained by the schools. Schools did not reveal truths, they concealed them. Perhaps they must be burned away so that the heart of this thing might be known.

Unfit for the schools, and in good measure wanting to be unfit for them, and lacking the savvy I needed to master the streets, I felt there could be no escape for me or, honestly, anyone else. The fearless boys and girls who would knuckle up, call on cousins and crews, and, if it came to it, pull guns seemed to have mastered the streets. But their knowledge peaked at seventeen, when they ventured out of their parents' homes and discovered that America had guns and cousins, too. I saw their futures in the tired faces of mothers dragging themselves onto the 28 bus, swatting and cursing at three-year-olds; I saw their futures in the men out on the corner yelling obscenely at some young girl because she would not smile. Some of them stood outside liquor stores waiting on a few dollars for a bottle. We would hand them a twenty and tell them to keep the change. They would dash inside and return with Red Bull, Mad Dog, or Cisco.[6] Then we would walk to the house of someone whose mother worked nights, play "Fuck tha Police," and drink to our

---

[6] **Red Bull, Mad Dog, or Cisco:** Potent stimulant drinks. —EDS.

youth. We could not get out. The ground we walked was trip-wired. The air we breathed was toxic. The water stunted our growth. We could not get out.

A year after I watched the boy with the small eyes pull out a gun, my   15 father beat me for letting another boy steal from me. Two years later, he beat me for threatening my ninth-grade teacher. Not being violent enough could cost me my body. Being too violent could cost me my body. We could not get out. I was a capable boy, intelligent, well-liked, but powerfully afraid. And I felt, vaguely, wordlessly, that for a child to be marked off for such a life, to be forced to live in fear was a great injustice. And what was the source of this fear? What was hiding behind the smoke screen of streets and schools? And what did it mean that number 2 pencils, conjugations without context, Pythagorean theorems, handshakes, and head nods were the difference between life and death, were the curtains drawing down between the world and me?

The Reader's Presence

1. Coates describes the "worlds" he remembers in cosmic terms. He writes, for instance, "Somewhere out there beyond the firmament, past the asteroid belt, there were other worlds where children did not regularly fear for their bodies" (paragraph 5). What do you think Coates gains and risks by choosing to frame his perspective on his experience in this way? What implications can you draw from Coates's using language of the "firmament" and the "body" for the scope and focus of the story he tells—and the points he explains? Consider Coates's use of figurative language (words or expressions with a meaning different from the literal interpretation—such as metaphor, analogy, allusion). Identify two or three examples, and explain what effects Coates's use of figurative language has on your understanding and appreciation of his writing.

2. This selection is drawn from *Between the World and Me*, written as a letter to Coates's son. What does Coates gain by addressing his son directly rather than the reader? How does this shape or alter your perception of his narrative, of the significance he expects his readers to draw from it? Support each point you make with a detailed analysis of specific passages. What response does Coates elicit from his readers by mentioning Michael Brown (killed by the police on August 9, 2014, in Ferguson, Missouri) and Trayvon Martin (shot by George Zimmerman on February 26, 2012, in Sanford, Florida)?

3. **CONNECTIONS:** Compare and contrast Coates's view of schools with John Taylor Gatto's in "Against School" (page 517). Coates observes, for example, "If the streets shackled my right leg, the schools shackled my left" (paragraph 11). What consequences does Coates recount as the consequences of being "shackled" by each? Which forms of being shackled does he "prefer"? Explain why. In what specific ways are their descriptions of schools similar? Different? As you develop your answer, consider the relationship between the educational system Gatto describes and the need for personal security expressed by Coates.

The Writer at Work

Ta-Nehisi Coates on the Culture of Scholastic Achievement

Dave Allocca/StarPix/REX/Shutterstock.com

In the summer of 2014, in preparation for a fellowship that would take him to Paris, Ta-Nehisi Coates enrolled in a French immersion program at Middlebury College in Vermont. In the following excerpt from a long essay he published in the *Atlantic*, Coates describes his struggles to improve his French and relates them to the larger educational struggles of underprepared minority students who lack a "culture of scholastic achievement." For another perspective on learning French, please see David Sedaris "Me Talk Pretty One Day" (page 210).

❝I spent the majority of this summer at Middlebury College, studying at l'École Française. I had never been to Vermont. I have not been many places at all. I did not have an adult passport until I was 37 years old. Sometimes I regret this. And then sometimes not. Learning to travel when you're older allows you to be young again, to touch the childlike amazement that is so often dulled away by adult things. In the past year, I have seen more of the world than at any point before, and thus, I have been filled with that juvenile feeling more times then I can count—at a train station in Strasbourg, in an old Parisian bookstore, on a wide avenue in Lawndale. It was no different in Vermont where the green mountains loomed like giants. I would stare at these mountains out of the back window of the Davis Family Library. I would watch the clouds, which, before the rain, drooped over the mountains like lampshades, and I would wonder what, precisely, I had been doing with my life.

I was there to improve my French. My study consisted of four hours of class work and four hours of homework.

I was forbidden from reading, writing, speaking, or hearing English. I watched films in French, tried to read a story in *Le Monde* each day, listened to RFI and a lot of Barbara and Karim Oeullet.[1] At every meal I spoke French, and over the course of the seven weeks I felt myself gradually losing touch with the broader world. This was not a wholly unpleasant feeling. In the moments I had to speak English (calling my wife, interacting with folks in town or at the book store), my mouth felt alien and my ear slightly off.

And there were the latest developments, the likes of which I perceived faintly through the French media. I had some vague sense that King James had done something grand, that the police were killing black men over cigarette sales, that a passenger plane had been shot out the sky, and that powerful people in the world still believed that great problems could be ultimately solved with great armaments. In sum, I knew that very little had changed. And

---

[1] *Barbara and Karim Ouellet:* popular singers on Radio France International. —EDS.

I knew this even with my feeble French eyes, which turned the news of the world into an exercise in impressionism. Everything felt distorted. I understood that things were happening out there, but their size and scope mostly eluded me.

Acquiring a second language is hard. I have been told that it is easier for children, but I am not so sure if this is for reasons of biology or because adults have so much more to learn. Still, it remains true that the vast majority of students at Middlebury were younger than me, and not just younger, but fiercer. My classmates were, in the main, the kind of high-achieving college students who elect to spend their summer vacation taking on eight hours a day of schoolwork. There was no difference in work ethic between us. If I spent more time studying than my classmates, that fact should not be taken as an accolade but as a marker of my inefficiency.

They had something over me, and that something was a culture, which is to say a suite of practices so ingrained as to be ritualistic. The scholastic achievers knew how to quickly memorize a poem in a language they did not understand. They knew that recopying a handout a few days before an exam helped them digest the information. They knew to bring a pencil, not a pen, to that exam. They knew that you could (with the professor's permission) record lectures and take pictures of the blackboard.

This culture of scholastic achievement had not been acquired yesterday. The same set of practices had allowed my classmates to succeed in high school, and had likely been reinforced by other scholastic achievers around them. I am sure many of them had parents who were scholastic high-achievers. This is how social capital reinforces itself and compounds. It is not merely one high-achieving child, but a flock of high-achieving children, each backed by high-achieving parents. I once talked to a woman who spoke German, English, and French and had done so since she was a child. How did this happen, I asked? "Everyone in my world spoke multiple languages," she explained. "It was just what you did."

There were five tiers of French students, starting with those who could barely speak a word and scaling upward to those who were pursuing a master's degree. I was in the second tier, meaning I could order a coffee, recount a story with some difficulty, write a short note (sans verb and gender agreement), and generally understand a French speaker provided he or she talked to me really slowly. The majority of people I interacted with spoke better, wrote better, read better, and heard better than me. There was no escape from my ineptitude. At every waking hour, someone said something to me that I did not understand. At every waking hour, I mangled some poor Frenchman's lovely language. For the entire summer, I lived by two words: "Désolé, encore."[2]

Compared with my classmates on the second tier, my test scores were on the lower end. Each week, in my literature class, we were responsible for the recitation of some French poems (Baudelaire, Verlaine, Lamartine) from memory, and each day we had to recite a stanza. This sort of exercise may well be familiar to readers of *The Atlantic*, but the rituals required to master it were totally new to me. I had never been a high-achieving student. Indeed, during my 15 or so years in school, I was a remarkably low-achieving student.

---

[2] *"Désolé, encore":* "Sorry, again." —EDS.

> There were years when I failed the majority of my classes. This was not a matter of my being better suited for the liberal arts than sciences. I was an English minor in college. I failed American Literature, British Literature, Humanities, and (voilà) French. The record of failure did not end until I quit college to become a writer. My explanation for this record is unsatisfactory: I simply never saw the point of school. I loved the long process of understanding. In school, I often felt like I was doing something else.
>
> Like many black children in this country, I did not have a culture of scholastic high achievement around me. There were very few adults around me who'd been great students and were subsequently rewarded for their studiousness. The phrase "Ivy League" was an empty abstraction to me. I mostly thought of school as a place one goes so as not to be eventually killed, drugged, or jailed. These observations cannot be disconnected from the country I call home, nor from the government to which I swear fealty. **"**

Amy Cunningham
WHY WOMEN SMILE

AMY CUNNINGHAM (b. 1955) has been writing on psychological issues and modern life for magazines such as *Redbook, Glamour*, and the *Washington Post Magazine* since she graduated from the University of Virginia in 1977 with a BA in English. Cunningham says that the essay reprinted here grew out of her own experience as an "easy to get along with person" who was raised by southerners in the suburbs of Chicago. She also recalls that when writing it, "I was unhappy with myself for taking too long, for not being efficient the way I thought a professional writer should be—but the work paid off and now I think it is one of the best essays I've written." "Why Women Smile" originally appeared in *Lear's* in 1993.

> **"Good writing has less to do with talent and more to do with the discipline of staying seated . . . in front of the computer and getting the work done."**

Looking back on her writing career, Cunningham notes, "When I was younger I thought if you had talent you would make it as a writer. I'm surprised to realize now that good writing has less to do with talent and more to do with the discipline of staying seated in the chair, by yourself, in front of the computer and getting the work done."

AFTER SMILING BRILLIANTLY for nearly four decades, I now find myself trying to quit. Or, at the very least, seeking to lower the wattage a bit.

Not everyone I know is keen on this. My smile has gleamed like a cheap plastic night-light so long and so reliably that certain friends and relatives worry that my mood will darken the moment my smile dims. "Gee," one says, "I associate you with your smile. It's the essence of you. I should think you'd want to smile more!" But the people who love me best agree that my smile—which springs forth no matter where I am or how I feel—hasn't been serving me well. Said my husband recently, "Your smiling face and unthreatening demeanor make people like you in a fuzzy way, but that doesn't seem to be what you're after these days."

Smiles are not the small and innocuous things they appear to be: Too many of us smile in lieu of showing what's really on our minds. Indeed, the success of the women's movement might be measured by the sincerity—and lack of it—in our smiles. Despite all the work we American women have done to get and maintain full legal control of our bodies, not to mention our destinies, we still don't seem to be fully in charge of a couple of small muscle groups in our faces.

We smile so often and so promiscuously—when we're angry, when we're tense, when we're with children, when we're being photographed, when we're interviewing for a job, when we're meeting candidates to employ—that the Smiling Woman has become a peculiarly American archetype. This isn't entirely a bad thing, of course. A smile lightens the load, diffuses unpleasantness, redistributes nervous tension. Women doctors smile more than their male counterparts, studies show, and are better liked by their patients.

Oscar Wilde's[1] old saw that "a woman's face is her work of fiction" is often   5
quoted to remind us that what's on the surface may have little connection to what we're feeling. What is it in our culture that keeps our smiles on automatic pilot? The behavior seems to be an equal blend of nature and nurture. Research has demonstrated that since females often mature earlier than males and are less irritable, girls smile more than boys from the very beginning. But by adolescence, the differences in the smiling rates of boys and girls are so robust that it's clear the culture has done more than its share of the dirty work. Just think of the mothers who painstakingly embroidered the words ENTER SMILING on little samplers, and then hung their handiwork on doors by golden chains. Translation: "Your real emotions aren't welcome here."

Clearly, our instincts are another factor. Our smiles have their roots in the greetings of monkeys, who pull their lips up and back to show their fear of attack, as well as their reluctance to vie for a position of dominance. And like the opossum caught in the light by the clattering garbage cans, we, too, flash toothy grimaces when we make major mistakes. By declaring ourselves nonthreatening, our smiles provide an extremely versatile means of protection.

---

[1] *Oscar Wilde* (1854–1900): An Irish writer, poet, aesthete, and popular playwright in the early 1890s remembered for his epigrams and his early death. —EDS.

Our earliest baby smiles are involuntary reflexes having only the vaguest connection to contentment or comfort. In short, we're genetically wired to pull on our parents' heartstrings. As Desmond Morris[2] explains in *Babywatching*, this is our way of attaching ourselves to our caretakers, as truly as baby chimps clench their mothers' fur. Even as babies we're capable of projecting onto others (in this case, our parents) the feelings we know we need to get back in return.

Bona fide social smiles occur at two-and-a-half to three months of age, usually a few weeks after we first start gazing with intense interest into the faces of our parents. By the time we are six months old, we are smiling and laughing regularly in reaction to tickling, feedings, blown raspberries, hugs, and peekaboo games. Even babies who are born blind intuitively know how to react to pleasurable changes with a smile, though their first smiles start later than those of sighted children.

Psychologists and psychiatrists have noted that babies also smile and laugh with relief when they realize that something they thought might be dangerous is not dangerous after all. Kids begin to invite their parents to indulge them with "scary" approach-avoidance games; they love to be chased or tossed up into the air. (It's interesting to note that as adults, we go through the same gosh-that's-shocking-and-dangerous-but-it's-okay-to-laugh-and-smile cycles when we listen to raunchy stand-up comics.)

From the wilds of New Guinea to the sidewalks of New York, smiles are   10 associated with joy, relief, and amusement. But smiles are by no means limited to the expression of positive emotions: People of many different cultures smile when they are frightened, embarrassed, angry, or miserable. In Japan, for instance, a smile is often used to hide pain or sorrow.

Psychologist Paul Ekman, the head of the University of California's Human Interaction Lab in San Francisco, has identified 18 distinct types of smiles, including those that show misery, compliance, fear, and contempt. The smile of true merriment, which Dr. Ekman calls the Duchenne Smile, after the nineteenth-century French doctor who first studied it, is characterized by heightened circulation, a feeling of exhilaration, and the employment of two major facial muscles: the zygomaticus major of the lower face, and the orbicularis oculi, which crinkles the skin around the eyes. But since the average American woman's smile often has less to do with her actual state of happiness than it does with the social pressure to smile no matter what, her baseline social smile isn't apt to be a felt expression that engages the eyes like this. Ekman insists that if people learned to read smiles, they could see the sadness, misery, or pain lurking there, plain as day.

Evidently, a woman's happy, willing deference is something the world wants visibly demonstrated. Woe to the waitress, the personal assistant or receptionist, the flight attendant, or any other woman in the line of public service whose

---

[2] **Desmond Morris** (b. 1928): Distinguished zoologist and author of the best-selling *The Naked Ape* (1967) and *Babywatching* (1992). —EDS.

Paul D. Ekman, PHD.

Paul D. Ekman, PHD.

These photos from Paul Ekman's study show the difference between the social smile (left) and the true enjoyment smile (right).

smile is not offered up to the boss or client as proof that there are no storm clouds—no kids to support, no sleep that's been missed—rolling into the sunny workplace landscape. Women are expected to smile no matter where they line up on the social, cultural, or economic ladder: College professors are criticized for not smiling, political spouses are pilloried for being too serious, and women's roles in films have historically been smiling ones. It's little wonder that men on the street still call out, "Hey, baby, smile! Life's not *that* bad, is it?" to women passing by, lost in thought.

A friend remembers being pulled aside by a teacher after class and asked, "What is wrong, dear? You sat there for the whole hour looking so sad!" "All I could figure," my friend says now, "is that I wasn't smiling. And the fact that *she* felt sorry for me for looking normal made me feel horrible."

Ironically, the social laws that govern our smiles have completely reversed themselves over the last two thousand years. Women weren't always expected to seem animated and responsive; in fact, immoderate laughter was once considered one of the more conspicuous vices a woman could have, and mirth was downright sinful. Women were kept apart, in some cultures even veiled, so that they couldn't perpetuate Eve's seductive, evil work. The only smile deemed appropriate on a privileged woman's face was the serene, inward smile of the Virgin Mary at Christ's birth, and even that expression was best directed exclusively at young children. Cackling laughter and wicked glee were the kinds of sounds heard only in hell.

What we know of women's facial expressions in other centuries comes   15
mostly from religious writings, codes of etiquette, and portrait paintings. In fifteenth century Italy, it was customary for artists to paint lovely, blank-faced women in profile. A viewer could stare endlessly at such a woman, but she

could not gaze back. By the Renaissance, male artists were taking some pleasure in depicting women with a semblance of complexity, Leonardo da Vinci's
Mona Lisa,[3] with her veiled enigmatic smile, being the most famous example.

The Golden Age of the Dutch Republic[4] marks a fascinating period for
studying women's facial expressions. While we might expect the drunken
young whores of Amsterdam to smile devilishly (unbridled sexuality and
lasciviousness were *supposed* to addle the brain), it's the faces of the Dutch
women from fine families that surprise us. Considered socially more free,
these women demonstrate a fuller range of facial expressions than their
European sisters. Frans Hals's[5] 1622 portrait of Stephanus Geraerdt and
Isabella Coymans, a married couple, is remarkable not just for the full,
friendly smiles on each face but for the frank and mutual pleasure the couple
take in each other.

Art Resource

3 ***Mona Lisa:*** Widely recognized as one of the most important works of art in history, this
sixteenth-century portrait painted in oil by Leonardo di ser Piero da Vinci (1452–1519) is on
display at the Musée du Louvre in Paris as "Portrait of Lisa Gherardini, wife of Francesco del
Giocondo." —EDS.

4 ***Golden Age of the Dutch Republic:*** A period in Dutch history, ranging across the seventeenth
century, in which Dutch achievements in trade, science, art, and military were highly acclaimed. —EDS.

5 ***Frans Hals*** (c. 1582/83–1666): One of the most celebrated painters during the Dutch Golden
Age. —EDS.

In the 1800s, sprightly, pretty women began appearing in advertisements for everything from beverages to those newfangled Kodak Land cameras.[6] Women's faces were no longer impassive, and their willingness to bestow status, to offer, proffer, and yield, was most definitely promoted by their smiling images. The culture appeared to have turned the smile, originally a bond shared between intimates, into a socially required display that sold capitalist ideology as well as kitchen appliances. And female viewers soon began to emulate these highly idealized pictures. Many longed to be more like her, that perpetually smiling female. She seemed so beautiful. So content. So whole.

By the middle of the nineteenth century, the bulk of America's smile burden was falling primarily to women and African-American slaves, providing a very portable means of protection, a way of saying, "I'm harmless. I won't assert myself here." It reassured those in power to see signs of gratitude and contentment in the faces of subordinates. As long ago as 1963, adman David Ogilvy declared the image of a woman smiling approvingly at a product clichéd, but we've yet to get the message. Cheerful Americans still appear in ads today, smiling somewhat less disingenuously than they smiled during the middle of the century, but smiling broadly nonetheless.

Other countries have been somewhat reluctant to import our "Don't worry, be happy" American smiles. When McDonald's opened in Moscow not long ago [1990] and when EuroDisney debuted in France last year [1992], the Americans involved in both business ventures complained that they couldn't get the natives they'd employed to smile worth a damn.

Europeans visiting the United States for the first time are often surprised   20 at just how often Americans smile. But when you look at our history, the relentless good humor (or, at any rate, the pretense of it) falls into perspective. The American wilderness was developed on the assumption that this country had a shortage of people in relation to its possibilities. In countries with a more rigid class structure or caste system, fewer people are as captivated by the idea of quickly winning friends and influencing people. Here in the States, however, every stranger is a potential associate. Our smiles bring new people on board. The American smile is a democratic version of a curtsy or doffed hat, since, in this land of free equals, we're not especially formal about the ways we greet social superiors.

The civil rights movement never addressed the smile burden by name, but activists worked on their own to set new facial norms. African-American males stopped smiling on the streets in the 1960s, happily aware of the unsettling effect this action had on the white population. The image of the simple-minded, smiling, white-toothed black was rejected as blatantly racist, and it gradually retreated into the distance. However, like the women of Sparta and the wives of samurai, who were expected to look happy upon learning their sons or husbands had died in battle, contemporary American women have yet to unilaterally declare their faces their own property.

6 *Kodak Land camera:* An instant camera, invented by American scientist Edwin Land and first sold in 1948. —EDS.

For instance, imagine a woman at a morning business meeting being asked if she could make a spontaneous and concise summation of a complicated project she's been struggling to get under control for months. She might draw the end of her mouth back and clench her teeth—Eek!—in a protective response, a polite, restrained expression of her surprise, not unlike the expression of a conscientious young schoolgirl being told to get out paper and pencil for a pop quiz. At the same time, the woman might be feeling resentful of the supervisor who sprang the request, but she fears taking that person on. So she holds back a comment. The whole performance resolves in a weird grin collapsing into a nervous smile that conveys discomfort and unpreparedness. A pointed remark by way of explanation or self-defense might've worked better for her—but her mouth was otherwise engaged.

We'd do well to realize just how much our smiles misrepresent us, and swear off for good the self-deprecating grins and ritual displays of deference. Real smiles have beneficial physiological effects, according to Paul Ekman. False ones do nothing for us at all.

"Smiles are as important as sound bites on television," insists producer and media coach Heidi Berenson, who has worked with many of Washington's most famous faces. "And women have always been better at understanding this than men. But the smile I'm talking about is not a cutesy smile. It's an authoritative smile. A genuine smile. Properly timed, it's tremendously powerful."

To limit a woman to one expression is like editing down an orchestra to one instrument. And the search for more authentic means of expression isn't easy in a culture in which women are still expected to be magnanimous smilers, helpmates in crisis, and curators of everybody else's morale. But change is already floating in the high winds. We see a boon in assertive female comedians who are proving that women can *dish out* smiles, not just wear them. Actress Demi Moore has stated that she doesn't like to take smiling roles. Nike is running ads that show unsmiling women athletes sweating, reaching, pushing themselves. These women aren't overly concerned with issues of rapport; they're not being "nice" girls—they're working out. 25

If a woman's smile were truly her own, to be smiled or not, according to how the *woman* felt, rather than according to what someone else needed, she would smile more spontaneously, without ulterior, hidden motives. As Rainer Maria Rilke[7] wrote in *The Journal of My Other Self*, "Her smile was not meant to be seen by anyone and served its whole purpose in being smiled."

That smile is my long-term aim. In the meantime, I hope to stabilize on the smile continuum somewhere between the eliciting grin of Farrah Fawcett[8] and the haughty smirk of Jeane Kirkpatrick.[9] ■

---

[7] **Rainer Maria Rilke** (1875–1926): Austrian poet, art critic, and author of *Letters to a Young Poet* (1929) and *The Journal of My Other Self* (1930). —EDS.

[8] **Farrah Fawcett** (1947–2009): American actress who became an international celebrity after appearing in the television series *Charlie's Angels* in 1976. —EDS.

[9] **Jeane Kirkpatrick** (1926–2006): An American ambassador to the United Nations during the administration of President Ronald Reagan. —EDS.

IIIIIIIIIIIIIIIIIIIIIIIIIIIIIIIIIIIIIIIIIIIIIIIIIIIIIIIIIIIIIIIIIIIIIIIIIIIIIIIIIIIIIIIIIIIIIIIIIIIIIIIIIIIIIIIIIIIIIIIIIIIIIIIIIIIIIIIIIIIII▶

The Reader's Presence

1. Cunningham presents an informative précis of the causes and effects of smiling in Western culture. Consider the points of view from which she addresses this subject. Summarize and evaluate her treatment of smiling from psychological, physiological, sociological, and historical points of view. Which do you find most incisive? Why? What other points of view does she introduce into her discussion of smiling? What effects do they create? What does she identify as the benefits (and the disadvantages) of smiling?

2. At what point in this essay does Cunningham address the issue of gender? Characterize the language she uses to introduce this issue. She distinguishes between the different patterns—and the consequences—experienced by men and women who smile. Summarize these differences and assess the nature and the extent of the evidence she provides for each of her points. What more general distinctions does she make about various kinds of smiles? What are their different purposes and degrees of intensity? What information does she provide about smiling as an issue of nationality and race? What is the overall purpose of this essay? Where—and how—does Cunningham create and sustain a sense of her own presence in this essay? What does she set as her personal goal in relation to smiling?

3. **VISUAL PRESENCE:** Compare the two photographs from Paul Ekman's study (page 342) with the *Mona Lisa* (page 343). The Ekman study photos demonstrate the difference between the "social smile" and the "true enjoyment smile." To which category does the *Mona Lisa* belong? Explain why.

4. **CONNECTIONS:** Cunningham explains the causes of an activity that few of her readers are likely to think about in both scientific and historical terms. Compare her use of science and history to that of Steven Pinker in "Violence Vanquished" (page 591). How does each writer establish her or his authority in these fields? Point to specific examples to support each point you make. Summarize the nature of each writer's presentation. To what extent does each writer rely on factual evidence?

Edwidge Danticat
MESSAGE TO MY DAUGHTERS

Born in Haiti under a dictator who ordered the police to murder thousands of civilians, **EDWIDGE DANTICAT** (b. 1969) is no stranger to the abuses of power. At the age of twelve, she arrived in the United States, where she would encounter abuses of another kind due to the color of her skin. In "Message to My Daughters," the author describes the acts of racial violence that marked the years after she came to America and her hopes for the future.

A prolific writer of fiction, Danticat has earned critical acclaim for her novels and short stories. At the age of twenty-seven, she was named one of the Best Young American Novelists in *Granta* literary magazine for her first novel, *Breath, Eyes, Memory* (1994). Her memoir, *Brother, I'm Dying* (2007), received the National Book Critics Circle Award. She has taught at New York University and the University of Miami. Her most recent novels are *Claire of the Sea Light* (2013) and *Untwine* (2015).

> **"I am a writer who is shaped by everything that I have experienced and loved, including Haiti."**

Danticat's prose reflects a strong affinity for her birthplace: "I am a writer who is shaped by everything that I have experienced and loved, including Haiti. I think that is probably true for all writers," she says. "The trick is how to get that out of you and turn it into something truly worth sharing with others."

SOON AFTER THE ONE-YEAR ANNIVERSARY of the fatal shooting of Michael Brown[1] by the Ferguson police officer Darren Wilson, I was in Haiti, at the southernmost end of the country's border with the Dominican Republic, where hundreds of Haitian refugees had either been deported or driven out of the Dominican Republic by intimidation or threats. Many of these men and women had very little warning that they were going to be picked up or chased away and most of them had fled with nothing but the clothes on their backs.

It was a bright sunny day, but the air was thick with dust. As some friends and I walked through the makeshift resettlement camps on the Haitian side of the border, in a place called Pak Kado, it felt as though we, along with the residents of the camps, were floating through clouds. Around us were lean-tos made of cardboard boxes and sheets. Dust-covered children walked around looking dazed even while playing with pebbles that stood in for marbles, or while flying plastic bags as kites. Elderly people stood on the edge of food and clothes distribution lines, some too weak to wade into the crowd. Later the elderly, along with pregnant women and the disabled, would be given special consideration by the priest and nuns who were giving out the only food available to the camp dwellers, but the food would always run out before they could get to everyone.

A few days after leaving Haiti and returning to the United States, I read a Michael Brown anniversary opinion piece in *The Washington Post* written by Raha Jorjani, an immigration attorney and law professor. In her essay, Jorjani argues that African Americans living in the United States could easily

---

[1] **Michael Brown:** On August 9, 2014, Michael Brown, an eighteen-year-old black man, was fatally shot by a white Ferguson, Missouri, police officer, after Brown reportedly robbed a convenience store. The controversial circumstances of the shooting resulted in national protests and civic unrest in the predominantly black city, north of St. Louis. —Eds.

qualify as refugees. Citing many recent cases of police brutality and killings of unarmed black men, women, and children, she wrote:

> Suppose a client walked into my office and told me that police officers in his country had choked a man to death over a petty crime. Suppose he said police fatally shot another man in the back as he ran away. That they arrested a woman during a traffic stop and placed her in jail, where she died three days later. That a 12-year-old boy in his country was shot and killed by the police as he played in the park.
>
> Suppose he told me that all of those victims were from the same ethnic community—a community whose members fear being harmed, tortured or killed by police or prison guards. And that this is true in cities and towns across his nation. At that point, as an immigration lawyer, I'd tell him he had a strong claim for asylum protection under U.S. law.

This is not the first time that the idea of African Americans as internal or external refugees has been floated or applied. The six-million-plus African Americans who migrated from the rural south to urban centers in the northern United States for more than half a century during the Great Migration were often referred to as refugees, as were those people internally displaced by Hurricane Katrina.

Having now visited many refugee and displacement camps, the label 5 "refugee" at first seemed an extreme designation to assign to citizens of one of the richest countries in the world, especially if it is assigned on a singular basis to those who are black. Still, compared to the relative wealth of the rest of the society, a particularly run-down Brooklyn public housing project where a childhood friend used to live had all the earmarks of a refugee camp. It occupied one of the least desirable parts of town and provided only the most basic necessities. A nearby dilapidated school, where I attended junior high, could have easily been on the edge of that refugee settlement, where the primary daily task was to keep the children occupied, rather than engaged and learning. Aside from a few overly devoted teachers, we were often on our own. We, immigrant blacks and African Americans alike, were treated by those who housed us, and were in charge of schooling us, as though we were members of a group in transit. The message we always heard from those who were meant to protect us: that we should either die or go somewhere else. This is the experience of a refugee.

I have seen state abuses up close, both in Haiti, where I was born under a ruthless dictatorship, and in New York, where I migrated to a working-class and predominantly African, African American, and Caribbean neighborhood in Brooklyn at the age of twelve. In the Haiti of the 1970s and early '80s, the violence was overtly political. Government detractors were dragged out of their homes, imprisoned, beaten, or killed. Sometimes their bodies were left out in the streets, in the hot sun, for extended periods, to intimidate neighbors.

In New York, the violence seemed a bit more subtle, though no less pervasive. When I started riding the city bus to high school, I observed that a muffled radio message from an annoyed bus driver—about someone talking too loud or not having the right fare—was all it took to make the police rush in, drag a young man off the bus, and beat him into submission on the sidewalk. There were no cell phone cameras back then to record such abuse, and most of us were too terrified to demand a badge number.

Besides, many of us had fled our countries as exiles, migrants, and refugees just to escape this kind of military or police aggression; we knew how deadly a confrontation with an armed and uniformed authoritarian figure could be. Still, every now and then a fellow traveler would summon his or her courage and, dodging the swaying baton, or screaming from a distance, would yell some variation of "Stop it! This is a child! A child!"

Of course, not all of the police's victims were children. Abner Louima, a family friend, was thirty years old when he was mistaken for someone who had punched a police officer outside a Brooklyn nightclub, on August 9, 1997, sixteen years to the day before Michael Brown was killed. Abner was arrested, beaten with fists, as well as with police radios, flashlights, and nightsticks, and then sexually assaulted with the wooden handle of a toilet plunger or a broom inside a precinct bathroom. After Abner, there was Amadou Diallo, a Guinean immigrant, who was hit by nineteen of the forty-one bullets aimed at him as he retrieved his wallet from his pocket. Then there was Patrick Dorismond, the U.S.-born child of Haitian immigrants, who died trying to convince undercover cops that he was not a drug dealer.

These are only a few among the cases from my era that made the news. 10 There was also sixty-six-year-old Eleanor Bumpurs, who, thirteen years before Abner's assault, was killed by police with a twelve-gauge shotgun inside her own apartment. I have no doubt there were many others. We marched for all of them in the Louima/Diallo/Dorismond decade. We carried signs and chanted "No Justice! No Peace!" and "Whose Streets? Our Streets!" even while fearing the latter would never be true. The streets belonged to the people with the uniforms and the guns. The streets were never ours. Our sons and brothers, fathers and uncles, our mothers and sisters, daughters and nieces, our neighbors were, and still are, prey.

My father, a Brooklyn cab driver, used to half joke that police did not beat him up because, at sixty-five years old, he was too skinny and too old, and not worth the effort. Every now and then, when he was randomly stopped by a police officer and deigned to ask why, rather than a beating, he would be given a handful of unwarranted traffic citations that would wipe out a few weeks' hard-earned wages. Today, one might generously refer to such acts as micro-aggressions. That is, until they turn major and deadly, until other unarmed black bodies, with nowhere to go for refuge, find themselves in the path of yet another police officer's or armed vigilante's gun.

When it was announced that Darren Wilson would not be indicted for the killing of Michael Brown, I kept thinking of Abner Louima, whose assault took place when Michael Brown was just eighteen months old. Abner and I have known each other for years. Both our families have attended the same Creole-speaking church for decades, so I called him to hear his thoughts about Michael Brown's killer going free. If anyone could understand all those broken hearts, all the rage, all the desperation, the yearning for justice, what it is to be a member of a seemingly marooned and persecuted group, I thought, he would.

Scott Olson/Getty Images News/Getty Images

To mark the first anniversary of his son's death after being shot by a Ferguson police officer, Michael Brown Sr. led a march from the location where his son was killed to the high school where his son was a student.

Abner Louima, unlike Michael Brown, had survived. He went on with his life, moved from New York City to south Florida, started businesses. He has a daughter and two sons. One son was eighteen years old when we spoke, the same age Michael Brown was when he died.

How does he feel, I asked him, each time he hears that yet another black person was killed or nearly killed by police?

"It reminds me that our lives mean nothing," he replied.   15

We are in America because our lives meant nothing to those in power in the countries where we came from. Yet we come here to realize that our lives also mean nothing here. Some of us try to distance ourselves from this reality, thinking that because we are another type of "other"—immigrants, migrants, refugees—this is not our problem, nor one we can solve. But ultimately we realize the precarious nature of citizenship here: that we too are prey, and that those who have been in this country for generations—walking, living, loving in the same skin we're in—they too can suddenly become refugees.

Parents are often too nervous to broach difficult subjects with their children. Love. Sex. Death. Race. But some parents are forced to have these conversations early. Too early. A broken heart might lead to questions we'd rather not answer, as might an inappropriate gesture, the death of a loved one, or the murder of a stranger.

Each time a black person is killed in a manner that's clearly racially motivated, either by a police officer or a vigilante civilian, I ask myself if the time has come for me to talk to my daughters about Abner Louima and the long list of dead that have come since. My daughters have met Abner, but I have never told them about his past, even though his past is a future they might have to face.

Why don't I tell them? My decision is about more than avoiding a difficult conversation. The truth is, I do not want my daughters to grow up as I did, terrified of the country and the world they live in. But is it irresponsible of me to not alert them to the potentially life-altering, or even life-ending horrors they might face as young black women?

The night President Barack Obama was first elected (would he too qualify   20
for refugee status?), my oldest daughter was three and I was in the last weeks of my pregnancy with my second. When President Obama was inaugurated for the first time, I was cradling both my little girls in my arms.

To think, I remember telling my husband, our daughters will never know a world in which the president of their country has not been black. Indeed, as we watched President Obama's inaugural speech, my oldest daughter was shocked that no woman had ever been president of the United States. That day, the world ahead for my girls seemed full of greater possibility—if not endless possibilities, then at least greater than those for generations past. Many more doors suddenly seemed open to my girls, and the "joyous day-break" evoked by Martin Luther King, Jr., in his "I Have a Dream" speech, a kind of jubilee, seemed to have emerged. However, it quickly became clear that this one man was not going to take all of us with him into the postracial promised land. Or that he even had full access to it. Constant talk of "wanting him to fail" was racially tinged, as were the "birther" investigations, and the bigoted commentaries and jokes by both elected officials and ordinary folk. One of the most consistent attacks against the president, was that, like my husband and myself, he was born elsewhere and was not *really* American.

Like Barack Obama's father, many of us had brought our black bodies to America from somewhere else. Some of us, like the president, were the children of such people. We are people who need to have two different talks with our black offspring: one about why we're here and the other about why it's not always a promised land for people who look like us.

In his own version of "The Talk," James Baldwin wrote to his nephew James in "My Dungeon Shook," "You were born in a society which spelled out with brutal clarity, and in as many ways as possible that you were a worthless human being."

That same letter could have been written to a long roster of dead young men and women, whose dungeons shook, but whose chains did not com-pletely fall off. Among these very young people are Oscar Grant, Aiyana Stanley-Jones, Rekia Boyd, Kimani Gray, Renisha McBride, Trayvon Martin, Michael Bell, Tamir Rice, Michael Brown, Sandra Bland, and counting. It's sad to imagine what these young people's letters from their loved ones may have said. Had their favorite uncle notified them that they could qualify for refugee status within their own country? Did their mother or father, grand-mother or grandfather warn them to not walk in white neighborhoods, to, impossibly, avoid police officers, to never play in a public park, to stay away from neighborhood watchmen, to never go to a neighbor's house, even if to seek help from danger?

I am still, in my own mind, drafting a "My Dungeon Shook" letter to my   25 daughters. It often begins like this. *Dear Mira and Leila, I've put off writing this letter to you for as long as I can, but I don't think I can put it off any longer. Please know that there will be times when some people might be hostile or even violent to you for reasons that have nothing to do with your beauty, your humor, or your grace, but only your race and the color of your skin. Please don't let this restrict your freedom, break your spirit, or kill your joy. And if possible do everything you can to change the world so that your generation of brown and black men, women, and children will be the last who experience all this. And please do live your best lives and achieve your full potential. Love deeply. Be joyful. In Jubilee, Mom.*

To my draft of this letter, I often add snippets of Baldwin.

"I tell you this because I love you and please don't you ever forget it," Baldwin reminded his James. "Know whence you came. If you know whence you came, there is no limit to where you can go."

"The world is before you," I want to tell my daughters, "and you need not take it or leave it as it was when you came in."

I want to look happily forward. I want to be optimistic. I want to have a dream. I want to live in jubilee. I want my daughters to feel that they have the power to at least try to change things, even in a world that resists change with more strength than they have. I want to tell them they can overcome everything, if they are courageous, resilient, and brave. Paradoxically, I also want to tell them their crowns have already been bought and paid for and that all they have to do is put them on their heads. But the world keeps tripping me up. My certainty keeps flailing.

So I took them to the border, the one between Haiti and the Dominican   30 Republic, where hundreds of refugees were living, or rather existing. There they saw and helped comfort men, women, and children who look like them, but are stateless, babies with not even a bedsheet between them and a dirt floor, young people who may not be killed by bullets but by the much slower assault of disease.

"These are all our causes," I tried to both tell and show them, brown and black bodies living with "certain uncertainty," to use Frantz Fanon's[2] words, black bodies fleeing oppression, persecution, and poverty, wherever they are.

"You think your pain and your heartbreak are unprecedented in the history of the world, but then you read," James Baldwin wrote. Or you see. Or you weep. Or you pray. Or you speak. Or you write. Or you fight so that one day everyone will be able to walk the earth as though they, to use Baldwin's words, have "a right to be here." May that day come, Mira and Leila, when you can finally claim those crowns of yours and put them on your heads. When that day of jubilee finally arrives, all of us will be there with you, walking, heads held high, crowns a-glitter, because we do have a right to be here. ●

2 *Franz Fanon* (1925–1961): West Indian psychoanalyst and philosopher whose writings about race influenced post-colonial critical theory. —EDS.

The Reader's Presence

1. Refugees are generally viewed as people fleeing their home or country to avoid disaster or violence. Danticat suggests that African Americans could be viewed as refugees within their own country. What examples does she draw on to strengthen this overarching point of her essay? What strategies as a writer does she use to draw us deeply into her personal experience and that of her family—and especially her children? What new perspective and context does Danticat add to discussing the problem of racism in America? What can we learn from this perspective? She uses irony frequently to reinforce her point. See, for example, the scene where she discusses her father (paragraph 11). Comment on her using "microaggression" to characterize her father's treatment by the police. Point to—and discuss—other examples of irony.

2. As the title indicates, the essay is framed as a message to Danticat's daughters. Why does she decide, in the end, to convey her message by bringing them to Haiti, rather than speaking directly about the victims of racial violence? Comment on the effectiveness of the specific strategies she employs to integrate her own experience into the essay. For example, she recounts what happens to Abner Louima, "a family friend," who, based on mistaken identity, was arrested, savagely beaten and then sexually assaulted inside a police bathroom (paragraph 9). Later, she tells us that "My daughters have met Abner, but I have never told them about his past, even though his past is a future they might have to face" (paragraph 18). What importance does the experiences of Haitian refugees convey in such a discussion?

3. **CONNECTIONS:** Danticat cites James Baldwin in her essay as she imagines writing a letter to her daughters. In "Notes of a Native Son" (page 40), Baldwin reflects on the death of his father and his own experiences with racism. How do specific aspects of Baldwin's essay—such as his relationship with his father—relate to the message Danticat wishes to convey to her daughters? Compare and contrast the ways in which violence is portrayed in both essays.

Joan Didion

THE SANTA ANA

The author of novels, short stories, screenplays, and essays, **JOAN DIDION** (b. 1934) began her career in 1956 as a staff writer at *Vogue* magazine in New York. In 1963, she published her first novel, *Run River*, and the following year returned to her native California. Didion's essays have appeared in periodicals ranging from *Mademoiselle* to the *National Review*. "The Santa Ana" first appeared in the *Saturday Evening Post* in 1967 and later appeared as a part of "Los Angeles Notebook," an essay collected in *Slouching Towards Bethlehem*. Didion's other nonfiction publications include *The White Album* (1979),

Salvador (1983), Miami (1987), After Henry (1992), Political Fictions (2001), Fixed Ideas: America since 9.11 (2003), and Where I Was from (2003). Her essays, written between 1968 and 2003, are collected in We Tell Ourselves Stories in Order to Live (2006). The Year of Magical Thinking (2005), Didion's account of grief and survival after the loss of her husband of forty years, John Gregory Dunne, and the near-fatal illness of their only child, won the 2005 National Book Award for Nonfiction; Didion adapted her tragic memoir into a play, which opened on Broadway in 2007, starring Vanessa Redgrave and directed by David Hare. Didion's Blue Nights (2011) is a memoir about aging and about her relationship with her daughter, who died in 2005.

> "I write entirely to find out what's on my mind, what I'm thinking, what I'm looking at, what I'm seeing and what it means, what I want and what I'm afraid of."

Didion has defined a writer as "a person whose most absorbed and passionate hours are spent arranging words on pieces of paper. I write entirely to find out what's on my mind, what I'm thinking, what I'm looking at, what I'm seeing and what it means, what I want and what I'm afraid of." She has also said that "all writing is an attempt to find out what matters, to find the pattern in disorder, to find the grammar in the shimmer. Actually I don't know whether you find the grammar in the shimmer or you impose a grammar on the shimmer, but I am quite specific about the grammar—I mean it literally. The scene that you see in your mind finds its own structure; the structure dictates the arrangement of the words. . . . All the writer has to do really is to find the words." However, she warns, "You have to be alone to do this."

THERE IS SOMETHING UNEASY in the Los Angeles air this afternoon, some unnatural stillness, some tension. What it means is that tonight a Santa Ana will begin to blow, a hot wind from the northeast whining down through the Cajon and San Gorgonio Passes, blowing up sand storms out along Route 66, drying the hills and the nerves to flash point. For a few days now we will see smoke back in the canyons, and hear sirens in the night. I have neither heard nor read that a Santa Ana is due, but I know it, and almost everyone I have seen today knows it too. We know it because we feel it. The baby frets. The maid sulks. I rekindle a waning argument with the telephone company, then cut my losses and lie down, given over to whatever it is in the air. To live with the Santa Ana is to accept, consciously or unconsciously, a deeply mechanistic view of human behavior.

I recall being told, when I first moved to Los Angeles and was living on an isolated beach, that the Indians would throw themselves into the sea when the bad wind blew. I could see why. The Pacific turned ominously glossy during a Santa Ana period, and one woke in the night troubled not only by the peacocks screaming in the olive trees but by the eerie absence of surf. The heat was surreal. The sky had a yellow cast, the kind of light sometimes called "earthquake weather." My only neighbor would not come out of her house for days, and there were no lights at night, and her husband roamed the place with a machete. One day he would tell me that he had heard a trespasser, the next a rattlesnake.

"On nights like that," Raymond Chandler[1] once wrote about the Santa Ana, "every booze party ends in a fight. Meek little wives feel the edge of the carving knife and study their husbands' necks. Anything can happen." That was the kind of wind it was. I did not know then that there was any basis for the effect it had on all of us, but it turns out to be another of those cases in which science bears out folk wisdom. The Santa Ana, which is named for one of the canyons it rushes through, is a *foehn* wind, like the *foehn* of Austria and Switzerland and the *hamsin* of Israel. There are a number of persistent malevolent winds, perhaps the best known of which are the mistral of France and the Mediterranean sirocco, but a *foehn* wind has distinct characteristics: it occurs on the leeward slope of a mountain range and, although the air begins as a cold mass, it is warmed as it comes down the mountain and appears finally as a hot dry wind. Whenever and wherever a *foehn* blows, doctors hear about headaches and nausea and allergies, about "nervousness," about "depression." In Los Angeles some teachers do not attempt to conduct formal classes during a Santa Ana, because the children become unmanageable. In Switzerland the suicide rate goes up during the *foehn*, and in the courts of some Swiss cantons the wind is considered a mitigating circumstance for crime. Surgeons are said to watch the wind, because blood does not clot normally during a *foehn*. A few years ago an Israeli physicist discovered that not only during such winds, but for the ten or twelve hours which precede them, the air carries an unusually high ratio of positive to negative ions. No one seems to know exactly why that should be; some talk about friction and others suggest solar disturbances. In any case the positive ions are there, and what an excess of positive ions does, in the simplest terms, is make people unhappy. One cannot get much more mechanistic than that.

Easterners commonly complain that there is no "weather" at all in Southern California, that the days and the seasons slip by relentlessly, numbingly bland. That is quite misleading. In fact the climate is characterized by infrequent but violent extremes: two periods of torrential subtropical rains which continue for weeks and wash out the hills and send subdivisions sliding toward the sea; about twenty scattered days a year of the Santa Ana, which, with its incendiary dryness, invariably means fire. At the first prediction of a Santa Ana, the Forest Service flies men and equipment from northern California into the southern forests, and the Los Angeles Fire Department cancels its ordinary nonfirefighting routines. The Santa Ana caused Malibu to burn the way it did in 1956, and Bel Air in 1961, and Santa Barbara in 1964. In the winter of 1966–67 eleven men were killed fighting a Santa Ana fire that spread through the San Gabriel Mountains.

Just to watch the front-page news out of Los Angeles during a Santa Ana   5
is to get very close to what it is about the place. The longest single Santa

---

[1] **Raymond Chandler** (1888–1959): American author best known for his detective novels featuring Philip Marlowe. —EDS.

||||||||||||||||||||||||||||||||||||||||||||||||||||||||||||||||||||||||||||||||||||||||||||||||||||||||||||||||||||||||||||||||||||||||||||||||

Ana period in recent years was in 1957, and it lasted not the usual three or four days but fourteen days, from November 21 until December 4. On the first day 25,000 acres of the San Gabriel Mountains were burning, with gusts reaching 100 miles an hour. In town, the wind reached Force 12, or hurricane force, on the Beaufort Scale; oil derricks were toppled and people ordered off the downtown streets to avoid injury from flying objects. On November 22 the fire in the San Gabriels was out of control. On November 24 six people were killed in automobile accidents, and by the end of the week the Los Angeles *Times* was keeping a box score of traffic deaths. On November 26 a prominent Pasadena attorney, depressed about money, shot and killed his wife, their two sons and himself. On November 27 a South Gate divorcée, twenty-two, was murdered and thrown from a moving car. On November 30 the San Gabriel fire was still out of control, and the wind in town was blowing eighty miles an hour. On the first day of December four people died violently, and on the third the wind began to break.

It is hard for people who have not lived in Los Angeles to realize how radically the Santa Ana figures in the local imagination. The city burning is Los Angeles's deepest image of itself. Nathanael West perceived that, in *The Day of the Locust*; and at the time of the 1965 Watts riots what struck the imagination most indelibly were the fires.[2] For days one could drive the Harbor Freeway and see the city on fire, just as we had always known it would be in the end. Los Angeles weather is the weather of catastrophe, of apocalypse, and, just as the reliably long and bitter winters of New England determine the way life is lived there, so the violence and the unpredictability of the Santa Ana affect the entire quality of life in Los Angeles, accentuate its impermanence, its unreliability. The wind shows us how close to the edge we are. ●

The Reader's Presence

1. Characterize the role of the "imagination" in relation to the effects of the Santa Ana winds. Didion writes scientifically about the wind, specifically the "excess of positive ions" (paragraph 3) in the air and how this supposedly leads to nervousness and depression, yet she also discusses the wind in fictional terms, citing Raymond Chandler (paragraph 3) and referencing Nathanael West's novel *The Day of the Locust* (paragraph 6). What do you see as the compositional advantages of Didion's blend of fiction and reality in her essay? In what specific way(s) does Didion's connection between the two point to the wind itself?

2. There's a determinism that pervades Didion's essay, exemplified by the last sentence of the first paragraph: "To live with the Santa Ana is to accept, consciously or unconsciously, a deeply mechanistic view of human behavior." Much like the mythos of the full moon, Didion connects erratic, unpredictable human behavior to the dry Santa Ana winds. To what extent do you share her "mechanistic" outlook, or do you view this connection as an expression of "the local imagination" (paragraph 6)?

2 *The Day of the Locust . . . Watts riots:* West's 1939 novel about Hollywood ends in riot and fire. The August 1965 disturbances in the Watts neighborhood of Los Angeles resulted in millions of dollars in damage from fires. —EDS.

3. Didion discusses associating Los Angeles with destruction and fire in some detail, referencing the "1965 Watts riots" and noting that "[t]he city burning is Los Angeles's deepest image of itself" (paragraph 6). In what specific ways does this volatile image of the city affect the "local imagination"? What specific images and associations does Didion's description of the "violence and unpredictability of the Santa Ana" evoke? What is she discussing that is of greater consequence than the weather? How does the wind "[show] us how close to the edge we are" (paragraph 6)?

4. **CONNECTIONS:** Review carefully Didion's essay "Why I Write" (below). What specifically does she say here about her own writing process that helps you to understand and appreciate what she has achieved compositionally in "The Santa Ana"? In this respect, compare and contrast Didion's observations about why she writes and what an essayist does with those of E. B. White ("E. B. White on the Essayist," page 262).

The Writer at Work

JOAN DIDION on Why I Write

Chris Felver/Getty Images

Contrary to popular belief, writers are not necessarily intellectuals, or even people especially interested in ideas. Quite a few writers may be intellectuals, but being an intellectual and being able to write well do not always proceed hand in hand. In this passage from a well-known essay, Joan Didion takes a close look at the motives behind her writing and shows how our abilities can sometimes be fostered by our inabilities, in her case a lack of interest in abstract thinking and a tendency to always focus on the particulars of her immediate environment.

As Didion admits from the start, her essay was inspired by George Orwell's famous essay of the same title (see page 201).

❝Of course I stole the title for this talk,[1] from George Orwell. One reason I stole it was that I like the sound of the words: Why I Write. There you have three short unambiguous words that share a sound, and the sound they share is this:

I

I

I

In many ways writing is the act of saying *I*, of imposing oneself upon other people, of saying *listen to me, see it my way, change your mind.* It's an aggressive, even a hostile act. You can disguise its aggressiveness all you want with veils of subordinate clauses and qualifiers and tentative subjunctives, with ellipses and evasions—with the whole manner of intimating rather than claiming, of alluding rather than stating—but there's no getting around the fact that setting words on paper is the tactic of a secret bully, an invasion, an imposition of the writer's sensibility on the reader's most private space.

[1]This essay is adapted from a Regents' Lecture delivered at the University of California, Berkeley.

I stole the title not only because the words sounded right but because they seemed to sum up, in a no-nonsense way, all I have to tell you. Like many writers I have only this one "subject," this one "area": the act of writing. I can bring you no reports from any other front. I may have other interests: I am "interested," for example, in marine biology, but I don't flatter myself that you would come out to hear me talk about it. I am not a scholar. I am not in the least an intellectual, which is not to say that when I hear the word "intellectual" I reach for my gun, but only to say that I do not think in abstracts. During the years when I was an undergraduate at Berkeley I tried, with a kind of hopeless late-adolescent energy, to buy some temporary visa into the world of ideas, to forge for myself a mind that could deal with the abstract.

In short I tried to think. I failed. My attention veered inexorably back to the specific, to the tangible, to what was generally considered, by everyone I knew then and for that matter have known since, the peripheral. I would try to contemplate the Hegelian dialectic and would find myself concentrating instead on a flowering pear tree outside my window and the particular way the petals fell on my floor. I would try to read linguistic theory and would find myself wondering instead if the lights were on in the bevatron[2] up the hill. When I say that I was wondering if the lights were on in the bevatron you might immediately suspect, if you deal in ideas at all, that I was registering the bevatron as a political symbol, thinking in shorthand about the military-industrial complex and its role in the university community, but you would be wrong. I was only wondering if the

[2]***bevatron:*** the enormous particle accelerator housed at Berkeley Lab from 1954–2009. —Eds.

lights were on in the bevatron, and how they looked. A physical fact.

I had trouble graduating from Berkeley, not because of this inability to deal with ideas—I was majoring in English, and I could locate the house-and-garden imagery in *The Portrait of a Lady* as well as the next person, "imagery" being by definition the kind of specific that got my attention—but simply because I had neglected to take a course in Milton. For reasons which now sound baroque I needed a degree by the end of that summer, and the English department finally agreed, if I would come down from Sacramento every Friday and talk about the cosmology of *Paradise Lost*, to certify me proficient in Milton. I did this. Some Fridays I took the Greyhound bus, other Fridays I caught the Southern Pacific's City of San Francisco on the last leg of its transcontinental trip. I can no longer tell you whether Milton put the sun or the earth at the center of his universe in *Paradise Lost*, the central question of at least one century and a topic about which I wrote 10,000 words that summer, but I can still recall the exact rancidity of the butter in the City of San Francisco's dining car, and the way the tinted windows on the Greyhound bus cast the oil refineries around Carquinez Straits into a grayed and obscurely sinister light. In short my attention was always on the periphery, on what I could see and taste and touch, on the butter, and the Greyhound bus. During those years I was traveling on what I knew to be a very shaky passport, forged papers: I knew that I was no legitimate resident in any world of ideas. I knew I couldn't think. All I knew then was what I couldn't do. All I knew then was what I wasn't, and it took me some years to discover what I was.

Which was a writer.**"**

Brian Doyle

A WRITING PORTFOLIO
Dawn and Mary / His Last Game / A Note on Mascots

Journalist, essayist, and editor **BRIAN DOYLE** (1956–2017) was born in New York, edu-cated "fitfully" at the University of Notre Dame, and was editor of *Portland Magazine* at the University of Portland. Doyle was noted for writing books with spiritual and religious themes, including *Credo: Essays on Grace, Altar Boys, Bees, Kneeling, Saints, the Mass, Priests, Strong Women, Epiphanies, a Wake, and the Haunting Thin Energetic Dusty Figure of Jesus the Christ* (1999); *Saints Passionate & Peculiar: Brief Exuberant Essays for Teens* (2002); *The Wet Engine: Exploring the Mad Wild Miracle of the Heart* (2005); and *The Thorny Grace of It: And Other Essays for Imperfect Catholics* (2013), among many others. His novel *Mink River* was published in 2010, and he wrote *The Adventures of John Carson in Several Quarters of the World* (2017). *The Plover* (2014) in response to readers asking what happened to one of the char-acters in *Mink River*. He edited the anthology *God Is Love: Essays from* Portland Magazine (2003), and his work has appeared in *Best American Essays*, *Best Spiritual Writing*, *Best Essays Northwest*, and in many other anthologies.

> **"I don't have a responsibility to edify. I think if you feel that way you're tending toward sermon and homily and lecture, which is basically the road to purgatory. Also, you know, the tendency to sermon and homily and lecture is basically boring."**

Doyle's essays and poems have appeared in numerous magazines, journals, and news-papers, including the *Atlantic Monthly*, *Harper's*, *Commonweal*, *American Scholar*, *Georgia Review*, the *Times of London*, the *Sydney Morning Herald*, the *Kansas City Star*, the *San Francisco Chronicle*, *Newsday*, and *Orion*.

Though Doyle often wrote on matters of faith and religion, he cautioned against writing that sermonizes. In an interview on Quotidiana.org, he said that, as a writer, he doesn't "have a responsibility to edify," adding that such writing tends "toward sermon and homily and lecture," a tendency he calls "boring."

DAWN AND MARY

EARLY ONE MORNING several teachers and staffers at a Connecticut grade school were in a meeting. The meeting had been underway for about five minutes when they heard a chilling sound in the hallway. (*We heard pop-pop-pop*, said one of the staffers later.)

Most of them dove under the table. That is the reasonable thing to do, what they were trained to do, and that is what they did.

But two of the staffers *jumped*, or *leapt*, or *lunged* out of their chairs and ran toward the sound of bullets. Which word you use depends on which news account of that morning you read, but the words all point in the same direction—toward the bullets.

One of the staffers was the principal. Her name was Dawn. She had two daughters. Her husband had proposed to her five times before she'd finally said yes, and they had been married for ten years. They had a vacation house on a lake. She liked to get down on her knees to paint with the littlest kids in her school.

The other staffer was a school psychologist named Mary. She had two 5 daughters. She was a football fan. She had been married for more than thirty years. She and her husband had a cabin on a lake. She loved to go to the theater. She was due to retire in one year. She liked to get down on her knees to work in her garden.

Dawn the principal told the teachers and the staffers to lock the door behind them, and the teachers and the staffers did so after Dawn and Mary ran out into the hall.

You and I have been in that hallway. We spent seven years of our childhood in that hallway. It's friendly and echoing, and when someone opens the doors at the end, a wind comes and flutters all the paintings and posters on the walls.

Dawn and Mary jumped, or leapt, or lunged toward the sound of bullets. Every fiber of their bodies—bodies descended from millions of years of bodies that had leapt away from danger—must have wanted to dive under the table. That's what they'd been trained to do. That's how you live to see another day. That's how you stay alive to paint with the littlest kids and work in the garden and hug your daughters and drive off laughing to your cabin on the lake.

But they leapt for the door, and Dawn said, *Lock the door after us*, and they lunged right at the boy with the rifle.

The next time someone says the word *hero* to you, you say this: There 10 once were two women. One was named Dawn, and the other was named Mary. They both had two daughters. They both loved to kneel down to care for small beings. They leapt from their chairs and ran right at the boy with the rifle, and if we ever forget their names, if we ever forget the wind in that hallway, if we ever forget what they did, if we ever forget that there is something in us beyond sense and reason that snarls at death and runs roaring at it to defend children, if we ever forget that all children are our children, then we are fools who have allowed memory to be murdered too, and what good are we then? *What good are we then?* ◼

The Reader's Presence

1. Doyle's essay is a startling and simple account of the bravery of two people who sacrificed themselves to protect the children they cared for at Sandy Hook Elementary School in Connecticut. How would you characterize the structure and length of Doyle's sentences as the essay unfolds? What reasonable inferences can you draw from the observations you make? What impact does Doyle's use of italics at the end of paragraph 1 and at the end of the essay have on your experience of reading his essay? What relationship does he establish between the words and sentences he italicizes? What does he accomplish by choosing to italicize *"hero"* in the opening sentence of the final paragraph? In what specific ways does this decision affect your reading?

2. Reread Doyle's brief essay aloud. How would you characterize the sound of the speaker's voice throughout this essay? Does the speaker's voice remain consistent throughout the essay? If not, where—and how—does it change? with what effects? Cite specific examples to support your response.

3. Doyle provides background information for Dawn and Mary—"She had two daughters" (paragraphs 4 and 5) and "She was a football fan" (paragraph 5). In what specific way(s) are those details important to the overall tone and purpose of Doyle's essay? How do these details impact your connection to the characters and to the overall influence of the essay? Doyle addresses the reader directly in paragraph 7, "You and I have been in that hallway." Why does he address the reader? What larger point is Doyle making here?

4. **CONNECTIONS:** After you have read Doyle's essay carefully several times, compare and contrast his attitudes and tone of voice when discussing violence with those of Steven Pinker in his essay "Violence Vanquished" (page 591) and of Jacob Ewing in his student essay on Pinker's argument (page 597). Who among these three writers creates the most evocative and compelling perspective on violence? Support your response with detailed references to each text.

HIS LAST GAME

◼ WE WERE SUPPOSED TO BE DRIVING to the pharmacy for his prescriptions, but he said just drive around for a while, my prescriptions aren't going anywhere without me, so we just drove around. We drove around the edges of the college where he had worked and we saw a blue heron in a field of stubble, which is not something you see every day, and we stopped for a while to see if the heron was fishing for mice or snakes, on which we bet a dollar, me taking mice and him taking snakes, but the heron glared at us and refused to work under scrutiny, so we drove on.

We drove through the arboretum checking on the groves of ash and oak and willow trees, which were still where they were last time we looked, and then we checked on the wood duck boxes in the pond, which still seemed sturdy and did not feature ravenous weasels that we noticed, and then we saw a kestrel hanging in the crisp air like a tiny helicopter, but as soon as we bet mouse or snake the kestrel vanished, probably for religious reasons, said my brother, probably a *lot* of kestrels are adamant that gambling is immoral, but we are just *not* as informed as we should be about kestrels.

We drove deeper into the city and I asked him why we were driving this direction, and he said I am looking for something that when I see it you will know what I am looking for, which made me grin, because he knew and I knew that I would indeed know, because we have been brothers for 50 years, and brothers have many languages, some of which are physical, like broken noses and fingers and teeth and punching each other when you want to say I love you but don't know how to say that right, and some of them are laughter, and some of them are roaring and spitting, and some of them are weeping in the bathroom, and some of them we don't have words for yet.

By now it was almost evening, and just as I turned on the car's running lights I saw what it was he was looking for, which was a basketball game in a park. I laughed and he laughed and I parked the car. There were six guys on the court, and to their credit they were playing full court. Five of the guys looked to be in their twenties, and they were fit and muscled, and one of them wore a porkpie hat. The sixth guy was much older, but he was that kind of older ballplayer who is comfortable with his age and he knew where to be and what not to try.

We watched for a while and didn't say anything but both of us noticed   5 that one of the young guys was not as good as he thought he was, and one was better than he knew he was, and one was flashy but essentially useless, and the guy with the porkpie hat was a worker, setting picks, boxing out, whipping outlet passes, banging the boards not only on defense but on offense, which is much harder. The fifth young guy was one of those guys who ran up and down yelling and waving for the ball, which he never got. This guy was supposed to be covering the older guy but he didn't bother, and the older guy gently made him pay for his inattention, scoring occasionally on backdoor cuts and shots from the corners on which he was so alone he could have opened a circus and sold tickets, as my brother said.

The older man grew visibly weary as we watched, and my brother said he's got one last basket in him, and I said I bet a dollar it's a shot from the corner, and my brother said no, he doesn't even have the gas for that, he'll snake the kid somehow, you watch, and just then the older man, who was bent over holding the hems of his shorts like he was exhausted, suddenly cut to the basket, caught a bounce pass, and scored, and the game ended, maybe because the park lights didn't go on even though the street lights did.

On the way home my brother and I passed the heron in the field of stubble again, and the heron stopped work again and glared at us until we turned the corner.

That is one *withering* glare, said my brother. That's a ballplayer glare if ever I saw one. That's the glare a guy gives another guy when the guy you were supposed to be covering scores on a backdoor cut and you thought your guy was ancient and near death but it turns out he snaked you good and you are an idiot. *I* know that glare. You owe me a dollar. We better go get my prescriptions. They are not going to do any good but we better get them anyway so they don't go to waste. One less thing for my family to do afterwards. That game was good but the heron was even better. I think the prescriptions are pointless now but we already paid for them so we might as well get them. They'll just get thrown out if we don't pick them up. That was a good last game, though. I'll remember the old guy, sure, but the kid with the hat banging the boards, that was cool. You hardly ever see a guy with a porkpie hat hammering the boards.

There's so much to love, my brother added. All the little things. Remember shooting baskets at night and the only way you could tell if the shot went in was the sound of the net? Remember the time we cut the fingertips off our gloves so we could shoot on icy days and dad was so angry he lost his voice and he was supposed to give a speech and had to gargle and mom laughed so hard we thought she was going to pee? Remember that? I remember that. What happens to what I remember? You remember it for me, okay? You remember the way that heron glared at us like he would kick our ass except he was working. And you remember that old man snaking that kid. *Stupid kid*, you could say, but that's the obvious thing. The *beautiful* thing is the little thing that the old guy knew full well he wasn't going to cut around picks and drift out into the corner again, that would burn his last gallon of gas, not to mention he would have to hoist up a shot from way out there, so he snakes the kid beautiful, he knows the kid thinks he's old, and the guy with the hat sees him cut, and gets him the ball on a dime, that's a beautiful thing because it's little, and we saw it and we knew what it meant. You remember that for me. You owe me a dollar. ●

The Reader's Presence

1. What expectations do most readers carry into reading the beginning of an essay? What responses does Doyle elicit from his readers by beginning his essay with the phrase "We were supposed to"? What implications does this phrase bear for the focus and direction of his essay? Point to specific words and phrases to support your response. Notice that Doyle repeats the word "just" in the opening sentence. What other words and phrases does he repeat in the essay? With what effect(s)? The final sentence of the opening paragraph presents another reversal of expectations: "the heron glared at us and refused to work under scrutiny, so we drove on." What do see as the significance of this line, and how does it help to frame Doyle's essay?

2. What is the narrative trajectory of Doyle's essay? Where does it start and end? What literally happens during the course of the essay? What does the title "His Last Game" allude to? What specific evidence can you summon to support your response? What do you think the narrator means when he says, "brothers have many languages,

some of which are physical" (paragraph 3)? Comment on Doyle's use of evocative detail, especially as the brothers observe—and then participate in—"a basketball game in a park" (paragraph 4)?

3. What role does figurative language—especially similes and metaphors—play in the essay? With what effect(s)? Consider, for example, the phrase "he snaked you" in paragraph 8. What are the effects of the three appearances of the heron as the narrative unfolds? What do you understand to be the point when the narrator observes "The *beautiful* thing is the little thing" (paragraph 9)? Ultimately, what do you think is the subject of Doyle's essay?

4. **CONNECTIONS:** Based on your reading of Doyle's essay, what would you identify as his implicit rules for writing? What importance do you think Doyle would assign to a writer's use of figurative language, especially similes and metaphors? What other features of writing effectively does Doyle accentuate in this essay and in the others printed here? Compare and contrast these compositional principles with those Stephen King articulates in "Everything You Need to Know About Writing Successfully—in Ten Minutes" (page 426). In what specific way(s) are Doyle and King kindred spirits when thinking and writing about writing?

A NOTE ON MASCOTS

THE FIRST SPORTS TEAM I REMEMBER loving as a child, in the dim dewy days when I was two or three years old and just waking up to things that were not milk and mama and dirt and dogs, was the Fighting Irish of the University of Notre Dame, who were on television every day, it seemed, in our bustling brick Irish Catholic house; and then, inasmuch as I was hatched and coddled near Manhattan, there were Metropolitans and Knickerbockers and Rangers and Islanders; and then, as I shuffled shyly into high school, there were, for the first time, snarling and roaring mammalian mascots, notably the Cougars of my own alma mater, which was plopped in marshlands where I doubt a cougar had been seen for three hundred years; but right about then I started paying attention to how we fetishize animals as symbols for our athletic adventures, and I have become only more attentive since, for I have spent nearly thirty years now working for colleges and universities, and you could earn a degree in zoology just by reading the college sports news, where roar and fly and sprint and lope and canter and gallop and prowl animals from anteater to wasp—among them, interestingly, armadillos, bees, boll weevils, herons, owls, koalas, turtles, moose, penguins, gulls, sea lions, and squirrels, none of which seem especially intimidating or prepossessing, although I know a man in North Carolina who once lost a fistfight with a heron, and certainly many of us have run away from angry bees and moose, and surely there are some among us who could relate stories of furious boll weevils, but perhaps this is not the time, although anyone who *has* a story like that should see me right after class.

There are vast numbers of canids (coyotes, foxes, huskies, salukis, great danes), felids (lions, tigers, panthers, lynx, bobcats), ruminants (bulls, chargers, broncs, broncos, and bronchoes, though no bronchials), mustelids (badgers, wolverine, otters), and denizens of the deep (dolphins, gators, sharks, sailfish, and "seawolves," or orca). There are two colleges which have an aggrieved camel as their mascot. There are schools represented by snakes and tomcats. There is a school whose symbol is a frog and one whose mascot is a large clam and one whose mascot famously is a slug. There is a school whose mascot is the black fly. There are the Fighting Turtles of the College of Insurance in New York. There are schools represented by lemmings and scorpions and spiders. There are the Fighting Stormy Petrels of Oglethorpe University in Georgia. There is a school represented by an animal that has never yet been seen in the Americas, the bearcat of Asia, although perhaps that is meant to be a wolverine, which did once inhabit southern Ohio, and may still live in Cincinnati, which has tough neighborhoods. The most popular mascot appears to be the eagle, especially if you count the fifteen schools represented by golden eagles, which brings us to a round total of eighty-two schools symbolized by a bird Benjamin Franklin considered "a bird of bad moral character, too lazy to fish for himself . . . like those among men who live by sharping & robbing he is generally poor and often very lousy. Besides he is a rank coward." But the two schools that Franklin helped establish are nicknamed the Quakers and the Diplomats, so we can safely ignore Ben on this matter.

This is not even to delve into the mysterious world of fantastical fauna — blue bears and blue tigers, crimson hawks, trolls, dragons and firebirds, griffins and griffons and gryphons, delta devils and jersey devils (there are a *lot* of devils, which says something interesting), jayhawks and kohawks and duhawks, green eagles and phoenixes, thunderhawks and thunderwolves — the mind reels, and then there is the whole subset of nicknamery that has to do with botany, as evidenced most memorably by the Fighting Violets of New York University, on which image we had better pull this whole essay to the side of the road and sit silently for a moment.

Beyond all the obvious reasons we choose animals as symbols for our sporting teams — their incredible energy and muscle, grace and strength, intelligence and verve, our ancient conviction of their power and magic, ancient associations as clan signs and tribal totems, even more ancient shivers perhaps of fear at animals who hunted and ate us, not to mention the way their images look cool on letterheads and sweatshirts and pennants and fundraising appeals — there is something else, something so deep and revelatory about human beings that I think we do not admit it because it is too sad.

I think we love animals as images because we miss them in the flesh, and 5 I think we love them as images because they matter to us spiritually in ways we cannot hope to articulate. The vast majority of us will never see a cougar or a wolverine, not to mention a boll weevil, but even wearing one on a shirt, or shouting the miracle of its name in a stadium, or grinning to see its rippling beauty on the window of a car, gives us a tiny subtle crucial electric jolt in the heart, connects us somehow to what we used to be with animals, which was thrilled and terrified. We've lost the salt of that feeling forever, but even a hint of it matters immensely to us as animals too. Maybe that's what we miss the most—the feeling that they are our cousins, and not clans of creatures who once filled the earth and now are shreds of memory, mere symbols, beings who used to be. ●

The Reader's Presence

1. The origins of the word *mascot* can be traced back to medieval France, where "mascotte" was used to signify a charm or talisman, an object thought to have magical powers and to bring good luck. The word first gained widespread attention in the late nineteenth century, when the French composer Edmond Audran wrote the popular operetta *La Mascotte*. What specific characteristics does Doyle attribute to modern-day sports mascots? What do you understand him to mean when he observes that mascots "matter to us spiritually" (paragraph 5)? In the final paragraph, Doyle suggests that "[w]e've lost the salt of that feeling forever." What "feeling" does he allude to here?

2. Consider carefully the structure of Doyle's essay. What do you notice about the sentence structure of the opening paragraph? What reasonable inferences can you draw from your observations? Now consider the pacing as well as the specific diction Doyle uses. What observations and inferences can you draw from the choices Doyle makes? Finally, what do you notice about his use of specific poetic devices in his opening paragraph? Repeat the same pattern of making careful observations and drawing reasonable inferences in each of the succeeding paragraphs. What additional compositional effects does Doyle introduce in each new paragraph? Point to specific words and phrases as the basis of your observations and inferences.

3. What does Doyle gain by introducing the quotation from Benjamin Franklin on the eagle: "a bird of bad moral character" (paragraph 2)? How would you characterize Doyle's tone of voice (his attitude toward his subject) in this essay? For example, does he position himself as superior to, equal with, or subservient to his subject? Point to specific word choices to verify your response. In a similar manner, comment on his use of irony and humor. What impression does Doyle leave his readers with when he says, "We've lost the salt of that feeling forever" and "[the mascots] are our cousins" (paragraph 5)?

4. **CONNECTIONS:** Compare and contrast the voice of Doyle's essay on mascots with that of David Foster Wallace in "Consider the Lobster" (page 649). In what specific ways do these writers seek to elicit similar responses from their readers? Support your responses with specific passages from each text as well as an analysis of each. What connections can you draw between both authors' views on how we perceive certain animals?

The Reader's Presence: Questions on Three Essays and an Interview

1. In his interview with the editors of this collection (page 368), Brian Doyle responded to our question "What are the most challenging aspects of writing for you?" by observing: "Avoiding self-absorbed self-indulgent sermonizing homilizing advice-giving-counsel-confiding muck. A constant battle. I am always reminding myself to just tell a story." Examine carefully two of three essays included in Doyle's portfolio, and

identify several instances in each essay where Doyle resists the temptation to indulge in sermonizing. What specific compositional strategies does Doyle use to let the story tell itself—without his editorializing or "sermonizing"? Support your response with an analysis of specific passages.

2. Doyle offered the following response to our question about what method he uses to start writing: "Make a note instantly when an idea or a line or a caught remark or a memory or an epiphany hits you suddenly in the kidney. INSTANTLY. . . . Then hustle to a keyboard as fast as you can and take the note out for a stroll and see what happens. Don't think. Just start typing and see what happens. Don't control it. Don't even think 'this will be an essay.' Just start. . . ." Choose one of the three essays reprinted here, and demonstrate how this spontaneity surfaces in Doyle's published essay(s). What specific evidence can you identify that illustrates Doyle's compositional belief?

3. When asked about the audience he imagines for his essays, Doyle declared: "I don't have a Reader in mind; for me it's more like a piece wants to be born and I have to try to catch it while it's ready and not edit or think much about it during the birthing hour." Select one of Doyle's essays in this portfolio and, after rereading it carefully, comment on the extent to which Doyle puts this principle for writing into practice. How is this belief evident in the structure and tone of his essay? Is his use of direct address in his essay "Dawn and Mary" a seeming exception? What does he gain as a writer in speaking directly to his readers in this instance? Comment on the effectiveness of direct address in this example. What other, similar, examples can you identify? With what effects?

The Writer at Work

BRIAN DOYLE on the Pleasures and Craft of Writing and Reading

Brian Doyle

Brian Doyle was one of America's most engaging and memorable essayists. Many of his essays begin with the simple act of observing carefully the people and objects in the world he inhabits. By focusing and sustaining his attention on the artful elegance of the immediate and seemingly mundane aspects of life, Doyle crafted essays fueled by his imaginative attentiveness and his lyrical and descriptive sensibility. He was also a widely admired teacher and editor, a writer who generously encouraged and advised other writers—from undergraduates at the University of Portland to professionals who submitted their work to *Portland*, the quarterly magazine he edited for the university. *Portland* continues to be widely recognized as one of the top-ten university magazines in the country.

Brian Doyle graciously agreed to provide responses to the following questions prepared by the editors of *The Writer's Presence*.

What are your earliest recollections of writing? of reading?

Reading first—I was raised in a house in New York crammed with books, newspapers, and magazines—my dad was a newspaperman and my mom a teacher, and we were Irish and Catholic and American, and so story-addled and story-mad and story-starving; and my parents—bless their souls—arranged the books by height access, as it were, so that the shelves you could reach when little were maps and cartoons and photo books, and then up you went to the myths and adventures shelf (Hans Christian Andersen, the Grimms, Jim Kjelgaard, Tolkien, *Kon-Tiki*), and the Irish shelf (Mary Lavin! Frank O'Connor! Yeats!) and the Catholic shelf (Flannery O'Connor! J. F. Powers! Walker Percy! Greene! Waugh!), and the American shelf (Twain, Steinbeck, Edwin O'Connor), and finally the shelf I never got tall enough to read. My brothers did, and so they read Proust and Churchill's war memoirs. As for writing, I vividly remember writing a short story at age 11, and while it was the worst short story ever written, I was totally nailed by the thought that THOSE WORDS HAD NEVER BEEN IN THAT ORDER EVER BEFORE IN THE HISTORY OF THE UNIVERSE, a feeling I still have with every piece of writing. We do not celebrate the sheer amazement of writing enough, I think.

How would you characterize yourself as a writer? What metaphor(s) would you use to characterize yourself as a writer?

Essayist first and foremost; it's the greatest form, I think, because it magpies all the other forms but is the most naked, the most direct and unadorned and unfiltered and most like the human voice and the human interior voice; but I have had enormous fun in recent years writing Big Fat Novels. Also my ambition is to write one of everything; so far I have published books of essays, stories, "proems," a novella, nonfiction books about wine and hearts and saints. If I could write a play and a comic book and a movie I am set.

What are the most challenging aspects of writing for you?

Avoiding self-absorbed self-indulgent sermonizing homilizing advice-giving counsel-confiding muck. A constant battle. I am always reminding myself to just tell a story. The best stories are about other people. Live there as a writer. Never give advice. Just catch and share stories and the world advances two inches.

What method of getting started is most successful for you?

Make a note instantly when an idea or a line or a caught remark or a memory or an epiphany hits you suddenly in the kidney. INSTANTLY. Use dollar bills and children's necks if necessary. (I once started an essay on my son Liam's neck at the beach.) Then hustle to a keyboard as fast as you can and take the note out for a stroll and see what happens. Don't think. Just start typing and see what happens. Don't control it. Don't even think "this will be an essay." Just start. I find that often the piece soon enough tells you what shape it wishes to take.

What specific strategies and/or tactics do you use to generate ideas for the essays you write?

Listening, above all. As my dad says, learn to ask a question and then shut your piehole and listen. People will tell amazing stories if you let them and invite them and be silent and dig them. People crave witness. Be a witness, and then report from the frontier of grace and pain and mercy and hilarity and terror and courage. Also I read wildly, especially newspapers, where you find an awful lot of stories that cry out to be explored.

Given your admirable productivity, procrastination doesn't seem to be an issue for you as a writer. If it is, what do you do to overcome it?

I am that lucky sort of man who knows full well he is an idiot and a turtle and a lazy-bone and so I am intent on writing every day, an hour a day if I can get it. I just show up and stuff happens. Talent has nothing to do with writing. Curiosity and typing and listening are the great tools. I usually have a Big Project on the griddle, and then happily do other things as they present themselves. I find that if you just show up every morning, a lot of stuff accumulates. I think of writing not at all as art but as craft. It's like carpentry and basketball—you put in your 10,000 hours of practice and then you stop thinking about doing it, you just do it. I don't think about art or quality or shoot for goals like *Best American Essays*; I just write, and then what happens happens. The cool stuff is all gravy to me. The best part about writing is connecting and being told by readers that your arrow landed. That's amazing and holy to me and I am humbled and thrilled and deeply moved by it. Even the insulting responses please me; at least the poor lunatics read the piece closely, heh heh heh. Although mostly those notes are from my brothers.

If someone walked into the room and observed you writing, what would he or she see?

Maniacal typing and shocking language issued by a large grizzled badger with an attitude and spectacles.

Describe the environment most conducive to you as a writer.

Actually I love working in the morning because it's quiet and the piece can present itself if I type fast enough to keep up.

For whom do you imagine that you are writing?

I don't have a Reader in mind; for me it's more like a piece wants to be born and I have to try to catch it while it's ready and not edit or think much about it during the birthing hour. Also I think I have developed some sort of subtle cadence antennae; the only revising and tinkering I do while writing is for swing and rhythm and cadence; I'll revise with a cold heart a day later. One of my personal rules is let a piece go cold for a day when I think I am finished and then go back to it with impersonal cruelty, looking to commit surgery.

What special habits do you have as a writer?

Muttering mumbling humming snarling grumbling groaning snickering burbling, with occasional snatches of song, mostly Miles Davis or the Beach Boys. If anyone ever heard me they would think I was mad.

What specific process do you follow when writing the first draft of an essay?

Bang it out. Follow its energy. Write like hell. DON'T THINK. Catch it as it wants to be. Tell a story. No "we should" or "we must . . ."—that's comment. No comment. Just catch and share a story, as much as you can in one burst.

How do you know when an essay is "finished"? What criteria do you use for making this decision?

Is it a whole story? Beginning and middle and end, as my dad says? did I get out of the way? is it lean and taut and direct? was I too playful or addicted to driving language too fast for my own amusement, which is one of my sins? Conversely is it too prim and normal? did I say anything real? is there bone and salt and song and humor? Is it naked? There's enough witless cocky arrogant pompous fatuous idiot opinion and lecture in the world—did I just add another drop to that foul ocean, or does this thing before me *matter*, will it make the reader laugh or cry or snarl in rage or kneel in prayer or ideally all at once, which would be a mess?

What role has reading played in your success as a writer?

No reading, no writing. You have got to hear lots of voices on the page to learn how to get voices onto pages. The best education for a young writer is wild wide reading. Read everything of all sorts. Get a sense of how stories can be shaped and shared. Then get your butt in the chair every day, "lower your standards," as the great Oregon poet William Stafford said, and type like a maniac.

What have you learned about writing as a result of your reading? What do you do when you read that helps you when you write?

I notice now that while writing a novel I cannot read any novelist whose voice will mess with or override mine, so when I am writing a novel I read a lot of books about the sea and about animals. Weird. Although I will note that when I feel clogged and stupid and fatuous as a writer, I happily reread the essays of E. B. White and Annie Dillard and Robert Louis Stevenson and Twain, and Mary Oliver's poems, and they clear the pipes with their attentiveness and humor and verve and honesty and artful artlessness. Also I read the New Testament and the Psalms in the King James translation a lot for the amazing shouldery prickly muscular language. I always feel taller.

What specific advice would you offer other, but less experienced, writers to help them strengthen their efforts to improve their writing?

Do it every day for at least 30 minutes to an hour. Don't think. Just write. Edit and revise later. Lower your standards. When you are done with a piece, get it off your desk and into the mail. Don't tinker forever. Finish a piece and then do another and then another and etc. Don't think about style. Just write. There are millions of stories waiting to be sensed and caught and shared. What are you waiting for? The best stories will come from other people. The best writing of all is witness. Be a witness. It's a holy and crucial job. If you have what my friend George Higgins called the "benign neurosis" of the itch to write, you are ready for the job. Get your butt in the chair today and do it. Don't expect money. Do hope you will shiver a heart here and there, or make people laugh. There's nothing as cool as that. If I can do it, by gawd you can do it, because I am a humming idiot. Do it again tomorrow. Best of luck. . . .

Lars Eighner

ON DUMPSTER DIVING

LARS EIGHNER (b. 1948) was born in Texas and attended the University of Texas at Austin. An essayist and a fiction writer, he contributes regularly to the *Threepenny Review*, *Advocate Men*, the *Guide*, and *Inches*. He has published several collections of short stories, essays, and gay erotica. His most recent publications include a camp novel, *Pawn to Queen Four* (1995); a collection of essays, *Gay Cosmos* (1995); an erotic short story collection, *Whispered in the Dark* (1995); and *WANK: The Tapes* (1998). Eighner writes a blog on his Web site, larseighner.com.

> "A writer needs talent, luck, and persistence. You can make do with two out of three, and the more you have of one, the less you need of the others."

Eighner became homeless in 1988, after he lost his job as a mental-hospital attendant. "On Dumpster Diving" is Eighner's prize-winning essay based on this experience, later reprinted as part of his full-length book about homelessness, *Travels with Lizbeth: Three Years on the Road and on the Streets* (1993). Eighner and Lizbeth, Eighner's dog, became homeless again in 1996. Friends organized a fund under the auspices of the *Texas Observer* and obtained an apartment for Eighner and Lizbeth in Austin. Lizbeth has since passed away.

On what is required to find success as a writer, Eighner has said, "I was not making enough money to support myself as a housed person, but I was writing well before I became homeless. . . . A writer needs talent, luck, and persistence. You can make do with two out of three, and the more you have of one, the less you need of the others."

LONG BEFORE I began Dumpster diving I was impressed with Dumpsters, enough so that I wrote the Merriam-Webster research service to discover what I could about the word "Dumpster." I learned from them that "Dumpster" is a proprietary word belonging to the Dempster Dumpster company.

Since then I have dutifully capitalized the word although it was lower-cased in almost all of the citations Merriam-Webster photocopied for me. Dempster's word is too apt. I have never heard these things called anything but Dumpsters. I do not know anyone who knows the generic name for these objects. From time to time, however, I hear a wino or hobo give some corrupted credit to the original and call them Dipsy Dumpsters.

I began Dumpster diving about a year before I became homeless.

I prefer the term "scavenging" and use the word "scrounging" when I mean to be obscure. I have heard people, evidently meaning to be polite, using the word "foraging," but I prefer to reserve that word for gathering nuts and berries and such which I do also according to the season and the opportunity. "Dumpster diving" seems to me to be a little too cute and, in my case, inaccurate because I lack the athletic ability to lower myself into the Dumpsters as the true divers do, much to their increased profit.

I like the frankness of the word "scavenging," which I can hardly think   5
of without picturing a big black snail on an aquarium wall. I live from the refuse of others. I am a scavenger. I think it a sound and honorable niche, although if I could I would naturally prefer to live the comfortable consumer life, perhaps—and only perhaps—as a slightly less wasteful consumer owing to what I have learned as a scavenger.

While my dog Lizbeth and I were still living in the house on Avenue B in Austin, as my savings ran out, I put almost all my sporadic income into rent. The necessities of daily life I began to extract from Dumpsters. Yes, we ate from Dumpsters. Except for jeans, all my clothes came from Dumpsters. Boom boxes, candles, bedding, toilet paper, medicine, books, a typewriter, a virgin male love doll, change sometimes amounting to many dollars: I acquired many things from the Dumpsters.

I have learned much as a scavenger. I mean to put some of what I have learned down here, beginning with the practical art of Dumpster diving and proceeding to the abstract.

What is safe to eat?

After all, the finding of objects is becoming something of an urban art. Even respectable employed people will sometimes find something tempting sticking out of a Dumpster or standing beside one. Quite a number of people, not all of them of the bohemian type, are willing to brag that they found this or that piece in the trash. But eating from Dumpsters is the thing that separates the dilettanti from the professionals.

Eating safely from the Dumpsters involves three principles: using the   10
senses and common sense to evaluate the condition of the found materials, knowing the Dumpsters of a given area and checking them regularly, and seeking always to answer the question "Why was this discarded?"

Perhaps everyone who has a kitchen and a regular supply of groceries has, at one time or another, made a sandwich and eaten half of it before discovering mold on the bread or got a mouthful of milk before realizing the milk had turned. Nothing of the sort is likely to happen to a Dumpster diver because he is constantly reminded that most food is discarded for a reason. Yet a lot of perfectly good food can be found in Dumpsters.

Canned goods, for example, turn up fairly often in the Dumpsters I frequent. All except the most phobic people would be willing to eat from a can even if it came from a Dumpster. Canned goods are among the safest of foods to be found in Dumpsters, but are not utterly foolproof.

Although very rare with modern canning methods, botulism is a possibility. Most other forms of food poisoning seldom do lasting harm to a healthy person. But botulism is almost certainly fatal and often the first symptom is death. Except for carbonated beverages, all canned goods should contain a slight vacuum and suck air when first punctured. Bulging, rusty, dented cans and cans that spew when punctured should be avoided, especially when the contents are not very acidic or syrupy.

Heat can break down the botulin, but this requires much more cooking than most people do to canned goods. To the extent that botulism occurs at all, of course, it can occur in cans on pantry shelves as well as in cans from Dumpsters. Need I say that home-canned goods found in Dumpsters are simply too risky to be recommended.

From time to time one of my companions, aware of the source of my 15 provisions, will ask, "Do you think these crackers are really safe to eat?" For some reason it is most often the crackers they ask about.

This question always makes me angry. Of course I would not offer my companion anything I had doubts about. But more than that I wonder why he cannot evaluate the condition of the crackers for himself. I have no special knowledge and I have been wrong before. Since he knows where the food comes from, it seems to me he ought to assume some of the responsibility for deciding what he will put in his mouth.

For myself I have few qualms about dry foods such as crackers, cookies, cereal, chips, and pasta if they are free of visible contaminants and still dry and crisp. Most often such things are found in the original packaging, which is not so much a positive sign as it is the absence of a negative one.

Raw fruits and vegetables with intact skins seem perfectly safe to me, excluding of course the obviously rotten. Many are discarded for minor imperfections which can be pared away. Leafy vegetables, grapes, cauliflower, broccoli, and similar things may be contaminated by liquids and may be impractical to wash.

Candy, especially hard candy, is usually safe if it has not drawn ants. Chocolate is often discarded only because it has become discolored as the cocoa butter de-emulsified. Candying after all is one method of food preservation because pathogens do not like very sugary substances.

All of these foods might be found in any Dumpster and can be evaluated 20 with some confidence largely on the basis of appearance. Beyond these are foods which cannot be correctly evaluated without additional information.

I began scavenging by pulling pizzas out of the Dumpster behind a pizza delivery shop. In general prepared food requires caution, but in this case I knew when the shop closed and went to the Dumpster as soon as the last of the help left.

Such shops often get prank orders, called "bogus." Because help seldom stays long at these places pizzas are often made with the wrong topping, refused on delivery for being cold, or baked incorrectly. The products to be discarded are boxed up because inventory is kept by counting boxes: A boxed pizza can be written off; an unboxed pizza does not exist.

I never placed a bogus order to increase the supply of pizzas and I believe no one else was scavenging in this Dumpster. But the people in the shop became suspicious and began to retain their garbage in the shop overnight.

While it lasted I had a steady supply of fresh, sometimes warm pizza. Because I knew the Dumpster I knew the source of the pizza, and because I visited the Dumpster regularly I knew what was fresh and what was yesterday's.

The area I frequent is inhabited by many affluent college students. I am not here by chance; the Dumpsters in this area are very rich. Students throw out many good things, including food. In particular they tend to throw everything out when they move at the end of a semester, before and after breaks, and around midterm when many of them despair of college. So I find it advantageous to keep an eye on the academic calendar.

The students throw food away around the breaks because they do not know whether it has spoiled or will spoil before they return. A typical discard is a half jar of peanut butter. In fact nonorganic peanut butter does not require refrigeration and is unlikely to spoil in any reasonable time. The student does not know that, and since it is Daddy's money, the student decides not to take a chance.

Opened containers require caution and some attention to the question "Why was this discarded?" But in the case of discards from student apartments, the answer may be that the item was discarded through carelessness, ignorance, or wastefulness. This can sometimes be deduced when the item is found with many others, including some that are obviously perfectly good.

Some students, and others, approach defrosting a freezer by chucking out the whole lot. Not only do the circumstances of such a find tell the story, but also the mass of frozen goods stays cold for a long time and items may be found still frozen or freshly thawed.

Yogurt, cheese, and sour cream are items that are often thrown out while they are still good. Occasionally I find a cheese with a spot of mold, which of course I just pare off, and because it is obvious why such a cheese was discarded, I treat it with less suspicion than an apparently perfect cheese found in similar circumstances. Yogurt is often discarded, still sealed, only because the expiration date on the carton had passed. This is one of my favorite finds because yogurt will keep for several days, even in warm weather.

Students throw out canned goods and staples at the end of semesters and when they give up college at midterm. Drugs, pornography, spirits, and the like are often discarded when parents are expected — Dad's day, for example. And spirits also turn up after big party weekends, presumably discarded by the newly reformed. Wine and spirits, of course, keep perfectly well even once opened.

My test for carbonated soft drinks is whether they still fizz vigorously. Many juices or other beverages are too acid or too syrupy to cause much concern provided they are not visibly contaminated. Liquids, however, require some care.

One hot day I found a large jug of Pat O'Brien's Hurricane mix. The jug had been opened, but it was still ice cold. I drank three large glasses before it became apparent to me that someone had added the rum to the mix, and not a little rum. I never tasted the rum and by the time I began to feel the effects I had already ingested a very large quantity of the beverage. Some divers would have considered this a boon, but being suddenly and thoroughly intoxicated in a public place in the early afternoon is not my idea of a good time.

I have heard of people maliciously contaminating discarded food and even handouts, but mostly I have heard of this from people with vivid imaginations who have had no experience with the Dumpsters themselves. Just before the pizza shop stopped discarding its garbage at night, jalapeños began showing up on most of the discarded pizzas. If indeed this was meant to discourage me it was a wasted effort because I am a native Texan.

For myself, I avoid game, poultry, pork, and egg-based foods whether I find them raw or cooked. I seldom have the means to cook what I find, but when I do I avail myself of plentiful supplies of beef which is often in very good condition. I suppose fish becomes disagreeable before it becomes dangerous. The dog is happy to have any such thing that is past its prime and, in fact, does not recognize fish as food until it is quite strong.

Home leftovers, as opposed to surpluses from restaurants, are very often   35
bad. Evidently, especially among students, there is a common type of personality that carefully wraps up even the smallest leftover and shoves it into the back of the refrigerator for six months or so before discarding it. Characteristic of this type are the reused jars and margarine tubs which house the remains.

I avoid ethnic foods I am unfamiliar with. If I do not know what it is supposed to look like when it is good, I cannot be certain I will be able to tell if it is bad.

No matter how careful I am I still get dysentery at least once a month, oftener in warm weather. I do not want to paint too romantic a picture. Dumpster diving has serious drawbacks as a way of life.

I learned to scavenge gradually, on my own. Since then I have initiated several companions into the trade. I have learned that there is a predictable series of stages a person goes through in learning to scavenge.

At first the new scavenger is filled with disgust and self-loathing. He is ashamed of being seen and may lurk around, trying to duck behind things, or he may try to dive at night.

(In fact, most people instinctively look away from a scavenger. By skulk-   40
ing around, the novice calls attention to himself and arouses suspicion. Diving at night is ineffective and needlessly messy.)

Every grain of rice seems to be a maggot. Everything seems to stink. He can wipe the egg yolk off the found can, but he cannot erase the stigma of eating garbage out of his mind.

That stage passes with experience. The scavenger finds a pair of running shoes that fit and look and smell brand new. He finds a pocket calculator in perfect working order. He finds pristine ice cream, still frozen, more than he can eat or keep. He begins to understand: People do throw away perfectly good stuff, a lot of perfectly good stuff.

At this stage, Dumpster shyness begins to dissipate. The diver, after all, has the last laugh. He is finding all manner of good things which are his for the taking. Those who disparage his profession are the fools, not he.

He may begin to hang onto some perfectly good things for which he has neither a use nor a market. Then he begins to take note of the things which are not perfectly good but are nearly so. He mates a Walkman with broken earphones and one that is missing a battery cover. He picks up things which he can repair.

At this stage he may become lost and never recover. Dumpsters are full 45 of things of some potential value to someone and also of things which never have much intrinsic value but are interesting. All the Dumpster divers I have known come to the point of trying to acquire everything they touch. Why not take it, they reason, since it is all free.

This is, of course, hopeless. Most divers come to realize that they must restrict themselves to items of relatively immediate utility. But in some cases the diver simply cannot control himself. I have met several of these packrat types. Their ideas of the values of various pieces of junk verge on the psychotic. Every bit of glass may be a diamond, they think, and all that glistens, gold.

I tend to gain weight when I am scavenging. Partly this is because I always find far more pizza and doughnuts than water-packed tuna, non-fat yogurt, and fresh vegetables. Also I have not developed much faith in the reliability of Dumpsters as a food source, although it has been proven to me many times. I tend to eat as if I have no idea where my next meal is coming from. But mostly I just hate to see food go to waste and so I eat much more than I should. Something like this drives the obsession to collect junk.

As for collecting objects, I usually restrict myself to collecting one kind of small object at a time, such as pocket calculators, sunglasses, or campaign buttons. To live on the street I must anticipate my needs to a certain extent: I must pick up and save warm bedding I find in August because it will not be found in Dumpsters in November. But even if I had a home with extensive storage space I could not save everything that might be valuable in some contingency.

I have proprietary feelings about my Dumpsters. As I have suggested, it is no accident that I scavenge from Dumpsters where good finds are common. But my limited experience with Dumpsters in other areas suggests to me that it is the population of competitors rather than the affluence of the dumpers that most affects the feasibility of survival by scavenging. The large number of competitors is what puts me off the idea of trying to scavenge in places like Los Angeles.

Curiously, I do not mind my direct competition, other scavengers, so much 50 as I hate the can scroungers.

People scrounge cans because they have to have a little cash. I have tried scrounging cans with an able-bodied companion. Afoot a can scrounger simply cannot make more than a few dollars a day. One can extract the necessities of life from the Dumpsters directly with far less effort than would be required to accumulate the equivalent value in cans.

Can scroungers, then, are people who *must* have small amounts of cash. These are drug addicts and winos, mostly the latter because the amounts of cash are so small.

Spirits and drugs do, like all other commodities, turn up in Dumpsters and the scavenger will from time to time have a half bottle of a rather good wine with his dinner. But the wino cannot survive on these occasional finds; he must have his daily dose to stave off the DTs. All the cans he can carry will buy about three bottles of Wild Irish Rose.

I do not begrudge them the cans, but can scroungers tend to tear up the Dumpsters, mixing the contents and littering the area. They become so specialized that they can see only cans. They earn my contempt by passing up change, canned goods, and readily hockable items.

There are precious few courtesies among scavengers. But it is a common   55
practice to set aside surplus items: pairs of shoes, clothing, canned goods, and such. A true scavenger hates to see good stuff go to waste and what he cannot use he leaves in good condition in plain sight.

Can scroungers lay waste to everything in their path and will stir one of a pair of good shoes to the bottom of a Dumpster, to be lost or ruined in the muck. Can scroungers will even go through individual garbage cans, something I have never seen a scavenger do.

Individual garbage cans are set out on the public easement only on garbage days. On other days going through them requires trespassing close to a dwelling. Going through individual garbage cans without scattering litter is almost impossible. Litter is likely to reduce the public's tolerance of scavenging. Individual garbage cans are simply not as productive as Dumpsters; people in houses and duplexes do not move as often and for some reason do not tend to discard as much useful material. Moreover, the time required to go through one garbage can that serves one household is not much less than the time required to go through a Dumpster that contains the refuse of twenty apartments.

But my strongest reservation about going through individual garbage cans is that this seems to me a very personal kind of invasion to which I would object if I were a householder. Although many things in Dumpsters are obviously meant never to come to light, a Dumpster is somehow less personal.

I avoid trying to draw conclusions about the people who dump in the Dumpsters I frequent. I think it would be unethical to do so, although I know many people will find the idea of scavenger ethics too funny for words.

Dumpsters contain bank statements, bills, correspondence, and other   60
documents, just as anyone might expect. But there are also less obvious sources of information. Pill bottles, for example. The labels on pill bottles contain the name of the patient, the name of the doctor, and the name of the drug. AIDS drugs and antipsychotic medicines, to name but two groups, are specific and are seldom prescribed for any other disorders. The plastic compacts for birth control pills usually have complete label information.

Despite all of this sensitive information, I have had only one apartment resident object to my going through the Dumpster. In that case it turned out the resident was a university athlete who was taking bets and who was afraid I would turn up his wager slips.

Occasionally a find tells a story. I once found a small paper bag containing some unused condoms, several partial tubes of flavored sexual lubricant, a partially used compact of birth control pills, and the torn pieces of a picture of a young man. Clearly she was through with him and planning to give up sex altogether.

Dumpster things are often sad—abandoned teddy bears, shredded wedding books, despaired-of sales kits. I find many pets lying in state in Dumpsters. Although I hope to get off the streets so that Lizbeth can have a long and comfortable old age, I know this hope is not very realistic. So I suppose when her time comes she too will go into a Dumpster. I will have no better place for her. And after all, for most of her life her livelihood has come from the Dumpster. When she finds something I think is safe that has been spilled from the Dumpster I let her have it. She already knows the route around the best Dumpsters. I like to think that if she survives me she will have a chance of evading the dog catcher and of finding her sustenance on the route.

Silly vanities also come to rest in the Dumpsters. I am a rather accomplished needleworker. I get a lot of materials from the Dumpsters. Evidently sorority girls, hoping to impress someone, perhaps themselves, with their mastery of a womanly art, buy a lot of embroider-by-number kits, work a few stitches horribly, and eventually discard the whole mess. I pull out their stitches, turn the canvas over, and work an original design. Do not think I refrain from chuckling as I make original gifts from these kits.

I find diaries and journals. I have often thought of compiling a book of literary found objects. And perhaps I will one day. But what I find is hopelessly commonplace and bad without being, even unconsciously, camp. College students also discard their papers. I am horrified to discover the kind of paper which now merits an A in an undergraduate course. I am grateful, however, for the number of good books and magazines the students throw out.

In the area I know best I have never discovered vermin in the Dumpsters, but there are two kinds of kitty surprise. One is alley cats which I meet as they leap, claws first, out of Dumpsters. This is especially thrilling when I have Lizbeth in tow. The other kind of kitty surprise is a plastic garbage bag filled with some ponderous, amorphous mass. This always proves to be used cat litter.

City bees harvest doughnut glaze and this makes the Dumpster at the doughnut shop more interesting. My faith in the instinctive wisdom of animals is always shaken whenever I see Lizbeth attempt to catch a bee in her mouth, which she does whenever bees are present. Evidently some birds find Dumpsters profitable, for birdie surprise is almost as common as kitty surprise of the first kind. In hunting season all kinds of small game turn up in Dumpsters, some of it, sadly, not entirely dead. Curiously, summer and winter, maggots are uncommon.

The worst of the living and near-living hazards of the Dumpsters are the fire ants. The food that they claim is not much of a loss, but they are vicious and aggressive. It is very easy to brush against some surface of the Dumpster and pick up half a dozen or more fire ants, usually in some sensitive area such as the underarm. One advantage of bringing Lizbeth along as I make Dumpster rounds is that, for obvious reasons, she is very alert to ground-based fire ants. When Lizbeth recognizes the signs of fire ant infestation around our feet she does the Dance of the Zillion Fire Ants. I have learned not to ignore this warning from Lizbeth, whether I perceive the tiny ants or not, but to remove ourselves at Lizbeth's first pas de bourrée.[1] All the more so because the ants are the worst in the months I wear flip-flops, if I have them.

(Perhaps someone will misunderstand the above. Lizbeth does the Dance of the Zillion Fire Ants when she recognizes more fire ants than she cares to eat, not when she is being bitten. Since I have learned to react promptly, she does not get bitten at all. It is the isolated patrol of fire ants that falls in Lizbeth's range that deserves pity. Lizbeth finds them quite tasty.)

By far the best way to go through a Dumpster is to lower yourself into it. Most of the good stuff tends to settle at the bottom because it is usually weightier than the rubbish. My more athletic companions have often demonstrated to me that they can extract much good material from a Dumpster I have already been over. 70

To those psychologically or physically unprepared to enter a Dumpster, I recommend a stout stick, preferably with some barb or hook at one end. The hook can be used to grab plastic garbage bags. When I find canned goods or other objects loose at the bottom of a Dumpster I usually can roll them into a small bag that I can then hoist up. Much Dumpster diving is a matter of experience for which nothing will do except practice.

Dumpster diving is outdoor work, often surprisingly pleasant. It is not entirely predictable; things of interest turn up every day and some days there are finds of great value. I am always very pleased when I can turn up exactly the thing I most wanted to find. Yet in spite of the element of change, scavenging more than most other pursuits tends to yield returns in some proportion to the effort and intelligence brought to bear. It is very sweet to turn up a few dollars in change from a Dumpster that has just been gone over by a wino.

The land is now covered with cities. The cities are full of Dumpsters. I think of scavenging as a modern form of self-reliance. In any event, after ten years of government service, where everything is geared to the lowest common denominator, I find work that rewards initiative and effort refreshing. Certainly I would be happy to have a sinecure again, but I am not heartbroken not to have one anymore.

I find from the experience of scavenging two rather deep lessons. The first is to take what I can use and let the rest go by. I have come to think that there is no value in the abstract. A thing I cannot use or make useful, perhaps by trading, has no value however fine or rare it may be. I mean useful in a broad sense—so, for example, some art I would think useful and valuable, but other art might be otherwise for me.

---

[1] *pas de bourrée:* A transitional ballet step. —EDS.

I was shocked to realize that some things are not worth acquiring, but   75
now I think it is so. Some material things are white elephants that eat up the
possessor's substance.

The second lesson is of the transience of material being. This has not
quite converted me to a dualist, but it has made some headway in that direction. I do not suppose that ideas are immortal, but certainly mental things are
longer-lived than other material things.

Once I was the sort of person who invests material objects with sentimental value. Now I no longer have those things, but I have the sentiments yet.

Many times in my travels I have lost everything but the clothes I was
wearing and Lizbeth. The things I find in Dumpsters, the love letters and
ragdolls of so many lives, remind me of this lesson. Now I hardly pick up a
thing without envisioning the time I will cast it away. This I think is a healthy
state of mind. Almost everything I have now has already been cast out at least
once, proving that what I own is valueless to someone.

Anyway, I find my desire to grab for the gaudy bauble has been largely
sated. I think this is an attitude I share with the very wealthy—we both know
there is plenty more where what we have came from. Between us are the rat-
race millions who have confounded their selves with the objects they grasp
and who nightly scavenge the cable channels looking for they know not what.

I am sorry for them. ●   80

The Reader's Presence

1. At the center of "On Dumpster Diving" is Eighner's effort to bring out from the
   shadows of contemporary American life the lore and practices of scavenging, what
   he calls "a modern form of self-reliance." His essay also provides a compelling
   account of his self-education as he took to the streets for "the necessities of daily
   life" (paragraph 6). Outline the stages in this process, and summarize the ethical and
   moral issues and the questions of decorum that Eighner confronted along the way.
   Show how this process reflects the structure of his essay, "beginning with the practical art of Dumpster diving and proceeding to the abstract" (paragraph 7).

2. One of the most remarkable aspects of Eighner's essay is the tone (the attitude) he
   expresses toward his subject. Select a paragraph from the essay. Read it aloud. How
   would you characterize the sound of his voice? Does he sound, for example, tough-
   minded? polite? strident? experienced? cynical? something else? Consider, for example, paragraph 34, where he notes: "For myself, I avoid game, poultry, pork, and
   egg-based foods whether I find them raw or cooked." Where have you heard talk
   like this before? Do you notice any changes as the essay develops, or does Eighner
   maintain the same tone in discussing his subject? What responses does he elicit from
   his readers when he speaks of scavenging as a "profession" and a "trade"?

3. Think about Eighner's relationship with his readers. Does he consider himself fundamentally different from or similar to his audience? In what specific ways? Consider,
   for example, the nature of the information Eighner provides in the essay. Does he
   expect his readers to be familiar with the information? How does he characterize
   his own knowledgeability about this often-noticed but rarely discussed activity in

urban America? Comment on Eighner's use of irony in presenting information about Dumpster diving and in anticipating his readers' responses to the circumstances within which he does the work of his trade.

4. **VISUAL PRESENCE:** Examine the photograph of Lars Eighner below. What features of the portrait help establish Eighner's presence? Support your answer with specific details from the picture.

5. **CONNECTIONS:** Compare Eighner's description of Dumpster diving to one of the most famous essays in the English language, Jonathan Swift's "A Modest Proposal" (page 630). Both essays deal with economics and the effects of poverty. In what ways does each author use humor and satire? How does each author introduce us to the grim realities of poverty? What role does food play in each essay? You might also compare Eighner's essay to Peter Singer's "The Singer Solution to World Poverty" (page 615). Discuss how applicable you find Singer's "solution" to Eighner's problems.

The Writer at Work

LARS EIGHNER on the Challenges of Writing While Homeless

Barbara Laing/Getty Images

Lars Eighner and Lizbeth.

In the summer of 1989, Lars Eighner, without a job and with no place to live, began writing about his experiences as a homeless person trying to survive in the college town of Austin, Texas. When one of his essays, "On Dumpster Diving," was published in the prestigious literary journal *The Threepenny Review* (Fall 1991), it became immediately clear that he had contributed one of the best and most authentic accounts of life on the American streets. The essay, now a modern classic and reprinted widely, was collected in *Travels with Lizbeth: Three Years on the Road and on the Streets* in 1993. For that volume, Eighner included an introduction (excerpted here) in which he discussed the challenges that confront a homeless writer.

❝ When I began this account I was living under a shower curtain in a stand of bamboo in a public park. I did not undertake to write about homelessness, but wrote what I knew, as an artist paints a still life, not because he is especially fond of fruit, but because the subject is readily at hand.

In the summer of 1989, when I was in the bamboo, I supposed interest in homelessness had peaked in the presidential election of the previous year. Moreover, I thought my experiences with homelessness were atypical.

I still think my experiences were atypical, but I have come to disbelieve in typical homelessness. I had some advantages and some disadvantages and I chose the course that seemed mostly likely to provide the survival of myself and my dog Lizbeth on the most comfortable terms of which our situation would admit.

I did not often associate with other homeless people. I avoided the homeless shelters and hobo jungles. I did not attempt to survive on the streets of a very large city, but made my way for the most part in a liberal and affluent area of an overgrown college town. Although I often despaired of improving my material situation, I seldom lacked for a feeling of self-worth or a sense of mission. On the other hand, I spent most of my time in Texas, where a general contempt for the poor is reflected in a useless, vestigial social welfare system. I handicapped myself by adopting from the first a policy of not stealing and not begging on the streets. And, of course, I would not be parted from Lizbeth. I do not pretend to speak for the homeless. I think no one could speak for all the various people who have in common the condition of being homeless. I do not know many of the homeless, but of the condition of being homeless I know something, and that is part of what I have written about.

In truth, becoming homeless was a long process that I can date only arbitrarily. I had been without a reliable income for about a year before I left the shack I had been living in. For about five months after I left the shack I traveled

and imposed on friends and strangers, so that I spent only part of the time on the streets. Moreover, throughout that first period I believed I had one prospect or another of improving my situation and I did not regard myself as truly homeless.

When I had the opportunity to get off the street for a week or a month or even for only a night, I did so; my object was not to explore homelessness but to get off the street. I have recounted these events in the ordinary narrative manner, but have only summarized the events of my longer stopovers. Eventually I became homeless enough to suit anyone's definition. In spite of the challenges that homelessness presented, the chief characteristic of my experience of homelessness was tedium. The days and nights that Lizbeth and I were literally without a roof over our heads, although by far the majority of the more than two years encompassed here, are represented by relatively few examples. One of those days was so much like each of the others that to call any of them typical would be an understatement. Our immediate needs I met with more or less trouble, but once that was done I could do no more. Day after day I could aspire, within reason, to nothing more than survival. Although the planets wandered among the stars and the moon waxed and waned, the identical naked barrenness of existence was exposed to me, day in and day out. I do not think I could write a narrative that would quite capture the unrelenting ennui of homelessness, but if I were to write it, no one could bear to read it. I spare myself as much as the reader in not attempting to recall so many empty hours. Every life has trivial occurrences, pointless episodes, and unresolved mysteries, but a homeless life has these and virtually nothing else. I have found it best in some parts to abandon a strictly chronological account and to treat in essay form experiences that relate to a single subject although they occurred in disparate times and places. **"**

Megan Garber

BARBIE'S HIPS DON'T LIE

Most toys are harmless sources of entertainment and a means of fostering creativity in children. Some, however, have attracted significant controversy in their capacity to impart and distort social values. In "Barbie's Hips Don't Lie," journalist **MEGAN GARBER** explores the motives surrounding Mattel's decision to make Barbie dolls more diverse. Barbie has often been met with criticism for setting unrealistic ideals for young women, so her newfound variety appears to be a much-needed step in the right direction. But diversity, according to Garber, is also "good business."

> **Journalist Megan Garber explores the motives surrounding Mattel's decision to make Barbie dolls more diverse.**

A staff writer at the *Atlantic*, Garber has written on subjects ranging from film and television to politics and the future of journalism. Previously an assistant editor for the Nieman Journalism Lab and a staff writer at *Columbia Journalism Review*, she received a Mirror Award for her work in journalism in 2010.

BARBIE BEGAN HER LIFE AS, essentially, a glorified sex toy. She—it's fair, given her influence over her gender and her culture, to refer to her as "she"—is modeled on a mid-century German doll and comic-book figure named Lilli. Sassy and buxom, Lilli was euphemistically prostitute-like, fond of breezy phrases like "I could do without balding old men, but my budget couldn't!" and, "The sunrise is so beautiful that I always stay late at the nightclub to see it!" Her doll—cartoonishly curvaceous, in the traditional manner of women-designed-by-men—was, in the mid-20th century, often given out as a joke at bachelor parties and similar gatherings. A funny thing ended up happening with those jokey, sex-infused pieces of plastic, though: Kids began to play with them. Girls, in particular. They liked dressing Lilli up. They liked grooming her hair. They liked imagining that, one day, they would be—they would look—like her.

It's that impulse of small humans—to treat dolls as vehicles not just of amusement, but of aspiration—that makes today's news such a big deal. Barbie, the doll that the Mattel co-founder Ruth Handler modeled after Lilli and introduced at the World's Fair in 1959, will now come in a variety of shapes and shades. (And also: a variety of hairstyles, and eye colors, and "face sculpts.") The doll will still be fairly cartoonish—this is Barbie, after all—but, from today, she can be bought in sizes "petite" and "tall" and "curvy." (The terms, *Time* notes—the English euphemisms, as well as their translations into other languages—were extensively debated by Mattel marketing executives.) She can also, just as importantly, be bought in seven different skin tones.

Which is to say that Barbie—that singular figure who has always carried pretensions toward broader cultural representation—is becoming, finally, more diverse. She is, in her highly limited way, trying to do a better job of representing the people who play with her. And a better job, at the same time, of affecting who those people will become.

That is, in its small way, big news. And good news! But the best news of all might just be the specific reasons Mattel has offered for the changes. To transform Barbie's body—to expand its offerings to include shapes and shades that more closely resemble the storied "Average American Woman"—was, after all, a large logistical challenge for the company. It required Mattel to create whole new sets of clothes to accommodate the dolls' body shapes. It required, even, the creation of new shoes that would accommodate wider feet.

Mattel did not make those changes, necessarily, because it wanted to be   5
a moral leader, *Time*'s Eliana Dockterman notes. It did so instead as part of a cynical business calculation—the kind of cynical business calculation any good company is expected to make on behalf of itself and its shareholders. The changes in Barbie's body may have arisen out of the company's desire to do good; mostly, though, they arose from its need to do well. This was that oldest and most American of things: cultural change by way of capitalism.

It went like this: Mattel's sales of its Barbie dolls have, recently, been plummeting. (They dropped 20 percent between 2012 and 2014, Dockterman reports, and continued their slide last year.) This is in part because Disney recently awarded its Princess business to Hasbro, taking that merchandise away from Mattel during The Age of Elsa. Also, though, the dive has to do with shifts taking place in the culture at large. Via broad demographic changes, and also via the various serendipities of celebrity, Hollywood and the media have been expanding their sense of the "ideal" feminine form. Waifs may still be prominent on catwalks and red carpets, but so are curvaceous women like Beyoncé and Kim Kardashian and Christina Hendricks and Amy Schumer. White women may be prominent in advertising and television and movies, but so, increasingly, are women like Lupita N'yongo and Gina Rodriguez and Maggie Q. Under their influence, and under the influence of a culture that so often equates progress with prestige, "traditional" beauty ideals have become boring beauty ideals.

In that sense, Barbie—as a cultural symbol, and as a commercial product—had to change. Ruth Handler may have designed the doll, in the 1950s, to be a progressive alternative to the baby doll, thereby expanding girls' vision of what their roles might be; what she also designed, however, was an impossible standard that would endure for generations. Barbie represented, from the outset, the freight of femininity. She represented the awkward disconnect between cultural expectation and physical reality. (That waist! Those hips! Those perma-heeled feet!)

Mattel/Splash News/Newscom/Splash News/New York/USA

Curvy Barbie

And as the women's movement arose—as feminism dissolved, quickly, into the culture at large—Barbie came to symbolize a tension between empowerment and subjugation. She came to be seen, by many commentators but also by many parents, as not only quaintly anti-quated, but also potentially damaging. And no company, of course, wants the purchase of their toys to become a matter of moral anxiety to their customers. Evelyn Mazzocco, *Time* notes, who heads the Barbie brand for Mattel, keeps a board behind her desk dotted with customer criticisms of the traditional Barbie doll. It includes phrases like "not diverse," "materialistic," and "out of touch."

So the varied-shaped and varied-shaded new Barbies are part of Mattel's attempt to make things right—with history, yes, but also with their shareholders. That the company may be able to do both at once is both revealing and encouraging. It would be churlish to compare a plastic doll to the broader discussions taking place across the culture right now—conversa-tions about diversity, and representation, and inclusion. Barbie is not a culture. Barbie is not a system. Barbie is not a series of decisions, tiny on their own yet determinative taken together, about who gets to participate, and be seen, and be heard.

In a very small way, though, Barbie *is* all of those things. Toys, after all—the objects we invite into children's lives to entertain them and also to shape them—reflect society's highest aspirations for itself. They're the way we teach the littlest humans what will be expected of them, and hoped for them, when they get bigger: bravery (G.I. Joe), curiosity (Dora the Explorer), creativity (Legos), empathy (Elsa), beauty (Barbie). They're myths, in the form of objects. They're lessons. They're proxies. They're the reason that toymakers, recently, have gone out of their way to send the "right" messages, both to kids and the adults who are buying things on their behalf.

Mattel's expansion of Barbie's look, in that sense, represents the basic, hopeful idea that diversity is valuable not just for diversity's sake (or, as Anna Holmes recently put it, as a kind of grudging obligation). Diversity is—much more pragmatically, much more transformatively—good business. If consumers can see themselves in their dolls, Mattel has calculated, they will be more likely to purchase those dolls. The company is taking a note from the American Girl dolls, which long ago realized that diversity is good business. And it is suggest-ing a path for Hollywood, and for the rest of us—one that allows "doing well" and "doing good" to complement, rather than conflict with, each other. Mattel is doing what capitalism, at its best, will do: transforming cynical self-interest into cultural progress.

The Reader's Presence

1. As you reread Megan Garber's essay, please note the playful character of her word choices and characterization of Barbie, along with her representation of male imaginings of female bodies. See, for example, the opening paragraph in which Barbie is described as an example of "the traditional manner of women-designed-by-men." Point to other examples and identify the stereotypes and sexist characterizations they represent. Garber distinguishes between a company doing "well" and doing "good" (paragraph 5). What does she mean by these terms, and why is the distinction important? How should we interpret Mattel's decision to make Barbie more diverse given these categories? What are the implications of the announcement that Barbie "will now come in a variety of shapes and shades. (And also: a variety of hairstyles, and eye colors, and 'face sculpts') (paragraph 2). Do you agree with Garber's assertion that "this was that oldest and most American of things: cultural change by way of capitalism"? Point to specific evidence in the essay to verify your response.

2. This essay appeared in the *Atlantic Daily*, an online affiliate of the *Atlantic*, was founded in 1857 and one of the nation's most celebrated monthly magazines. Both the daily and monthly publications cover the news and provide analyses of politics, business, culture, and technology, as well as other important aspects of American life. Based on your reading of "Barbie's Hips Don't Lie," what aspects of Garber's essay might have made it a more suitable topic for the daily rather than the monthly publication? Please support your response with specific evidence in Garber's essay.

3. **CONNECTIONS:** In "Why Boys Don't Play with Dolls" (page 478), Katha Pollitt observes, "Women's looks matter terribly in this society, and so Barbie, however ambivalently, must be passed along" (paragraph 7). In what ways does this ambivalence about Barbie resemble or differ from Garber's view of Mattel? To what extent does the company's "cynical self-interest" lessen the impact of Barbie's new diversity? What messages does Barbie convey, according to these authors? When formulating your answer, consider the meaning of the word "value" in both essays. Compare the role of diversity in Garber's essay with that of Walter Benn Michaels's "The Trouble with Diversity" (page 571). Can Barbie now be listed among what Michaels calls "diversity products"? At the end of her essay, Garber states that Mattel transforms "cynical self-interest into cultural progress." Would Michaels agree? Explain why.

Malcolm Gladwell

SMALL CHANGE: WHY THE REVOLUTION WILL NOT BE TWEETED

MALCOLM GLADWELL (b. 1963) is a best-selling author and staff writer for the *New Yorker*. Son of a British father and a Jamaican mother, Gladwell was born in England and moved to Canada as a child. He began his journalism career at the *American Spectator*, a conservative monthly magazine. He started writing for the *Washington Post* in 1987, serving as a science writer before becoming the paper's New York City bureau chief. He left the *Post* in 1996 to write for the *New Yorker*. Gladwell is known for his best-selling books *The Tipping Point: How Little Things Can Make a Big Difference* (2000), *Blink: The Power of Thinking Without Thinking* (2005), *Outliers: The Story of Success* (2008), and *What the Dog Saw: And Other Adventures* (2009). His most recent book is *David and Goliath* (2013), which draws on history, politics, business, and psychology to examine what causes the underdog to win (or lose). "Small Change: Why the Revolution Will Not Be Tweeted" first appeared in the October 4, 2010, issue of the *New Yorker*.

> **"Ideas and products and messages and behaviors spread just like viruses do."**

Gladwell's writing tends to be concerned with illuminating the patterns behind everyday life and identifying the origins of major events and the trends in minor ones. According to Gladwell, "Ideas and products and messages and behaviors spread just like viruses do." He was named one of *Time* magazine's 100 Most Influential People in 2005.

AT FOUR-THIRTY in the afternoon on Monday, February 1, 1960, four college students sat down at the lunch counter at the Woolworth's in downtown Greensboro, North Carolina. They were freshmen at North Carolina A. & T., a black college a mile or so away.

"I'd like a cup of coffee, please," one of the four, Ezell Blair, said to the waitress.

"We don't serve Negroes here," she replied.

The Woolworth's lunch counter was a long L-shaped bar that could seat sixty-six people, with a standup snack bar at one end. The seats were for whites. The snack bar was for blacks. Another employee, a black woman who worked at the steam table, approached the students and tried to warn them away. "You're acting stupid, ignorant!" she said. They didn't move. Around five-thirty, the front doors to the store were locked. The four still didn't move. Finally, they left by a side door. Outside, a small crowd had gathered, including a photographer from the Greensboro *Record*. "I'll be back tomorrow with A. & T. College," one of the students said.

By next morning, the protest had grown to twenty-seven men and four women, most from the same dormitory as the original four. The men were dressed in suits and ties. The students had brought their schoolwork, and studied as they sat at the counter. On Wednesday, students from Greensboro's "Negro" secondary school, Dudley High, joined in, and the number of protesters swelled to eighty. By Thursday, the protesters numbered three hundred, including three white women, from the Greensboro campus of the University of North Carolina. By Saturday, the sit-in had reached six hundred. People spilled out onto the street. White teenagers waved Confederate

5

The Granger Collection, NY

The four college students at the lunch counter at Woolworth's in downtown Greensboro, North Carolina, February 2, 1960.

flags. Someone threw a firecracker. At noon, the A. & T. football team arrived. "Here comes the wrecking crew," one of the white students shouted.

By the following Monday, sit-ins had spread to Winston-Salem, twenty-five miles away, and Durham, fifty miles away. The day after that, students at Fayetteville State Teachers College and at Johnson C. Smith College, in Charlotte, joined in, followed on Wednesday by students at St. Augustine's College and Shaw University, in Raleigh. On Thursday and Friday, the protest crossed state lines, surfacing in Hampton and Portsmouth, Virginia, in Rock Hill, South Carolina, and in Chattanooga, Tennessee. By the end of the month, there were sit-ins throughout the South, as far west as Texas. "I asked every student I met what the first day of the sitdowns had been like on his campus," the political theorist Michael Walzer wrote in *Dissent*. "The answer was always the same: 'It was like a fever. Everyone wanted to go.'" Some seventy thousand students eventually took part. Thousands were arrested and untold thousands more radicalized. These events in the early sixties became a civil-rights war that engulfed the South for the rest of the decade—and it happened without e-mail, texting, Facebook, or Twitter.

The world, we are told, is in the midst of a revolution. The new tools of social media have reinvented social activism. With Facebook and Twitter and the like, the traditional relationship between political authority and popular will has been upended, making it easier for the powerless to collaborate, coordinate, and give voice to their concerns. When ten thousand protesters took to the streets in Moldova in the spring of 2009 to protest against their country's Communist government, the action was dubbed the Twitter Revolution, because of the means by which the demonstrators had been brought together. A few months after that, when student protests rocked Tehran, the State Department took the unusual step of asking Twitter to suspend scheduled maintenance of its Web site, because the Administration didn't want such a critical organizing tool out of service at the height of the demonstrations. "Without Twitter the people of Iran would not have felt empowered and confident to stand up for freedom and democracy," Mark Pfeifle, a former national-security adviser, later wrote, calling for Twitter to be nominated for the Nobel Peace Prize. Where activists were once defined by their causes, they are now defined by their tools. Facebook warriors go online to push for change. "You are the best hope for us all," James K. Glassman, a former senior State Department official, told a crowd of cyber activists at a recent conference sponsored by Facebook, A.T.&T., Howcast, MTV, and Google. Sites like Facebook, Glassman said, "give the U.S. a significant competitive advantage over terrorists. Some time ago, I said that Al Qaeda was 'eating our lunch on the Internet.' That is no longer the case. Al Qaeda is stuck in Web 1.0. The Internet is now about interactivity and conversation."

These are strong, and puzzling, claims. Why does it matter who is eating whose lunch on the Internet? Are people who log on to their Facebook page really the best hope for us all? As for Moldova's so-called Twitter Revolution, Evgeny Morozov, a scholar at Stanford who has been the most persistent of digital evangelism's critics, points out that Twitter had scant internal significance in Moldova, a country where very few Twitter accounts exist. Nor does it seem to have been a revolution, not least because the protests—as Anne Applebaum suggested in the *Washington Post*—may well have been a bit of stagecraft cooked up by the government. (In a country paranoid about Romanian revanchism,[1] the protesters flew a Romanian flag over the Parliament building.) In the Iranian case, meanwhile, the people tweeting about the demonstrations were almost all in the West. "It is time to get Twitter's role in the events in Iran right," Golnaz Esfandiari wrote, this past summer, in *Foreign Policy*. "Simply put: There was no Twitter Revolution inside Iran." The cadre of prominent bloggers, like Andrew Sullivan, who championed the role of social media in Iran, Esfandiari continued, misunderstood the situation. "Western journalists who couldn't reach—or didn't bother reaching?—people on the ground in Iran simply scrolled through the English-language tweets post with tag #iranelection," she wrote. "Through

---

[1] **revanchism** (from the French *revanche*, "revenge"): A term used to describe a political policy of a nation or an ethnic group, intended to regain lost territory or standing. —EDS.

it all, no one seemed to wonder why people trying to coordinate protests in Iran would be writing in any language other than Farsi."

Some of this grandiosity is to be expected. Innovators tend to be solipsists. They often want to cram every stray fact and experience into their new model. As the historian Robert Darnton has written, "The marvels of communication technology in the present have produced a false consciousness about the past—even a sense that communication has no history, or had nothing of importance to consider before the days of television and the Internet." But there is something else at work here, in the outsized enthusiasm for social media. Fifty years after one of the most extraordinary episodes of social upheaval in American history, we seem to have forgotten what activism is.

Greensboro in the early nineteen-sixties was the kind of place where   10 racial insubordination was routinely met with violence. The four students who first sat down at the lunch counter were terrified. "I suppose if anyone had come up behind me and yelled 'Boo,' I think I would have fallen off my seat," one of them said later. On the first day, the store manager notified the police chief, who immediately sent two officers to the store. On the third day, a gang of white toughs showed up at the lunch counter and stood ostentatiously behind the protesters, ominously muttering epithets such as "burr-head nigger." A local Ku Klux Klan leader made an appearance. On Saturday, as tensions grew, someone called in a bomb threat, and the entire store had to be evacuated.

The dangers were even clearer in the Mississippi Freedom Summer Project of 1964, another of the sentinel campaigns of the civil-rights movement. The Student Nonviolent Coordinating Committee recruited hundreds of Northern, largely white unpaid volunteers to run Freedom Schools, register black voters, and raise civil-rights awareness in the Deep South. "No one should go *anywhere* alone, but certainly not in an automobile and certainly not at night," they were instructed. Within days of arriving in Mississippi, three volunteers—Michael Schwerner, James Chaney, and Andrew Goodman—were kidnapped and killed, and, during the rest of the summer, thirty-seven black churches were set on fire and dozens of safe houses were bombed; volunteers were beaten, shot at, arrested, and trailed by pickup trucks full of armed men. A quarter of those in the program dropped out. Activism that challenges the status quo—that attacks deeply rooted problems—is not for the faint of heart.

What makes people capable of this kind of activism? The Stanford sociologist Doug McAdam compared the Freedom Summer dropouts with the participants who stayed, and discovered that the key difference wasn't, as might be expected, ideological fervor. "*All* of the applicants—participants and withdrawals alike—emerge as highly committed, articulate supporters of the goals and values of the summer program," he concluded. What mattered more was an applicant's degree of personal connection to the civil-rights movement. All the volunteers were required to provide a list of personal contacts—the people they wanted kept apprised of their activities—and participants were far more likely than dropouts to have close friends who were also going to Mississippi. High-risk activism, McAdam concluded, is a "strong-tie" phenomenon.

This pattern shows up again and again. One study of the Red Brigades, the Italian terrorist group of the nineteen-seventies, found that seventy percent of recruits had at least one good friend already in the organization. The same is true of the men who joined the mujahideen in Afghanistan. Even revolutionary actions that look spontaneous, like the demonstrations in East Germany that led to the fall of the Berlin Wall, are, at core, strong-tie phenomena. The opposition movement in East Germany consisted of several hundred groups, each with roughly a dozen members. Each group was in limited contact with the others: at the time, only thirteen percent of East Germans even had a phone. All they knew was that on Monday nights, outside St. Nicholas Church in downtown Leipzig, people gathered to voice their anger at the state. And the primary determinant of who showed up was "critical friends"—the more friends you had who were critical of the regime the more likely you were to join the protest.

So one crucial fact about the four freshmen at the Greensboro lunch counter—David Richmond, Franklin McCain, Ezell Blair, and Joseph McNeil—was their relationship with one another. McNeil was a roommate of Blair's in A. & T.'s Scott Hall dormitory. Richmond roomed with McCain one floor up, and Blair, Richmond, and McCain had all gone to Dudley High School. The four would smuggle beer into the dorm and talk late into the night in Blair and McNeil's room. They would all have remembered the murder of Emmett Till in 1955, the Montgomery bus boycott that same year, and the showdown in Little Rock in 1957. It was McNeil who brought up the idea of a sit-in at Woolworth's. They'd discussed it for nearly a month. Then McNeil came into the dorm room and asked the others if they were ready. There was a pause, and McCain said, in a way that works only with people who talk late into the night with one another, "Are you guys chicken or not?" Ezell Blair worked up the courage the next day to ask for a cup of coffee because he was flanked by his roommate and two good friends from high school.

The kind of activism associated with social media isn't like this at all.   15 The platforms of social media are built around weak ties. Twitter is a way of following (or being followed by) people you may never have met. Facebook is a tool for efficiently managing your acquaintances, for keeping up with the people you would not otherwise be able to stay in touch with. That's why you can have a thousand "friends" on Facebook, as you never could in real life.

This is in many ways a wonderful thing. There is strength in weak ties, as the sociologist Mark Granovetter has observed. Our acquaintances—not our friends—are our greatest source of new ideas and information. The Internet lets us exploit the power of these kinds of distant connections with marvellous efficiency. It's terrific at the diffusion of innovation, interdisciplinary collaboration, seamlessly matching up buyers and sellers, and the logistical functions of the dating world. But weak ties seldom lead to high-risk activism.

In a new book called *The Dragonfly Effect: Quick, Effective, and Powerful Ways to Use Social Media to Drive Social Change*, the business consultant Andy Smith and the Stanford Business School professor Jennifer Aaker tell the story of Sameer Bhatia, a young Silicon Valley entrepreneur who came down with acute myelogenous leukemia. It's a perfect illustration of social media's strengths. Bhatia needed a bone-marrow transplant, but he could not find a match among his relatives and friends. The odds were best with a donor of his ethnicity, and there were few South Asians in the national bone-marrow database. So Bhatia's business partner sent out an e-mail explaining Bhatia's plight to more than four hundred of their acquaintances, who forwarded the e-mail to their personal contacts; Facebook pages and YouTube videos were devoted to the Help Sameer campaign. Eventually, nearly twenty-five thousand new people were registered in the bone-marrow database, and Bhatia found a match.

But how did the campaign get so many people to sign up? By not asking too much of them. That's the only way you can get someone you don't really know to do something on your behalf. You can get thousands of people to sign up for a donor registry, because doing so is pretty easy. You have to send in a cheek swab and—in the highly unlikely event that your bone marrow is a good match for someone in need—spend a few hours at the hospital. Donating bone marrow isn't a trivial matter. But it doesn't involve financial or personal risk; it doesn't mean spending a summer being chased by armed men in pickup trucks. It doesn't require that you confront socially entrenched norms and practices. In fact, it's the kind of commitment that will bring only social acknowledgment and praise.

The evangelists of social media don't understand this distinction; they seem to believe that a Facebook friend is the same as a real friend and that signing up for a donor registry in Silicon Valley today is activism in the same sense as sitting at a segregated lunch counter in Greensboro in 1960. "Social networks are particularly effective at increasing motivation," Aaker and Smith write. But that's not true. Social networks are effective at increasing *participation*—by lessening the level of motivation that participation requires. The Facebook page of the Save Darfur Coalition has 1,282,339 members, who have donated an average of nine cents apiece. The next biggest Darfur charity on Facebook has 22,073 members, who have donated an average of thirty-five cents. Help Save Darfur has 2,797 members, who have given, on average, fifteen cents. A spokesperson for the Save Darfur Coalition told *Newsweek*, "We wouldn't necessarily gauge someone's value to the advocacy movement based on what they've given. This is a powerful mechanism to engage this critical population. They inform their community, attend events, volunteer. It's not something you can measure by looking at a ledger." In other words, Facebook activism succeeds not by *motivating* people to make a real sacrifice but by motivating them to do the things that people do when they are not motivated enough to make a real sacrifice. We are a long way from the lunch counters of Greensboro.

The students who joined the sit-ins across the South during the winter   20
of 1960 described the movement as a "fever." But the civil-rights movement was more like a military campaign than like a contagion. In the late nineteen-fifties, there had been sixteen sit-ins in various cities throughout the South, fifteen of which were formally organized by civil-rights organizations like the NAACP and CORE. Possible locations for activism were scouted. Plans were drawn up. Movement activists held training sessions and retreats for would-be protesters, The Greensboro Four were a product of this groundwork: all were members of the NAACP Youth Council. They had close ties with the head of the local NAACP chapter. They had been briefed on the earlier wave of sit-ins in Durham, and had been part of a series of movement meetings in activist churches. When the sit-in movement spread from Greensboro throughout the South, it did not spread indiscriminately. It spread to those cities which had preexisting "movement centers" — a core of dedicated and trained activists ready to turn the "fever" into action.

The civil-rights movement was high-risk activism. It was also, crucially, strategic activism: a challenge to the establishment mounted with precision and discipline. The NAACP was a centralized organization, run from New York according to highly formalized operating procedures. At the Southern Christian Leadership Conference, Martin Luther King, Jr., was the unquestioned authority. At the center of the movement was the black church, which had, as Aldon D. Morris points out in his superb 1984 study, "The Origins of the Civil Rights Movement," a carefully demarcated division of labor, with various standing committees and disciplined groups. "Each group was task-oriented and coordinated its activities through authority structures," Morris writes. "Individuals were held accountable for their assigned duties, and important conflicts were resolved by the minister, who usually exercised ultimate authority over the congregation."

This is the second crucial distinction between traditional activism and its online variant: social media are not about this kind of hierarchical organization. Facebook and the like are tools for building *networks*, which are the opposite, in structure and character, of hierarchies. Unlike hierarchies, with their rules and procedures, networks aren't controlled by a single central authority. Decisions are made through consensus, and the ties that bind people to the group are loose.

This structure makes networks enormously resilient and adaptable in low-risk situations. Wikipedia is a perfect example. It doesn't have an editor, sitting in New York, who directs and corrects each entry. The effort of putting together each entry is self-organized. If every entry in Wikipedia were to be erased tomorrow, the content would swiftly be restored, because that's what happens when a network of thousands spontaneously devote their time to a task.

There are many things, though, that networks don't do well. Car companies sensibly use a network to organize their hundreds of suppliers, but not to
design their cars. No one believes that the articulation of a coherent design
philosophy is best handled by a sprawling, leaderless organizational system.
Because networks don't have a centralized leadership structure and clear
lines of authority, they have real difficulty reaching consensus and setting
goals. They can't think strategically; they are chronically prone to conflict
and error. How do you make difficult choices about tactics or strategy or
philosophical direction when everyone has an equal say?

The Palestine Liberation Organization originated as a network, and the   25
international-relations scholars Mette Eilstrup-Sangiovanni and Calvert
Jones argue in a recent essay in *International Security* that this is why it ran
into such trouble as it grew: "Structural features typical of networks—the
absence of central authority, the unchecked autonomy of rival groups, and
the inability to arbitrate quarrels through formal mechanisms—made the
P.L.O. excessively vulnerable to outside manipulation and internal strife."

In Germany in the nineteen-seventies, they go on, "the far more unified
and successful left-wing terrorists tended to organize hierarchically, with professional management and clear divisions of labor. They were concentrated
geographically in universities, where they could establish central leadership, trust, and camaraderie through regular, face-to-face meetings." They
seldom betrayed their comrades in arms during police interrogations. Their
counterparts on the right were organized as decentralized networks, and had
no such discipline. These groups were regularly infiltrated, and members,
once arrested, easily gave up their comrades. Similarly, Al Qaeda was most
dangerous when it was a unified hierarchy. Now that it has dissipated into a
network, it has proved far less effective.

The drawbacks of networks scarcely matter if the network isn't interested in systemic change—if it just wants to frighten or humiliate or make
a splash—or if it doesn't need to think strategically. But if you're taking on
a powerful and organized establishment you have to be a hierarchy. The
Montgomery bus boycott required the participation of tens of thousands
of people who depended on public transit to get to and from work each
day. It lasted a *year*. In order to persuade those people to stay true to the
cause, the boycott's organizers tasked each local black church with maintaining morale, and put together a free alternative private carpool service,
with forty-eight dispatchers and forty-two pickup stations. Even the White
Citizens Council, King later said, conceded that the carpool system moved
with "military precision." By the time King came to Birmingham, for the
climactic showdown with Police Commissioner Eugene (Bull) Connor, he
had a budget of a million dollars, and a hundred full-time staff members on
the ground, divided into operational units. The operation itself was divided
into steadily escalating phases, mapped out in advance. Support was maintained through consecutive mass meetings rotating from church to church
around the city.

Boycotts and sit-ins and nonviolent confrontations—which were the weapons of choice for the civil-rights movement—are high-risk strategies. They leave little room for conflict and error. The moment even one protester deviates from the script and responds to provocation, the moral legitimacy of the entire protest is compromised. Enthusiasts for social media would no doubt have us believe that King's task in Birmingham would have been made infinitely easier had he been able to communicate with his followers through Facebook, and contented himself with tweets from a Birmingham jail. But networks are messy: think of the ceaseless pattern of correction and revision, amendment and debate, that characterizes Wikipedia. If Martin Luther King, Jr., had tried to do a wiki-boycott in Montgomery, he would have been steamrollered by the white power structure. And of what use would a digital communication tool be in a town where ninety-eight percent of the black community could be reached every Sunday morning at church? The things that King needed in Birmingham—discipline and strategy—were things that online social media cannot provide.

The bible of the social-media movement is Clay Shirky's *Here Comes Everybody*. Shirky, who teaches at New York University, sets out to demonstrate the organizing power of the Internet, and he begins with the story of Evan, who worked on Wall Street, and his friend Ivanna, after she left her smart phone, an expensive Sidekick, on the back seat of a New York City taxicab. The telephone company transferred the data on Ivanna's lost phone to a new phone, whereupon she and Evan discovered that the Sidekick was now in the hands of a teenager from Queens, who was using it to take photographs of herself and her friends.

When Evan e-mailed the teenager, Sasha, asking for the phone back, she   30 replied that his "white ass" didn't deserve to have it back. Miffed, he set up a Web page with her picture and a description of what had happened. He forwarded the link to his friends, and they forwarded it to their friends. Someone found the MySpace page of Sasha's boyfriend, and a link to it found its way onto the site. Someone found her address online and took a video of her home while driving by; Evan posted the video on the site. The story was picked up by the news filter Digg. Evan was now up to ten e-mails a minute. He created a bulletin board for his readers to share their stories, but it crashed under the weight of responses. Evan and Ivanna went to the police, but the police filed the report under "lost," rather than "stolen," which essentially closed the case. "By this point millions of readers were watching," Shirky writes, "and dozens of mainstream news outlets had covered the story." Bowing to the pressure, the NYPD reclassified the item as "stolen." Sasha was arrested, and Evan got his friend's Sidekick back.

Shirky's argument is that this is the kind of thing that could never have happened in the pre-Internet age—and he's right. Evan could never have tracked down Sasha. The story of the Sidekick would never have been publicized. An army of people could never have been assembled to wage this fight.

The police wouldn't have bowed to the pressure of a lone person who had misplaced something as trivial as a cell phone. The story, to Shirky, illustrates "the ease and speed with which a group can be mobilized for the right kind of cause" in the Internet age.

Shirky considers this model of activism an upgrade. But it is simply a form of organizing which favors the weak-tie connections that give us access to information over the strong-tie connections that help us persevere in the face of danger. It shifts our energies from organizations that promote strategic and disciplined activity and toward those which promote resilience and adaptability. It makes it easier for activists to express themselves, and harder for that expression to have any impact. The instruments of social media are well suited to making the existing social order more efficient. They are not a natural enemy of the status quo. If you are of the opinion that all the world needs is a little buffing around the edges, this should not trouble you. But if you think that there are still lunch counters out there that need integrating it ought to give you pause.

Shirky ends the story of the lost Sidekick by asking, portentously, "What happens next?"—no doubt imagining future waves of digital protesters. But he has already answered the question. What happens next is more of the same. A networked, weak-tie world is good at things like helping Wall Streeters get phones back from teenage girls. *Viva la revolución.* ●

The Reader's Presence

1. Reread the first six paragraphs of Gladwell's essay. What do they lead you to believe will be the focus of his essay? Point to specific words and phrases to support your response. How does the scene that Gladwell describes relate to the point he is making in this essay? What are the effects of Gladwell's decision not to mention anything about social media until the end of this opening section?

2. Point to specific ways in which Gladwell recounts the events of the Greensboro lunch counter sit-in differently from the way he relates the story of the New Yorker who lost her Sidekick. What compositional strategies does Gladwell use to make the effects of reading about these two events seem so different?

3. **VISUAL PRESENCE:** Examine the 1960 photograph on page 388 of a lunch counter sit-in. How is this image similar to or different from more recent pictures of protests you have seen that were spread by social media? Use specific examples to support your response.

4. **CONNECTIONS:** Compare Gladwell's essay with Kwame Anthony Appiah's "Race in the Modern World" (page 291). How does each author use historical facts to support the points he is making? In what specific ways are the authors' uses of historical facts similar? How are they different? In what ways do their claims support each other? To what extent could either author's argument benefit from the other's?

Amanda Hess

MULTIPLE CHOICE

In a time when gender roles and identities are no longer understood in simple terms of male and female, pronouns have become a matter of public debate and confusion. In "Multiple Choice," journalist **AMANDA HESS** considers the limitations of the English language and how our vocabulary to identify gender might adapt to better represent those who do not identify with "he" or "she."

Hess is perhaps best known for her *Pacific Standard* article, "Why Women Aren't Welcome on the Internet," which won the Sidney Award as well as a National Magazine Award for Public Interest. She is currently a writer at the *New York Times* and was previously a staff writer for *Slate*.

> Journalist Amanda Hess considers the limitations of the English language and how our gender vocabulary might adapt to better represent those who do not identify with "he" or "she."

WE ARE WITNESSING a great explosion in the way that human beings are allowed to express their gender identities. We are also hearing a lot of awkward conversations. What are we supposed to . . . call everyone? A recent scene on HBO's "Girls" riffed on this problem, drawing a linguistic fault line down a Brooklyn street. On one side is a no-frills coffee joint run by Ray Ploshansky, the show's resident grumpy old man. (He's, like, 38.) Across the street, a hip new cafe springs up and instantly hoovers up Ray's clientele.

When Ray crosses the road to eyeball the competition, he encounters a barista he can't quite size up. First he calls the barista "sir," and the barista balks, "Why'd you feel the need to call me 'sir'?" So Ray tries "female?" and the barista says: "Oh, 'female'? You a biologist? You a biological essentialist? Are you a detective?" So Ray asks, "What's going on here?" and a second barista steps in to explain: "What's going on here is that you offended they, and you offended me, so I think it's best that you leave." He does. The baristas embrace.

The cafe clash took the language debate of the moment and personified its most extreme positions. On one side are people like Ray, who come off as clueless and offensive for failing to recalibrate their language to accommodate people who don't identify as "he" or "she." On the other side are "theys" like the barista, who can sound unreasonable and absurd when they try to police new rules of language that are still in flux. But in the subtext of the scene, a third figure emerged. The barista character was played by the younger sibling of Lena Dunham, the creator of "Girls": Grace Dunham, a young queer writer and performer who identifies as a "trans person with a vagina" and recently wrote on Twitter, "I hate, fear and am allergic to binaries"—and is also game for joking about how hard it can be to get everybody on the same page.

This registers as a modern problem, but gender-neutral pronouns have been proposed for centuries. In 1808, Samuel Taylor Coleridge suggested repurposing "it" and "which" "in order to avoid particularizing man or woman, or in order to express either sex indifferently." But only recently has mainstream pop culture entertained the idea of a neutral pronoun for referring to trans, genderqueer and even some feminist folks who either don't identify as "he" or "she" or are interested in demolishing that binary in speech. A flurry of totally new constructions has emerged to bridge the gap. On Tumblr, it's now typical for young people to pin their preferred pronouns to their pages: The writer behind a blog called "The Gayest Seabass" identifies as "Danny, xe/xim/xir or he/him/his or they/them/their, taken-ish, 20."

Lynn Liben, a psychologist at Penn State, has studied the effects of   5
gender-coded language—English weaves it in by way of pronouns (she, his) but also identifying nouns (girl, uncle) and honorifics (Mr. and Mrs.)—for about 15 years. In a pair of studies conducted in preschool classrooms in 2008 and 2010, Liben found that when teachers emphasize a gender divide in speech—like saying, "Good morning, boys and girls"—children adopt more intense stereotypes about what boys and girls are supposed to do, and become less likely to play with children of a different gender at recess. "When they see adults talk about gender as a category system," Liben says, "kids become more vigilant about making the distinction themselves." Jill Soloway, creator of the Amazon series "Transparent," is a fan of "they" as a corrective to that phenomenon. "A really interesting thought exercise is to say 'they' and 'them' for all genders," she told *The New Yorker* recently. "The promise of this revolution is not having to say, 'Men do this, women do this.'"

These gender-neutral constructions, which not so long ago may have sounded odd or even unthinkable to traditionalists, are becoming accepted as standard English. *The Washington Post* is one of the first to have taken up the cause, welcoming the singular "they" into the paper's stylebook late last year. And in January, the American Dialect Society voted the singular "they" its 2015 Word of the Year, noting its "emerging use as a pronoun to refer to a known person, often as a conscious choice by a person rejecting the traditional gender binary of he and she."

But central to the appeal of the singular "they" is that it's often deployed *unconsciously*. It's regularly repurposed as a linguistic crutch when an individual's gender is unknown or irrelevant. You might use it to refer to a hypothetical person who, say, goes to the store and forgets "their" wallet. That casual usage has a long history—it has appeared in Chaucer, Shakespeare, Austen and Shaw. It wasn't until 1745, when the schoolmistress-turned-grammar-expert

Ann Fisher proposed "he" as a universal pronoun for a person of unknown gender, that the use of "they" in the same circumstance was respun as grammatically incorrect. "The Masculine Person answers to the general Name, which comprehends both Male and Female; as, any Person who knows what he says," she wrote.

It's precisely the vagueness of "they" that makes it a not-so-ideal pronoun replacement. It can obscure a clear gender identification with a blurred one. Think of genderqueer people who are confident in their knowledge of their own gender identity as one that simply doesn't fit the boxes of "he" or "she": Calling all of them "they" can make it sound as if someone's gender is unknowable; it's the grammatical equivalent of a shrug. In December, the *Post* copy editor Bill Walsh called "they" "the only sensible solution to English's lack of a gender-neutral third-person singular personal pronoun," with "sensible" being the key word. The singular "they" gained favor with *The Post's* standard-bearer partly because the presumptive "he" "hasn't been palatable for decades," but also because a generic "she" feels "patronizing" and "attempts at made-up pronouns" — like "xe," "xim," and "xir" — strike Walsh as "silly." *The New York Times* hasn't officially adopted "they," but *The Times's* standards editor, Phillip B. Corbett, thinks it's likely to earn a place in the paper's stylebook as usage evolves. "Eventually, I assume, certain forms will become widely adopted, and that's the point when it would make sense for us to set out formal style rules," he told me. "My guess—just a guess—is that 'they' is far more likely to become the default pronoun in these cases, rather than 'xe' or other neologisms."

A 2014 dispatch in *The Economist* in favor of "they" argued that "pronouns (unlike nouns and verbs) are a 'closed class' of words, almost never admitting new members." (*The Economist's* style guide, by the way, still calls the honorific Ms. an "ugly" word.) If the point of the gender-neutral pronoun is to get hulking institutions like *The Washington Post* and *The Economist* to become comfortable with a concept that currently strikes traditional folks as incomprehensible—the rejection of the gender binary—then "they" feels a little bit like a shortcut on the way to acceptance. It represents a third option outside the binary, sure. But it doesn't compel people to make mental room for a new word.

The media guide for "transgender issues" by GLAAD, a lesbian, gay, bisexual and transgender advocacy group, advises reporters to use whatever pronoun their subjects prefer. If they don't prefer "they," using it anyway feels like an erasure of their own identity in favor of society's new standardized label. In a very real way, accepting the fluidity of gender requires rejecting standards in general. It means opening our "closed class" of pronouns. In "The Argonauts," Maggie Nelson's memoir of gender and language, she acknowledges "the Aristotelian, perhaps evolutionary need to put everything into categories," but embraces another need "to pay homage to the transitive, the flight, the great soup of being in which we actually live." It's hard to sum it all up in a word. ◼

10

The Reader's Presence

1. Amanda Hess introduces her essay by focusing on a scene from the television series *Girls*. What does she gain by beginning with an example from fiction? In what specific ways does this "cafe clash" (paragraph 3) set the stage for the rest of her essay? What does she gain by framing the gender issues she discusses as a "cafe clash"? What does the phrase imply about the limitations of expressing gender identity in conversation, especially when addressing strangers?

2. Discuss Hess's stance on "they" as a singular gender-neutral pronoun. What does she identify as the advantages and disadvantages of using this word? Why is "they" worth considering as an option, despite the potential downsides? Hess calls the word a "shortcut on the way to acceptance" (paragraph 9). To what extent do you agree with this assessment? Explain why or why not.

3. **CONNECTIONS:** After citing *The Economist*, Hess observes, "*The Economist's* style guide, by the way, still calls the honorific Ms. an 'ugly' word." Compare the use of sources in "Multiple Choice" with Eula Biss's "Sentimental Medicine" (page 304). In what ways does each author use, identify, and characterize sources they consider noncredible, outdated, or simply incorrect? What role do authority and expertise play in their essays? Compare and contrast the limitations of binary choices in matters of gender and ethnicity in Hess's essay with Wendy Willis's "Boxed In" (page 671).

Walter Isaacson
THE GREAT CONNECTORS

If you were born sometime between 1980 and 2000—the age demographic often referred to as the Millennials—then you arrived in the midst of the digital revolution. The Internet as we know it took shape as the World Wide Web in 1991. Now billions access the Internet on a daily basis via laptops, cell phones, and a myriad of other devices. It is easy to take our technology for granted without knowing the discoveries that made them possible. In "The Great Connectors," journalist and author **WALTER ISAACSON** (b. 1952) examines the innovations that powered the digital revolution.

> "[C]reativity is a collaborative endeavor and a team sport."

Isaacson is currently the president and CEO of the Aspen Institute, a nonprofit organization emphasizing nonpartisan dialogue about world issues. He has previously served as CEO of Cable News Network and as the managing editor of *Time* magazine. As a writer, Isaacson is perhaps best known for his biographies: he has written on the lives of Steve Jobs, Benjamin Franklin, Albert Einstein, and Henry Kissinger. His latest project is a biography of Leonardo da Vinci.

While Isaacson's biographies revolve around famous individuals, he emphasizes the collaborative nature of historical breakthroughs in "The Great Connectors." In an interview with the *Harvard Gazette*, he observed, "Those of us who write biographies know that to some extent we distort history. We make it seem like somebody in a garage or in a garret has a 'light-bulb moment' and the world changes, when in fact creativity is a collaborative endeavor and a team sport."

JUST AS THE INDUSTRIAL REVOLUTION was driven by combining the steam engine with ingenious machinery, the Digital Revolution has been driven by two great innovations: the personal computer and the Internet. The relationship between the two was standoffish at first, and it was only after their development became intertwined that the digital economy began to transform our lives. The result was a shift in influence from an old establishment led by bankers, wise men, and a corporate elite to a new establishment led by the pioneers of technology, information, and entertainment. This digital inflection point occurred in 1994, the year that this magazine [*Vanity Fair*] began publishing its New Establishment list.

The first personal computers had sprouted two decades earlier, led by the Altair, a solder-it-yourself kit created by Ed Roberts, an engineer and hobbyist in Albuquerque. When one was shown off at a meeting of the Homebrew Computer Club, a collection of hackers and geeks who met monthly in Silicon Valley, a college dropout named Steve Wozniak got so excited that he devised an even better circuit board that he integrated with a keyboard and monitor. He was so proud of it that he gave away the specifications for free until his best friend from down the street, Steve Jobs, convinced him they should assemble them in the Jobs family's garage and sell them. Thus was born the Apple I.

At that time, a new set of standards was being adopted for sending packets of information through digital networks. They were dubbed "Internet protocols" by their creators, Vint Cerf and Bob Kahn, and you generally had to be affiliated with a university or research institution to jack in.

It took a series of innovations to make it possible for the personal computer and Internet to meld into the combustible mix that fueled a revolution. One was creating a simple, consumer-friendly version of a modem, which could modulate and demodulate (hence the name) phone signals so they could carry digital data. That allowed electronic pioneers, such as the provocateur Stewart Brand and the marketer Steve Case, to create the WELL and AOL and other dial-up services that offered home-computer users e-mail, bulletin boards, chat rooms, and information. The wall between the P.C. and the Internet was breached by 1994, after AOL began allowing its members direct access to the Internet.

As ordinary folks began flooding onto the Internet, in 1994, another phenomenon exploded: the World Wide Web, a set of protocols that allowed people to post and access pages embedded with hypertext links, words, pictures, and eventually audio and video. It was created by Tim Berners-Lee, an Oxford-educated engineer who took a job at the CERN laboratory, in Switzerland, and

5

AP Photo/Atlanta Journal-Constitution, William Berry

Dr. Ed Roberts, with the Altair 8800 computer, 1997.

was looking for ways to keep track of projects and foster collaboration. He was inspired by his favorite book as a child, a Victorian almanac crammed with random wisdom titled *Enquire Within upon Everything*, and he set out to create a web of links that would allow users of a network to do just that. His web spread rapidly after Marc Andreessen, an undergraduate at the University of Illinois, created an easy-to-install browser that allowed personal-computer users to call up Web sites. In January 1994, there were 700 Web sites in the world. By the end of that year there were 10,000. The combination of personal computers and the Internet had spawned something amazing: anyone could get content from anywhere, distribute new creations everywhere, and enquire within upon everything.

As a result, 1994 also witnessed the birth of a whole new medium. Justin Hall, a freshman at Swarthmore, created a beguiling Web site that included a running log of his personal activities, random thoughts, deep beliefs, and intimate encounters. His Web log featured poems about his father's suicide, spiky musings about his diverse sexual desires, pictures of his penis, edgy stories about his stepfather, and other effusions that darted back and forth across the line of Too Much Information. By linking to others with similar logs he fostered a sense of community. Soon the phrase "Web log" had been shortened to "blog," and Justin Hall had become a founding scamp of the first wholly new form of content to be created for, and to take advantage of, personal-computer networks.

In the 20 years since then, new platforms, services, and social networks have increasingly enabled fresh opportunities for individual imagination and collaborative creativity. Four of these innovations were especially transformative.

The first was the concept of search, pioneered most successfully by Google. Larry Page and Sergey Brin harnessed the wisdom of the billions of humans who put links on their Web sites with the power of a recursive algorithm that could rank each page by calculating the number of links pointing to it and the relative importance of each of those links based on the rank of the pages that originated them. In doing so they created a world in which humans, computers, and networks were intimately linked.

The second was the idea of crowd-sourced collaboration, which found full expression in Wikipedia. Jimmy Wales, a serial entrepreneur from Huntsville, Alabama, took a piece of software that allowed readers to edit a Web page and applied it to his effort to create an encyclopedia. Anyone could edit a page, and the results would show up instantly. Sure, that meant vandals could mess up pages. So could idiots or ideologues. But the software kept track of every version. If a bad edit appeared, others in the community could simply get rid of it by clicking on a "revert" link. That sometimes led to disputes. Wars have been fought with less intensity than the reversion battles on Wikipedia. But, somewhat amazingly, the forces of reason regularly triumphed. Wikipedia thus pioneered a Web 2.0 that was a place for open, peer-to-peer collaboration and crowd-sourced content.

The third seminal innovation was the migration to mobile. Steve Jobs   10 paved the way by launching the iPhone in 2007. It included little pieces of application software, known as apps, for surfing the Web and other tasks. But initially Jobs wouldn't allow outsiders to create apps for the iPhone, because he thought they might infect it with viruses or pollute its integrity. After pressure from his inner circle, Jobs figured out a way to have the best of both worlds. He would permit outsiders to write apps, but they would have to be approved by Apple and sold through the iTunes Store. The result was a new app economy, with 1.2 million apps available from Apple and a comparable number for Android systems.

And finally there was the creation of social networks. Early versions emerged around the time of the seminal year of 1994, with the advent of Geocities, The-Globe, and Tripod. But the real wave began 10 years later with the rise of Friendster, MySpace, and LinkedIn, followed by Facebook, Foursquare, Tumblr, and Twitter.

The next phase of the Digital Revolution will bring a fuller fusion of technology with the creative industries, such as media, fashion, music, entertainment, education, literature, and the arts. Much of the early innovation involved pouring old wine—books, newspapers, opinion pieces, journals, songs, television shows, movies—into new, digital bottles. But now completely new forms of expression and media formats are emerging. Role-playing games and interactive plays are merging with collaborative modes of storytelling and augmented realities. People are creating multimedia books that can be crowd-sourced and wikified but also curated. Instead of pursuing mere artificial intelligence, people are finding ways to partner the power of the computer with that of the human mind.

In this new era, the primary role for humans will be the same as it was 20 years ago. Human entrepreneurs and innovators will supply the imagination, the creativity, and the ability, as Steve Jobs would say, to think different. The people who succeed will be the ones who can link beauty to engineering, humanity to technology, and poetry to processors. In other words, it will come from creators like those on this year's list, who can flourish where the arts intersect with the sciences and who have a rebellious sense of wonder that opens them to the beauty of both. ▪

The Reader's Presence

1. Near the end of paragraph 7, Walter Isaacson declares, "The combination of personal computers and the Internet had spawned something amazing." Identify — and comment on — the specific features of computers and the Internet that, when joined together, changed for those who had access to these tools, enabling them to explore and respond to their experience as well as giving them access to worlds larger than their own. How would you articulate the impact these two innovations have had on your life? Be as concrete and specific as possible. Consider how your life would be different without access to the Internet. Consider the significance of the title of Isaacson's essay in your response.

2. Isaacson calls attention to certain individuals who contributed to starting and shaping the digital revolution, including Ed Roberts and Steve Jobs. What role did "ordinary folks," as Isaacson calls them, play in this revolution? To what extent does Isaacson suggest that the "great connectors" are the inventors? their inventions? something else? Support your responses by pointing to and analyzing specific passages from the essay.

3. **CONNECTIONS:** Compare and contrast Isaacson's essay with Malcolm Gladwell's essay "Small Change: Why the Revolution Will Not Be Tweeted" (page 386). What do Isaacson and Gladwell envision as the role of social media in political activism? Identify — and analyze — specific passages in each essay, and apply them to any recent incident where personal computers and the Internet have had a significant impact on the outcome of political events.

Pico Iyer

THE TERMINAL CHECK

PICO IYER (b. 1957) is the British-born son of Indian philosopher Raghavan N. Iyer and religious scholar Nandini Nanak Mehta. When Iyer was seven years old, his family left Oxford, England, for California. He returned to Oxford for his own degree, graduating with the highest marks in his class, then went on to teach writing and literature at Harvard University before joining *Time* magazine in 1982 to write on world affairs. Known primarily as a travel writer, he has written several books of fiction and nonfiction, including novels *Cuba and the Night* (1995) and *Abandon* (2003), as well as

> As an Indian born in England and raised predominantly in the United States, Iyer has said that "being an outsider, as I always was, proved to be a perfect background, and launching pad, for writing (and for traveling)."

numerous books of essays and travelogues, including *Video Night in Kathmandu: And Other Reports from the Not-So-Far East* (1988), *The Lady and the Monk: Four Seasons in Kyoto* (1991), *Falling Off the Map: Some Lonely Places of the World* (1993), and *The Open Road: The Global Journey of the Fourteenth Dalai Lama* (2008), an extended journalistic analysis of the Tibetan spiritual leader. Iyer's latest books are *The Man Within My Head* (2012), a memoir that tracks his fascination with and the strange parallels shared with his literary hero, the novelist Graham Greene, and *The Art of Stillness: Adventures in Going Nowhere* (2014). "The Terminal Check" first appeared in *Granta* in 2011.

As an Indian born in England and raised predominantly in the United States, Iyer has said that "being an outsider, as I always was, proved to be a perfect background, and launching pad, for writing (and for traveling)."

I'M SITTING IN THE EXPANSIVE SPACES of Renzo Piano's four-story airport outside Osaka, sipping an Awake tea from Starbucks and waiting for my bus home. I've chosen to live in Japan for the past twenty years, and I know its rites as I know the way I need tea when feeling displaced, or to head for a right-hand window seat as soon as I enter a bus. A small, round-faced Japanese man in his early thirties, accompanied by a tall and somewhat cadaverous man of the same age, approaches me.

"Excuse me," says the small, friendly-seeming one; they look like newborn salarymen in their not-quite-perfect suits. "May I see your passport?"

When I look up, surprised, he flashes me a badge showing that he's a plain-clothes policeman. Dazed after crossing sixteen time zones (from California), I hand him my British passport.

"What are you doing in Japan?"

"I'm writing about it." I pull out my business card with the red embossed   5
logo of *Time* magazine.

"*Time* magazine?" says the smiling cop, strangely impressed. "He works for *Time* magazine," he explains to his lanky and impassive partner. "Very famous magazine," he assures me. "High prestige!"

Then he asks for my address and phone number and where I plan to be for the next eighty-nine days. "If there is some unfortunate incident," he explains, "some terrorist attack," (he's sotto voce now) "then we will know you did it."

Six months later, I fly back to the country I love once more. This time I need to withdraw some yen[1] from an ATM as I stumble out of my trans-Pacific plane, in order to pay for my bus home.

"You're getting some money?" says an attractive young Japanese woman, suddenly appearing beside me with a smile.

"I am. To go back to my apartment."   10

"You live here?" Few Japanese women have ever come up to me in public, let alone without an introduction, and shown such interest.

"I do."

---

[1] **yen:** Monetary unit used in Japan. —EDS.

"May I see your passport?" she asks sweetly, flashing a badge at me, much as the pair of questioners had done two seasons before.

"Just security," she says, anxious not to put me out, as my Japanese neighbors stream, unconcerned, towards the Gakuenmae bus that's about to pull out of its bay.

I tell my friends back in California about these small disruptions and 15 they look much too knowing. It's 9/11, they assure me. Over the past decade, security has tightened around the world, which means that insecurity has increased proportionally. Indeed, in recent years Japan has introduced finger-printing for all foreign visitors arriving at its airports, and takes photographs of every outsider coming across its borders; a large banner on the wall behind the immigration officers in Osaka—as angry-looking with its red-and-black hand-lettering as a student banner—explains the need for heightened mea-sures in the wake of threats to national order.

But the truth of the matter is that, for those of us with darker skins, and from nations not materially privileged, it was ever thus. When I was eighteen, I was held in custody in Panama's airport (because of the Indian passport I then carried) and denied formal entry to the nation, while the roguish English friend from high school with whom I was traveling was free to enter with impunity and savor all the dubious pleasures of the Canal Zone. On my way into Hong Kong—a transit lounge of a city if ever there was one, a duty-free zone whose only laws seem to be those of the marketplace—I was hauled into a special cabin for a lengthy interrogation because my face was deemed not to match my (by then British) passport. In Japan I was strip-searched every time I returned to the country, three or four times a year—my lifelong tan moving the authorities to assume that I must be either Saddam Hussein's cousin or an illegal Iranian (or, worst of all, what I really am, a wandering soul with Indian forebears). Once I was sent to a small room in Tokyo reserved for anyone of South Asian ancestry (where bejewelled women in saris loudly complained in exaggerated Oxbridge accents about being taken for common criminals).

Another time, long before my Japanese neighbors had heard of Osama bin Laden, I was even detained on my way *out* of Osaka—and the British Embassy hastily faxed on a Sunday night—as if any male with brown skin, passable English, and a look of shabby quasi-respectability must be doing something wrong if he's crossing a border.

But now, having learned over decades to accept such indignities or injus-tices, I walk into a chorus of complaints every time I return to California, from my pale-skinned, affluent neighbors. They're patting us down now, my friends object, and they're confiscating our contact-lens fluid. They're forcing us to travel with tiny tubes of toothpaste and moving us to wear loafers when usually we'd prefer lace-ups. They're taking away every bottle of water—but only after bottles of water have been shown to be weapons of mass destruc-tion; they're feeling us up with blue gloves, even here in Santa Barbara, now that they know that underwear can be a lethal weapon.

I listen to their grousing and think that the one thing the 9/11 attacks have achieved, for those of us who spend too much time in airports, is to make suspicion universal; fear and discomfort are equal-opportunity employers now. The world is flat in ways the high-flying global theoreticians don't always acknowledge; these days, even someone from the materially fortunate parts of the world—a man with a ruddy complexion, a woman in a Prada suit—is pulled aside for what is quixotically known as "random screening."

It used to be that the rich corners of the world seemed relatively safe,   20 protected, and the poor ones too dangerous to enter. Now, the logic of the terrorist attacks on New York and Washington has reversed all that. If anything, it's the rich places that feel unsettled. It used to be that officials would alight on people who look like me—from nations of need, in worn jeans, bearing the passports of more prosperous countries—as likely troublemakers; now they realize that even the well-born and well-dressed may not always be well-intentioned.

I understand why my friends feel aggrieved to be treated as if they came from Nigeria or Mexico or India. But I can't really mourn too much that airports, since 9/11, have become places where everyone may be taken to be guilty until proven innocent. The world is all mixed up these days, and America can no longer claim immunity. On 12 September 2001, *Le Monde* ran its now famous headline: WE ARE ALL AMERICANS. On 12 September 2011, it might more usefully announce: WE ARE ALL INDIANS. ●

The Reader's Presence

1. What does Iyer mean when he laments that "[t]he world is all mixed up" (paragraph 21) after the events of September 11, 2001? How do Iyer's friends explain his treatment abroad? What is his response to their explanation? Does he find some solace and justice in everyone's being subjected to the same treatment he describes in Japan? To what extent do you think his point that "fear and discomfort" are becoming "equal-opportunity employers" (paragraph 19) responds appropriately to the current circumstances for traveling, or does this attitude reinscribe the injustices described by Iyer? Explain your response. What does Iyer mean when he writes "WE ARE ALL INDIANS" (paragraph 21)?

2. The experiences Iyer describes in Japan of being subjected to not-so-random searches have occurred with such frequency that he has "learned over decades to accept such indignities or injustices" (paragraph 18). How do you reconcile Iyer's acceptance of these events with the innocuous complaints of his "pale-skinned, affluent neighbors" (paragraph 18)? Do you think they have no right to complain? Why or why not? To what extent does Iyer lament his experiences? Explain your answer.

3. **CONNECTIONS:** In what specific ways does the sense of uneasiness and "unsettled[ness]" Iyer describes in modern America relate to Laila Lalami's essay "My Life as a Muslim in the West's 'Gray Zone'" (page 154)? Compare and contrast Iyer's attitudes toward stereotyping people with those expressed by Lalami. How does the "gray zone" from Lalami's essay play into the universal suspicion described by Iyer?

MEHER AHMAD
My Homeland Security Journey

Meher Ahmad

When she wrote "My Homeland Security Journey," Meher Ahmad was a senior majoring in Middle Eastern studies at the University of Wisconsin–Madison. The essay was originally published in the *Progressive* magazine, where she served as an intern. She is currently a producer at VICE Media, Inc. When asked about her writing, she emphasized the importance of revision, saying she "wrote two drafts before submitting it to the editors at the *Progressive*, and that it was edited about three times after that." She goes on to say that subsequently she "revised it several times and reorganized several portions of it multiple times. The revisions allowed for a more continuous and direct narrative."

I grew up in a suburb of Indianapolis called Carmel and never found myself to be any different from my predominantly white friends, except for the odd unibrow joke and clarifying the pronunciation of my name during roll call.

On 9/11, hours after our teacher choked back tears to tell our fourth grade class the Twin Towers had been attacked, we all sat watching the news on the television. Some of us were crying, but we didn't quite comprehend why. A clip came on of people cheering around the world. First there was a reel of young Palestinians clamoring for the camera's attention. Someone in class pointed to the TV and said, "They did it!" I thought, "Why would they be celebrating when all these people are covered in ash and my teacher is crying?"

Then the newscast cut to a similar crowd of Pakistani boys jumping on cars in the street. Whoever pointed at the Palestinians was still pointing at the TV, this time suggesting that Pakistanis had done it. I could not even begin to grasp why Pakistanis would be happy about the attack, let alone what they had to do with all of the people running from a collapsing building in New York. Even if no one turned to me after the clip ended, I was acutely aware of the fact that I was Pakistani and not American.

> Establishes how her sense of identity changed after the 9/11 attacks she witnessed on television as a child.

Nearly eleven years after 9/11, virtually every Pakistani family in the area has a Homeland Security tale to tell.

My Homeland Security journey began in the summer of 2002, the first time I flew since 9/11 for a family vacation to Hawaii. I was eleven years old. At the airport waiting to check in, I was playing Game Boy with my kid brother on the floor, ignoring the exchange the airline official was having with my parents.

But when I looked up, the attendant was flustered and scared, I could tell. A feeling of panic reached my stomach, which only worsened when a police officer showed up. My brother and I wondered, "Why are we under arrest?" "What's happening?" "What's wrong?" We tugged at our parents' pant legs, and they told us sweetly in Urdu that we weren't under arrest and to please stop bothering them, be quiet, and sit over there, for God's sake.

My parents tell me now that the FBI was crosschecking our names, and while we waited for hours at the check-in desk, an agent in the Washington, D.C., office verified our identities. After a while, a friendly looking man in a white shirt and blue jeans escorted us to our newly booked flight, as our original one had taken off long ago. He told us it was most likely my name that had set off the security flag.

The man we sat next to on the flight wasn't an ordinary passenger. My mom murmured to me as we squeezed past him that it figures she would be the one person next to such a big man on the long flight. He answered in perfect Urdu, our secret language for making fun of strangers in public. With a visage not unlike Brad Pitt's, he was the last person I would think to speak Urdu fluently, but after describing to us his time in Islamabad as a former CIA agent, I could see why he did. Strange as it was, we arrived in Hawaii, and I shelved the journey in the back of my mind.

Suspicion greeted us every time we traveled, and in my teenage years I responded with sarcasm. I'd ask the TSA agent why I was being stopped, just so I could roll my eyes when they repeated it was a random search.

A few years of that bratty attitude didn't bring me any satisfaction, and now as an experienced navigator of airport security, I remain as polite and cooperative as possible. After all, it isn't the fault of the TSA agent, who probably just wants

Switches narrative to more recent times and provides a concrete instance of encountering airport security.

to go home, that I'm being stopped. Instead of a smirk, I sport a smile. I know the drill, so let's get this over with.

As I approached the row of agents in Chicago O'Hare this winter, I made bets with my father and brother about my chances of getting stopped. We reached the desk and slipped our passports through the glass. A few minutes after looking through my family's passports, the immigration officer finally picked mine up. He glanced up at me; I was staring intently back at him so as to signal complete confidence, a cover for the self-consciousness seasoned with a hint of doubt that creeps into my head every time I hand my passport over to American immigration. It's like slowing down when you see a cop car in the rearview mirror even if you're driving five below.

I ran a reel of situations through my head that the agent might misconstrue. What if my interviews with women in the Islamic Action Front in Jordan could be used against me? What if the fact that I was in Cairo after the Coptic riots was misconstrued? I went to the West Bank; could that be it?

The immigration officer made a brief phone call to a shadowy figure that I liken to the Wizard of Oz. I won the bet. We were escorted to the cubicle-like office of O'Hare's Homeland Security.

I tried to make myself comfortable on the impossibly narrow benches in the waiting room and glanced at a few posters with waving American flags that reminded me of my rights within that space. I was a suspect yet again.

A month before I landed in O'Hare, I found myself in a similarly tiny cordoned-off area where unsightly travelers like myself were corralled at the Allenby Bridge into Israel from Jordan. Surrounded by Arabs, mostly Palestinians who had likely been waiting for more than an hour before I joined them, I noticed the crowd wasn't frustrated or defeated. They were playing games on their cell phones, reading the newspaper, conversing with their neighbors. It didn't seem to bother them that they had been waiting for so long; it was the norm.

I had known that I was going to join them in their wait when the Israeli immigration officer opened my passport. I'm used to the disappointed look on security personnel's faces when I hand them my passport because before 2004, I carried a Pakistani one. Pakistani passports are notoriously easy to forge. On my old passport, my name was misspelled (written in ballpoint pen), crossed out, and rewritten with an arrow pointing to the correct spelling. I could understand why its validity was always in question.

But now, with a fresh American passport and citizenship, I expected to be presumed innocent. This thing has holograms and chips in it: What more could you want? But my passport isn't the kind an immigration officer likes to see:

> Name: Ahmad, Noor Meher
> Birthplace: Islamabad, Pakistan
> Places Traveled: Pakistan, Jordan, Egypt, Turkey,
>   Lebanon, Israel, United Kingdom

In Israel, they didn't pretend that the thorough and condescending questioning of my identity was random, as I'm always assured in the United States. It was blatantly discriminatory, and as I waved to my Caucasian American friends, who told me before they would wait in solidarity outside of the terminal, I was strangely comforted by the openly racist security policy of the IDF.

Back in O'Hare, the scene was tenser. My flight had come from Istanbul and it was full of people that ended up in the same waiting room as us. Though nobody told us not to talk, everyone kept quiet and spoke only in hushed tones. After an hour of anxiously watching the clock get closer to the time our connecting flight departed, I saw the Homeland Security agent come toward me to give me my passport back. He was smiling as if he just handed me a steaming apple pie.

> Provides yet another example of a security delay to drive home her main point about profiling in airports.

After sprinting through the terminal, we ended up missing our flight, and that's when the helplessness of our situation hit me. There was nothing I could have done to get out of that gray waiting room faster. I couldn't prove to the agent that I was an all-American girl, that I drink Coca-Cola and frequently indulge in *The Real Housewives* series. I couldn't avoid my own identity.

> Concludes by returning to her opening description of 9/11 and explaining how the years have not altered the experience of being uncomfortably different."

Eleven years after my classmate pointed his finger at Pakistanis celebrating 9/11, I've now encountered a growing mass of finger-pointers. It used to be the only place I felt uncomfortably different was at an Arby's in rural Indiana. Now, I can sense the glares on my back as agents search my bags in plain view of my fellow passengers. It doesn't feel like they'll stop pointing any time soon.

Hope Jahren

FROM *LAB GIRL*

For biologist and author **HOPE JAHREN** (b. 1969), the life of plants is not so different from human life. "Science has taught me," she explains, "that everything is more complicated than we first assume, and that being able to derive happiness from discovery is a recipe for a beautiful life." In this chapter from her award-winning memoir, *Lab Girl* (2016), Jahren writes about a specific tree from her childhood and imagines the life it led.

A highly respected scientist, Jahren has received numerous honors for her research in geobiology, including three Fulbright Awards. She currently teaches at the University of Oslo in Norway.

> **"Science has taught me that everything is more complicated than we first assume, and that being able to derive happiness from discovery is a recipe for a beautiful life."**

LIKE MOST PEOPLE, I have a particular tree that I remember from my childhood. It was a blue-tinged spruce (*Picea pungens*) that stood defiantly green through the long months of bitter winter. I remember its needles as sharp and angry against the white snow and gray sky; it seemed a perfect role model for the stoicism being cultivated in me. In the summer I hugged it and climbed it and talked to it, and fantasized that it knew me and that I was invisible when I was underneath it, watching ants carry dead needles back and forth, damned to some lower circle of insect Hell. As I got older I realized that the tree didn't actually care about me, and I was taught that it could make its own food from water and air. I knew that my climbing constituted (at most) a vibration beneath notice, and that pulling branches off for my forts was akin to pulling single hairs off of my own head. And yet, each night for several more years, I slept ten feet away from that tree, separated only by a glass window. Then I went to college and began the long process of leaving my hometown, and my childhood, behind.

Since then, I have realized that my tree had been a child once too. The embryo that became my tree sat on the ground for years, caught between the danger of waiting too long and the danger of leaving the seed too early. Any mistake would surely have led to death, and to being swallowed up by a seething, unforgiving world capable of rotting even the strongest leaf in a matter of days. My tree had also been a teenager. It went through a ten-year period where it grew wildly, with little regard

FotoLesnik/Fotosearch LBRF/AGE Fotostock

Blue Spruce.

for the future. Between ages ten and twenty it doubled in size, and it was often ill prepared for the new challenges and responsibilities that came with such height. It strove to keep up with its peers and occasionally dared to outdo them by brazenly claiming the odd pocket of full sun. Focused solely on growth, it was incapable of making seeds yet prone to fits and starts of the necessary hormones. it marked the year as did the other teenagers: it shot up tall in the spring, it made new needles for the summer season, and it stretched its roots in the fall, until it reluctantly settled into a boring winter.

From the teenagers' perspective, the grown-up trees presented a future that was as stultifying as it was interminable. Nothing but fifty, eighty, maybe a hundred years of just trying not to fall down, unpunctuated by the piecemeal toil of replacing fallen needles every morning and shutting down enzymes every night. No more rush of nutrients to signal the conquering of new territory underground, just the droop of a reliable, worn taproot into last winter's new cracks. The adults grew a bit thicker around the middle each year, with little else to show for the passing decades. In their branches they stingily dangled hard-won nutrients above the perpetually hungry younger generations. Good neighborhoods, rich with water, thick soil, and—most important—full sunlight, give rise to trees that reach their maximum potential. In contrast, trees in bad neighborhoods never achieve half of that height, never have much of a teenage growth spurt, but focus instead on just holding on, growing at less than half the rate of the more fortunate.

During its eighty-odd years my tree was likely sick several times. Unable to run away from the constant barrage of animals and insects eager to dismantle it for shelter and food, it preempted attacks by armoring itself with sharp points and toxic, inedible sap. Its roots were the most at risk, smothered and vulnerable within a blanket of rotting plant tissue. The cost of maintaining these defenses came out of my tree's meager savings that were intended for happier uses: each drop of sap was a seed that didn't happen; each thorn was a leaf that wouldn't be made.

In 2013 my tree made a terrible mistake. Assuming that winter was over,   5
it stretched its branches and grew a new crop of lush needles in anticipation
of the summer. But then an unusual May brought a rare spring blizzard, and
a copious amount of snow came down in just one weekend. Conifer trees can
stand heavy snow, but the added weight of the foliage proved too much. The
branches first bowed and then broke off, leaving a tall, bare trunk. My parents euthanized my tree by cutting it down and grinding out its roots. When
they mentioned it on the phone months later, I was standing in the dazzling
sunshine, living more than four thousand miles away in a place where it never
snows. I think of the irony that I fully appreciated that my tree was alive only
just in time to hear that it had died. But it's more than that—my spruce tree
was not only alive; it had a *life*, similar to but different from my own. It passed
its own milestones. My tree had its time, and time changed it.

Time has also changed me, my perception of my tree, and my perception
of my tree's perception of itself. Science has taught me that everything is more
complicated than we first assume, and that being able to derive happiness
from discovery is a recipe for a beautiful life. It has also convinced me that
carefully writing everything down is the only real defense we have against
forgetting something important that once was and is no more, including the
spruce tree that should have outlived me but did not. ■

The Reader's Presence

1. Hope Jahren identifies "a blue-tinged spruce (*Picea pungens)* that stood defiantly
   green through the long months of bitter winter" as "a perfect role model for the
   stoicism being cultivated in me" (paragraph 1). Point to other moments in her
   essay when she deliberately associates herself with what happens to the tree as
   both mature. Which of these features of the tree's maturing did you find most
   engaging? Explain why, supporting your response with specific references in the
   text. Why is it useful for her to write about the tree in this way, as if it were a person? What do we learn from these descriptions that would be lost if told in purely
   objective, scientific terms?

2. In the final paragraph, Jahren concludes by observing not only that "time has also
   changed me" but also that "science has taught me that everything is more complicated than we first assume, and that being able to derive happiness from discovery
   is a recipe for a beautiful life." At what specific moments in her essay does Jahren
   exemplify this point? Point to specific words and phrases as you formulate your
   response. In closing her essay, Jahren says ". . . carefully writing everything down is
   the only real defense we have against forgetting something that once was and is no
   more." Consider an example of when "carefully writing everything down" made a
   significant difference in your own experience of nature or the world around you.

3. **CONNECTIONS:** Compare and contrast Hope Jahren's essay to Virginia Woolf's "The
   Death of the Moth" (page 499). How are their representations of life and death
   similar? What are the specific ways in which each author relates with her subject?

Leslie Jamison

MARK MY WORDS. MAYBE.

"I am human; nothing human is alien to me." This is the epigraph of **LESLIE JAMISON'S** acclaimed collection of essays *The Empathy Exams* (2014), and it is also the message tattooed on her left forearm in Latin. The words hold a deeply personal meaning for the author. And yet, much like personal essays, tattoos invite us to participate in their meaning and interpret them for ourselves. Jamison (b. 1983) writes about this transformation of personal meaning as it enters the public view in "Mark My Words. Maybe."

In addition to her essay collection, which won the Graywolf Press Nonfiction Prize, Jamison has also written a novel, *The Gin Closet* (2010). She studied at Harvard University and the Iowa Writers' Workshop before earning her PhD in English literature at Yale University. She is a columnist for the *New York Times Book Review* and teaches at Columbia University. She served as the guest editor of *Best American Essays 2017*.

> **Much like personal essays, tattoos invite us to participate in their meaning and interpret them for ourselves.**

MY TATTOO kept getting delayed by other people's weddings: a bachelorette party in Vegas, cliff-top vows in Zion, a ceremony in Westchester. I wasn't just attending the ceremony in Westchester, I was officiating at the ceremony in Westchester. I couldn't picture giving my blessing in front of 200 people while my left arm glistened under Saran Wrap. I felt the slightest twinge of resentment. My life seemed perpetually tucked into the pockets of time created between the milestones of other lives.

I was getting the tattoo, in part, to mark a break from the man with whom I'd spent four years building and then dismantling a life. I was branding myself to mark a new era: my body was no longer entwined with someone else's. It was mine alone again. I was moving to a new city and I had a new book coming out, and the tattoo would be its epigraph: "I am human: nothing human is alien to me."

The quotation belongs to Terence, the Roman playwright. In the original Latin, it reads: homo sum: humani nil a me alienum puto. When I first came upon it, I felt its force beyond rational explanation. I knew it was something I needed to keep saying.

I got the job done by an artist who worked in a converted fire station. His walls were lined with giant beetles in jars of formaldehyde, taxidermied birds and bright oil paintings full of wizards and dragons. "Sure you don't want anything drawn?" he asked, gesturing to his art. I pictured a dragon with a thought bubble: "nothing human is alien to me . . ." I said I was fine with just words. He wrote them in a cursive line from elbow to wrist. "I'm going to do this so we miss your veins," he said. I said that sounded great.

It hurt just enough to make me feel like something was happening. There   5
was a sense of deserving—that I'd earned this by hurting for it. It was an old logic I hadn't felt in a while: Pain justifies ownership. It scared me, a bit. It also thrilled me. I left with Very Serious Aftercare Instructions and an arm encased like a pale sausage in plastic wrap.

The woman at the drugstore where I bought my Very Serious Aftercare supplies immediately wanted to know what the tattoo said. When I told her, she looked at me for a long time. "I think there is so much evil in this world," she said, "and so much good."

From now on, I realized, my body would basically be asking every stranger, "What do you think about the possibilities of human understanding?" During the months that followed, I found myself explaining the tattoo to a parade of strangers and acquaintances. It's about empathy and camaraderie, I would say. Or else, it's a denial of this lifelong obsession I've had with singularity and exceptionality.

We often think of tattoos as declarations of selfhood: this is what I am, love, believe. But there are other things we might inscribe on ourselves: what we fear, what we hate, what we hope to be but can't yet manage.

"I am human; nothing human is alien to me" — my tattoo wasn't true for me, not yet. But it was what I most needed to hear, an asymptote,[1] a horizon.

On a hot day near the end of summer, another drugstore clerk reached   10
for my arm with a searching look on his face.

He was a large man, imposing.

When I told him what the tattoo meant, he shook his head. "There are people going through things in this world that are really bad," he said. "Do you understand that?"

I tried to explain about aspiration, asymptote, attempt.

"You will leave a little piece of your self with everyone you imagine," he said. "You will get exhausted trying to give yourself away."

I didn't know what to say to this. I felt exhausted by *him*. I felt how much   15
I needed, from him and everyone, a certain kind of response: to feel inspired by the tat, and tell me so.

"You tried to give me something," he said, pointing at my arm. "But I blocked it. I blocked what you were giving me."

He was interrupting the ticktock rhythm of my righteousness, saying something about the easy aphorism on my arm: how it didn't go down easy for him and shouldn't go down easy for me, either.

He wasn't the only one with questions. My father wrote from the Rwanda Genocide Memorial: Did I really believe what my tattoo said, even about perpetrators of genocide? And on a first date, a man asked me whether my

---

1 *asymptote:* A technical term from mathematics that in a broad sense suggests anything that approaches something closely but never meets it. —Eds.

tattoo could even apply to evil? We never went out again. But there were other dates, other men wanting translations, running their fingers along the script. It started to feel uncomfortably like philosophy as accessory, something to match a certain kind of intellectual posture.

Before these men, there was a moment with the original man, the one from whom the tattoo marked my liberation. I ran into him on an ordinary afternoon, about a week after I got the tattoo and a week before I moved away from the city we shared. He was surprised to see my arm holding something it hadn't held before.

I realized how different things were now. Something could happen to my 20 body and it would be weeks or months before he knew about it. The tattoo was supposed to represent a new freedom but in that moment it felt like a shackle. It showed me how much it still hurt to feel the new distance between us. I felt that loss of proximity like a flesh wound.

It's like being pregnant, people would tell me. Your body is a conversation-starter. Eventually I started drawing the comparison myself. But the truth was it didn't feel like being pregnant at all. I was alone; my body was my own. It was a deep privacy, an autonomy tinged with sadness. It was the opposite of pregnancy, the residue of intimacy.

I'd always insisted I didn't get the tattoo so that people would talk to me about it. In fact, I told myself I wanted nothing less. But at a certain point I've had to admit to a desire for contact I couldn't own at first: It's there and it isn't.

The script is full of vectors pointing in opposite directions, a statement both aspirational and self-scolding, a desire to be seen and a desire to be left alone; a desire to have my body admired and a desire for my body to need nothing but itself, to need no affirmation from anyone. The tattoo holds an idea and its refutation, a man and his absence, a vote of confidence from the world and—in that downtown drugstore, on that humid day in summer—something more like the opposite. ●

The Reader's Presence

1. What does Jamison gain by telling the story of getting her tattoo, rather than simply writing about the words themselves? Why do "other people" feature so prominently in her story? In what specific ways do they influence how she sees her tattoo? What does her tattoo mean to you?

2. One of the clerks tells Jamison, "I blocked what you were giving me" (paragraph 16). What do you think this means? What does this encounter suggest about the way tattoos are perceived in public? In your answer, consider the possible reasons the author chose to add "Maybe" to the title.

3. **CONNECTIONS:** Compare and contrast Jamison's text with Simon Tam's "Trademark Offense" (page 638). Consider the degree to which both Jamison's tattoo and Tam's band name are expressions of personal identity and also parts of a larger conversation. What do their experiences have in common? How do they address the problems arising when their messages are rejected or misinterpreted? To what degree are their messages distorted as a direct result of being purchased—as a tattoo or as a trademark—into public view?

Jon Kerstetter

TRIAGE

A veteran of three tours in Iraq, **JON KERSTETTER** served in the United States Army as a combat physician and flight surgeon. In "Triage," he examines the troubling choices doctors must make in times of war to preserve as many lives as possi- ble, even if that means allowing some soldiers who might otherwise be saved to go untreated. The process of triage, Kerstetter writes, "obli- gates doctors and medics, whose principal duty is to save lives, to perform tasks which share in the brutality and the ugliness of war." Originally published in *River Teeth*, "Triage" also appeared in *Best American Essays 2013.*

> Kerstetter examines the troubling choices doctors must make in times of war to preserve as many lives as possible, even if that means allowing some soldiers who might otherwise be saved to go untreated.

Kerstetter, who grew up in poverty on the Oneida Reservation in Wisconsin, has taught emergency medicine in Rwanda, Bosnia, Kosovo, and Honduras. He directed the Johns Hopkins residency in Emergency Medicine at the University of Pristina in Kosovo. In addition to his degree as a doctor of medicine, he holds an MS in business and an MFA in creative nonfiction. An injury and stroke sustained during his third tour led him to retire from both medicine and the military in 2009, and he now lives in Iowa City with his wife. His memoir, *Crossings: A Doctor-Soldier's Story*, was published in 2017.

OCTOBER 2003, BAGHDAD, IRAQ. Major General Jon Gallinetti, U.S. Marine Corps, chief of staff of CJTF7, the operational command unit of coalition forces in Iraq, accompanied me on late-night clinical rounds in a combat surgical hospital. We visited soldiers who were injured in multiple IED[1] attacks throughout Baghdad just hours earlier. I made this mental note: *Soldier died tonight. IED explosion. Held him. Prayed. Told his commander to stay focused.*

In the hospital, the numbers of wounded that survived the attacks created a backlog of patients who required immediate surgery. Surgeons, nurses, medics, and hospital staff moved from patient to patient at an exhausting pace. When one surgery was finished, another began immediately. Several operating rooms were used simultaneously. Medical techs shuttled post-op patients from surgery to the second-floor ICU[2], where the numbers of beds quickly became inadequate. Nurses adjusted their care plans to accommodate

---

1 **IED:** Improvised explosive device, often a roadside bomb. —EDS.
2 **ICU:** Intensive care unit. —EDS.

the rapid influx. A few less critical patient beds lined the halls just outside the ICU.

The general wanted to visit the hospital to encourage the patients and the medical staff. We made a one-mile trip to the hospital compound late at night, unannounced, with none of the fanfare that usually accompanies a visit by a general officer in the military. After visiting the patients in the ICU, we walked down the hallway to the triage room.

One patient occupied the triage room: a young soldier, private first class. He had a ballistic head injury. His elbows flexed tightly in spastic tension, drawing his forearms to his chest; his hands made stonelike fists; his fingers coiled together as if grabbing an imaginary rope attached to his sternum. His breathing was slow and sporadic. He had no oxygen mask. An intravenous line fed a slow drip of saline and painkiller. He was what is known in military medicine as *expectant.*

Some of his fellow soldiers gathered at the foot of his bed. A few of   5
them had been injured in the same attack and had already been treated and bandaged in the emergency room. These fellow soldiers stood watch over the expectant patient. The general and I stood watch over them. One soldier had a white fractal of body salt edging the collar of his uniform. One wept. One prayed. Another quietly said "Jesus" over and over and kept shaking his head from side to side. And another had no expression at all: he simply stared a blank stare into the empty space above the expectant patient's head. A young sergeant, hands shaking, stammered as he tried to explain what had happened. The captain in charge of the expectant soldier's unit told the general and me that this was their first soldier to be killed—then he corrected himself and said this was the first soldier in their unit to be assigned to triage. He told us that the soldier was a good soldier. The general nodded in agreement and the room was suddenly quiet.

The general laid his hand on the expectant soldier's leg—the leg whose strength I imagined was drifting like a shape-shifting cloud moving against a dark umber sky—strength retreating into a time before it carried a soldier. And I watched the drifting of a man back into the womb of his mother, toward a time when a leg was not a leg, a body not a body, toward a time when a soldier was only the laughing between two young lovers—a man and a woman who could never imagine that a leg-body-man-soldier would one day lie expectant and that that soldier would be their son.

As I watched the soldiers at the foot of the bed, I noted their sanded faces, their trembling mouths, their hollow-stare eyes. I watched them watch the shallow breathing and the intermittent spasm of seizured limbs and the pale gray color of expectant skin. I took clinical notes in my mind. I noted the soldiers—noted the patient. I noted all the things that needed to be noted: the size of the triage room, the frame of the bed, the tiles of the ceiling, and the dullness of the overhead light. I noted the taut draw of the white linen sheets and the shiny polished metal of the hospital fixtures. A single ceiling fan rotated slowly. The walls were off-white. There were no windows. The floor was spotless, the smell antiseptic. A drab-green wool army blanket covered each bed. Three beds lay empty. I noted the absence of noise and chaos, the absence of nurses rushing to prepare surgical instruments, and the absence of teams of doctors urgently exploring wounds and calling out orders. There was an absence of the hurried sounds and the hustle of soldiers in the combat emergency room one floor down. Nobody yelled "medic" or "doc." Nobody called for the chaplain. Medics did not cut off clothing or gather dressings. Ambulances and medevac helicopters did not arrive with bleeding soldiers.

The *American Heritage Dictionary* defines *triage* as "a process for sorting injured people into groups based on their need for or likely benefit from immediate medical treatment. Triage is used in hospital emergency rooms, on battlefields, and at disaster sites when limited medical resources must be allocated." All dictionary definitions refer to the origin of the word *triage* as deriving from the French verb *trier,* to sort. The essence of the meaning is in the sorting. In the context of battle, a soldier placed in a triage room as *expectant* has been literally sorted from a group of other injured soldiers whose probability of survival was deduced by a sort of battlefield calculus implemented by a medical officer or a triage officer. The sorting occurs rather quickly—usually with minimal, if any, deliberation.

A military physician trains for triage situations. I trained to make combat medical decisions based on the developing battlefield situation and limited medical resources. I read about triage. I role-played it in combat exercises. When I first learned about the role of triage in combat, I reasoned, *Of course, triage is necessary. It's part of war. You do it as part of the job of a medical officer.*

More than twenty years ago, when I was a newly minted captain, 10 I attended the two-week Combat Casualty Care Course at Camp Bullis, Texas. The course was designed to teach medical officers combat trauma care and field triage techniques. The capstone exercise included a half-day mass casualty scenario complete with percussion grenades, smoke bombs, and simulated enemy forces closing on the casualty collection point. The objective was to give medical officers a realistic setting in which to perform triage decisions and to initiate medevac protocols according to standard operating procedures. About twenty moulaged[3] patients mimicked battlefield casualties ranging from the minimally injured to those requiring immediate surgery. Each medical officer in training was given five minutes to perform the triage exercise and to prepare an appropriate medevac request. Providing treatment was not an option: the exercise focused exclusively on making triage decisions.

All the participants could have easily completed the role-play within the time limit. Nothing, of course, is that straightforward in army training. There is always some built-in element of surprise to test how well trainees cope with chaos. In this case, the element of the "unexpected" was a simulated psychiatric patient who was brandishing an M16 rifle and holding a medic hostage while threatening to commit suicide. In order to maintain the element of surprise, the doctors who had finished their turn were whisked out

---

3 ***moulaged:*** Patients with mock injuries used for training purposes. —EDS.

the back of the triage tent, not to be seen again until the after-action review some hours later.

My turn. I entered the tent at the shove of my evaluator. The mock psych patient was screaming and threatening to kill a nearby medic. Other medics were pleading with the disturbed patient to lay his weapon down and let the wounded get on a helicopter. I was to take charge and get control. I did. I approached the screaming patient with quick, confident steps. I got about halfway through the triage tent when he pointed his rifle directly at his hostage medic and yelled, "One more step and the medic is dead." I backed off slowly, turned sideways, and quietly pulled my pistol. In an abrupt and instantaneous movement, I reeled around and shot the psych patient with my blank ammunition. "Bang—you're dead!" I yelled. A nearby evaluator took his weapon and made him play dead. One out-of-control psycho eliminated. I finished the triage exercise within the five-minute time limit. My evaluator laughed. "Damn," he said.

I felt great. I had control.

In the after-action review, I was asked about my decision to shoot. "Time," I answered. "I only had five minutes, so I maximized my effectiveness by eliminating a threat. It's combat," I argued.

One fellow doc asked if I would really shoot a patient in combat. A debate   15 ensued as to the ethics of my decision. Nobody else had shot the psych case. Nobody else finished the exercise in the allotted time. Some trainees had considered shooting the crazed soldier but had failed to act. Some managed to talk the psych patient into giving up his weapon. Those physicians had taken nearly fifteen minutes to complete the exercise—minutes in which some of the simulated patients died a simulated death. In the end, it was decided that my decision to shoot, while potentially serving a greater need, may have been a bit aggressive, but that it was in fact *my* decision, and my decision met the needs of the mission. All ethical considerations aside, I felt that I understood the necessity and the theory of triage. I understood it as part of my job.

Military triage classifications are based on NATO[4] guidelines and are published in numerous websites and Department of Defense publications. The triage categories in the third edition of *Emergency War Surgery*, the Department of Defense bible of military medicine, are listed below:

> **Immediate:** This group includes those soldiers requiring lifesaving surgery. The surgical procedures in this category should not be time consuming and should concern only those patients with high chances of survival.
> **Delayed:** This group includes those wounded who are badly in need of time-consuming surgery but whose general condition permits delay in surgical treatment without unduly endangering life. Sustaining treatment will be required.
> **Minimal:** These casualties have relatively minor injuries . . . and can effectively care for themselves or can be helped by nonmedical personnel.

---

[4] **NATO:** North Atlantic Treaty Organization, an alliance of North American and European nations formed in 1949 for mutual defense. —EDS.

> **Expectant:** Casualties in this category have wounds that are so extensive that even if they were the sole casualty and had the benefit of optimal medical resource application, their survival would be unlikely. The expectant casualty should not be abandoned, but should be separated from the view of other casualties. . . . Using a minimal but competent staff, provide comfort measures for these casualties.

The text of *Emergency War Surgery* further notes, "The decision to withhold care from a wounded soldier, who in another less overwhelming situation might be salvaged, is difficult for any surgeon or medic. Decisions of this nature are infrequent, even in mass casualty situations. Nonetheless, this is the essence of military triage." Triage requires assigning patients to those various categories based upon a rather quick and semi-objective assessment of a patient's injuries. If the triage officer calculates that a patient falls into the *expectant* category, treatment is withheld in order to allow medical teams to concentrate more efficiently on those soldiers with potentially survivable injuries. Preserving the fighting force is the central tenet of the process.

I have read and reread the official triage definition. I suppose I might have used it in a classroom of medics that I instructed. I am intimately familiar with the words that describe each category and with the professional commentary about the mechanics and ethics of sorting injured patients, yet I repeatedly come back to those words that try to clarify exactly what might be involved in the process of triage. I find the words weak and innocuous. They undercut the gravity and scope of a real-time triage experience. Here's the rub: the official commentary about the decision process focuses on the essence of triage as being the *difficulty* of making that decision. The difficulty is a given, but I think there is more. I think the essence of military triage is the *necessity* of making the decision when the combat situation demands it. It is the necessity of triage that requires medical staff to assign expectant soldiers to their death in order to provide an accommodation to a calculated greater good—a cause measured by the number of combat survivors. It is an accommodation that has not changed since the trench warfare of World War I.

Modern military medicine provides battlefield casualties with more sophisticated treatment and much faster aeromedical evacuation than in prior wars, but the process of triage remains essentially raw and unrefined as a standard combat operating procedure. Combat physicians encounter an overwhelming number or complexity of casualties. They make a rapid medical assessment, render a decision based on incomplete information, assign a triage category, and move to the next patient. Done. If they are particularly adept, they can triage several critical patients simultaneously.

Saving lives is the endpoint of all triage. Let one life go, save three others, or five, or maybe ten. The ratios don't matter, the benefits do. And a benefit in war always comes at a cost. On the surface, of course, the ultimate cost of a triage decision is a soldier's life. One decision, one life; perhaps one decision, several lives. But there are other costs not so easily calculated, like the   20 emotional cost to survivors or the psychological cost to soldiers who make triage decisions. Textbook definitions are silent on how military physicians prepare for, or react to, the demands of making a triage decision. No chapter in a military textbook instructs combat physicians in the multidimensional complexity of decision making that serves to deny lifesaving interventions for soldiers. There are chapters on why triage decisions must be made and chapters on how to apply established medical criteria in making those decisions. But what to do next, after the triage decision has been made — not covered. And that vacuum of knowledge leads to a feeling of exposure and vulnerability, both of which cannot be tolerated in war.

The act of triage is subsumed under the assigned duties of medics and physicians. I am not suggesting that the process fall to someone else or that the criteria used to make triage decisions should be discarded for a different process. I know of no other way of quickly sorting and categorizing patients when the critical nature of combat demands that it be done. I am, however, declaring that the practice of triage obligates doctors and medics, whose principal duty is the saving of lives, to perform tasks which share in the brutality and the ugliness of war — tasks that are tantamount to pulling a trigger on fellow soldiers.

In the final analysis, the decision to withhold medical care is not a decision that can be practiced, and rehearsed, and fully prepared for, outside of the realm of combat. How could that ever be accomplished with any modicum of reality? Could a medical officer simply say, as I did in training, "Bang, you're dead" or "Put the black tag on this one," and with that feel the same gut-ripping tension that combat evokes? No, the reality of triage tends to hit more like the force of a bomb blast. In an instant, fragments of stone and metal explode through the air with such velocity that when they hit a human target, even if the target is not killed, it is stunned and bleeding and breathless. It is that environment in which a military doctor or medic makes a live-fire triage decision and then must stand against the ballistic force of its consequences.

Somewhere in the process of making notes about the expectant patient, I paused and moved toward the middle of the bed. I put my hand on the patient's l.he general had done. I laid it there, let it linger. From where I stood, I stared directly into the expectant soldier's face. I watched his agonal breathing,[5] a long sighed breath followed by an absence of movement, and that followed by three to four shallow breaths. I matched his breathing with my own breathing. I timed the slowing pattern with my watch. I made some mental calculations, then looked away. Once again I noted the quiet of the room and the whiteness of the walls. I noted the empty beds, and the ceiling, and the antiseptic smell. Again I watched the expectant soldier, who was oblivious to all of my watching.

---

[5] **agonal breathing:** Medical term for gasping or labored breathing that could indicate someone's final moments. —EDS.

I stood at the triage bedside thinking if this were my son, I would want soldiers to gather in his room—listen to his breathing. I would want them to break stride from their war routines, perhaps to weep, perhaps to pray. And if he called out for his dad, I would want them to become a father to a son. Simply that: nothing more, nothing less—procedures not in Department of Defense manuals or war theory classes or triage exercises.

I moved to the head of the bed, placed my right hand on the chest of the   25 patient. And my hand rested there with barely any movement. I turned to the other soldiers, gave them an acknowledgment with a slight upturned purse of my lips, then looked away. I lifted my hand to the patient's right shoulder and let my weight shift as if trying to gently hold him in place. I half kneeled, half bent—closed the distance between our bodies. I noted the weave of the fabric in his skullcap dressing and the faint show of blood that tainted its white cotton edges. I lingered. I prayed for God to take him in that very instant. I whispered, so only he could hear, "You're a good soldier. You're finished here. It's okay to go home now." I waited. I watched. I saw the faces of my own sons in his: was glad they were not soldiers.

I finished, stood up, and walked to the foot of the bed. One of the soldiers asked me if there wasn't something I could do. I said no. I meant no. I wanted my answer to be yes. I faced the captain and put my hand on his shoulder, told him that we were finished, that his soldier did not feel pain, that he would be gone soon, and that everybody had done everything they could. The tone of my voice was neither comforting nor encouraging, neither sorrowful nor hopeful. It was, as I remember, military and professional.

I think about that expectant soldier so often. I know I would have seen his name in his hospital chart or been told his name by his commander. I did not take the time to write it down anywhere, and that bothers me. It bothers me because years later he remains nameless—just like so many other soldier-patients I encountered—and I think I equate that namelessness with a form of abandonment for which I feel personally responsible. I do understand, in a professional sense, that the patient was not abandoned, that his triage was purposeful, and that it allowed an ascent to medical efficiency which, in the end, saved other soldiers' lives. But I also understand that the theoretical basis of triage quickly erodes when confronted with the raw, emotional, human act of sorting through wounded patients and assigning triage categories. In my mind, the theoretical and the practical wage a constant battle, so that whenever I participate in a triage decision, part of me says *yes*, and part of me says *no*.

I sometimes find myself wanting to speak with the expectant soldier's mother and father. I want to tell them that their son did not die alone in a triage bed—that he was not simply abandoned or left as hopeless in a secluded corner room of a distant combat hospital. I want to assure them that he died in the company of men who stood watch over him as if guarding an entire battalion and that we tried to give everything we could give—that we tried to be more than soldiers or generals or doctors.

When I tell the story of this particular soldier to my medical colleagues, I always mention that triage is a necessary part of war. I tell them it's a matter of compassionate medical necessity and the entrenched reality of combat—that it's the exercise of a soldier's final duty.

Occasionally, though, I think about telling them how I wished I could have done something, anything. But then I realize I cannot tell them that, because in fact I did do something, and I am left with the nameless face of an expectant soldier and countless sheets of history filled with decisions made by doctors at war. I am left with my own understanding that we who are soldiers are all triaged.

I want to remember the expectant soldier as a person with a name, but I have come to accept that I cannot. I remember instead the triage room. I recall the general who placed his hand on a young man. And I see the drifting once again—the fading of a soldier back into the womb from which he was born into life. I see him loved. He is a soldier. Wounded. Triaged. Expectant. ●

The Reader's Presence

1. Jon Kerstetter's essay recounts the process and consequences of observation on matters of life and death on the front lines of combat. He details how military physicians carefully "read" their patients' wounds to determine whether they will receive medical attention or die. In the opening paragraph, Kerstetter mentions having made a note about the death of a soldier. What impact does this fact have on your reading as the essay proceeds? Be as specific as possible in your response to this telling moment. For example, how does this notation compare and contrast to the scene when he shouts "Bang—you're dead" when eliminating the "out-of-control psycho" (paragraph 12)? Kerstetter builds momentum in his narrative by focusing on telling details. Choose a scene and explain how attending to detail generates a gravitational force propelling the essay forward.

2. "Triage" is also an essay about the "art" of war. What specific strategies does Kerstetter use as a writer to accelerate and intensify the pace of his prose? Point to—and analyze—specific examples. His essay is also an exercise in definition. In what specific ways does Kerstetter use this writing strategy to raise larger ethical issues? What distinctions, for example, does he imply between "difficulty" and "necessity" (paragraph 18)? What are the consequences of this distinction? How does he complicate the meaning of "battle" as the essay unfolds? How would you characterize the tone he uses? To what extent does it remain consistent? Comment on the final paragraph. In what specific ways does it address the issues and questions Kerstetter posed through the essay?

3. **CONNECTIONS:** "Triage" provides an excellent opportunity to identify and explore the thematic and compositional similarities in several essays. See, for example, Christopher Hitchens's "Believe Me, It's Torture" (page 531) and Steven Pinker's "Violence Vanquished" (page 591), as well as Virginia Woolf's "The Death of a Moth" (page 499). Identify—and characterize—the similarities and differences in their approaches to talking about violence and death. Which writer do you believe is more artfully engaging when talking about violence and death? Explain the basis for your judgment and identify specific evidence to support your conclusion.

Stephen King

Everything You Need to Know About Writing Successfully — In Ten Minutes

STEPHEN KING was born in 1947 in Portland, Maine. He began writing stories early in his life, but it was his discovery of a box of horror and science fiction novels in the attic of his aunt's house that made him decide to pursue a career as a writer. He published his first short stories in pulp horror magazines while in high school. After graduating from the University of Maine at Orono in 1970, King, while working at a low-paying job in a laundry, began writing his first novel, *Carrie* (1974). *Carrie* was followed by some fifty more novels, including a series written under the pen name Richard Bachman, as well as numerous novellas, short story collections, and screenplays. His critically acclaimed work of nonfiction, *On Writing* (2000), the source of the following essay, was completed while he was recovering painfully from a much-publicized accident.

> Stephen King's discovery of horror and science fiction novels in his aunt's attic prompted him to pursue a writing career.

Stephen King has commented that, as a creative writer, he always hopes for "that element of inspiration which lifts you past the point where the characters are just you, where you do achieve something transcendental and the people are really people in the story."

I. THE FIRST INTRODUCTION

THAT'S RIGHT. I know it sounds like an ad for some sleazy writers' school, but I really am going to tell you everything you need to pursue a successful and financially rewarding career writing fiction, and I really am going to do it in ten minutes, which is exactly how long it took me to learn. It will actually take you twenty minutes or so to read this article, however, because I have to tell you a story, and then I have to write a second introduction. But these, I argue, should not count in the ten minutes.

II. THE STORY, OR, HOW STEPHEN KING LEARNED TO WRITE

When I was a sophomore in high school, I did a sophomoric thing which got me in a pot of fairly hot water, as sophomoric didoes often do. I wrote and published a small satiric newspaper called *The Village Vomit*. In this little paper I lampooned a number of teachers at Lisbon (Maine) High School, where I was under instruction. These were not very gentle lampoons; they ranged from the scatological to the downright cruel.

Eventually, a copy of this paper found its way into the hands of a faculty member, and since I had been unwise enough to put my name on it (a fault, some critics would argue, of which I have still not been entirely cured). I was brought into the office. The sophisticated satirist had by that time reverted to what he really was: a fourteen-year-old kid who was shaking in his boots and wondering if he was going to get a suspension . . . what we called a "three-day vacation" in those dim days of 1964.

I wasn't suspended. I was forced to make a number of apologies—they were warranted, but they tasted like dog-dirt in my mouth—and spent a week in detention hall. And the guidance counselor arranged what he no doubt thought of as a more constructive channel for my talents. This was a job—contingent upon the editor's approval—writing sports for the Lisbon Enterprise, a twelve-page weekly of the sort with which any small-town resident will be familiar. This editor was the man who taught me everything I know about writing in ten minutes. His name was John Gould—not the famed New England humorist or the novelist who wrote *The Greenleaf Fires*, but a relative of both, I believe.

He told me he needed a sports writer, and we could "try each other out,"   5
if I wanted.

I told him I knew more about advanced algebra than I did sports.

Gould nodded and said, "You'll learn."

I said I would at least try to learn. Gould gave me a huge roll of yellow paper and promised me a wage of 1/2 ¢ per word. The first two pieces I wrote had to do with a high school basketball game in which a member of my school team broke the Lisbon High scoring record. One of these pieces was a straight piece of reportage. The second was a feature article.

I brought them to Gould the day after the game, so he'd have them for the paper, which came out Fridays. He read the straight piece, made two minor corrections, and spiked it. Then he started in on the feature piece with a large black pen and taught me all I ever needed to know about my craft. I wish I still had the piece,—it deserves to be framed, editorial corrections and all—but I can remember pretty well how it went and how it looked when he had finished with it. Here's an example:

> Last night, in the ~~well-loved~~ gymnasium of Lisbon   10
> High School, partisans and Jay Hills fans alike were
> stunned by an athletic performance unequalled in
> school history: Bob Ransom, ~~known as Bullet Bob~~
> ~~for both his size and accuracy,~~ scored thirty-seven
> points. Yes, you heard me right. ~~Plus~~ he did it with
> grace, and speed ... and with an odd courtesy as
> well, committing only two personal fouls in his
> ~~knight-like~~ quest for a record which has eluded Lis-
> bon ~~thinclad~~ since ~~the years of Korea~~ . .
>   players   1953

When Gould finished marking up my copy in the manner I have indicated above, he looked up and must have seen something on my face. I think he must have thought it was horror, but it was not: It was revelation.

"I only took out the bad parts, you know," he said. "Most of it's pretty good."

"I know," I said, meaning both things; yes, most of it was good, and yes, he had only taken out the bad parts. "I won't do it again."

"If that's true," he said, "you'll never have to work again. You can do this for a living."

Then he threw back his head and laughed.

And he was right: I am doing this for a living, and as long as I can keep   15
on, I don't expect ever to have to work again.

III. THE SECOND INTRODUCTION

All of what follows has been said before. If you are interested enough in writing to be a purchaser of this magazine [*Writer*], you will have either heard or read all (or almost all) of it before. Thousands of writing courses are taught across the United States each year; seminars are convened; guest lecturers talk, then answer questions, and it all boils down to what follows.

I am going to tell you these things again because often people will only listen—really listen—to someone who makes a lot of money doing the thing he's talking about. This is sad but true. And I told you the story above not to make myself sound like a character out of a Horatio Alger novel but to make a point: I saw, I listened, and I learned. Until that day in John Gould's little office, I had been writing first drafts of stories that might run 2,500 words. The second drafts were apt to run 3,300 words. Following that day, my 2,500-word first drafts became 2,200-word second drafts. And two years after that, I sold the first one.

So here it is, with all the bark stripped off. It'll take ten minutes to read, and you can apply it right away . . . if you listen.

IV. EVERYTHING YOU NEED TO KNOW ABOUT WRITING SUCCESSFULLY

1. Be talented

This, of course, is the killer. What is talent? I can hear someone shouting, and here we are, ready to get into a discussion right up there with "What is the meaning of life?" for weighty pronouncements and total uselessness. For the purposes of the beginning writer, talent may as well be defined as eventual success—publication and money. If you wrote something for which someone sent you a check, if you cashed the check and it didn't bounce, and if you then paid the light bill with the money, I consider you talented.

Now some of you are really hollering. Some of you are calling me one   20
crass money-fixated creep. Nonsense. Worse than nonsense, off the subject.

We're not talking about good or bad here. I'm interested in telling you how to get your stuff published, not in critical judgments of who's good or bad. As a rule, the critical judgments come after the check's been spent, anyway. I have my own opinions, but most times I keep them to myself. People who are published steadily and are paid for what they are writing may be either saints or trollops, but they are clearly reaching a great many someones who want what they have. Ergo, they are communicating. Ergo, they are talented. The biggest part of writing successfully is being talented, and in the context of marketing, the only bad writer is one who doesn't get paid. If you're not talented, you won't succeed. And if you're not succeeding, you should know when to quit.

When is that? I don't know. It's different for each writer. Not after six rejection slips, certainly, nor after sixty. But after six hundred? Maybe. After six thousand? My friend, after six thousand pinks, it's time you tried painting or computer programming.

Further, almost every aspiring writer knows when he is getting warmer — you start getting little jotted notes on your rejection slips, or personal letters . . . maybe a commiserating phone call. It's lonely out there in the cold, but there are encouraging voices . . . unless there is nothing in your words that warrants encouragement. I think you owe it to yourself to skip as much of the self-illusion as possible. If your eyes are open, you'll know which way to go . . . or when to turn back.

2. Be neat

Type. Double-space. Use a nice heavy white paper. If you've marked your manuscript a lot, do another draft.

3. Be self-critical

If you haven't marked up your manuscript a lot, you did a lazy job. Only God gets things right the first time. Don't be a slob.

4. Remove every extraneous word

You want to get up on a soapbox and preach? Fine. Get one, and try your local park. You want to write for money? Get to the point. And if you remove the excess garbage and discover you can't find the point, tear up what you wrote and start all over again . . . or try something new.

5. Never look at a reference book while doing a first draft

You want to write a story? Fine. Put away your dictionary, your encyclopedias, your *World Almanac*, and your thesaurus. Better yet, throw your thesaurus into the wastebasket. The only things creepier than a thesaurus are those little paperbacks college students too lazy to read the assigned novels buy around exam time. Any word you have to hunt for in a thesaurus is the wrong word. There are no exceptions to this rule. You think you might have misspelled a word? O.K., so here is your choice: Either look it up in the dictionary, thereby making sure you have it right — and breaking your train of thought and the writer's trance in the bargain—or just spell it phonetically and correct it later. Why not? Did you think it was going to go somewhere? And if you need to know the largest city in Brazil and you find you don't have it in your head, why not write in Miami, or Cleveland? You can check it . . . but later. When you sit down to write, write. Don't do anything else except go to the bathroom, and only do that if it absolutely cannot be put off.

6. Know the markets

Only a dimwit would send a story about giant vampire bats surrounding a high school to *McCall's*. Only a dimwit would send a tender story about a mother and daughter making up their differences on Christmas Eve to *Playboy* . . . but people do it all the time. I'm not exaggerating; I have seen such stories in the slush piles of the actual magazines. If you write a good story, why send it out in an ignorant fashion? Would you send your kid out in a snowstorm dressed in Bermuda shorts and a tank top? If you like science fiction, read science fiction novels and magazines. If you want to write mysteries, read the magazines. And so on. It isn't just a matter of knowing what's right for the present story; you can begin to catch on, after a while, to overall rhythms, editorial likes and dislikes, a magazine's slant. Sometimes your reading can influence the next story, and create a sale.

7. Write to entertain

Does this mean you can't write "serious fiction"? It does not. Somewhere along the line pernicious critics have invested the American reading and writing public with the idea that entertaining fiction and serious ideas do not overlap. This would have surprised Charles Dickens, not to mention Jane Austen, John Steinbeck, William Faulkner, Bernard Malamud, and hundreds of others. But your serious ideas must always serve your story, not the other way around. I repeat: If you want to preach, get a soapbox.

8. Ask yourself frequently, "Am I having fun?"

The answer needn't always be yes. But if it's always no, it's time for a new project or a new career.

9. How to evaluate criticism

Show your piece to a number of people—ten, let us say. Listen carefully to what they tell you. Smile and nod a lot. Then review what was said very carefully. If your critics are all telling you the same thing about some facet of your story—a plot twist that doesn't work, a character who rings false, stilted narrative, or half a dozen other possibles—change it. It doesn't matter if you really like that twist or that character; if a lot of people are telling you something is wrong with your piece, it is. If seven or eight of them are hitting on that same thing, I'd still suggest changing it. But if everyone—or even most everyone—is criticizing something different, you can safely disregard what all of them say. 30

10. Observe all rules for proper submission

Return postage, self-addressed envelope, etc.

11. An agent? Forget it. For now.

Agents get 10 percent to 15 percent of monies earned by their clients. Fifteen percent of nothing is nothing. Agents also have to pay the rent. Beginning writers do not contribute to that or any other necessity of life. Flog your stories around yourself. If you've done a novel, send around query letters to publishers, one by one, and follow up with sample chapters and/or the complete manuscript. And remember Stephen King's First Rule of Writers and Agent, learned by bitter personal experience: You don't need one until you're making enough for someone to steal . . . and if you're making that much, you'll be able to take your pick of good agents.

12. If it's bad, kill it

When it comes to people, mercy killing is against the law. When it comes to fiction, it is the law.

That's everything you need to know. And if you listened, you can write everything and anything you want. Now I believe I will wish you a pleasant day and sign off.

My ten minutes are up. ●   35

The Reader's Presence

1. Why does King include sections I through III, even though they are not part of the "ten minutes"? What does the first introduction actually introduce? the second? How effectively does section II work with section IV? For example, how many rules did King learn when John Gould edited his story? Which rules does he break in his own essay? Why do you think he breaks them?

2. King is best known for writing horror novels, stories that scare people. What fears does he play on throughout this essay? How does he go about setting up suspenseful situations? What does he do to frighten people in this essay? If the rules are monsters, which ones do you think are the most frightening? Why?

3. By King's definition, a talented author is one who has been paid for his or her writing. Pick an author in this collection whom you consider talented and evaluate him or her according to King's rules. How successful should this writer be according to King? What other rules of success does the writer's essay suggest should be added to King's list?

4. **CONNECTIONS:** King's essay represents an approach to an ongoing debate between money and art. Signaled by terms like *practicality* and *popularity*, the money side holds that you should write to make money. Signaled by phrases like "art for art's sake" or "selling out," the art side holds that you should write to please yourself. George Orwell in "George Orwell on the Four Reasons for Writing" (page 195) represents another approach to this debate when he lists "four great motives for

writing" (paragraph 1). Read Orwell's essay and determine how well each motive would lead to the kind of successful writing that King imagines. For example, how well—or how poorly—does Orwell's desire to "share an experience which one feels is valuable" (paragraph 3) lead to King's "eventual success—publication and money" (paragraph 19)?

Naomi Klein

THE CHANGE WITHIN

The products of human industry can have far-reaching consequences for life on earth. Most of us are aware of climate change in one way or another: we recycle, buy hybrid cars, or ride bikes to reduce our carbon "footprint." Or perhaps we prefer not to think about the environment at all. In "The Change Within," Canadian author and activist **NAOMI KLEIN** (b. 1970) reflects on the ways in which human society is specifically *not* equipped to handle this global issue unless we make significant changes. "If the ideas that rule our culture are stopping us from saving ourselves," she writes, "then it is within our power to change those ideas."

> "If the ideas that rule our culture are stopping us from saving ourselves, then it is within our power to change those ideas."

Originally published by the *Nation*, Klein's essay discusses some of the ideas found in her book *This Changes Everything: Capitalism vs. The Climate* (2014), a *New York Times* bestseller. Her other titles, *No Is Not Enough* (2017), *The Shock Doctrine: The Rise of Disaster Capitalism* (2007), and *No Logo* (2000), were both international bestsellers. She has published articles in the *New Yorker* and *Harper's Magazine*, and her work has been featured in several documentaries.

THIS IS A STORY ABOUT BAD TIMING. One of the most disturbing ways that climate change is already playing out is through what ecologists call "mismatch" or "mistiming." This is the process whereby warming causes animals to fall out of step with a critical food source, particularly at breeding times, when a failure to find enough food can lead to rapid population losses.

The migration patterns of many songbird species, for instance, have evolved over millennia so that eggs hatch precisely when food sources such as caterpillars are at their most abundant, providing parents with ample nourishment for their hungry young. But because spring now often arrives early, the caterpillars are hatching earlier too, which means that in some areas they are less plentiful when the chicks hatch, threatening a number of health and fertility impacts. Similarly, in West Greenland, caribou are arriving at their calving grounds only to find themselves out of sync with the forage plants they have relied on for thousands of years, now growing earlier thanks to rising temperatures. That is leaving female caribou with less energy for lactation, reproduction and feeding their young, a mismatch that has been linked to sharp decreases in calf births and survival rates.

Scientists are studying cases of climate-related mistiming among dozens of species, from Arctic terns to pied flycatchers. But there is one important species they are missing — us. *Homo sapiens.* We too are suffering from a terrible case of climate-related mistiming, albeit in a cultural-historical, rather than a biological, sense. Our problem is that the climate crisis hatched in our laps at a moment in history when political and social conditions were uniquely hostile to a problem of this nature and magnitude — that moment being the tail end of the go-go '80s, the blastoff point for the crusade to spread deregulated capitalism around the world. Climate change is a collective problem demanding collective action the likes of which humanity has never actually accomplished. Yet it entered mainstream consciousness in the midst of an ideological war being waged on the very idea of the collective sphere.

This deeply unfortunate mistiming has created all sorts of barriers to our ability to respond effectively to this crisis. It has meant that corporate power was ascendant at the very moment when we needed to exert unprecedented controls over corporate behavior in order to protect life on earth. It has meant that regulation was a dirty word just when we needed those powers most. It has meant that we are ruled by a class of politicians who know only how to dismantle and starve public institutions, just when they most need to be fortified and reimagined. And it has meant that we are saddled with an apparatus of "free trade" deals that tie the hands of policy-makers just when they need maximum flexibility to achieve a massive energy transition.

Confronting these various structural barriers to the next economy is the critical work of any serious climate movement. But it's not the only task at hand. We also have to confront how the mismatch between climate change and market domination has created barriers within our very selves, making it harder to look at this most pressing of humanitarian crises with anything more than furtive, terrified glances. Because of the way our daily lives have been altered by both market and technological triumphalism, we lack many of the observational tools necessary to convince ourselves that climate change is real — let alone the confidence to believe that a different way of living is possible.

And little wonder: just when we needed to gather, our public sphere was disintegrating; just when we needed to consume less, consumerism took over virtually every aspect of our lives; just when we needed to slow down and notice, we sped up; and just when we needed longer time horizons, we were able to see only the immediate present.

This is our climate change mismatch, and it affects not just our species, but potentially every other species on the planet as well.

The good news is that, unlike reindeer and songbirds, we humans are blessed with the capacity for advanced reasoning and therefore the ability to adapt more deliberately—to change old patterns of behavior with remarkable speed. If the ideas that rule our culture are stopping us from saving ourselves, then it is within our power to change those ideas. But before that can happen, we first need to understand the nature of our personal climate mismatch.

• **Climate change demands that we consume less, but being consumers is all we know.** Climate change is not a problem that can be solved simply by changing what we buy—a hybrid instead of an SUV, some carbon offsets when we get on a plane. At its core, it is a crisis born of overconsumption by the comparatively wealthy, which means the world's most manic consumers are going to have to consume less.

The problem is not "human nature," as we are so often told. We weren't   10 born having to shop this much, and we have, in our recent past, been just as happy (in many cases happier) consuming far less. The problem is the inflated role that consumption has come to play in our particular era.

Late capitalism teaches us to create ourselves through our consumer choices: shopping is how we form our identities, find community and express ourselves. Thus, telling people that they can't shop as much as they want to because the planet's support systems are overburdened can be understood as a kind of attack, akin to telling them that they cannot truly be themselves. This is likely why, of the original "Three Rs"—reduce, reuse, recycle—only the third has ever gotten any traction, since it allows us to keep on shopping as long as we put the refuse in the right box. The other two, which require that we consume less, were pretty much dead on arrival.

• **Climate change is slow, and we are fast.** When you are racing through a rural landscape on a bullet train, it looks as if everything you are passing is standing still: people, tractors, cars on country roads. They aren't, of course. They are moving, but at a speed so slow compared with the train that they appear static.

So it is with climate change. Our culture, powered by fossil fuels, is that bullet train, hurtling forward toward the next quarterly report, the next election cycle, the next bit of diversion or piece of personal validation via our smartphones and tablets. Our changing climate is like the landscape out the window: from our racy vantage point, it can appear static, but it is moving, its slow progress measured in receding ice sheets, swelling waters and incremental temperature rises. If left unchecked, climate change will most certainly speed up enough to capture our fractured attention—island nations wiped off the map, and city-drowning superstorms, tend to do that. But by then, it may be too late for our actions to make a difference, because the era of tipping points will likely have begun.

• **Climate change is place-based, and we are everywhere at once.** The problem is not just that we are moving too quickly. It is also that the terrain on which the changes are taking place is intensely local: an early blooming of a particular flower, an unusually thin layer of ice on a lake, the late arrival of a migratory bird. Noticing those kinds of subtle changes requires an intimate connection to a specific ecosystem. That kind of communion happens only when we know a place deeply, not just as scenery but also as sustenance, and when local knowledge is passed on with a sense of sacred trust from one generation to the next.

But that is increasingly rare in the urbanized, industrialized world. We   15
tend to abandon our homes lightly—for a new job, a new school, a new love. And as we do so, we are severed from whatever knowledge of place we managed to accumulate at the previous stop, as well as from the knowledge amassed by our ancestors (who, at least in my case, migrated repeatedly themselves).

Even for those of us who manage to stay put, our daily existence can be disconnected from the physical places where we live. Shielded from the elements as we are in our climate-controlled homes, workplaces and cars, the changes unfolding in the natural world easily pass us by. We might have no idea that a historic drought is destroying the crops on the farms that surround our urban homes, since the supermarkets still display miniature mountains of imported produce, with more coming in by truck all day. It takes something huge—like a hurricane that passes all previous high-water marks, or a flood destroying thousands of homes—for us to notice that something is truly amiss. And even then we have trouble holding on to that knowledge for long, since we are quickly ushered along to the next crisis before these truths have a chance to sink in.

Climate change, meanwhile, is busily adding to the ranks of the rootless every day, as natural disasters, failed crops, starving livestock and climate-fueled ethnic conflicts force yet more people to leave their ancestral homes. And with every human migration, more crucial connections to specific places are lost, leaving yet fewer people to listen closely to the land.

• **Climate pollutants are invisible, and we have stopped believing in what we cannot see.** When BP's Macondo well ruptured in 2010, releasing torrents of oil into the Gulf of Mexico, one of the things we heard from company CEO Tony Hayward was that "the Gulf of Mexico is a very big ocean. The amount of volume of oil and dispersant we are putting into it is tiny in relation to the total water volume." The statement was widely ridiculed at the time, and rightly so, but Hayward was merely voicing one of our culture's most cherished beliefs: that what we can't see won't hurt us and, indeed, barely exists.

So much of our economy relies on the assumption that there is always an "away" into which we can throw our waste. There's the away where our garbage goes when it is taken from the curb, and the away where our waste goes when it is flushed down the drain. There's the away where the minerals and metals that make up our goods are extracted, and the away where those raw materials are turned into finished products. But the lesson of the BP spill, in the words of ecological theorist Timothy Morton, is that ours is "a world in which there is no 'away.'"

When I published *No Logo* a decade and a half ago, readers were 20 shocked to learn of the abusive conditions under which their clothing and gadgets were manufactured. But we have since learned to live with it—not to condone it, exactly, but to be in a state of constant forgetfulness. Ours is an economy of ghosts, of deliberate blindness.

Air is the ultimate unseen, and the greenhouse gases that warm it are our most elusive ghosts. Philosopher David Abram points out that for most of human history, it was precisely this unseen quality that gave the air its power and commanded our respect. "Called Sila, the wind-mind of the world, by the Inuit; Nilch'i, or Holy Wind, by the Navajo; Ruach, or rushing-spirit, by the ancient Hebrews," the atmosphere was "the most mysterious and sacred dimension of life." But in our time, "we rarely acknowledge the atmosphere as it swirls between two persons." Having forgotten the air, Abram writes, we have made it our sewer, "the perfect dump site for the unwanted by-products of our industries. . . . Even the most opaque, acrid smoke billowing out of the pipes will dissipate and disperse, always and ultimately dissolving into the invisible. It's gone. Out of sight, out of mind."

Another part of what makes climate change so very difficult for us to grasp is that ours is a culture of the perpetual present, one that deliberately severs itself from the past that created us as well as the future we are shaping with our actions. Climate change is about how what we did generations in the past will inescapably affect not just the present, but generations in the future. These time frames are a language that has become foreign to most of us.

This is not about passing individual judgment, nor about berating ourselves for our shallowness or rootlessness. Rather, it is about recognizing that we are products of an industrial project, one intimately, historically linked to fossil fuels.

And just as we have changed before, we can change again. After listening to the great farmer-poet Wendell Berry deliver a lecture on how we each have a duty to love our "homeplace" more than any other, I asked him if he had any advice for rootless people like me and my friends, who live in our computers and always seem to be shopping for home. "Stop somewhere," he replied. "And begin the thousand-year-long process of knowing that place."

That's good advice on lots of levels. Because in order to win this fight of 25 our lives, we all need a place to stand. ●

The Reader's Presence

1. Naomi Klein begins: "This is a story about bad timing." As you reread her essay, discuss the importance of time in her writing. How, more specifically, does our perception of time as humans make it difficult to respond to climate change? Point to—and analyze—specific examples to support your response. Klein portrays climate change as a social problem, demanding a collective effort to solve. What specific assertions and solutions does Klein offer, and which do you think are most logical and persuasive? Explain why. Which assertions and solutions do you find less convincing? Describe the kind of society that would respond effectively to climate change. Be specific.

2. Klein supports her analysis by drawing on figurative language—simile, metaphor, and analogy—to increase the accessibility of her points. Here's an example: "Our changing climate is like the landscape out the window: from our racy vantage point, it can appear static, but it is moving, its slow progress measured in receding ice sheets, swelling waters and incremental temperature rises" (paragraph 13). Analyze the effectiveness of this example, and characterize the overall effectiveness of using figurative language to make her points. For instance, Klein uses the word "just" numerous times in her essay. "Just" is often characterized as an "empty word," one with so many different, colloquial meanings that it finally lacks specific meaning. Identify the numerous instances of "just" in Klein's essay and comment on the relative effectiveness of each. What word do you suggest substituting for "just" in each instance? Explain why.

3. **CONNECTIONS:** Both Naomi Klein and Hope Jahren (see "Lab Girl," page 412) address the impact of climate change. Given the different scope of each essay, which do you find more engaging? Explain why by examining each essay in convincing detail.

MADDY PERELLO
Climate Change: A Serious Threat

Courtesy of Maddy Perello

Maddy Perello was a student at San Diego State University when she wrote the following column for the school newspaper, the *Daily Aztec*, in 2015. Although not an expert on the topic, she had done sufficient research to establish her claim that a major problem surrounding the topic of climate change is the serious lack of knowledge most people bring to the issue. When asked what inspired her to write the essay, she responded: "I started realizing that many people don't know about the climate change crisis, and if you don't understand it, can you really care?"

Human use of natural resources coal, oil and gas could melt all the ice on the planet in as little as 5,000 years, according to *National Geographic's* interactive "Rising Sea Levels" map.

Essay opens with an authoritative source

When that happens, San Diego, the Central Valley, and the entire Eastern Seaboard of the U.S. will be underwater, and the average global temperature will go from 58 to 80 degrees Fahrenheit. Luckily for us, it is doubtful that most species will survive that long, anyway. As a *National Geographic* article by Nadia Drake estimates, "As many as three-quarters of animal species could be extinct within several human lifetimes."

Quotes an authoritative article

We are facing constant threats of climate change all over the world. Human carbon dioxide emissions are contributing to ocean acidification, global warming, extreme weather, sea-level rise, species extinction and disease. That sentence alone should be enough to spur action toward change. Instead, climate change has fallen victim to political polarization and doubt.

Expresses her main point

A recent study by the Yale School of Forestry and Environmental Studies reports that 63 percent of Americans know that climate change is happening, but only 8 percent "have knowledge equivalent to an A or B, 40 percent would receive a C or D, and 52 percent would get an F" (Leiserowitz, et al. 3).

Cites a prestigious study

Everyone, but college students especially, should have an understanding of the problems we are going to inherit from older generations and pass on to younger ones.

The basics of climate change are as follows: The sun radiates heat to Earth, and Earth radiates heat back into outer space. Greenhouse gasses in the atmosphere trap some of that heat and it warms up the planet. This is known as the greenhouse effect and is largely natural and precisely balanced.

Summarizes the science of climate change

In fact, without the greenhouse effect, Earth would be too cold to sustain life. Fluctuations in this balance are also natural and have happened throughout the planet's 4.6-billion-year history (think ice ages and periods of extreme heat). Humans are disrupting the balance with excessive carbon dioxide emissions.

CO_2 accounts for 0.035 percent of Earth's atmosphere naturally. Between the constant burning of fossil fuels, agriculture and deforestation, humans emit seven gigatons of CO_2 per year (about the weight of 1 billion elephants), and have brought this number up to 0.04 percent, according to a Teacher's TV video.

It is estimated that the average temperature of the planet will be 2–6 degrees warmer by the end of the century. In all of the planet's recorded history, the temperature has never changed by more than 2 degrees in 100 years, so there is no doubt that humans are accelerating the global warming process.

Anthropogenic climate change has environmental, social and economic implications. It is a vast and multifaceted issue that will affect all life on the planet. This is the world that today's college students are graduating into.

August 13 was Overshoot Day—the day on which humans have used the amount of natural resources Earth can produce in 12 months—according to the World Wildlife Fund. That means we are using more than the planet can support and replenish.

There is a famous anonymous quote, "We do not inherit the Earth from our ancestors; we borrow it from our children."

Concludes with a famous quotation and returns to her main point.

People have an obligation to limit the damage done to the Earth because it provides every essential resource that humans and all other living things need to survive.

This is merely an overview of the huge, all-encompassing fields of environmental science and sustainability. Amongst many complex problems, one thing is clear: Something needs to change. Since less than half of the population of the U.S. is knowledgeable about climate change, education is step one.

Works Cited

Drake, Nadia. "Will Humans Survive the Sixth Great Extinction?" *National Geographic*, 23 June 2015, news.nationalgeographic. com/2015/06/150623-sixth-extinction-kolbert-animals-conservation-science-world.

Leiserowitz, Anthony, et al. *America's Knowledge of Climate Change. Yale Project on Climate Change Communication, Yale University*, 12 Oct. 2010, http://climatecommunication.yale.edu/wp-content/uploads/2016/02/2010_10_Americans%E2%80%99-Knowledge-of-Climate-Change.pdf.

"Teachers TV: Climate Change – the Causes." *YouTube*, 9 Dec. 2012. www.youtube.com/watch?v=RHrFBOUl6-8.

"What the World Would Look Like If All the Ice Melted." *National Geographic*, www.nationalgeographic.com/magazine/2013/09/rising-seas-ice-melt-new-shoreline-maps. Accessed 9 Sept. 2015.

Alan Lightman

OUR PLACE IN THE UNIVERSE

ALAN LIGHTMAN (b. 1948) is unique among American fiction writers in that he is also a respected physicist. In fact, he was the first professor ever to receive a joint appointment in the sciences and the humanities from the Massachusetts Institute of Technology. Born in Memphis, Tennessee, he demonstrated an unusual talent for both science and English at an early age, winning statewide science fairs and English awards in high school. As a scientist, his research has focused largely on gravity: he is particularly well known for positing that, because all falling objects accelerate at the same speed, gravity must be described as a geometrical warping of time and space.

> **Alan Lightman's most famous novel, *Einstein's Dreams* (1992), depicts Albert Einstein as a young man, developing the theory of relativity, plagued by dreams about time.**

Lightman's most famous novel, *Einstein's Dreams* (1992), depicts Albert Einstein as a young man, developing the theory of relativity, plagued by dreams about time. It was an international best-seller and has been translated into thirty languages. Lightman has written several novels since then, including *Reunion* (2003) and *Ghost* (2007), as well as a number of essay collections and books about science, including *Dance for Two* (1996) and *Great Ideas in Physics: The Conservation of Energy, the Second Law of Thermodynamics, the Theory of Relativity, and Quantum Mechanics*, originally published in 1992 and now in its third edition. His most recent novel, *Mr g* (2012), is the story of creation told from the perspective of God. He has described "the history of science . . . as the recasting of phenomena that were once thought to be accidents as phenomena that can be understood in terms of fundamental causes and principles," and suggested that, because of findings that "have led some of the world's premier physicists to propose . . . that some of the most basic features of our particular universe are indeed mere *accidents* . . . there [may be] no hope of ever explaining our universe's particular features in terms of fundamental causes and principles." Lightman's most recent nonfiction books are *The Accidental Universe* (2014) and a memoir, *Screening Room* (2015). The following essay, "Our Place in the Universe," was originally published in *Harper's* in 2012.

MY MOST VIVID ENCOUNTER with the vastness of nature occurred years ago on the Aegean Sea. My wife and I had chartered a sailboat for a two-week holiday in the Greek islands. After setting out from Piraeus, we headed south and hugged the coast, which we held three or four miles to our port. In the thick summer air, the distant shore appeared as a hazy beige ribbon—not entirely solid, but a reassuring line of reference. With binoculars, we could just make out the glinting of houses, fragments of buildings.

Then we passed the tip of Cape Sounion and turned west toward Hydra. Within a couple of hours, both the land and all other boats had disappeared. Looking around in a full circle, all we could see was water, extending out and out in all directions until it joined with the sky. I felt insignificant, misplaced, a tiny odd trinket in a cavern of ocean and air.

Naturalists, biologists, philosophers, painters, and poets have labored to express the qualities of this strange world that we find ourselves in. Some things are prickly, others are smooth. Some are round, some jagged. Luminescent or dim. Mauve colored. Pitter-patter in rhythm. Of all these aspects of things, none seems more immediate or vital than *size*. Large versus small. Consciously and unconsciously, we measure our physical size against the dimensions of other people, against animals, trees, oceans, mountains. As brainy as we think ourselves to be, our bodily size, our bigness, our simple volume and bulk are what we first present to the world. Somewhere in our fathoming of the cosmos, we must keep a mental inventory of plain size and scale, going from atoms to microbes to humans to oceans to planets to stars. And some of the most impressive additions to that inventory have occurred at the high end. Simply put, the cosmos has gotten larger and larger. At each new level of distance and scale, we have had to contend with a different conception of the world that we live in.

The prize for exploring the greatest distance in space goes to a man named Garth Illingworth, who works in a ten-by-fifteen-foot office at the University of California, Santa Cruz. Illingworth studies galaxies so distant that their light has traveled through space for more than 13 billion years to get here. His office is packed with tables and chairs, bookshelves, computers, scattered papers, issues of *Nature*, and a small refrigerator and a microwave to fuel research that can extend into the wee hours of the morning.

Like most professional astronomers these days, Illingworth does not look   5 directly through a telescope. He gets his images by remote control—in his case, quite remote. He uses the Hubble Space Telescope, which orbits Earth once every ninety-seven minutes, high above the distorting effects of Earth's atmosphere. Hubble takes digital photographs of galaxies and sends the images to other orbiting satellites, which relay them to a network of earth-bound antennae; these, in turn, pass the signals on to the Goddard Space Flight Center in Greenbelt, Maryland. From there the data is uploaded to a secure website that Illingworth can access from a computer in his office.

The most distant galaxy Illingworth has seen so far goes by the name UDFj-39546284 and was documented in early 2011. This galaxy is about 100,000,000,000,000,000,000,000 miles away from Earth, give or take. It appears as a faint red blob against the speckled night of the distant universe—red because the light has been stretched to longer and longer wavelengths as the galaxy has made its lonely journey through space for billions of years. The actual color of the galaxy is blue, the color of young, hot stars, and it is twenty times smaller than our galaxy, the Milky Way. UDFj-39546284 was one of the first galaxies to form in the universe.

"That little red dot is hellishly far away," Illingworth told me recently. At sixty-five, he is a friendly bear of a man, with a ruddy complexion, thick strawberry-blond hair, wire-rimmed glasses, and a broad smile. "I sometimes think to myself: What would it be like to be out there, looking around?"

One measure of the progress of human civilization is the increasing scale of our maps. A clay tablet dating from about the twenty-fifth century B.C. found near what is now the Iraqi city of Kirkuk depicts a river valley with a plot of land labeled as being 354 *iku* (about thirty acres) in size. In the earliest recorded cosmologies, such as the Babylonian *Enuma Elish*, from around 1500 B.C., the oceans, the continents, and the heavens were considered finite, but there were no scientific estimates of their dimensions. The early Greeks, including Homer, viewed Earth as a circular plane with the ocean enveloping it and Greece at the center, but there was no understanding of scale. In the early sixth century B.C., the Greek philosopher Anaximander, whom historians consider the first mapmaker, and his student Anaximenes proposed that the stars were attached to a giant crystalline sphere. But again there was no estimate of its size.

The first large object ever accurately measured was Earth, accomplished in the third century B.C. by Eratosthenes, a geographer who ran the Library of Alexandria. From travelers, Eratosthenes had heard the intriguing report that at noon on the summer solstice, in the town of Syene, due south of Alexandria, the sun casts no shadow at the bottom of a deep well. Evidently the sun is directly overhead at that time and place. (Before the invention of the clock, noon could be defined at each place as the moment when the sun was highest in the sky, whether that was exactly vertical or not.) Eratosthenes knew that the sun was not overhead at noon in Alexandria. In fact, it was tipped 7.2 degrees from the vertical, or about one fiftieth of a circle—a fact he could determine by measuring the length of the shadow cast by a stick planted in the ground. That the sun could be directly overhead in one place and not another was due to the curvature of Earth. Eratosthenes reasoned that if he knew the distance from Alexandria to Syene, the full circumference of the planet must be about fifty times that distance. Traders passing through Alexandria told him that camels could make the trip to Syene in about fifty days, and it was known that a camel could cover one hundred stadia (almost eleven and a half miles) in a day. So the ancient geographer estimated that Syene and Alexandria were about 570 miles apart. Consequently, the complete circumference of Earth he figured to be about 50 × 570 miles, or 28,500 miles. This number was within 15 percent of the modern measurement, amazingly accurate considering the imprecision of using camels as odometers.

As ingenious as they were, the ancient Greeks were not able to calculate the size of our solar system. That discovery had to wait for the invention of the telescope, nearly two thousand years later. In 1672, the French

10

astronomer Jean Richer determined the distance from Earth to Mars by measuring how much the position of the latter shifted against the background of stars from two different observation points on Earth. The two points were Paris (of course) and Cayenne, French Guiana. Using the distance to Mars, astronomers were also able to compute the distance from Earth to the sun, approximately 100 million miles.

A few years later, Isaac Newton managed to estimate the distance to the nearest stars. (Only someone as accomplished as Newton could have been the first to perform such a calculation and have it go almost unnoticed among his other achievements.) If one assumes that the stars are similar objects to our sun, equal in intrinsic luminosity, Newton asked, how far away would our sun have to be in order to appear as faint as nearby stars? Writing his computations in a spidery script, with a quill dipped in the ink of oak galls, Newton correctly concluded that the nearest stars are about 100,000 times the distance from Earth to the sun, about 10 trillion miles away. Newton's calculation is contained in a short section of his *Principia* titled simply "On the distance of the stars."

Newton's estimate of the distance to nearby stars was larger than any distance imagined before in human history. Even today, nothing in our experience allows us to relate to it. The fastest most of us have traveled is about 500 miles per hour, the cruising speed of a jet. If we set out for the nearest star beyond our solar system at that speed, it would take us about 5 million years to reach our destination. If we traveled in the fastest rocket ship ever manufactured on Earth, the trip would last 100,000 years, at least a thousand human life spans.

But even the distance to the nearest star is dwarfed by the measurements made in the early twentieth century by Henrietta Leavitt, an astronomer at the Harvard College Observatory. In 1912, she devised a new method for determining the distances to faraway stars. Certain stars, called Cepheid variables, were known to oscillate in brightness. Leavitt discovered that the cycle times of such stars are closely related to their intrinsic luminosities. More luminous stars have longer cycles. Measure the cycle time of such a star and you know its intrinsic luminosity. Then, by comparing its intrinsic luminosity with how bright it appears in the sky, you can infer its distance, just as you could gauge the distance to an approaching car at night if you knew the wattage of its headlights. Cepheid variables are scattered throughout the cosmos. They serve as cosmic distance signs in the highway of space.

Using Leavitt's method, astronomers were able to determine the size of the Milky Way, a giant congregation of about 200 billion stars. To express such mind-boggling sizes and distances, twentieth-century astronomers adopted a new unit called the light-year, the distance that light travels in a year—about 6 trillion miles. The nearest stars are several light-years away. The diameter of the Milky Way has been measured at about 100,000 light-years. In other words, it takes a ray of light 100,000 years to travel from one side of the Milky Way to the other.

There are galaxies beyond our own. They have names like Andromeda   15
(one of the nearest), Sculptor, Messier 87, Malin 1, IC 1101. The average distance between galaxies, again determined by Leavitt's method, is about twenty
galactic diameters, or 2 million light-years. To a giant cosmic being leisurely
strolling through the universe and not limited by distance or time, galaxies
would appear as illuminated mansions scattered about the dark countryside of
space. As far as we know, galaxies are the largest objects in the cosmos. If we
sorted the long inventory of material objects in nature by size, we would start
with subatomic particles like electrons and end up with galaxies.

Over the past century, astronomers have been able to probe deeper and
deeper into space, looking out to distances of hundreds of millions of light-
years and farther. A question naturally arises: Could the physical universe be
unending in size? That is, as we build bigger and bigger telescopes sensitive
to fainter and fainter light, will we continue to see objects farther and farther
away—like the third emperor of the Ming Dynasty, Yongle, who surveyed
his new palace in the Forbidden City and walked from room to room to room,
never reaching the end?

Here we must take into account a curious relationship between distance
and time. Because light travels at a fast (186,000 miles per second) but not
infinite speed, when we look at a distant object in space we must remember
that a significant amount of time has passed between the emission of the light
and the reception at our end. The image we see is what the object looked like
when it emitted that light. If we look at an object 186,000 miles away, we see
it as it appeared one second earlier; at 1,860,000 miles away, we see it as it
appeared ten seconds earlier; and so on. For extremely distant objects, we
see them as they were millions or billions of years in the past.

Now the second curiosity. Since the late 1920s we have known that the
universe is expanding, and that as it does so it is thinning out and cooling.
By measuring the current rate of expansion, we can make good estimates of
the moment in the past when the expansion began—the Big Bang—which
was about 13.7 billion years ago, a time when no planets or stars or galaxies
existed and the entire universe consisted of a fantastically dense nugget of
pure energy. No matter how big our telescopes, we cannot see beyond the
distance light has traveled since the Big Bang. Farther than that, and there
simply hasn't been enough time since the birth of the universe for light to get
from there to here. This giant sphere, the maximum distance we can see, is
only the *observable* universe. But the universe could extend far beyond that.

In his office in Santa Cruz, Garth Illingworth and his colleagues have
mapped out and measured the cosmos to the edge of the observable universe.
They have reached out almost as far as the laws of physics allow. All that
exists in the knowable universe—oceans and sky; planets and stars; pulsars,
quasars, and dark matter; distant galaxies and clusters of galaxies; and great
clouds of star-forming gas—has been gathered within the cosmic sensorium
gauged and observed by human beings.

"Every once in a while," says Illingworth, "I think: By God, we are study-   20
ing things that we can never physically touch. We sit on this miserable little
planet in a midsize galaxy and we can characterize most of the universe. It

is astonishing to me, the immensity of the situation, and how to relate to it in terms we can understand."

The idea of Mother Nature has been represented in every culture on Earth. But to what extent is the new universe, vastly larger than anything conceived of in the past, part of *nature*? One wonders how connected Illingworth feels to this astoundingly large cosmic terrain, to the galaxies and stars so distant that their images have taken billions of years to reach our eyes. Are the little red dots on his maps part of the same landscape that Wordsworth and Thoreau described, part of the same environment of mountains and trees, part of the same cycle of birth and death that orders our lives, part of our physical and emotional conception of the world we live in? Or are such things instead digitized abstractions, silent and untouchable, akin to us only in their (hypothesized) makeup of atoms and molecules? And to what extent are we human beings, living on a small planet orbiting one star among billions of stars, part of that same nature?

The heavenly bodies were once considered divine, made of entirely different stuff than objects on Earth. Aristotle argued that all matter was constituted from four elements: earth, fire, water, and air. A fifth element, ether, he reserved for the heavenly bodies, which he considered immortal, perfect, and indestructible. It wasn't until the birth of modern science, in the seventeenth century, that we began to understand the similarity of heaven and Earth. In 1610, using his new telescope, Galileo noted that the sun had dark patches and blemishes, suggesting that the heavenly bodies are not perfect. In 1687, Newton proposed a universal law of gravity that would apply equally to the fall of an apple from a tree and to the orbits of planets around the sun. Newton then went further, suggesting that all the laws of nature apply to phenomena in the heavens as well as on Earth. In later centuries, scientists used our understanding of terrestrial chemistry and physics to estimate how long the sun could continue shining before depleting its resources of energy; to determine the chemical composition of stars; to map out the formation of galaxies.

Yet even after Galileo and Newton, there remained another question: Were living things somehow different from rocks and water and stars? Did animate and inanimate matter differ in some fundamental way? The "vitalists" claimed that animate matter had some special essence, an intangible spirit or soul, while the "mechanists" argued that living things were elaborate machines and obeyed precisely the same laws of physics and chemistry as did inanimate material. In the late nineteenth century, two German physiologists, Adolf Eugen Fick and Max Rubner, each began testing the mechanistic hypothesis by painstakingly tabulating the energies required for muscle contraction, body heat, and other physical activities and comparing these energies against the chemical energy stored in food. Each gram of fat, carbohydrate, and protein had its energy equivalent. Rubner concluded that the amount of energy used by a living creature was exactly equal to the energy it consumed in its food. Living things were to be viewed as complex arrangements of biological pulleys and levers, electric currents, and chemical impulses. Our bodies are made of the same atoms and molecules as stones, water, and air.

And yet many had a lingering feeling that human beings were somehow separate from the rest of nature. Such a view is nowhere better illustrated than in the painting *Tallulah Falls* (1841), by George Cooke, an artist associated with the Hudson River School. Although this group of painters celebrated nature, they also believed that human beings were set apart from the natural world. Cooke's painting depicts tiny human figures standing on a small promontory above a deep canyon. The people are dwarfed by tree-covered mountains, massive rocky ledges, and a waterfall pouring down to the canyon below. Not only insignificant in size compared with their surroundings, the human beings are mere witnesses to a scene they are not part of and never could be. Just a few years earlier, Ralph Waldo Emerson had published his famous essay "Nature," an appreciation of the natural world that nonetheless held humans separate from nature, at the very least in the moral and spiritual domain: "Man is fallen; nature is erect."

Today, with various back-to-nature movements attempting to resist the dislocations brought about by modernity, and with our awareness of Earth's precarious environmental state ever increasing, many people feel a new sympathy with the natural world on this planet. But the gargantuan cosmos beyond remains remote. We might understand at some level that those tiny points of light in the night sky are similar to our sun, made of atoms identical to those in our bodies, and that the cavern of outer space extends from our galaxy of stars to other galaxies of stars, to distances that would take light billions of years to traverse. We might understand these discoveries in intellectual terms, but they are baffling abstractions, even disturbing, like the notion that each of us once was the size of a dot, without mind or thought. Science has vastly expanded the scale of our cosmos, but our emotional reality is still limited by what we can touch with our bodies in the time span of our lives. George Berkeley, the eighteenth-century Irish philosopher, argued that the entire cosmos is a construct of our minds, that there is no material reality outside our thoughts. As a scientist, I cannot accept that belief. At the emotional and psychological level, however, I can have some sympathy with Berkeley's views. Modern science has revealed a world as far removed from our bodies as colors are from the blind.

Very recent scientific findings have added yet another dimension to the question of our place in the cosmos. For the first time in the history of science, we are able to make plausible estimates of the rate of occurrence of life in the universe. In March 2009, NASA launched a spacecraft called *Kepler* whose mission was to search for planets orbiting in the "habitable zone" of other stars. The habitable zone is the region in which a planet's surface temperature is not so cold as to freeze water and not so hot as to boil it. For many reasons, biologists and chemists believe that liquid water is required for the emergence of life, even if that life may be very different from life on Earth. Dozens of candidates for such planets have been found, and we can make a rough preliminary calculation that something like 3 percent of all stars are accompanied by a potentially life-sustaining planet. The totality of living matter on Earth—humans and animals, plants, bacteria, and pond scum—makes up 0.00000001 percent of the mass of the planet. Combining this figure with the results from the *Kepler* mission, and assuming that all potentially life-sustaining planets do indeed have life, we can estimate that the fraction of stuff in the visible universe that exists in living form is something like 0.000000000000001 percent, or one millionth of one billionth of 1 percent. If some cosmic intelligence created the universe, life would seem to have been only an afterthought. And if life emerges by random processes, vast amounts of lifeless material are needed for each particle of life. Such numbers cannot help but bear upon the question of our significance in the universe.

Decades ago, when I was sailing with my wife in the Aegean Sea, in the midst of unending water and sky, I had a slight inkling of infinity. It was a sensation I had not experienced before, accompanied by feelings of awe, fear, sublimity, disorientation, alienation, and disbelief. I set a course for 255°, trusting in my compass—a tiny disk of painted numbers with a sliver of rotating metal—and hoped for the best. In a few hours, as if by magic, a pale ocher smidgen of land appeared dead ahead, a thing that drew closer and closer, a place with houses and beds and other human beings. ■

The Reader's Presence

1. Lightman addresses the centuries-old question of whether we exist within the framework of the natural world or are observers of a universe in which we have an insignificant place: "The idea of Mother Nature has been represented in every culture on Earth. But to what extent is the new universe, vastly larger than anything conceived of in the past, part of *nature*? . . . And to what extent are we human beings, living on a small planet orbiting one star among billions of stars, part of that same nature?" (paragraph 21). What are the compositional advantages of Lightman's decision to begin and end his essay by writing about a personal "encounter with the vastness of nature" (paragraph 1)? In what specific ways do your own experiences in and with nature, on both a large and small scale, affect your own sense of place in the universe?

2. To what extent do you agree with Lightman's assertion that our conception of the "size and scale" (paragraph 3) of the world impacts how we think about our lives? What was your first reaction when you read that the distance of the galaxy UDFj-39546284 is 100,000,000,000,000,000,000,000 miles from Earth (paragraph 6)? How is your reaction related to what Lightman calls your "physical and emotional conception of the world" (paragraph 21)? What is your response to Lightman's question, "[T]o what extent is the new universe, vastly larger than anything conceived of in the past, part of *nature*?" (paragraph 21)? Lightman relies on analogies to help us make sense of the massive scale of the universe. Which of his examples do you find most helpful? Explain why.

3. **CONNECTIONS:** Compare Lightman's essay to Naomi Klein's "The Change Within" (page 432). How consistent is Klein's view of nature with the cosmic perspective offered by Lightman? Does Lightman's more expansive look at our world's place in the universe raise any issues pertinent to Klein's argument? Why or why not? How do you think Klein would relate to Lightman's statement, "Science has vastly expanded the scale of our cosmos, but our emotional reality is still limited by what we can touch with our bodies in the time span of our lives" (paragraph 25)?

Abraham Lincoln

GETTYSBURG ADDRESS

ABRAHAM LINCOLN (1809–1865), the sixteenth president of the United States, led the country through a bloody civil war in which one side "would *make* war rather than let the nation survive; and the other would *accept* war rather than let it perish." During his presidency, Lincoln, who is still widely admired as both a political figure and a writer, wrote notable documents such as the Emancipation Proclamation and several poignant and moving speeches, including the Gettysburg Address.

Four months after the Battle of Gettysburg, Lincoln joined in a dedication of a national cemetery on the battlefield. The Gettysburg Address, delivered on November

> **"A house divided against itself cannot stand."**

19, 1863, would become one of the most famous—and one of the shortest—speeches given by a U.S. president. The text that follows has been widely accepted as the "final" version of the Gettysburg Address. It comes from the "Bliss copy" of the speech—the fifth and final version of the text that Lincoln copied out by hand, probably sometime in early 1864.

FOUR SCORE and seven years ago our fathers brought forth on this continent, a new nation, conceived in Liberty, and dedicated to the proposition that all men are created equal.

Now we are engaged in a great civil war, testing whether that nation, or any nation so conceived and so dedicated, can long endure. We are met on a great battle-field of that war. We have come to dedicate a portion of that field, as a final resting place for those who here gave their lives that that nation might live. It is altogether fitting and proper that we should do this.

But, in a larger sense, we can not dedicate—we can not consecrate—we can not hallow—this ground. The brave men, living and dead, who struggled here, have consecrated it, far above our poor power to add or detract. The world will little note, nor long remember what we say here, but it can never forget what they did here. It is for us the living, rather, to be dedicated here to the unfinished work which they who fought here have thus far so nobly advanced. It is rather for us to be here dedicated to the great task remaining before us—that from these honored dead we take increased devotion to that cause for which they gave the last full measure of devotion—that we here highly resolve that these dead shall not have died in vain—that this nation, under God, shall have a new birth of freedom—and that government of the people, by the people, for the people, shall not perish from the earth. ▪

The Reader's Presence

1. What historical event does Lincoln refer to at the beginning and end of the Gettysburg Address? Why do you think he chose to place this information in a position of such prominence? Why is this event relevant to the dedication of a cemetery?

2. Consider Lincoln's strategy of repetition. What phrases and sentence structures does he repeat? What is the effect of the repetition? Read the speech aloud. Do you find the repetition more or less effective when the words are spoken? Why?

3. **CONNECTIONS:** Compare and contrast Lincoln's Gettysburg Address to Thomas Jefferson's draft of The Declaration of Independence (page 537). Focus on their respective uses of such rhetorical devices as repetition, parallel structure, alliteration, and antithesis (a figure of speech in which an opposition or a contrast of ideas is expressed by parallelism of words that are the opposites of, or strongly contrasted with, each other). Which writer uses these rhetorical devices more successfully? Support your response by pointing to specific examples of each rhetorical device.

The Writer at Work

ABRAHAM LINCOLN'S Hay Draft of the Gettysburg Address

Alexander Hesler/Contributor/Getty Images

Abraham Lincoln, 1860.

Two of the five surviving versions of the Gettysburg Address in Lincoln's own handwriting were written down just before or just after he gave the speech on November 19, 1863. Scholars disagree about whether one of these two drafts — known as the "Nicolay Draft" and the "Hay Draft" — might have been the pages Lincoln read from on the field at Gettysburg; both drafts differ somewhat from contemporary accounts of the speech that the president delivered that day. Both also differ from the final "Bliss copy" that has become the standard version of the Gettysburg Address (see previous page).

The images on the following pages show the pages of the Hay Draft of the Gettysburg Address, the second version that Lincoln wrote. Note the additions and changes Lincoln has made to this draft of his speech. Compare this version, written very close to the time of the speech's delivery, with the final version made several months later. As the fame of the Gettysburg Address continued to grow, Lincoln kept revising the words for an increasingly wide audience that had not been present to hear him speak. What do Lincoln's continuing revisions suggest about his hopes for this text? Which version do you find more compelling?

Four score and seven years ago our fathers brought forth, upon this continent, a new nation, conceived in Liberty, and dedicated to the proposition that all men are created equal.

Now we are engaged in a great civil war, testing whether that nation, or any nation, so conceived, and so dedicated, can long endure. We are met here on a great battle-field of that war. We have come to dedicate a portion of it as a final resting place for those who here gave their lives that that nation might live. It is altogether fitting and proper that we should do this.

But in a larger sense we can not dedicate— we can not consecrate— we can not hallow this ground. The brave men, living and dead, who struggled here, have consecrated it far above our poor power to add or detract. The world will little note, nor long remember, what we say here, but can never forget what they did here. It is for us, the living, rather to be dedicated here to the unfinished work which they have, thus far, so nobly carried on. It is rather

There are five known manuscript versions of Lincoln's Gettysburg Address. This manuscript, known as the Hay Draft, features Lincoln's handwritten corrections. It was discovered in 1906, during a search for the "original manuscript" of the address among the papers of John Hay, Lincoln's personal secretary.

James McBride

Hip-Hop Planet

Writer, journalist, and musician **JAMES McBRIDE** (b. 1957) grew up in Harlem in New York City, the son of a black father and a white, Jewish mother, and the eighth of twelve siblings. The title of his best-selling memoir, *The Color of Water: A Black Man's Tribute to His White Mother* (1996), refers to the answer his mother gave him when he asked about the color of God's skin. McBride's first novel, *Miracle of St. Anna* (2002), has been made into a film by Spike Lee. His second novel, *Song Yet Sung* (2008), set in pre–Civil War Maryland, is the story of a slave girl who can see the future, and his most recent book, released in 2013, is a comic novel called *The Good Lord Bird*. It won the 2013 National Book Award for fiction. *Kill 'Em and Leave: Searching for James Brown and the American Soul* appeared in 2016.

> "The nice thing about rap music, . . . good rap that's straight ahead and deals with truth really gets to the point and takes you places, just like a good book will. . . . It's all storytelling."

McBride began his dual career as journalist and musician early, studying composition at the Oberlin Conservatory of Music in Ohio and receiving his master's in journalism from Columbia University in New York at age twenty two. He has been a staff writer for the *Washington Post, People* magazine, and the *Boston Globe*, and he has written articles for the *New York Times, Essence, Rolling Stone*, and *National Geographic*, where his essay "Hip-Hop Planet" appeared in April 2007. McBride is a composer, lyricist, producer, and performer, playing tenor saxophone. He has written for such music luminaries as Anita Baker, Grover Washington Jr., and Gary Burton, and he has recorded and performed with numerous jazz and pop artists. His collaboration with Ed Shockly on the musical *Bobos* won the Stephen Sondheim Award and the Richard Rodgers Foundation Horizon Award. He holds several honorary doctorates and was appointed a Distinguished Writer in Residence at New York University in 2005. He is married with three children and lives in Pennsylvania and New York.

McBride often talks about writing in the context of music, likening writing fiction to playing jazz and, in an interview with Powell's Books, rap music to storytelling: "The nice thing about rap music, and I know people give rap a bad rap, good rap that's straight ahead and deals with truth really gets to the point and takes you places, just like a good book will. And it's all valid. It's no more or less valid than Def Leppard or Henri Salvador, the French singer. It's all storytelling."

THIS IS MY NIGHTMARE: My daughter comes home with a guy and says, "Dad, we're getting married." And he's a rapper, with a mouthful of gold teeth, a do-rag on his head, muscles popping out of his arms, and a thug attitude. And then the nightmare gets deeper, because before you know it, I'm hearing the pitter-patter of little feet, their offspring, cascading through my living room, cascading through my life, drowning me with the sound of my own hypocrisy, because when I was young, I was a knucklehead, too, hearing my own music, my own sounds. And so I curse the day I saw his face, which is a reflection of my own, and I rue the day I heard his name, because I realize to my horror that rap—music seemingly without melody, sensibility, instruments, verse, or harmony, music with no beginning, end, or middle, music that doesn't even seem to be music—rules the world. It is no longer my world. It is his world. And I live in it. I live on a hip-hop planet.

HIGH-STEPPING

I remember when I first heard rap. I was standing in the kitchen at a party in Harlem. It was 1980. A friend of mine named Bill had just gone on the blink. He slapped a guy, a total stranger, in the face right in front of me. I can't remember why. Bill was a fellow student. He was short-circuiting. Problem was, the guy he slapped was a big guy, dude wearing a do-rag who'd crashed the party with three friends, and, judging by the fury on their faces, there would be no Martin Luther King moments in our immediate future.

There were no white people in the room, though I confess I wished there had been, if only to hide the paleness of my own frightened face. We were black and Latino students about to graduate from Columbia University's journalism school, having learned the whos, whats, wheres, and whys of American reporting. But the real storytellers of the American experience came from the world of the guy that Bill had just slapped. They lived less than a mile from us in the South Bronx. They had no journalism degrees. No money. No credibility. What they did have, however, was talent.

Earlier that night, somebody tossed a record on the turntable, which sent my fellow students stumbling onto the dance floor, howling with delight, and made me, a jazz lover, cringe. It sounded like a broken record. It was a version of an old hit record called "Good Times," the same four bars looped over and over. And on top of this loop, a kid spouted a rhyme about how he was the best disc jockey in the world. It was called "Rapper's Delight." I thought it was the most ridiculous thing I'd ever heard. More ridiculous than Bill slapping that stranger.

Bill survived that evening, but in many ways, I did not. For the next 26 years, I high-stepped past that music the way you step over a crack in the sidewalk. I heard it pounding out of cars and alleyways from Paris to Abidjan, yet I never listened. It came rumbling out of boomboxes from Johannesburg to Osaka, yet I pretended not to hear. I must have strolled past the corner of St. James Place and Fulton Street in my native Brooklyn where a fat kid named Christopher Wallace, aka Biggie Smalls, stood amusing friends with rhyme, a hundred times, yet I barely noticed. I high-stepped away from that music for 26 years because it was everything I thought it was, and more than I ever dreamed it would be, but mostly, because it held everything I wanted to leave behind.

In doing so, I missed the most important cultural event of my lifetime.

Not since the advent of swing jazz in the 1930s has an American music exploded across the world with such overwhelming force. Not since the Beatles invaded America and Elvis packed up his blue suede shoes has a music crashed against the world with such outrage. This defiant culture of song, graffiti, and dance, collectively known as hip-hop, has ripped popular

5

music from its moorings in every society it has permeated. In Brazil, rap rivals samba in popularity. In China, teens spray-paint graffiti on the Great Wall. In France it has been blamed, unfairly, for the worst civil unrest that country has seen in decades.

Its structure is unique, complex, and at times bewildering. Whatever music it eats becomes part of its vocabulary, and as the commercial world falls into place behind it to gobble up the powerful slop in its wake, it metamorphoses into the Next Big Thing. It is a music that defies definition, yet defines our collective societies in immeasurable ways. To many of my generation, despite all attempts to exploit it, belittle it, numb it, classify it, and analyze it, hip-hop remains an enigma, a clarion call, a cry of "I am" from the youth of the world. We'd be wise, I suppose, to start paying attention.

BURNING MAN

Imagine a burning man. He is on fire. He runs into the room. You put out the flames. Then another burning man arrives. You put him out and go about your business. Then two, three, four, five, ten appear. You extinguish them all, send them to the hospital. Then imagine no one bothers to examine why the men caught fire in the first place. That is the story of hip-hop.

It is a music dipped in the boiling cauldron of race and class, and for   10
that reason it is clouded with mystics, snake oil salesmen, two-bit scholars, race-baiters, and sneaker salesmen, all professing to know the facts, to be "real," when the reality of race is like shifting sand, dependent on time, place, circumstance, and who's telling the history. Here's the real story: In the mid-1970s, New York City was nearly broke. The public school system cut funding for the arts drastically. Gone were the days when you could wander into the band room, rent a clarinet for a minimal fee, and march it home to squeal on it and drive your parents nuts.

The kids of the South Bronx and Harlem came up with something else. In the summer of 1973, at 1595 East 174th Street in the Bronx River Houses, a black teenager named Afrika Bambaataa stuck a speaker in his mother's first-floor living room window, ran a wire to the turntable in his bedroom, and set the housing project of 3,000 people alight with party music. At the same time, a Jamaican teenager named Kool DJ Herc was starting up the scene in the East Bronx, while a technical whiz named Grandmaster Flash was rising to prominence a couple of miles south. The Bronx became a music magnet for Puerto Ricans, Jamaicans, Dominicans, and black Americans from the surrounding areas. Fab 5 Freddy, Kurtis Blow, and Melle Mel were only a few of the pioneers. Grand Wizard Theodore, Kool DJ AJ, the Cold Crush Brothers, Spoony Gee, and the Rock Steady Crew of B-boys showed up to "battle"—dance, trade quips and rhymes, check out each other's records and equipment—not knowing as they strolled through the doors of the community center near Bambaataa's mother's apartment that they were writing musical history. Among them was an MC named Lovebug Starski, who was said to utter the phrase "hip-hop" between breaks to keep time.

This is how it worked: One guy, the DJ, played records on two turntables. One guy—or girl—served as master of ceremonies, or MC. The DJs learned to move the record back and forth under the needle to create a "scratch," or to drop the needle on the record when the beat was the hottest, playing "the break" over and over to keep the folks dancing. The MCs "rapped" over the music to keep the party going. One MC sought to outchat the other. Dance styles were created — "locking" and "popping" and "breaking." Graffiti artists spread the word of the "I" because the music was all about identity: I am the best. I spread the most love in the Bronx, in Harlem, in Queens. The focus initially was not on the MCs, but on the dancers, or B-boys. Commercial radio ignored it. DJs sold mix tapes out of the back of station wagons. "Rapper's Delight" by the Sugarhill Gang—the song I first heard at that face-slapping party in Harlem—broke the music onto radio in 1979.

That is the short history.

The long history is that spoken-word music made its way here on slave ships from West Africa centuries ago: Ethnomusicologists trace hip-hop's roots to the dance, drum, and song of West African griots, or storytellers, its pairing of word and music the manifestation of the painful journey of slaves who survived the middle passage. The ring shouts, field hollers, and spirituals[1] of early slaves drew on common elements of African music, such as call and response and improvisation. "Speech-song has been part of black culture for a long, long time," says Samuel A. Floyd, director of the Center for Black Music Research at Columbia College in Chicago. The "dozens," "toasts," and "signifying" of black Americans—verbal dueling, rhyming, self-deprecating tales, and stories of blacks outsmarting whites—were defensive, empowering strategies.

You can point to jazz musicians such as Oscar Brown, Jr., Edgar "Eddie" Jefferson, and Louis Armstrong, and blues greats such as John Lee Hooker, and easily find the foreshadowing of rap music in the verbal play of their work. Black performers such as poet Nikki Giovanni and Gil Scott-Heron, a pianist and vocalist who put spoken political lyrics to music (most famously in "The Revolution Will Not Be Televised"), elevated spoken word to a new level.   15

But the artist whose work arguably laid the groundwork for rap as we know it was Amiri Baraka, a beat poet out of Allen Ginsberg's Greenwich Village scene. In the 1950s and '60s, Baraka performed with shrieks, howls, cries, stomps, verse floating ahead of or behind the rhythm, sometimes in staccato syncopation. It was performance art, delivered in a dashiki and Afro, in step with the anger of a bold and sometimes frightening nationalistic black movement, and it inspired what might be considered the first rap group, the Last Poets.

I was 13 when I first heard the Last Poets in 1970. They scared me. To black America, they were like the relatives you hoped wouldn't show up at your barbecue because the boss was there—the old Aunt Clementine who

---

[1] **ring shouts, field hollers, and spirituals:** Various types of music and circle dances that drew from African sources but were adapted by slave communities as they developed new forms of expression in the pre–Civil War American South. —Eds.

The Sugarhill Gang, an American rap group active since the 1970s: (left to right) Michael "Wonder Mike" Wright, Guy "Master Gee" O'Brien, and Henry "Big Bank Hank" Jackson.

would arrive, get drunk, and pull out her dentures. My parents refused to allow us to play their music in our house—so my siblings waited until my parents went to work and played it anyway. They were the first musical group I heard to use the N-word on a record, with songs like "N------ Are Scared of Revolution." In a world where blacks were evolving from "Negroes" to "blacks," and the assassinations of civil rights leaders Malcolm X and Martin Luther King, Jr., still reverberated in the air like a shotgun blast, the Last Poets embodied black power. Their records consisted of percussion and spoken-word rhyme. They were wildly popular in my neighborhood. Their debut recording sold 400,000 records in three months, says Last Poet member Umar Bin Hassan. "No videos, no radio play, strictly word of mouth." The group's demise coincided with hip-hop's birth in the 1970s.

It's unlikely that the Last Poets ever dreamed the revolution they sang of would take the form it has. "We were about the movement," Abiodun Oyewoke, a founder of the group, says. "A lot of today's rappers have talent. But a lot of them are driving the car in the wrong direction."

THE CROSSOVER

Highways wrap around the city of Dayton, Ohio, like a ribbon bowtied on a box of chocolates from the local Esther Price candy factory. They have six ladies at the plant who do just that: Tie ribbons around boxes all day. Henry Rosenkranz can tell you about it. "I love candy," says Henry, a slim white teenager in glasses and a hairnet, as he strolls the factory, bucket in hand. His full-time after-school job is mopping the floors.

Henry is a model American teenager—and the prototypical consumer at 20 which the hip-hop industry is squarely aimed, which has his parents sitting up in their seats. The music that was once the purview of black America has gone white and gone commercial all at once. A sea of white faces now rises up to greet rap groups as they perform, many of them teenagers like Henry, a NASCAR fanatic and self-described redneck. "I live in Old North Dayton," he says. "It's a white, redneck area. But hip-hop is so prominent with country people . . . if you put them behind a curtain and hear them talk, you won't know if they're black or white. There's a guy I work with, when Kanye West sings about a gold digger, he can relate because he's paying alimony and child support."

Obviously, it's not just working-class whites, but also affluent, suburban kids who identify with this music with African-American roots. A white 16-year-old hollering rap lyrics at the top of his lungs from the driver's seat of his dad's late-model Lexus may not have the same rationale to howl at the moon as a working-class kid whose parents can't pay for college, yet his own anguish is as real to him as it gets. What attracts white kids to this music is the same thing that prompted outraged congressmen to decry jazz during the 1920s and Tipper Gore[2] to campaign decades later against violent and sexually explicit lyrics: life on the other side of the tracks; its "cool" or illicit factor, which black Americans, like it or not, are always perceived to possess.

Hip-hop has continually changed form, evolving from party music to social commentary with the 1982 release of Grandmaster Flash and the Furious Five's "The Message." Today, alternative hip-hop artists continue to produce socially conscious songs, but most commercial rappers spout violent lyrics that debase women and gays. Beginning with the so-called gangsta rap of the '90s, popularized by the still unsolved murders of rappers Biggie Smalls and Tupac Shakur, the genre has become dominated by rappers who brag about their lives of crime. 50 Cent, the hip-hop star of the moment, trumpets his sexual exploits and boasts that he has been shot nine times.

"People call hip-hop the MTV music now," scoffs Chuck D., of Public Enemy, known for its overtly political rap. "It's Big Brother controlling you. To slip something in there that's indigenous to the roots, that pays homage to the music that came before us, it's the Mount Everest of battles."

Most rap songs unabashedly function as walking advertisements for luxury cars, designer clothes, and liquor. Agenda Inc., a "pop culture brand strategy agency" listed Mercedes-Benz as the number one brand mentioned in *Billboard*'s top 20 singles in 2005. Hip-hop sells so much Hennessy cognac, listed at number six, that the French makers, deader than yesterday's beer a decade ago, are now rolling in suds. The company even sponsored a contest to win a visit to its plant in France with a famous rapper.

---

[2] ***Tipper Gore:*** Mary Elizabeth ("Tipper") Gore is the ex-wife of former U.S. vice president Al Gore. In 1985, she founded an organization that advocated putting warning labels on albums with explicit lyrics. —EDS.

In many ways, the music represents an old dream. It's the pot of gold to   25
millions of kids like Henry, who quietly agonizes over how his father slaves
14 hours a day at two tool-and-die machine jobs to make ends meet. Like
teenagers across the world, he fantasizes about working in the hip-hop business and making millions himself.

"My parents hate hip-hop," Henry says, motoring his 1994 Dodge Shadow
through traffic on the way home from work on a hot October afternoon. "But
I can listen to Snoop Dogg and hear him call women whores, and I know he
has a wife and children at home. It's just a fantasy. Everyone has the urge
deep down to be a bad guy or a bad girl. Everyone likes to talk the talk, but
not everyone will walk the walk."

FULL CIRCLE

You breathe in and breathe out a few times and you are there. Eight hours
and a wake-up shake on the flight from New York, and you are on the tar-
mac in Dakar, Senegal. Welcome to Africa. The assignment: Find the roots of
hip-hop. The music goes full circle. The music comes home to Africa. That
whole bit. Instead it was the old reporter's joke: You go out to cover a story
and the story covers you. The stench of poverty in my nostrils was so strong
it pulled me to earth like a hundred-pound ring in my nose. Dakar's Sandaga
market is full of "local color" — unless you live there. It was packed and filthy,
stalls full of new merchandise surrounded by shattered pieces of life everywhere, broken pipes, bicycle handlebars, fruit flies, soda bottles, beggars,
dogs, cell phones. A teenager beggar, his body malformed by polio, crawled
by on hands and feet, like a spider. He said, "Hey brother, help me." When
I looked into his eyes, they were a bottomless ocean.

The Hotel Teranga is a fortress, packed behind a concrete wall where
beggars gather at the front gate. The French tourists march past them, the
women in high heels and stonewashed jeans. They sidle through downtown Dakar like royalty, haggling in the market, swimming in the hotel pool
with their children, a scene that resembles Birmingham, Alabama, in the
1950s — the blacks serving, the whites partying. Five hundred yards away,
Africans eat off the sidewalk and sell peanuts for a pittance. There is a restlessness, a deep sense of something gone wrong in the air.

The French can't smell it, even though they've had a mouthful back
home. A good amount of the torching of Paris suburbs in October 2005 was
courtesy of the children of immigrants from former French African colonies,
exhausted from being bottled up in housing projects for generations with
no job prospects. They telegraphed the punch in their music — France is the
second largest hip-hop market in the world — but the message was ignored.
Around the globe, rap music has become a universal expression of outrage,
its macho pose borrowed from commercial hip-hop in the U.S.

In Dakar, where every kid is a microphone and turntable away from squalor,   30
and American rapper Tupac Shakur's picture hangs in market stalls of folks

who don't understand English, rap is king. There are hundreds of rap groups in Senegal today. French television crews troop in and out of Dakar's nightclubs filming the kora harp lute[3] and *tama*[4] talking drum with regularity. But beneath the drumming and the dance lessons and the jingling sound of tourist change, there is a quiet rage, a desperate fury among the Senegalese, some of whom seem to bear an intense dislike of their former colonial rulers.

"We know all about French history," says Abdou Ba, a Senegalese producer and musician. "We know about their kings, their castles, their art, their music. We know everything about them. But they don't know much about us."

Assane N'Diaye, 19, loves hip-hop music. Before he left his Senegalese village to work as a DJ in Dakar, he was a fisherman, just like his father, like his father's father before him. Tall, lean, with a muscular build and a handsome chocolate face, Assane became a popular DJ, but the equipment he used was borrowed, and when his friend took it back, success eluded him. He has returned home to Toubab Dialaw, about 25 miles south of Dakar, a village marked by a huge boulder, perhaps 40 feet high, facing the Atlantic Ocean.

About a century and a half ago, a local ruler led a group of people fleeing slave traders to this place. He was told by a white trader to come here, to Toubab Dialaw. When he arrived, the slavers followed. A battle ensued. The ruler fought bravely but was killed. The villagers buried him by the sea and marked his grave with a small stone, and over the years it is said to have sprouted like a tree planted by God. It became a huge, arching boulder that stares out to sea, protecting the village behind it. When the fishermen went deep out to sea, the boulder was like a lighthouse that marked the way home. The Great Rock of Toubab Dialaw is said to hold a magic spirit, a spirit that Assane N'Diaye believes in.

In the shadow of the Great Rock, Assane has built a small restaurant, Chez Las, decorated with hundreds of seashells. It is where he lives his hip-hop dream. At night, he and his brother and cousin stand by the Great Rock and face the sea. They meditate. They pray. Then they write rap lyrics that are worlds away from the bling-bling culture of today's commercial hip-hoppers. They write about their lives as village fishermen, the scarcity of catch forcing them to fish in deeper and deeper waters, the hardship of fishing for 8, 10, 14 days at a time in an open pirogue in rainy season, the high fee they pay to rent the boat, and the paltry price their catches fetch on the market. They write about the humiliation of poverty, watching their town sprout up around them with rich Dakarians and richer French. And they write about the relatives who leave in the morning and never return, surrendered to the sea, sharks, and God.

The dream, of course, is to make a record. They have their own demo,   35 their own logo, and their own name, Salam T. D. (for Toubab Dialaw). But

---

[3] **kora harp lute:** In West Africa, a popular 21-string instrument played with both hands and used by storytellers and bards. —EDS.

[4] **tama:** A flexible West African drum, known as a "talking drum," popular in Senegal; it is placed under the shoulder and can be manipulated to produce a wide range of tones and sounds. —EDS.

rap music represents a deeper dream: a better life. "We want money to help our parents," Assane says over dinner. "We watch our mothers boil water to cook and have nothing to put in the pot."

He fingers his food lightly. "Rap doesn't belong to American culture," he says. "It belongs here. It has always existed here, because of our pain and our hardships and our suffering."

On this cool evening in a restaurant above their village, these young men, clad in baseball caps and T-shirts, appear no different from their African-American counterparts, with one exception. After a dinner of chicken and rice, Assane says something in Wolof[5] to the others. Silently and without ceremony, they take every bit of the leftover dinner—the half-eaten bread, rice, pieces of chicken, the chicken bones—and dump them into a plastic bag to give to the children in the village. They silently rise from the table and proceed outside. The last I see of them, their regal figures are outlined in the dim light of the doorway, heading out to the darkened village, holding on to that bag as though it held money.

THE CITY OF GODS

Some call the Bronx River Houses the City of Gods, though if God has been by lately, he must've slipped out for a chicken sandwich. The 10 drab, red-brick buildings spread out across 14 acres, coming into view as you drive east across the East 174th Street Bridge. The Bronx is the hallowed holy ground of hip-hop, the place where it all began. Visitors take tours through this neighborhood now, care of a handful of fortyish "old-timers," who point out the high and low spots of hip-hop's birthplace.

It is a telling metaphor for the state of America's racial landscape that you need a permit to hold a party in the same parks and playgrounds that produced the music that changed the world. The rap artists come and go, but the conditions that produced them linger. Forty percent of New York City's black males are jobless. One in three black males born in 2001 will end up in prison. The life expectancy of black men in the U.S. ranks below that of men in Sri Lanka and Colombia. It took a massive hurricane in New Orleans for the United States to wake up to its racial realities.

That is why, after 26 years, I have come to embrace this music I tried so   40
hard to ignore. Hip-hop culture is not mine. Yet I own it. Much of it I hate. Yet I love it, the good of it. To confess a love for a music that, at least in part, embraces violence is no easy matter, but then again our national anthem talks about bombs bursting in air, and I love that song, too. At its best, hip-hop lays bare the empty moral cupboard that is our generation's legacy. This music that once made visible the inner culture of America's greatest social problem, its legacy of slavery, has taken the dream deferred to a global scale. Today, 2 percent of the Earth's adult population owns more than 50 percent of its

---

5 **Wolof:** The most widely used language in Senegal; "banana" is a Wolof word. —EDS.

household wealth, and indigenous cultures are swallowed with the rapidity of a teenager gobbling a bag of potato chips. The music is calling. Over the years, the instruments change, but the message is the same. The drums are pounding out a warning. They are telling us something. Our children can hear it.

The question is: Can we? ●

The Reader's Presence

1. "Hip-Hop Planet" features a popular topic covered by an experienced journalist. What characteristics of the selection seem to belong to the personal essay? What characteristics seem to belong to a journalistic article? How are these two components of the selection brought together? Would you prefer if the selection used only a single method — for example, interviews and information told in the third person without a personal response? Explain why or why not.

2. Discuss McBride's attitude toward hip-hop. Why did he dislike it at first? What did he come to admire about it? What does McBride still not like about the music? What does he think about today's commercial rap artists? In what ways do they differ from the groups McBride enjoys most? How would you describe the differences? Do those differences matter to you?

3. **CONNECTIONS:** Compare McBride's evaluation of hip-hop culture to Ta-Nehisi Coates's evaluation of black youth in "Between the World and Me" (page 330). After reading each essay carefully, consider the points on which McBride and Coates would agree. What do you think would be their major points of disagreement? Which account of youth do you find more engaging and convincing? Support your points with specific references to each text.

Azar Nafisi

FROM READING LOLITA IN TEHRAN

AZAR NAFISI (b. 1950) was raised in Tehran, Iran, and educated in England and the United States. Having returned to Iran in the 1970s to teach English literature, she experienced firsthand the revolution and its aftermath, when strict Islamic religious codes were imposed; the harshest restrictions were placed on women. Nafisi has said that "before the revolution I had an image of myself as a woman, as a writer, as an academician, as a person with a set of values." Afterward, even the smallest public gestures were forbidden, from kissing her husband in public to shaking hands with a colleague. Fearing she would "become someone who was a stranger to herself," Nafisi resigned her university position in 1995 and for two years took a group of her best students "underground" for weekly discussions of Western authors, including Vladimir Nabokov, the author of *Lolita* and the subject of Nafisi's scholarly work.

Reading Lolita in Tehran (2003), the book she wrote about her experiences, has been translated into thirty-two languages, won multiple awards, and spent more than one hundred weeks on the *New York Times* best-seller list. She is also the author of *The Republic of Imagination: America in Three Books* (2014).

> "I think if a civilization or a culture does not take its own works of literature seriously it goes downhill. You need imagination in order to imagine a future that doesn't exist."

"Unfortunately you have to be deprived of something in order to understand its worth," Nafisi told an interviewer. "I think if a civilization or a culture does not take its own works of literature seriously it goes downhill. You need imagination in order to imagine a future that doesn't exist."

Nafisi left Iran with her family in 1997. She is currently a Visiting Fellow at the Foreign Policy Institute of the Johns Hopkins University School of Advanced International Studies and the director of the Dialogue Project, an education and policy initiative for the development of democracy and human rights in the Muslim world. This essay, adapted from *Reading Lolita in Tehran* (2003), first appeared in the *Chronicle of Higher Education*. She has since published a second memoir, *Things I've Been Silent About: Memories of a Prodigal Daughter* (2008), which focuses on her family.

IN THE FALL OF 1995, after resigning from my last academic post, I decided to indulge myself and fulfill a dream. I chose seven of my best and most committed students and invited them to come to my home every Thursday morning to discuss literature. They were all women—to teach a mixed class in the privacy of my home was too risky, even if we were discussing harmless works of fiction.

For nearly two years, almost every Thursday morning, rain or shine, they came to my house, and almost every time, I could not get over the shock of seeing them shed their mandatory veils and robes and burst into color. When my students came into that room, they took off more than their scarves and robes. Gradually, each one gained an outline and a shape, becoming her own inimitable self. Our world in that living room with its window framing my beloved Elburz Mountains became our sanctuary, our self-contained universe, mocking the reality of black-scarved, timid faces in the city that sprawled below.

The theme of the class was the relationship between fiction and reality. We would read Persian classical literature, such as the tales of our own lady of fiction, Scheherazade, from *A Thousand and One Nights*, along with Western classics—*Pride and Prejudice, Madame Bovary, Daisy Miller, The Dean's*

December, and *Lolita*, the work of fiction that perhaps most resonated with our lives in the Islamic Republic of Iran. For the first time in many years, I felt a sense of anticipation that was not marred by tension: I would not need to go through the tortuous rituals that had marked my days when I taught at the university—rituals governing what I was forced to wear, how I was expected to act, the gestures I had to remember to control.

Life in the Islamic Republic was as capricious as the month of April, when short periods of sunshine would suddenly give way to showers and storms. It was unpredictable: The regime would go through cycles of some tolerance, followed by a crackdown. Now, in the mid-1990s, after a period of relative calm and so-called liberalization, we had again entered a time of hardships. Universities had once more become the targets of attack by the cultural purists, who were busy imposing stricter sets of laws, going so far as to segregate men and women in classes and punishing disobedient professors.

The University of Allameh Tabatabai, where I had been teaching since   5
1987, had been singled out as the most liberal university in Iran. It was rumored that someone in the Ministry of Higher Education had asked, rhetorically, if the faculty at Allameh thought they lived in Switzerland. Switzerland had somehow become a byword for Western laxity. Any program or action that was deemed un-Islamic was reproached with a mocking reminder that Iran was by no means Switzerland.

The pressure was hardest on the students. I felt helpless as I listened to their endless tales of woe. Female students were being penalized for running up the stairs when they were late for classes, for laughing in the hallways, for talking to members of the opposite sex. One day Sanaz had barged into class near the end of the session, crying. In between bursts of tears, she explained that she was late because the female guards at the door, finding a blush in her bag, had tried to send her home with a reprimand.

Why did I stop teaching so suddenly? I had asked myself this question many times. Was it the declining quality of the university? The ever-increasing indifference among the remaining faculty members and students? The daily struggle against arbitrary rules and restrictions?

I often went over in my mind the reaction of the university officials to my letter of resignation. They had harassed and limited me in all manner of ways, monitoring my visitors, controlling my actions, refusing my long-overdue tenure; and when I resigned, they infuriated me by suddenly commiserating and by refusing to accept my resignation. The students had threatened to boycott classes, and it was of some satisfaction to me to find out later that despite threats of reprisals, they in fact did boycott my replacement. Everyone thought I would break down and eventually return. It took two more years before they finally accepted my resignation.

Teaching in the Islamic Republic, like any other vocation, was subservient to politics and subject to arbitrary rules. Always, the joy of teaching was marred by diversions and considerations forced on us by the regime—how well could one teach when the main concern of university officials was not the quality of one's work but the color of one's lips, the subversive potential of a single strand of hair? Could one really concentrate on one's job when what preoccupied the faculty was how to excise the word "wine" from a Hemingway story, when they decided not to teach Brontë because she appeared to condone adultery?

In selecting students for study in my home, I did not take into consider- 10
ation their ideological or religious backgrounds. Later, I would count it as the class's great achievement that such a mixed group, with different and at times conflicting backgrounds, personal as well as religious and social, remained so loyal to its goals and ideals. One reason for my choice of these particular girls was the peculiar mixture of fragility and courage I sensed in them. They were what you would call loners, who did not belong to any particular group or sect. I admired their ability to survive not despite but in some ways because of their solitary lives.

One of the first books we read was Nabokov's *Invitation to a Beheading*. Nabokov creates for us in this novel not the actual physical pain and torture of a totalitarian regime but the nightmarish quality of living in an atmosphere of perpetual dread. Cincinnatus C. is frail, he is passive, he is a hero without knowing or acknowledging it: He fights with his instincts, and his acts of writing are his means of escape. He is a hero because he refuses to become like all the rest.

We formed a special bond with Nabokov despite the difficulty of his prose. This went deeper than our identification with his themes. His novels are shaped around invisible trapdoors, sudden gaps that constantly pull the carpet from under the reader's feet. They are filled with mistrust of what we call everyday reality, an acute sense of that reality's fickleness and frailty. There was something, both in his fiction and in his life, that we instinctively related to and grasped, the possibility of a boundless freedom when all options are taken away.

Nabokov used the term "fragile unreality" to explain his own state of exile; it also describes our existence in the Islamic Republic of Iran. We lived in a culture that denied any merit to literary works, considering them important only when they were handmaidens to something seemingly more urgent—namely, ideology. This was a country where all gestures, even the most private, were interpreted in political terms. The colors of my head scarf or my father's tie were symbols of Western decadence and imperialist tendencies. Not wearing a beard, shaking hands with members of the opposite sex, clapping or whistling in public meetings, were likewise considered Western and therefore decadent, part of the plot by imperialists to bring down our culture.

Our class was shaped within this context. There, in that living room, we rediscovered that we were also living, breathing human beings; and no matter how repressive the state became, no matter how intimidated and frightened we were, like Lolita we tried to escape and to create our own little pockets of freedom. And, like Lolita, we took every opportunity to flaunt our insubordination: by showing a little hair from under our scarves, insinuating a little color into the drab uniformity of our appearances, growing our nails, falling in love, and listening to forbidden music.

How can I create this other world outside the room? I have no choice   15
but to appeal to your imagination. Let's imagine one of the girls, say Sanaz, leaving my house, and let us follow her from there to her final destination. She says her goodbyes and puts on her black robe and scarf over her orange shirt and jeans, coiling her scarf around her neck to cover her huge gold earrings. She directs wayward strands of hair under the scarf, puts her notes into her large bag, straps it on over her shoulder, and walks out into the hall. She pauses for a moment on top of the stairs to put on thin, lacy, black gloves to hide her nail polish.

We follow Sanaz down the stairs, out the door, and into the street. You might notice that her gait and her gestures have changed. It is in her best interest not to be seen, not to be heard or noticed. She doesn't walk upright, but bends her head toward the ground and doesn't look at passers-by. She walks quickly and with a sense of determination. The streets of Tehran and other Iranian cities are patrolled by militia, who ride in white Toyota patrols—four gun-carrying men and women, sometimes followed by a mini-bus. They are called the Blood of God. They patrol the streets to make sure that women like Sanaz wear their veils properly, do not wear makeup, do not walk in public with men who are not their fathers, brothers, or husbands. If she gets on a bus, the seating is segregated. She must enter through the rear door and sit in the back seats, allocated to women.

You might well ask, What is Sanaz thinking as she walks the streets of Tehran? How much does this experience affect her? Most probably, she tries to distance her mind as much as possible from her surroundings. Perhaps she is thinking of her distant boyfriend and the time when she will meet him in Turkey. Does she compare her own situation with her mother's when she was the same age? Is she angry that women of her mother's generation could walk the streets freely, enjoy the company of the opposite sex, join the police force, become pilots, live under laws that were among the most progressive in the world regarding women? Does she feel humiliated by the new laws, by the fact that after the revolution, the age of marriage was lowered from eighteen to nine, that stoning became once more the punishment for adultery and prostitution?

In the course of nearly two decades, the streets have been turned into a war zone, where young women who disobey the rules are hurled into patrol cars, taken to jail, flogged, fined, forced to wash the toilets and humil-iated—and, as soon as they leave, they go back and do the same thing. Is she aware, Sanaz, of her own power? Does she realize how dangerous she can be when her every stray gesture is a disturbance to public safety? Does she think how vulnerable are the Revolutionary Guards, who for over eighteen years have patrolled the streets of Tehran and have had to endure young women like herself, and those of other generations, walking, talking, showing a strand of hair just to remind them that they have not converted?

These girls had both a real history and a fabricated one. Although they came from very different backgrounds, the regime that ruled them had tried to make their personal identities and histories irrelevant. They were never free of the regime's definition of them as Muslim women.

Take the youngest in our class, Yassi. There she is, in a photograph I have of the students, with a wistful look on her face. She is bending her head to one side, unsure of what expression to choose. She is wearing a thin white-and-gray scarf, loosely tied at the throat—a perfunctory homage to her family's strict religious background. Yassi was a freshman who audited my graduate courses in my last year of teaching. She felt intimidated by the older students, who, she thought, by virtue of their seniority, were blessed not only with greater knowledge and a better command of English but also with more wisdom. Although she understood the most difficult texts better than many of the graduate students, and although she read the texts more dutifully and with more pleasure than most, she felt secure only in her terrible sense of insecurity.

About a month after I had decided privately to leave Allameh Tabatabai, Yassi and I were standing in front of the green gate at the entrance of the university. What I remember most distinctly about the university now is that green gate. I owe my memory of that gate to Yassi: She mentioned it in one of her poems. The poem is called "How Small Are the Things That I Like." In it, she describes her favorite objects—an orange backpack, a colorful coat, a bicycle just like her cousin's—and she also describes how much she likes to enter the university through the green gate. The gate appears in this poem, and in some of her other writings, as a magical entrance into the forbidden world of all the ordinary things she had been denied in life.

Yet that green gate was closed to her, and to all my girls. Next to the gate there was a small opening with a curtain hanging from it. Through this opening all the female students went into a small, dark room to be inspected. Yassi would describe later what was done to her in this room: "I would first be checked to see if I have the right clothes: the color of my coat, the length of my uniform, the thickness of my scarf, the form of my shoes, the objects in my bag, the visible traces of even the mildest makeup, the size of my rings and their level of attractiveness, all would be checked before I could enter the campus of the university, the same university in which men also study. And to them the main door, with its immense portals and emblems and flags, is generously open."

In the sunny intimacy of our encounter that day, I asked Yassi to have an ice cream with me. We went to a small shop, where, sitting opposite each other with two tall *cafés glacés* between us, our mood changed. We became, if not somber, quite serious. Yassi came from an enlightened religious family that had been badly hurt by the revolution. They felt the Islamic Republic was a betrayal of Islam rather than its assertion. At the start of the revolution, Yassi's mother and older aunt joined a progressive Muslim women's group that, when the new government started to crack down on its former supporters, was forced to go underground. Yassi's mother and aunt went into hiding for a long time. This aunt had four daughters, all older than Yassi, all of whom in one way or another supported an opposition group that was popular with young religious Iranians. They were all but one arrested, tortured, and jailed. When they were released, every one of them married within a year. They married almost haphazardly, as if to negate their former rebellious selves. Yassi felt that they had survived the jail but could not escape the bonds of traditional marriage.

To me, Yassi was the real rebel. She did not join any political group or organization. As a teenager she had defied family traditions and, in the face of strong opposition, had taken up music. Listening to any form of nonreligious music, even on the radio, was forbidden in her family, but Yassi forced her will. Her rebellion did not stop there: She did not marry the right suitor at the right time and instead insisted on leaving her hometown, Shiraz, to go to college in Tehran. Now she lived partly with her older sister and husband and partly in the home of an uncle with fanatical religious leanings. The university, with its low academic standards, its shabby morality, and its ideological limitations, had been a disappointment to her.

What could she do? She did not believe in politics and did not want to   25
marry, but she was curious about love. That day, she explained why all the normal acts of life had become small acts of rebellion and political insubordination to her and to other young people like her. All her life she was shielded. She was never let out of sight; she never had a private corner in which to think, to feel, to dream, to write. She was not allowed to meet any young men on her own. Her family not only instructed her on how to behave around men, but seemed to think they could tell her how she should feel about them as well. What seems natural to someone like you, she said, is so strange and unfamiliar to me.

Again she repeated that she would never get married. She said that for her a man always existed in books, that she would spend the rest of her life with Mr. Darcy[1] — even in the books, there were few men for her. What was wrong with that? She wanted to go to America, like her uncles, like me. Her mother and her aunts had not been allowed to go, but her uncles were given the chance. Could she ever overcome all the obstacles and go to America? Should she go to America? She wanted me to advise her; they all wanted that. But what could I offer her, she who wanted so much more from life than she had been given?

There was nothing in reality that I could give her, so I told her instead about Nabokov's "other world." I asked her if she had noticed how in most of Nabokov's novels, there was always the shadow of another world, one that was attainable only through fiction. It is this world that prevents his heroes and heroines from utter despair, that becomes their refuge in a life that is consistently brutal.

---

[1] **Mr. Darcy:** The leading male character in Jane Austen's classic novel *Pride and Prejudice* (1813). —Eds.

Take *Lolita*. This was the story of a twelve-year-old girl who had nowhere to go. Humbert had tried to turn her into his fantasy, into his dead love, and he had destroyed her. The desperate truth of Lolita's story is not the rape of a twelve-year-old by a dirty old man but the confiscation of one individual's life by another. We don't know what Lolita would have become if Humbert had not engulfed her. Yet the novel, the finished work, is hopeful, beautiful even, a defense not just of beauty but of life, ordinary everyday life, all the normal pleasures that Lolita, like Yassi, was deprived of.

Warming up and suddenly inspired, I added that, in fact, Nabokov had taken revenge against our own solipsizers; he had taken revenge on the Ayatollah Khomeini and those like him. They had tried to shape others according to their own dreams and desires, but Nabokov, through his portrayal of Humbert, had exposed all solipsists who take over other people's lives. She, Yassi, had much potential; she could be whatever she wanted to be — a good wife or a teacher and poet. What mattered was for her to know what she wanted.

I want to emphasize that we were not Lolita, the Ayatollah was not 30 Humbert, and this republic was not what Humbert called his princedom by the sea. *Lolita* was not a critique of the Islamic Republic, but it went against the grain of all totalitarian perspectives.

At some point, the truth of Iran's past became as immaterial to those who had appropriated it as the truth of Lolita's is to Humbert. It became immaterial in the same way that Lolita's truth, her desires and life, must lose color before Humbert's one obsession, his desire to turn a twelve-year-old unruly child into his mistress.

This is how I read *Lolita*. Again and again as we discussed *Lolita* in that class, our discussions were colored by my students' hidden personal sorrows and joys. Like tear stains on a letter, these forays into the hidden and the personal shaded all our discussions of Nabokov.

Humbert never possesses his victim; she always eludes him, just as objects of fantasy are always simultaneously within reach and inaccessible. No matter how they may be broken, the victims will not be forced into submission.

This was on my mind one Thursday evening after class, as I was looking at the diaries my girls had left behind, with their new essays and poems. At the start of our class, I had asked them to describe their image of themselves. They were not ready then to face that question, but every once in a while I returned to it and asked them again. Now, as I sat curled up on the love seat, I looked at dozens of pages of their recent responses.

I have one of these responses in front of me. It belongs to Sanaz, who 35 handed it in shortly after a recent experience in jail, on trumped-up morality charges. It is a simple drawing in black and white, of a naked girl, the white of her body caught in a black bubble. She is crouched in an almost fetal position, hugging one bent knee. Her other leg is stretched out behind her. Her long, straight hair follows the same curved line as the contour of her back, but her face is hidden. The bubble is lifted in the air by a giant bird with long black talons. What interests me is a small detail: the girl's hand reaches out of the bubble and holds on to the talon. Her subservient nakedness is dependent on that talon, and she reaches out to it.

The drawing immediately brought to my mind Nabokov's statement in his famous afterword to *Lolita*, about how the "first little throb of Lolita" went through him in 1939 or early 1940, when he was ill with a severe attack of intercostal neuralgia. He recalls that "the initial shiver of inspiration was somehow prompted by a newspaper story about an ape in the Jardin des Plantes, who, after months of coaxing by a scientist, produced the first drawing ever charcoaled by an animal: this sketch showed the bars of the poor creature's cage."

The two images, one from the novel and the other from reality, reveal a terrible truth. Its terribleness goes beyond the fact that in each case an act of violence has been committed. It goes beyond the bars, revealing the victim's proximity and intimacy with its jailer. Our focus in each is on the delicate spot where the prisoner touches the bar, on the invisible contact between flesh and cold metal.

Most of the other students expressed themselves in words. Manna saw herself as fog, moving over concrete objects, taking on their form but never becoming concrete herself. Yassi described herself as a figment. Nassrin, in one response, gave me the *Oxford English Dictionary*'s definition of the word "paradox." Implicit in almost all of their descriptions was the way they saw themselves in the context of an outside reality that prevented them from defining themselves clearly and separately.

Manna had once written about a pair of pink socks for which she was reprimanded by the Muslim Students' Association. When she complained to a favorite professor, he started teasing her about how she had already ensnared and trapped her man, Nima, and did not need the pink socks to entrap him further.

These students, like the rest of their generation, were different from my 40 generation in one fundamental aspect. My generation complained of a loss, the void in our lives that was created when our past was stolen from us, making us exiles in our own country. Yet we had a past to compare with the present; we had memories and images of what had been taken away. But my girls spoke constantly of stolen kisses, films they had never seen, and the wind they had never felt on their skin. This generation had no past. Their memory was of a half-articulated desire, something they never had. It was this lack, their sense of longing for the ordinary, taken-for-granted aspects of life, that gave their words a certain luminous quality akin to poetry.

I had asked my students if they remembered the dance scene in *Invitation to a Beheading*: The jailer invites Cincinnatus to a dance. They begin a waltz and move out into the hall. In a corner they run into a guard: "They described a circle near him and glided back into the cell, and now Cincinnatus regretted that the swoon's friendly embrace had been so brief." This movement in circles is the main movement of the novel. As long as he accepts the sham world the jailers impose upon him, Cincinnatus will remain their prisoner and will move within the circles of their creation. The worst crime committed by totalitarian mind-sets is that they force their citizens, including their victims, to become complicit in their crimes. Dancing with your jailer, participating in your own execution, that is an act of utmost brutality. My students witnessed it in show trials on television and enacted it every time they went out into the streets dressed as they were told to dress. They had not become part of the crowd who watched the executions, but they did not have the power to protest them, either.

The only way to leave the circle, to stop dancing with the jailer, is to find a way to preserve one's individuality, that unique quality which evades description but differentiates one human being from the other. That is why, in their world, rituals—empty rituals—become so central.

There was not much difference between our jailers and Cincinnatus's executioners. They invaded all private spaces and tried to shape every gesture, to force us to become one of them, and that in itself is another form of execution.

In the end, when Cincinnatus is led to the scaffold, and as he lays his head on the block, in preparation for his execution, he repeats the magic mantra: "by myself." This constant reminder of his uniqueness, and his attempts to write, to articulate and create a language different from the one imposed upon him by his jailers, saves him at the last moment, when he takes his head in his hands and walks away toward voices that beckon him from that other world, while the scaffold and all the sham world around him, along with his executioner, disintegrate. ■

The Reader's Presence

1. What does literature represent to Nafisi's students? How do the young women's experiences in Iran shape their interpretations and understandings of Nabokov?

2. Why is Cincinnatus's execution a metaphor Nafisi's students can relate to? What is the meaning of Cincinnatus's mantra "by myself" (paragraph 44)? How does Cincinnatus "save" himself in the end? Is this ending hopeful for Nafisi's students? Why or why not?

3. **CONNECTIONS:** Compare and contrast the idea of "other worlds" in Nafisi's essay with Yiyun Li's "To Speak Is to Blunder" (page 159). In what ways does Li's abandonment of her native language relate to the situation of Nafisi's students? What insights can you draw between Nafisi's concept of execution and that of suicide in Li's essay?

Danielle Ofri

SAT

DANIELLE OFRI (b. 1965) demonstrates that it is possible to be a productive writer while pursuing a busy life or career. With an MD and a PhD, Ofri is an attending physician at Bellevue Hospital and assistant professor of medicine at New York University School of Medicine. She is also editor in chief and co-founder of the *Bellevue Literary Review* and the associate chief editor of the award-winning medical textbook *The Bellevue Guide to Outpatient Medicine*. Her essays have appeared in the *New York Times*, the *Los Angeles Times, Best American Essays, Best American Science Writing*, the *New England Journal of Medicine*, the *Missouri Review, Tikkun*, the *Journal of the American Medical Association*, and the *Lancet*. Her

> Danielle Ofri demonstrates that it is possible to be a productive writer while pursuing a busy life or career. In addition to professionally editing and writing, she is an attending physician at Bellevue Hospital and assistant professor of medicine at New York University School of Medicine.

Web site, danielleofri.com, explores the relationship between literature and medicine. A frequent guest on National Public Radio, Ofri lives in New York City with her husband and three children.

Her first collection, *Singular Intimacies: Becoming a Doctor at Bellevue* (2003), was described by physician/author Perri Klass as "a beautiful book about souls and bodies, sadness and healing at a legendary hospital." Ofri co-edited with her colleagues *The Best of the Bellevue Literary Review* (2008), a collection of writings from that journal. Her essay, "SAT," is taken from her 2005 book, *Incidental Findings: Lessons from My Patients in the Art of Medicine*. A *New York Times* profile reports, "To Dr. Ofri every patient's history is a mystery story, a narrative that unfolds full of surprises, exposing the vulnerability at the human core." Her most recent books are *What Doctors Feel: How Emotions Affect the Practice of Medicine* (2013) and *What Patients Say, What Doctors Hear* (2017).

"NEMESIO RIOS?" I called out to the crowded waiting room of our medical clinic. I'd just finished a long stint attending on the wards and I was glad to be back to the relatively sane life of the clinic. "Nemesio Rios?" I called out again.

"Yuh," came a grunt, as a teenaged boy in baggy jeans with a ski hat pulled low over his brow hoisted himself up. He sauntered into my office and slumped into the plastic chair next to my desk.

"What brings you to the clinic today?"

He shrugged. "Feel all right, but they told me to come today," he said, slouching lower into the chair, his oversize sweatshirt reaching nearly to his knees. The chart said he'd been in the ER two weeks ago for a cough.

"How about a regular checkup?" He shrugged again. His eyes were deep 5
brown, tucked deep beneath his brow.

Past medical history? None. Past surgical history? None. Meds? None. Allergies? None. Family history? None.

"Where were you born?" I asked, wanting to know his nationality.

"Here."

"Here in New York?"

"Yeah, in this hospital." 10

"A Bellevue baby!" I said with a grin, noticing that his medical record number had only six digits (current numbers had nine digits). "A genuine Bellevue baby."

There was a small smile, but I could see him working hard to suppress it. "My mom's from Mexico."

"Have you ever been there?" I asked, curious.

"You sound like my mom." He rolled his eyes. "She's always trying to get me to go. She's over there right now visiting her sisters."

"You don't want to go visit?" 15

"Mexico? Just a bunch of corrupt politicians." Nemesio shifted his unlaced sneakers back and forth on the linoleum floor, causing a dull screech each time.

I asked about his family. In a distracted voice, as though he'd been through this a million times before, he told me that he was the youngest of eight, but now that his sister got married, it was only he and his mother left in the house. I asked about his father.

"He lives in Brooklyn." Nemesio poked his hand in and out of the pocket of his sweatshirt. "He's all right, I guess, but he drinks a lot," he said, his voice trailing off. "Doesn't do anything stupid, but he drinks."

"Are you in school now?"

"Me?" he said, his voice perking up for the first time from his baseline 20
mumble. "I'm twenty. I'm done! Graduated last year."

"What are you doing now?"

"Working in a kitchen. It's all right, I guess."

"Any thoughts about college?"

"You sound like my cousin in Connecticut. He's in some college there and he's always bugging me about going to college. But I'm lazy. No one to kick my lazy butt."

"What do you want to do when you grow up?" 25

"What I *really* want to do? I want to play basketball." He gave a small laugh. "But they don't take five-foot-seven guys in the NBA."

"Anything else besides basketball?"

He thought for a minute. "Comics. I like to draw comics. I guess I could be an artist that draws comics." His eye caught the tiny Monet poster I'd taped above the examining table. "That's pretty cool, that painting."

"There are a lot of great art schools here in New York." My comment floated off into empty space. We were silent for a few minutes. I made a few notes in the chart.

"That stuff about peer pressure is a bunch of crap," he said abruptly,   30
forcefully, sitting up in his chair, speaking directly toward the poster in front of him.

I leaned closer toward Nemesio, trying to figure out what this sudden outburst was related to. But he continued, staring straight forward, lecturing at the empty room, as if I weren't there.

"Anyone who tells you they do something because of peer pressure is full of crap." He was even more animated now, even angry. "People always asking me to do stuff, but I can make my own mind up." His hands came out of his sweatshirt pocket and began gesticulating in the air. "My brother and his friends, they're always drinking beer. But I don't like the taste of it. I don't believe in peer pressure."

Speech ended, Nemesio settled back into his chair, resumed his slouched posture, and repositioned his hands into his pockets. Then he glanced up at the ceiling and added quietly, almost wistfully, "But if beer tasted like apple juice, I might be drinking it every day."

He was quiet for a few minutes. One hand slid out of his pocket and started fiddling with the zipper on his sweatshirt.

Without warning he swiveled in his chair to face me directly, his whole   35
body leaning into my desk. "You ever face peer pressure, Doc?"

His eyes were right on mine, and I was caught off guard by this sudden shift in his voice and body language. I felt unexpectedly on the spot. Who does he see? I wondered. Do I represent the older generation or the medical profession or women or non-Hispanic whites? Or all of the above?

Nemesio refused to let my gaze wander off his. He demanded an answer to his question, and our doctor–patient encounter had obviously taken an abrupt turn. I could tell that a lot was riding on my answer, though I wasn't sure what exactly was at stake. Did he need me to provide a reassuring socie-tal answer about how bad drugs are? Or did he need me to identify with him, to say that I've been where he's been, even if that was not exactly the truth?

"Yes," I said, after debating in my head for a moment, trying to think of something sufficiently potent to satisfy the question but not so sordid as to embarrass myself. "I have."

He stared at me, waiting for me to continue. His eyes looked younger and younger.

"In my first year of college," I said. "In the very first week. Everyone was   40
sitting in the stairwell and they were passing a joint around. Everyone took a drag. When it came to me I hesitated. I wasn't really interested in smoking, but everyone else was doing it."

"So what did you do?"

"I didn't want anyone to think I was a little kid, so I took a drag too."

"Did you like it?"

"No, I just hacked and coughed. I didn't even *want* the stupid joint to begin with, and I couldn't believe I was doing it just because everyone else was."

"That peer pressure is crap." Nemesio stated it as a fact and then sank back into his seat.

"You're right. It is. It took me a little while to figure that out."

He pushed the ski hat back from his brow a few inches. "In my high school there was this teacher that was always on my case. She was always bugging me to study and take the tests. What a pain in the butt she was." He pulled the hat all the way off. "But now there's no one around to kick my lazy butt. I could get to college easy, but I'm just lazy."

My mind wandered back to a crisp autumn day in my second month of medical school. Still overwhelmed by the pentose-phosphate shunt and other minutiae of biochemistry, our Clinical Correlation group—led by two fourth-year students—promised us first-year students a taste of clinical medicine.

The CC student leaders had obtained permission for a tour of the New York City medical examiner's office. All suspicious deaths—murders, suicides, and the like—were investigated here.

The autumn sun dazzled against the bright turquoise bricks of the ME building, which stood out in sharp contrast to the gray concrete buildings lining First Avenue. We congregated on the steps, endeavoring to look nonchalant.

The security guard checked our ID cards as well as our letter of entry. We followed him through the metal detector, down the whitewashed concrete hallway, into the unpainted service elevator with a hand-pulled metal grate.

We stared at our sneakers as the elevator lurched downward. It creaked past several floors and landed with a jolt. Out we spilled, gingerly, onto the raw concrete floor. Our first stop was the morgue. The cavernous walk-in refrigerator was icy and silent. There was a Freon smell, the kind I recalled from the frozen food departments in grocery stores. As a child, when I went shopping with my mother I used to lean into the bins of ice cream and frozen waffles and inhale that curiously appealing, vaguely sweet, chemical fragrance. But here the odor was intensified—magnified by the rigid chill and bleak soundlessness of the room.

Nine naked corpses lay on shelves, their wizened bodies covered with skin that glowed a ghastly green from the low-wattage fluorescent lights. These were the unclaimed bodies, mostly elderly men found on the streets. The ones that were never identified, never claimed by relatives. The ones that were sent next door to the medical school. These were the subjects of our first-year anatomy course.

From there we were herded into the autopsy room. Loosely swinging doors delivered us into a shock of cacophonous noise and harsh bright lights. We stumbled into each other, a discombobulated mass at the entranceway, blinking to adjust from the stark silence of the morgue. The autopsy room was long and rectangular. The high ceilings and brisk yellow walls lent an odd air of cheeriness. Seven metal tables lay parallel in the center. Six of them were surrounded by groups of pathology residents performing autopsies. The residents wore long rubber gloves and industrial-strength aprons. The sound of their voices and their clanking instruments echoed in the room.

The only body I had ever opened was my cadaver in anatomy lab, which 55 was preserved in formaldehyde and completely dried out. I'd never actually seen blood. In the autopsy room there was blood everywhere. Residents were handling organs—weighing hearts, measuring kidneys, taking samples from livers—then replacing them in the open corpses. Their aprons were spotted with scarlet streaks. Blood streamed down the troughs that surrounded each table.

It was disgusting, but I wasn't nauseated. These bodies didn't look like people anymore. It was more like a cattle slaughterhouse: cows and pigs lined up to be transformed into sterile packages of cellophane-wrapped chopped meat. The slaughterhouse that compelled you to vow lifetime vegetarianism, a resolve that lasted only until the next barbecue with succulent, browned burgers that looked nothing like the disemboweled carcasses you'd seen earlier.

Then I spied the last table, the only one without a sea of activity around it. Lying on the metal table was a young boy who didn't look older than twelve. He was wearing new Nikes and one leg of his jeans was rolled up to the knee. His bright red basketball jersey was pushed up, revealing a smooth brown chest. He looked as if he were sleeping.

I tiptoed closer. Could he really be dead? There was not a mark on his body. Every part was in its place. His clothes were crisp and clean. There was no blood, no dirt, no sign of struggle. He wasn't anything like the gutted carcasses on the other tables. His expression was serene, his face without blemish. His skin was plump. He was just a beautiful boy sleeping.

I wanted to rouse him, to tell him to get out of this house of death, quick, before the rubber-aproned doctors got to him. There is still time, I wanted to say. Get out while you can!

I leaned over his slender, exposed, adolescent chest. I peered closer. 60 There, just over his left nipple, was a barely perceptible hole. Smaller than the tip of my little finger. A tiny bullet hole.

I stared at that hole. That ignominious hole. That hole that stole this boy's life. I wanted to rewind the tape, to give him a chance to dodge six inches to the right. That's all he'd need—just six inches. Who would balk over six inches?

Somebody pulled on my arm. Time to go.

For months after my visit to the medical examiner's office, I had nightmares. But they weren't about bloody autopsies or refrigerated corpses. I dreamt only about the boy, that beautiful, untouched, intact boy. The one who'd had the misfortune to fall asleep in the autopsy room.

At night, he would creep into my bed. On the street, I could feel his breath on the back of my neck. In the library, while I battled the Krebs cycle and the branches of the trigeminal nerve, he would slip silently into the pages of my book. His body was so perfect, so untouched.

Except for that barely perceptible hole. 65

Now I looked at Nemesio Rios sitting before me; his beautiful body adrift in the uncertainty of adolescence, made all the rockier by the unfair burdens of urban poverty. Research has shown that health status and life expectancy are directly correlated with socioeconomic status and earning power. Whether this is related to having health insurance, or simply to having more knowledge to make healthier lifestyle choices, there is no doubt that being poor is bad for your health.

As I scribbled in his chart, an odd thought dawned on me: the best thing that I, as a physician, could recommend for Nemesio's long-term health would be to take the SAT and get into college. Too bad I couldn't just write a prescription for that.

"Have you taken the SAT yet?" I asked Nemesio.

"Nah. I can't stand U.S. history. What's the point of knowing U.S. history?"

I twisted my stethoscope around my finger. "Ever hear of McCarthy?" 70

He shrugged. "Yeah, maybe."

"McCarthy tried to intimidate people to turn in their friends and coworkers. Anyone who might believe differently from him. I'd hate to see that part of U.S. history repeated."

He nodded slowly. "Yeah, I guess. I wouldn't want nobody to tell me what to think. That peer pressure is crap."

"Besides," I added, "there's no U.S. history on the SAT."

Nemesio turned toward me, his eyes opened wide. "Yeah? No U.S. his- 75 tory?" His cheeks were practically glowing.

"No history. Just math and English."

"Wow," he said. "No U.S. history. That's pretty cool." His tone of voice changed abruptly as his gaze plummeted to the floor. "But damn, I can't remember those fractions and stuff."

"Sure you can," I said. "It's all the same from high school. If you review it, it'll all come back to you."

In medical school, I had taught an SAT prep course on the weekends to help pay my living expenses. For kids in more affluent neighborhoods, these courses were standard. But it didn't seem fair, because for Nemesio, his health depended on it.

"Listen," I said. "I'll make you a deal. You go out and buy one of those 80 SAT review books and bring it to our next appointment. I bet we can brush you up on those fractions."

He shifted in his seat and I could just detect a hint of a swagger in his torso. "Okay, Doc. I'll take you on."

Nemesio stood up to go and then turned quickly back to me. "College ain't so bad, but what I really want is to play basketball."

Now it was my turn to nod. "There's nothing like a good ballgame. I played point guard in college."

"You? You even shorter than me."

"That's why I had to find another career."

He grinned. "You and me both." Nemesio put his ski hat on and pulled it carefully down over his forehead. Then he slouched out the door.

Nemesio and I met three times over the next two months. While my stethoscope and blood pressure cuff sat idle, we reviewed algebra, analogies, geometry, and reading comprehension. With only a little prodding, Nemesio was able to recall what he had learned in high school. And he thought it was "really cool" when I showed him the tricks and shortcuts that I recalled from the SAT prep course.

I lost touch with Nemesio after that. Many days I thought about him, wondering how things turned out. If this were a movie, he'd score a perfect 1600 and be off to Princeton on full scholarship. But Harlem isn't Hollywood, and the challenges in real life are infinitely more complex. I don't know if Nemesio ever got into college—any college—or if he even took the SAT exam. But he did learn a bit more about fractions, and I learned a bit more about the meaning of preventative medicine. At the end of each visit, I would face the clinic billing sheet. The top fifty diagnoses were listed—the most common and important medical issues, according to Medicaid, that faced our patients. I scrutinized them each time, because I was required to check one off, to check off Nemesio Rios's most salient medical diagnosis and treatment, to identify the most pressing issues for his health, to categorize the medical interventions deemed necessary for this patient's well-being, otherwise the clinic wouldn't get reimbursed.

SAT prep was not among them. ●

The Reader's Presence

1. Ofri uses dialogue extensively throughout the essay. What are the effects of this choice? How would the essay be different if she had not used her patient's own words?

2. Why does Ofri juxtapose the material about Nemesio Rios with the material about her experiences in the morgue? Is the fact that Ofri does not reveal the outcome of Nemesio's story disturbing? Does this uncertainty make the essay more or less believable? Why?

3. **CONNECTIONS:** Ofri argues that continuing his education is the best step her patient can take to safeguard his health. Do you agree? Read John Taylor Gatto's "Against School" (page 517). Does Gatto's argument apply to a case like that of Ofri's young patient? Why or why not?

Katha Pollitt

WHY BOYS DON'T PLAY WITH DOLLS

KATHA POLLITT was born in 1949 in New York City and is considered one of the leading poets of her generation. Her 1982 collection of poetry, *Antarctic Traveller*, won a National Book Critics Circle Award. Her poetry has appeared in such publications as the *Atlantic* and the *New Yorker*, and she has received a Guggenheim Fellowship and a National Endowment for the Arts grant. She published a second collection of poetry, *The Mind-Body Problem*, in 2009.

Pollitt also writes essays, and she has gained a reputation for incisive analysis and persuasive argument. She contributes reviews, essays, and social commentary to numerous national publications, many of which are collected in *Reasonable Creatures: Essays on Women and Feminism* (1994). Her collections

> **"What I want in a poem . . . is not an argument, it's not a statement, it has to do with language."**

of essays, *Subject to Debate: Sense and Dissents on Women, Politics, and Culture* (2001) and *Virginity or Death! And Other Social and Political Issues of Our Time* (2006), draw on her column called "Subject to Debate," which is printed twice monthly in the *Nation*, where she has been a writer, an associate editor, and a columnist since 1980. She won the American Book Award's Lifetime Achievement Award in 2010. Her latest collection of personal essays is *Learning to Drive: And Other Life Stories* (2008). She has also written *Pro: Reclaiming Abortion Rights* (2015). "Why Boys Don't Play with Dolls" appeared in the *New York Times Magazine* in 1995.

Pollitt thinks of writing poems and political essays as two distinct endeavors. "What I want in a poem—one that I read or one that I write—is not an argument, it's not a statement, it has to do with language. . . . There isn't that much political poetry that I find I even want to read once, and almost none that I would want to read again."

IT'S TWENTY-EIGHT YEARS since the founding of NOW,[1] and boys still like trucks and girls still like dolls. Increasingly, we are told that the source of these robust preferences must lie outside society—in prenatal hormonal influences, brain chemistry, genes—and that feminism has reached its natural limits. What else could possibly explain the love of preschool girls for party dresses or the desire of toddler boys to own more guns than Mark from Michigan?[2]

---

[1] **NOW:** The National Organization for Women was founded in 1966. —EDS.

[2] **Mark from Michigan:** Mark Koernke, a former right-wing talk-show host who supports the militia movement's resistance to federal government. —EDS.

True, recent studies claim to show small cognitive differences between the sexes: he gets around by orienting himself in space, she does it by remembering landmarks. Time will tell if any deserve the hoopla with which each is invariably greeted, over the protests of the researchers themselves. But even if the results hold up (and the history of such research is not encouraging), we don't need studies of sex-differentiated brain activity in reading, say, to understand why boys and girls still seem so unalike.

The feminist movement has done much for some women, and something for every woman, but it has hardly turned America into a playground free of sex roles. It hasn't even got women to stop dieting or men to stop interrupting them.

Instead of looking at kids to "prove" that differences in behavior by sex are innate, we can look at the ways we raise kids as an index to how unfinished the feminist revolution really is, and how tentatively it is embraced even by adults who fully expect their daughters to enter previously male-dominated professions and their sons to change diapers.

I'm at a children's birthday party. "I'm sorry," one mom silently mouths to   5
the mother of the birthday girl, who has just torn open her present—Tropical Splash Barbie. Now, you can love Barbie or you can hate Barbie, and there are feminists in both camps. But *apologize* for Barbie? Inflict Barbie, against your own convictions, on the child of a friend you know will be none too pleased?

Every mother in that room had spent years becoming a person who had to be taken seriously, not least by herself. Even the most attractive, I'm willing to bet, had suffered over her body's failure to fit the impossible American ideal. Given all that, it seems crazy to transmit Barbie to the next generation. Yet to reject her is to say that what Barbie represents—being sexy, thin, stylish—is unimportant, which is obviously not true, and children know it's not true.

Women's looks matter terribly in this society, and so Barbie, however ambivalently, must be passed along. After all, there are worse toys. The Cut and Style Barbie styling head, for example, a grotesque object intended to encourage "hair play." The grown-ups who give that probably apologize, too.

How happy would most parents be to have a child who flouted sex conventions? I know a lot of women, feminists, who complain in a comical, eyeball-rolling way about their sons' passion for sports: the ruined weekends, obnoxious coaches, macho values. But they would not think of discouraging their sons from participating in this activity they find so foolish. Or do they? Their husbands are sports fans, too, and they like their husbands a lot.

Could it be that even sports-resistant moms see athletics as part of manliness? That if their sons wanted to spend the weekend writing up their diaries, or reading, or baking, they'd find it disturbing? Too antisocial? Too lonely? Too gay?

Theories of innate differences in behavior are appealing. They let parents   10
off the hook—no small recommendation in a culture that holds moms, and sometimes even dads, responsible for their children's every misstep on the road to bliss and success.

They allow grown-ups to take the path of least resistance to the dominant culture, which always requires less psychic effort, even if it means more actual work: just ask the working mother who comes home exhausted and nonetheless finds it easier to pick up her son's socks than make him do it himself. They let families buy for their children, without *too* much guilt, the unbelievably sexist junk that the kids, who have been watching commercials since birth, understandably crave.

But the thing that theories do most of all is tell adults that the *adult* world—in which moms and dads still play by many of the old rules even as they question and fidget and chafe against them—is the way it's supposed to be. A girl with a doll and a boy with a truck "explain" why men are from Mars and women are from Venus, why wives do housework and husbands just don't understand.

The paradox is that the world of rigid and hierarchical sex roles evoked by determinist theories is already passing away. Three-year-olds may indeed insist that doctors are male and nurses female, even if their own mother is a physician. Six-year-olds know better. These days, something like half of all medical students are female, and male applications to nursing school are inching upward. When tomorrow's three-year-olds play doctor, who's to say how they'll assign the roles?

With sex roles, as in every area of life, people aspire to what is possible, and conform to what is necessary. But these are not fixed, especially today. Biological determinism may reassure some adults about their present, but it is feminism, the ideology of flexible and converging sex roles, that fits our children's future. And the kids, somehow, know this.

That's why, if you look carefully, you'll find that for every kid who fits a   15
stereotype, there's another who's breaking one down. Sometimes it's the same kid—the boy who skateboards *and* takes cooking in his afterschool program; the girl who collects stuffed animals *and* A-pluses in science.

Feminists are often accused of imposing their "agenda" on children. Isn't that what adults always do, consciously and unconsciously? Kids aren't born religious, or polite, or kind, or able to remember where they put their sneakers. Inculcating these behaviors, and the values behind them, is a tremendous amount of work, involving many adults. We don't have a choice, really, about *whether* we should give our children messages about what it means to be male and female—they're bombarded with them from morning till night.

The question, as always, is what do we want those messages to be? ●

The Reader's Presence

1. Pollitt notes in her opening paragraph, "It's twenty-eight years since the founding of NOW, and boys still like trucks and girls still like dolls." What does Pollitt identify as the competing theories to explain these differences between boys and girls? Which theory does Pollitt prefer, and how does she express her support of it?

2. As you reread the essay, consider carefully the role of the media in upholding the status quo with regard to differentiated roles for girls and boys. As you develop a response to this question, examine carefully both the media directed principally to children and the media targeted at adults. In the latter category, for instance,

Pollitt refers to the media version of scientific research studies into gender differences (paragraph 2) and alludes to popular books that discuss the differences between men and women, such as *Men Are from Mars, Women Are from Venus*, and *You Just Don't Understand* (paragraph 12). Drawing on Pollitt's essay and on your own experience, identify—and discuss—the specific social responsibilities you would like to see America's mass media take more seriously.

3. **CONNECTIONS:** How would you characterize Pollitt's stance toward today's parents? What are some of the reasons she gives to explain parents' choices and actions? Consider Pollitt's argument in light of both Amy Chua's "Parents and Children" (page 514) and the excerpt from Margo Jefferson's "Negroland" (page 124). How do these selections offer readers a portrait of parents and parenting? Drawing on all three essays, consider the ways parenting figures in the transmission of beliefs and practices? Note that two of the essays present parenting from ethnic and racial perspectives. In your opinion, do these diverse perspectives challenge or confirm Pollitt's views on parenting?

Eric Schlosser
WHY MCDONALD'S FRIES TASTE SO GOOD

Investigative reporter and author **ERIC SCHLOSSER** was born in New York City in 1959. A correspondent for the *Atlantic* and a contributor to *Rolling Stone* and the *New Yorker*, he has won numerous journalistic honors and awards. His two-part *Atlantic Monthly* series, "Reefer Madness" and "Marijuana and the Law," won the National Magazine Award in 1994 and became the basis for his best-selling collection of essays, *Reefer Madness: Sex, Drugs, and Cheap Labor in the American Black Market* (2003), an exposé of America's underground economy. *Fast Food Nation: The Dark Side of the All-American Meal* (2001), Schlosser's controversial and influential first book, prompted a reexamination of practices in the meat-processing industry. A best-seller,

> **Fast Food Nation: The Dark Side of the All-American Meal (2001), Eric Schlosser's first book, prompted a reexamination of practices in the meat-processing industry.**

the book was adapted and released as a motion picture in 2006, followed by a companion book for young people, *Chew on This: Everything You Don't Want to Know About Fast Food* (2006). His most recent book, *Command and Control: Nuclear Weapons, the Damascus Accident, and the Illusion of Safety*, was published in 2013.

Of writing *Fast Food Nation*, Schlosser said, "I care about the literary aspects of the book. I tried to make it as clear as possible, and make it an interesting thing to read, but I sacrificed some of that, ultimately, in order to get this out to people and let them know what's going on."

THE FRENCH FRY was "almost sacrosanct for me," Ray Kroc, one of the founders of McDonald's, wrote in his autobiography, "its preparation a ritual to be followed religiously." During the chain's early years french fries were made from scratch every day. Russet Burbank potatoes were peeled, cut into shoestrings, and fried in McDonald's kitchens. As the chain expanded nationwide, in the mid-1960s, it sought to cut labor costs, reduce the number of suppliers, and ensure that its fries tasted the same at every restaurant. McDonald's began switching to frozen french fries in 1966—and few customers noticed the difference. Nevertheless, the change had a profound effect on the nation's agriculture and diet. A familiar food had been transformed into a highly processed industrial commodity. McDonald's fries now come from huge manufacturing plants that can peel, slice, cook, and freeze two million pounds of potatoes a day. The rapid expansion of McDonald's and the popularity of its low-cost, mass-produced fries changed the way Americans eat. In 1960 Americans consumed an average of about eighty-one pounds of fresh potatoes and four pounds of frozen french fries. In 2000 they consumed an average of about fifty pounds of fresh potatoes and thirty pounds of frozen fries. Today McDonald's is the largest buyer of potatoes in the United States.

The taste of McDonald's french fries played a crucial role in the chain's success—fries are much more profitable than hamburgers—and was long praised by customers, competitors, and even food critics. James Beard loved McDonald's fries. Their distinctive taste does not stem from the kind of potatoes that McDonald's buys, the technology that processes them, or the restaurant equipment that fries them: other chains use Russet Burbanks, buy their french fries from the same large processing companies, and have similar fryers in their restaurant kitchens. The taste of a french fry is largely determined by the cooking oil. For decades McDonald's cooked its french fries in a mixture of about 7 percent cottonseed oil and 93 percent beef tallow. The mixture gave the fries their unique flavor—and more saturated beef fat per ounce than a McDonald's hamburger.

In 1990, amid a barrage of criticism over the amount of cholesterol in its fries, McDonald's switched to pure vegetable oil. This presented the company with a challenge: how to make fries that subtly taste like beef without cooking them in beef tallow. A look at the ingredients in McDonald's french fries suggests how the problem was solved. Toward the end of the list is a seemingly innocuous yet oddly mysterious phrase: "natural flavor." That ingredient helps to explain not only why the fries taste so good but also why most fast food—indeed, most of the food Americans eat today—tastes the way it does.

Advertising poster for the 2004 award-winning documentary
by Morgan Spurlock that examined the consequences of
surviving for one month entirely on meals from McDonald's.

Open your refrigerator, your freezer, your kitchen cupboards, and look
at the labels on your food. You'll find "natural flavor" or "artificial flavor" in
just about every list of ingredients. The similarities between these two broad
categories are far more significant than the differences. Both are man-made
additives that give most processed food most of its taste. People usually buy
a food item the first time because of its packaging or appearance. Taste usually determines whether they buy it again. About 90 percent of the money
that Americans now spend on food goes to buy processed food. The canning, freezing, and dehydrating techniques used in processing destroy most
of food's flavor—and so a vast industry has arisen in the United States to

make processed food palatable. Without this flavor industry today's fast food would not exist. The names of the leading American fast-food chains and their best-selling menu items have become embedded in our popular culture and famous worldwide. But few people can name the companies that manufacture fast food's taste.

The flavor industry is highly secretive. Its leading companies will not   5
divulge the precise formulas of flavor compounds or the identities of clients. The secrecy is deemed essential for protecting the reputations of beloved brands. The fast-food chains, understandably, would like the public to believe that the flavors of the food they sell somehow originate in their restaurant kitchens, not in distant factories run by other firms. A McDonald's french fry is one of countless foods whose flavor is just a component in a complex manufacturing process. The look and the taste of what we eat now are frequently deceiving — by design.

THE FLAVOR CORRIDOR

The New Jersey Turnpike runs through the heart of the flavor industry, an industrial corridor dotted with refineries and chemical plants. International Flavors & Fragrances (IFF), the world's largest flavor company, has a manufacturing facility off Exit 8A in Dayton, New Jersey; Givaudan, the world's second-largest flavor company, has a plant in East Hanover. Haarmann & Reimer, the largest German flavor company, has a plant in Teterboro, as does Takasago, the largest Japanese flavor company. Flavor Dynamics has a plant in South Plainfield; Frutarom is in North Bergen; Elan Chemical is in Newark. Dozens of companies manufacture flavors in the corridor between Teaneck and South Brunswick. Altogether the area produces about two-thirds of the flavor additives sold in the United States.

The IFF plant in Dayton is a huge pale-blue building with a modern office complex attached to the front. It sits in an industrial park, not far from a BASF plastics factory, a Jolly French Toast factory, and a plant that manufactures Liz Claiborne cosmetics. Dozens of tractor-trailers were parked at the IFF loading dock the afternoon I visited, and a thin cloud of steam floated from a roof vent. Before entering the plant, I signed a nondisclosure form, promising not to reveal the brand names of foods that contain IFF flavors. The place reminded me of Willy Wonka's chocolate factory. Wonderful smells drifted through the hallways, men and women in neat white lab coats cheerfully went about their work, and hundreds of little glass bottles sat on laboratory tables and shelves. The bottles contained powerful but fragile flavor chemicals, shielded from light by brown glass and round white caps shut tight. The long chemical names on the little white labels were as mystifying to me as medieval Latin. These odd-sounding things would be mixed and poured and turned into new substances, like magic potions.

I was not invited into the manufacturing areas of the IFF plant, where, it was thought, I might discover trade secrets. Instead I toured various laboratories and pilot kitchens, where the flavors of well-established brands are tested or adjusted, and where whole new flavors are created. IFF's snack-and-savory lab is responsible for the flavors of potato chips, corn chips, breads, crackers, breakfast cereals, and pet food. The confectionary lab devises flavors for ice cream, cookies, candies, toothpastes, mouthwashes, and antacids. Everywhere I looked, I saw famous, widely advertised products sitting on laboratory desks and tables. The beverage lab was full of brightly colored liquids in clear bottles. It comes up with flavors for popular soft drinks, sports drinks, bottled teas, and wine coolers, for all-natural juice drinks, organic soy drinks, beers, and malt liquors. In one pilot kitchen I saw a dapper food technologist, a middle-aged man with an elegant tie beneath his crisp lab coat, carefully preparing a batch of cookies with white frosting and pink-and-white sprinkles. In another pilot kitchen I saw a pizza oven, a grill, a milk-shake machine, and a french fryer identical to those I'd seen at innumerable fast-food restaurants.

In addition to being the world's largest flavor company, IFF manufactures the smells of six of the ten best-selling fine perfumes in the United States, including Estée Lauder's Beautiful, Clinique's Happy, Lancôme's Trésor, and Calvin Klein's Eternity. It also makes the smells of household products such as deodorant, dishwashing detergent, bath soap, shampoo, furniture polish, and floor wax. All these aromas are made through essentially the same process: the manipulation of volatile chemicals. The basic science behind the scent of your shaving cream is the same as that governing the flavor of your TV dinner.

"NATURAL" AND "ARTIFICIAL"

Scientists now believe that human beings acquired the sense of taste as a   10 way to avoid being poisoned. Edible plants generally taste sweet, harmful ones bitter. The taste buds on our tongues can detect the presence of half a dozen or so basic tastes, including sweet, sour, bitter, salty, astringent, and umami, a taste discovered by Japanese researchers—a rich and full sense of deliciousness triggered by amino acids in foods such as meat, shellfish, mushrooms, potatoes, and seaweed. Taste buds offer a limited means of detection, however, compared with the human olfactory system, which can perceive thousands of different chemical aromas. Indeed, "flavor" is primarily the smell of gases being released by the chemicals you've just put in your mouth. The aroma of a food can be responsible for as much as 90 percent of its taste.

The act of drinking, sucking, or chewing a substance releases its volatile gases. They flow out of your mouth and up your nostrils, or up the passageway in the back of your mouth, to a thin layer of nerve cells called the olfactory epithelium, located at the base of your nose, right between your eyes. Your brain combines the complex smell signals from your olfactory epithelium with the simple taste signals from your tongue, assigns a flavor to what's in your mouth, and decides if it's something you want to eat.

A person's food preferences, like his or her personality, are formed during the first few years of life, through a process of socialization. Babies innately prefer sweet tastes and reject bitter ones; toddlers can learn to enjoy hot and spicy food, bland health food, or fast food, depending on what the people around them eat. The human sense of smell is still not fully understood. It is greatly affected by psychological factors and expectations. The mind focuses intently on some of the aromas that surround us and filters out the overwhelming majority. People can grow accustomed to bad smells or good smells; they stop noticing what once seemed overpowering. Aroma and memory are somehow inextricably linked. A smell can suddenly evoke a long-forgotten moment. The flavors of childhood foods seem to leave an indelible mark, and adults often return to them, without always knowing why. These "comfort foods" become a source of pleasure and reassurance—a fact that fast-food chains use to their advantage. Childhood memories of Happy Meals, which come with french fries, can translate into frequent adult visits to McDonald's. On average, Americans now eat about four servings of french fries every week.

The human craving for flavor has been a largely unacknowledged and unexamined force in history. For millennia royal empires have been built, unexplored lands traversed, and great religions and philosophies forever changed by the spice trade. In 1492 Christopher Columbus set sail to find seasoning. Today the influence of flavor in the world marketplace is no less decisive. The rise and fall of corporate empires—of soft-drink companies, snack-food companies, and fast-food chains—is often determined by how their products taste.

The flavor industry emerged in the mid-nineteenth century, as processed foods began to be manufactured on a large scale. Recognizing the need for flavor additives, early food processors turned to perfume companies that had long experience working with essential oils and volatile aromas. The great perfume houses of England, France, and the Netherlands produced many of the first flavor compounds. In the early part of the twentieth century Germany took the technological lead in flavor production, owing to its powerful chemical industry. Legend has it that a German scientist discovered methyl anthranilate, one of the first artificial flavors, by accident while mixing chemicals in his laboratory. Suddenly the lab was filled with the sweet smell of grapes. Methyl anthranilate later became the chief flavor compound in grape Kool-Aid. After World War II much of the perfume industry shifted from Europe to the United States, settling in New York City near the garment district and the fashion houses. The flavor industry came with it, later moving to New Jersey for greater plant capacity. Man-made flavor additives were used mostly in baked goods, candies, and sodas until the 1950s, when sales of processed food began to soar. The invention of gas chromatographs and mass spectrometers—machines capable of detecting volatile gases at low levels—vastly increased the number of flavors that could be synthesized. By the mid-1960s flavor companies were churning out compounds to supply the taste of Pop Tarts, Bac-Os, Tab, Tang, Filet-O-Fish sandwiches, and literally thousands of other new foods.

The American flavor industry now has annual revenues of about   15
$1.4 billion. Approximately 10,000 new processed-food products are intro-
duced every year in the United States. Almost all of them require flavor
additives. And about nine out of ten of these products fail. The latest flavor
innovations and corporate realignments are heralded in publications such
as *Chemical Market Reporter*, *Food Chemical News*, *Food Engineering*, and
Food Product Design. The progress of IFF has mirrored that of the flavor
industry as a whole. IFF was formed in 1958, through the merger of two small
companies. Its annual revenues have grown almost fifteenfold since the early
1970s, and it currently has manufacturing facilities in twenty countries.

Today's sophisticated spectrometers, gas chromatographs, and headspace-
vapor analyzers provide a detailed map of a food's flavor components, detecting chemical aromas present in amounts as low as one part per billion. The
human nose, however, is even more sensitive. A nose can detect aromas
present in quantities of a few parts per trillion—an amount equivalent to
about 0.000000000003 percent. Complex aromas, such as those of coffee and
roasted meat, are composed of volatile gases from nearly a thousand different
chemicals. The smell of a strawberry arises from the interaction of about 350
chemicals that are present in minute amounts. The quality that people seek
most of all in a food—flavor—is usually present in a quantity too infinitesimal
to be measured in traditional culinary terms such as ounces or teaspoons. The
chemical that provides the dominant flavor of bell pepper can be tasted in
amounts as low as 0.02 parts per billion; one drop is sufficient to add flavor to
five average-size swimming pools. The flavor additive usually comes next to
last in a processed food's list of ingredients and often costs less than its packaging. Soft drinks contain a larger proportion of flavor additives than most
products. The flavor in a twelve-ounce can of Coke costs about half a cent.

The color additives in processed foods are usually present in even smaller
amounts than the flavor compounds. Many of New Jersey's flavor companies
also manufacture these color additives, which are used to make processed
foods look fresh and appealing. Food coloring serves many of the same decorative purposes as lipstick, eye shadow, mascara—and is often made from
the same pigments. Titanium dioxide, for example, has proved to be an especially versatile mineral. It gives many processed candies, frostings, and icings
their bright white color; it is a common ingredient in women's cosmetics; and
it is the pigment used in many white oil paints and house paints. At Burger
King, Wendy's, and McDonald's coloring agents have been added to many
of the soft drinks, salad dressings, cookies, condiments, chicken dishes, and
sandwich buns.

Studies have found that the color of a food can greatly affect how its
taste is perceived. Brightly colored foods frequently seem to taste better than
bland-looking foods, even when the flavor compounds are identical. Foods
that somehow look off-color often seem to have off tastes. For thousands of

years human beings have relied on visual cues to help determine what is edible. The color of fruit suggests whether it is ripe, the color of meat whether it is rancid. Flavor researchers sometimes use colored lights to modify the influence of visual cues during taste tests. During one experiment in the early 1970s people were served an oddly tinted meal of steak and french fries that appeared normal beneath colored lights. Everyone thought the meal tasted fine until the lighting was changed. Once it became apparent that the steak was actually blue and the fries were green, some people became ill.

The federal Food and Drug Administration does not require companies to disclose the ingredients of their color or flavor additives so long as all the chemicals in them are considered by the agency to be GRAS ("generally recognized as safe"). This enables companies to maintain the secrecy of their formulas. It also hides the fact that flavor compounds often contain more ingredients than the foods to which they give taste. The phrase "artificial strawberry flavor" gives little hint of the chemical wizardry and manufacturing skill that can make a highly processed food taste like strawberries.

A typical artificial strawberry flavor, like the kind found in a Burger King   20
strawberry milk shake, contains the following ingredients: amyl acetate, amyl butyrate, amyl valerate, anethol, anisyl formate, benzyl acetate, benzyl isobutyrate, butyric acid, cinnamyl isobutyrate, cinnamyl valerate, cognac essential oil, diacetyl, dipropyl ketone, ethyl acetate, ethyl amyl ketone, ethyl butyrate, ethyl cinnamate, ethyl heptanoate, ethyl heptylate, ethyl lactate, ethyl methylphenylglycidate, ethyl nitrate, ethyl propionate, ethyl valerate, heliotropin, hydroxyphenyl-2-butanone (10 percent solution in alcohol), α-ionone, isobutyl anthranilate, isobutyl butyrate, lemon essential oil, maltol, 4-methylacetophenone, methyl anthranilate, methyl benzoate, methyl cinnamate, methyl heptine carbonate, methyl naphthyl ketone, methyl salicylate, mint essential oil, neroli essential oil, nerolin, neryl isobutyrate, orris butter, phenethyl alcohol, rose, rum ether, γ-undecalactone, vanillin, and solvent.

Although flavors usually arise from a mixture of many different volatile chemicals, often a single compound supplies the dominant aroma. Smelled alone, that chemical provides an unmistakable sense of the food. Ethyl-2-methyl butyrate, for example, smells just like an apple. Many of today's highly processed foods offer a blank palette: whatever chemicals are added to them will give them specific tastes. Adding methyl-2-pyridyl ketone makes something taste like popcorn. Adding ethyl-3-hydroxy butanoate makes it taste like marshmallow. The possibilities are now almost limitless. Without affecting appearance or nutritional value, processed foods could be made with aroma chemicals such as hexanal (the smell of freshly cut grass) or 3-methyl butanoic acid (the smell of body odor).

The 1960s were the heyday of artificial flavors in the United States. The synthetic versions of flavor compounds were not subtle, but they did not have to be, given the nature of most processed food. For the past twenty years food processors have tried hard to use only "natural flavors" in their products. According to the FDA, these must be derived entirely from natural sources—from herbs, spices, fruits, vegetables, beef, chicken, yeast, bark, roots, and so forth. Consumers prefer to see natural flavors on a label, out of a belief that they are more healthful. Distinctions between artificial and natural flavors can be arbitrary and somewhat absurd, based more on how the flavor has been made than on what it actually contains.

"A natural flavor," says Terry Acree, a professor of food science at Cornell University, "is a flavor that's been derived with an out-of-date technology." Natural flavors and artificial flavors sometimes contain exactly the same chemicals, produced through different methods. Amyl acetate, for example, provides the dominant note of banana flavor. When it is distilled from bananas with a solvent, amyl acetate is a natural flavor. When it is produced by mixing vinegar with amyl alcohol and adding sulfuric acid as a catalyst, amyl acetate is an artificial flavor. Either way it smells and tastes the same. "Natural flavor" is now listed among the ingredients of everything from Health Valley Blueberry Granola Bars to Taco Bell Hot Taco Sauce.

A natural flavor is not necessarily more healthful or purer than an artificial one. When almond flavor—benzaldehyde—is derived from natural sources, such as peach and apricot pits, it contains traces of hydrogen cyanide, a deadly poison. Benzaldehyde derived by mixing oil of clove and amyl acetate does not contain any cyanide. Nevertheless, it is legally considered an artificial flavor and sells at a much lower price. Natural and artificial flavors are now manufactured at the same chemical plants, places that few people would associate with Mother Nature.

A TRAINED NOSE AND A POETIC SENSIBILITY

The small and elite group of scientists who create most of the flavor in most   25
of the food now consumed in the United States are called "flavorists." They draw on a number of disciplines in their work: biology, psychology, physiology, and organic chemistry. A flavorist is a chemist with a trained nose and a poetic sensibility. Flavors are created by blending scores of different chemicals in tiny amounts—a process governed by scientific principles but demanding a fair amount of art. In an age when delicate aromas and microwave ovens do not easily co-exist, the job of the flavorist is to conjure illusions about processed food and, in the words of one flavor company's literature, to ensure "consumer likeability." The flavorists with whom I spoke were discreet, in keeping with the dictates of their trade. They were also charming, cosmopolitan, and ironic. They not only enjoyed fine wine but could identify the chemicals that give each grape its unique aroma. One flavorist compared his work to composing music. A well-made flavor compound will have a "top note" that is often followed by a "dry-down" and a "leveling-off," with different chemicals responsible for each stage. The taste of a food can be radically altered by minute changes in the flavoring combination. "A little odor goes a long way," one flavorist told me.

In order to give a processed food a taste that consumers will find appealing, a flavorist must always consider the food's "mouthfeel"—the unique combination of textures and chemical interactions that affect how the flavor is perceived. Mouthfeel can be adjusted through the use of various fats, gums, starches, emulsifiers, and stabilizers. The aroma chemicals in a food can be precisely analyzed, but the elements that make up mouthfeel are much harder to measure. How does one quantify a pretzel's hardness, a french fry's crispness? Food technologists are now conducting basic research in rheology, the branch of physics that examines the flow and deformation of materials. A number of companies sell sophisticated devices that attempt to measure mouthfeel. The TA.XT2i Texture Analyzer, produced by the Texture Technologies Corporation, of Scarsdale, New York, performs calculations based on data derived from as many as 250 separate probes. It is essentially a mechanical mouth. It gauges the most-important rheological properties of a food—bounce, creep, breaking point, density, crunchiness, chewiness, gumminess, lumpiness, rubberiness, springiness, slipperiness, smoothness, softness, wetness, juiciness, spreadability, springback, and tackiness.

Some of the most important advances in flavor manufacturing are now occurring in the field of biotechnology. Complex flavors are being made using enzyme reactions, fermentation, and fungal and tissue cultures. All the flavors created by these methods—including the ones being synthesized by fungi—are considered natural flavors by the FDA. The new enzyme-based processes are responsible for extremely true-to-life dairy flavors. One company now offers not just butter flavor but also fresh creamy butter, cheesy butter, milky butter, savory melted butter, and super-concentrated butter flavor, in liquid or powder form. The development of new fermentation techniques, along with new techniques for heating mixtures of sugar and amino acids, have led to the creation of much more realistic meat flavors.

The McDonald's Corporation most likely drew on these advances when it eliminated beef tallow from its french fries. The company will not reveal the exact origin of the natural flavor added to its fries. In response to inquiries from *Vegetarian Journal*, however, McDonald's did acknowledge that its fries derive some of their characteristic flavor from "an animal source." Beef is the probable source, although other meats cannot be ruled out. In France, for example, fries are sometimes cooked in duck fat or horse tallow.

Other popular fast foods derive their flavor from unexpected ingredients. McDonald's Chicken McNuggets contain beef extracts, as does Wendy's Grilled Chicken Sandwich. Burger King's BK Broiler Chicken Breast Patty contains "natural smoke flavor." A firm called Red Arrow Products specializes in smoke flavor, which is added to barbecue sauces, snack foods, and processed meats. Red Arrow manufactures natural smoke flavor by charring sawdust and capturing the aroma chemicals released into the air. The smoke is captured in water and then bottled, so that other companies can sell food that seems to have been cooked over a fire.

The Vegetarian Legal Action Network recently petitioned the FDA 30 to issue new labeling requirements for foods that contain natural flavors.

The group wants food processors to list the basic origins of their flavors on their labels. At the moment vegetarians often have no way of knowing whether a flavor additive contains beef, pork, poultry, or shellfish. One of the most widely used color additives—whose presence is often hidden by the phrase "color added"—violates a number of religious dietary restrictions, may cause allergic reactions in susceptible people, and comes from an unusual source. Cochineal extract (also known as carmine or carminic acid) is made from the desiccated bodies of female *Dactylopius coccus Costa*, a small insect harvested mainly in Peru and the Canary Islands. The bug feeds on red cactus berries, and color from the berries accumulates in the females and their unhatched larvae. The insects are collected, dried, and ground into a pigment. It takes about 70,000 of them to produce a pound of carmine, which is used to make processed foods look pink, red, or purple. Dannon strawberry yogurt gets its color from carmine, and so do many frozen fruit bars, candies, and fruit fillings, and Ocean Spray pink-grapefruit juice drink.

In a meeting room at IFF, Brian Grainger let me sample some of the company's flavors. It was an unusual taste test—there was no food to taste. Grainger is a senior flavorist at IFF, a soft-spoken chemist with graying hair, an English accent, and a fondness for understatement. He could easily be mistaken for a British diplomat or the owner of a West End brasserie with two Michelin stars. Like many in the flavor industry, he has an Old World, old-fashioned sensibility. When I suggested that IFF's policy of secrecy and discretion was out of step with our mass-marketing, brand-conscious, self-promoting age, and that the company should put its own logo on the countless products that bear its flavors, instead of allowing other companies to enjoy the consumer loyalty and affection inspired by those flavors, Grainger politely disagreed, assuring me that such a thing would never be done. In the absence of public credit or acclaim, the small and secretive fraternity of flavor chemists praise one another's work. By analyzing the flavor formula of a product, Grainger can often tell which of his counterparts at a rival firm devised it. Whenever he walks down a supermarket aisle, he takes a quiet pleasure in seeing the well-known foods that contain his flavors.

Grainger had brought a dozen small glass bottles from the lab. After he opened each bottle, I dipped a fragrance-testing filter into it—a long white strip of paper designed to absorb aroma chemicals without producing off notes. Before placing each strip of paper in front of my nose, I closed my eyes. Then I inhaled deeply, and one food after another was conjured from the glass bottles. I smelled fresh cherries, black olives, sautéed onions, and shrimp. Grainger's most remarkable creation took me by surprise. After closing my eyes, I suddenly smelled a grilled hamburger. The aroma was uncanny, almost miraculous—as if someone in the room were flipping burgers on a hot grill. But when I opened my eyes, I saw just a narrow strip of white paper and a flavorist with a grin. ▰

The Reader's Presence

1. What do McDonald's french fries have to do with Schlosser's primary aim in this selection? Why does he feature them in the title and use them in the opening to the essay? Why, in your opinion, didn't he use a different example?

2. Describe Schlosser's attitude toward "natural" and "artificial" flavoring (paragraph 4). Does he think one is superior to the other? Why or why not? How critical does he appear toward food additives in general? Do you read his essay as a condemnation of fast food? How does his account of his laboratory visit color your response? Overall, were his laboratory experiences positive or negative? Explain what in his account makes you feel one way or the other.

3. **VISUAL PRESENCE:** Examine carefully the film poster for *Super Size Me* on page 483. What message does this poster convey about the fast-food industry? What specific features in the poster illustrate that message? How does the poster relate to Schlosser's points about food flavoring?

4. **CONNECTIONS:** Compare and contrast Schlosser's investigative techniques with those of Amy Cunningham in "Why Women Smile" (page 339). How does each writer establish a question to investigate, provoke your interest in the issue, gather information, and conduct the investigation? How important are sources and interviews? What information about sources and interviews is omitted from the essays?

Rebecca Solnit

MEN EXPLAIN THINGS TO ME

Between sexual assault and the suppression of free speech, there is a common thread of gendered violence. Feminism has made great strides in the past century, yet gender inequality continues to manifest itself in a number of ways, some more subtle than others. In "Men Explain Things to Me," **REBECCA SOLNIT** (b. 1961) recalls some of her own experiences as she examines the continued struggles of women fighting to be heard in the modern world.

> **"Write bad stuff because the road to good writing is made of words and not all of them are well-arranged words."**

Author of twenty books, Solnit is a prolific essayist, journalist, and historian. She has written on a wide range of subjects, from the history of walking to photography and natural disaster. She is a columnist at *Harper's Magazine*, and her writing has appeared in many other publications, including the *Los Angeles Times* and the *London Review of Books*.

Solnit advises those interested in writing to practice often. "Write. There is no substitute," she says. "Write bad stuff because the road to good writing is made of words and not all of them are well-arranged words."

I STILL DON'T KNOW why Sallie and I bothered to go to that party in the forest slope above Aspen. The people were all older than us and dull in a distinguished way, old enough that we, at forty-ish, passed as the occasion's young ladies. The house was great—if you like Ralph Lauren-style chalets—a rugged luxury cabin at 9,000 feet complete with elk antlers, lots of kilims, and a wood-burning stove. We were preparing to leave, when our host said, "No, stay a little longer so I can talk to you." He was an imposing man who'd made a lot of money.

He kept us waiting while the other guests drifted out into the summer night, and then sat us down at his authentically grainy wood table and said to me, "So? I hear you've written a couple of books."

I replied, "Several, actually."

He said, in the way you encourage your friend's seven-year-old to describe flute practice, "And what are they about?"

They were actually about quite a few different things, the six or seven   5 out by then, but I began to speak only of the most recent on that summer day in 2003, *River of Shadows: Eadweard Muybridge and the Technological Wild West,* my book on the annihilation of time and space and the industrialization of everyday life.

He cut me off soon after I mentioned Muybridge. "And have you heard about the *very important* Muybridge book that came out this year?"

So caught up was I in my assigned role as ingénue that I was perfectly willing to entertain the possibility that another book on the same subject had come out simultaneously and I'd somehow missed it. He was already telling me about the very important book—with that smug look I know so well in a man holding forth, eyes fixed on the fuzzy far horizon of his own authority.

Here, let me just say that my life is well sprinkled with lovely men, with a long succession of editors who have, since I was young, listened to and encouraged and published me, with my infinitely generous younger brother, with splendid friends of whom it could be said—like the Clerk in *The Canterbury Tales* I still remember from Mr. Pelen's class on Chaucer—"gladly would he learn and gladly teach." Still, there are these other men, too. So, Mr. Very Important was going on smugly about this book I should have known when Sallie interrupted him, to say, "That's her book." Or tried to interrupt him anyway.

But he just continued on his way. She had to say, "That's her book" three or four times before he finally took it in. And then, as if in a nineteenth-century novel, he went ashen. That I was indeed the author of the very important book it turned out he hadn't read, just read about in the *New York Times Book Review* a few months earlier, so confused the neat categories into which his world was sorted that he was stunned speechless—for a moment, before he began holding forth again. Being women, we were politely out of earshot before we started laughing, and we've never really stopped.

III

I like incidents of that sort, when forces that are usually so sneaky and   10
hard to point out slither out of the grass and are as obvious as, say, an ana-
conda that's eaten a cow or an elephant turd on the carpet.

THE SLIPPERY SLOPE OF SILENCINGS

Yes, people of both genders pop up at events to hold forth on irrelevant things
and conspiracy theories, but the out-and-out confrontational confidence of
the totally ignorant is, in my experience, gendered. Men explain things to
me, and other women, whether or not they know what they're talking about.
Some men.

Every woman knows what I'm talking about. It's the presumption that
makes it hard, at times, for any woman in any field; that keeps women from
speaking up and from being heard when they dare; that crushes young
women into silence by indicating, the way harassment on the street does,
that this is not their world. It trains us in self-doubt and self-limitation just as
it exercises men's unsupported overconfidence.

I wouldn't be surprised if part of the trajectory of American politics since
2001 was shaped by, say, the inability to hear Coleen Rowley, the FBI woman
who issued those early warnings about al-Qaeda, and it was certainly shaped
by a Bush administration to which you couldn't tell anything, including that Iraq
had no links to al-Qaeda and no WMDs,[1] or that the war was not going to be a
"cakewalk." (Even male experts couldn't penetrate the fortress of its smugness.)

Arrogance might have had something to do with the war, but this syndrome is a war that nearly every woman faces every day, a war within herself
too, a belief in her superfluity, an invitation to silence, one from which a fairly
nice career as a writer (with a lot of research and facts correctly deployed)
has not entirely freed me. After all, there was a moment there when I was
willing to let Mr. Important and his overweening confidence bowl over my
more shaky certainty.

Don't forget that I've had a lot more confirmation of my right to think and   15
speak than most women, and I've learned that a certain amount of self-doubt is
a good tool for correcting, understanding, listening, and progressing—though
too much is paralyzing and total self-confidence produces arrogant idiots.
There's a happy medium between these poles to which the genders have been
pushed, a warm equatorial belt of give and take where we should all meet.

More extreme versions of our situation exist in, for example, those Middle
Eastern countries where women's testimony has no legal standing: so that a
woman can't testify that she was raped without a male witness to counter the
male rapist. Which there rarely is.

Credibility is a basic survival tool. When I was very young and just
beginning to get what feminism was about and why it was necessary, I had
a boyfriend whose uncle was a nuclear physicist. One Christmas, he was

---

[1] **WMDs:** weapons of mass destruction. —EDS.

telling—as though it were a light and amusing subject—how a neighbor's wife in his suburban bomb-making community had come running out of her house naked in the middle of the night screaming that her husband was trying to kill her. How, I asked, did you know that he wasn't trying to kill her? He explained, patiently, that they were respectable middle-class people. Therefore, her-husband-trying-to-kill-her was simply not a credible explanation for her fleeing the house yelling that her husband was trying to kill her. That she was crazy, on the other hand. . . .

Even getting a restraining order—a fairly new legal tool—requires acquiring the credibility to convince the courts that some guy is a menace and then getting the cops to enforce it. Restraining orders often don't work anyway. Violence is one way to silence people, to deny their voice and their credibility, to assert your right to control over their right to exist. About three women a day are murdered by spouses or ex-spouses in this country. It's one of the main causes of death for pregnant women in the United States. At the heart of the struggle of feminism to give rape, date rape, marital rape, domestic violence, and workplace sexual harassment legal standing as crimes has been the necessity of making women credible and audible.

I tend to believe that women acquired the status of human beings when these kinds of acts started to be taken seriously, when the big things that stop us and kill us were addressed legally from the mid-1970s on; well after, that is, my birth. And for anyone about to argue that workplace sexual intimidation isn't a life-or-death issue, remember that Marine Lance Corporal Maria Lauterbach, age twenty, was apparently killed by her higher-ranking colleague one winter's night while she was waiting to testify that he raped her. The burned remains of her pregnant body were found in the fire pit in his backyard.

Being told that, categorically, he knows what he's talking about and she   20
doesn't, however minor a part of any given conversation, perpetuates the ugliness of this world and holds back its light. After my book *Wanderlust* came out in 2000, I found myself better able to resist being bullied out of my own perceptions and interpretations. On two occasions around that time, I objected to the behavior of a man, only to be told that the incidents hadn't happened at all as I said, that I was subjective, delusional, overwrought, dishonest—in a nutshell, female.

Most of my life, I would have doubted myself and backed down. Having public standing as a writer of history helped me stand my ground, but few women get that boost, and billions of women must be out there on this seven-billion-person planet being told that they are not reliable witnesses to their own lives, that the truth is not their property, now or ever. This goes way beyond Men Explaining Things, but it's part of the same archipelago of arrogance.

Men explain things to me, still. And no man has ever apologized for explaining, wrongly, things that I know and they don't. Not yet, but according to the actuarial tables, I may have another forty-something years to live, more or less, so it could happen. Though I'm not holding my breath.

WOMEN FIGHTING ON TWO FRONTS

A few years after the idiot in Aspen, I was in Berlin giving a talk when the Marxist writer Tariq Ali invited me out to a dinner that included a male writer and translator and three women a little younger than me who would remain deferential and mostly silent throughout the dinner. Tariq was great. Perhaps the translator was peeved that I insisted on playing a modest role in the conversation, but when I said something about how Women Strike for Peace, the extraordinary, little-known antinuclear and antiwar group founded in 1961, helped bring down the communist-hunting House Committee on Un-American Activities, HUAC, Mr. Very Important II sneered at me. HUAC, he insisted, didn't exist by the early 1960s and, anyway, no women's group played such a role in HUAC's downfall. His scorn was so withering, his confidence so aggressive, that arguing with him seemed a scary exercise in futility and an invitation to more insult.

I think I was at nine books at that point, including one that drew from primary documents about and interviews with a key member of Women Strike for Peace. But explaining men still assume I am, in some sort of obscene impregnation metaphor, an empty vessel to be filled with their wisdom and knowledge. A Freudian would claim to know what they have and I lack, but intelligence is not situated in the crotch—even if you can write one of Virginia Woolf's long mellifluous musical sentences about the subtle subjugation of women in the snow with your willie. Back in my hotel room, I searched online a bit and found that Eric Bentley in his definitive history of the House Committee on Un-American Activities credits Women Strike for Peace with "striking the crucial blow in the fall of HUAC's Bastille." In the early 1960s.

So I opened an essay (on Jane Jacobs, Betty Friedan, and Rachel Carson) for the *Nation* with this interchange, in part as a shout-out to one of the more unpleasant men who have explained things to me: Dude, if you're reading this, you're a carbuncle on the face of humanity and an obstacle to civilization. Feel the shame.

The battle with Men Who Explain Things has trampled down many women—of my generation, of the up-and-coming generation we need so badly, here and in Pakistan and Bolivia and Java, not to speak of the countless women who came before me and were not allowed into the laboratory, or the library, or the conversation, or the revolution, or even the category called human.

After all, Women Strike for Peace was founded by women who were tired of making the coffee and doing the typing and not having any voice or decision-making role in the antinuclear movement of the 1950s. Most women fight wars on two fronts, one for whatever the putative topic is and one simply for the right to speak, to have ideas, to be acknowledged to be in possession of facts and truths, to have value, to be a human being. Things have gotten better, but this war won't end in my lifetime. I'm still fighting it, for myself certainly, but also for all those younger women who have something to say, in the hope that they will get to say it. ■

The Reader's Presence

1. Rebecca Solnit opens with a personal anecdote and adds several as her essay unfolds. How is the substance and structure of her essay shaped by these memories? What specific compositional purpose does each anecdote serve? How do the narrative elements of the essay complement the historical discourse about women?

2. Solnit notes that her status as a published author influenced her ability to assert herself. "I found myself better able to resist being bullied out of my own perceptions and interpretations," she writes (paragraph 20). What roles do authority and credibility play in the essay? Consider the reasons why Solnit chooses to address these topics, given that many women do not have the same level of public standing.

3. **CONNECTIONS:** "Violence is one way to silence people, to deny their voice and their credibility," Solnit writes (paragraph 18). Examine the relationship between violence and voice in Roxane Gay's "The Careless Language of Sexual Violence" (page 525) and apply this to a reading of Solnit's essay. What does sexual violence as portrayed in media imply about the nature of relationships between men and women? How does rape culture, as Gay defines it, shape Solnit's experiences?

The Writer at Work

"It Struck a Chord:" On Writing "Men Explain Things to Me"

David Butow/Redux

When Rebecca Solnit included her essay "Men Explain Things to Me" in her collection of that name in 2014, she added a "Postscript" recounting how the essay originated and found an audience. "The point of the essay," she writes, "was never to suggest that I think I am notably oppressed. It was to take these conversations as the narrow end of the wedge that opens up space for men and closes it off for women, space to speak, to be heard, to have rights, to participate, to be respected, to be a full and free human being." Although the essay is now closely associated with what came to be called "mansplaining," Solnit acknowledges here that she played no role in coining that term.

❝One evening over dinner in March 2008, I began to joke, as I often had before, about writing an essay called "Men Explain Things to Me." Every writer has a stable of ideas that never make it to the racetrack, and I'd been trotting this pony out recreationally once in a while. My houseguest, the brilliant theorist and activist Marina Sitrin,[1] insisted that I had to write it down because people like her younger sister Sam needed to read it. Young women, she said, needed to know that being belittled wasn't the result

[1]*Marina Sitrin:* A self-described "writer, lawyer, teacher, organizer, militant, and dreamer." —EDS.

of their own secret failings; it was the boring old gender wars, and it happened to most of us who were female at some point or other.

I wrote it in one sitting early the next morning. When something assembles itself that fast, it's clear it's been composing itself somewhere in the unknowable back of the mind for a long time. It wanted to be written; it was restless for the racetrack; it galloped along once I sat down at the computer. Since Marina slept in later than me in those days, I served it for breakfast and later that day sent it to Tom Engelhardt[2] at TomDispatch, who published it online soon after. It spread quickly, as essays put up at Tom's site do, and has never stopped going around, being reposted and shared and commented upon. It's circulated like nothing else I've done.

It struck a chord. And a nerve.

Some men explained why men explaining things to women wasn't really a gendered phenomenon. Usually, women then pointed out that, in insisting on their right to dismiss the experiences women say they have, men succeeded in explaining in just the way I said they sometimes do. (For the record, I do believe that women have explained things in patronizing ways, to men among others. But that's not indicative of the massive power differential that takes far more sinister forms as well or of the broad pattern of how gender works in our society.)

Other men got it and were cool. This was, after all, written in the era when male feminists had become a more meaningful presence, and feminism was funnier than ever. Not everyone knew they were funny, however. At TomDispatch in 2008, I got an email from an older man in Indianapolis, who wrote in to tell me that he had "never personally

or professionally shortchanged a woman" and went on to berate me for not hanging out with "more regular guys or at least do a little homework first." He then gave me some advice about how to run my life and commented on my "feelings of inferiority." He thought that being patronized was an experience a woman chooses to have, or could choose not to have—and so the fault was all mine.

A website named "Academic Men Explain Things to Me" arose, and hundreds of university women shared their stories of being patronized, belittled, talked over, and more. The term "mansplaining" was coined soon after the piece appeared, and I was sometimes credited with it. In fact, I had nothing to do with its actual creation, though my essay, along with all the men who embodied the idea, apparently inspired it. (I have doubts about the word and don't use it myself much; it seems to me to go a little heavy on the idea that men are inherently flawed this way, rather than that some men explain things they shouldn't and don't hear things they should. If it's not clear enough in the piece, I love it when people explain things to me they know and I'm interested in but don't yet know; it's when they explain things to me I know and they don't that the conversation goes wrong.) By 2012, the term "mansplained"—one of the *New York Times*'s words of the year for 2010—was being used in mainstream political journalism.

Alas, this was because it dovetailed pretty well with the times. TomDispatch reposted "Men Explain Things" in August 2012, and fortuitously, more or less simultaneously, Representative Todd Akin (R-Missouri) made his infamous statement that we don't need abortion for women who are raped, because "if it's a legitimate rape, the female body has ways to try to shut the whole thing down." That electoral season was peppered by the crazy pro-rape, anti-fact statements of male conservatives. And salted with feminists

---

[2] *Thomas M. Engelhardt* (b. 1944): An American writer and editor and creator of the Nation Institute's tomdispatch.com, an online blog. —EDS.

pointing out why feminism is necessary and why these guys are scary. It was nice to be one of the voices in that conversation; the piece had a big revival.

Chords, nerves: the thing is still circulating as I write. The point of the essay was never to suggest that I think I am notably oppressed. It was to take these conversations as the narrow end of the wedge that opens up space for men and closes it off for women, space to speak, to be heard, to have rights, to participate, to be respected, to be a full and free human being. This is one way that, in polite discourse, power is expressed—the same power that in impolite discourse and in physical acts of intimidation and violence, and very often in how the world is organized—silences and erases and annihilates women, as equals, as participants, as human beings with rights, and far too often as living beings.

The battle for women to be treated like human beings with rights to life, liberty, and the pursuit of involvement in cultural and political arenas continues, and it is sometimes a pretty grim battle.

I surprised myself when I wrote the essay, which began with an amusing incident and ended with rape and murder. That made clear to me the continuum that stretches from minor social misery to violent silencing and violent death (and I think we would understand misogyny and violence against women even better if we looked at the abuse of power as a whole rather than treating domestic violence separately from rape and murder and harassment and intimidation, online and at home and in the workplace and in the streets; seen together, the pattern is clear).

Having the right to show up and speak are basic to survival, to dignity, and to liberty. I'm grateful that, after an early life of being silenced, sometimes violently, I grew up to have a voice, circumstances that will always bind me to the rights of the voiceless.

Virginia Woolf
THE DEATH OF THE MOTH

One of the most important writers of the twentieth century, **VIRGINIA WOOLF** (1882–1941) explored innovations in indirect narration and the impressionistic use of language that are now considered hallmarks of the modern novel and continue to influence novelists on both sides of the Atlantic. Together with her husband, Leonard Woolf, she founded the Hogarth Press, which published many experimental works that have now become classics, including her own. A central figure in the Bloomsbury group of writers, Woolf established her reputation with the novels *Mrs. Dalloway* (1925), *To the Lighthouse* (1927), and *The Waves* (1931). The feminist movement has helped to focus attention on her work, and Woolf's nonfiction has provided the basis for several important lines of argument in contemporary feminist theory. *A Room of One's Own* (1929), *Three Guineas* (1938), and *The Common Reader* (1938) are the major works of nonfiction published in Woolf's lifetime; posthumously, her essays have been gathered together in *The Death of the Moth* (1942) (where the essay reprinted here appears) and in the four-volume *Collected Essays* (1967).

> **"The novelist—it is his distinction and his danger—is terribly exposed to life. . . . He can no more cease to receive impressions than a fish in mid-ocean can cease to let the water rush through his gills."**

Reflecting on her own writing life, Woolf wrote, "The novelist—it is his distinction and his danger—is terribly exposed to life. . . . He can no more cease to receive impressions than a fish in mid-ocean can cease to let the water rush through his gills." To turn those impressions into writing, Woolf maintained, requires solitude and the time for thoughtful selection. Given tranquility, a writer can, with effort, discover art in experience. "There emerges from the mist something stark, formidable and enduring, the bone and substance upon which our rush of indiscriminating emotion was founded."

MOTHS THAT FLY BY DAY are not properly to be called moths; they do not excite that pleasant sense of dark autumn nights and ivy-blossom which the commonest yellow-underwing asleep in the shadow of the curtain never fails to rouse in us. They are hybrid creatures, neither gay like butterflies nor somber like their own species. Nevertheless the present specimen, with his narrow hay-colored wings, fringed with a tassel of the same color, seemed to be content with life. It was a pleasant morning, mid-September, mild, benignant, yet with a keener breath than that of the summer months. The plough was already scoring the field opposite the window, and where the share had been, the earth was pressed flat and gleamed with moisture. Such vigor came rolling in from the fields and the down beyond that it was difficult to keep the eyes strictly turned upon the book. The rooks too were keeping one of their annual festivities; soaring round the tree tops until it looked as if a vast net with thousands of black knots in it had been cast up into the air; which, after a few moments sank slowly down upon the trees until every twig seemed to have a knot at the end of it. Then, suddenly, the net would be thrown into the air again in a wider circle this time, with the utmost clamor and vociferation, as though to be thrown into the air and settle slowly down upon the tree tops were a tremendously exciting experience.

The same energy which inspired the rooks, the ploughmen, the horses, and even, it seemed, the lean bare-backed downs, sent the moth fluttering from side to side of his square of the windowpane. One could not help watching him. One was, indeed, conscious of a queer feeling of pity for him. The possibilities of pleasure seemed that morning so enormous and so various that to have only a moth's part in life, and a day moth's at that, appeared a hard fate, and his zest in enjoying his meager opportunities to the full, pathetic. He flew vigorously to one corner of his compartment, and after waiting there a second, flew across to the other. What remained for him but to fly to a third corner and then to a fourth? That was all he could do, in spite of the size of the downs, the width of the sky, the far-off smoke of houses, and the romantic voice, now and then, of a steamer out at sea. What he could do he did. Watching him, it seemed as if a fiber, very thin but pure, of the enormous energy of the world had been thrust into his frail and diminutive body. As often as he crossed the pane, I could fancy that a thread of vital light became visible. He was little or nothing but life.

Yet, because he was so small, and so simple a form of the energy that was rolling in at the open window and driving its way through so many narrow and intricate corridors in my own brain and in those of other human beings, there was something marvelous as well as pathetic about him. It was as if someone had taken a tiny bead of pure life and decking it as lightly as possible with down and feathers, had set it dancing and zigzagging to show us the true nature of life. Thus displayed one could not get over the strangeness of it. One is apt to forget all about life, seeing it humped and bossed and garnished and cumbered so that it has to move with the greatest circumspection and dignity. Again, the thought of all that life might have been had he been born in any other shape caused one to view his simple activities with a kind of pity.

After a time, tired by his dancing apparently, he settled on the window ledge in the sun, and, the queer spectacle being at an end, I forgot about him. Then, looking up, my eye was caught by him. He was trying to resume his dancing, but seemed either so stiff or so awkward that he could only flutter to the bottom of the windowpane; and when he tried to fly across it he failed. Being intent on other matters I watched these futile attempts for a time without thinking, unconsciously waiting for him to resume his flight, as one waits for a machine, that has stopped momentarily, to start again without considering the reason of its failure. After perhaps a seventh attempt he slipped from the wooden ledge and fell, fluttering his wings, on to his back on the windowsill. The helplessness of his attitude roused me. It flashed upon me that he was in difficulties; he could no longer raise himself; his legs struggled vainly. But, as I stretched out a pencil, meaning to help him to right himself, it came over me that the failure and awkwardness were the approach of death. I laid the pencil down again.

The legs agitated themselves once more. I looked as if for the enemy against which he struggled. I looked out of doors. What had happened there? Presumably it was midday, and work in the fields had stopped. Stillness and quiet had replaced the previous animation. The birds had taken themselves off to feed in the brooks. The horses stood still. Yet the power was there all the same, massed outside, indifferent, impersonal, not attending to anything in particular. Somehow it was opposed to the little hay-colored moth. It was useless to try to do anything. One could only watch the extraordinary efforts made by those tiny legs against an oncoming doom which could, had it chosen, have submerged an entire city, not merely a city, but masses of human beings; nothing, I knew had any chance against death. Nevertheless after a pause of exhaustion the legs fluttered again. It was superb this last protest, and so frantic that he succeeded at last in righting himself. One's sympathies,

5

of course, were all on the side of life. Also, when there was nobody to care or to know, this gigantic effort on the part of an insignificant little moth, against a power of such magnitude, to retain what no one else valued or desired to keep, moved one strangely. Again, somehow, one saw life, a pure bead. I lifted the pencil again, useless though I knew it to be. But even as I did so, the unmistakable tokens of death showed themselves. The body relaxed, and instantly grew stiff. The struggle was over. The insignificant little creature now knew death. As I looked at the dead moth, this minute wayside triumph of so great a force over so mean an antagonist filled me with wonder. Just as life had been strange a few minutes before, so death was now as strange. The moth having righted himself now lay most decently and uncomplainingly composed. O yes, he seemed to say, death is stronger than I am. ●

The Reader's Presence

1. Woolf calls her essay "The Death of the Moth." What effect(s) does her decision to use a definite article ("the" rather than "a" moth) have? What quality does the definite article add to the essay?

2. Reread the essay, paying special attention not to the moth but to the writer. What presence does Woolf establish for herself in the essay? How does the act of writing itself get introduced? Of what significance is the pencil? Can you discover any connection between the essay's subject and its composition?

3. **CONNECTIONS:** Read Virginia Woolf's "The Death of the Moth" in conjunction with Anne Fadiman's "Under Water" (page 91). What characteristics of style do the two essays share? In what ways does imagery play a significant role in each essay? What similarities do you find between each author's final paragraph?

The Writer at Work

VIRGINIA WOOLF on the Practice of Freewriting

George C. Beresford/Getty Images

At the time of her death (1941), Virginia Woolf, one of modern literature's outstanding creative voices, left twenty-six volumes of a handwritten diary that she had started in 1915. Her diary records her daily activities, social life, reading, and, most important, her thoughts about the writing process. In 1953, her husband, Leonard Woolf, extracted her remarks about writing and published them in a separate volume called *A Writer's Diary*. Here, just having completed a newspaper article on the novelist Daniel Defoe, Woolf decides to take a break and think about the different ways she composes when she writes in her diary as opposed to when she writes more formally for publication.

This Loose, Drifting Material of Life
Easter Sunday, April 20, 1919

In the idleness which succeeds any long article, and Defoe is the second leader this month, I got out this diary and read, as one always does read one's own writing, with a kind of guilty intensity. I confess that the rough and random style of it, often so ungrammatical, and crying for a word altered, afflicted me somewhat. I am trying to tell whichever self it is that reads this hereafter that I can write very much better; and take no time over this; and forbid her to let the eye of man behold it. And now I may add my little compliment to the effect that it has a slapdash and vigor and sometimes hits an unexpected bull's eye. But what is more to the point is my belief that the habit of writing thus for my own eye only is good practice. It loosens the ligaments. Never mind the misses and the stumbles. Going at such a pace as I do I must make the most direct and instant shots at my object, and thus have to lay hands on words, choose them and shoot them with no more pause than is needed to put my pen in the ink. I believe that during the past year I can trace some increase of ease in my professional writing which I attribute to my casual half hours after tea. Moreover there looms ahead of me the shadow of some kind of form which a diary might attain to. I might in the course of time learn what it is that one can make of this loose, drifting material of life; finding another use for it than the use I put it to, so much more consciously and scrupulously, in fiction. What sort of diary should I like mine to be? Something loose knit and yet not slovenly, so elastic that it will embrace anything, solemn, slight, or beautiful that comes into my mind. I should like it to resemble some deep old desk, or capacious hold-all, in which one flings a mass of odds and ends without looking them through. I should like to come back, after a year or two, and find that the collection had sorted itself and refined itself and coalesced, as such deposits so mysteriously do, into a mold, transparent enough to reflect the light of our life, and yet steady, tranquil compounds with the aloofness of a work of art. The main requisite, I think on re-reading my old volumes, is not to play the part of censor, but to write as the mood comes or of anything whatever; since I was curious to find how I went for things put in haphazard, and found the significance to lie where I never saw it at the time. But looseness quickly becomes slovenly. A little effort is needed to face a character or an incident which needs to be recorded.**

PART 3

ARGUMENTATIVE WRITING
Contending with Issues

" ————————————————

Good writing does not succeed or fail on the strength of its ability to persuade. It succeeds or fails on the strength of its ability to engage you, to make you think, to give you a glimpse into someone else's head.

Malcolm Gladwell
(b. 1963, Canadian author)

——————————————— **"**

WHAT IS ARGUMENTATIVE WRITING?

Argument—whether written or spoken—is an inescapable part of our cultural environment, from newspaper editorials, blogs, and magazine articles to talk radio, commercials, and the evening news shows. In most forms of public argument today, someone is either defending or attacking a controversial position—gun control, government surveillance, the death penalty, climate change, and so on. These topics are commonly known as "issues"; an issue is basically a topic that is in dispute, one that people take various positions on, and one that is often a matter of contentious public debate. In this part, we look at how some highly regarded writers contend with issues: how they attempt to persuade you that one policy is better than another, that a certain course of action would lead to desirable or disastrous outcomes, or that certain choices are more ethically or morally correct than others.

Thinking about and writing an argument can seem overwhelming, but constructing arguments is a basic operation of the mind. As you'll discover when you dig deeper into any topic, even experts in a field disagree, and convincing reasons and evidence can too often be supplied for the many conflicting opinions we encounter daily. This is true not only with respect to public policy and political or legal debate but also with conflicts in our own life as we conduct "inner debates" with ourselves about decisions we must make or courses of action we wish to pursue. We construct arguments all the time—in our thoughts, in our informal conversations with friends—but we don't always examine how we arrive at our beliefs and convictions, nor do we normally pay close attention to the intricacies of our reasoning. Reading the essays in this part and drafting your own will help you slow down and think about how arguments are put together and what makes them persuasive.

Argumentative essays, as you will see in this part, come in all shapes and sizes. Regardless of length, style, and approach, however, arguments usually depend on four main features: **presenting the issue**, **making a claim**, **building a case**, and **coming to a conclusion**. Argumentative strategies may vary according to how much an author believes his or her audience knows about a topic or other matters of context, but these four features will very likely be present in most argumentative essays.

STRATEGIES FOR PRESENTING THE ISSUE

Even if the writer believes his or her opinions on a hotly debated topic represent an ideal solution—with all other opinions considered wrong—the issue doesn't go away but remains debated and discussed. For example, the fact that one believes that climate change or the Second Amendment's right to bear arms is an indisputable fact does not mean that the argument is over. No matter how meritorious our position may appear to ourselves, there will undoubtedly be others who disagree. So we need to supply reasons and evidence even for positions we assume are unarguable. And because we're speaking to those who may not agree, we must be careful how we present the issue.

Short argumentative essays—the kind we see in editorials and blogs—usually present the issue in the opening paragraph; it's generally a good idea not to leave your reader wondering what you're planning to discuss. In longer arguments, however, the writer may gradually set the stage for the essay's central issue. For example, the greatly admired novelist and essayist David Foster Wallace spends several pages describing a Maine lobster festival with its enormous lobster cooker before introducing the ethical issue at the heart of his essay:

> So then here is a question that's all but unavoidable at the World's Largest Lobster Cooker, and may arise in kitchens across the US: Is it all right to boil a sentient creature alive just for our gustatory pleasure? **David Foster Wallace**, "Consider the Lobster" (page 649)

Wallace's question works well precisely because we've been led through pages of a well-told (but perhaps faintly alarming) description of the festival. We don't get the sense that his answer to this question was necessarily made up before he arrived, the question itself is well asked and doesn't overly predetermine its answer in the way it's phrased, and it pinpoints a turning point in the essay: from here on out, he's going to explore the answer. Because Wallace has engaged our interest and proven himself to be a knowledgeable guide, we agree to come along as he does so.

When you present your own topic, no matter how passionately you feel about it, it's wise to check your emotions on the subject at first, and present your topic in a similarly levelheaded tone. You likely won't have the time or the luxury of an audience engaged enough to spend several pages getting to your point. You'll probably want to do that in the first few paragraphs. But you can present yourself as a curious and logical speaker on the subject, one who will be laying out all the relevant pieces of the argument and coming to a justified and persuasive conclusion. There might be appropriate space in your conclusion for more emotion, but we'll get to that.

STRATEGIES FOR MAKING A CLAIM

Once the issue at stake has been established, it's time to make a claim about that issue. Our claim is our position. It is essentially where we stand, what we are arguing for. Claims usually fall into four categories: claims about policy, about value, about outcomes, and about a situation or condition.

Claims about policy often take the form of proposals, which recommend a course of action; for example, an educational psychologist proposing a better way of keeping public schools safe from gun violence or an activist arguing that nuclear power plants are a poor source of energy and should be abolished.

Claims about value argue whether something is good or bad, moral or immoral. A writer may claim that it is wrong to kill and eat living creatures. Value claims can also include social and cultural opinions, such as "Facebook is cheapening the concept of friendship" or "*Breaking Bad* is the best television series ever filmed."

Claims about outcomes usually examine what will happen if we pursue a certain course of action or adopt a particular position. For example, one could argue that if we banned automobiles from inner cities, we would create more livable urban communities; or one could argue that if college athletes were paid, only football and basketball players would truly benefit.

Claims about a situation or condition usually depend heavily on facts, research, and evidence. An author, for example, attempts to identify a trend or a state of affairs—that television shows are growing increasingly pornographic or that televised news reports are now being shaped by social media. Note how the distinguished Harvard psychologist Steven Pinker expresses such a claim in his essay on violence. Disputing the commonly held idea that the world was a better, less-violent place in the past, he writes:

> Believe it or not, the world of the past was *much* worse. Violence has been in decline for thousands of years, and today we may be living in the most peaceable era in the existence of our species. **Steven Pinker**, "Violence Vanquished" (page 591)

Pinker's claim, and many of these other kinds of claims, works best when they argue something unexpected. Just by walking around in the world and watching the news, we've ingested the sense that our own era is exceptionally violent, and Pinker's claim quickly taps into those cultural assumptions and rattles them, preparing us for his argument.

As you read the essays in this section, it might help to identify which kind of claim the author is making and how the author conveys a sense of urgency to that particular kind of argument. Maybe you'll be able to identify which type of argument works best on you: Are you more persuaded by claims about value—this or that is wrong or immoral? Or are you more persuaded by claims that are carefully built with facts and evidence, like a claim about a situation or condition? When it comes time to write your own essay, think about which of these claims best suits your subject and use similar essays in this section to model how professional writers do what you're setting out to do.

STRATEGIES FOR BUILDING A CASE

It is relatively easy to make a claim but harder to back it up with reasons and evidence. Without support, Pinker's statement about the decline of world violence would be a mere assertion. His claim demands some level of proof before we can take it seriously. Pinker's essay goes on to cite historical records, statistics, and biological science as evidence to support his claim, and that kind of authoritative evidence might be what your essay calls for, too.

Writers rely on a number of different ways to support their claims and build a case for their opinions. Following are some of the most common: citing experts and authorities, using examples, providing statistics, presenting analogies, sharing personal experience, and anticipating objections.

Writers may **cite experts and authorities** when they'd like to add credibility to their own opinions. This strategy says, "See! Even experts agree with me," and it's a persuasive—though not always necessary—addition to an argument. For example, a writer supports his contention that the First Amendment of the U.S. Constitution does not grant individual citizens the right to free speech by quoting a prominent law professor who has written several books on the subject. Or, in attempting to prove that a lobster can experience pain, Wallace cites the author of a book about lobsters (page 660). When you come across a reference to or quotation by an expert in the essays that follow, consider the claim without that support. How would it change the way you respond to the argument?

Using examples to illustrate a key point can serve as another effective means of support. For example (we'll use this strategy to illustrate this point, too), a writer hoping to show that memoirs today are becoming increasingly unreliable refers to several recent books criticized for containing lies and fabrications. Peter Singer's argument in which he proposes a solution to world poverty depends entirely on examples ("The Singer Solution to World Poverty," page 615).

Statistics (figures and data) from reputable sources provide the basis of many arguments, especially in the sciences and social sciences. For example, an author who wants to impress upon her readers the urgency of the negative impact of climate change might cite data from leading climatologists. In "The Tyranny of Choice," Barry Schwartz cites a recent study in the *Journal of the American Medical Association* to suggest that the incidence of clinical depression is increasing in the United States (page 608).

An **analogy** in which we compare the similarities of two different things to make our point can be an effective way to build an argument. A writer may want to show the benefits of communal cooperation by comparing a human society to a bee colony. Or, in "The Pitfalls of Plastic Surgery" (page 584), note how Camille Paglia begins her essay with an analogy that will inform her entire argument: the comparison between cosmetic surgery and the fine arts. "Plastic surgery is living sculpture: a triumph of modern medicine. As a revision of nature, cosmetic surgery symbolizes the conquest of biology by human free will. With new faces and bodies, people have become their own works of art."

Persuasive arguments can be constructed from **personal experience**. A disabled student may argue for better campus facilities by citing his personal difficulties. This chapter contains a number of essays that argue from personal experience, perhaps most memorably Christopher Hitchens's account of his voluntarily undergoing "waterboarding" to prove that it constitutes torture ("Believe Me, It's Torture," page 531).

Though it's slightly different from other kinds of evidence, **anticipating objections** should be considered a necessary part of building your case if it's at all applicable to your topic. In constructing a case to support their claim, conscientious writers realize the importance of taking into account opposing opinions and testimony. Good debaters know the importance of understanding all sides of an issue and, like an effective courtroom attorney, prepare themselves for rebuttal and counterarguments. But writers rarely get the chance to hear objections to their arguments. Therefore, it is important in building a case within an essay to think carefully through the main objections that someone may bring to your argument and respond to them as you proceed to make your points. This strategy not only helps you to construct your case more effectively but also indicates to the reader that you have reasonably considered other points of view.

For example, in "Violence Vanquished," Pinker realizes how his notion that violence is decreasing worldwide must strike readers familiar with reports of horrific daily events. So shortly after he states his main point, Pinker writes: "This claim, I know, invites skepticism, incredulity, and sometimes anger." He then proceeds to acknowledge the scenes of violence we encounter in the media and how these may affect our "impressions." By anticipating our initial resistance to a surprising claim, a writer is able to disarm our immediate objections and prepare us for a systematic presentation of his or her case. However, if a writer ignores the other side of the argument entirely or doesn't seem to be aware of how a surprising claim will impact a reader, the writer appears less trustworthy—we're not sure we want to hear what he or she has to say.

STRATEGIES FOR COMING TO A CONCLUSION

In essays that argue a position and support it with reasoning and evidence, conclusions can be quite important. For one thing, you may need to reiterate or summarize your points for emphasis, especially if in a longer paper or research report you have provided a significant amount of supporting evidence. But a summary should not be a verbatim repetition of what you've already said. A good summarizing paragraph can be a pithy reminder to the reader of your issue's importance and the reasonableness of your position or opinion.

Some persuasive conclusions consist of **calls to action** that often take the form of a collaboration of writer and reader to do something together—advance a cause, resist a poor policy, join a movement, and so on. Note the way Howard Zinn concludes his essay criticizing Hollywood films for their inadequate depictions of social and political realities. He begins by briefly reminding his readers of some of the types of films he would like to see produced and then finishes with a call to action:

> If such films are made—about war, about class conflict, about the history of governmental lies, about broken treaties and official violence—if those stories reach the public, we might produce a new generation. As a teacher, I'm not interested in just reproducing class after class of graduates who will get out, become successful, and take their obedient places in the slots that society has prepared for them. What we

> must do—whether we teach or write or make films—is educate a new generation to do this very modest thing: change the world. **Howard Zinn**, "Stories Hollywood Never Tells" (page 676)

Zinn's conclusion works well because it's both possible (we can imagine films on topics like these) and overly ambitious (can changing the world really be taught?). This reminds and grounds the reader in what's come before and sends the reader forward, continuing to think about Zinn's ideas and the scope of film's influence. Zinn's may be a good model for your own essays: think about both solidifying your reader in what you've argued and urging the reader to join you in acting on larger ideas.

Another type of conclusion is admonitory; that is, the author **issues a warning** about unfortunate outcomes if a recommended course of action is not accepted. Here is how Schwartz ends his essay on what he calls the "tyranny of choice," the limitations people may come to feel when they experience too much choice:

> There is a *New Yorker* cartoon that depicts a parent goldfish and an offspring in a small goldfish bowl. "You can be anything you want to be—no limit," says the myopic parent, not realizing how limited an existence the fishbowl allows. I'd like to suggest that perhaps the parent is not so myopic. Freedom without limits, choice within constraints, is indeed liberating. But if the fishbowl gets shattered—if the constraints disappear—freedom of choice can turn into a tyranny of choice. **Barry Schwartz**, "The Tyranny of Choice" (page 608)

Schwartz's final three words match the title of the essay, bringing us back to the beginning and reinforcing that ominous word—*tyranny*. You might think about creating a similar circle in your own essay, using the conclusion to touch back on what you discussed in your introduction. You might also consider creating the kind of tone Schwartz creates: a serious tone emphasizes the seriousness of the issue you discuss and warns your reader to consider your argument carefully.

Effective conclusions do not need to neatly wrap up the argument. They can suggest new thoughts or perspectives that can expand the discussion or even change course. One way to conclude an argumentative essay that moves the reader in a new direction is to **end with a question**. In an essay that takes a close hard look at the imprisoning aspects of modern romantic relationships, Laura Kipnis ("Against Love," page 546) concludes by asking her readers: "But isn't it a little depressing to think we are somehow incapable of inventing forms of emotional life based on anything other than subjugation?" Her question at once echoes the topic of the entire essay yet directs the discussion into a new direction, asking the reader to continue thinking about all she's presented.

READING ARGUMENTATIVE ESSAYS: A Checklist

✔ Can you approach the argument with an open mind? Do the author's opinions differ so much from yours that you cannot give the essay a fair hearing?

✔ Does the writer appear credible? Does she or he demonstrate a solid knowledge of the topic? Are the information and evidence derived from personal and professional expertise or is the writer relying on other authorities?

✔ Has the writer presented the issue clearly and fairly? Has he or she stayed on topic? Do you feel it is a genuine issue or do you feel it has been contrived to suit the author's purposes?

✔ Has the writer strayed off issue to attack opponents personally by insulting, name-calling, or associating them with unpopular groups? Does the author appear morally and ethically superior while those disagreed with are portrayed as ignorant or contemptible?

✔ Does the writer appear to be "preaching before the choir" — that is, arguing a point to an audience who already accepts it?

✔ Does the argument appear to be based on oversimplifications: reducing a complex situation to an either/or possibility or explaining a complicated series of events by a single cause that cannot be determined?

✔ To what extent does the author use emotions to persuade a reader? Does the essay try to inspire negative feelings of fear, anger, disgust, or resentment?

✔ To what extent does the author use figurative language—images, metaphors, symbols—to influence the reader? Does the figurative language feel appropriate or manipulative?

✔ Has the author depended on generalizations that you feel are unjustified? Do you think that his or her generalizations are based on too few examples or too little evidence?

✔ Do the reasons the author provides to support his or her position seem consistent and coherent? Can you locate any inconsistencies or contradictory comments in the author's reasoning?

✔ Has the writer demonstrated an awareness of different opinions on the issue? Do you feel he or she has attempted to fairly state or summarize other opinions and perspectives?

✔ How does the writer's tone of voice strike you: strident? preachy? stuffy? snooty? sarcastic? ironic? Do you detect any ways of speaking that make the author appear unreasonable or not credible?

✔ Does the writer clearly identify sources of information such as statistical data, testimony of experts, or quotations? Do you feel the information being provided to support the opinion is trustworthy?

Amy Chua

TOUGH LOVE: PARENTS AND CHILDREN

AMY CHUA (b. 1962) became the subject of national attention in the wake of her memoir, *Battle Hymn of the Tiger Mother* (2011), in which she recounts her experiences raising her two daughters. The book drew considerable praise *and* criticism, sparking debate about the differences between Western and Eastern parenting styles. "All decent parents want to do what's best for their children," Chua writes. "The Chinese just have a totally different idea of how to do that."

A graduate of Harvard Law, Chua practiced law on Wall Street before she started teaching at Duke University. She is currently the John M. Duff, Jr. Professor of Law at Yale Law School. Her career as an author began with two critically acclaimed books on globalization and ethnic divisions, *World on Fire* (2002) and *Day of Empire* (2009). In 2014, she co-authored with her Yale Law School colleague (and husband) Jed Rubenfeld *The Triple Package: How Three Unlikely Traits Explain the Rise and Fall of Cultural Groups in America*.

> Chua's book drew considerable praise *and* criticism, sparking debate about the differences between Western and Eastern parenting styles.

HERE'S A STORY IN FAVOR OF COERCION, Chinese-style. Lulu was about seven, still playing two instruments, and working on a piano piece called "The Little White Donkey" by the French composer Jacques Ibert. The piece is really cute—you can just imagine a little donkey ambling along a country road with its master—but it's also incredibly difficult for young players because the two hands have to keep schizophrenically different rhythms.

Lulu couldn't do it. We worked on it nonstop for a week, drilling each of her hands separately, over and over. But whenever we tried putting the hands together, one always morphed into the other, and everything fell apart. Finally, the day before her lesson, Lulu announced in exasperation that she was giving up and stomped off.

"Get back to the piano now," I ordered.

"You can't make me."

"Oh yes I can."

5

Back at the piano, Lulu made me pay. She punched, thrashed, and kicked. She grabbed the music score and tore it to shreds. I taped the score back together and encased it in a plastic shield so that it could never be destroyed again. Then I hauled Lulu's dollhouse to the car and told her I'd donate it to the Salvation Army piece by piece if she didn't have "The Little White Donkey" perfect by the next day. When Lulu said, "I thought you were going to the Salvation Army, why are you still here?" I threatened her with no lunch, no dinner, no Christmas or Hanukkah presents, no birthday parties for two, three, four years. When she still kept playing it wrong, I told her she was purposely working herself into a frenzy because she was secretly afraid she couldn't do it. I told her to stop being lazy, cowardly, self-indulgent, and pathetic.

My husband Jed took me aside. He told me to stop insulting Lulu—which I wasn't even doing, I was just motivating her—and that he didn't think threatening Lulu was helpful. Also, he said, maybe Lulu really just couldn't do the technique—perhaps she didn't have the coordination yet—had I considered that possibility?

"You just don't believe in her," I accused.

"That's ridiculous," Jed said scornfully. "Of course I do."

"Sophia could play the piece when she was this age."   10

"But Lulu and Sophia are different people," Jed pointed out.

Motherhood is the strangest thing; it can be like being one's own Trojan horse.

> —*Rebecca West, 1959*

"Oh no, not this," I said, rolling my eyes. "Everyone is special in their special own way," I mimicked sarcastically. "Even losers are special in their own special way. Well don't worry, you don't have to lift a finger. I'm willing to put in as long as it takes, and I'm happy to be the one hated. And you can be the one they adore because you make them pancakes and take them to Yankees games."

I rolled up my sleeves and went back to Lulu. I used every weapon and tactic I could think of. We worked right through dinner into the night, and I wouldn't let Lulu get up, not for water, not even to go to the bathroom. The house became a war zone, and I lost my voice yelling, but still there seemed to be only negative progress, and even I began to have doubts.

Then, out of the blue, Lulu did it. Her hands suddenly came together—her right and left hands each doing their own imperturbable thing—just like that.

Lulu realized it the same time I did. I held my breath. She tried it ten-   15 tatively again. Then she played it more confidently and faster, and still the rhythm held. A moment later, she was beaming. "Mommy, look—it's easy!" After that, she wanted to play the piece over and over and wouldn't leave the piano. That night, she came to sleep in my bed, and we snuggled and hugged, cracking each other up. When she performed "The Little White Donkey" at a recital a few weeks later, parents came up to me and said, "What a perfect piece for Lulu—it's so spunky and so *her*."

Even Jed gave me credit for that one. Western parents worry a lot about their children's self-esteem. But as a parent, one of the worst things you can do for your child's self-esteem is to let them give up. On the flip side, there's nothing better for building confidence than learning you can do something you thought you couldn't.

There are all these new books out there portraying Asian mothers as scheming, callous, overdriven people indifferent to their kids' true interests. For their part, many Chinese secretly believe that they care more about their children and are willing to sacrifice much more for them than Westerners, who seem perfectly content to let their children turn out badly. I think it's a misunderstanding on both sides. All decent parents want to do what's best for their children. The Chinese just have a totally different idea of how to do that.

Western parents try to respect their children's individuality, encouraging them to pursue their true passions, supporting their choices, and providing positive reinforcement and a nurturing environment. By contrast, the Chinese believe that the best way to protect their children is by preparing them for the future, letting them see what they're capable of and arming them with skills, work habits, and inner confidence that no one can ever take away. ●

The Reader's Presence

1. Amy Chua opens her essay on a bold assertion: "Here's a story in favor of coercion, Chinese-style." Why might she introduce her story in such strong terms? How does Chua portray coercion in the essay? Which of her various acts of coercion do you find most memorable? Explain why, supporting your reasoning by analyzing specific examples. To what extent does Chua's diction reflect her escalating threats against her daughter's resistance to playing "The Little White Donkey" by Jacques Ibert? Summarize the "Chinese-style" of parenting represented in the text. How does Chua want us to view Chinese parenting when compared to Western parenting?

2. Characterize the tone of Chua's essay. Who do you envision as her intended audience? Support your response by pointing to—and analyzing—specific passages. To what extent is her story designed to be instructional? playful? ironic? sarcastic? How would you characterize Chua's self-awareness? For example, what distinctions does Chua draw between "insulting" and "motivating" her daughter (paragraph 5)? What effect did Chua's citing Rebecca West's axiom *"Motherhood is the strangest thing; it can be like being one's own Trojan Horse"* have on your response to her essay? What does Chua gain or lose by positioning it near the middle of her essay? How do you react to the distinction she draws between Chinese and Western parents in the final two paragraphs? What message about parenting do you think she conveys, and does she accomplish that goal? Why or why not? In your answer, consider how your own childhood experiences affect your perception of Chua's methods.

3. **CONNECTIONS:** Chua's story touches on the concept of self-esteem. Compare self-esteem as Chua describes it with the version presented in Lauren Slater's "The Trouble with Self-Esteem" (page 621). What distinctions does Chua draw between how Western and Eastern parenting promote self-esteem in children? Consider, for example, how Slater distinguishes self-esteem and discipline. Which of these ideas does Chua's parenting method seem to support? Explain why, and support your response by analyzing specific words and phrases in each text.

John Taylor Gatto

AGAINST SCHOOL

"I've taught public school for twenty-six years but I just can't do it anymore," began an impassioned op-ed piece published in the *Wall Street Journal* in 1991. Its author, **JOHN TAYLOR GATTO** (b. 1935), continued, "I've come slowly to understand what it is I really teach: A curriculum of confusion, class position, arbitrary justice, vulgarity, rudeness, disrespect for privacy, indifference to quality, and utter dependency. I teach how to fit into a world I don't want to live in." With the headline "I May Be a Teacher but I'm Not an Educator," the essay set off a fierce debate among parents, teachers, and politicians about the system of public education in the United States. It also launched Gatto's career as a speaker, consultant, and writer.

> "I've come slowly to understand what it is I really teach: A curriculum of confusion, class position, arbitrary justice, vulgarity, rudeness, disrespect for privacy, indifference to quality, and utter dependency. I teach how to fit into a world I don't want to live in."

After graduating from Columbia University, Gatto worked as a scriptwriter, a songwriter, and an ad writer; drove a cab; sold hot dogs; and, finally, began a distinguished career as a schoolteacher. He was recognized as New York City Teacher of the Year for three years in a row. In 1991, the year he resigned in protest from his position as a seventh-grade teacher at the Booker T. Washington School in New York City, he was named New York State Teacher of the Year. He has edited and written many books on education, including *Dumbing Us Down: The Hidden Curriculum of Compulsory Schooling* (1992), *The Exhausted School* (1993), *A Different Kind of Teacher: Solving the Crisis of American Schooling* (2000), and *The Underground History of American Education: A Schoolteacher's Intimate Investigation into the Prison of Modern Schooling* (2001). *Weapons of Mass Instruction: A Schoolteacher's Journey Through the Dark World of Compulsory Schooling* (2010) focuses on the ways in which compulsory schooling cripples the imagination. His essay "Against School" first appeared in *Harper's* magazine in 2001.

I TAUGHT FOR THIRTY YEARS in some of the worst schools in Manhattan, and in some of the best, and during that time I became an expert in boredom. Boredom was everywhere in my world, and if you asked the kids, as I often did, *why* they felt so bored, they always gave the same answers: They said the work was stupid, that it made no sense, that they already knew it. They said they wanted to be doing something real, not just sitting around. They said teachers didn't seem to know much about their subjects and clearly weren't interested in learning more. And the kids were right: their teachers were every bit as bored as they were.

Boredom is the common condition of schoolteachers, and anyone who has spent time in a teachers' lounge can vouch for the low energy, the whining, the dispirited attitudes, to be found there. When asked why *they* feel bored, the teachers tend to blame the kids, as you might expect. Who wouldn't get bored teaching students who are rude and interested only in grades? If even that. Of course, teachers are themselves products of the same twelve-year compulsory school programs that so thoroughly bore their students, and as school personnel they are trapped inside structures even more rigid than those imposed upon the children. Who, then, is to blame?

We all are. My grandfather taught me that. One afternoon when I was seven I complained to him of boredom, and he batted me hard on the head. He told me that I was never to use that term in his presence again, that if I was bored it was my fault and no one else's. The obligation to amuse and instruct myself was entirely my own, and people who didn't know that were childish people, to be avoided if possible. Certainly not to be trusted. That episode cured me of boredom forever, and here and there over the years I was able to pass on the lesson to some remarkable student. For the most part, however, I found it futile to challenge the official notion that boredom and childishness were the natural state of affairs in the classroom. Often I had to defy custom, and even bend the law, to help kids break out of this trap.

The empire struck back, of course; childish adults regularly conflate opposition with disloyalty. I once returned from a medical leave to discover that all evidence of my having been granted the leave had been purposely destroyed, that my job had been terminated, and that I no longer possessed even a teaching license. After nine months of tormented effort I was able to retrieve the license when a school secretary testified to witnessing the plot unfold. In the meantime my family suffered more than I care to remember. By the time I finally retired in 1991, I had more than enough reason to think of our schools — with their long-term, cell-block–style, forced confinement of both students and teachers — as virtual factories of childishness. Yet I honestly could not see *why* they had to be that way. My own experience had revealed to me what many other teachers must learn along the way, too, yet keep to themselves for fear of reprisal: if we wanted to we could easily and inexpensively jettison the old, stupid structures and help kids *take* an education rather than merely *receive* a schooling. We could encourage the best qualities of youthfulness — curiosity, adventure, resilience, the capacity for surprising insight — simply by being more flexible about time, texts, and tests, by introducing kids to truly competent adults, and by giving each student what autonomy he or she needs in order to take a risk every now and then.

But we don't do that. And the more I asked why not, and persisted in thinking about the "problem" of schooling as an engineer might, the more I missed the point: What if there is no "problem" with our schools? What if   5 they are the way they are, so expensively flying in the face of common sense and long experience in how children learn things, not because they are doing something wrong but because they are doing something right? Is it possible that George W. Bush accidentally spoke the truth when he said we would "leave no child behind"? Could it be that our schools are designed to make sure not one of them ever really grows up?

Do we really need school? I don't mean education, just forced schooling: six classes a day, five days a week, nine months a year, for twelve years. Is this deadly routine really necessary? And if so, for what? Don't hide behind reading, writing, and arithmetic as a rationale, because two million happy homeschoolers have surely put that banal justification to rest. Even if they hadn't, a considerable number of well-known Americans never went through the twelve-year wringer our kids currently go through, and they turned out all right. George Washington, Benjamin Franklin, Thomas Jefferson, Abraham Lincoln? Someone taught them, to be sure, but they were not products of a school *system*, and not one of them was ever "graduated" from a secondary school. Throughout most of American history, kids generally didn't go to high school, yet the unschooled rose to be admirals, like Farragut; inventors, like Edison; captains of industry, like Carnegie and Rockefeller; writers, like Melville and Twain and Conrad; and even scholars, like Margaret Mead.[1] In fact, until pretty recently people who reached the age of thirteen weren't looked upon as children at all. Ariel Durant, who co-wrote an enormous, and very good, multivolume history of the world with her husband, Will, was happily married at fifteen, and who could reasonably claim that Ariel Durant was an uneducated person? Unschooled, perhaps, but not uneducated.

We have been taught (that is, schooled) in this country to think of "success" as synonymous with, or at least dependent upon, "schooling," but historically that isn't true in either an intellectual or a financial sense. And plenty of people throughout the world today find a way to educate themselves without resorting to a system of compulsory secondary schools that all too often resemble prisons. Why, then, do Americans confuse education with just such a system? What exactly is the purpose of our public schools?

Mass schooling of a compulsory nature really got its teeth into the United States between 1905 and 1915, though it was conceived of much earlier and pushed for throughout most of the nineteenth century. The reason given for this enormous upheaval of family life and cultural traditions was, roughly speaking, threefold:

1. To make good people.

2. To make good citizens.

3. To make each person his or her personal best.

---

[1] **Margaret Mead** (1901–1978): Became the most famous anthropologist in the world, best known for *Coming of Age in Samoa* (1928), a book that analyzed cultural influence on adolescence. —EDS.

These goals are still trotted out today on a regular basis, and most of us accept them in one form or another as a decent definition of public education's mission, however short schools actually fall in achieving them. But we are dead wrong. Compounding our error is the fact that the national literature holds numerous and surprisingly consistent statements of compulsory schooling's true purpose. We have, for example, the great H. L. Mencken,[2] who wrote in *The American Mercury* for April 1924 that the aim of public education is not

> to fill the young of the species with knowledge and awaken their intelligence. . . . Nothing could be further from the truth. The aim . . . is simply to reduce as many individuals as possible to the same safe level, to breed and train a standardized citizenry, to put down dissent and originality. That is its aim in the United States . . . and that is its aim everywhere else.

Because of Mencken's reputation as a satirist, we might be tempted to dismiss this passage as a bit of hyperbolic sarcasm. His article, however, goes on to trace the template for our own educational system back to the now vanished, though never to be forgotten, military state of Prussia. And although he was certainly aware of the irony that we had recently been at war with Germany, the heir to Prussian thought and culture, Mencken was being perfectly serious here. Our educational system really is Prussian in origin, and that really is cause for concern.

The odd fact of a Prussian provenance for our schools pops up again and   10 again once you know to look for it. William James[3] alluded to it many times at the turn of the century. Orestes Brownson, the hero of Christopher Lasch's 1991 book, *The True and Only Heaven*, was publicly denouncing the Prussianization of American schools back in the 1840s. Horace Mann's[4] "Seventh Annual Report" to the Massachusetts State Board of Education in 1843 is essentially a paean to the land of Frederick the Great and a call for its schooling to be brought here. That Prussian culture loomed large in America is hardly surprising, given our early association with that utopian state. A Prussian served as Washington's aide during the Revolutionary War, and so many German-speaking people had settled here by 1795 that Congress considered publishing a German-language edition of the federal laws. But what shocks is that we should so eagerly have adopted one of the very worst aspects of Prussian culture: an educational system deliberately designed to produce mediocre intellects, to hamstring the inner life, to deny students appreciable leadership skills, and to ensure docile and incomplete citizens—all in order to render the populace "manageable."

---

2 *H[enry] L[ouis] Mencken* (1880–1956): An influential journalist, essayist, magazine editor, satirist, and critic of American life and culture.—EDS.

3 *William James* (1842–1910): One of America's most important psychologists and philosophers. Trained as a medical doctor, he wrote important books on psychology, and particularly on education and religious experience, as well as on the philosophy of pragmatism. The brother of novelist Henry James and of diarist Alice James.—EDS.

4 *Horace Mann* (1796–1859): A celebrated American education reformer and also a member of the U.S. House of Representatives (Massachusetts) from 1848 to 1853.—EDS.

It was from James Bryant Conant—president of Harvard for twenty years, WWI poison-gas specialist, WWII executive on the atomic-bomb project, high commissioner of the American zone in Germany after WWII, and truly one of the most influential figures of the twentieth century—that I first got wind of the real purposes of American schooling. Without Conant, we would probably not have the same style and degree of standardized testing that we enjoy today, nor would we be blessed with gargantuan high schools that warehouse 2,000 to 4,000 students at a time, like the famous Columbine High in Littleton, Colorado. Shortly after I retired from teaching I picked up Conant's 1959 book-length essay, *The Child, the Parent and the State*, and was more than a little intrigued to see him mention in passing that the modern schools we attend were the result of a "revolution" engineered between 1905 and 1930. A revolution? He declines to elaborate, but he does direct the curious and the uninformed to Alexander Inglis's 1918 book, *Principles of Secondary Education*, in which "one saw this revolution through the eyes of a revolutionary."

Inglis, for whom a lecture in education at Harvard is named, makes it perfectly clear that compulsory schooling on this continent was intended to be just what it had been for Prussia in the 1820s: a fifth column into the burgeoning democratic movement that threatened to give the peasants and the proletarians a voice at the bargaining table. Modern, industrialized, compulsory schooling was to make a sort of surgical incision into the prospective unity of these underclasses. Divide children by subject, by age-grading, by constant rankings on tests, and by many other more subtle means, and it was unlikely that the ignorant mass of mankind, separated in childhood, would ever re-integrate into a dangerous whole.

Inglis breaks down the purpose—the *actual* purpose—of modern schooling into six basic functions, any one of which is enough to curl the hair of those innocent enough to believe the three traditional goals listed earlier:

1. The *adjustive or adaptive* function. Schools are to establish fixed habits of reaction to authority. This, of course, precludes critical judgment completely. It also pretty much destroys the idea that useful or interesting material should be taught, because you can't test for *reflexive* obedience until you know whether you can make kids learn, and do, foolish and boring things.

2. The *integrating* function. This might well be called "the conformity function," because its intention is to make children as alike as possible. People who conform are predictable, and this is of great use to those who wish to harness and manipulate a large labor force.

3. The *diagnostic and directive* function. School is meant to determine each student's proper social role. This is done by logging evidence mathematically and anecdotally on cumulative records. As in "your permanent record." Yes, you do have one.

4. The *differentiating* function. Once their social role has been "diagnosed," children are to be sorted by role and trained only so far as

their destination in the social machine merits—and not one step further. So much for making kids their personal best.

5. The *selective* function. This refers not to human choice at all but to Darwin's theory of natural selection as applied to what he called "the favored races." In short, the idea is to help things along by consciously attempting to improve the breeding stock. Schools are meant to tag the unfit—with poor grades, remedial placement, and other punishments—clearly enough that their peers will accept them as inferior and effectively bar them from the reproductive sweepstakes. That's what all those little humiliations from first grade onward were intended to do: wash the dirt down the drain.

6. The *propaedeutic* function. The societal system implied by these rules will require an elite group of caretakers. To that end, a small fraction of the kids will quietly be taught how to manage this continuing project, how to watch over and control a population deliberately dumbed down and declawed in order that government might proceed unchallenged and corporations might never want for obedient labor.

That, unfortunately, is the purpose of mandatory public education in this country. And lest you take Inglis for an isolated crank with a rather too cynical take on the educational enterprise, you should know that he was hardly alone in championing these ideas. Conant himself, building on the ideas of Horace Mann and others, campaigned tirelessly for an American school system designed along the same lines. Men like George Peabody, who funded the cause of mandatory schooling throughout the South, surely understood that the Prussian system was useful in creating not only a harmless electorate and a servile labor force but also a virtual herd of mindless consumers. In time a great number of industrial titans came to recognize the enormous profits to be had by cultivating and tending just such a herd via public education, among them Andrew Carnegie and John D. Rockefeller.

There you have it. Now you know. We don't need Karl Marx's[5] conception of a grand warfare between the classes to see that it is in the interest of complex management, economic or political, to dumb people down, to demoralize them, to divide them from one another, and to discard them if they don't conform. Class may frame the proposition, as when Woodrow Wilson, then president of Princeton University, said the following to the New York City School Teachers Association in 1909: "We want one class of persons to have a liberal education, and we want another class of persons, a very much larger class, of necessity, in every society, to forgo the privileges of a liberal education and fit themselves to perform specific difficult manual tasks." But the motives behind the disgusting decisions that bring about these ends need not be class-based at all. They can stem purely from fear, or from the by now

15

---

5 *Karl Marx* (1818–1883): Often identified as the father of communism, Marx was a philosopher, political economist, sociologist, political theorist, and revolutionary.—EDS.

familiar belief that "efficiency" is the paramount virtue, rather than love, liberty, laughter, or hope. Above all, they can stem from simple greed.

There were vast fortunes to be made, after all, in an economy based on mass production and organized to favor the large corporation rather than the small business or the family farm. But mass production required mass consumption, and at the turn of the twentieth century most Americans considered it both unnatural and unwise to buy things they didn't actually need. Mandatory schooling was a godsend on that count. School didn't have to train kids in any direct sense to think they should consume nonstop, because it did something even better: it encouraged them not to think at all. And that left them sitting ducks for another great invention of the modern era—marketing.

Now, you needn't have studied marketing to know that there are two groups of people who can always be convinced to consume more than they need to: addicts and children. School has done a pretty good job of turning our children into addicts, but it has done a spectacular job of turning our children into children. Again, this is no accident. Theorists from Plato to Rousseau to our own Dr. Inglis knew that if children could be cloistered with other children, stripped of responsibility and independence, encouraged to develop only the trivializing emotions of greed, envy, jealousy, and fear, they would grow older but never truly grow up. In the 1934 edition of his once well-known book *Public Education in the United States*, Ellwood P. Cubberley detailed and praised the way the strategy of successive school enlargements had extended childhood by two to six years, and forced schooling was at that point still quite new. This same Cubberley—who was dean of Stanford's School of Education, a textbook editor at Houghton Mifflin, and Conant's friend and correspondent at Harvard—had written the following in the 1922 edition of his book *Public School Administration*: "Our schools are . . . factories in which the raw products (children) are to be shaped and fashioned. . . . And it is the business of the school to build its pupils according to the specifications laid down."

It's perfectly obvious from our society today what those specifications were. Maturity has by now been banished from nearly every aspect of our lives. Easy divorce laws have removed the need to work at relationships; easy credit has removed the need for fiscal self-control; easy entertainment has removed the need to learn to entertain oneself; easy answers have removed the need to ask questions. We have become a nation of children, happy to surrender our judgments and our wills to political exhortations and commercial blandishments that would insult actual adults. We buy televisions, and then we buy the things we see on the television. We buy computers, and then we buy the things we see on the computer. We buy $150 sneakers whether we need them or not, and when they fall apart too soon we buy another pair. We drive SUVs and believe the lie that they constitute a kind of life insurance, even when we're upside-down in them. And, worst of all, we don't bat an eye when Ari Fleischer[6]

---

[6] ***Ari Fleischer:*** White House press secretary under President George W. Bush from 2001 to 2003. —EDS.

tells us to "be careful what you say," even if we remember having been told somewhere back in school that America is the land of the free. We simply buy that one too. Our schooling, as intended, has seen to it.

Now for the good news. Once you understand the logic behind modern schooling, its tricks and traps are fairly easy to avoid. School trains children to be employees and consumers; teach your own to be leaders and adventurers. School trains children to obey reflexively; teach your own to think critically and independently. Well-schooled kids have a low threshold for boredom; help your own to develop an inner life so that they'll never be bored. Urge them to take on the serious material, the *grown-up* material, in history, literature, philosophy, music, art, economics, theology—all the stuff schoolteachers know well enough to avoid. Challenge your kids with plenty of solitude so that they can learn to enjoy their own company, to conduct inner dialogues. Well-schooled people are conditioned to dread being alone, and they seek constant companionship through the TV, the computer, the cell phone, and through shallow friendships quickly acquired and quickly abandoned. Your children should have a more meaningful life, and they can.

First, though, we must wake up to what our schools really are: laboratories   20
of experimentation on young minds, drill centers for the habits and attitudes that corporate society demands. Mandatory education serves children only incidentally; its real purpose is to turn them into servants. Don't let your own have their childhoods extended, not even for a day. If David Farragut could take command of a captured British warship as a preteen, if Thomas Edison could publish a broadsheet at the age of twelve, if Ben Franklin could apprentice himself to a printer at the same age (then put himself through a course of study that would choke a Yale senior today), there's no telling what your own kids could do. After a long life, and thirty years in the public school trenches, I've concluded that genius is as common as dirt. We suppress our genius only because we haven't yet figured out how to manage a population of educated men and women. The solution, I think, is simple and glorious. Let them manage themselves. ■

The Reader's Presence

1. Would you agree with Gatto that compulsory schooling has the effect of creating conformity and obedience to authority? Why or why not? To what extent does schooling attempt to form citizens? To what extent are students trained to be consumers?

2. Gatto makes a distinction between "education" and "schooling" (paragraph 4). What is significant about this distinction? What are the consequences of conflating the two?

3. **CONNECTIONS:** Gatto argues that compulsory schooling can—and often does—effectively prevent students from becoming independent thinkers. Read his essay in light of Lukianoff and Haidt's "The Coddling of the American Mind" (page 542). Although the selections have different educational purposes and use different types of evidence, in what ways do they arrive at similar conclusions? Explain which essay, in your opinion, delves more deeply into today's educational issues?

Roxane Gay

THE CARELESS LANGUAGE OF SEXUAL VIOLENCE

How should we write about sexual violence? How should we portray it in film and television? "I am troubled," writes essayist and author **ROXANE GAY**, "by how we have allowed intellectual distance between violence and the representation of violence." In her essay "The Careless Language of Sexual Violence," Gay (b. 1974) challenges the casual language employed by media that strips away the terror and reality of rape and other violent acts.

Gay has authored two collections of short stories, a collection of essays, and a novel. Her work has appeared in *Best American Mystery Stories 2014*, *Best American Short Stories 2012*, *McSweeney's*, and *Virginia Quarterly Review*, among others. She teaches creative writing at Purdue University, writes opinion pieces for the *New York Times*, and is a writer for Marvel's Black Panther spinoff series, *World of Wakanda*. Her latest title is the memoir *Hunger* (2017).

> **Gay challenges the casual language employed by media that strips away the terror and reality of rape and other violent acts.**

THERE ARE CRIMES and then there are crimes and then there are atrocities. These are, I suppose, matters of scale. I read an article in the *New York Times* about an eleven-year-old girl who was gang raped by eighteen men in Cleveland, Texas. The levels of horror to this story are many, from the victim's age to what is known about what happened to her, to the number of attackers, to the public response in that town, to how it is being reported. There is video of the attack too, because this is the future. The unspeakable will be televised.

The *Times* article was entitled "Vicious Assault Shakes Texas Town," as if the victim in question was the town itself. James McKinley Jr., the article's author, focused on how the men's lives would be changed forever, how the town was being ripped apart, how those poor boys might never be able to return to school. There was discussion of how the eleven-year-old girl, the child, dressed like a twenty-year-old, implying that there is a realm of possibility where a woman can "ask for it" and that it's somehow understandable that eighteen men would rape a child. There were even questions about the whereabouts of the mother, given, as we all know, that a mother must be with her child at all times or whatever ill may befall the child is clearly the mother's fault. Strangely, there were no questions about the whereabouts of the father while this rape was taking place.

Vicious Assault Shakes Texas Town	
By JAMES C. McKINLEY Jr. MARCH 8, 2011	

Headline of the newspaper article reporting on the gang rape of an eleven-year-old.

The overall tone of the article was what a shame it all was, how so many lives were affected by this one terrible event. Little addressed the girl, the child. It was an eleven-year-old girl whose body was ripped apart, not a town. It was an eleven-year-old girl whose life was ripped apart, not the lives of the men who raped her. It is difficult for me to make sense of how anyone could lose sight of that and yet it isn't.

We live in a culture that is very permissive where rape is concerned. While there are certainly many people who understand rape and the damage of rape, we also live in a time that necessitates the phrase "rape culture." This phrase denotes a culture where we are inundated, in different ways, by the idea that male aggression and violence toward women is acceptable and often inevitable. As Lynn Higgins and Brenda Silver ask in their book *Rape and Representation*, "How is it that in spite (or perhaps because) of their erasure, rape and sexual violence have been so ingrained and so rationalized through their representations as to appear 'natural' and inevitable, to women as men?" It is such an important question, trying to understand how we have come to this. We have also, perhaps, become immune to the horror of rape because we see it so often and discuss it so often, many times without acknowledging or considering the gravity of rape and its effects. We jokingly say things like, "I just took a rape shower," or "My boss totally just raped me over my request for a raise." We have appropriated the language of rape for all manner of violations, great and small. It is not a stretch to imagine why James McKinley Jr. is more concerned about the eighteen men than one girl.

The casual way in which we deal with rape may begin and end with   5
television and movies where we are inundated with images of sexual and domestic violence. Can you think of a dramatic television series that has not incorporated some kind of rape storyline? There was a time when these storylines had a certain educational element to them, à la *A Very Special Episode*. I remember, for example, the episode of *Beverly Hills 90210* where Kelly Taylor discussed being date raped at a slumber party, surrounded, tearfully, by her closest friends. For many young women that episode created a space where they could have a conversation about rape as something that did not only happen with strangers. Later in the series, when the show was on its last legs, Kelly would be raped again, this time by a stranger. We watched the familiar trajectory of violation, trauma, disillusion, and finally vindication, seemingly forgetting we had sort of seen this story before.

Every other movie aired on Lifetime or Lifetime Movie Network features some kind of violence against women. The violence is graphic and gratuitous while still being strangely antiseptic where more is implied about the actual act than shown. We consume these representations of violence and do so eagerly. There is a comfort, I suppose, to consuming violence contained in 90-minute segments and muted by commercials for household goods and communicated to us by former television stars with feathered bangs.

While once rape as entertainment fodder may have also included an element of the didactic, such is no longer the case. Rape, these days, is good for ratings. *Private Practice*, on ABC, recently aired a story arc where Charlotte King, the iron-willed, independent, and sexually adventurous doctor was brutally raped. This happened, of course, just as February sweeps were beginning. The depiction of the assault was as graphic as you might expect from prime-time network television. For several episodes we saw the attack and its aftermath, how the once vibrant Charlotte became a shell of herself, how she became sexually frigid, how her body bore witness to the physical damage of rape. Another character on the show, Violet, bravely confessed she too had been raped. The show was widely applauded for its sensitive treatment of a difficult subject.

The soap opera *General Hospital*[1] is currently airing a rape storyline, and the height of that story arc occurred, yes, during sweeps. *General Hospital*, like most soap operas, incorporates a rape storyline every five years or so when they need an uptick in viewers. Before the current storyline, Emily Quartermaine was raped and before Emily, Elizabeth Webber was raped, and long before Elizabeth Webber, Laura of Luke and Laura was raped by Luke but that rape was okay because Laura ended up marrying Luke so her rape doesn't really count. Every woman, *General Hospital* wanted us to believe, loves her rapist. The current rape storyline has a twist. This time the victim is a man, Michael Corinthos Jr., son of Port Charles mob boss Sonny Corinthos, himself no stranger to violence against women. While it is commendable to see the show's producers trying to address the issue of male rape and prison rape, the subject matter is still handled carelessly, is still a source of titillation, and is still packaged neatly between commercials for cleaning products and baby diapers.

Of course, if we are going to talk about rape and how we are inundated by representations of rape and how, perhaps, we've become numb to rape, we have to discuss *Law & Order: SVU*, which deals, primarily, in all manner of sexual assault against women, children, and once in a great while, men. Each week the violation is more elaborate, more lurid, more unspeakable. When the show first aired, Rosie O'Donnell, I believe, objected quite vocally when one of the stars appeared on her show. O'Donnell said she didn't understand why such a show was needed. People dismissed her objections and the incident was quickly forgotten. The series is in its 12th season and shows no

---

[1] *General Hospital:* The longest-running American soap opera in production and the third longest running in American history after *Guiding Light* and *As the World Turns.* —EDS.

signs of ending anytime soon. When O'Donnell objected to *SVU*'s premise, when she dared to suggest that perhaps a show dealing so explicitly with sexual assault was unnecessary, was too much, people treated her like she was the crazy one, the prude censor. I watch *SVU* religiously, have actually seen every single episode. I am not sure what that says about me.

I am trying to connect my ideas here. Bear with me.   10

It is rather ironic that only a couple weeks ago, the *Times* ran an editorial about the War on Women. This topic is, obviously, one that matters to me. I recently wrote an essay about how, as a writer who is also a woman, I increasingly feel that to write is a political act whether I intend it to be or not because we live in a culture where McKinley's article is permissible and publishable. I am troubled by how we have allowed intellectual distance between violence and the representation of violence. We talk about rape but we don't talk about rape, not carefully.

We live in a strange and terrible time for women. There are days, like today, where I think it has always been a strange and terrible time to be a woman. It is nothing less than horrifying to realize we live in a culture where the "paper of record" can write an article that comes off as sympathetic to eighteen rapists while encouraging victim blaming. Have we forgotten who an eleven-year-old is? An eleven-year-old is very, very young, and somehow, that amplifies the atrocity, at least for me. I also think, perhaps, people do not understand the trauma of gang rape. While there's no benefit to creating a hierarchy of rape where one kind of rape is worse than another because rape is, at the end of day, rape, there is something particularly insidious about gang rape, about the idea that a pack of men feed on each other's frenzy and both individually and collectively believe it is their right to violate a woman's body in such an unspeakable manner.

Gang rape is a difficult experience to survive physically and emotionally. There is the exposure to unwanted pregnancy and sexually transmitted diseases, vaginal and anal tearing, fistula and vaginal scar tissue. The reproductive system is often irreparably damaged. Victims of gang rape, in particular, have a higher chance of miscarrying a pregnancy. Psychologically, there are any number of effects including PTSD, anxiety, fear, coping with the social stigma, and coping with shame, and on and on. The actual rape ends but the aftermath can be very far reaching and even more devastating than the rape itself. We rarely discuss these things, though. Instead, we are careless. We allow ourselves that rape can be washed away as neatly as it is on TV and in the movies where the trajectory of victimhood is neatly defined.

I cannot speak universally but given what I know about gang rape, the experience is wholly consuming and a never-ending nightmare. There is little point in pretending otherwise. Perhaps McKinley Jr. is, like so many people today, anesthetized or somehow willfully distanced from such brutal realities. Perhaps it is that despite this inundation of rape imagery, where we are immersed in a rape culture, that not enough victims of gang rape speak out about the toll the experience exacts. Perhaps the right stories are not being told or we're not writing enough about the topic of rape. Perhaps we are writing too many stories about rape. It is hard to know how such things come to pass.

I am approaching this topic somewhat selfishly. I write about sexual   15
violence a great deal in my fiction. The why of this writerly obsession doesn't matter but I often wonder why I come back to the same stories over and over. Perhaps it is simply that writing is cheaper than therapy or drugs. When I read articles such as McKinley's, I start to wonder about my responsibility as a writer. I'm finishing my novel right now. It's the story of a brutal kidnapping in Haiti and part of the story involves gang rape. Having to write that kind of story requires going to a dark place. At times, I have made myself nauseous with what I'm writing and what I am capable of writing and imagining, my ability to *go there*.

As I write any of these stories, I wonder if I am being gratuitous. I want to *get it right*. How do you get this sort of thing right? How do you write violence authentically without making it exploitative? There are times when I worry I am contributing to the kind of cultural numbness that would allow an article like the one in the *Times* to be written and published, that allows rape to be such rich fodder for popular culture and entertainment. We cannot separate violence in fiction from violence in the world no matter how hard we try. As Laura Tanner notes in her book *Intimate Violence*, "The act of reading a representation of violence is defined by the reader's suspension between the semiotic and the real, between a representation and the material dynamics of violence which it evokes, reflects, or transforms." She also goes on to say that "the distance and detachment of a reader who must leave his or her body behind in order to enter imaginatively into the scene of violence make it possible for representations of violence to obscure the material dynamics of bodily violation, erasing not only the victim's body but his or her pain." The way we currently represent rape, in books, in newspapers, on television, on the silver screen, often allows us to ignore the material realities of rape, the impact of rape, the meaning of rape.

While I have these concerns, I also feel committed to telling the truth, to saying these violences happen even if bearing such witness contributes to a spectacle of sexual violence. When we're talking about race or religion or politics, it is often said we need to speak carefully. These are difficult topics where we need to be vigilant not only in what we say but how we express ourselves. That same care, I would suggest, has to be extended to how we write about violence, and sexual violence in particular.

In the *Times* article, the phrase "sexual assault" is used, as is the phrase "the girl had been forced to have sex with several men." The word "rape" is only used twice and not really in connection with the victim. That is not the careful use of language. Language, in this instance, and far more often than makes sense, is used to buffer our sensibilities from the brutality of rape, from the extraordinary nature of such a crime. Feminist scholars have long called for a rereading of rape. Higgins and Silver note that "the act of rereading rape involves more than listening to silences; it requires restoring rape to the literal, to the body: restoring, that is, the violence—the physical, sexual violation." I would suggest we need to find new ways, whether in fiction or creative nonfiction or journalism, for not only rereading rape but rewriting rape as well, ways of rewriting that restore the actual violence to these crimes and that make it impossible for men to be excused for committing atrocities and that make it impossible for articles like McKinley's to be written, to be published, to be considered acceptable.

An eleven-year-old girl was raped by eighteen men. The suspects ranged in age from middle-schoolers to a 27-year-old. There are pictures and videos. Her life will never be the same. The *New York Times*, however, would like you to worry about those boys, who will have to live with this for the rest of their lives. That is not simply the careless language of violence. It is the criminal language of violence. ●

The Reader's Presence

1. Near the end of her essay, Roxane Gay declares: "The way we currently represent rape, in books, in newspapers, on television, on the silver screen, often allows us to ignore the material realities of rape, the impact of rape, the meaning of rape" (paragraph 16). As you reread her essay, list and analyze the specific points Gay unpacks to make her case that Americans are living in what she calls a "rape culture," a term she defines at the outset of her essay as "a culture where we are inundated in different ways, by the idea that male aggression and violence toward women is acceptable and often inevitable" (paragraph 4). In addition to the article she cites from the *New York Times*, Gay provides numerous examples of sexual violence in television, fiction, and advertising. What is the specific nature of Gay's criticism of these media in portraying rape and its consequences? What is the relationship between the fictional scenes of rape Gay refers to and the language used to describe actual rape?

2. Gay urges that "we need to find new ways, whether in fiction or creative nonfiction or journalism, for not only rereading rape but rewriting rape as well." (paragraph 17). To what extent does she provide examples of such writing? With what effects? What specific changes in news accounts of rape does she advocate? Consider, for example, her conviction that articles about rape should be written "to restore the actual violence." How would this change the significance and impact of the article, and what message would it convey about the nature of sexual violence against women?

3. **CONNECTIONS:** Evaluate the argument of Steven Pinker's "Violence Vanquished" (page 591) in terms of the language he uses to describe violence. How might Gay respond to the diction and substance of his essay? To what extent does Pinker's perspective on the history of human violence affect your reading of Gay's argument? Support your response with specific examples—and analysis—of both essays.

Christopher Hitchens

BELIEVE ME, IT'S TORTURE

One of the world's most public intellectuals, **CHRISTOPHER HITCHENS** (1949–2011) was known for making controversial arguments. His 2007 book, for example, *God Is Not Great: How Religion Poisons Everything*, argues that religion is immoral, contributing to everything from ignorance to terrorism to sexual repression. In another book, *The Missionary Position: Mother Teresa in Theory and Practice* (1995), he took the very unpopular position that the Catholic nun was more interested in furthering Catholic doctrine and "becoming a saint" than she was in genuinely helping the poor. Although his views on religion and sexuality were typically associated with the political left, Hitchens was not reluctant to criticize liberal politicians: his 1999 book, *No One Left to Lie To: The Values of the Worst Family*, was a scathing attack on the Clinton family. His last books included *Hitch-22* (2010), a candid memoir of his personal life and political philosophy, and *Mortality* (2012), published posthumously, a collection of essays describing his struggle with esophageal cancer, which claimed his life in 2011.

> One of the world's most public intellectuals, Christopher Hitchens was known for making controversial arguments.

HERE IS THE MOST chilling way I can find of stating the matter. Until recently, "waterboarding" was something that Americans did to other Americans. It was inflicted, and endured, by those members of the Special Forces who underwent the advanced form of training known as SERE (Survival, Evasion, Resistance, Escape). In these harsh exercises, brave men and women were introduced to the sorts of barbarism that they might expect to meet at the hands of a lawless foe who disregarded the Geneva Conventions. But it was something that Americans were being trained to resist, not to *inflict*.

Exploring this narrow but deep distinction, on a gorgeous day last May I found myself deep in the hill country of western North Carolina, preparing to be surprised by a team of extremely hardened veterans who had confronted their country's enemies in highly arduous terrain all over the world. They knew about everything from unarmed combat to enhanced interrogation and, in exchange for anonymity, were going to show me as nearly as possible what real waterboarding might be like.

It goes without saying that I knew I could stop the process at any time, and that when it was all over I would be released into happy daylight rather than returned to a darkened cell. But it's been well said that cowards die many times before their deaths, and it was difficult for me to completely forget the clause in the contract of indemnification that I had signed. This document (written by one who knew) stated revealingly: "'Water boarding' is a potentially dangerous activity in which the participant can receive serious and permanent (physical, emotional and psychological) injuries and even death, including injuries and death due to the respiratory and neurological systems of the body." As the agreement went on to say, there would be safeguards provided "during the 'water boarding' process, however, these measures may fail and even if they work properly they may not prevent Hitchens from experiencing serious injury or death."

On the night before the encounter I got to sleep with what I thought was creditable ease, but woke early and knew at once that I wasn't going back to any sort of doze or snooze. The first specialist I had approached with the scheme had asked my age on the telephone and when told what it was (I am 59) had laughed out loud and told me to forget it. Waterboarding is for Green Berets in training, or wiry young jihadists whose teeth can bite through the gristle of an old goat. It's not for wheezing, paunchy scribblers. For my current "handlers" I had had to produce a doctor's certificate assuring them that I did not have asthma, but I wondered whether I should tell them about the 15,000 cigarettes I had inhaled every year for the last several decades. I was feeling apprehensive, in other words, and beginning to wish I hadn't given myself so long to think about it.

I have to be opaque about exactly where I was later that day, but there   5
came a moment when, sitting on a porch outside a remote house at the end of a winding country road, I was very gently yet firmly grabbed from behind, pulled to my feet, pinioned by my wrists (which were then cuffed to a belt), and cut off from the sunlight by having a black hood pulled over my face. I was then turned around a few times, I presume to assist in disorienting me, and led over some crunchy gravel into a darkened room. Well, mainly darkened: there were some oddly spaced bright lights that came as pinpoints through my hood. And some weird music assaulted my ears. (I'm no judge of these things, but I wouldn't have expected former Special Forces types to be so fond of New Age techno-disco.) The outside world seemed very suddenly very distant indeed.

Arms already lost to me, I wasn't able to flail as I was pushed onto a sloping board and positioned with my head lower than my heart. (That's the main point: the angle can be slight or steep.) Then my legs were lashed together so that the board and I were one single and trussed unit. Not to bore you with my phobias, but if I don't have at least two pillows I wake up with acid reflux and mild sleep apnea, so even a merely supine position makes me uneasy. And, to tell you something I had been keeping from myself as well as from my new experimental friends, I do have a fear of drowning that comes from a bad childhood moment on the Isle of Wight, when I got out of my depth.

As a boy reading the climactic torture scene of *1984*,[1] where what is in Room 101 is the worst thing in the world, I realize that somewhere in my version of that hideous chamber comes the moment when the wave washes over me. Not that that makes me special: I don't know anyone who *likes* the idea of drowning. As mammals we may have originated in the ocean, but water has many ways of reminding us that when we are in it we are out of our element. In brief, when it comes to breathing, give me good old air every time.

You may have read by now the official lie about this treatment, which is that it "simulates" the feeling of drowning. This is not the case. You feel that you are drowning because you *are* drowning—or, rather, being drowned, albeit slowly and under controlled conditions and at the mercy (or otherwise) of those who are applying the pressure. The "board" is the instrument, *not* the method. You are not being boarded. You are being watered. This was very rapidly brought home to me when, on top of the hood, which still admitted a few flashes of random and worrying strobe light to my vision, three layers of enveloping towel were added. In this pregnant darkness, head downward, I waited for a while until I abruptly felt a slow cascade of water going up my nose. Determined to resist if only for the honor of my navy ancestors who had so often been in peril on the sea, I held my breath for a while and then had to exhale and—as you might expect—inhale in turn. The inhalation brought the damp cloths tight against my nostrils, as if a huge, wet paw had been suddenly and annihilatingly clamped over my face. Unable to determine whether I was breathing in or out, and flooded more with sheer panic than with mere water, I triggered the pre-arranged signal and felt the unbelievable relief of being pulled upright and having the soaking and stifling layers pulled off me. I find I don't want to tell you how little time I lasted.

This is because I had read that Khalid Sheikh Mohammed, invariably referred to as the "mastermind" of the atrocities of September 11, 2001, had impressed his interrogators by holding out for upward of two minutes before cracking. (By the way, this story is not confirmed. My North Carolina friends jeered at it. "Hell," said one, "from what I heard they only washed his damn face before he babbled.") But, hell, I thought in my turn, no Hitchens is going to do worse than *that*. Well, O.K., I admit I didn't outdo him. And so then I said, with slightly more bravado than was justified, that I'd like to try it one more time. There was a paramedic present who checked my racing pulse and warned me about adrenaline rush. An interval was ordered, and then I felt the mask come down again. Steeling myself to remember what it had been like last time, and to learn from the previous panic attack, I fought down the first, and some of the second, wave of nausea and terror but soon found that I was an abject prisoner of my gag reflex. The interrogators would hardly have had time to ask me any questions, and I knew that I would quite readily have agreed to supply any answer. I still feel ashamed when I think about it. Also, in case it's of interest, I have since woken up trying to

---

[1] ***Nineteen Eighty-Four*** (also written as ***1984***): George Orwell's novel (published 1948) depicting a world of constant warfare, government surveillance, and public mind control, a world in which the individual is subordinated to the state ("Big Brother").—EDS.

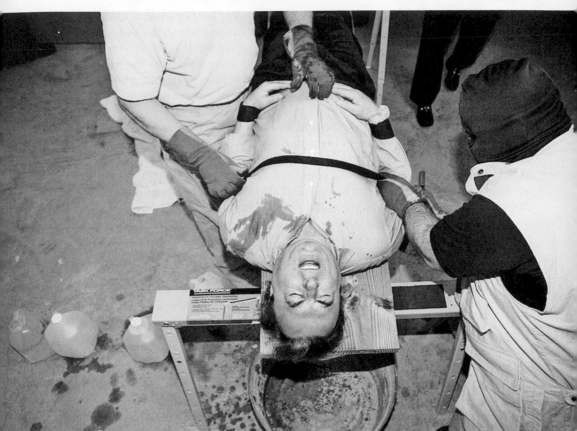

Gasper Tringale Photography

Christopher Hitchens undergoing waterboarding "treatment."

push the bedcovers off my face, and if I do anything that makes me short of breath I find myself clawing at the air with a horrible sensation of smothering and claustrophobia. No doubt this will pass. As if detecting my misery and shame, one of my interrogators comfortingly said, "Any time is a long time when you're breathing water." I could have hugged him for saying so, and just then I was hit with a ghastly sense of the sadomasochistic dimension that underlies the relationship between the torturer and the tortured. I apply the Abraham Lincoln test for moral casuistry:[2] "If slavery is not wrong, nothing is wrong." Well, then, if waterboarding does not constitute torture, then there is no such thing as torture.

   I am somewhat proud of my ability to "keep my head," as the saying goes, and to maintain presence of mind under trying circumstances. I was completely convinced that, when the water pressure had become intolerable, I had firmly uttered the pre-determined code word that would cause it to cease. But my interrogator told me that, rather to his surprise, I had not spoken a word. I had activated the "dead man's handle" that signaled the onset

2 ***casuistry:*** Using clever but unsound reasoning, especially in relation to moral questions.—EDS.

of unconsciousness. So now I have to wonder about the role of false memory and delusion. What I do recall clearly, though, is a hard finger feeling for my solar plexus as the water was being poured. What was that for? "That's to find out if you are trying to cheat, and timing your breathing to the doses. If you try that, we can outsmart you. We have all kinds of enhancements." I was briefly embarrassed that I hadn't earned or warranted these refinements, but it hit me yet again that this is certainly the *language* of torture.

Maybe I am being premature in phrasing it thus. Among the veterans   10 there are at least two views on all this, which means in practice that there are two opinions on whether or not "waterboarding" constitutes torture. I have had some extremely serious conversations on the topic, with two groups of highly decent and serious men, and I think that both cases have to be stated at their strongest.

The team who agreed to give me a hard time in the woods of North Carolina belong to a highly honorable group. This group regards itself as out on the front line in defense of a society that is too spoiled and too ungrateful to appreciate those solid, underpaid volunteers who guard us while we sleep. These heroes stay on the ramparts at all hours and in all weather, and if they make a mistake they may be arraigned in order to scratch some domestic political itch. Faced with appalling enemies who make horror videos of torture and beheadings, they feel that they are the ones who confront denunciation in our press, and possible prosecution. As they have just tried to demonstrate to me, a man who has been waterboarded may well emerge from the experience a bit shaky, but he is in a mood to surrender the relevant information and is unmarked and undamaged and indeed ready for another bout in quite a short time. When contrasted to actual torture, waterboarding is more like foreplay. No thumbscrew, no pincers, no electrodes, no rack. Can one say this of those who have been captured by the tormentors and murderers of (say) Daniel Pearl? On this analysis, any call to indict the United States for torture is therefore a lame and diseased attempt to arrive at a moral equivalence between those who defend civilization and those who exploit its freedoms to hollow it out, and ultimately to bring it down. I myself do not trust anybody who does not clearly understand this viewpoint.

Against it, however, I call as my main witness Mr. Malcolm Nance. Mr. Nance is not what you call a bleeding heart. In fact, speaking of the coronary area, he has said that, in battlefield conditions, he "would personally cut bin Laden's heart out with a plastic M.R.E. spoon."[3] He was to the fore on September 11, 2001, dealing with the burning nightmare in the debris of the Pentagon. He has been involved with the SERE program since 1997. He speaks Arabic and has been on al Qaeda's tail since the early 1990s. His most recent book, *The Terrorists of Iraq* [2007], is a highly potent analysis both of the jihadist threat in Mesopotamia and of the ways in which we have made its life easier. I passed one of the most dramatic evenings of my life listening

---

[3] After searching for Osama bin Laden for nearly a decade following the attacks of September 11, 2001, Osama bin Laden was killed by American special military forces on May 2, 2011. —EDS.

to his cold but enraged denunciation of the adoption of waterboarding by the United States. The argument goes like this:

1. Waterboarding is a deliberate torture technique and has been prosecuted as such by our judicial arm when perpetrated by others.

2. If we allow it and justify it, we cannot complain if it is employed in the future by other regimes on captive U.S. citizens. It is a method of putting American prisoners in harm's way.

3. It may be a means of extracting information, but it is also a means of extracting junk information. (Mr. Nance told me that he had heard of someone's being compelled to confess that he was a hermaphrodite. I later had an awful twinge while wondering if I myself could have been "dunked" this far.) To put it briefly, even the CIA sources for the *Washington Post* story on waterboarding conceded that the information they got out of Khalid Sheikh Mohammed was "not all of it reliable." Just put a pencil line under that last phrase, or commit it to memory.

4. It opens a door that cannot be closed. Once you have posed the notorious "ticking bomb" question, and once you assume that you are in the right, what will you *not* do? Waterboarding not getting results fast enough? The terrorist's clock still ticking? Well, then, bring on the thumbscrews and the pincers and the electrodes and the rack.

Masked by these arguments, there lurks another very penetrating point. Nance doubts very much that Khalid Sheikh Mohammed lasted that long under the water treatment (and I am pathetically pleased to hear it). It's also quite thinkable, *if* he did, that he was trying to attain martyrdom at our hands. But even if he endured so long, and since the United States has in any case bragged that *in fact* he did, one of our worst enemies has now become one of the founders of something that will someday disturb your sleep as well as mine. To quote Nance:

> Torture advocates hide behind the argument that an open discussion about specific American interrogation techniques will aid the enemy. Yet, convicted Al Qaeda members and innocent captives who were released to their host nations have already debriefed the world through hundreds of interviews, movies and documentaries on exactly what methods they were subjected to and how they endured. Our own missteps have created a cadre of highly experienced lecturers for Al Qaeda's own virtual SERE school for terrorists.

Which returns us to my starting point, about the distinction between training *for* something and training to resist it. One used to be told—and surely with truth—that the lethal fanatics of al Qaeda were schooled to lie, and instructed to claim that they had been tortured and maltreated whether they had been tortured and maltreated or not. Did we notice what a frontier we had crossed when we admitted and even proclaimed that their stories might in fact be true? I had only a very slight encounter on that frontier, but I still wish that my experience were the only way in which the words "waterboard" and "American" could be mentioned in the same (gasping and sobbing) breath.

The Reader's Presence

1. How would you characterize the tone of voice Hitchens uses in this essay? Pay particular attention to the passages where he describes the sensation of being waterboarded. How would you describe the sound of his voice in these passages? What other approaches could he have taken with equal plausibility, given the subject matter? Why do you think Hitchens takes the approach that he does?

2. Hitchens writes: "As if detecting my misery and shame, one of my interrogators comfortingly said, 'Any time is a long time when you're breathing water.' I could have hugged him for saying so, and just then I was hit with a ghastly sense of the sadomasochistic dimension that underlies the relationship between the torturer and the tortured" (paragraph 8). What does Hitchens mean by this? What is the effect of Hitchens's having made this observation so close to the end of the essay? With what impression does Hitchens leave the reader at the end of his essay?

3. **VISUAL PRESENCE:** What details attract your attention in the photograph of Hitchens as he subjects himself to a waterboarding "treatment" (page 534)? In what specific way(s) does the angle of the camera reinforce the effects of this image? What does the photographer gain by positioning the camera at this angle? What is "lost" in this decision? Be as specific as possible in your response.

4. **CONNECTIONS:** Compare Hitchens's essay to the passages from Michihiko Hachiya's "Hiroshima Diary" (page 105). What similarities (and differences) do you notice about the way the two writers tell their stories? Consider, for example, their respective tones of voice, sentence lengths, rhythms, and interjections of personal opinion. How do those similarities and differences affect your understanding of what each writer experienced? How did your visceral reaction to each essay differ?

Thomas Jefferson
THE DECLARATION OF INDEPENDENCE

THOMAS JEFFERSON (1743–1826) was born and raised in Virginia and attended William and Mary College. After being admitted to the bar, he entered politics and served in the Virginia House of Burgesses and the Continental Congress of 1775. During the Revolutionary War he was elected governor of Virginia, and after independence he was appointed special minister to France and later secretary of state. As the nation's third president, he negotiated the Louisiana Purchase. Of all his accomplishments as an inventor, an architect, a diplomat, a scientist, and a politician, Jefferson counted his work in designing the University of Virginia among the most important, along with his efforts to establish separation of church and state and the composition of the Declaration of Independence.

In May and June 1776, the Continental Congress had been vigorously debating the dangerous idea of independence and felt the need to issue a document that clearly pointed out the colonial grievances against Great Britain. A committee was appointed to "prepare a declaration" that would summarize the specific reasons for colonial discontent. The committee of five included Thomas Jefferson, Benjamin Franklin, and John Adams. Jefferson, who was noted for his skills in composition and, as Adams put it, "peculiar felicity of expression," was chosen to write the first draft. The assignment took Jefferson about two weeks, and he submitted the draft first to the committee, which made a few verbal alterations, and then on June 28 to Congress, where, after further alterations mainly relating to slavery, it was finally approved on July 4, 1776.

> **Thomas Jefferson intended the Declaration of Independence "to be an expression of the American mind, and to give to that expression the proper tone and spirit called for by the occasion."**

Jefferson claims to have composed the document without research, working mainly from ideas he felt were commonly held at the time. As Jefferson recalled many years later, he drafted the document as "an appeal to the tribunal of the world" and hoped "to place before mankind the common sense of the subject, in terms so plain and firm as to command their assent." He claims that "neither aiming at originality of principle or sentiment . . . it was intended to be an expression of the American mind, and to give to that expression the proper tone and spirit called for by the occasion."

WHEN IN THE COURSE of human events, it becomes necessary for one people to dissolve the political bands which have connected them with another, and to assume among the Powers of the earth, the separate and equal station to which the Laws of Nature and of Nature's God entitle them, a decent respect to the opinions of mankind requires that they should declare the causes which impel them to the separation.

We hold these truths to be self-evident, that all men are created equal, that they are endowed by their Creator with certain inalienable Rights, that among these are Life, Liberty and the pursuit of Happiness. That to secure these rights, Governments are instituted among Men, deriving their just powers from the consent of the governed. That whenever any Form of Government becomes destructive of these ends, it is the Right of the People to alter or to abolish it, and to institute new Government, laying its foundation on such principles and organizing its powers in such form, as to them shall seem most likely to effect their Safety and Happiness. Prudence, indeed, will dictate that Governments long established should not be changed for light and transient causes; and accordingly all experience hath shown, that mankind are more disposed to suffer, while evils are sufferable, than to right themselves by abolishing the forms to which they are accustomed. But when a long train of abuses and usurpations, pursuing invariably the same Object evinces a design to reduce them under absolute Despotism, it is their right, it is their duty, to throw off such Government, and to provide new Guards for their future security. — Such has been the patient sufferance of these Colonies; and such is now the necessity which constrains them to alter their former Systems of Government. The history of the present King of Great Britain is a history of repeated injuries and usurpations, all having in direct object the establishment of an absolute Tyranny over these States. To prove this, let Facts be submitted to a candid world.

He has refused his Assent to Laws, the most wholesome and necessary for the public good.

He has forbidden his Governors to pass Laws of immediate and pressing importance, unless suspended in their operation till his Assent should be obtained; and when so suspended, he has utterly neglected to attend to them.

He has refused to pass other laws for the accommodation of large districts   5
of people, unless those people would relinquish the right of Representation in the Legislature, a right inestimable to them and formidable to tyrants only.

He has called together legislative bodies at places unusual, uncomfortable, and distant from the depository of their Public Records, for the sole purpose of fatiguing them into compliance with his measures.

He has dissolved Representative Houses repeatedly, for opposing with manly firmness his invasions on the rights of the people.

He has refused for a long time, after such dissolutions, to cause others to be elected; whereby the Legislative Powers, incapable of Annihilation, have returned to the People at large for their exercise; the State remaining in the mean time exposed to all the dangers of invasion from without, and convulsions within.

He has endeavoured to prevent the population of these States;[1] for that purpose obstructing the Laws for Naturalization of Foreigners; refusing to pass others to encourage their migration hither, and raising the conditions of new Appropriations of Lands.

He has obstructed the Administration of Justice, by refusing his Assent   10
to Laws for establishing Judiciary Powers.

He has made Judges dependent on his Will alone, for the tenure of their offices, and the amount and payment of their salaries.

He has erected a multitude of New Offices, and sent hither swarms of Officers to harass our People, and eat out their substance.

He has kept among us, in times of peace, Standing Armies without the Consent of our legislature.

He has affected to render the Military independent of and superior to the Civil Power.

He has combined with others to subject us to a jurisdiction foreign to our   15
constitution, and unacknowledged by our laws; giving his Assent to their acts of pretended Legislation:

For quartering large bodies of armed troops among us:

For protecting them, by a mock Trial, from Punishment for any Murders which they should commit on the Inhabitants of these States:

---

[1] ***prevent the population of these States:*** This meant limiting emigration to the Colonies, thus controlling their growth. —EDS.

For cutting off our Trade with all parts of the world:

For imposing taxes on us without our Consent:

For depriving us in many cases, of the benefits of Trial by Jury: 20

For transporting us beyond Seas to be tried for pretended offenses:

For abolishing the free System of English Laws in a neighboring Province, establishing therein an Arbitrary government, and enlarging its Boundaries so as to render it at once an example and fit instrument for introducing the same absolute rule into these Colonies:

For taking away our Charters, abolishing our most valuable Laws, and altering fundamentally the Forms of our Governments:

For suspending our own Legislatures, and declaring themselves invested with Power to legislate for us in all cases whatsoever.

He has abdicated Government here, by declaring us out of his Protection   25 and waging War against us.

He has plundered our seas, ravaged our Coasts, burnt our towns, and destroyed the lives of our people.

He is at this time transporting large armies of foreign mercenaries to compleat the works of death, desolation and tyranny, already begun with circumstances of Cruelty & perfidy scarcely paralleled in the most barbarous ages, and totally unworthy of the Head of a civilized nation.

He has constrained our fellow Citizens taken Captive on the high Seas to bear Arms against their Country, to become the executioners of their friends and Brethren, or to fall themselves by their Hands.

He has excited domestic insurrections amongst us, and has endeavoured to bring on the inhabitants of our frontiers, the merciless Indian Savages, whose known rule of warfare, is an undistinguished destruction of all ages, sexes and conditions.

In every stage of these Oppressions We have Petitioned for Readdress in   30 the most humble terms: Our repeated Petitions have been answered only by repeated injury. A Prince, whose character is thus marked by every act which may define a Tyrant, is unfit to be the ruler of a free People.

Nor have We been wanting in attention to our British brethren. We have warned them from time to time of attempts by their legislature to extend an unwarrantable jurisdiction over us. We have reminded them of the circumstances of our emigration and settlement here. We have appealed to their native justice and magnanimity, and we have conjured them by the ties of our common kindred to disavow these usurpations, which would inevitably interrupt our connections and correspondence. They too have been deaf to the voice of justice and of consanguinity. We must, therefore, acquiesce in the necessity, which denounces our Separation, and hold them, as we hold the rest of mankind, Enemies in War, in Peace Friends.

We, therefore, the Representatives of the United States of America, in General Congress, Assembled, appealing to the Supreme Judge of the world for the rectitude of our intentions, do in the Name, and by Authority of the good People of these Colonies, solemnly publish and declare, That these United Colonies are, and of Right ought to be Free and Independent States, that they are Absolved from all Allegiance to the British Crown, and that all political connection between them and the State of Great Britain, is and ought to be totally dissolved; and that as Free and Independent States, they have full Power to levy War, conclude Peace, contract Alliances, establish Commerce, and to do all other Acts and Things which Independent States may of right do. And for the support of this Declaration, with a firm reliance on the Protection of Divine Providence, we mutually pledge to each other our Lives, our Fortunes and our sacred Honor. ●

The Reader's Presence

1. How does Jefferson seem to define *independence*? Whom does the definition include? Whom does it exclude? How does Jefferson's definition of *independence* differ from your own? It has been pointed out that Jefferson disregards "interdependence." Can you formulate an argument contrary to Jefferson's?

2. Examine the Declaration's first sentence. Who is the speaker here? What is the effect of the omniscient tone of the opening? Why does the first paragraph have no personal pronouns or references to specific events? What might Jefferson's argument stand to gain in generalizing the American situation?

3. **CONNECTIONS:** *The Writer's Presence* features two of the greatest documents in American history, both written by presidents famous for their writing ability and rhetorical power. Compare Jefferson's "Declaration of Independence" with Abraham Lincoln's "Gettysburg Address" (page 448). What rhetorical features do you find common to both? Lincoln's address was composed many years after the Declaration; see if you can identify some instances where Lincoln appears influenced by Jefferson's language and style.

The Writer at Work

Thomas Jefferson, 1776 (oil on canvas)/
Peale, Charles Willson (1741–1827) (after)/
HUNTINGTON ART COLLECTIONS
/Huntington Library and Art Gallery, San
Marino, CA, USA/Bridgeman Images

Another Draft of the Declaration of Independence

The "original Rough draught" of the Declaration of Independence is one of the foundational documents in American history. The following reproduction of the opening paragraphs of the Declaration illustrates how the text evolved from the initial draft by Thomas Jefferson to the final text adopted by Congress on the morning of July 4, 1776.

❝A Declaration by the Representatives of the United States of America, in General Congress assembled.

When in the course of human events, it becomes necessary for one people to dissolve the political bands which have connected them with another, and to assume among the powers of the earth the separate and equal station to which the laws of nature and of nature's God entitle them, a decent respect to the opinions of mankind requires that they should declare the causes which impel them to the separation.

We hold these truths to be self-evident: that all men are created equal; that they are endowed by their Creator with [inherent and] inalienable rights; that among these are life, liberty, and the pursuit of happiness; that to secure these rights, governments are instituted among men, deriving their just powers from the consent of the governed; that whenever any form of government becomes destructive of these ends, it is the right of the people to alter or to abolish it, and to institute new government, laying its foundation on such principles, and organizing its powers in such form, as to them shall seem most likely to effect their safety and happiness. Prudence, indeed, will dictate that governments long established should not be changed for light and transient causes; and accordingly all experience hath shown that mankind are more disposed to suffer while evils are sufferable, than to right themselves by abolishing the forms to which they are accustomed. But when a long train of abuses and usurpations, [begun at a distinguished period and] pursuing invariably the same object, evinces a design to reduce them under absolute despotism, it is their right, it is their duty to throw off such government, and to provide new guards for their future security. Such has been the patient sufferance of these colonies; and such is now the necessity which constrains them to [expunge] their former systems of government. The history of the present king of Great Britain is a history of [unremitting] injuries and usurpations, [among which appears no solitary fact to contradict the uniform tenor of the rest, but all have] in direct object the establishment of an absolute tyranny over these states. To prove this, let facts be submitted to a candid world [for the truth of which we pledge a faith yet unsullied by falsehood.] . . .❞

Greg Lukianoff and Jonathan Haidt

FROM *THE CODDLING OF THE AMERICAN MIND*

Where should colleges and universities stand on the issue of free expression? Should they—as a matter of course—let all speech flow freely in the interest of allowing a wide diversity of viewpoints to be heard, thus reinforcing a permissive attitude once considered an ideal of a liberal society? Or, given the contentious nature of our times, does the university bear a responsibility to protect vulnerable students from offensive and hateful speech? Today, such protections often take the form of trigger warnings, the availability of "safe spaces" on campus, and, at times, a deliberate implementation of speech codes, all of which have been covered extensively in the news media by both those who see such measures to be necessary safeguards to civil discourse or serious restrictions on individual liberty.

> **Where should colleges and universities stand on the issue of free expression?**

One of the most controversial arguments opposed to the restriction of speech on campus appeared to much publicity in the fall of 2015. Written by **GREG LUKIANOFF** (a lawyer and advocate of individual educational rights, b. 1974) and **JONATHAN HAIDT** (a social psychologist at New York University's Stern School of Business, b. 1963), "The Coddling of the American Mind" attacked what the authors viewed as a misguided attempt to protect students from "psychological harm." The originally published essay, which set out a list of reasons why such campus measures to protect students were actually harming them, was too long to conveniently reprint in this collection. We have, therefore, included only the opening section that contains a summary of the educational situation, some key terms, and the authors' position. For those interested in the entire argument, the full article can be found in the *Atlantic*, September 2015.

SOMETHING STRANGE IS happening at America's colleges and universities. A movement is arising, undirected and driven largely by students, to scrub campuses clean of words, ideas, and subjects that might cause discomfort or give offense. Last December, Jeannie Suk wrote in an online article for *The New Yorker* about law students asking her fellow professors at Harvard not to teach rape law—or, in one case, even use the word *violate* (as in "that violates the law") lest it cause students distress. In February, Laura Kipnis, a professor at Northwestern University, wrote an essay in *The Chronicle of Higher Education* describing a new campus politics of sexual paranoia—and was then subjected to a long investigation after students who were offended by the article and by a tweet she'd sent filed Title IX[1] complaints against her. In June, a professor protecting himself with a pseudonym wrote an essay for Vox describing how gingerly he now has to teach. "I'm a Liberal Professor, and My Liberal Students Terrify Me," the headline said. A number of popular comedians, including Chris Rock, have stopped performing on college campuses. Jerry Seinfeld and Bill Maher have publicly condemned the oversensitivity of college students, saying too many of them can't take a joke.

Two terms have risen quickly from obscurity into common campus parlance. *Microaggressions* are small actions or word choices that seem on their face to have no malicious intent but that are thought of as a kind of violence

---

[1] **Title IX:** The federal law that forbids discrimination on the basis of sex in any educational setting that is federally funded. —EDS.

||||||||||||||||||||||||||||||||||||||||||||||||||||||||||||||||||||||||||||||||||||||||||||||||||||||||||||||||||||||||||||||||||||||||||

nonetheless. For example, by some campus guidelines, it is a microaggression to ask an Asian American or Latino American "Where were you born?," because this implies that he or she is not a real American. *Trigger warnings* are alerts that professors are expected to issue if something in a course might cause a strong emotional response. For example, some students have called for warnings that Chinua Achebe's *Things Fall Apart* describes racial violence and that F. Scott Fitzgerald's *The Great Gatsby* portrays misogyny and physical abuse, so that students who have been previously victimized by racism or domestic violence can choose to avoid these works, which they believe might "trigger" a recurrence of past trauma.

Some recent campus actions border on the surreal. In April, at Brandeis University, the Asian American student association sought to raise awareness of microaggressions against Asians through an installation on the steps of an academic hall. The installation gave examples of microaggressions such as "Aren't you supposed to be good at math?" and "I'm colorblind! I don't see race." But a backlash arose among other Asian American students, who felt that the display itself was a microaggression. The association removed the installation, and its president wrote an e-mail to the entire student body apologizing to anyone who was "triggered or hurt by the content of the microaggressions."

This new climate is slowly being institutionalized, and is affecting what can be said in the classroom, even as a basis for discussion. During the 2014–15 school year, for instance, the deans and department chairs at the 10 University of California system schools were presented by administrators at faculty leader-training sessions with examples of microaggressions. The list of offensive statements included: "America is the land of opportunity" and "I believe the most qualified person should get the job."

The press has typically described these developments as a resurgence   5
of political correctness. That's partly right, although there are important differences between what's happening now and what happened in the 1980s and '90s. That movement sought to restrict speech (specifically hate speech aimed at marginalized groups), but it also challenged the literary, philosophical, and historical canon, seeking to widen it by including more-diverse perspectives. The current movement is largely about emotional well-being. More than the last, it presumes an extraordinary fragility of the collegiate psyche, and therefore elevates the goal of protecting students from psychological harm. The ultimate aim, it seems, is to turn campuses into "safe spaces" where young adults are shielded from words and ideas that make some uncomfortable. And more than the last, this movement seeks to punish anyone who interferes with that aim, even accidentally. You might call this impulse *vindictive protectiveness*. It is creating a culture in which everyone must think twice before speaking up, lest they face charges of insensitivity, aggression, or worse.

We have been studying this development for a while now, with rising alarm. (Greg Lukianoff is a constitutional lawyer and the president and CEO of the Foundation for Individual Rights in Education, which defends free speech and academic freedom on campus, and has advocated for students and faculty involved in many of the incidents this article describes; Jonathan Haidt is a social psychologist who studies the American culture wars. The stories of how we each came to this subject can be read on theatlantic.com.) The dangers that these trends pose to scholarship and to the quality of American universities are significant; we could write a whole essay detailing them. But in this essay we focus on a different question: What are the effects of this new protectiveness *on the students themselves*? Does it benefit the people it is supposed to help? What exactly are students learning when they spend four years or more in a community that polices unintentional slights, places warning labels on works of classic literature, and in many other ways conveys the sense that words can be forms of violence that require strict control by campus authorities, who are expected to act as both protectors and prosecutors?

There's a saying common in education circles: Don't teach students *what* to think; teach them *how* to think. The idea goes back at least as far as Socrates. Today, what we call the Socratic method is a way of teaching that fosters critical thinking, in part by encouraging students to question their own unexamined beliefs, as well as the received wisdom of those around them. Such questioning sometimes leads to discomfort, and even to anger, on the way to understanding.

But vindictive protectiveness teaches students to think in a very different way. It prepares them poorly for professional life, which often demands intellectual engagement with people and ideas one might find uncongenial or wrong. The harm may be more immediate, too. A campus culture devoted to policing speech and punishing speakers is likely to engender patterns of thought that are surprisingly similar to those long identified by cognitive behavioral therapists as causes of depression and anxiety. The new protectiveness may be teaching students to think pathologically. ■

The Reader's Presence

1. The authors are generally opposed to the movement (as they say) to "scrub campuses clean of words, ideas, and subjects that might cause discomfort or give offense." As a result of their position, do you think they define fairly the meaning and significance of such key terms as "microaggressions," "trigger warnings," and "safe spaces"? Explain why or why not you agree with their definitions and examples.

2. In your opinion, what does "political correctness" mean? Is it a good or bad thing to be "politically correct"? Why do the authors believe the current movements on campus are only in part a matter of political correctness (see paragraph 6)? To them, what is the larger issue behind the trends on college campuses today?

3. **CONNECTIONS:** Read Lukianoff and Haidt's essay in conjunction with Simon Tam's "Trademark Offense" (page 638). What do the two selections have in common? In your opinion is "Trademark Offense" about something larger than "political correctness"? Explain how you think Lukianoff and Haidt would respond to Tam's position on words that give offense.

Laura Kipnis

AGAINST LOVE

LAURA KIPNIS (b. 1956) is a cultural theorist, an author, and a former videographer whose work blends academic theory, social criticism, and witty analysis, all "richly informed by her post-Marxist, post-structuralist, post-feminist, post-everything sense of humor," according to a recent biography. A professor in the school of communications at Northwestern University in Evanston, Illinois, Kipnis is the author of several books, including *Ecstasy Unlimited: On Sex, Capital, Gender, and Aesthetics* (1993), *Bound and Gagged: Pornography and the Politics of Fantasy in America* (1996), *Against Love: A Polemic* (2003), and *The Female Thing: Dirt, Sex, Envy, Vulnerability* (2006). Kipnis's video essays—including *Ecstasy Unlimited: The Interpenetrations of Sex and Capital* (1985), *A Man's Woman* (1988), and *Marx: The Video* (1990)—have been screened in such venues as the Museum of Modern Art, the American Film Institute, and the Whitney Museum. Kipnis has also written essays and reviews for *Slate*, the *Village Voice*, *Harper's*, *Critical Inquiry*, *Wide Angle*, and the *New York Times Magazine*, where "Against Love" appeared in 2001. Her recent books include *Men: Notes from an Ongoing Investigation* (2014) and *Unwanted Advances: Sexual Paranoia Comes to Campus* (2017).

> "It's a polemic, so there are certain questions I don't have to address, or complications I don't have to go into. I can be completely irresponsible. I love it."

Kipnis's work has evolved over time, shifting from what was once a strictly academic tone to her more recent playful and casual style. In an interview with the editor of the *Minnesota Review*, she admits that she has developed a growing interest in "creativity" over "theory." She explains, "I trace it back to my art school origins. I started as a painter, actually, and there's something about the writing I've been doing lately which has gotten really intricate and worked over, that reminds me of my origins as a painter. I've started to write in a painterly way, dabbing at it, endlessly revising."

In a discussion of *Against Love* in 2001, Kipnis pointed out that "the voice isn't precisely 'me,' it's some far more vivacious and playful version of me. It's a polemic, so there are certain questions I don't have to address, or complications I don't have to go into. I can be completely irresponsible. I love it."

LOVE IS, as we know, a mysterious and controlling force. It has vast power over our thoughts and life decisions. It demands our loyalty, and we, in turn, freely comply. Saying no to love isn't simply heresy; it is tragedy—the failure to achieve what is most essentially human. So deeply internalized is our obedience to this most capricious despot that artists create passionate odes to its cruelty, and audiences seem never to tire of the most deeply unoriginal mass spectacles devoted to rehearsing the litany of its torments, fixating their very beings on the narrowest glimmer of its fleeting satisfactions.

Yet despite near total compliance, a buzz of social nervousness attends the subject. If a society's lexicon of romantic pathologies reveals its particular anxieties, high on our own list would be diagnoses like "inability to settle down" or "immaturity," leveled at those who stray from the norms of domestic coupledom either by refusing entry in the first place or, once installed, pursuing various escape routes: excess independence, ambivalence, "straying," divorce. For the modern lover, "maturity" isn't a depressing signal of impending decrepitude but a sterling achievement, the sine qua non of a lover's qualifications to love and be loved.

This injunction to achieve maturity—synonymous in contemporary usage with thirty-year mortgages, spreading waistlines, and monogamy—obviously finds its raison d'être in modern love's central anxiety, that structuring social contradiction the size of the San Andreas Fault: namely, the expectation that romance and sexual attraction can last a lifetime of coupled togetherness despite much hard evidence to the contrary.

Ever optimistic, heady with love's utopianism, most of us eventually pledge ourselves to unions that will, if successful, far outlast the desire that impelled them into being. The prevailing cultural wisdom is that even if sexual desire tends to be a short-lived phenomenon, "mature love" will kick in to save the day when desire flags. The issue that remains unaddressed is whether cutting off other possibilities of romance and sexual attraction for the more muted pleasures of mature love isn't similar to voluntarily amputating a healthy limb: a lot of anesthesia is required and the phantom pain never entirely abates. But if it behooves a society to convince its citizenry that wanting change means personal failure or wanting to start over is shameful or simply wanting more satisfaction than what you have is an illicit thing, clearly grisly acts of self-mutilation will be required.

There hasn't always been quite such optimism about love's longevity.   5
For the Greeks, inventors of democracy and a people not amenable to being pushed around by despots, love was a disordering and thus preferably brief experience. During the reign of courtly love, love was illicit and usually fatal. Passion meant suffering: the happy ending didn't yet exist in the cultural imagination. As far as togetherness as an eternal ideal, the 12th-century advice manual "De Amore et Amoris Remedio" ("On Love and the Remedies of Love") warned that too many opportunities to see or chat with the beloved would certainly decrease love.

The innovation of happy love didn't even enter the vocabulary of romance until the 17th century. Before the 18th century—when the family was primarily an economic unit of production rather than a hothouse of Oedipal tensions—marriages were business arrangements between families; participants had little to say on the matter. Some historians consider romantic love a learned behavior that really only took off in the late 18th century along with the new fashion for reading novels, though even then affection between a husband and wife was considered to be in questionable taste.

Historians disagree, of course. Some tell the story of love as an eternal and unchanging essence; others, as a progress narrative over stifling social conventions. (Sometimes both stories are told at once; consistency isn't required.) But has modern love really set us free? Fond as we are of projecting our own emotional quandaries back through history, construing vivid costume dramas featuring medieval peasants or biblical courtesans sharing their feelings with the post-Freudian savvy of lifelong analysands, our amatory predecessors clearly didn't share all our particular aspirations about their romantic lives.

We, by contrast, feel like failures when love dies. We believe it could be otherwise. Since the cultural expectation is that a state of coupled permanence is achievable, uncoupling is experienced as crisis and inadequacy—even though such failures are more the norm than the exception.

As love has increasingly become the center of all emotional expression in the popular imagination, anxiety about obtaining it in sufficient quantities—and for sufficient duration—suffuses the population. Everyone knows that as the demands and expectations on couples escalated, so did divorce rates. And given the current divorce statistics (roughly 50 percent of all marriages end in divorce), all indications are that whomever you love today—your beacon of hope, the center of all your optimism—has a good chance of becoming your worst nightmare tomorrow. (Of course, that 50 percent are those who actually leave their unhappy marriages and not a particularly good indication of the happiness level or nightmare potential of those who remain.) Lawrence Stone, a historian of marriage, suggests—rather jocularly, you can't help thinking—that today's rising divorce rates are just a modern technique for achieving what was once taken care of far more efficiently by early mortality.

Love may or may not be a universal emotion, but clearly the social forms it takes are infinitely malleable. It is our culture alone that has dedicated itself to allying the turbulence of romance and the rationality of the long-term couple, convinced that both love and sex are obtainable from one person over the course of decades, that desire will manage to sustain itself for thirty or forty or fifty years and that the supposed fate of social stability is tied to sustaining a fleeting experience beyond its given life span.

Of course, the parties involved must "work" at keeping passion alive (and we all know how much fun that is), the presumption being that even after living in close proximity to someone for a historically unprecedented length of time, you will still muster the requisite desire to achieve sexual congress on a regular basis. (Should passion fizzle out, just give up sex. Lack of desire for a mate is never an adequate rationale for "looking elsewhere.") And it is true, many couples do manage to perform enough psychic retooling to reshape the anarchy of desire to the confines of the marriage bed, plugging away at the task year after year (once a week, same time, same position) like diligent assembly-line workers, aided by the occasional fantasy or two to help get the old motor to turn over, or keep running, or complete the trip. And so we have the erotic life of a nation of workaholics: if sex seems like work, clearly you're not working hard enough at it.

But passion must not be allowed to die! The fear—or knowledge—that it does shapes us into particularly conflicted psychological beings, perpetually in search of prescriptions and professional interventions, regardless of cost or consequence. Which does have its economic upside, at least. Whole new sectors of the economy have been spawned, with massive social investment in new technologies from Viagra to couples' porn: capitalism's Lourdes[1] for dying marriages.

There are assorted low-tech solutions to desire's dilemmas too. Take advice. In fact, take more and more advice. Between print, airwaves, and the therapy industry, if there were any way to quantify the GNP in romantic counsel, it would be a staggering number. Desperate to be cured of love's temporality, a love-struck populace has molded itself into an advanced race of advice receptacles, like some new form of miracle sponge that can instantly absorb many times its own body weight in wetness.

Inexplicably, however, a rebellious breakaway faction keeps trying to leap over the wall and emancipate themselves, not from love itself—unthinkable!—but from love's domestic confinements. The escape routes are well trodden—love affairs, midlife crises—though strewn with the left-behind luggage of those who encountered unforeseen obstacles along the way (panic, guilt, self-engineered exposures) and beat self-abashed retreats to their domestic gulags, even after pledging body and soul to new-found loves in the balmy utopias of nondomesticated romances. Will all the adulterers in the audience please stand up? You know who you are. Don't be embarrassed! Adulterers aren't just "playing around." These are our homegrown closet social theorists, because adultery is not just a referendum on the sustainability of monogamy; it is a veiled philosophical discussion about the social contract itself. The question on the table is thus "How much renunciation of desire does society demand of us, versus the degree of gratification it provides?" Clearly, the adulterer's answer, following a long line of venerable social critics, would be, "Too much."

But what exactly is it about the actual lived experience of modern domes- 15 tic love that would make flight such a compelling option for so many? Let us briefly examine those material daily life conditions.

Fundamentally, to achieve love and qualify for entry into that realm of salvation and transcendence known as the couple (the secular equivalent of

---

[1] **Lourdes:** Notre Dame de Lourdes in France has been a site of Catholic pilgrimage ever since a fourteen-year-old girl reportedly received a vision there in 1858. —EDS.

entering a state of divine grace), you must *be* a lovable person. And what precisely does being lovable entail? According to the tenets of modern love, it requires an advanced working knowledge of the intricacies of *mutuality*.

Mutuality means recognizing that your partner has needs and being prepared to meet them. This presumes, of course, that the majority of those needs can and should be met by one person. (Question this, and you question the very foundations of the institution. So don't.) These needs of ours run deep, a tangled underground morass of ancient, gnarled roots, looking to ensnarl any hapless soul who might accidentally trod upon their outer radices.

Still, meeting those needs is the most effective way to become the object of another's desire, thus attaining intimacy, which is required to achieve the state known as psychological maturity. (Despite how closely it reproduces the affective conditions of our childhoods, since trading compliance for love is the earliest social lesson learned; we learn it in our cribs.)

You, in return, will have your own needs met by your partner in matters large and small. In practice, many of these matters turn out to be quite small. Frequently, it is the tensions and disagreements over the minutiae of daily living that stand between couples and their requisite intimacy. Taking out the garbage, tone of voice, a forgotten errand—these are the rocky shoals upon which intimacy so often founders.

Mutuality requires *communication*, since in order to be met, these needs   20 must be expressed. (No one's a mind reader, which is not to say that many of us don't expect this quality in a mate. Who wants to keep having to tell someone what you need?) What you need is for your mate to understand you—your desires, your contradictions, your unique sensitivities, what irks you. (In practice, that means what about your mate irks you.) You, in turn, must learn to understand the mate's needs. This means being willing to hear what about yourself irks your mate. Hearing is not a simple physiological act performed with the ears, as you will learn. You may think you know how to *hear*, but that doesn't mean that you know how to *listen*.

With two individuals required to coexist in enclosed spaces for extended periods of time, domesticity requires substantial quantities of compromise and adaptation simply to avoid mayhem. Yet with the post-Romantic ideal of unconstrained individuality informing our most fundamental ideas of the self, this can prove a perilous process. Both parties must be willing to jettison whatever aspects of individuality might prove irritating while being simultaneously allowed to retain enough individuality to feel their autonomy is not being sacrificed, even as it is being surgically excised.

Having mastered mutuality, you may now proceed to *advanced intimacy*. Advanced intimacy involves inviting your partner "in" to your most interior self. Whatever and wherever our "inside" is, the widespread—if somewhat metaphysical—belief in its existence (and the related belief that whatever is in there is dying to get out) has assumed a quasi-medical status. Leeches once served a similar purpose. Now we "express our feelings" in lieu of our fluids because everyone knows that those who don't are far more prone to cancer, ulcers or various dire ailments.

With love as our culture's patent medicine, prescribed for every ill (now even touted as a necessary precondition for that other great American obsession, longevity), we willingly subject ourselves to any number of arcane procedures in its quest. "Opening up" is required for relationship health, so lovers fashion themselves after doctors wielding long probes to penetrate the tender regions. Try to think of yourself as one big orifice: now stop clenching and relax. If the procedure proves uncomfortable, it just shows you're not open enough. Psychotherapy may be required before sufficient dilation can be achieved: the world's most expensive lubricant.

Needless to say, this opening-up can leave you feeling quite vulnerable, lying there psychically spread-eagled and shivering on the examining table of your relationship. (A favored suspicion is that your partner, knowing exactly where your vulnerabilities are, deliberately kicks you there—one reason this opening-up business may not always feel as pleasant as advertised.) And as anyone who has spent much time in—or just in earshot of—a typical couple knows, the "expression of needs" is often the Trojan horse of intimate warfare, since expressing needs means, by definition, that one's partner has thus far failed to meet them.

In any long-term couple, this lexicon of needs becomes codified over time   25 into a highly evolved private language with its own rules. Let's call this couple grammar. Close observation reveals this as a language composed of one recurring unit of speech: the interdiction—highly nuanced, mutually imposed commands and strictures extending into the most minute areas of household affairs, social life, finances, speech, hygiene, allowable idiosyncrasies and so on. From bathroom to bedroom, car to kitchen, no aspect of coupled life is not subject to scrutiny, negotiation and codes of conduct.

A sample from an inexhaustible list, culled from interviews with numerous members of couples of various ages, races and sexual orientations:

You can't leave the house without saying where you're going. You can't not say what time you'll return. You can't go out when the other person feels like staying at home. You can't be a slob. You can't do less than 50 percent of the work around the house, even if the other person wants to do 100 percent more cleaning than you find necessary or even reasonable. You can't leave the dishes for later, load them the way that seems best to you, drink straight from the carton or make crumbs. You can't leave the bathroom door open—it's offensive. You can't leave the bathroom door closed—your partner needs to get in. You can't not shave your underarms or legs. You can't gain weight. You can't watch soap operas. You can't watch infomercials or the pregame show or Martha Stewart. You can't eat what you want—goodbye Marshmallow Fluff; hello tofu meatballs. You can't spend too much time on the computer. And stay out of those chat rooms. You can't take risks, unless they are agreed-upon risks, which somewhat limits the concept of "risk." You can't make major purchases alone, or spend money on things the other person considers excesses. You can't blow money just because you're in a bad mood, and you can't be in a bad mood without being required to explain it. You can't begin a sentence with "You always. . . ." You can't begin a sentence with "I never. . . ." You can't be simplistic, even when things are simple. You can't say what you really think of that outfit or color combination or cowboy hat. You can't be cynical about things the other person is sincere about. You can't drink without the other person counting your drinks. You can't have the wrong laugh. You can't bum cigarettes when you're out because it embarrasses your mate, even though you've explained the unspoken fraternity between smokers. You can't tailgate, honk or listen to talk radio in the car. And so on. The specifics don't matter. What matters is that the operative word is "can't."

Thus is love obtained.

Certainly, domesticity offers innumerable rewards: companionship, child-rearing convenience, reassuring predictability and many other benefits too varied to list. But if love has power over us, domesticity is its enforcement wing: the iron dust mop in the velvet glove. The historian Michel Foucault[2] has argued that modern power made its mark on the world by inventing new types of enclosures and institutions, places like factories, schools, barracks, prisons and asylums, where individuals could be located, supervised, processed and subjected to inspection, order and the clock. What current social institution is more enclosed than modern intimacy? What offers greater regulation of movement and time, or more precise surveillance of body and thought, to a greater number of individuals?

Of course, it is your choice—as if any of us could really choose not to desire love or not to feel like hopeless losers should we fail at it. We moderns are beings yearning to be filled, yearning to be overtaken by love's mysterious power. We prostrate ourselves at love's portals, like social strivers waiting at the rope line outside some exclusive club hoping to gain admission and thereby confirm our essential worth. A life without love lacks an organizing narrative. A life without love seems so barren, and it might almost make you consider how empty the rest of the world is, as if love were vital plasma and everything else just tap water.

Exchanging obedience for love comes naturally—after all, we all were once children whose survival depended on the caprices of love. And there you have the template for future intimacies. If you love me, you'll do what I want—or need, or demand—and I'll love you in return. We all become household dictators, petty tyrants of the private sphere, who are, in our turn, dictated to.

And why has modern love developed in such a way as to maximize submission and minimize freedom, with so little argument about it? No doubt a citizenry schooled in renouncing desire instead of imagining there could be something more would be, in many respects, advantageous. After all, wanting more is the basis for utopian thinking, a path toward dangerous social demands, even toward imagining the possibilities for altogether different social arrangements. But if the most elegant forms of social control are those

30

---

2 *Michel Foucault* (1926–1984): French philosopher and historian who questioned assumptions about the constitution of power and knowledge.—EDS.

that came packaged in the guise of individual needs and satisfactions, so wedded to the individual psyche that any opposing impulse registers as the anxiety of unlovability, who needs a soldier on every corner? We are more than happy to police ourselves and those we love and call it living happily ever after. Perhaps a secular society needed another metaphysical entity to subjugate itself to after the death of God, and love was available for the job. But isn't it a little depressing to think we are somehow incapable of inventing forms of emotional life based on anything other than subjugation? ◼

The Reader's Presence

1. How does Kipnis reevaluate the meaning of adultery and midlife crises? What sort of evidence are these phenomena, in her opinion?

2. What elements of Kipnis's writing mark this essay as a scholarly argument? Do you agree that it is also a "polemic," as the subtitle of her book indicates? Is it more effective as a scholarly argument or as a polemic? Why?

3. **CONNECTIONS:** Kipnis suggests that society benefits from convincing its populace to marry and that people have been brainwashed into believing that these long-term arrangements are natural. What benefits does society gain from long-term relationships? What, in Kipnis's opinion, do individuals give up? Read John Taylor Gatto's "Against School" (page 517). What, according to his argument, does the individual lose in submitting to compulsory schooling? Who, according to Gatto, benefits from it?

Bill McKibben

A MORAL ATMOSPHERE

BILL McKIBBEN (b. 1960) advocates human behavior toward earth that is "sound and elegant and civilized and respectful of community." Born in Palo Alto, California, and raised in Massachusetts, he now lives with his family in New York's Adirondack Mountains. After graduating from Harvard University in 1982, McKibben immediately went to work as a writer, and later as an editor, at the *New Yorker*, where he wrote more than four hundred articles for the magazine's "Talk of the Town" column. His essays, reporting, and criticism appear regularly in publications such as the *Atlantic Monthly*, *Harper's*, the *New York Review of Books*, the *New York Times*, *Orion*, *Rolling Stone*, and *Outside*. McKibben is currently the Schumann Distinguished Scholar in Environmental Studies at Middlebury College in Vermont.

McKibben's 1989 book, *The End of Nature*, sounded one of the earliest alarms about climate change and catalyzed an international debate on the issue that is still ongoing. His long list of books catalogs his concerns about the health of our global ecosystem, particularly the relationship between humanity and nature and the impact of our consumer society on both. His recent books include *The Age of Missing Information* (2006), *Deep Economy: The Wealth of Communities and the Durable Future* (2007), *Fight Global Warming Now: The Handbook for Taking Action in Your Community* (2007), *Eaarth: Making a Life on a Tough New Planet* (2010), *Oil and Honey: The Education of an Unlikely Activist* (2013), and *Radio Free Vermont: A Fable of Resistance* (2017). His collected essays, *The Bill McKibben Reader*, was published in 2008. He's organized several massive global protests calling for attention to the issue of climate change, including the 350.org protests in 2009, which involved 5,200 simultaneous demonstrations in 181 countries. He received the Gandhi Peace Award in 2013, and he holds honorary degrees from a dozen colleges.

> **"What we call the environmental crisis is really a crisis of desire. We're losing the battle to offer people an alternative set of things to desire."**

In a 1999 interview, McKibben discussed the competing visions of what is good for people and the planet: "The market forces pushing convenience, individualism, and comfort are still stronger than the attraction of community, fellowship, and connection with the natural world. . . . What we call the environmental crisis is really a crisis of desire. We're losing the battle to offer people an alternative set of things to desire."

McKibben's essay "A Moral Atmosphere" is another call to action concerning climate change, dismissing the idea that we can't take action until we can do so without hypocrisy. It was first published in *Orion* in 2013.

THE LIST OF REASONS for not acting on climate change is long and ever-shifting. First it was "there's no problem"; then it was "the problem's so large there's no hope." There's "China burns stuff too," and "it would hurt the economy," and, of course, "it would hurt the economy." The excuses are getting tired, though. Post Sandy (which hurt the economy to the tune of $100 billion) and the drought[1] ($150 billion), 74 percent of Americans have decided they're very concerned about climate change and want something to happen.

But still, there's one reason that never goes away, one evergreen excuse not to act: "you're a hypocrite." I've heard it ten thousand times myself—how can you complain about climate change and drive a car/have a house/turn on a light/raise a child? This past fall, as I headed across the country on a bus tour to push for divestment from fossil fuels, local newspapers covered each

[1] **Sandy . . . drought:** Hurricane Sandy ravaged the entire East Coast of the United States in late October 2012; the North American drought has continued since 2012 to impact much of the central and western United States.—EDS.

stop. I could predict, with great confidence, what the first online comment from a reader following each account would be: "Do these morons not know that their bus takes gasoline?" In fact, our bus took biodiesel—as we headed down the East Coast, one job was watching the web app that showed the nearest station pumping the good stuff. But it didn't matter, because the next comment would be: "Don't these morons know that the plastic fittings on their bus, and the tires, and the seats are all made from fossil fuels?"

Actually, I do know—even a moron like me. I'm fully aware that we're embedded in the world that fossil fuel has made, that from the moment I wake up, almost every action I take somehow burns coal and gas and oil. I've done my best, at my house, to curtail it: we've got solar electricity, and solar hot water, and my new car runs on electricity—I can plug it into the roof and thus into the sun. But I try not to confuse myself into thinking that's helping all that much: it took energy to make the car, and to make everything else that streams into my life. I'm still using far more than any responsible share of the world's vital stuff.

And, in a sense, that's the point. If those of us who are trying really hard are still fully enmeshed in the fossil fuel system, it makes it even clearer that what needs to change are not individuals but precisely that system. We simply can't move fast enough, one by one, to make any real difference in how the atmosphere comes out. Here's the math, obviously imprecise: maybe 10 percent of the population cares enough to make strenuous efforts to change—maybe 15 percent. If they all do all they can, in their homes and offices and so forth, then, well . . . nothing much shifts. The trajectory of our climate horror stays about the same.

But if 10 percent of people, once they've changed the light bulbs, work all-out to change the system? That's enough. That's more than enough. It would be enough to match the power of the fossil fuel industry, enough to convince our legislators to put a price on carbon. At which point none of us would be required to be saints. We could all be morons, as long as we paid attention to, say, the price of gas and the balance in our checking accounts. Which even dummies like me can manage.

I think more and more people are coming to realize this essential truth. Ten years ago, half the people calling out hypocrites like me were doing it from the left, demanding that we do better. I hear much less of that now, mostly, I think, because everyone who's pursued those changes in good faith has come to realize both their importance and their limitations. Now I hear it mostly from people who have no intention of changing but are starting to feel some psychic tension. They feel a little guilty, and so they dump their guilt on Al Gore because he has two houses. Or they find even lamer targets.

For instance, as college presidents begin to feel the heat about divestment, I've heard from several who say, privately, "I'd be more inclined to listen to kids if they didn't show up at college with cars." Which in one sense is fair enough. But in another sense it's avoidance at its most extreme. Young people are asking college presidents to stand up to oil companies. (And the ones doing the loudest asking are often the most painfully idealistic, not to

5

Alan Schein Photography/Getty Images

The fossil fuel system is difficult to avoid.

mention the hardest on themselves.) If as a college president you *do* stand up to oil companies, then you stand some chance of changing the outcome of the debate, of weakening the industry that has poured billions into climate denial and lobbying against science. The action you're demanding of your students—less driving—can't rationally be expected to change the outcome. The action they're demanding of you has at least some chance. That makes you immoral, not them.

Yes, they should definitely take the train to school instead of drive. But unless you're the president of Hogwarts, there's a pretty good chance there's no train that goes there. Your students, in other words, by advocating divestment, have gotten way closer to the heart of the problem than you have. They've taken the lessons they've learned in physics class and political science and sociology and economics and put them to good use. And you—because it would be uncomfortable to act, because you don't want to get crosswise with the board of trustees—have summoned a basically bogus response. If you're a college president making the argument that you won't act until your students stop driving cars, then clearly you've failed morally, but you've also failed intellectually. Even if you just built an energy-efficient fine arts center, and installed a bike path, and dedicated an acre of land to a college garden, you've failed. Even if you drive a Prius, you've failed.

Maybe especially if you drive a Prius. Because there's a certain sense in which Prius-driving can become an out, an excuse for inaction, the twenty-first-century equivalent of "I have a lot of black friends." It's nice to walk/drive the talk; it's much smarter than driving a semi-military vehicle to get your groceries. But it's become utterly clear that doing the right thing in your personal life, or even on your campus, isn't going to get the job done in time; and it may be providing you with sufficient psychic comfort that you don't feel the need to do the hard things it will take to get the job done. It's in our role as citizens—of campuses, of nations, of the planet—that we're going to have to solve this problem. We each have our jobs, and none of them is easy. ⬤

The Reader's Presence

1. McKibben observes that the argument asserting activists' hypocrisy for using fossil fuels is simply one example in a long "list of reasons for not acting on climate change" (paragraph 1). What other reasons does he enumerate for not taking action to address this global problem? How does McKibben deal with the fact that he, too, is "embedded in the world that fossil fuel has made" (paragraph 3)? What does McKibben mean when he writes, "everyone who's pursued . . . changes in good faith has come to realize both their importance and their limitations" (paragraph 6)?

2. McKibben discusses the fossil fuel system, a vast commercial network that touches nearly every facet of modern life. How does he address the issue of individual use in such a vast system? What moral and ethical reasons does McKibben summon to reinforce the need for an individual corrective action? What role(s) does he imply students should play in addressing this global problem? What role should college presidents play? On what grounds does McKibben criticize college presidents? How convincing do you find his argument? How might McKibben strengthen this aspect of his argument? What other examples would you use to strengthen or refute his claims?

3. According to McKibben, why is driving a hybrid car not enough action to solve the problem of climate change? Why might choosing to drive a hybrid hinder rather than help the problem? What distinctions does McKibben make between the terms "moral" and "intellectual" with regard to choices we make in response to climate change? To what extent do you agree with the arguments in McKibben's essay? Support your response by summoning specific reasons and evidence.

4. **VISUAL PRESENCE:** Given the spirit and substance of McKibben's argument in "A Moral Atmosphere," what specific words and phrases can you envision that he would adapt from his essay to characterize the parking lot shown above? Be as specific as possible in identifying—and explaining—the appropriateness of the word choices you make.

5. **CONNECTIONS:** Consider the nature and extent of the arguments McKibben enumerates to advocate for individual and collective action in responding to the global problem of climate change. Compare and contrast McKibben's arguments with those Peter Singer offers to address world poverty ("The Singer Solution to World Poverty," page 615). Which writer presents the more convincing and compelling case? Explain why.

John McWhorter

THICK OF TONGUE

What does it mean to "sound" black or white? The question holds special meaning for linguist **JOHN McWHORTER** (b. 1965), a black man who has often been told he sounds white. In "Thick of Tongue," he explores the nature of black speech in America and the ways we interpret different sounds and patterns. "The black sound is, though we don't usually use the term this way, an accent," he explains.

McWhorter writes frequently on language and race and has authored many books, including *The Power of Babel* (2001), *Our Magnificent Bastard Tongue* (2008), and *Talking Back, Talking Black* (2017). He contributes articles to *Time* magazine, CNN, and the *Atlantic*, and his work has appeared in numerous publications, including the *Wall Street Journal*, the *New York Times*, and *Forbes*. Despite the reservations about his voice expressed in "Thick of Tongue," McWhorter—a professor at Columbia University—has spoken at TED and been interviewed several times on National Public Radio.

> **What does it mean to "sound" black or white?**

GIVEN THAT I am the kind of black person who is often termed "articulate," it may seem surprising that I spend much of my life feeling quite thick of tongue. I am one of those unfortunate black people who sound white. It is, of all things, a social handicap.

"So *white* . . .!", then, I seemed, years ago, to a black administrative assistant. I was told of the assessment some time later by an acquaintance of hers, but I could sense that this lady couldn't stand me as soon as we met. This was long before I had any public notoriety for unconventional views about race issues; I was an utterly anonymous new professor of linguistics. That she found me so disagreeable must have had something to do with me as a person. I arrived into the situation with good intentions and was interested in ingratiating myself as much as possible with everyone there, so I have reason to assume that what repelled her is the way I talk, which does indeed sound "so white."

Some will say that this woman was especially narrow-minded or ignorant, but she wasn't—that's just the thing. I could tell countless similar stories, about the couple of black listeners who liked my recorded linguistic courses in the Great Courses series but complained about the way I speak, one of them adding that a friend heard me and thought I lacked "swagger." When I was twelve, a cousin of mine, not yet three, remarked that my sister and

I didn't sound like everybody else he knew. This kind of thing, for me, is and has always been just part of living.

I hardly consider myself significantly oppressed on this score. It is well documented that sounding black on the phone makes you less likely to be shown an apartment or house or to get a job interview. A black kid who uses Black English in school is often criticized by teachers and thought less intelligent. Classic experiments have shown that people's evaluation of someone reading a passage changes according to whether it's read by a white or black person. The black voice is rated less favorably—considered less bright, less friendly. My burden, in comparison, is a mere personal cross to bear, worse than having a hard-to-spell name but hardly on the order of being denied services and thought dim. Yet to an extent that few would have reason to know, I suffer.

When you're black and you sound just like a white person, it puts a lot of 5 black people off. The vast majority of black Americans, including educated ones, are identifiable as black from their speech; the "black sound" is a subconscious but near-universal hallmark of black American culture. This means that if you are black, upon meeting you, a great many black people will tacitly expect that the two of you will speak more similarly to one another—at the very least in terms of that certain "sound"—than either of you do to white people. That similarity is an index of acceptance and warmth in a society that looks askance on black people in so many ways. Then it turns out that you don't sound similar, despite your black face. The wrong voice is coming out of you.

Although the expectation that you were going to sound black was not conscious, the fact that you don't is processed quite consciously: it's the discrepancy that elicits attention. You are heard as talking "like that," though you know no other way to talk. It seems, perhaps, that you purposefully distanced yourself from the normal black way of talking in a quest to join whites. More certainly, you sound snooty, chilly, not like the type anyone would want to have a beer (or anything else!) with. To a black person who knows only other black people who speak with the same sound, your different sound is not just peculiar but, because it is a "white sound," snobbish. The matter is not one of perplexity or discomfort, but irritation, even contempt.

Plus, these days, the "black sound" has acquired a certain cachet in mainstream society through the popularity of hip hop, so increasingly someone like me finds that even whites below a certain age process him as "square." Call it stereotyping or call it progress, but a lot of white people happily anticipate a certain hipness, "realness," from a black person. We're so "down," so approachable, so "the shit," apparently. In talking to these people, just as to so many black people, I disappoint. I offend.

* * *

One of the hardest things about this is that so many people would be inclined to say that the problem—being read as not sounding black—doesn't exist.

During the O.J. Simpson trial, in response to one witness who claimed to have heard a "black voice" at the scene of the murder of Simpson's wife

and her friend, lawyer Johnnie Cochran objected: "What's a black voice?"
The mostly black jury assented. Cochran was implying that the very idea that
black speech has a particular sound is racist; often, people making the claim
insist that black people simply talk like Southerners.

Most any American knows that a white Southerner is unlikely to sound   10
like Chris Rock while a black person is unlikely to sound like Paula Deen.[1]
Black and Southern English overlap, but just that. Did the Reverend Martin
Luther King and the white police officers beating and arresting him speak the
same dialect? Yet the notion of a "black sound" smells like it could bring on
accusations of stereotyping, so one is inclined to just step around the issue.

Black people's own ticklish orientation when it comes to acknowledging
a black way of speech is understandable for two reasons. The first is the racist
past (and present) of this country—so often, that which is black is trashed as
deficient; one becomes permanently wary. Then also, Black English is primarily associated with what are considered errors—*ain't*, *he be*, *aks*, and so
on. Naturally, one worries that any characterization of black people's speech
will be a critique rather than a neutral description. To many, the idea that
even educated black people have this sound will seem like a prelude to the
claim that even educated black people are incapable of mastering "proper
language."

But the same people who hotly deny that there is such a thing as a black
sound will notice immediately when a black person "sounds white," as countless black people teased about this as children can attest to. Logic dictates
that if a black person can sound white—and this accusation is uncontrover-
sial in black America—then the norm must be for black people to sound
something else.

* * *

So what exactly is this "black sound" I am insisting exists?

I am not referring to black slang. Plenty of black people use little street
slang and yet still have a black *sound*. The question is why you could tell
most black people were black if they read you a shopping list over the phone.

Scholarship has confirmed what most of us sense intuitively: whites and   15
blacks are very good at identifying black voices, even from an isolated word.
The black sound is, though we don't usually use the term this way, an accent.
It differs from standard English's sound in the same way that other dialects
do, in certain shadings of vowels, aspects of intonation, and also that elusive
thing known as timbre, most familiar to singers—degrees of breathiness,
grain, huskiness, "space."

Contrary to how some may read me here, I am not bragging about how
"well" I speak. I'm not. The black sound has nothing whatsoever to do with
whether one is capable of expressing their feelings elegantly, convincing
others to their point of view, weaving an engaging story. It's just a matter of

---

1 ***Paula Deen:*** An American celebrity chef and cooking show television host who resides in
Savannah, Georgia. —EDS.

some vowels—it's like the difference between one carpet color and another, nothing more.

But *why* is there a black sound? Well, in actuality, there is nothing inherently "black" about it. It isn't genetic, of course, and it isn't a degradation or departure from standard English. When English came to America, it developed in many directions, of which today's standard and black varieties are but two. Black and standard English share the relationship of two sisters, not that of a mother and her wayward daughter. Sisters begin as different people, and over time become even more different. Dialects of a common language behave the same way. This is why actors in old movies sound increasingly weird to us; people who learned to speak in 1900 picked up sounds at a different stage of drift than they're at now. Fred Astaire proclaims "This is revo-LYEW-tion!" where we would say "revo-LOO-tion." William Powell as The Thin Man prepares to round up what he calls the "sus-PECTS" instead of the "SUS-pects."

Sounds change. An *ah* might become an *aw* or an *ay*. A *t* might become a *d* or a *ch*. The way a sound progresses is no more meaningful in itself than changing hemlines, the fact that the fadeout on pop recordings went out of fashion, or that avocado was such a popular color in home décor for a while. But when these random changes happen at the same time to two different dialects, over long periods, they'll seem more and more distinct. This is why black people have a different sound than whites.

The differences between the white sound and the black sound that tip an American listener off to a speaker's race are subtle. I am not talking here about obvious, bluesy things, like saying *thang* for *thing* or *mo* for *more*, which are patterns less likely of educated people. One difference is that the *eh* sound before *m* or *n* sounds a little more like *ih*, so that, for example, *mention* sounds not exactly but to a whisper of an extent like *mintion*. Or, the *er* sound is slightly distinct: *bird* will sound a touch like *buh-urd*—not in a drawly way, but enough to alert the American brain. Then there is the timbre, fine-grained differences in vocal placement and texture that analysts have yet to characterize in detail, though the ear and mind can pick them up easily enough.

As dry as such details are in isolation, together they are why you might   20
sometimes have heard a voice on National Public Radio and known the person was black, no matter whether they were talking about the latest doings in Congress or tomorrow's weather. If you have ever had that impression, you may well have felt guilty about it, especially if you're white.

The dominant conception is that only racism could create the impression that black people have a particular way of speaking. The assumption, roughly, is that educated black people talk just like educated white people, while less educated black people usually (but not always) speak a combination of Southern English and bad grammar. There is little room in our public discourse for the reality, which is that (1) almost all black people code-switch between standard and Black (not Southern) English to varying degrees, (2) even the most educated black people typically talk with vowel colorings and a general cadence that most Americans readily hear as "black" (and not "Southern") after a few sentences, and (3) there isn't a thing wrong with that.

* * *

The result of all of this, for me, is an ongoing cognitive dissonance in my relations with other people. Yet I stopped bringing it up long ago. You just hit a wall trying.

Though I often wish I did, I don't have the vowels and cadence of the "blaccent." I have lost count of how many times callers-in to radio shows I appeared on have assumed I was white (including plenty of black ones) or asked whether I was. Radio hosts often gently advise me to, when commenting on racial issues, mention my race on air—which indicates that it's not evident from my voice that I'm black. Several listeners to my Great Courses lectures have written to me and mentioned that they didn't know I was black until they saw my photograph. Once, answering the phone for a white roommate, I listened as an old man drifted, when a news event came up, into a diatribe about "niggers" coming over the horizon; clearly, he did not hear blackness in my voice. I barely code-switch—after drinks, awakened in the middle of the night, talking to my daughters, amused or angry, I sound pretty much the same: boring Mid-Atlantic American. I have written here and there about the fact that black Americans have a larger English than most white Americans. Alas, my English isn't large at all.

My noting that I don't have a black-sounding voice has, on a couple of occasions, seemed to peeve the black person I was talking to. I think they were wondering whether I was claiming that, unlike other black people, I speak "properly." I mean no such thing—though much of what made it seem like I did was surely my "white" voice and the subconscious associations it brings up.

There has also been the occasional white person who has sincerely suggested that I just take on a black sound if I feel so uncomfortable. But they were unclear as to what I meant when I referred to "sounding black." One white woman said, while making vaguely vernacular street gestures, "Can't you just, like, 'Heyyy . . .'?" Well, I suppose I could "Heyyy"—but, for one thing, it would be stepping outside of my natural self. The fluently "Ebonic" guy expected to speak standard English does not need to adopt a foreign code to do so—any black person can speak standard as well as Black English, even if they would rather dwell in the latter. I didn't grow up saying "Heyyy," and Rosetta Stone offers no materials that might instruct me in the art.

Accent is the hardest thing to pick up in a new way of speaking after the age of about fourteen. The colorings that constitute a blaccent are subtle, deeply ingrained, and even *harder* to master for someone whose home base is standard English, precisely because Black English and standard English are so similar. And no, my being a linguist doesn't help: we have neither the training nor the inherent talent that would make us better at this than other people. It's professional actors who wangle it—Idris Elba and Thandie Newton have, dazzlingly, managed to learn a light blaccent for their roles

25

despite growing up outside of the United States. I could no more master a subtle blaccent than I could learn to blink, lift a fork, or laugh differently. Your accent is your you.

* * *

Why do I sound so white when I talk? It's a good question. Both of my parents were black (some people ask, and they must be spurred on by my voice, as I'm not that light-skinned). I grew up around plenty of black people—in an integrated Philadelphia neighborhood where my friends were all black kids, and then all-black Lawnside, New Jersey. Most of my friends were black until adolescence; my best friend had a working-class black Philadelphian accent himself. Neither of my parents were given to code-switching to full-blown Black English—but both of them used a somewhat more Black English-inflected way of speaking when talking comfortably with black people.

Yet somehow I came out sounding like an announcer in a 1940s newsreel. I'm tempted to say that as an inveterate nerd I identified more with the teachers and students at the private schools I attended, who were mostly white. But plenty of middle-class black kids—of whom, by the 1970s, there were more every year—went to school with whites and played at home with blacks and emerged sounding like home, not school.

I'm not a joiner, and people around me are more likely to pick up speech habits from me than I am to pick up speech habits from them. But then, my sister is more of a joiner than I am, and also had a richness of black experience at all-black Spelman College that I never had. She had an extremely light blaccent that she developed in those years to identify with her friends, but that was just a phase; on the whole, she has always spoken exactly like me. Truth to tell, I'm not quite sure why I sound like this. But I do.

* * *

It is more my curse than it is my sister's. I know that, especially in school, black girls get teased for "talking white" as much as black boys do. But I submit that, particularly in adulthood, not having a black voice is less of a social stain for a black woman than a black man. Linguists have discovered that with almost eerie consistency, across societies, women tend to speak more "properly" than men. Certainly women use slang and profanity and say *singin'* instead of *singing*—but less than men do. For this reason, the black woman's "white" speech can be processed, for better or worse, as "ladylike," sophisticated. However, sounding white is not associated with masculinity—if anything, when it pertains to a man it can be heard as suggesting effeminacy. 30

I thwart expectations in glum little ways. It comes down to the idea that black equals funky. A white woman I dated in the nineties watched me play a semi-classical piece on the piano and then smiled, "I'm waiting to see you really get into it." "Into it"? It turned out she was waiting for me to play some blues. Of course, a black man isn't "really" playing the piano until he "jams." In the same way, another woman I dated said, about my lack of a blaccent,

"I've been waiting for you to do it." To her, my actual voice was preliminary, public, stiff. She assumed that once comfortable I would glide from *Word!* into "Wuh-urd!" —from *no* into "naw," from *hold on* into a little "hode on." I already was comfortable—and was talking the way I am comfortable talking. But to her, my vocal comfort zone constituted "not really getting into it."

One of the strangest things about being a white-sounding black person is that, in one regard and only in that regard, I would have felt more comfortable in the past. Until the 1960s, the linguistic landscape in America was prissier than it is now. In public, language was to be presented in its Sunday best, and casual speech was only for off-time with intimates. Even grade school inculcated hardcore spelling and grammar rules, such that modestly educated soldiers during the Civil War wrote letters that sound practically Shakespearian (and sometimes quote the man). This divide between "high" and "low" was maintained as strictly in the black community as anywhere else, and what it meant was that it was not considered odd for an educated black person to not "sound black" at all.

One of the oddest things about listening to recordings of Booker T. Washington, educator Mary McLeod Bethune, civil rights titan A. Phillip Randolph, or operatic contralto Marian Anderson is that, in their public speech, at least, they did not have, or barely had, blaccents, where their equivalents today would. This is true of countless educated black people of the time, who surprise the modern ear listening to oral histories and other late-in-life interviews in that they sound so utterly white.

The social boundaries of Black English, which has existed since at least the early 1700s, expanded starting in the late sixties, when the counterculture encouraged a new informality and black activists and intellectuals taught black America to be proud of its vernacular heritage. A friend of mine, who was young at the time and has no blaccent, recalls a party in 1968 during which she sensed the change in the black linguistic landscape. Two black men of modest education teased her for not being able to enunciate "motherfucker" as they thought she should; she wasn't speaking "blackly" enough. That scene would have been much less likely ten years earlier, and just about impossible twenty years before that. Newly, this woman was heard as sounding white rather than just well-spoken.

I certainly do not yearn for a return to the time when one had to work so 35 hard on one's speech patterns to be heard by wider society. Or to the time when black people were subject to such decisive segregation there was no question as to whether any black person "knew they were black" or not, no matter how they spoke. But I do envy that black people did not have a tacit expectation that all people of their color, regardless of education level, temperament, or socioeconomic background, would share a way of speaking. I would like to be able to have a conversation with a black person of whatever social position without worrying that he thinks I don't sound black or that I think I'm better than him. I don't think I'm better than anybody and am quite aware that I am not white.

Am I oversimplifying the problem? Maybe—I suspect many would say that the issue isn't only that I sound white, but that I am reserved. That's true; I know black men without blaccents who are heartier types than I am and who probably put black people off less than I do vocally. But: a reserved black man who does have the black vowels and cadence is read as contained, as keeping his own counsel, not as cold, unfriendly, classist, uptight.

* * *

Though my speaking voice often feels like a club foot, I do not hate myself. I also have black friends who do not hear froideur[2] in the way I talk, sometimes because they themselves lack blaccents, and sometimes because they are just wired differently than that administrative assistant. And, as I am rounding fifty, my voice will increasingly come off as the fussiness of an "older" gent, quaint rather than offensive. I'm already sensing this with people younger than twenty-five. It's the sole facet of aging I'm enjoying.

Still, when I read that Jewish immigrants at the turn of the twentieth century learning English felt like they might open their mouths to speak only for shards of glass to fall out, I identify. I all but stopped doing live talks on race years ago despite the money I could earn, out of a sense that using my "white" voice to have such discussions was ineffective and makes me sound disconnected from the issues. I mainly write on race instead; on paper my vowels and cadence don't distort my message.

Sounding black? What's *that* all about? Well, that. A minor problem in the grand scheme, I know. But I'm just saying. (Luckily, in print.) ●

The Reader's Presence

1. McWhorter closes his essay by identifying with the challenges Jewish immigrants faced at the turn of the twentieth century: "[They] felt like they might open their mouths to speak only for shards of glass to fall out." He then observes: "I identify. I all but stopped doing live talks on race years ago despite the money I could earn, out of a sense that using my 'white' voice to have discussions was ineffective and makes me sound disconnected from the issues. I mainly write on race instead; on paper my vowels and cadence don't distort my message" (paragraph 38). As you reconsider the scope of McWhorter's essay, what writing strategies does he invoke to lead his readers to this conclusion? Be as specific as possible in your response, analyzing examples where he demonstrates what he calls "blaccent" (paragraph 23). How does McWhorter separate the concept of "black sound" from stereotyping and racism? Why does he draw this distinction? Why does he believe his "white" voice distorts his ability to give talks on race, given his description of the voices of individuals like Booker T. Washington?

2. McWhorter opens his essay by identifying himself as "the kind of black person who is often termed 'articulate.'" What effect(s) are implied when he places "articulate" in quotation marks? Show how this statement underpins the direction and structure of his essay. McWhorter provides several examples of each point he makes, some from personal experience and others from history and media. Which do you find most

---

[2] **froideur:** an aloof manner or cold attitude. —EDS.

convincing, and why? How would you characterize McWhorter's voice in this essay? How would you characterize his diction and tone in his closing paragraph: "Sounding black? What's *that* all about? A minor problem in the grand scheme, I know. But I'm just saying. (Luckily, in print.)"? How "thick" is his "tongue" here?

3. **CONNECTIONS:** Compare the "black sound" of McWhorter's essay to the idea of blackness in Thomas Chatterton Williams's "Black and Blue and Blond" (page 272). How similar are the experiences of these writers in failing to be recognized as black? How are they different? Compare McWhorter's situation as a black man with a "white" voice to that of Williams's daughter. Support each point with a detailed analysis of specific passages.

Marisa Meltzer
THE LAST FEMINIST TABOO

Can a woman go on a diet because of personal concerns over weight issues and be a good feminist at the same time? Does a concern about being "overweight" indicate that you have bought into male ideas about how a woman should look? The following essay, "The Last Feminist Taboo," delicately explores the tensions between politics and dieting, as the author wonders why it is so difficult for feminists to admit and discuss their personal diets. The essay is an attempt to confront the issue and to open up for liberated women "the complicated politics involved in food, fat, and their bodies."

> **This essay delicately explores the tensions between politics and dieting.**

A writer based in New York City, **MARISA MELTZER** has contributed to many nationally known periodicals as both an author and editor. She is the co-author of *How Sassy Changed My Life* (2007) and author of *Girl Power* (2010). Her work appears regularly in the *New York Times Magazine*, the *Wall Street Journal*, *Slate*, and *Teen Vogue*. "The Last Feminist Taboo" originally appeared in *Elle*.

UNLIKE CERTAIN B-LIST CELEBS, who take to the covers of tabloids to trumpet their diet success stories, I'm hoping no one will comment on the fact that I've lost more than 60 pounds in the past eight months. Dieting is my biggest secret. I wish I could say it's a thrilling one, like dating your college TA, but it's more like waxing my lip—I don't ever want to talk about it, and I'd rather people thought I never had to worry about it in the first place.

As the pounds started coming off, physically I felt lighter. I slept well. I was in a better mood. But I also felt strangely furtive and isolated. I've told exactly one friend about my weight loss. (It's probably no coincidence that she's a fellow chronic dieter and lives across the country from me.) Trading secrets late one night outside a bar, a particularly willowy friend recently admitted to me that she'd struggled with her weight in college. And yet even then, I—who can speak freely about anything: abortions, boys, Rihanna—could not confess that I've been tallying calories for months. "It's a bargain I make with myself," agrees Wendy McClure, a friend and the author of the weight-loss memoir *I'm Not the New Me.* "It's okay as long as I'm off doing this by myself."

For as long as I can remember having an identity at all, I've considered myself a feminist, graduating from *Free to Be . . . You and Me* to *Ms.* magazine to Naomi Wolf, who wrote in 1991's *The Beauty Myth* that "a cultural fixation on female thinness is not an obsession about female beauty, but an obsession about female obedience. Dieting is the most potent political sedative in women's history; a quietly mad population is a tractable one." Good feminists, in short, do not diet. Or if they do, they don't talk about it.

When I was growing up, the same mother who took me to protests against the Miss California pageant and to lectures by Gloria Steinem also never ate more than half of anything on her plate. Neither she nor my father, a gourmand who has made halfhearted attempts to lose 20 pounds for the past 30 years, have ever had real problems with weight. As the only child of divorced parents busy with their careers and love lives, I don't recall having a lot of sit-down, well-balanced family meals. I'm not sure I ever got the opportunity to learn proper eating habits; I also happened to be blessed with a sluggish metabolism.

My parents put me on my first diet in kindergarten. In photos from the 5
time, I'm only mildly chubby, but they wanted me to be happy and healthy, and to shield me from ridicule. Their intentions were pure enough, but having to diet at my parents' behest felt like a punishment. I spent several summers at a hellish, boot camp-like Junior Lifeguard program where one particularly sadistic fellow camper nicknamed me "Chubs" in my regulation red swimsuit. At 10, I was sent to a fat camp in Santa Barbara, where we attended four hours of exercise classes a day and our bags were searched for contraband candy. By high school, I lived a kind of dual feminist-dieter life, surviving on oatmeal, salads, and frozen yogurt while singing along to "as a woman I was taught to always be hungry" at Bikini Kill concerts.

You can trace my life's trajectory through my weight. Here I am as a teenager, constantly hungry, weighing myself daily to make sure I don't waver above my all-time low of 125 pounds. At Evergreen State College in Olympia, Washington, subsisting on pints of Alaskan Amber and $5 pizzas—weighing in at 170 pounds but enjoying the break from hypervigilance. In Paris my senior year, down to 140, jogging laps around the moat of Château de Vincennes and thrilled to fit into French sizes. In San Francisco postgraduation, going from overweight to obese on burrito lunches and topping the 200-pound mark.

By the time I turned 35 last year, I was living in Brooklyn, going through a breakup, and diagnosed with clinical depression for the first time in my life. Food was the most reliable comfort I could find: cookie-dough breakfasts washed down with Coke and the kind of delivery orders where the restaurant packs four sets of plastic utensils. The cocktail of pills I took—Lexapro, Abilify, Pristiq, Lamictal, Wellbutrin—helped lift me out of the dark fog, but they also elevated my weight. I hit 250, my highest ever.

I tried to wear my heaviness with a certain hard-won pride. It was a kiss-off to the years of calorie counting my parents had subjected me to, I told myself. Dating while fat? A way to filter out shallow men. (Though after one potential online suitor inquired as to whether I was fat or "merely chubby"—evidently my picture didn't spell it out clearly enough—I gave up on men altogether; my self-esteem couldn't withstand further blows.) I flirted with fat acceptance, tried to believe that weight should not define who I am, that beauty comes in different packages. But the truth was that I was neither healthy nor happy. I weighed more than my father, who is seven inches taller than me; my blood pressure, taken during a long-delayed visit to my doctor, was becoming worrisome.

It would be technically accurate to say that dieting was necessary for my health, but ultimately it came down to how I looked. I was scared of heart disease, yes, but was perhaps even more afraid of never fitting into Isabel Marant[1] again. My shapeless Marni dresses were suddenly tight. I could no longer fit into certain pairs of shoes. My stomach grazed the table when I slid into booths. And my career was affected: A national morning news show invited me to pontificate about young feminists (my own adolescent riot grrrl years having made me something of an expert), but I turned it down because I didn't like my appearance.

In late February 2013, I decided to make a change. Weight-loss surgery 10 was out of the question—insurance didn't cover it, and I worried I'd have to tell friends why I was recuperating from major surgery and eating tiny portions. Meal delivery felt too restrictive; logging every morsel on Weight Watchers, too tedious. My doctor devised a plan high in plant-based foods and protein. After I weighed in with her each month, she'd say, in her thick Romanian accent, "You are going to look like model." I certainly missed fish and chips and meatball heros, but I started getting used to—even craving—kale and cauliflower and chickpeas. Now I eat more vegetables than I previously thought possible, grill salmon sans oil, and avoid white flour and sugar. I go to spin classes and hot yoga. I've lost track of the last time I ate a cheeseburger.

But I do it all in private.

Odds are, I'm not the only one in my set on a diet: 64 percent of American women are considered overweight or obese, with a BMI above 25. According to one major study, roughly 45 million Americans diet each year, spending some $33 billion on weight-loss products.

---

1 ***Isabel Marant:*** French house of fashion founded in 1994.—Eds.

Now that I'm among them, the guilt I once felt about what I ate has been replaced by guilt over being the wrong kind of feminist—or maybe no kind of feminist: a woman pursuing something as pedestrian and frankly boring as losing weight. I fear that instead of fighting for a world where all bodies are admired, I'm pandering, reshaping my body to make it acceptable to the world around me. And I'm not alone: Jessica Wakeman, a writer for the blog The Frisky, recently came out as a dieter in a post called "True Story: A Feminist Joins Weight Watchers." This is a woman who's written casually about attending an orgy, but dieting required a lengthy justification.

There's a thread of old-school feminist thought that says taking pleasure in being admired for our looks is participating in our own oppression, minimizing our brains and power. But by the time I came of age in the '90s, feminism had shifted to include, if not embrace, such girly frivolities as lipstick and high heels: Picture Liz Phair singing "The fire that you like so much in me / is the mark of someone adamantly free"—all pissed off and righteous and yet feminine as you please in miniskirts and baby tees. Still, altering your body in any way that could read as conformity—that was different. Dieting, specifically, was choosing denial and self-abnegation over letting yourself enjoy all the lusty pleasures of life. It was selling out. (Nobody thought to ask exactly how Liz fit in those minis, but whatever.) Feminist writer Kate Harding, coauthor of *Lessons From the Fat-o-sphere: Quit Dieting and Declare a Truce With Your Body,* compares dieting to taking your husband's last name. "You can be a feminist and make a nonfeminist choice," she tells me. "But what drives me nuts is trying to make it a feminist act."

But there's also a strain of ambivalence that's more nebulous and apolitical: the notion that evolved girls simply don't need to diet. The modern woman, after all, is that highly capable, have-it-all creature to whom career success, confidence, and effortless style—and, oh yeah, the yoga body and the eco-conscious, preservative-free diet—come naturally. She's too damn smart and balanced to overeat in the first place. If anything, she's already healthy and getting ever healthier. So juice fasts and Goop[2] cleanses and barre classes? All fine as part of a vague "healthy lifestyle" of "clean eating." Losing weight for your wedding day? Okay, you get a free pass on that one. But the daily slog of dieting—all that calorie counting and dessert skipping and cardio bingeing? That's not at all chic.

So whether you brand it feminism or not—and plenty don't; according to one recent survey, only 23 percent of women identify themselves as feminist—liberated women are hip to the complicated politics involved in food, fat, and their bodies. We know how corrupt the diet industry is; we take to Twitter to applaud brands like ASOS for expanding their plus-size lines. Most of us agree that the insurance charts for what is considered a healthy weight are unrealistic, that the standard definition of beauty is narrow. We have a surplus of knowledge, and perhaps because of this, the only

15

---

2 **Goop:** A lifestyle brand launched by actress and singer Gwyneth Paltrow in 2008 as a weekly email newsletter. —Eds.

publicly acceptable message is one of body positivity and self-acceptance. Kudos to Melissa McCarthy, Rebel Wilson, Octavia Spencer for being, as Lena Dunham has put it, "freed from the prison" of Hollywood beauty standards. Props to Dunham, that paragon of Gen-Y feminism and achievement, who told an interviewer: "I ate cake for breakfast on the day of the Emmys, I ate cake for dinner, my workout didn't require Spanx, and I still feel like I looked better than people expected me to. It was amazing. I could feel the envy of every woman in the Sunset Tower."[3]

But for most women, that attitude is just a front. The French-born photographer and fashion blogger Garance Doré has voiced her frustration with fashion lovers who pretend to fit effortlessly into their leather microshorts. She writes, "For every friend who can eat whatever she wants and still stay thin, 10 of us have to pay a little more attention to our eating habits (like me) (and I'm not talking about being anorexic or anything, but just using moderation and maybe not eating a giant piece of carrot cake after a big lunch. It's no small task). And lying about the subject, now that I have a problem with." A few years ago, Julianne Moore said, "I still battle with my deeply boring diet of, essentially, yogurt and breakfast cereal and granola bars. I hate dieting. I hate having to do it to be the 'right' size." Moore's admission was far enough afield from the standard actress line of "Oh, I just ate a cheeseburger on the way here" to make headlines. Femininity, I guess, is still supposed to be wrapped up in mystery.

I look at all the cute, smart girls where I live in Brooklyn, where boutiques rarely stock sizes over 8 and rail-thin Michelle Williams[4] is the ideal, and I wonder if they diet too. Every time I order a salad — so often these days — and have just one glass of wine at dinner, I worry that someone will comment. But as I started writing this and talking to women about what they eat, I got a rare glimpse behind the curtain, where apparently quite a few of us are doing sad but poignant things to hide our dieting. Sarah Hepola, a writer I know who lost 45 pounds two years ago on a prepackaged diet, told me that she "lived in terror that a gentleman caller was going to open up my freezer for, say, an ice cube and be confronted with direct evidence of my weakness." McClure, the aforementioned memoirist, weighs her portions on the postal scale in her office. "The scale is in a high-traffic area, and we're a laid-back office, but I never, ever want anyone to catch me weighing a handful of cashews."

I decided to go to the source and call Naomi Wolf. Twenty-two years after *The Beauty Myth,* she's still critical of the kind of nitpicky thinking that dieting encourages. "Women are always tasked with surveilling, evaluating, judging. There is something about the culture asking us to be in that part of our brains all the time that dials down passion and intuition," she says. I brace myself for what comes next — is she going to chastise me, tell me I'm betraying the cause? But Wolf is surprisingly laissez-faire on the subject

---

3 *Sunset Tower:* Historic hotel located on the Sunset Strip in West Hollywood. —EDS.

4 *Michelle Williams:* American actress known for her television, film, and Broadway performances. —EDS.

of individual choice. "Feminism often gets into an unappealing cul-de-sac where there's this set of practices or beliefs that you have to be part of to be a good feminist. Interestingly, that's not very different from more conventional forms of social policing. I don't think there's anything wrong with taking care of your body. I just want to know you're feeling beautiful and important at whatever weight you want."

By losing weight, I am putting more value on my thinner body, which 20 becomes smaller every day as I continue to try to shed the last 30 or so pounds. I admit I feel more comfortable in this new body, which in turn has made me more confident in the choice I made to lose weight. What remains is for me to open up about it to the women I know; it's a discussion I hope to initiate. Among my friends, the conversation is just beginning. ■

The Reader's Presence

1. Consider the author's central argument carefully: do you think there is an inherent contradiction between being a good feminist and being conscious and careful of one's weight? Explain why or why not. To what extent do you think the issue argued in this essay is more a personal concern of the author's than a political concern of feminism?

2. Aside from personal experiences, what evidence does Meltzer offer to support her contention that dieting and feminist values can be at odds with one another? How, for example, does she use statistics? How does she use the quotations of various celebrities? What do you take away from the evidence supplied by celebrities?

3. **CONNECTIONS:** Read Meltzer's argument in conjunction with Camille Paglia's "The Pitfalls of Plastic Surgery" (page 584). In what ways would the acceptance of plastic surgery encounter the same feminist arguments as dieting? How does each author bring feminist values to the body image–related processes of dieting and plastic surgery? How might Meltzer respond to Paglia's arguments?

Walter Benn Michaels
THE TROUBLE WITH DIVERSITY

WALTER BENN MICHAELS (b. 1948) entered a swirl of controversy—from both right and left—with his 2006 book, *The Trouble with Diversity: How We Learned to Love Identity and Ignore Equality*, his polemic against identity politics and economic inequality on college campuses and in the greater society. In his book, he argues that the thorniest problem in American society is not racism or sexism or any of the other isms but the "increasing gap between the rich and the poor." Michaels received his PhD at the University of California, Santa Barbara, and taught English at the University of California, Berkeley, and at Johns Hopkins University before joining the faculty at the University of Illinois at Chicago, where he has taught American literature and literary theory since 2001. His books and monographs include *The Gold Standard and the Logic of Naturalism: American Literature at the Turn of the Century* (1987), *Our America: Nativism, Modernism, and Pluralism* (1995), *The Shape of the Signifier: 1967 to the End of History*

> **Walter Benn Michaels argues that the thorniest problem in American society is not racism or sexism or any of the other isms but the "increasing gap between the rich and the poor."**

(2004), and *The Beauty of a Social Problem: Photography, Autonomy, Economy* (2015). His essay "The Trouble with Diversity," excerpted from his 2006 book, appeared in the *American Prospect* in 2006.

In a 2004 essay in the *New York Times Magazine*, Michaels argued that focusing on diversity keeps our eyes off the real problem. "As long as we think that our best universities are fair if they are appropriately diverse, we don't have to worry that most people can't go to them, while others get to do so because they've had the good luck to be born into relatively wealthy families. In other words, as long as the left continues to worry about diversity, the right won't have to worry about inequality."

"THE RICH are different from you and me" is a famous remark supposedly made by F. Scott Fitzgerald to Ernest Hemingway, although what made it famous — or at least made Hemingway famously repeat it — was not the remark itself but Hemingway's reply: "Yes, they have more money." In other words, to Hemingway, the rich really aren't very different from you and me. Fitzgerald's mistake, he thought, was that he mythologized or sentimentalized the rich, treating them as if they were a different kind of person instead of the same kind of person with more money. It was as if, according to Fitzgerald, what made rich people different was not what they *had* — their money — but what they *were*, "a special glamorous race."

To Hemingway, this difference — between what people owned and what they were — seemed obvious. No one cares much about Robert Cohn's money in *The Sun Also Rises*, but everybody feels the force of the fact that he's a "race conscious . . . little kike." And whether or not it's true that Fitzgerald sentimentalized the rich, it's certainly true that he, like Hemingway, believed that the fundamental differences — the ones that really mattered — ran deeper than the question of how much money you had. That's why in *The Great Gatsby*, the fact that Gatsby has made a great deal of money isn't quite enough to win Daisy Buchanan back. Rich as he has become, he's still "Mr. Nobody from Nowhere," not Jay Gatsby but Jimmy Gatz. The change of name is what matters. One way to look at *The Great Gatsby* is as a story about a poor boy who makes good, which is to say, a poor boy who becomes rich—the so-called American Dream. But *Gatsby* is not really about someone who makes a lot of money; it is instead about someone who tries and fails to change who he is. Or, more precisely, it's about someone who pretends to be something he's not; it's about Jimmy Gatz pretending to be Jay Gatsby. If, in the end, Daisy Buchanan is very different from Jimmy Gatz, it's not because she's rich and he isn't but because Fitzgerald treats them as if they really belong to different races, as if poor boys who made a lot of money were only "passing" as rich. "We're all white here," someone says, interrupting one of Tom Buchanan's racist outbursts. Jimmy Gatz isn't quite white enough.

What's important about *The Great Gatsby*, then, is that it takes one kind of difference (the difference between the rich and the poor) and redescribes it as another kind of difference (the difference between the white and the not-so-white). To put the point more generally, books like *The Great Gatsby* (and there have been a great many of them) give us a vision of our society divided into races rather than into economic classes. And this vision has proven to be extraordinarily attractive. Indeed, it has survived even though what we used to think were the races have not. In the 1920s, racial science was in its heyday; now very few scientists believe that there are any such things as races. But many of those who are quick to remind us that there are no biological entities called races are even quicker to remind us that races have not disappeared; they should just be understood as social entities instead. And these social entities have turned out to be remarkably tenacious, both in ways we know are bad and in ways we have come to think of as good. The bad ways involve racism, the inability or refusal to accept people who are different from us. The good ways involve just the opposite: embracing difference, celebrating what we have come to call diversity.

Indeed, in the United States, the commitment to appreciating diversity emerged out of the struggle against racism, and the word diversity itself began to have the importance it does for us today in 1978 when, in *Bakke v. Board of Regents*, the Supreme Court ruled that taking into consideration the race of an applicant to the University of California (the medical school at UC Davis, in this case) was acceptable if it served "the interest of diversity." The Court's point here was significant. It was not asserting that preference in admissions could be given, say, to black people because they had previously been discriminated against. It was saying instead that universities had a legitimate interest in taking race into account in exactly the same way they had a legitimate interest in taking into account what part of the country an applicant came from or what his or her nonacademic interests were. They had, in other words, a legitimate interest in having a "diverse student body," and racial diversity, like geographic diversity, could thus be an acceptable goal for an admissions policy.

Two things happened there. First, even though the concept of diversity   5
was not originally connected with race (universities had long sought diverse student bodies without worrying about race at all), the two now came to be

firmly associated. When universities publish their diversity statistics today, they're not talking about how many kids come from Oregon. My university — the University of Illinois at Chicago — is ranked as one of the most diverse in the country, but well over half the students in it come from Chicago. What the rankings measure is the number of African Americans and Asian Americans and Latinos we have, not the number of Chicagoans.

And, second, even though the concept of diversity was introduced as a kind of end run around the historical problem of racism (the whole point was that you could argue for the desirability of a diverse student body without appealing to the history of discrimination against blacks and so without getting accused by people like Alan Bakke of reverse discrimination against whites), the commitment to diversity became deeply associated with the struggle against racism. Indeed, the goal of overcoming racism — of creating a "color-blind" society — was now reconceived as the goal of creating a diverse, that is, a color-conscious, society. Instead of trying to treat people as if their race didn't matter, we would not only recognize but celebrate racial identity. Indeed, race has turned out to be a gateway drug for all kinds of identities, cultural, religious, sexual, even medical. To take what may seem like an extreme case, advocates for the disabled now urge us to stop thinking of disability as a condition to be "cured" or "eliminated" and to start thinking of it instead on the model of race: We don't think black people should want to stop being black; why do we assume the deaf want to hear?

Our commitment to diversity has thus redefined the opposition to discrimination as the appreciation (rather than the elimination) of difference. So with respect to race, the idea is not just that racism is a bad thing (which of course it is) but that race itself is a good thing.

And what makes it a good thing is that it's not class. We love race — we love identity — because we don't love class. We love thinking that the differences that divide us are not the differences between those of us who have money and those who don't but are instead the differences between those who are black and those who are white or Asian or Latino or whatever. A world where some of us don't have money is a world where the differences between us present a problem: the need to get rid of inequality or to justify it. A world where some of us are black and some of us are white — or biracial or Native American or transgendered — is a world where the differences between us present a solution: appreciating our diversity. So we like to talk about the differences we can appreciate, and we don't like to talk about the ones we can't. Indeed, we don't even like to acknowledge that they exist. As survey after survey has shown, Americans are very reluctant to identify themselves as belonging to the lower class and even more reluctant to identify themselves as belonging to the upper class. The class we like is the middle class.

But the fact that we all like to think of ourselves as belonging to the same class doesn't, of course, mean that we actually do belong to the same class. In reality, we obviously and increasingly don't. "The last few decades," as *The Economist* puts it, "have seen a huge increase in inequality in America."

The rich *are* different from you and me, and one of the ways they're different is that they're getting richer and we're not. And while it's not surprising that most of the rich and their apologists on the intellectual right are unperturbed by this development, it is at least a little surprising that the intellectual left has managed to remain almost equally unperturbed. Giving priority to issues like affirmative action and committing itself to the celebration of difference, the intellectual left has responded to the increase in economic inequality by insisting on the importance of cultural identity. So for 30 years, while the gap between the rich and the poor has grown larger, we've been urged to respect people's identities—as if the problem of poverty would be solved if we just appreciated the poor. From the economic standpoint, however, what poor people want is not to contribute to diversity but to minimize their contribution to it—they want to stop being poor. Celebrating the diversity of American life has become the American left's way of accepting their poverty, of accepting inequality.

Our current notion of cultural diversity—trumpeted as the repudiation   10
of racism and biological essentialism—in fact grew out of and perpetuates the very concepts it congratulates itself on having escaped. The American love affair with race—especially when you can dress race up as culture—has continued and even intensified. Almost everything we say about culture (that the significant differences between us are cultural, that such differences should be respected, that our cultural heritages should be perpetuated, that there's a value in making sure that different cultures survive) seems to me mistaken. We must shift our focus from cultural diversity to economic equality to help alter the political terrain of contemporary American intellectual life.

In the last year, it has sometimes seemed as if this terrain might in fact be starting to change, and there has been what at least looks like the beginning of a new interest in the problem of economic inequality. Various newspapers have run series noticing the growth of inequality and the decline of class mobility; it turns out, for example, that the Gatsby-style American Dream—poor boy makes good, buys beautiful, beautiful shirts—now has a better chance of coming true in Sweden than it does in America, and as good a chance of coming true in western Europe (which is to say, not very good) as it does here. People have begun to notice also that the intensity of interest in the race of students in our universities has coincided with more or less complete indifference to their wealth. We're getting to the point where there are more black people than poor people in elite universities (even though there are still precious few black people). And Hurricane Katrina—with its televised images of the people left to fend for themselves in drowning New Orleans—provided both a reminder that there still are poor people in America and a vision of what the consequences of that poverty can be.

At the same time, however, the understanding of these issues has proven to be more a symptom of the problem than a diagnosis. In the *Class Matters* series in the *New York Times*, for example, the differences that mattered most turned out to be the ones between the rich and the really rich and between the old rich and the new rich. Indeed, at one point, the *Times* started treating class not as an issue to be addressed in addition to race but as itself a version of race, as if the rich and poor really were different races and so as if the occasional marriage between them were a kind of interracial marriage.

But classes are not like races and cultures, and treating them as if they were—different but equal—is one of our strategies for managing inequality rather than minimizing or eliminating it. White is not better than black, but rich is definitely better than poor. Poor people are an endangered species in elite universities not because the universities put quotas on them (as they did with Jews in the old days) and not even because they can't afford to go to them (Harvard will lend you or even give you the money you need to go there) but because they can't get into them. Hence the irrelevance of most of the proposed solutions to the systematic exclusion of poor people from elite universities, which involve ideas like increased financial aid for students who can't afford the high tuition, support systems for the few poor students who manage to end up there anyway, and, in general, an effort to increase the "cultural capital" of the poor. Today, says David Brooks, "the rich don't exploit the poor, they just out-compete them." And if out-competing people means tying their ankles together and loading them down with extra weight while hiring yourself the most expensive coaches and the best practice facilities, he's right. The entire U.S. school system, from pre-K up, is structured from the very start to enable the rich to out-compete the poor, which is to say, the race is fixed. And the kinds of solutions that might actually make a difference—financing every school district equally, abolishing private schools, making high-quality child care available to every family—are treated as if they were positively un-American.

But it's the response to Katrina that is most illuminating for our purposes, especially the response from the left, not from the right. "Let's be honest," Cornel West told an audience at the Paul Robeson Student Center at Rutgers University, "we live in one of the bleakest moments in the history of black people in this nation." "Look at the Super Dome," he went on to say. "It's not a big move from the hull of the slave ship to the living hell of the Super Dome." This is what we might call the "George Bush doesn't care about black people" interpretation of the government's failed response to the catastrophe. But nobody doubts that George Bush cares about Condoleezza Rice, who is very much a black person and who is fond of pointing out that she's been black since birth. And there are, of course, lots of other black people—like Clarence Thomas[1] and Thomas Sowell[2] and Janice Rogers Brown[3] and, at least once upon a time, Colin Powell—for whom George Bush almost certainly has warm feelings. But what American liberals want is for our conservatives to be

[1] **Clarence Thomas** (b. 1948): Associate justice of the Supreme Court of the United States since 1991 and the second African American to serve on the Supreme Court, after Justice Thurgood Marshall.—EDS.

[2] **Thomas Sowell** (b. 1930): An American economist, social commentator, author of numerous books, and a senior fellow of the Hoover Institution.—EDS.

[3] **Janice Rogers Brown** (b. 1949): A federal judge on the United States Court of Appeals for the District of Columbia Circuit and previously an associate justice of the California Supreme Court.—EDS.

racists. We want the black people George Bush cares about to be "some of my best friends are black" tokens. We want a fictional George Bush who doesn't care about black people rather than the George Bush we've actually got, one who doesn't care about poor people.

Although that's not quite the right way to put it. First because, for all I 15 know, George Bush does care about poor people; at least he cares as much about poor people as anyone else does. What he doesn't care about—and what Bill Clinton, judging by his eight years in office, didn't much care about, and what John Kerry, judging from his presidential campaign, doesn't much care about, and what we on the so-called left, judging by our own willingness to accept Kerry as the alternative to Bush, don't care about either—is taking any steps to get them to stop being poor. We would much rather get rid of racism than get rid of poverty. And we would much rather celebrate cultural diversity than seek to establish economic equality.

Indeed, diversity has become virtually a sacred concept in American life today. No one's really against it; people tend instead to differ only in their degrees of enthusiasm for it and their ingenuity in pursuing it. Microsoft, for example, is very ingenious indeed. Almost every company has the standard racial and sexual "employee relations groups," just as every college has the standard student groups: African American, Black and Latino Brotherhood, Alliance of South Asians, Chinese Adopted Sibs (this one's pretty cutting-edge), and the standard GLBTQ (the Q is for *Questioning*) support center. But (as reported in a 2003 article in *Workforce Management*) Microsoft also includes groups for "single parents, dads, Singaporean, Malaysian, Hellenic, and Brazilian employees, and one for those with attention deficit disorder." And the same article goes on to quote Patricia Pope, CEO of a diversity management firm in Cincinnati, describing companies that "tackle other differences" like "diversity of birth order" and, most impressive of all, "diversity of thought." If it's a little hard to imagine the diversity of birth order workshops (all the oldest siblings trying to take care of each other, all the youngest competing to be the baby), it's harder still to imagine how the diversity of thought workshops go. What if the diversity of thought is about your sales plan? Are you supposed to reach agreement (but that would eliminate diversity) or celebrate disagreement (but that would eliminate the sales plan)?

Among the most enthusiastic proponents of diversity, needless to say, are the thousands of companies providing "diversity products," from diversity training (a $10-billion-a-year industry) to diversity newsletters (I subscribe to *Diversity Inc.*, but there are dozens of them) to diversity rankings to diversity gifts and clothing—you can "show your support for multiculturalism" *and* "put an end to panty lines" with a "Diversity Rocks Classic Thong" ($9.99). The "Show Me the Money Diversity Venture Capital Conference" says what needs to be said here. But it's not all about the benjamins.[4] There's no money for the government in proclaiming Asian Pacific American Heritage

---

[4] **benjamins:** 100-dollar bills; so called because the face of Benjamin Franklin is on the bill.—Eds.

III

Month (it used to be just a week, but the first President Bush upgraded it) or in Women's History Month or National Disability Employment Awareness Month or Black History Month or American Indian Heritage Month. And there's no money for the Asians, Indians, blacks, and women whose history gets honored.

In fact, the closest thing we have to a holiday that addresses economic inequality instead of identity is Labor Day, which is a product not of the multicultural cheerleading at the end of the 20th century but of the labor unrest at the end of the 19th. The union workers who took a day off to protest President Grover Cleveland's deployment of 12,000 troops to break the Pullman strike weren't campaigning to have their otherness respected. And when, in 1894, their day off was made official, the president of the American Federation of Labor, Samuel Gompers, looked forward not just to a "holiday" but to "the day for which the toilers in past centuries looked forward, when their rights and wrongs would be discussed." The idea was not that they'd celebrate their history but that they'd figure out how to build a stronger labor movement and make the dream of economic justice a reality.

Obviously, it didn't work out that way, either for labor (which is weaker than it's ever been) or for Labor Day (which mainly marks the end of summer). You get bigger crowds, a lot livelier party and a much stronger sense of solidarity for Gay Pride Day. But Gay Pride Day isn't about economic equality, and celebrating diversity shouldn't be an acceptable alternative to seeking economic equality.

In an ideal universe we wouldn't be celebrating diversity at all—we wouldn't even be encouraging it—because in an ideal universe the question of who you wanted to sleep with would be a matter of concern only to you and to your loved (or unloved) ones. As would your skin color; some people might like it, some people might not, but it would have no political significance whatsoever. Diversity of skin color is something we should happily take for granted, the way we do diversity of hair color. No issue of social justice hangs on appreciating hair color diversity; no issue of social justice hangs on appreciating racial or cultural diversity.   20

If you're worried about the growing economic inequality in American life, if you suspect that there may be something unjust as well as unpleasant in the spectacle of the rich getting richer and the poor getting poorer, no cause is less worth supporting, no battles are less worth fighting, than the ones we fight for diversity. While some cultural conservatives may wish that everyone should be assimilated to their fantasy of one truly American culture, and while the supposed radicals of the "tenured left" continue to struggle for what they hope will finally become a truly inclusive multiculturalism, the really radical idea of redistributing wealth becomes almost literally unthinkable. In the early 1930s, Senator Huey Long of Louisiana proposed a law making it illegal for anyone to earn more than $1 million a year and for anyone to inherit more than $5 million. Imagine the response if—even suitably adjusted for inflation—any senator were to propose such a law today, cutting off incomes at, say, $15 million a year and inheritances at $75 million. It's not just the numbers that wouldn't fly; it's the whole concept. Long's proposal never became law, but it was popular and debated with some seriousness. Today, such a restriction would seem as outrageous and unnatural as interracial—not to mention gay—marriage would have seemed then. But we don't need to purchase our progress in civil rights at the expense of a commitment to economic justice. More fundamentally still, we should not allow—or we should not continue to allow—the phantasm of respect for difference to take the place of that commitment to economic justice. Commitment to diversity is at best a distraction and at worst an essentially reactionary position that prevents us from putting equality at the center of the national agenda.

Our identity is the least important thing about us. And yet, it is the thing we have become most committed to talking about. From the standpoint of a left politics, this is a profound mistake since what it means is that the political left—increasingly invested in the celebration of diversity and the redress of historical grievance—has converted itself into the accomplice rather than the opponent of the right. Diversity has become the left's way of doing neoliberalism, and antiracism has become the left's contribution to enhancing market efficiency. The old Socialist leader Eugene Debs used to be criticized for being unwilling to interest himself in any social reform that didn't involve attacking economic inequality. The situation now is almost exactly the opposite; the left obsessively interests itself in issues that have nothing to do with economic inequality.

And, not content with pretending that our real problem is cultural difference rather than economic difference, we have also started to treat economic difference as if it were cultural difference. So now we're urged to be more respectful of poor people and to stop thinking of them as victims, since to treat them as victims is condescending—it denies them their "agency." And if we can stop thinking of the poor as people who have too little money and start thinking of them instead as people who have too little respect, then it's our attitude toward the poor, not their poverty, that becomes the problem to be solved, and we can focus our efforts of reform not on getting rid of classes but on getting rid of what we like to call classism. The trick, in other words, is to stop thinking of poverty as a disadvantage, and once you stop thinking of it as a disadvantage then, of course, you no longer need to worry about getting rid of it. More generally, the trick is to think of inequality as a consequence of our prejudices rather than as a consequence of our social system and thus to turn the project of creating a more egalitarian society into the project of getting people (ourselves and, especially, others) to stop being racist, sexist, classist homophobes. The starting point for a progressive politics should be to attack that trick. ◼

The Reader's Presence

1. According to Michaels, why does celebrating diversity distract us from minimizing inequality? Specifically, how does Michaels establish connections between race and class? What would happen if we followed his advice and focused only on economic inequalities? For example, describe how colleges would be affected if they did not take the diversity of their student body into account during the admissions process. Michaels is not specific about how eliminating race as a political category will eliminate class as a social misery. Applying Michaels's logic to his Hurricane Katrina example (paragraph 14), how would ignoring race have led to a better response for the hurricane's victims?

2. Michaels skillfully uses wit and humor at strategic moments in his essay. Consider, for example, such lines as "what poor people want is not to contribute to diversity but to minimize their contribution to it" (paragraph 9). What are the effects of using wit and humor to write about such a serious subject? What risks does Michaels take in doing so? How effectively would his essay read if such wit and humor were omitted? In formulating your response, identify a few humorous or witty moments and rewrite them with a serious tone. How did changing the tone affect the argument? Do you think a reader would be more—or less—convinced by an argument that was formulated without wit and humor? Explain why.

3. **CONNECTIONS:** Compare and contrast Michaels's argument about "The Trouble with Diversity" with David Brooks's ideas in "People Like Us" (page 324). For example, contrast the opening two sentences in Brooks's essay — "Maybe it's time to admit the obvious. We don't really care about diversity all that much in America, even though we talk about it a great deal" — with the tone and direction Michaels sets for his readers in the opening of his essay. What would Brooks make of Michaels's assertion that "no issue of social justice hangs on appreciating racial or cultural diversity" (paragraph 20)? What standards of evidence and argument do Michaels and Brooks use to evaluate cultural claims about race and class? Which essay do you find more informative? More convincing? Explain why by pointing to specific passages from each essay.

Walter Mosley

GET HAPPY

WALTER MOSLEY (b. 1952) is best known for his popular crime novels, but he is also one of the most versatile writers in contemporary American literature, penning literary fiction as well as science fiction, political writing, young adult novels, and plays. He is the author of over forty books, which have been translated into more than twenty languages worldwide. He is the recipient of PEN America's Lifetime Achievement Award, and his essays have appeared in magazines such as the *New York Times Magazine* and the *Nation*. His mother was Jewish, the daughter of Russian immigrants, and his father was African American, and he has said that he identifies with both groups. Growing up in the Los Angeles area in the 1950s and 1960s, he was witness to a great deal of racial conflict, and he is an outspoken critic of race relations in the United States. He recently said, "Things seem better, but there are serious cracks in the veneer of our progress. Injustices such as the one committed against Trayvon Martin have reared their ugly heads since before Emmett Till's murder in 1955." This concern with racial injustice often appears in the context of his fiction and nonfiction. He has cited Langston Hughes and Raymond Chandler among his influences. "Get Happy" originally appeared in the *Nation* in October 2009.

> **"There are serious cracks in the veneer of our progress."**

> *We hold these truths to be self-evident, that all men are created equal, that they are endowed by their Creator with certain unalienable rights, that among these are Life, Liberty, and the pursuit of Happiness.*

AMERICANS ARE AN UNHAPPY, UNHEALTHY LOT. From the moment we declared our independence from the domination of British rule, we have included the people's right to pursue happiness as one of the primary privileges of our citizens and the responsibility of our government. Life and liberty are addressed to one degree or another by our executive, legislative and judicial branches, but our potential for happiness has lagged far behind.

As the quote above says (and does not say), freedom was once the province of white men; now the lack of that freedom and the subsequent loss of the potential for happiness belongs to all of us. Our happiness is kept from us by prisonlike schools and meaningless jobs, un(der)employment and untreated physical and psychological ailments, by political leaders who scare the votes out of us and corporate "persons" that buy up all the resources that have been created and defined by our labor.

Citizens are not treated like members of society but more like employees who can be cut loose for any reason large or small, whether that reason be an individual action or some greater event like the downturn of the stock market. We are lied to by our leaders and the mass media to such a great extent that it's almost impossible to lay a finger on one thing that we can say, unequivocally, is true. We wage a "war on drugs" while our psychiatrists prescribe mood-altering medicines at an alarming rate. We eat and drink and smoke too much, and sleep too little. We worry about health and taxes and the stock market until one of the three finally drags us down. We fall for all sorts of get-rich-quick schemes, from the stock market to the lottery. We practice rampant consumerism, launch perpetual wars and seek out meaningless sex.

Through these studies we create aberrant citizens who glean their empty and impossible hopes from television, the Internet and stadium sports. These issues, and others, form the seat of our discontent, a throne of nails under a crown of thorns.

Happiness is considered by most to be a subset of wealth, which is not necessarily true. But even if it was true, most Americans are not wealthy, and most of those who are will lose that wealth before they die. Besides, money cannot buy happiness. It can buy bigger TVs and comelier sex partners; it can pay for liposuction and enough fossil fuel to speed away from smog-filled urban sprawls. Money can influence court verdicts, but it cannot buy justice. And without the bedrock of justice, how can any American citizen be truly happy? 5

Happiness is a state of mind cultivated under a sophisticated understanding of a rapidly changing world. In times gone by the world didn't change so fast. As recently as the early twentieth century it would take a generation or more for knowledge to double; now the sum total of our knowledge doubles each year, perhaps even less than that. As technology and technique change, so does our world and our reactions to it. The Internet, gene-splicing, transportation, overpopulation and other vast areas of ever-growing knowledge and experience force significant changes in our lifestyles every few years.

The pursuit of happiness implies room to move, but the definition of that space has changed—from open fields to Internet providers, from talk with a friend or religious leader to psychotherapy and antidepresssion drugs.

If you are reading this essay and believe that you and the majority of your fellows are happy, content, satisfied and generally pleased with the potentials presented to you and others, then you don't have to continue reading. I certainly do not wish to bring unhappiness to anyone who feels they fit into this world like a pampered foot into a sheepskin slipper.

Some of us are naturally happy; others have had the good fortune to be born at the right moment, in the right place. But many of us suffer under a corporatized bureaucracy where homelessness, illiteracy, poverty, malnourishment (both physical and spiritual) and an unrelenting malaise are not only possible but likely.

One cure—for those who feel that their pursuit of happiness has been sent on a long detour through the labor camps of American and international capitalism—is the institution of a government department that has as its only priority the happiness of all Americans. 10

At first blush this might seem like a frivolous suggestion. Each and every American is responsible for her or his own happiness, whatever that is, you might say. Furthermore, even if a government department was designed to monitor, propagate and ensure the happiness of our citizens, that department should not have the power or even the desire to enforce its conclusions on anyone.

But the suggestion here is to expand the possibilities for happiness, not to codify or impose these possibilities. Our Declaration of Independence says that the pursuit of happiness is an "unalienable right." This language seems to make the claim that it is a government responsibility to ensure that all Americans, or as many as possible, are given a clear path toward that pursuit.

This is not and cannot be some rocky roadway through a barren landscape. Our world is more like the tropics, crowded by a lush forest of fast-growing knowledge. The path must be cleared every day. How can a normal person be happy with herself in this world, when the definition of the world is changing almost hourly?

What we need is a durable and yet flexible definition (created by study and consensus) that will impact the other branches of government. If we can, through a central agency, begin to come to a general awareness of what we need to clear the path to the pursuit of happiness, I believe that the lives we are living stand a chance of being more satisfying. If we can have a dialogue based on our forefathers' declaration, I believe that we can tame the shadowy government and corporate incursions into our lives.

What do we need to be assured of our own path to a contented existence? 15 Enough food to eat? Health? Help with childcare? A decent, fulfilling educa-tion? Should we feel that the land we stand on is ours? Or that our welfare is the most important job of a government that is made up by our shared citizenship?

These simple interrogations are complex in their nature. All paths are not the same; many conflict. But we need a government that assures us the prom-ise of the Declaration of Independence. We need to realize that the ever more convoluted world of knowledge can flummox even the greatest minds. We need to concentrate on our own happiness if we expect to make a difference in the careening technological and slovenly evolving social world of the twenty-first century. ▪

The Reader's Presence

1. What does Mosley gain by including as an epigraph the opening lines from the Declaration of Independence? To what extent do you agree with Mosley that in com-parison to life and liberty, "our potential for happiness has lagged far behind" (para-graph 1)? How does Mosley's definition of happiness ("a state of mind cultivated under a sophisticated understanding of a rapidly changing world," paragraph 6) relate to the fact that the "pursuit of happiness has been sent on a long detour" (paragraph 10)?

2. What is your reaction to Mosley's invitation to stop reading in the eighth paragraph? Were you tempted to stop reading? Explain why or why not. What does Mosley potentially gain or lose by suggesting this proposition in his essay? Do you think he intends his offer to be taken seriously, or is he being facetious? What evidence can you identify to support your response? What larger point does he make here about our general sense of unhappiness?

3. How convincing do you find Mosley's suggestion that a government department be established to help Americans in their "pursuit of happiness"? To what extent do you think the happiness/unhappiness Mosley discusses is the same as that mentioned in the Declaration of Independence? Explain your response.

4. **CONNECTIONS:** Read Mosley's essay with direct reference to the document that is central to his argument: the Declaration of Independence (page 537). At one point Mosley maintains that the "language" of the Declaration "seems to make the claim that it is a government responsibility to ensure that all Americans, or as many as

possible, are given a clear path toward that pursuit [of happiness]" (paragraph 12). What do you think of Mosley's point in light of the specific language of the Declaration? Do you think he takes the notion of the "pursuit of happiness" out of its original context? Or do you think the Declaration clearly suggests that the happiness of its citizens is the responsibility of government? Be sure to explain the reasons behind your answer.

Camille Paglia
THE PITFALLS OF PLASTIC SURGERY

CAMILLE PAGLIA (b. 1947), academic, author, and *Salon*'s "fave pop intellectual," earned her PhD at Yale University and taught at Bennington College, Wesleyan University, and Yale University. In 1984, she joined the faculty at the University of the Arts in Philadelphia, where she is professor of humanities and media studies. Her academic study, and first book, *Sexual Personae: Art and Decadence from Nefertiti to Emily Dickinson* (1990) caused heated debate and launched her career as a noted feminist, cultural critic, and social commentator. By early 1991, she was featured on the cover of *New York Magazine*, under the headline "Woman Warrior." In 1992, her second book, *Sex, Art, and American Culture*, was published, followed by *Vamps & Tramps* (1994). In 1998, she published a volume about Alfred Hitchcock's

> **"That 700-page tome was a round-the-clock operation, requiring a fanaticism of attention and persistence that could not possibly have been combined with a responsible family life."**

film *The Birds*, for the British Film Institute Films Classics series. Her latest books are *Break, Blow, Burn: Camille Paglia Reads Forty-Three of the World's Best Poems* (2005), *Glittering Images: A Journey Through Art from Egypt to Star Wars* (2012), and *Free Women, Free Men: Sex, Gender, Feminism* (2017). Paglia is a founding contributor to *Salon*; and she writes about art, literature, culture, media, and politics for numerous publications throughout the world, including the *Advocate*, the *New York Times*, the *Independent* of London, the *American Enterprise*, and *Harper's Bazaar*, where "The Pitfalls of Plastic Surgery" appeared in 2005.

Paglia describes her life after turning sixty and becoming a parent, with her partner, of a baby boy—and reveals the trials of writing her first book. "I'm deeply enjoying being a parent—which I certainly would not have been able to do while I was writing *Sexual Personae* for 20 years," she told an interviewer. "That 700-page tome was a round-the-clock operation, requiring a fanaticism of attention and persistence that could not possibly have been combined with a responsible family life."

PLASTIC SURGERY is living sculpture: a triumph of modern medicine. As a revision of nature, cosmetic surgery symbolizes the conquest of biology by human free will. With new faces and bodies, people have become their own works of art.

Once largely confined to the entertainment and fashion industries, plastic surgery has become routine in the corporate workplace in the U.S., even for men. A refreshed, youthful look is now considered essential for job retention and advancement in high-profile careers. As cosmetic surgery has become more widespread and affordable, it has virtually become a civil right, an equal-opportunity privilege once enjoyed primarily by a moneyed elite who could fly to Brazil for a discreet nip and tuck.

The questions raised about plastic surgery often have a moralistic hue. Is cosmetic surgery a wasteful frivolity, an exercise in narcissism? Does the pressure for alteration of face and body fall more heavily on women because of endemic sexism? And are coercive racist stereotypes at work in the trend among black women to thin their noses and among Asian women to "Westernize" their eyes?

All these ethical issues deserve serious attention. But nothing, I submit, will stop the drive of the human species toward beauty and the shimmering illusion of perfection. It is one of our deepest and finest instincts. From pre-history on, tribal peoples flattened their skulls, pierced their noses, elongated their necks, stretched their earlobes and scarred or tattooed their entire bodies to achieve the most admired look. Mutilation is in the eye of the beholder.

Though cosmetic surgery is undoubtedly an unstoppable movement, we   5
may still ask whether its current application can be improved. I have not had surgery and have no plans to do so, on the theory that women intellectuals, at least, should perhaps try to hold out. (On the other hand, one doesn't want to scare the horses!) Over the past 15 years, I have become increasingly uneasy about ruling styles of plastic surgery in the U.S. What norms are being imposed on adult or aging women?

I would suggest that the current models upon which many American surgeons are basing their reworking of the female face and body are far too parochial. The eye can be retrained over time, and so we have come to accept a diminished and even demeaning view of woman as ingenue, a perky figure of ingratiating girliness. Neither sex bomb nor dominatrix, she is a cutesy sex kitten without claws.

In the great era of the Hollywood studio system, from the 1920s to the early '60s, pioneering makeup techniques achieved what plastic surgery does now to remold the appearance of both male and female stars. For example, the mature Lana Turner[1] of *Imitation of Life* or *Peyton Place* was made to look like a superglamorous and ravishingly sensual version of a woman of Turner's own age. The problem today is that Hollywood expects middle-aged female actors to look 20 or even 30 years younger than they are. The ideal has become the bouncy Barbie doll or simpering nymphet, not a sophisticated woman of the

---

[1] **Lana Turner** (1921–1995): One of Hollywood's most glamorous stars in the 1940s and 1950s, Turner appeared in countless films, including *Peyton Place* (1957) and *Imitation of Life* (1959). — EDS.

world. Women's faces are erased, blanked out as in a cartoon. In Europe, in contrast, older women are still considered sexy: Women are granted the dignity of accumulated experience. The European woman has a reserve or mystique because of her assumed mastery of the esoteric arts of love.

Why this cultural discrepancy? Many of the founders of Hollywood, from studio moguls to directors, screenwriters, makeup artists, and composers, were European émigrés whose social background ranged from peasant to professional. European models of beauty are based on classical precedents: on luminous Greek sculpture, with its mathematical symmetry and proportion, or on Old Master oil paintings, with their magnificent portraiture of elegant aristocrats and hypnotic femme fatales. As an upstart popular form with trashy roots in nickelodeons and penny arcades, Hollywood movies strove to elevate their prestige by invoking a noble past. The studios presented their stable of stars as a Greek pantheon of resurrected divinities, sex symbols with an unattainable grandeur.

But Hollywood's grounding in great art has vanished. In this blockbuster era of computerized special effects and slam-bang action-adventure films, few producers and directors root their genre in the ancestry of the fine arts. On the contrary, they are more likely to be inspired by snarky television sitcoms or holographic video games, with their fantasy cast of overmuscled heroes and pneumatic vixens. The profound influence of video games can be seen in the redefining of today's ultimate female body type, inspired by Amazonian superheroines like Lara Croft: large breasts with a flat midriff and lean hips, a hormonally anomalous profile that few women can attain without surgical intervention and liposuction.

Maximizing one's attractiveness and desirability is a justifiable aim in any society, except for the most puritanical. But it is worrisome that the American standard of female sexual allure may be regressing. In the post-1960s culture of easy divorce on demand, middle-aged women have found themselves competing with nubile women in their 20s, who are being scooped up as trophy second wives by ambitious men having a midlife crisis. Cosmetic surgery seems to level the playing field. But at what cost?   10

Good surgery discovers and reveals personality; bad surgery obscures or distorts it. The facial mask should not be frozen or robotic. We still don't know what neurological risks there might be in long term use of nonsurgical Botox, a toxin injected subcutaneously to paralyze facial muscles and smooth out furrows and wrinkles. What is clear, however, is that unskilled practitioners are sometimes administering Botox in excessive amounts, so that even major celebrities in their late 30s and 40s can be seen at public events with frighteningly waxen, mummified foreheads. Actors who overuse Botox are forfeiting the mobile expressiveness necessary to portray character. We will probably never again see "great faces" among accomplished older women — the kind of severe, imperious, craggy look of formidable visionaries like Diana Vreeland or Lillian Hellman.[2]

---

2 **Diana Vreeland or Lillian Hellman:** Vreeland (1903–1989), the celebrated fashion editor of *Vogue* magazine, and Hellman (1905–1984), the well-known American playwright, were known for their strikingly craggy facial features. —EDS.

The urgent problem is that today's cosmetic surgeons are drawing from too limited a repertoire of images. Plastic surgery is an art form: Therefore, surgeons need training in art as well as medicine. Without a broader visual vocabulary, too many surgeons will continue to homogenize women, divesting them of authority and reducing them to a generic cookie-cutter sameness. And without a gift for psychology, surgeons cannot intuit and reinforce a woman's unique personality.

For cosmetic surgery to maintain or regain subtlety and nuance, surgeons should meditate on great painting and sculpture. And women themselves must draw the line against seeking and perpetuating an artificial juvenility that obliterates their own cultural value. ■

The Reader's Presence

1. How would you describe Paglia's attitude toward cosmetic surgery? What ethical issues does it raise for her? In what ways does cosmetic surgery affect Paglia's artistic sensibility? What distinction does she make between good surgery and bad surgery?

2. How does Paglia connect the popularity of cosmetic surgery today to the history of the American film industry? How did changes in the movie industry alter American notions of what is beautiful? According to Paglia, what are the sources of today's standards of attractiveness and how are they affecting cosmetic surgery? Do you find her analysis persuasive? Why or why not?

3. **CONNECTIONS:** Although both sexes may opt for cosmetic surgery, Camille Paglia focuses primarily on women and the idea of beauty. Compare Paglia's ideas on beauty with those of another essay on that subject, Alice Walker's "Beauty: When the Other Dancer Is the Self" (page 232). In what ways does Walker's essay challenge Paglia's assumptions about beauty? Which essay do you think best explores the concept of beauty? Why?

SABRINA VERCHOT
A Response to Camille Paglia's "The Pitfalls of Plastic Surgery"

Sabrina Verchot was a senior at Emerson College in Boston, working toward her BFA in writing, literature, and publishing. After graduating, in spring 2011, she took the summer off to work on writing projects, both fiction and nonfiction. She lives in Massachusetts.

Sabrina Verchot

In her essay, "The Pitfalls of Plastic Surgery," Camille Paglia explores the growing practice of cosmetic surgery and how it has both influenced and been influenced by American culture. She examines the idea that plastic surgery is simply a form of sculpture for Hollywood actresses who want their bodies to conform to the sexist ideal promoted by American media. She suggests that conformity to this ideal has also become the norm for many other Americans, and now plays a critical role in job retention as well as marriage retention. Although Paglia's argument is in many ways sensible, there are a few points I take issue with, such as the idea that Hollywood has perpetuated a sexist ideal of women through plastic surgery.

Plastic surgery was indeed made popular by Hollywood. Most of the news coverage of plastic surgery typically involves Hollywood actresses, particularly those who have undergone extreme cosmetic surgery or who have had multiple operations. Paglia is certainly right about that detail. Even so, in the past few years, Hollywood has not encouraged surgically enhanced sexist images. In fact, casting directors have gone in the opposite direction and some refuse to cast anyone who looks as though she has been transformed by plastic surgery. For example, the casting director of *Pirates of the Caribbean 4*, now underway, specifically requested auditions from those with "natural-looking breasts only" (Fagen). Clearly, there has been a distinct switch in Hollywood thinking when it comes to surgical enhancement and the media's vision of the ideal woman.

Paglia states that "plastic surgery is living sculpture" [paragraph 1]. She is literally correct. The word *plastic* comes from the Greek *Plastikos*, to make or form, so even the very root of the word suggests that to opt for plastic surgery is to be *formed* into something other than what you are. However, that does not necessarily mean that if you elect such surgery you will automatically become a carbon copy of everyone else who has done the same. Paglia complains that plastic surgeons "homogenize women, divesting them of authority and reducing them to a generic cookie-cutter sameness" [paragraph 12]. But the process of plastic surgery actually takes place over a number of different medical sessions to make sure that the person undergoing surgery will receive the expected results, not some generic face or body that the surgeon has pre-selected for all of his or her patients.

There are women in Hollywood who undergo massive amounts of surgery to achieve the "perfect body," the homogenized version of a woman Paglia talks about. But most of those women are actually addicted to plastic surgery and have body dysmorphic disorder, which causes them to see their own bodies as unappealing. They might see themselves as fat even if they are thin, and they'll pick up on the tiniest imperfection and feel that they have to fix it. Michael Jackson is the most well-known case of body dysmorphic disorder in Hollywood, but Kelly Osbourne is another case, and there is quite a bit of debate over whether Heidi Montag has the disease, considering her recent venture into plastic surgery in which she had ten operations done in one day (Goldman).

By introducing the example of Michael Jackson she suggests the issue isn't only about women.

Although some patients, particularly those with body dysmorphic disorder, may want to be the "perfect" woman, displaying—as Paglia observes — "large breasts with a flat midriff and lean hips" [paragraph 9], that certainly isn't every woman's ideal. Some simply want to soften harsh features or even out bodily proportions. Not to mention that there are—usually to the surprise of many men—women unhappy with large breasts who willingly undergo breast-reduction surgery. Not all women want implants. Even Hollywood seems to be getting the idea that women do not require oversized breasts to be sexually appealing. Drew Barrymore, Queen Latifah, and Kelly Osbourne have all either openly discussed the idea of having breast-reduction surgery or are planning to undergo the surgery, and not just for the cosmetic reasons Paglia seems to focus on when she criticizes plastic surgery (Stewart). Reducing breast size can actually be medically beneficial for some women and can eliminate back pain and headaches (Ray). Additionally, studies have suggested that breast-reduction surgery can reduce the risk of breast cancer, especially in women over the age of fifty (Hage).

Cites two medical studies that claim plastic surgery can be beneficial.

Medically, a huge number of benefits can result from successful plastic surgery, and each of these benefits is particular to the patient and the problem he or she would like to remedy. Plastic surgery isn't confined to Hollywood, as Paglia notes, but it is also not confined to the "corporate workplace" for "job retention and advancement in high-profile careers" [paragraph 2]. Plastic surgery is practiced in hospitals all over the world on normal, everyday

Points out
how plastic
surgery is
used routinely
in hospitals
and cites a
particular case.

people who need a life-changing procedure. In Boston, just a few years ago, James Maki fell onto the subway tracks. Half of his face was burnt off, his nose was completely gone, his upper lips and cheeks were missing. He survived miraculously, but once he was out of the hospital he wouldn't leave his house for fear of how neighbors would react. In 2009, he returned to Brigham and Women's Hospital in Boston for plastic surgery to reconstruct his face. The procedure was a success and dramatically changed his life for the better. The surgery gave him a life outside of the confines of his home (Kowalczyk).

Though Paglia is certainly right on many counts, there is clearly much more to plastic surgery than its "pitfalls." When examining the costs and benefits of cosmetic surgery we must look carefully at the whole picture. That picture includes not just how plastic surgery perpetuates the media's version of a "perfect body" but also how it can give hope to all the people in hospitals today desperately looking for a better life.

Concludes
by conceding
Paglia is
"right on
many counts"
but that her
argument
overlooks
the many
advantages of
plastic surgery.

WORKS CITED

Fagen, Cynthia R. "Disney Wants Women with Natural Breasts for New 'Pirate' Movie." *New York Post,* 21 Mar. 2010, nypost.com/2010/03/21/disney-wants-women-with-natural-breasts-for-new-pirates-movie/.

Goldman, Leslie. "Celebs and Body Dysmorphic Disorder." *Today,* NBC, 1 Mar. 2010, www.today.com.

Hage, Joris J., and Refaat B. Karim. "Risk of Breast Cancer among Reduction Mammaplasty Patients and the Strategies Used by Plastic Surgeons to Detect Such Cancer." *Plastic and Reconstructive Surgery,* vol. 117, no. 3, Mar. 2006, pp. 727–35.

Kowalczyk, Liz. "His Tragic Accident behind Him, New England's First Face Transplant Patient Tells of an Arduous Journey and a Life Renewed." *The Boston Globe,* 21 May 2009, archive.boston.com/news/local/massachusetts/articles/2009/05/21/his_tragic_accident_behind_him_new_englands_first_face_transplant_patient_tells_of_an_arduous_journey_and_a_life_renewed/.

Paglia, Camille. "The Pitfalls of Plastic surgery." *The Writer's Presence: A Pool of Readings,* edited by Robert Atwan and Donald McQuade, 9th ed., Bedford/St. Martin's, 2018, pp. 691–94.

Ray, Lynn. "Breast Reduction May Be Covered by Your Insurance Plan." *Examiner.com,* AXS Digital Group, 6 Aug. 2010, www.examiner.com/article/breast-reduction-may-be-covered-by-your-insurance-plan.

Stewart, Colin. "Smaller Breasts Are in Style." *Orange County Register,* 8 Sept. 2009, www.ocregister.com/articles/implants-28547-breast-women.html.

Steven Pinker

VIOLENCE VANQUISHED

STEVEN PINKER (b. 1954) is an author, a psychologist, a linguist, and a Harvard professor. He was born in Montreal, Quebec, Canada, and received his PhD in experimental psychology from Harvard University in 1979. He taught at the Massachusetts Institute of Technology and Stanford University before returning to Harvard in 2008. He is well known for his belief that the mind is an information-processing system, much like a computer, and that thinking is, therefore, a kind of computation. This theory, called "computational theory of mind," informs much of his work and celebrity. He is also a proponent of evolutionary psychology, which presumes that many of our psychological traits—such as the ability to deduce

> **"All our behaviors are a result of neurophysiological activity in the brain."**

the emotions of others, cooperate, and recognize our relatives—are, in fact, adaptations that helped human beings survive in our ancestral environments. Pinker has argued specifically that language is the result of natural selection.

He is the author of numerous books, including *The Language Instinct* (1994), *How the Mind Works* (1997), *The Blank Slate* (2002), *The Better Angels of Our Nature* (2011), and *The Sense of Style: The Thinking Person's Guide to Writing in the 21st Century* (2014), to name just a few. He is the chair of the usage panel of *The American Heritage Dictionary* and has received numerous prizes for his writing, including the Los Angeles Times Science Book Prize and the William James Book Prize, which he has had the distinguished honor of winning three times. He has also received a number of awards for his scientific research, notably the Troland Research Award from the National Academy of Sciences and the Henry Dale Prize from the Royal Institution of Great Britain. He was the Humanist of the Year in 2006 and the recipient of the Innovations for Humanity Award from La Ciudad de las Ideas in Mexico in 2008. He was named one of the 100 most influential scientists and thinkers in the world by *Time* magazine in 2008. In line with his ideas regarding evolutionary psychology and computational theory of mind, he has said, "All our behaviors are a result of neurophysiological activity in the brain." The following article, "Violence Vanquished," originally appeared in the *Wall Street Journal* in September 2011.

ON THE DAY THIS ARTICLE APPEARS, you will read about a shocking act of violence. Somewhere in the world there will be a terrorist bombing, a senseless murder, a bloody insurrection. It's impossible to learn about these catastrophes without thinking, "What is the world coming to?"

But a better question may be, "How bad was the world in the past?"

Believe it or not, the world of the past was *much* worse. Violence has been in decline for thousands of years, and today we may be living in the most peaceable era in the existence of our species.

The decline, to be sure, has not been smooth. It has not brought violence down to zero, and it is not guaranteed to continue. But it is a persistent historical development, visible on scales from millennia to years, from the waging of wars to the spanking of children.

This claim, I know, invites skepticism, incredulity, and sometimes anger.   5 We tend to estimate the probability of an event from the ease with which we can recall examples, and scenes of carnage are more likely to be beamed into our homes and burned into our memories than footage of people dying of old age. There will always be enough violent deaths to fill the evening news, so people's impressions of violence will be disconnected from its actual likelihood.

Evidence of our bloody history is not hard to find. Consider the genocides in the Old Testament and the crucifixions in the New, the gory mutilations in Shakespeare's tragedies and Grimm's fairy tales, the British monarchs who beheaded their relatives, and the American founders who dueled with their rivals.

Today the decline in these brutal practices can be quantified. A look at the numbers shows that over the course of our history, humankind has been blessed with six major declines of violence.

The first was a process of pacification: the transition from the anarchy of the hunting, gathering, and horticultural societies in which our species spent most of its evolutionary history to the first agricultural civilizations, with cities and governments, starting about 5,000 years ago.

For centuries, social theorists like Hobbes and Rousseau speculated from their armchairs about what life was like in a "state of nature." Nowadays we can do better. Forensic archeology—a kind of "CSI: Paleolithic"—can estimate rates of violence from the proportion of skeletons in ancient sites with bashed-in skulls, decapitations, or arrowheads embedded in bones. And ethnographers can tally the causes of death in tribal peoples that have recently lived outside of state control.

These investigations show that, on average, about 15% of people in   10 prestate eras died violently, compared to about 3% of the citizens of the earliest states. Tribal violence commonly subsides when a state or empire imposes control over a territory, leading to the various "paxes" (Romana, Islamica, Brittanica, and so on) that are familiar to readers of history.

It's not that the first kings had a benevolent interest in the welfare of their citizens. Just as a farmer tries to prevent his livestock from killing one another, so a ruler will try to keep his subjects from cycles of raiding and feuding. From his point of view, such squabbling is a dead loss— forgone opportunities to extract taxes, tributes, soldiers, and slaves.

The second decline of violence was a civilizing process that is best documented in Europe. Historical records show that between the late Middle

Ages and the 20th century, European countries saw a 10- to 50-fold decline in their rates of homicide.

The numbers are consistent with narrative histories of the brutality of life in the Middle Ages, when highwaymen made travel a risk to life and limb and dinners were commonly enlivened by dagger attacks. So many people had their noses cut off that medieval medical textbooks speculated about techniques for growing them back.

Historians attribute this decline to the consolidation of a patchwork of feudal territories into large kingdoms with centralized authority and an infrastructure of commerce. Criminal justice was nationalized, and zero-sum plunder gave way to positive-sum trade. People increasingly controlled their impulses and sought to cooperate with their neighbors.

The third transition, sometimes called the Humanitarian Revolution, took off with the Enlightenment. Governments and churches had long maintained order by punishing nonconformists with mutilation, torture, and gruesome forms of execution, such as burning, breaking, disembowelment, impalement, and sawing in half. The 18th century saw the widespread abolition of judicial torture, including the famous prohibition of "cruel and unusual punishment" in the eighth Amendment of the U.S. Constitution. 15

At the same time, many nations began to whittle down their list of capital crimes from the hundreds (including poaching, sodomy, witchcraft, and counterfeiting) to just murder and treason. And a growing wave of countries abolished blood sports, dueling, witch hunts, religious persecution, absolute despotism, and slavery.

The fourth major transition is the respite from major interstate war that we have seen since the end of World War II. Historians sometimes refer to it as the Long Peace.

Today we take it for granted that Italy and Austria will not come to blows, nor will Britain and Russia. But centuries ago, the great powers were almost

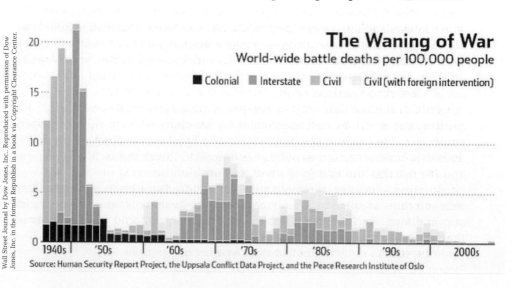

The Waning of War
World-wide battle deaths per 100,000 people

■ Colonial ■ Interstate ■ Civil Civil (with foreign intervention)

1940s   '50s   '60s   '70s   '80s   '90s   2000s

Source: Human Security Report Project, the Uppsala Conflict Data Project, and the Peace Research Institute of Oslo

Wall Street Journal by Dow Jones, Inc. Reproduced with permission of Dow Jones, Inc. in the format Republish in a book via Copyright Clearance Center.

always at war, and until quite recently, Western European countries tended to initiate two or three new wars every year. The cliché that the 20th century was "the most violent in history" ignores the second half of the century (and may not even be true of the first half, if one calculates violent deaths as a proportion of the world's population).

Though it's tempting to attribute the Long Peace to nuclear deterrence, non-nuclear developed states have stopped fighting each other as well. Political scientists point instead to the growth of democracy, trade, and international organizations—all of which, the statistical evidence shows, reduce the likelihood of conflict. They also credit the rising valuation of human life over national grandeur—a hard-won lesson of two world wars.

The fifth trend, which I call the New Peace, involves war in the world   20
as a whole, including developing nations. Since 1946, several organizations have tracked the number of armed conflicts and their human toll world-wide. The bad news is that for several decades, the decline of interstate wars was accompanied by a bulge of civil wars, as newly independent countries were led by inept governments, challenged by insurgencies, and armed by the cold war superpowers.

The less bad news is that civil wars tend to kill far fewer people than wars between states. And the best news is that, since the peak of the cold war in the 1970s and '80s, organized conflicts of all kinds—civil wars, genocides, repression by autocratic governments, terrorist attacks—have declined throughout the world, and their death tolls have declined even more precipitously.

The rate of documented direct deaths from political violence (war, terrorism, genocide, and warlord militias) in the past decade is an unprecedented few hundredths of a percentage point. Even if we multiplied that rate to account for unrecorded deaths and the victims of war-caused disease and famine, it would not exceed 1%.

The most immediate cause of this New Peace was the demise of communism, which ended the proxy wars in the developing world stoked by the superpowers and also discredited genocidal ideologies that had justified the sacrifice of vast numbers of eggs to make a utopian omelet. Another contributor was the expansion of international peacekeeping forces, which really do keep the peace—not always, but far more often than when adversaries are left to fight to the bitter end.

Finally, the postwar era has seen a cascade of "rights revolutions"—a growing revulsion against aggression on smaller scales. In the developed world, the civil rights movement obliterated lynchings and lethal pogroms, and the women's-rights movement has helped to shrink the incidence of rape and the beating and killing of wives and girlfriends.

In recent decades, the movement for children's rights has significantly   25
reduced rates of spanking, bullying, paddling in schools, and physical and sexual abuse. And the campaign for gay rights has forced governments in the developed world to repeal laws criminalizing homosexuality and has had some success in reducing hate crimes against gay people.

Why has violence declined so dramatically for so long? Is it because violence has literally been bred out of us, leaving us more peaceful by nature?

This seems unlikely. Evolution has a speed limit measured in generations, and many of these declines have unfolded over decades or even years. Toddlers continue to kick, bite, and hit; little boys continue to play-fight; people of all ages continue to snipe and bicker, and most of them continue to harbor violent fantasies and to enjoy violent entertainment.

It's more likely that human nature has always comprised inclinations toward violence and inclinations that counteract them — such as self-control, empathy, fairness, and reason — what Abraham Lincoln called "the better angels of our nature." Violence has declined because historical circumstances have increasingly favored our better angels.

The most obvious of these pacifying forces has been the state, with its monopoly on the legitimate use of force. A disinterested judiciary and police can defuse the temptation of exploitative attack, inhibit the impulse for revenge, and circumvent the self-serving biases that make all parties to a dispute believe that they are on the side of the angels.

We see evidence of the pacifying effects of government in the way that   30 rates of killing declined following the expansion and consolidation of states in tribal societies and in medieval Europe. And we can watch the movie in reverse when violence erupts in zones of anarchy, such as the Wild West, failed states, and neighborhoods controlled by mafias and street gangs, who can't call 911 or file a lawsuit to resolve their disputes but have to administer their own rough justice.

Another pacifying force has been commerce, a game in which everybody can win. As technological progress allows the exchange of goods and ideas over longer distances and among larger groups of trading partners, other people become more valuable alive than dead. They switch from being targets of demonization and dehumanization to potential partners in reciprocal altruism.

For example, though the relationship today between America and China is far from warm, we are unlikely to declare war on them or vice versa. Morality aside, they make too much of our stuff, and we owe them too much money.

A third peacemaker has been cosmopolitanism — the expansion of people's parochial little worlds through literacy, mobility, education, science, history, journalism, and mass media. These forms of virtual reality can prompt people to take the perspective of people unlike themselves and to expand their circle of sympathy to embrace them.

These technologies have also powered an expansion of rationality and objectivity in human affairs. People are now less likely to privilege their own interests over those of others. They reflect more on the way they live and consider how they could be better off. Violence is often reframed as a problem to be solved rather than as a contest to be won. We devote ever more of our brainpower to guiding our better angels. It is probably no coincidence that the Humanitarian Revolution came on the heels of the Age of Reason and the

Enlightenment, that the Long Peace and rights revolutions coincided with the electronic global village.

Whatever its causes, the implications of the historical decline of violence   35
are profound. So much depends on whether we see our era as a nightmare of crime, terrorism, genocide, and war or as a period that, in the light of the historical and statistical facts, is blessed by unprecedented levels of peaceful coexistence.

Bearers of good news are often advised to keep their mouths shut, lest they lull people into complacency. But this prescription may be backward. The discovery that fewer people are victims of violence can thwart cynicism among compassion-fatigued news readers who might otherwise think that the dangerous parts of the world are irredeemable hell holes. And a better understanding of what drove the numbers down can steer us toward doing things that make people better off rather than congratulating ourselves on how moral we are.

As one becomes aware of the historical decline of violence, the world begins to look different. The past seems less innocent, the present less sinister. One starts to appreciate the small gifts of coexistence that would have seemed utopian to our ancestors: the interracial family playing in the park, the comedian who lands a zinger on the commander in chief, the countries that quietly back away from a crisis instead of escalating to war.

For all the tribulations in our lives, for all the troubles that remain in the world, the decline of violence is an accomplishment that we can savor—and an impetus to cherish the forces of civilization and enlightenment that made it possible. ●

The Reader's Presence

1. Summarize the points that inform Pinker's claim that "[v]iolence has been in decline for thousands of years" (paragraph 3). What does Pinker identify as one of the earliest lifestyle changes that led to a more-peaceful coexistence? What kinds of past violence does he focus on, and how does he use this information to build his case? Pinker recognizes that his argument is often met with "skepticism, incredulity, and sometimes anger" (paragraph 5). Why do you think his claim provokes such strong reactions? What was your reaction to reading paragraph 3? How is—or isn't—your reaction consistent with Pinker's argument about the incessant coverage of violence in the media?

2. What reasons does Pinker provide for humankind's historical "process of pacification" (paragraph 8)? Although violence is declining, as Pinker writes, how do you explain our cultural fascination with violence throughout history, including "the Old Testament and the crucifixions in the New, the gory mutilations in Shakespeare's tragedies and Grimm's fairy tales, [and] the British monarchs who beheaded their relatives and the American founders who dueled with their rivals" (paragraph 6)? Pinker discusses other factors in the "declines of violence" (paragraph 7). What important areas might he have overlooked? What correlation, if any, can you establish between the decline of violence and the prevalence of violence in the arts?

3. Trade and commerce play an important role in Pinker's argument about the historical decline of violence; violence is, he observes, "a dead loss—forgone opportunities to extract taxes" (paragraph 11), and "people become more valuable alive than dead" (paragraph 31). To what extent can this assertion be viewed as a form of "reciprocal altruism" (paragraph 31)? To what extent do you find the reliance on money for peace to be troubling? What sorts of issues surface when people view each other in monetary terms?

4. **CONNECTIONS:** Consider the substance of Pinker's points about viewing people in monetary terms, and then compare and contrast these points with Andre Dubus III's treatment of similar issues in "The Land of No: Love in a Class-riven America" (page 83). Which writer's view of the relationship between identity and money do you find most convincing? Explain why. Support your response by analyzing specific passages from each text in detail.

Student Essay

JACOB EWING
Steven Pinker and the Question of Violence

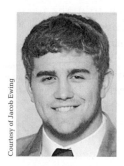

Courtesy of Jacob Ewing

At the time he wrote "Steven Pinker and the Question of Violence," Jacob Ewing was a junior at Ashland University in Ohio, where he majored in English and Spanish. In preparing to write, Ewing admits he thought Pinker's tone had "an air of finality, as though no arguments could be made to the contrary. I wanted to ask a few more questions before we closed the discussion."

His essay was in response to the following assignment:

Steven Pinker's book *The Better Angels of Our Nature: Why Violence Has Declined* has provoked a great deal of discussion. After reading carefully the essay, "Violence Vanquished," adapted from the book by the *Wall Street Journal*, join the controversy by writing a response to Pinker in which you confirm and/or challenge some of his findings and conclusions. Be sure to select several specific claims that Pinker makes and systematically point out their merits or weaknesses. You may bring in additional readings to support your own.

In his essay "Violence Vanquished," which appeared in the *Wall Street Journal* (September 24, 2011), the Harvard Professor of Psychology, Steven Pinker, claims that the modern era is the most peaceful time in the history of the human species. He says that now more than ever before, we are less likely to die a violent death at the hands of another

Opens his essay by citing the specific publication he is responding to and then summarizing Pinker's central claim.

human being. He cites statistics that show how violence of all kinds—murder, war, genocide, and so on—have decreased across the board.

Pinker is aware that this fact seems not only unlikely but blatantly wrong, especially in light of the seemingly end-less acts of violence that characterize so much of today's news. Yet, despite the horrors in Darfur, Syria, and Iraq and in virtually every major American city, Pinker is likely right in his general claim that violence is diminishing across the globe. It would be hard to argue with his statistics that prove that violence among human beings is at its lowest point in history.

But there are still some major issues to consider when evaluating Pinker's position. For instance, what exactly constitutes violence in this argument? It would first be help-ful to analyze the author's definition. Throughout the piece, he discusses violence in terms of how likely one is to die at the hands of another human being. This is a convenient statistic, especially for an argument as numbers-driven as Pinker's, but violence extends well beyond just murder or warfare. Rape, assault, bullying—these are all ways in which human beings act violent toward one another, yet none of these phenomena are mentioned in his article.

There are still other types of violence that permeate soci-ety. Most young boys have, at a certain point in their child-hood, gotten into a wrestling match or a fist fight, often with someone very close to them—a brother, a cousin, a best friend. Now, this type of violence is not on par with murder, but it is certainly an aspect of our society that goes unmen-tioned by Pinker's analysis. Violence manifests itself in modern society in a variety of ways, many of which Pinker ignores and some of which are not extreme enough to even be on his radar.

In the latter half of the article, Pinker attempts to deter-mine what exactly has caused the decline in violence he has described. He appeals first to modern governments, saying, "The most obvious of these pacifying forces has been the state, with its monopoly on the legitimate use of force." Here again, Pinker's point is not as simple as it appears. The state's ability to monopolize the use of force has absolutely helped quell vig-ilante justice and personal vendettas, but it has also created a potential for violence that is absolutely unprecedented.

Concedes that Pinker's statistics are probably correct, so will not argue with that aspect of the essay.

Shows various ways we can define violence that Pinker ignores.

Indeed, one could assume that at this moment, several of the world's major powers have the ability to launch a nuclear attack with weapons far more powerful than those used on Japan at the end of the Second World War, when a single plane dropping one atomic bomb over Hiroshima left over 100,000 human beings dead. The number of deaths that could result in a nuclear attack today is unthinkable. With modern weapons that absolutely dwarf the original atomic bomb, and with so many states having access to such weapons, Pinker's assertion that the state has brought about an alleviation of violence becomes less evident. He would be quick to point out that such an attack has not happened; it might be better to say that such an attack has not happened yet. As Robert Jervis says in his article "Pinker the Prophet," "If we think we're playing Russian roulette, then the fact that we were lucky does not count quite so strongly for our living in a less violent time."[1]

> *Reinforces his point about state violence by citing supporting view.*

Pinker also cites the global market as a source for this newfound peace. He points out how unlikely it is for a war to break out between the United States and China because "they make too much of our stuff, and we owe them too much money." But the fallacy of this point comes a paragraph earlier, when Pinker describes commerce as "a game in which everybody can win." This sentiment holds true when considering two nations like the United States and China—strong centralized governments, stable economies, freedom from internal conflict. This allows trade to occur between these two nations in a peaceful, mutually-beneficial manner.

> *Supplies example of diamond trade violence to counter Pinker's point about global commerce.*

But what about countries that aren't fortunate enough to be a world power? What about countries where the extraction of precious natural resources has resulted in some of the most gruesome violence of the twentieth century? One only need analyze the history of the diamond trade in Africa to realize the type of violence that can come as a direct result of commerce. Diamonds are a precious commodity, and any opportunity to make money in a place like Sierra Leone is likely to end in violence. Even more recently, the mining of coltan—a mineral used in most cell phones and laptops—has been the source for violence in the Democratic Republic of Congo. In these cases, commerce and trade have actually created violence—not alleviated it.

---

[1] *The National Interest*, Issue 116, Nov./Dec. 2011, p. 57.—EDS.

Confronts Pinker's point about the Enlightenment with counterexamples of today's violence.

Pinker is constantly alluding to the Enlightenment as another source for what he calls "the most peaceable era in the existence of our species." It would be hard to argue that the Enlightenment didn't at least help people realize that killing one another may not be the best thing to do. That seems obvious now. But what about people who are raised in our enlightened society, taught about playing nice and the sanctity of life and the golden rule, yet still kill people? The list of school-shootings over the past twenty years is already terrifying and growing by the year. These acts are carried out by people who are presumably enlightened, products of our education system, who have had the opportunity to learn how important and beautiful and sacred life is; yet the shootings still happen.

Pinker is quick to mention how "about 15% of people in prestate eras died violently," but fails to mention that the populations of these societies were savages by contemporary standards. Death happened at a much higher rate, but these people were wholly unable to comprehend the philosophical implications of the deaths they were causing. It was their way of life, and they didn't have the advanced knowledge to consider that life might be lived some other way. The same cannot be said about modern day murderers. If our society is truly as enlightened as Pinker likes to think it is — as we all like to think it is — then the fact that so many people still function outside of the collective societal reasoning, the fact that murders happen every day, should be far more shocking than the fact unenlightened savages killed one another at a higher rate than we do today.

Pinker's assertion that violence is in consistent decline is both intriguing and inspiring, but is not as solid as it appears on the surface. To his credit, Pinker readily concedes that violence still has an enormous presence in human society. But the way in which he measures violence — human death caused by another human being — is not necessarily the full story on the matter. Furthermore, his desire to appeal to state power, global commerce, and the modern enlightened mind all have some important implications, as noted above, to which his article does not do justice.

Summarizes his objections to the way Pinker "measures" violence.

The final claim that Pinker never addresses is an omission for which no one could blame him. One of the most frequent instances of violence over the past decade has been natural disasters—earthquakes, tsunamis, hurricanes, and so on. The amount of human life lost as a result is enormous, yes, but it wouldn't have anything to do with an assessment like Pinker's. Or would it? If one day, the world of science comes to discover that these patterns in extreme weather were caused by human beings, by the way modern society functions, is Pinker's argument changed at all? Are we considerably more violent if that is the case, even if it is unintentional? This is undoubtedly speculative, but if Pinker's project is to consider how violence works on the macro-level, it might not be a bad idea to at least consider the possibility that human beings kill one another in more ways than we realize.

> Instead of concluding with a summary, he effectively introduces a new question about violence and human responsibility that Pinker never addresses.

Michael J. Sandel

WHAT ISN'T FOR SALE?

MICHAEL J. SANDEL (b. 1953) is the Anne T. and Robert M. Bass Professor of Government at Harvard University, where he has taught political philosophy since 1980. He is well known for his "Justice" course, which has over the past two decades become one of the most widely attended courses offered by the renowned university. It was recorded in the fall semester of 2005 and condensed into a twelve-hour mini-series for WGBH public television. The series has been broadcast around the world and is particularly popular in Japan, where the companion book, *Justice: What's the Right Thing to Do?* (2009), became a best-seller. Sandel's course is also offered through edX, the non-profit collection of free Internet courses (or MOOCs—Massive Open Online Courses) from major universities. In 2012, Sandel published *What Money Can't Buy: The Moral Limits of Markets*. "What Isn't for Sale?" follows a similar theme as this most recent book and was originally published in *The Atlantic* in 2012.

> "The responsibility of political philosophy that tries to engage with practice is to be clear, or at least accessible—clear enough that its arguments and concerns can be accessible to a nonacademic public."

Sandel is known for being an excellent lecturer, drawing on clear examples from everyday life to make his arguments. He has said that "the responsibility of political philosophy that tries to engage with practice is to be clear, or at least accessible—clear enough that its arguments and concerns can be accessible to a nonacademic public. Otherwise, it's not possible really for political philosophers to generate debate that could possibly challenge existing understandings."

THERE ARE SOME THINGS money can't buy—but these days, not many. Almost everything is up for sale. For example:

- **A prison-cell upgrade: $90 a night.** In Santa Ana, California, and some other cities, nonviolent offenders can pay for a clean, quiet jail cell, without any non-paying prisoners to disturb them.

- **Access to the carpool lane while driving solo: $8.** Minneapolis, San Diego, Houston, Seattle, and other cities have sought to ease traffic congestion by letting solo drivers pay to drive in carpool lanes, at rates that vary according to traffic.

- **The services of an Indian surrogate mother: $8,000.** Western couples seeking surrogates increasingly outsource the job to India, and the price is less than one-third the going rate in the United States.

- **The right to shoot an endangered black rhino: $250,000.** South Africa has begun letting some ranchers sell hunters the right to kill a limited number of rhinos, to give the ranchers an incentive to raise and protect the endangered species.

- **Your doctor's cellphone number: $1,500 and up per year.** A growing number of "concierge" doctors offer cellphone access and same-day appointments for patients willing to pay annual fees ranging from $1,500 to $25,000.

- **The right to emit a metric ton of carbon dioxide into the atmosphere: $10.50.** The European Union runs a carbon-dioxide-emissions market that enables companies to buy and sell the right to pollute.

- **The right to immigrate to the United States: $500,000.** Foreigners who invest $500,000 and create at least 10 full-time jobs in an area of high unemployment are eligible for a green card that entitles them to permanent residency.

Not everyone can afford to buy these things. But today there are lots of new ways to make money. If you need to earn some extra cash, here are some novel possibilities:

- **Sell space on your forehead to display commercial advertising: $10,000.** A single mother in Utah who needed money for her son's education was paid $10,000 by an online casino to install a permanent tattoo of the casino's Web address on her forehead. Temporary tattoo ads earn less.

- **Serve as a human guinea pig in a drug-safety trial for a pharmaceutical company: $7,500.** The pay can be higher or lower, depending on the invasiveness of the procedure used to test the drug's effect and the discomfort involved.

- **Fight in Somalia or Afghanistan for a private military contractor: up to $1,000 a day.** The pay varies according to qualifications, experience, and nationality.

- **Stand in line overnight on Capitol Hill to hold a place for a lobbyist who wants to attend a congressional hearing: $15–$20 an hour.** Lobbyists pay line-standing companies, who hire homeless people and others to queue up.

- **If you are a second-grader in an underachieving Dallas school, read a book: $2.** To encourage reading, schools pay kids for each book they read.

We live in a time when almost everything can be bought and sold. Over the past three decades, markets—and market values—have come to govern our lives as never before. We did not arrive at this condition through any deliberate choice. It is almost as if it came upon us.

As the Cold War ended, markets and market thinking enjoyed unrivaled prestige, and understandably so. No other mechanism for organizing the production and distribution of goods had proved as successful at generating affluence and prosperity. And yet even as growing numbers of countries around the world embraced market mechanisms in the operation of their economies, something else was happening. Market values were coming to play a greater and greater role in social life. Economics was becoming an imperial domain. Today, the logic of buying and selling no longer applies to material goods alone. It increasingly governs the whole of life.

The years leading up to the financial crisis of 2008 were a heady time 5 of market faith and deregulation—an era of market triumphalism. The era began in the early 1980s, when Ronald Reagan and Margaret Thatcher proclaimed their conviction that markets, not government, held the key to prosperity and freedom. And it continued into the 1990s with the market-friendly liberalism of Bill Clinton and Tony Blair, who moderated but consolidated the faith that markets are the primary means for achieving the public good.

Today, that faith is in question. The financial crisis did more than cast doubt on the ability of markets to allocate risk efficiently. It also prompted a widespread sense that markets have become detached from morals, and that we need to somehow reconnect the two. But it's not obvious what this would mean, or how we should go about it.

Some say the moral failing at the heart of market triumphalism was greed, which led to irresponsible risk-taking. The solution, according to this view, is to rein in greed, insist on greater integrity and responsibility among bankers and Wall Street executives, and enact sensible regulations to prevent a similar crisis from happening again.

This is, at best, a partial diagnosis. While it is certainly true that greed played a role in the financial crisis, something bigger was and is at stake. The most fateful change that unfolded during the past three decades was not an increase in greed. It was the reach of markets, and of market values, into spheres of life traditionally governed by nonmarket norms. To contend with this condition, we need to do more than inveigh against greed; we need to have a public debate about where markets belong—and where they don't.

Consider, for example, the proliferation of for-profit schools, hospitals, and prisons, and the outsourcing of war to private military contractors. (In Iraq and Afghanistan, private contractors have actually outnumbered U.S. military troops.) Consider the eclipse of public police forces by private security firms—especially in the U.S. and the U.K., where the number of private guards is almost twice the number of public police officers.

Or consider the pharmaceutical companies' aggressive marketing of pre-   10 scription drugs directly to consumers, a practice now prevalent in the U.S. but prohibited in most other countries. (If you've ever seen the television commercials on the evening news, you could be forgiven for thinking that the greatest health crisis in the world is not malaria or river blindness or sleeping sickness but an epidemic of erectile dysfunction.)

Consider too the reach of commercial advertising into public schools, from buses to corridors to cafeterias; the sale of "naming rights" to parks and civic spaces; the blurred boundaries, within journalism, between news and advertising, likely to blur further as newspapers and magazines struggle to survive; the marketing of "designer" eggs and sperm for assisted reproduction; the buying and selling, by companies and countries, of the right to pollute; a system of campaign finance in the U.S. that comes close to permitting the buying and selling of elections.

These uses of markets to allocate health, education, public safety, national security, criminal justice, environmental protection, recreation, procreation, and other social goods were for the most part unheard-of 30 years ago. Today, we take them largely for granted.

Why worry that we are moving toward a society in which everything is up for sale?

For two reasons. One is about inequality, the other about corruption. First, consider inequality. In a society where everything is for sale, life is harder for those of modest means. The more money can buy, the more affluence—or the lack of it—matters. If the only advantage of affluence were the ability to afford yachts, sports cars, and fancy vacations, inequalities of income and wealth would matter less than they do today. But as money comes to buy more and more, the distribution of income and wealth looms larger.

The second reason we should hesitate to put everything up for sale is 15 more difficult to describe. It is not about inequality and fairness but about the corrosive tendency of markets. Putting a price on the good things in life can corrupt them. That's because markets don't only allocate goods; they express and promote certain attitudes toward the goods being exchanged. Paying kids to read books might get them to read more, but might also teach them to regard reading as a chore rather than a source of intrinsic satisfaction. Hiring foreign mercenaries to fight our wars might spare the lives of our citizens, but might also corrupt the meaning of citizenship.

Economists often assume that markets are inert, that they do not affect the goods being exchanged. But this is untrue. Markets leave their mark. Sometimes, market values crowd out nonmarket values worth caring about.

When we decide that certain goods may be bought and sold, we decide, at least implicitly, that it is appropriate to treat them as commodities, as instruments of profit and use. But not all goods are properly valued in this way. The most obvious example is human beings. Slavery was appalling because it treated human beings as a commodity, to be bought and sold at auction. Such treatment fails to value human beings as persons, worthy of dignity and respect; it sees them as instruments of gain and objects of use.

Something similar can be said of other cherished goods and practices. We don't allow children to be bought and sold, no matter how difficult the process of adoption can be or how willing impatient prospective parents might be. Even if the prospective buyers would treat the child responsibly, we worry that a market in children would express and promote the wrong way of valuing them. Children are properly regarded not as consumer goods but as beings worthy of love and care. Or consider the rights and obligations of citizenship. If you are called to jury duty, you can't hire a substitute to take your place. Nor do we allow citizens to sell their votes, even though others might be eager to buy them. Why not? Because we believe that civic duties are not private property but public responsibilities. To outsource them is to demean them, to value them in the wrong way.

These examples illustrate a broader point: some of the good things in life are degraded if turned into commodities. So to decide where the market belongs, and where it should be kept at a distance, we have to decide how to value the goods in question—health, education, family life, nature, art, civic duties, and so on. These are moral and political questions, not merely economic ones. To resolve them, we have to debate, case by case, the moral meaning of these goods, and the proper way of valuing them.

This is a debate we didn't have during the era of market triumphalism. 20 As a result, without quite realizing it—without ever deciding to do so—we drifted from having a market economy to being a market society.

The difference is this: A market economy is a tool—a valuable and effective tool—for organizing productive activity. A market society is a way of life in which market values seep into every aspect of human endeavor. It's a place where social relations are made over in the image of the market.

The great missing debate in contemporary politics is about the role and reach of markets. Do we want a market economy, or a market society? What role should markets play in public life and personal relations? How can we decide which goods should be bought and sold, and which should be governed by nonmarket values? Where should money's writ not run?

Even if you agree that we need to grapple with big questions about the morality of markets, you might doubt that our public discourse is up to the task. It's a legitimate worry. At a time when political argument consists mainly of shouting matches on cable television, partisan vitriol on talk radio, and ideological food fights on the floor of Congress, it's hard to imagine a reasoned public debate about such controversial moral questions as the right way to value procreation, children, education, health, the environment, citizenship, and other goods. I believe such a debate is possible, but only if we are willing to broaden the terms of our public discourse and grapple more explicitly with competing notions of the good life.

In hopes of avoiding sectarian strife, we often insist that citizens leave their moral and spiritual convictions behind when they enter the public square. But the reluctance to admit arguments about the good life into politics has had an unanticipated consequence. It has helped prepare the way for market triumphalism, and for the continuing hold of market reasoning.

In its own way, market reasoning also empties public life of moral argu-   25
ment. Part of the appeal of markets is that they don't pass judgment on the preferences they satisfy. They don't ask whether some ways of valuing goods are higher, or worthier, than others. If someone is willing to pay for sex, or a kidney, and a consenting adult is willing to sell, the only question the economist asks is "How much?" Markets don't wag fingers. They don't discriminate between worthy preferences and unworthy ones. Each party to a deal decides for him- or herself what value to place on the things being exchanged.

This nonjudgmental stance toward values lies at the heart of market reasoning, and explains much of its appeal. But our reluctance to engage in moral and spiritual argument, together with our embrace of markets, has exacted a heavy price: it has drained public discourse of moral and civic energy, and contributed to the technocratic, managerial politics afflicting many societies today.

A debate about the moral limits of markets would enable us to decide, as a society, where markets serve the public good and where they do not belong. Thinking through the appropriate place of markets requires that we reason together, in public, about the right way to value the social goods we prize. It would be folly to expect that a more morally robust public discourse, even at its best, would lead to agreement on every contested question. But it would make for a healthier public life. And it would make us more aware of the price we pay for living in a society where everything is up for sale. ■

The Reader's Presence

1. Sandel's essay revolves around his claim that market thinking so permeates contemporary life that we hardly notice it anymore. He further suggests that our market society has evolved as an unintentional progression: "[i]t is almost as if it came upon us" (paragraph 3). How does Sandel account for our evolving from a market economy to a market society in which everything is a commodity? Characterize the differences between a "market economy" and a "market society." What is "the price we pay for living in a society where everything is up for sale" (paragraph 27)? What is Sandel's view of the possibility of managing the reach of markets?

2. Explain what Sandel means by "the corrosive tendency of markets" (paragraph 15). To what extent do you think markets can answer the moral and political questions we face in society? What is your response to Sandel's observation that "market reasoning . . . empties public life of moral argument" (paragraph 25)? How does this relate to American society's "reluctance to engage in moral and spiritual argument" (paragraph 26)? What is your response to Sandel's argument encouraging citizens to "leave their moral and spiritual convictions behind when they enter the public square" (paragraph 24)? Near the end of his essay, Sandel claims that "[e]ven if you agree that we need to grapple with big questions about the morality of markets, you might doubt that our public discourse is up to the task" (paragraph 23). Explain why you agree—or disagree—with Sandel's point that public discourse has become ineffective. Draw on one of the three areas Sandel mentions—television, talk radio, and Congress—as the focus of your response.

3. **CONNECTIONS:** Compare Sandel's essay to Steven Pinker's "Violence Vanquished" (page 591), in which Pinker writes about the role of expanding international markets as a means to usher in a period of reduced violence never before seen in human history. How would Sandel respond to Pinker's claim that through markets "people become more valuable alive than dead" (paragraph 31)?

Barry Schwartz
THE TYRANNY OF CHOICE

Author and professor **BARRY SCHWARTZ** (b. 1946) has taught psychology and economics at Swarthmore College in Pennsylvania since receiving his PhD from the University
of Pennsylvania in 1971. He is currently the Dorwin Cartwright Professor of Social Theory
and Social Action, and his classes and seminars focus on the process of thinking and decision
making, the interaction of morality and self-interest, work satisfaction, and the intersection
of psychology and economics—all subjects
found in his many writings and books. In
addition to co-writing a number of textbooks
on the psychology of learning, memory,
and behaviorism, he has written *The Battle
for Human Nature: Science, Morality and
Modern Life* (1987), *The Costs of Living: How
Market Freedom Erodes the Best Things in
Life* (2000), and *The Paradox of Choice: Why
More Is Less* (2003), in which he explores how choice overload in the marketplace can lead to
anxiety and the inability to choose anything at all. *Why We Work* appeared in 2015. Schwartz
has written articles for numerous professional journals and mainstream periodicals, including
the *New York Times Magazine*, *USA Today*, *Scientific American*, and the *Chronicle of Higher
Education*, where his essay "The Tyranny of Choice" appeared in January 2004.

> Barry Schwartz's book, *The
> Paradox of Choice: Why More Is
> Less* (2003), explores how choice
> overload in the marketplace can
> lead to anxiety and the inability
> to choose anything at all.

THE MODERN UNIVERSITY has become a kind of intellectual shopping mall. Universities offer a wide array of different "goods" and allow,
even encourage, students—the "customers"— to shop around until they find
what they like. Individual customers are free to "purchase" whatever bundles
of knowledge they want, and the university provides whatever its customers
demand. In some rather prestigious institutions, this shopping-mall view has
been carried to an extreme. In the first few weeks of classes, students sample
the merchandise. They go to a class, stay 10 minutes to see what the professor
is like, then walk out, often in the middle of the professor's sentence, to try
another class. Students come and go in and out of classes just as browsers go
in and out of stores in a mall.

This explosion of choice in the university is a reflection of a pervasive
social trend. Americans are awash in choice, not only in the courses they take,
but also in the products they buy (300 kinds of cereal, 50 different cellphones,

thousands of mutual funds) and in virtually all aspects of life. Increasingly, people are free to choose when and how they will work, how they will worship, where they will live, and what they will look like (thanks to liposuction, Botox, and cosmetic surgery of every description), and what kind of romantic relationships they will have. Further, freedom of choice is greatly enhanced by increased affluence. In the last 40 years, the inflation-adjusted, per capita income of Americans has more than doubled. The proportion of homes with dishwashers has increased from 9 to 50 percent, with clothes dryers from 20 to 70 percent, and with air-conditioning from 15 to 73 percent. And of course, no one had cable TV, home computers, or the Internet in 1964. This increased affluence contributes to freedom of choice by giving people the means to act on their various goals and desires, whatever they may be.

Does increased affluence and increased choice mean we have more happy people? Not at all. Three recently published books—by the psychologist David Myers, the political scientist Robert E. Lane, and the journalist Gregg Easterbrook—point out how the growth of material affluence has not brought with it an increase in subjective well-being. Indeed, they argue that we are actually experiencing a *decrease* in well-being. In the last 30 years, the number of Americans describing themselves as "very happy" declined by 5 percent, which means that about 14 million fewer people report being very happy today than in 1974. And, as a recent study published in the *Journal of the American Medical Association* indicates, the rate of serious clinical depression has more than tripled over the last two generations, and increased by perhaps a factor of 10 from 1900 to 2000. Suicide rates are also up, not only in the United States, but in almost every developed country. And both serious depression and suicide are occurring among people younger than ever before. Deans at virtually every college and university in the United States can testify to this malaise, as they witness a demand for psychological services that they are unable to meet.

Why are people increasingly unhappy even as they experience greater material abundance and freedom of choice? Recent psychological research suggests that increased choice may itself be part of the problem.

It may seem implausible that there can be too much choice. As a matter   5
of logic, it would appear that adding options will make no one worse off and is bound to make someone better off. If you're content choosing among three different kinds of breakfast cereal, or six television stations, you can simply ignore the dozens or hundreds that get added to your supermarket shelves or cable provider's menu. Meanwhile, one of those new cereals or TV stations may be just what some other person was hoping for. Given the indisputable fact that choice is good for human well-being, it seems only logical that if some choice is good, more choice is better.

Logically true, yes. Psychologically true, no. My colleagues and I, along with other researchers, have begun amassing evidence—both in the laboratory and in the field—that increased choice can lead to *decreased* well-being. This is especially true for people we have termed "maximizers," people whose goal is to get the best possible result when they make decisions. Choice overload is also a problem for people we call "satisficers," people who seek only "good enough" results from their choices, but the problem is greatly magnified for maximizers. Much of the relevant research is summarized in my book, *The Paradox of Choice: Why More Is Less*. Here are some examples:

- Shoppers who confront a display of 30 jams or varieties of gourmet chocolate are less likely to purchase *any* than when they encounter a display of six.

- Students given 30 topics from which to choose to write an extra-credit essay are less likely to write one than those given six. And if they do write one, it tends to be of lower quality.

- The majority of medical patients do not want the decision authority that the canons of medical ethics have thrust upon them. Responsibility for medical decisions looks better to people in prospect than in actuality: Sixty-five percent of respondents say that if they were to get cancer, they would want to be in charge of treatment decisions, but among those who actually have cancer, only 12 percent want that control and responsibility.

- The more funds employers offer their employees in 401(k) retirement plans, the less likely the employees are to invest in any, even though in many cases, failing to do so costs them employer-matching funds of up to several thousand dollars a year.

- When maximizers, as opposed to satisficers, go shopping for big items or small ones, they spend more time looking, have a harder time deciding, look around more at what others are buying, and are less satisfied with their purchases.

- Maximizing college seniors send out more résumés, investigate more different fields, go on more job interviews, and get better, higher-paying jobs than satisficers. But they are less satisfied with their jobs, and are much more stressed, anxious, frustrated, and unhappy in the process.

These examples paint a common picture: Increasing options does not increase well-being, especially for maximizers, even when it enables choosers to do better by some objective standard. We have identified several processes that help explain why increased choice decreases satisfaction. Greater choice:

- Increases the burden of gathering information to make a wise decision.

- Increases the likelihood that people will regret the decisions they make.

- Increases the likelihood that people will *anticipate* regretting the decision they make, with the result that they can't make a decision at all.

- Increases the feeling of missed opportunities, as people encounter the attractive features of one option after another that they are rejecting.

- Increases expectations about how good the chosen option should be. Since assessments of the quality of a choice are almost always made relative to one's expectations, as expectations rise, actual choices have a rising standard to meet if they are to produce satisfaction.

- Increases the chances that people will blame themselves when their choices fail to live up to expectations. After all, with so many options out there, there is really no excuse for a disappointing choice.

To illustrate these last two points, I recall buying a bottle of wine to accompany dinner when I was vacationing with my family in a seaside cottage in a small town in Oregon. The tiny general store had about five options from which to choose. The wine I chose wasn't very good, but I didn't expect it to be, and I knew that I couldn't really have done much better. Contrast that with how it would feel to bring home a disappointing bottle of wine from a store that offered thousands of bottles from which to choose.

What are the implications of an abundance of choice for higher education today? College students don't have to worry about choosing 401(k) plans, and most of them don't have major health issues to make decisions about. Nonetheless, the world of the modern college student is so laden with choice, much of it extremely consequential, that for many, it has become overwhelming, perhaps contributing to the rush of students to university counseling services.

When I went to college, 35 years ago, there were almost two years' worth 10 of general-education requirements that all students had to complete. We had *some* choices among courses that met those requirements, but they were rather narrow. Almost every department had a single, introductory course that prepared the student for more advanced work in the field. You could be fairly certain, if you ran into a fellow student you didn't know, that the two of you would have at least a year's worth of courses in common to discuss. In the shopping mall that is the modern university, the chances that any two students have significant intellectual experiences in common are much reduced.

About 30 years ago, somewhat dismayed that their students no longer shared enough common intellectual experiences, the Harvard faculty revised its general-education requirements to form a "core curriculum." With this new curriculum (which is currently undergoing another revision), students take at least one course in each of 11 different broad areas of inquiry. But among those areas, there are dozens and dozens of courses from which to choose. What are the odds that two random students will have courses in common to discuss?

At the advanced end of the curriculum, Harvard offers about 40 majors. For students with interdisciplinary interests, these can be combined into an almost endless array of joint majors. If that doesn't do the trick, students can create their own degree plan. And within majors, at least many of them, internal structure has largely disappeared. Students can begin almost anywhere in the curriculum and end almost anywhere.

Harvard is not unusual. Princeton offers its students a choice of several hundred courses from which to satisfy its general-education requirements. Stanford, which has a larger student body, offers even more. Even at my small college, Swarthmore, with only 1,350 students, we offer about 120 courses to meet our version of the general-education requirement, from which students must select nine. And don't think that this range of choices is peculiar to elite, private institutions. At Pennsylvania State University, for example, liberal-arts students can choose from more than 40 majors and from hundreds of courses intended to meet basic requirements.

Within classes, the digital revolution has made access to information unbelievably easy. The Internet and the "digital library" can be a term-paper writer's blessing. But they can also be a curse. With so much information so readily available, when do you stop looking? There is no excuse for failing to examine all of it.

And outside the classroom, the range of recreational and extracurricular   15
activities afforded to students has become mind-boggling. As elite universities compete with one another for elite students (an example of social waste that I think rivals the SUV), the institutions engage in an arms race of amenity provision—fitness centers, indoor rock-climbing walls, hot tubs that accommodate dozens of people at once, espresso bars—in their effort to attract every student they want. The result is a set of choices of things to do outside of class that makes one's head spin.

There are many benefits to expanded educational opportunities. The traditional bodies of knowledge transmitted from teachers to students in the past were constraining and often myopic. The tastes and interests of the idiosyncratic students often were stifled and frustrated. In the modern university, each individual student is free to pursue almost any interest, without having to be harnessed to what his intellectual ancestors thought was worth knowing. Moreover, the advent of the digital age has opened up the intellectual world to all students, even those at resource-poor institutions.

But this freedom comes at a price. Now, students are required to make many choices about education that will affect them for the rest of their lives, and they are forced to make them at a point in their intellectual development when many students lack the wisdom to choose intelligently. In my own experience I see this manifested in several ways. Advisees ask me to approve course selections that have no rhyme or reason behind them and that the advisees themselves can't justify. Students are eager to have double and triple majors, partly, I know, to pad their résumés, but also because they can't figure out which discipline they really want to commit to. And I learned some time ago that "What are you doing when you graduate?" is not a friendly question to ask many college seniors.

In addition, students are faced with all this curricular choice while also trying to figure out what kinds of people they are going to be. Matters of ethnic, religious, and sexual identity are up for grabs. So are issues of romantic intimacy (to marry or not to marry; to have kids or not to have kids; to have kids early or to wait until careers are established). Students can live and work anywhere after they graduate, and in a wired world, they can work at any time, from any place. Of course it is true that students have always had to make these kinds of life decisions. College is an unsettled, and often unsettling, time. But in the past, in virtually each of these areas of life, there was a "default" option that was so powerful that many decisions didn't *feel* like decisions, because alternatives to the default weren't seriously considered. Nowadays, almost nothing is decided by default.

The result is a generation of students who use university counseling services and antidepressants in record numbers, and who provide places like Starbucks with the most highly educated minimum-wage work force in the world, as they bide their time hoping that the answer to the "what should I be when I grow up" question will eventually emerge. Choice overload is certainly not the only reason for the anxiety and uncertainty experienced by modern college students, but I believe it is an important one. I believe that by offering our students this much freedom of choice, we are doing them no favor. Indeed, I think that this obsession with choice constitutes an abdication of responsibility by university faculty members and administrators to provide college students with the guidance they badly need.

In an important respect, the "liberation" of the university experience mirrors the embrace of choice in American society at large. The dominant political trend in the last 25 years, influenced by the principles and assumptions of neoclassical economics, has been to stop trying to have the government provide services that serve the welfare of citizens and instead offer citizens choices so that each of us can pursue our own welfare. The push to privatize Social Security, to offer senior citizens choice among prescription-drug plans, and to offer parents choice in the public education their children receive—these are all instances of the view that choice cannot help but make people better off. And so it is with the modern university. What I have tried to indicate is that though all this choice no doubt makes *some* people better off, it makes *many* people worse off, even when their choices work out well.

If enhanced freedom of choice and increased affluence don't enhance well-being, what does? The most important factor seems to be close social relations. People who are married, who have good friends, and who are close to their families are happier than those who are not. People who participate in religious communities are happier than those who do not. Being connected to others seems to be more important to well-being than being rich or "keeping your options open."

In the context of this discussion of choice, it is important to note that, in many ways, social ties actually *decrease* freedom of choice. Marriage, for example, is a commitment to a particular other person that curtails freedom of choice of sexual or emotional partners. Serious friendship also entails weighty responsibilities and obligations that at times may limit one's own freedom. The same is true, obviously, of family. And most religious institutions call on their members to live their lives in a certain way, and to take responsibility for the well-being of their fellow congregants. So, counterintuitive as it may appear, what seems to contribute most to happiness binds us rather than liberates us.

Yet more than a quarter of Americans report being lonely, and loneliness seems to come not from being alone, but from lack of intimacy. We spend less

20

time visiting with neighbors. We spend less time visiting with our parents, and much less time visiting with other relatives. Partly this is because we *have* less time, since we are busy trying to determine what choices to make in other areas of life. But partly this is because close social relations have themselves become matters of choice. As Robert Lane writes: "What was once given by neighborhood and work now must be achieved; people have had to make their own friends . . . and actively cultivate their own family connections." In other words, our social fabric is no longer a birthright but has become a series of deliberate and demanding choices.

Universities should acknowledge the role they have played in creating a world of choice overload and move from being part of the problem to being a part of the solution. The "culture wars" over the canon that rocked college campuses for years have subsided, and most of us were not sorry to see them go. It is deeply troubling to face up to the fact that you and your colleagues can't agree on something as basic as what a college curriculum should consist of. There were no winners in these wars; they subsided, I think, because people got tired of fighting them. And they subsided because giving students choice seemed like a benign resolution of what were sometimes virulent conflicts. Some choice is good, we thought, so more choice is better. Let students choose and we never have to figure out what to choose for them.

But offering more choice is *not* benign. It is a major source of stress, uncertainty, anxiety—even misery. It is not serving our students well. They would be better served by a faculty and an institution that offered choice within limits, freedom within constraints. The poet and essayist Katha Pollitt observed some years ago that the real reason why battles over the curriculum were so intense—the reason that the stakes seemed so high—is that faculty members knew that for the vast majority of students, the last serious book they would *ever* read would be the last book they read in their college careers. I think we are less likely to turn our students off to the life of the mind if we offer them curricular options that are well structured and coherent than if we simply let them choose whatever they want on their own.

There is a *New Yorker* cartoon that depicts a parent goldfish and an offspring in a small goldfish bowl. "You can be anything you want to be—no limits," says the myopic parent, not realizing how limited an existence the fishbowl allows. I'd like to suggest that perhaps the parent is not so myopic. Freedom without limits, choice within constraints, is indeed liberating. But if the fishbowl gets shattered—if the constraints disappear—freedom of choice can turn into a tyranny of choice. ∎

The Reader's Presence

1. Schwartz, a professor of psychology and economics at Swarthmore College, begins his essay with the provocative assertion: "The modern university has become a kind of intellectual shopping mall." Explore the nature of this metaphor. What aspects of it do you find most—and least—convincing? Explain why. If "increased choice" leads to a "*decrease* in well-being," as Schwartz argues (paragraph 3), then to what extent should we decrease curriculum choice to increase our educational well-being?

Which parts of Schwartz's essay support eliminating our opportunity to choose college courses? Would Schwartz endorse the recommendation that all students should take the same classes through their undergraduate years? Explain why or why not. Develop a counterargument that defends increased choice, taking care to reply to each of Schwartz's points. In your judgment, what are some reasons to keep a university as "a kind of intellectual shopping mall" (paragraph 1)?

2. Identify—and comment on the effectiveness of—the different kinds of evidence Schwartz draws on to make his points (for example, statistics, stories, logic). In what circumstances—and why—does he use one kind of proof rather than another? For example, why do the statistics that begin the essay disappear toward the end? Which kinds of proof are the most convincing to support his points? Reread Schwartz's account of choosing a bottle of wine. These are personal facts, but this is the only personal story Schwartz tells. Why does he choose to tell it here? How is it more or less persuasive than citing another statistic or research study?

3. **CONNECTIONS:** What might Schwartz say about people who have no choices? For example, read Lars Eighner's "On Dumpster Diving" (page 371), which partly tells about what happens when we can no longer exercise choice about where we get our food and what we eat. As Schwartz predicts, Eighner comes to "a healthy state of mind" (Eighner, paragraph 78) by losing his material choices (food, cable channels, etc.). But explain the extent to which Eighner's mental well-being increases because he has lost his choices.

Peter Singer

THE SINGER SOLUTION TO WORLD POVERTY

PETER SINGER, born in 1946 in Melbourne, Australia, has had a long career as an animal rights activist and is one of today's most controversial contemporary philosophers. He is the DeCamp Professor of Bioethics at Princeton University's Center for Human Values and a laureate professor at the University of Melbourne. His book *Animal Liberation*, first published in 1975 and reprinted many times since, has become a basic sourcebook for animal rights activists, and his book *Practical Ethics* (1979) is one of the most widely recognized works of applied ethics. He has also written *Rethinking Life and Death: The Collapse of Our Traditional Ethics*, which received an award from the National Book Council in 1995. He is president of Animal Rights International, vice president of the United Kingdom's Royal

> **"For Singer, living ethically is living a meaningful life. It is a life that makes a difference in the world. It is a life that reduces the sum total of suffering."**

Society for the Prevention of Cruelty to Animals, and he serves on the advisory board of several organizations. Singer has written or edited more than thirty books, including *One World: The Ethics of Globalization* (2002), *Pushing Time Away: My Grandfather and the Tragedy of Jewish Vienna* (2003), and *The Life You Can Save: Acting Now to End World Poverty* (2009). He co-wrote with Jim Mason *The Ethics of What We Eat: Why Our Food Choices Matter* (2006) and co-edited the *Cambridge Textbook of Bioethics*, published in 2008. *Ethics in the Real World: 82 Brief Essays on Things That Matter* appeared in 2016. "The Singer Solution to World Poverty" was first published in the *New York Times* in September 1999.

A reviewer of *Writings on an Ethical Life* (1994) commented: "Singer argues that value judgments should be matters of rational scrutiny and not matters of taste about which argument is futile. . . . For Singer, living ethically is living a meaningful life. It is a life that makes a difference in the world. It is a life that reduces the sum total of suffering."

IN THE BRAZILIAN FILM *Central Station*, Dora is a retired schoolteacher who makes ends meet by sitting at the station writing letters for illiterate people. Suddenly she has an opportunity to pocket $1,000. All she has to do is persuade a homeless nine-year-old boy to follow her to an address she has been given. (She is told he will be adopted by wealthy foreigners.) She delivers the boy, gets the money, spends some of it on a television set, and settles down to enjoy her new acquisition. Her neighbor spoils the fun, however, by telling her that the boy was too old to be adopted—he will be killed and his organs sold for transplantation. Perhaps Dora knew this all along, but after her neighbor's plain speaking, she spends a troubled night. In the morning Dora resolves to take the boy back.

Suppose Dora had told her neighbor that it is a tough world, other people have nice new TVs too, and if selling the kid is the only way she can get one, well, he was only a street kid. She would then have become, in the eyes of the audience, a monster. She redeems herself only by being prepared to bear considerable risks to save the boy.

At the end of the movie, in cinemas in the affluent nations of the world, people who would have been quick to condemn Dora if she had not rescued the boy go home to places far more comfortable than her apartment. In fact, the average family in the United States spends almost one-third of its income on things that are no more necessary to them than Dora's new TV was to her. Going out to nice restaurants, buying new clothes because the old ones are no longer stylish, vacationing at beach resorts—so much of our income is spent on things not essential to the preservation of our lives and health. Donated to one of a number of charitable agencies, that money could mean the difference between life and death for children in need.

All of which raises a question: In the end, what is the ethical distinction between a Brazilian who sells a homeless child to organ peddlers and an American who already has a TV and upgrades to a better one—knowing that the money could be donated to an organization that would use it to save the lives of kids in need?

Of course, there are several differences between the two situations that 5 could support different moral judgments about them. For one thing, to be able to consign a child to death when he is standing right in front of you takes a chilling kind of heartlessness; it is much easier to ignore an appeal for money to help children you will never meet. Yet for a utilitarian philosopher like myself—that is, one who judges whether acts are right or wrong by their consequences—if the upshot of the American's failure to donate the money is that one more kid dies on the streets of a Brazilian city, then it is, in some sense, just as bad as selling the kid to the organ peddlers. But one doesn't need to embrace my utilitarian ethic to see that, at the very least, there is a troubling incongruity in being so quick to condemn Dora for taking the child to the organ peddlers while, at the same time, not regarding the American consumer's behavior as raising a serious moral issue.

In his 1996 book, *Living High and Letting Die*, the New York University philosopher Peter Unger presented an ingenious series of imaginary examples designed to probe our intuitions about whether it is wrong to live well without giving substantial amounts of money to help people who are hungry, malnourished, or dying from easily treatable illnesses like diarrhea. Here's my paraphrase of one of these examples:

Bob is close to retirement. He has invested most of his savings in a very rare and valuable old car, a Bugatti, which he has not been able to insure. The Bugatti is his pride and joy. In addition to the pleasure he gets from driving and caring for his car, Bob knows that its rising market value means that he will always be able to sell it and live comfortably after retirement. One day when Bob is out for a drive, he parks the Bugatti near the end of a railway siding and goes for a walk up the track. As he does so, he sees that a runaway train, with no one aboard, is running down the railway track. Looking farther down the track, he sees the small figure of a child very likely to be killed by the runaway train. He can't stop the train and the child is too far away to warn of the danger, but he can throw a switch that will divert the train down the siding where his Bugatti is parked. Then nobody will be killed—but the train will destroy his Bugatti. Thinking of his joy in owning the car and the financial security it represents, Bob decides not to throw the switch. The child is killed. For many years to come, Bob enjoys owning his Bugatti and the financial security it represents.

Bob's conduct, most of us will immediately respond, was gravely wrong. Unger agrees. But then he reminds us that we, too, have opportunities to save the lives of children. We can give to organizations like UNICEF or Oxfam America. How much would we have to give one of these organizations to have a high probability of saving the life of a child threatened by easily preventable diseases? (I do not believe that children are more worth saving than adults, but since no one can argue that children have brought their poverty on themselves, focusing on them simplifies the issues.) Unger called up some experts and used the information they provided to offer some plausible estimates that include the cost of raising money, administrative expenses, and the cost of delivering aid where it is most needed. By his calculation, $200 in donations would help a sickly two-year-old transform into a healthy six-year-old — offering safe passage through childhood's most dangerous years. To show how practical philosophical argument can be, Unger even tells his readers that they can easily donate funds by using their credit card and calling one of these toll-free numbers: (800) 367-5437 for UNICEF; (800) 693-2687 for Oxfam America.

Now you, too, have the information you need to save a child's life. How should you judge yourself if you don't do it? Think again about Bob and his Bugatti. Unlike Dora, Bob did not have to look into the eyes of the child he was sacrificing for his own material comfort. The child was a complete stranger to him and too far away to relate to in an intimate, personal way. Unlike Dora, too, he did not mislead the child or initiate the chain of events imperiling him. In all these respects, Bob's situation resembles that of people able but unwilling to donate to overseas aid and differs from Dora's situation.

If you still think that it was very wrong of Bob not to throw the switch that 10 would have diverted the train and saved the child's life, then it is hard to see how you could deny that it is also very wrong not to send money to one of the organizations listed above. Unless, that is, there is some morally important difference between the two situations that I have overlooked.

Is it the practical uncertainties about whether aid will really reach the people who need it? Nobody who knows the world of overseas aid can doubt that such uncertainties exist. But Unger's figure of $200 to save a child's life was reached after he had made conservative assumptions about the proportion of the money donated that will actually reach its target.

One genuine difference between Bob and those who can afford to donate to overseas aid organizations but don't is that only Bob can save the child on the tracks, whereas there are hundreds of millions of people who can give $200 to overseas aid organizations. The problem is that most of them aren't doing it. Does this mean that it is all right for you not to do it?

Suppose that there were more owners of priceless vintage cars — Carol, Dave, Emma, Fred, and so on, down to Ziggy — all in exactly the same situation as Bob, with their own siding and their own switch, all sacrificing the child in order to preserve their own cherished car. Would that make it all right for Bob to do the same? To answer this question affirmatively is to endorse follow-the-crowd ethics — the kind of ethics that led many Germans to look away when the Nazi atrocities were being committed. We do not excuse them because others were behaving no better.

We seem to lack a sound basis for drawing a clear moral line between Bob's situation and that of any reader of this article with $200 to spare who does not donate it to an overseas aid agency. These readers seem to be acting at least as badly as Bob was acting when he chose to let the runaway train hurtle toward the unsuspecting child. In the light of this conclusion, I trust that many readers will reach for the phone and donate that $200. Perhaps you should do it before reading further.

Now that you have distinguished yourself morally from people who put 15 their vintage cars ahead of a child's life, how about treating yourself and your partner to dinner at your favorite restaurant? But wait. The money you will spend at the restaurant could also help save the lives of children overseas! True, you weren't planning to blow $200 tonight, but if you were to give up dining out just for one month, you would easily save that amount. And what is one month's dining out, compared to a child's life? There's the rub. Since there are a lot of desperately needy children in the world, there will always be another child whose life you could save for another $200. Are you therefore obliged to keep giving until you have nothing left? At what point can you stop?

Hypothetical examples can easily become farcical. Consider Bob. How far past losing the Bugatti should he go? Imagine that Bob had got his foot stuck in the track of the siding, and if he diverted the train, then before it rammed the car it would also amputate his big toe. Should he still throw the switch? What if it would amputate his foot? His entire leg?

As absurd as the Bugatti scenario gets when pushed to extremes, the point it raises is a serious one: Only when the sacrifices become very signif-icant indeed would most people be prepared to say that Bob does nothing wrong when he decides not to throw the switch. Of course, most people could be wrong; we can't decide moral issues by taking opinion polls. But consider for yourself the level of sacrifice that you would demand of Bob, and then think about how much money you would have to give away in order to make a sacrifice that is roughly equal to that. It's almost certainly much, much more than $200. For most middle-class Americans, it could easily be more like $200,000.

Isn't it counterproductive to ask people to do so much? Don't we run the risk that many will shrug their shoulders and say that morality, so conceived, is fine for saints but not for them? I accept that we are unlikely to see, in the near or even medium-term future, a world in which it is normal for wealthy Americans to give the bulk of their wealth to strangers. When it comes to praising or blaming people for what they do, we tend to use a standard that is relative to some conception of normal behavior. Comfortably off Americans who give, say, 10 percent of their income to overseas aid organizations are so far ahead of most of their equally comfortable fellow citizens that I wouldn't go out of my way to chastise them for not doing more. Nevertheless, they should be doing much more, and they are in no position to criticize Bob for failing to make the much greater sacrifice of his Bugatti.

At this point various objections may crop up. Someone may say: "If every citizen living in the affluent nations contributed his or her share I wouldn't have to make such a drastic sacrifice, because long before such levels were reached, the resources would have been there to save the lives of all those children dying from lack of food or medical care. So why should I give more than my fair share?" Another, related objection is that the government ought to increase its overseas aid allocations, since that would spread the burden more equitably across all taxpayers.

Yet the question of how much we ought to give is a matter to be decided 20 in the real world—and that, sadly, is a world in which we know that most people do not, and in the immediate future will not, give substantial amounts to overseas aid agencies. We know, too, that at least in the next year, the United States government is not going to meet even the very modest United Nations—recommended target of 0.7 percent of gross national product; at the moment it lags far below that, at 0.09 percent, not even half of Japan's 0.22 percent or a tenth of Denmark's 0.97 percent. Thus, we know that the money we can give beyond that theoretical "fair share" is still going to save lives that would otherwise be lost. While the idea that no one need do more than his or her fair share is a powerful one, should it prevail if we know that others are not doing their fair share and that children will die preventable deaths unless we do more than our fair share? That would be taking fairness too far.

Thus, this ground for limiting how much we ought to give also fails. In the world as it is now, I can see no escape from the conclusion that each one of us with wealth surplus to his or her essential needs should be giving most of it to help people suffering from poverty so dire as to be life-threatening. That's right: I'm saying that you shouldn't buy that new car, take that cruise, redecorate the house, or get that pricey new suit. After all, a $1,000 suit could save five children's lives.

So how does my philosophy break down in dollars and cents? An American household with an income of $50,000 spends around $30,000 annually on necessities, according to the Conference Board, a nonprofit economic research organization. Therefore, for a household bringing in $50,000 a year, donations to help the world's poor should be as close as possible to $20,000. The $30,000 required for necessities holds for higher incomes as well. So a household making $100,000 could cut a yearly check for $70,000. Again, the formula is simple: Whatever money you're spending on luxuries, not necessities, should be given away.

Now, evolutionary psychologists tell us that human nature just isn't sufficiently altruistic to make it plausible that many people will sacrifice so much for strangers. On the facts of human nature, they might be right, but they would be wrong to draw a moral conclusion from those facts. If it is the case that we ought to do things that, predictably, most of us won't do, then let's face that fact head-on. Then, if we value the life of a child more than going to fancy restaurants, the next time we dine out we will know that we could have done something better with our money. If that makes living a morally decent life extremely arduous, well, then that is the way things are. If we don't do it, then we should at least know that we are failing to live a morally decent life—not because it is good to wallow in guilt but because knowing where we should be going is the first step toward heading in that direction.

When Bob first grasped the dilemma that faced him as he stood by that railway switch, he must have thought how extraordinarily unlucky he was to be placed in a situation in which he must choose between the life of an innocent child and the sacrifice of most of his savings. But he was not unlucky at all. We are all in that situation. ■

The Reader's Presence

1. How convincing do you find Singer's hypothetical examples, such as Bob and his uninsured Bugatti? Do you think the examples support Singer's basic argument or weaken it? Explain your response.

2. Singer defines a utilitarian philosopher as "one who judges whether acts are right or wrong by their consequences" (paragraph 5). Can you think of utilitarian solutions other than Singer's to the problems of world poverty? For example, would population-control methods that drastically reduced the number of impoverished children born into the world also be a utilitarian solution? Would donations to organizations that fund population control be more effective than charitable donations that directly assist children? If Singer's solution were adopted and more and more children were assisted, would that eventually encourage higher birth rates and thus worsen the very problem Singer wants to solve?

3. **CONNECTIONS:** Consider Singer's essay in conjunction with Jonathan Swift's classic satirical essay on poverty, "A Modest Proposal" (page 630). In what ways does Swift's essay also take a utilitarian position? How do you think Swift would react to Singer's solution to world poverty?

Lauren Slater

THE TROUBLE WITH SELF-ESTEEM

LAUREN SLATER (b. 1963) began her writing career after earning a doctorate in clinical psychology from Boston University. Her first book, *Welcome to My Country: A Therapist's Memoir of Madness* (1996), tells the stories of some of the patients she treated over the course of her eleven-year career. She is perhaps best known, however, for her accounts of her own mental illness and recovery, *Prozac Diary* (1998) and *Lying: A Metaphorical Memoir* (2000). Discussing the difference between writing about her patients and about herself, Slater explains, "I think I found it easier to write about other people, about patients, because I could portray the

> "In writing about myself, I feel much more constricted. I worry about solipsism, shortsightedness, self-aggrandizement, self-denigration, and all the other treacherous territories that come with the fascinating pursuit of autobiography."

enormity and dignity of their suffering without risking self-absorption, or blatant narcissism. In writing about myself, I feel much more constricted. I worry about solipsism, shortsightedness, self-aggrandizement, self-denigration, and all the other treacherous territories that come with the fascinating pursuit of autobiography."

Slater has also published numerous books combining scientific research, a professional's perspective, and personal experience, including *Love Works Like This: Moving from One Kind of Life to Another* (2002), *Opening Skinner's Box: Great Psychological Experiments of the Twentieth Century* (2004), and *Blue Beyond Blue* (2005), a collection of stories told as fairy tales. She has contributed pieces to the *New York Times*, *Harper's*, *Elle*, and *Nerve*, and her essays are found in numerous anthologies, including *Best American Essays of 1994, 1997*, and *2008*, *Best American Science Writing 2002*, and *Best American Magazine Writing 2002*. She has also published *The $60,000 Dog: My Life with Animals* (2012) and *Playing House: Notes of a Reluctant Mother* (2013). Her essay "The Trouble with Self-Esteem" appeared in the *New York Times Magazine* in 2002.

TAKE THIS TEST:

1. On the whole I am satisfied with myself.

2. At times I think that I am no good at all.

3. I feel that I have a number of good qualities.

4. I am able to do things as well as most other people.

5. I feel I do not have much to be proud of.

6. I certainly feel useless at times.

7. I feel that I am a person of worth, at least the equal of others.

8. I wish I could have more respect for myself.

9. All in all, I am inclined to feel that I am a failure.

10. I take a positive attitude toward myself.

Devised by the sociologist Morris Rosenberg, this questionnaire is one of the most widely used self-esteem assessment scales in the United States. If your answers demonstrate solid self-regard, the wisdom of the social sciences predicts that you are well adjusted, clean and sober, basically lucid, without criminal record and with some kind of college cum laude under your high-end belt. If your answers, on the other hand, reveal some inner shame, then it is obvious: you were, or are, a teenage mother; you are prone to social deviance; and if you don't drink, it is because the illicit drugs are bountiful and robust.

It has not been much disputed, until recently, that high self-esteem—defined quite simply as liking yourself a lot, holding a positive opinion of your actions and capacities—is essential to well-being and that its opposite is responsible for crime and substance abuse and prostitution and murder and rape and

even terrorism. Thousands of papers in psychiatric and social-science literature suggest this, papers with names like "Characteristics of Abusive Parents:
A Look at Self-Esteem" and "Low Adolescent Self-Esteem Leads to Multiple
Interpersonal Problems." In 1990, David Long published "The Anatomy of
Terrorism," in which he found that hijackers and suicide bombers suffer from
feelings of worthlessness and that their violent, fluorescent acts are desperate
attempts to bring some inner flair to a flat mindscape.

This all makes so much sense that we have not thought to question it. The
less confidence you have, the worse you do; the more confidence you have,
the better you do; and so the luminous loop goes round. Based on our beliefs,
we have created self-esteem programs in schools in which the main objective
is, as Jennifer Coon-Wallman, a psychotherapist based in Boston, says, "to
dole out huge heapings of praise, regardless of actual accomplishment." We
have a National Association for Self-Esteem with about a thousand members,
and in 1986, the State Legislature of California founded the "California Task
Force to Promote Self-Esteem and Personal and Social Responsibility." It was
galvanized by Assemblyman John Vasconcellos, who fervently believed that
by raising his citizens' self-concepts, he could divert drug abuse and all sorts
of other social ills.

It didn't work.   5

In fact, crime rates and substance abuse rates are formidable, right along
with our self-assessment scores on paper-and-pencil tests. (Whether these tests
are valid and reliable indicators of self-esteem is a subject worthy of inquiry
itself, but in the parlance of social-science writing, it goes "beyond the scope
of this paper.") In part, the discrepancy between high self-esteem scores and
poor social skills and academic acumen led researchers like Nicholas Emler of
the London School of Economics and Roy Baumeister of Case Western Reserve
University to consider the unexpected notion that self-esteem is overrated and
to suggest that it may even be a culprit, not a cure.

"There is absolutely no evidence that low self-esteem is particularly
harmful," Emler says. "It's not at all a cause of poor academic performance;
people with low self-esteem seem to do just as well in life as people with
high self-esteem. In fact, they may do better, because they often try harder."
Baumeister takes Emler's findings a bit further, claiming not only that low
self-esteem is in most cases a socially benign if not beneficent condition but
also that its opposite, high self-regard, can maim and even kill. Baumeister
conducted a study that found that some people with favorable views of themselves were more likely to administer loud blasts of ear-piercing noise to a
subject than those more tepid, timid folks who held back the horn. An earlier
experiment found that men with high self-esteem were more willing to put
down victims to whom they had administered electric shocks than were their
low-level counterparts.

Last year alone there were three withering studies of self-esteem released
in the United States, all of which had the same central message: people with
high self-esteem pose a greater threat to those around them than people with

low self-esteem and feeling bad about yourself is not the cause of our country's biggest, most expensive social problems. The research is original and compelling and lays the groundwork for a new, important kind of narrative about what makes life worth living — if we choose to listen, which might be hard. One of this country's most central tenets, after all, is the pursuit of happiness, which has been strangely joined to the pursuit of self-worth. Shifting a paradigm is never easy. More than 2,000 books offering the attainment of self-esteem have been published; educational programs in schools designed to cultivate self-esteem continue to proliferate, as do rehabilitation programs for substance abusers that focus on cognitive realignment with self-affirming statements like, "Today I will accept myself for who I am, not who I wish I were." I have seen therapists tell their sociopathic patients to say "I adore myself" every day or to post reminder notes on their kitchen cabinets and above their toilet-paper dispensers, self-affirmations set side by side with waste.

Will we give these challenges to our notions about self-esteem their due or will the research go the way of the waste? "Research like that is seriously flawed," says Stephen Keane, a therapist who practices in Newburyport, Mass. "First, it's defining self-esteem according to very conventional and problematic masculine ideas. Second, it's clear to me that many violent men, in particular, have this inner shame; they find out early in life they're not going to measure up, and they compensate for it with fists. We need, as men, to get to the place where we can really honor and expand our natural human grace."

Keane's comment is rooted in a history that goes back hundreds of years, 10 and it is this history that in part prevents us from really tussling with the insights of scientists like Baumeister and Emler. We have long held in this country the Byronic[1] belief that human nature is essentially good or graceful, that behind the sheath of skin is a little globe of glow to be harnessed for creative uses. Benjamin Franklin, we believe, got that glow, as did Joseph Pulitzer and scads of other, lesser, folks who eagerly caught on to what was called, in the 19th century, "mind cure."

Mind cure augurs New Age healing, so that when we lift and look at the roots, New Age is not new at all. In the 19th century, people fervently believed that you were what you thought. Sound familiar? Post it above your toilet paper. You are what you think. What you think. What you think. In the 1920's, a French psychologist, Émile Coué, became all the rage in this country; he proposed the technique of autosuggestion and before long had many citizens repeating, "Day by day in every way I am getting better and better."

But as John Hewitt says in his book criticizing self-esteem, it was maybe Ralph Waldo Emerson more than anyone else who gave the modern self-esteem movement its most eloquent words and suasive philosophy. Emerson died more than a century ago, but you can visit his house in Concord, Mass., and see his bedroom slippers cordoned off behind plush velvet ropes and his eyeglasses, surprisingly frail, the frames of thin gold, the ovals of shine,

---

1 **Byronic:** After the English poet George Gordon, Lord Byron (1788–1824). —EDS.

perched on a beautiful desk. It was in this house that Emerson wrote his famous transcendentalist essays like "On Self-Reliance," which posits that the individual has something fresh and authentic within and that it is up to him to discover it and nurture it apart from the corrupting pressures of social influence. Emerson never mentions "self-esteem" in his essay, but his every word echoes with the self-esteem movement of today, with its romantic, sometimes silly and clearly humane belief that we are special, from head to toe.

Self-esteem, as a construct, as a quasi-religion, is woven into a tradition that both defines and confines us as Americans. If we were to deconstruct self-esteem, to question its value, we would be, in a sense, questioning who we are, nationally and individually. We would be threatening our self-esteem. This is probably why we cannot really assimilate research like Baumeister's or Emler's; it goes too close to the bone and then threatens to break it. Imagine if you heard your child's teacher say, "Don't think so much of yourself." Imagine your spouse saying to you, "You know, you're really not so good at what you do." We have developed a discourse of affirmation, and to deviate from that would be to enter another arena, linguistically and grammatically, so that what came out of our mouths would be impolite at best, unintelligible at worst.

Is there a way to talk about the self without measuring its worth? Why, as a culture, have we so conflated the two quite separate notions—(a) self and (b) worth? This may have as much to do with our entrepreneurial history as Americans, in which everything exists to be improved, as it does, again, with the power of language to shape beliefs. How would we story the self if not triumphantly, redemptively, enhanced from the inside out? A quick glance at amazon.com titles containing the word "self" shows that a hefty percentage also have -improvement or -enhancement tucked into them, oftentimes with numbers—something like 101 ways to improve your self-esteem or 503 ways to better your outlook in 60 days or 604 ways to overcome negative self-talk. You could say that these titles are a product of a culture, or you could say that these titles and the contents they sheathe shape the culture. It is the old argument: do we make language or does language make us? In the case of self-esteem, it is probably something in between, a synergistic loop-the-loop.

On the subject of language, one could, of course, fault Baumeister and Emler for using "self-esteem" far too unidimensionally, so that it blurs and blends with simple smugness. Baumeister, in an attempt at nuance, has tried to shade the issue by referring to two previously defined types: high *unstable* self-esteem and high *well-grounded* self-esteem. As a psychologist, I remember once treating a murderer, who said, "The problem with me, Lauren, is that I'm the biggest piece of [expletive] the world revolves around." He would have scored high on a self-esteem inventory, but does he really "feel good" about himself? And if he doesn't really feel good about himself, then does it not follow that his hidden low, not his high, self-esteem leads to violence? And yet as Baumeister points out, research has shown that people with overt low self-esteem aren't violent, so why would low self-esteem cause violence only when it is hidden? If you follow his train of thinking, you could come up with the sort of silly conclusion that covert low self-esteem causes aggression,

15

but overt low self-esteem does not, which means concealment, not cockiness, is the real culprit. That makes little sense.

"The fact is," Emler says, "we've put antisocial men through every self-esteem test we have, and there's *no* evidence for the old psychodynamic concept that they secretly feel bad about themselves. These men are racist or violent because they don't feel bad *enough* about themselves." Baumeister and his colleagues write: "People who believe themselves to be among the top 10 percent on any dimension may be insulted and threatened whenever anyone asserts that they are in the 80th or 50th or 25th percentile. In contrast, someone with lower self-esteem who regards himself or herself as being merely in the top 60 percent would only be threatened by the feedback that puts him or her at the 25th percentile. . . . In short, the more favorable one's view of oneself, the greater the range of external feedback that will be perceived as unacceptably low."

Perhaps, as these researchers are saying, pride really is dangerous, and too few of us know how to be humble. But that is most likely not the entire reason why we are ignoring flares that say, "Look, sometimes self-esteem can be bad for your health." There are, as always, market forces, and they are formidable. The psychotherapy industry, for instance, would take a huge hit were self-esteem to be re-examined. After all, psychology and psychiatry are predicated upon the notion of the self, and its enhancement is the primary purpose of treatment. I am by no means saying mental health professionals have any conscious desire to perpetuate a perhaps simplistic view of self-esteem, but they are, we are (for I am one of them, I confess), the "cultural retailers" of the self-esteem concept, and were the concept to falter, so would our pocketbooks.

Really, who would come to treatment to be taken down a notch? How would we get our clients to pay to be, if not insulted, at least uncomfortably challenged? There is a profound tension here between psychotherapy as a business that needs to retain its customers and psychotherapy as a practice that has the health of its patients at heart. Mental health is not necessarily a comfortable thing. Because we want to protect our patients and our pocketbooks, we don't always say this. The drug companies that underwrite us never say this. Pills take you up or level you out, but I have yet to see an advertisement for a drug of deflation.

If you look at psychotherapy in other cultures, you get a glimpse into the obsessions of our own. You also see what a marketing fiasco we would have on our hands were we to dial down our self-esteem beliefs. In Japan, there is a popular form of psychotherapy that does not focus on the self and its worth. This psychotherapeutic treatment, called Morita, holds as its central premise that neurotic suffering comes, quite literally, from extreme self-awareness. "The most miserable people I know have been self-focused," says David Reynolds, a Morita practitioner in Oregon. Reynolds writes, "Cure is not defined by the alleviation of discomfort or the attainment of some ideal state (which is impossible) but by taking constructive action in one's life which helps one to live a full and meaningful existence and not be ruled by one's emotional state."

Morita therapy, which emphasizes action over reflection, might have some trouble catching on here, especially in the middle-class West, where folks would be hard pressed to garden away the 50-minute hour. That's what Morita patients do; they plant petunias and practice patience as they wait for them to bloom.

Like any belief system, Morita has its limitations. To detach from feelings carries with it the risk of detaching from their significant signals, which carry important information about how to act: reach out, recoil. But the current research on self-esteem does suggest that we might benefit, if not fiscally then at least spiritually, from a few petunias on the Blue Cross bill. And the fact that we continue, in the vernacular, to use the word "shrink" to refer to treatment means that perhaps unconsciously we know we sometimes need to be taken down a peg.

Down to . . . what? Maybe self-control should replace self-esteem as a primary peg to reach for. I don't mean to sound puritanical, but there is something to be said for discipline, which comes from the word "disciple," which actually means to comprehend. Ultimately, self-control need not be seen as a constriction; restored to its original meaning, it might be experienced as the kind of practiced prowess an athlete or an artist demonstrates, muscles not tamed but trained, so that the leaps are powerful, the spine supple and the energy harnessed and shaped.

There are therapy programs that teach something like self-control, but predictably they are not great moneymakers and they certainly do not attract the bulk of therapy consumers, the upper middle class. One such program, called Emerge, is run by a psychologist named David Adams in a low-budget building in Cambridge, Mass. Emerge's clients are mostly abusive men, 75 percent of them mandated by the courts. "I once did an intake on a batterer who had been in psychotherapy for three years, and his violence wasn't getting any better," Adams told me. "I said to him, 'Why do you think you hit your wife?' He said to me, 'My therapist told me it's because I don't feel good about myself inside.'" Adams sighs, then laughs. "We believe it has *nothing* to do with how good a man feels about himself. At Emerge, we teach men to evaluate their behaviors honestly and to interact with others using empathy and respect." In order to accomplish these goals, men write their entire abuse histories on 12-by-12 sheets of paper, hang the papers on the wall and read them. "Some of the histories are so long, they go all around the room," Adams says. "But it's a powerful exercise. It gets a guy to really concretely *see*." Other exercises involve having the men act out the abuse with the counselor as the victim. Unlike traditional "suburban" therapies, Emerge is under no pressure to keep its customers; the courts do that for them. In return, they are free to pursue a path that has to do with "balanced confrontation," at the heart of which is critical reappraisal and self—no, not esteem—responsibility.

While Emerge is for a specific subgroup of people, it might provide us with a model for how to reconfigure treatment—and maybe even life—if we do decide the self is not about how good it feels but how well it does, in work and love. Work and love. That's a phrase fashioned by Freud himself, who once said the successful individual is one who has achieved meaningful work and meaningful love. Note how separate this sentence is from the notion of self. We blame Freud for a lot of things, but we can't blame that cigar-smoking Victorian for this particular cultural obsession. It was Freud, after all, who said that the job of psychotherapy was to turn neurotic suffering into ordinary suffering. Freud never claimed we should be happy, and he never claimed confidence was the key to a life well lived.

I remember the shock I had when I finally read this old analyst in his   25 native tongue. English translations of Freud make him sound maniacal, if not egomaniacal, with his bloated words like id, ego and superego. But in the original German, id means under-I, ego translates into I and superego is not super-duper but, quite simply, over-I. Freud was staking a claim for a part of the mind that watches the mind, that takes the global view in an effort at honesty. Over-I. I can see. And in the seeing, assess, edit, praise and prune. This is self-appraisal, which precedes self-control, for we must first know both where we flail and stumble, and where we are truly strong, before we can make disciplined alterations. Self-appraisal. It has a certain sort of rhythm to it, does it not? Self-appraisal may be what Baumeister and Emler are actually advocating. If our lives are stories in the making, then we must be able to edit as well as advertise the text. Self-appraisal. If we say self-appraisal again and again, 101 times, 503 times, 612 times, maybe we can create it. And learn its complex arts. ●

The Reader's Presence

1. How does Slater establish her credibility? Identify techniques, words, phrases, and evidence that enhance your view of her as an expert. What makes establishing credibility especially important in this essay?

2. In Slater's opinion, how is self-esteem tied to American identity? What have Americans invested in the idea of self-esteem? What might be lost if self-esteem were no longer seen as valuable?

3. **CONNECTIONS:** In refuting the idea that self-esteem is highly valuable, Slater honestly addresses what would be threatened by such a change in perspective. How does Slater address each of these threats? Compare Slater's technique of arguing against a widely accepted ideal to Laura Kipnis's argument in "Against Love" (page 546) and John Taylor Gatto's in "Against School" (page 517). Which argument(s) do you find most convincing? Why?

The Writer at Work

LAUREN SLATER on Writing Groups

Many professional writers find it stimulating and inspiring to share their work with friends and colleagues. They prefer to do this while the writing is in progress so that they can discover problems they haven't anticipated, take note of alternate directions they might pursue, or simply obtain a "gut reaction" from a supportive audience. For Slater, a key advantage of working with a writing group is the impetus provided by a dialogue: "You feel like you're really involved in a dialogue as opposed to a monologue. I do better in engaging in dialogues" (paragraph 2). These comments on writing groups are part of an interview Slater did with Alys Culhane that appeared in the creative nonfiction journal *Fourth Genre* in spring 2005.

Culhane: I recently read that your writing group is integral to your writing process. Is this so? And if so, what's its history?

Slater: It's been quite critical. I was 24 when I started working with this group and I've just turned 40. My writing group has shortened or abolished the state between writer and reader. It can be weeks on end that you are writing, and when you send something out, weeks on end before you hear anything back. But you can bring something to group, and people will hear it right away. This provides a real impetus. You feel like you're really involved in a dialogue as opposed to a monologue. I do better in engaging in dialogues.

Culhane: Why do you think this is?

Slater: Probably everything I write is kind of a co-construction of what I think and what other people think and I just don't see myself as being someone who's pulling ideas out of her own head. I dialogue with people, with books, with pictures, with everything—the world is always giving me things and I'm always taking them and turning them over. I often feel like a quilt maker—and the members of my writing group have, in a way, provided me with ways of thinking about a design and given me some of the squares. So have other friends, other writers, other books. I'm a very derivative writer and I rely heavily on other texts.

Culhane: Can you provide a specific instance where a reliance upon other texts appears in your work?

Slater: Yes. I just finished a book of fairy tales, *Blue Beyond Blue*. In this book I take established fairy tales and established fairy-tale characters and tell the story of Snow White through the eyes of the stepmother, Hansel and Gretel through the eyes of the witch.

Culhane: How has the structure of your writing group changed over time?

Slater: It's always been very loose. There's been considerable discussion about life issues that have changed over the years, from getting a boyfriend, to having breast cancer, to having kids or not having kids; the issues have changed as we've changed. In terms of structure, we have always followed the same set of "rules." We convene around 8:30 p.m. every Thursday night. We eat. We talk. At around about 11 p.m. we start to read our work. We stay for as long as it takes for everyone who has work to read it. After a person is finished reading, we go around the room and give our own comments on the piece. When this is done, we plunge into a discussion. We're all very tired on Fridays.

Culhane: Now after many years of sharing your writing with the same people do you find that you anticipate their response when you're writing?

Slater: Yes. For example, to some degree I know that one person is going to feel that a particular, say, meditative or internal beginning is slow because her writing style favors very action-oriented scenes. Others are more partial to memoir, or to fiction. Some of us adhere to the "Show, Don't Tell" rule whereas others are more likely to analyze and interpret.

Culhane: Do you anticipate their specific responses?

Slater: Yes. As a writer, what I'm really looking for is a very visceral kind of response; I take visceral reactions much more to heart than studious ones. I ask myself, did they connect with this piece, does it resonate? What I should do with this paragraph or that paragraph isn't an issue to me.

Jonathan Swift

A MODEST PROPOSAL

For Preventing the Children of Poor People in Ireland from Being a Burden to Their Parents or Country, and for Making Them Beneficial to the Public

JONATHAN SWIFT (1667–1745) was born and raised in Ireland, the son of English parents. He was ordained an Anglican priest and, although as a young man he lived a literary life in London, he was appointed against his wishes to be dean of St. Patrick's Cathedral in Dublin. Swift wrote excellent poetry but is remembered principally for his essays and political pamphlets, most of which were published under pseudonyms. Swift received payment for only one work in his entire life, *Gulliver's Travels* (1726). Swift's political pamphlets were very influential in his day; among other issues, he spoke out against English exploitation of the Irish. Some of Swift's more important publications include *A Tale of a Tub* (1704), *The Importance of the Guardian Considered* (1713), *The Public Spirit of the Whigs* (1714), and *A Modest Proposal* (1729).

> **"The chief end I propose to myself in all my labors is to vex the world rather than divert it."**

Writing to his friend Alexander Pope, Swift commented that "the chief end I propose to myself in all my labors is to vex the world rather than divert it, and if I could compass that design without hurting my own person or Fortune I would be the most Indefatigable writer you have ever seen."

IT IS A MELANCHOLY OBJECT to those who walk through this great town[1] or travel in the country, when they see the streets, the roads, and cabin doors, crowded with beggars of the female sex, followed by three, four, or six children, all in rags and importuning every passenger for an alms. These mothers instead of being able to work for their honest livelihood, are forced to employ all their time in strolling to beg sustenance for their helpless infants: who as they grow up either turn thieves for want of work, or leave their dear native country to fight for the pretender in Spain,[2] or sell themselves to the Barbadoes.[3]

I think it is agreed by all parties that this prodigious number of children in the arms, or on the backs, or at the heels of their mothers, and frequently of their fathers, is in the present deplorable state of the kingdom a very great additional grievance; and, therefore, whoever could find out a fair, cheap, and easy method of making these children sound, useful members of the commonwealth, would deserve so well of the public as to have his statute set up for a preserver of the nation.

But my intention is very far from being confined to provide only for the children of professed beggars; it is of a much greater extent, and shall take in the whole number of infants at a certain age who are born of parents in effect as little able to support them as those who demand our charity in the streets.

As to my own part, having turned my thoughts for many years upon this important subject, and maturely weighed the several schemes of our projectors,[4] I have always found them grossly mistaken in their computation. It is true, a child just dropped from its dam may be supported by her milk for a solar year, with little other nourishment; at most not above the value of 2s.,[5]

---

[1] ***this great town:*** Dublin. —EDS.

[2] ***pretender in Spain:*** James Stuart (1688–1766); exiled in Spain, he laid claim to the English crown and had the support of many Irishmen who had joined an army hoping to restore him to the throne. —EDS.

[3] ***the Barbadoes:*** Inhabitants of the British colony in the Caribbean where Irishmen emigrated to work as indentured servants in exchange for their passage. —EDS.

[4] ***projectors:*** Planners. —EDS.

[5] ***2s.:*** Two shillings; in Swift's time one shilling was worth less than twenty-five cents. Other monetary references in the essay are to pounds sterling ("£"), pence ("d."), a crown, and a groat. A pound consisted of twenty shillings; a shilling of twelve pence; a crown was five shillings; a groat was worth a few cents. —EDS.

which the mother may certainly get, or the value in scraps, by her lawful occupation of begging; and it is exactly at one year old that I propose to provide for them in such a manner as instead of being a charge upon their parents or the parish, or wanting food and raiment for the rest of their lives, they shall on the contrary contribute to the feeding, and partly to the clothing, of many thousands.

There is likewise another great advantage in my scheme, that it will pre-   5
vent those voluntary abortions, and that horrid practice of women murdering their bastard children, alas! too frequent among us! sacrificing the poor inno-cent babes I doubt more to avoid the expense than the shame, which would move tears and pity in the most savage and inhuman breast.

The number of souls in this kingdom being usually reckoned one million and a half, of these I calculate there may be about 200,000 couple whose wives are breeders; from which number I subtract 30,000 couple who are able to maintain their own children (although I apprehend there cannot be so many, under the present distress of the kingdom); but this being granted, there will remain 170,000 breeders. I again subtract 50,000 for those women who miscarry, or whose children die by accident or disease within the year. There only remain 120,000 children of poor parents annually born. The ques-tion therefore is, how this number shall be reared and provided for? which, as I have already said, under the present situation of affairs, is utterly impos-sible by all the methods hitherto proposed. For we can neither employ them in handicraft or agriculture; we neither build houses (I mean in the country) nor cultivate land; they can very seldom pick up a livelihood by stealing, till they arrive at six years old, except where they are of towardly parts,[6] although I confess they learn the rudiments much earlier; during which time they can, however, be properly looked upon only as probationers; as I have been informed by a principal gentleman in the county of Cavan, who protested to me that he never knew above one or two instances under the age of six, even in a part of the kingdom so renowned for the quickest proficiency in that art.

I am assured by our merchants, that a boy or a girl before twelve years old is no salable commodity; and even when they come to this age they will not yield above 3£. or 3£. 2s. 6d. at most on the exchange; which cannot turn to account either to the parents or kingdom, the charge of nutriment and rags having been at least four times that value.

I shall now therefore humbly propose my own thoughts, which I hope will not be liable to the least objection.

I have been assured by a very knowing American of my acquaintance in London, that a young healthy child well nursed is at a year old a most delicious, nourishing, and wholesome food, whether stewed, roasted, baked, or broiled; and I make no doubt that it will equally serve in a fricassee or a ragout.[7]

---

6 **towardly parts:** Natural abilities. —EDS.
7 **ragout:** A stew. —EDS.

I do therefore humbly offer it to public consideration that of the 120,000   10
children already computed, 20,000 may be reserved for breed, whereof only
one-fourth part to be males; which is more than we allow to sheep, black
cattle, or swine; and my reason is, that these children are seldom the fruits of
marriage, a circumstance not much regarded by our savages; therefore one
male will be sufficient to serve four females. That the remaining 100,000 may,
at a year old, be offered in sale to the persons of quality and fortune through
the kingdom; always advising the mother to let them suck plentifully in the
last month, so as to render them plump and fat for a good table. A child will
make two dishes at an entertainment for friends; and when the family dines
alone, the fore and hind quarter will make a reasonable dish, and seasoned
with a little pepper or salt will be very good boiled on the fourth day, especially in winter.

I have reckoned upon a medium that a child just born will weigh
12 pounds, and in a solar year, if tolerably nursed, will increase to 28 pounds.

I grant this food will be somewhat dear, and therefore very proper for
landlords, who, as they have already devoured most of the parents, seem to
have the best title to the children.

Infants' flesh will be in season throughout the year, but more plentiful
in March, and a little before and after: for we are told by a grave author, an
eminent French physician,[8] that fish being a prolific diet, there are more
children born in Roman Catholic countries about nine months after Lent than
at any other season; therefore, reckoning a year after Lent, the markets will
be more glutted than usual, because the number of popish infants is at least
three to one in this kingdom: and therefore it will have one other collateral
advantage, by lessening the number of papists among us.

I have already computed the charge of nursing a beggar's child (in which
list I reckon all cottagers, laborers, and four-fifths of the farmers) to be about
2s. per annum, rags included; and I believe no gentleman would repine to
give 10s. for the carcass of a good fat child, which, as I have said, will make
four dishes of excellent nutritive meat, when he has only some particular
friend or his own family to dine with him. Thus the squire will learn to be a
good landlord, and grow popular among the tenants; the mother will have
8s. net profit, and be fit for work till she produces another child.

Those who are more thrifty (as I must confess the times require) may flay   15
the carcass; the skin of which artificially[9] dressed will make admirable gloves
for ladies, and summer boots for fine gentlemen.

As to our city of Dublin, shambles[10] may be appointed for this purpose
in the most convenient parts of it, and butchers we may be assured will not

---

8 **French physician:** François Rabelais (c. 1483–1553), the great Renaissance humanist and
author of the comic masterpiece *Gargantua and Pantagruel.* Swift is being ironic in calling Rabelais
"grave." —EDS.

9 **artificially:** Artfully. —EDS.

10 **shambles:** Slaughterhouses. —EDS.

be wanting: although I rather recommend buying the children alive, and dressing them hot from the knife as we do roasting pigs.

A very worthy person, a true lover of his country, and whose virtues I highly esteem, was lately pleased in discoursing on this matter to offer a refinement upon my scheme. He said that many gentlemen of this kingdom, having of late destroyed their deer, he conceived that the want of venison might be well supplied by the bodies of young lads and maidens, not exceeding fourteen years of age nor under twelve; so great a number of both sexes in every country being now ready to starve for want of work and service; and these to be disposed of by their parents, if alive, or otherwise by their nearest relations. But with due deference to so excellent a friend and so deserving a patriot, I cannot be altogether in his sentiments; for as to the males, my American acquaintance assured me from frequent experience that their flesh was generally tough and lean, like that of our schoolboys by continual exercise, and their taste disagreeable; and to fatten them would not answer the charge. Then as to the females, it would, I think, with humble submission be a loss to the public, because they soon would become breeders themselves: and besides, it is not improbable that some scrupulous people might be apt to censure such a practice (although indeed very unjustly), as a little bordering upon cruelty; which, I confess, has always been with me the strongest objection against any project, how well soever intended.

But in order to justify my friend, he confessed that this expedient was put into his head by the famous Psalmanazar[11] a native of the island Formosa, who came from thence to London about twenty years ago: and in conversation told my friend, that in his country when any young person happened to be put to death, the executioner sold the carcass to persons of quality as a prime dainty; and that in his time the body of a plump girl of fifteen, who was crucified for an attempt to poison the emperor, was sold to his imperial majesty's prime minister of state, and other great mandarins of the court, in joints from the gibbet, at 400 crowns. Neither indeed can I deny, that if the same use were made of several plump young girls in this town, who without one single groat to their fortunes cannot stir abroad without a chair,[12] and appear at the playhouse and assemblies in foreign fineries which they never will pay for, the kingdom would not be the worse.

Some persons of a desponding spirit are in great concern about the vast number of poor people, who are aged, diseased, or maimed, and I have been desired to employ my thoughts what course may be taken to ease the nation of so grievous an encumbrance. But I am not in the least pain upon that matter, because it is very well known that they are every day dying and rotting by cold and famine, and filth and vermin, as fast as can be reasonably expected. And as to the young laborers, they are now in as hopeful condition: They cannot get work, and consequently pine away for want of nourishment, to a degree that if at any time they are accidentally hired to common labor,

---

11 **Psalmanazar** (George; c. 1679–1763): A Frenchman who tricked London society into believing he was a native of Formosa (now Taiwan). —EDS.

12 **a chair:** A sedan chair in which one is carried about. —EDS.

they have not strength to perform it; and thus the country and themselves are happily delivered from the evils to come.

I have too long digressed, and therefore shall return to my subject. I think   20 the advantages by the proposal which I have made are obvious and many, as well as of the highest importance.

For first, as I have already observed, it would greatly lessen the number of papists, with whom we are yearly overrun, being the principal breeders of the nation as well as our most dangerous enemies; and who stay at home on purpose to deliver the kingdom to the Pretender, hoping to take their advantage by the absence of so many good Protestants, who have chosen rather to leave their country than stay at home and pay tithes against their conscience to an Episcopal curate.

Secondly, The poor tenants will have something valuable of their own, which by law may be made liable to distress[13] and help to pay their landlord's rent, their corn and cattle being already seized, and money a thing unknown.

Thirdly, Whereas the maintenance of 100,000 children from two years old and upward, cannot be computed at less that 10s. a-piece per annum, the nation's stock will be thereby increased £50,000 per annum, beside the profit of a new dish introduced to the tables of all gentlemen of fortune in the kingdom who have any refinement in taste. And the money will circulate among ourselves, the goods being entirely of our own growth and manufacture.

Fourthly, The constant breeders beside the gain of 8s. sterling per annum by the sale of their children, will be rid of the charge of maintaining them after the first year.

Fifthly, This food would likewise bring great custom to taverns, where   25 the vintners will certainly be so prudent as to procure the best receipts[14] for dressing it to perfection, and consequently have their houses frequented by all the fine gentlemen, who justly value themselves upon their knowledge in good eating; and a skillful cook who understands how to oblige his guests, will contrive to make it as expensive as they please.

Sixthly, This would be a great inducement to marriage, which all wise nations have either encouraged by rewards or enforced by laws and penalties. It would increase the care and tenderness of mothers toward their children, when they were sure of a settlement for life to the poor babes, provided in some sort by the public, to their annual profit instead of expense. We should see an honest emulation among the married women, which of them would bring the fattest child to the market. Men would become as fond of their wives during the time of their pregnancy as they are now of their mares in foal, their cows in calf, their sows when they are ready to farrow; nor offer to beat or kick them (as is too frequent a practice) for fear of a miscarriage.

Many other advantages might be enumerated. For instance, the addition of some thousand carcasses in our exportation of barreled beef, the propagation of swine's flesh, and improvement in the art of making good bacon, so much wanted among us by the great destruction of pigs, too frequent at our

---

13 **distress:** Seizure for payment of debt.—EDS.
14 **receipts:** Recipes.—EDS.

table; which are no way comparable in taste or magnificence to a well-grown, fat, yearling child, which roasted whole will make a considerable figure at a lord mayor's feast or any other public entertainment. But this and many others I omit, being studious of brevity.

Supposing that 1,000 families in this city would be constant customers for infants' flesh, besides others who might have it at merry-meetings, particularly at weddings and christenings, I compute that Dublin would take off annually about 20,000 carcasses; and the rest of the kingdom (where probably they will be sold somewhat cheaper) the remaining 80,000.

I can think of no one objection that will possibly be raised against this proposal unless it should be urged that the number of people will be thereby much lessened in the kingdom. This I freely own, and it was indeed one principal design in offering it to the world. I desire the reader will observe, that I calculate my remedy for this one individual kingdom of Ireland and for no other that ever was, is, or I think ever can be upon earth. Therefore let no man talk to me of other expedients: of taxing our absentees at 5s. a pound: of using neither clothes nor household furniture except what is of our own growth and manufacture: of utterly rejecting the materials and instruments that promote foreign luxury: of curing the expensiveness of pride, vanity, idleness, and gaming in our women: of introducing a vein of parsimony, prudence, and temperance: of learning to love our country, in the want of which we differ even from Laplanders and the inhabitants of Topinamboo:[15] of quitting our animosities and factions, nor acting any longer like the Jews, who were murdering one another at the very moment their city was taken:[16] of being a little cautious not to sell our country and conscience for nothing: of teaching landlords to have at least one degree of mercy toward their tenants: lastly, of putting a spirit of honesty, industry, and skill into our shopkeepers; who, if a resolution could now be taken to buy only our native goods, would immediately unite to cheat and exact upon us in the price the measure, and the goodness, nor could ever yet be brought to make one fair proposal of just dealing, though often and earnestly invited to it.

Therefore I repeat, let no man talk to me of these and the like expedients, 30 till he has at least some glimpse of hope that there will be ever some hearty and sincere attempt to put them in practice.

But as to myself, having been wearied out for many years with offering vain, idle, visionary thoughts, and at length utterly despairing of success, I fortunately fell upon this proposal; which, as it is wholly new, so it has something solid and real, of no expense and little trouble, full in our own power, and whereby we can incur no danger in disobliging England. For this kind of commodity will not bear exportation, the flesh being of too tender a consistence to admit a long continuance in salt, although perhaps I could name a country which would be glad to eat up our whole nation without it.

After all, I am not so violently bent upon my own opinion as to reject any offer proposed by wise men, which shall be found equally innocent, cheap,

---

15 **Laplanders and the inhabitants of Topinamboo:** Lapland is the area of Scandinavia above the Arctic Circle; Topinamboo, in Brazil, was known in Swift's time for the savagery of its tribes. —EDS.
16 **was taken:** A reference to the Roman seizure of Jerusalem (70 CE). —EDS.

easy, and effectual. But before something of that kind shall be advanced in contradiction to my scheme, and offering a better, I desire the author or authors will be pleased maturely to consider two points. First, as things now stand, how they will be able to find food and raiment for 100,000 useless mouths and backs. And secondly, there being a round million of creatures in human figure throughout this kingdom, whose subsistence put into a common stock would leave them in debt 2,000,000£. sterling, adding those who are beggars by profession to the bulk of farmers, cottagers, and laborers, with the wives and children who are beggars in effect; I desire those politicians who dislike my overture, and may perhaps be so bold as to attempt an answer, that they will first ask the parents of these mortals, whether they would not at this day think it a great happiness to have been sold for food at a year old in the manner I prescribe, and thereby have avoided such a perpetual scene of misfortunes as they have since gone through by the oppression of landlords, the impossibility of paying rent without money or trade, the want of common sustenance, with neither house nor clothes to cover them from the inclemencies of the weather, and the most inevitable prospect of entailing the like or greater miseries upon their breed for ever.

I profess, in the sincerity of my heart, that I have not the least personal interest in endeavoring to promote this necessary work, having no other motive than the public good of my country, by advancing our trade, providing for infants, relieving the poor, and giving some pleasure to the rich. I have no children by which I can propose to get a single penny; the youngest being nine years old, and my wife past childbearing. ●

The Reader's Presence

1. Consider Swift's title. In what sense is the proposal "modest"? What is modest about it? What synonyms would you use for *modest* that appear in the essay? In what sense is the essay a "proposal"? Does it follow any format that resembles a proposal? If so, what type of format? What aspects of its language seem to resemble proposal writing?

2. For this essay Swift invents a speaker, an unnamed, fictional individual who "humbly" proposes a plan to relieve poverty in Ireland. What attitudes and beliefs in the essay do you attribute to the speaker? Which do you attribute to Swift, the author? Having considered two authors (the speaker of the proposal and Swift), now consider two readers—the reader the speaker imagines and the reader Swift imagines. How do these two readers differ? Reread the final paragraph of the essay from the perspective of each of these readers. How do you think each reader is expected to respond?

3. **CONNECTIONS:** In the introductory comment, Swift is quoted as wanting "to vex the world rather than divert it" with his writing. Where in the essay do you find Swift most vexing? How does he attempt to provoke the reader's outrage? Where does the first, most visceral indication of the speaker's plan appear? Does he heighten the essay's effect after this point? If so, where and how? How does Swift mount a serious political argument in the midst of such hyperbole? Read "Against Love" by Laura Kipnis (page 546). How does Kipnis use hyperbole or satire in the presentation of her argument? Does she make a serious point? Why or why not?

Simon Tam

TRADEMARK OFFENSE

SIMON TAM (b. 1981) is the founder of the Slants, "the world's first and only all–Asian American dance rock band." Despite the success of their music, the history of the band is marked by a legal battle over the right to register their band's name with the U.S. Patent and Trademark Office. "Ironically," Tam says, "our band was too Asian to use the word *slant*." The word has been used as a racial slur and continues to be an obstacle in efforts to promote the rights of Asian Americans and other minorities, as he explains in "Trademark Offense."

> Simon Tam is the founder of the Slants, "the world's first and only all–Asian American dance rock band."

In addition to his role as bassist of the Slants, Tam is an activist and the author of two books on the music business. His band has been featured in the *New York Times*, *Time* magazine, and *Rolling Stone*, and he has contributed his own writing to the *Huffington Post*. He speaks frequently on matters of race and social justice and has made many public appearances, from giving talks at TED and Stanford University to performing at Comic-Con.

Months after this article appeared in *Oregon Humanities* in 2015, a federal court found the law barring Tam's ability to trademark the band's name unconstitutional. In June 2017, the United States Supreme Court also sided with Tam and ruled that the Asian rock band has the legal right to use a disparaging name. In 2017, the Slants released an EP titled *The Band Who Must Not Be Named*.

A FEW YEARS AGO, my band, the Slants, was invited to perform at the Oregon State Penitentiary. To many, sending an all–Asian American dance rock band into a prison with a significant neo-Nazi population seemed like an invitation for disaster. However, I didn't question the decision until we actually showed up and were handed bright-orange vests to wear over our clothes. Our singer asked if it would be okay to take them off mid-concert, since our suits and vests could get quite warm.

"Sure," the guard said, "but if an incident occurs, the orange vests let the sentry towers know who to avoid shooting." Got it: keep the safety gear on.

We continued through security with significant precautions at every step. There were bars and armed guards everywhere. The clanging of the doors would echo loudly for a while every time one was opened or shut. It was a place designed for containment, not comfort.

The Slants performing.

Eventually, we stepped onto a large field surrounded by concrete walls—a place called "the big yard." The stage was set up at one end with a thin line of plastic police tape stretched across the front—the only thing separating us from nearly two thousand convicted criminals. We'd been scheduled to perform the year before, but a large riot had put the place on lockdown, so they'd postponed the concert. This fact didn't do much to settle my nerves. I admit I was making assumptions about the kinds of people who are sent to maximum-security prison: murderers, rapists, and drug dealers.

While we played, a small crowd assembled in front of the stage, and a   5
larger one walked around the yard, getting the only hour of outdoor time they'd have for the day. As we launched into our cover of "Paint It Black,"[1] hundreds of prisoners jumped and cheered.

At the end of the concert, a small group of shirtless white men approached the police tape. Several of them were completely covered in swastikas and white pride tattoos. A large man in front came up, towering over me. He seemed nervous as he handed me a piece of paper and asked for an autograph.

"It's for my daughter," he said. "I want to tell her that I met the band."

He went on: "I know I have these tattoos, and I know what you must be thinking. I've made a lot of mistakes in my life, and they're mistakes that I don't want my little girl to make." He said he wanted to show that he could learn, that he could change his heart and mind even if he couldn't change what was stained into his skin.

That concert was one of the most powerful experiences of my life. I went in with all kinds of assumptions, but those changed when we talked with the prisoners.

I started the Slants nearly a decade ago because I wanted to change   10
people's assumptions. I remember watching Quentin Tarantino's *Kill Bill* on DVD in 2004. I paused the film during the iconic scene of O-Ren Ishii

---

[1] *"Paint It Black":* A song by the Rolling Stones. —EDS.

and her gang of Crazy 88s walking into a restaurant—not because of the gore or the soundtrack, but because I realized it was the first American-produced film I'd seen that depicted Asians in a cool and confident manner. The film industry was bad, but the music industry may have been worse: I couldn't think of a single mainstream Asian American music artist.

I wanted to change that with the Slants, the world's first and only all–Asian American dance rock band. Not only did we create our own brand of '80s-inspired synth pop, but we also got involved with social justice: we toured the country fighting stereotypes about Asian Americans, leading workshops, raising money for charities, and sharing our culture through our music. Letters of support from marginalized communities poured in.

During this time, our attorney recommended that we register the trademark on our band name, something that's commonly done for national acts. However, the U.S. Patent and Trademark Office, or USPTO, swiftly rejected our application, claiming our name was disparaging to Asians. To support their claim, officials used sources like UrbanDictionary.com, a photo of Miley Cyrus pulling her eyes back in a derogatory gesture, and anonymous posts on Internet message boards using the word *slant* as a racial slur.

I named the band the Slants because it represented our perspective—or slant—on life as people of color. It was a deliberate act of claiming an identity as well as a nod to Asian American activists who had been using the term for decades.

I've been fighting in courts to register our name for the past five years. I've supplied thousands of pages of evidence, including letters of support from community leaders and Asian American organizations, independent national surveys, and an etymology report from one of the country's leading linguistics professors. The trademark office was not swayed. They called our effort "laudable, but not influential." With just a few keystrokes, they wiped away the voices of thousands of Asian Americans.

We started digging deeper. Rather than focusing on whether or not Asian 15 Americans actually believed our use of the word to be disparaging, we started questioning why the USPTO accused us of using a racial slur to begin with. After all, slant can mean any number of things, and the racial connotation was relatively obscure. In fact, over the years, the trademark office has received eight hundred applications that include variations of the word, but not one was rejected for being racist toward Asians—until an Asian applied.

Trademark officials admitted they considered the word a racial slur in our application because "it is uncontested that applicant is a founding member of a band composed of members of Asian descent." They then presented evidence, including photographs of Asian people on our website, a "stylized dragon" on an album cover, and an illustration of an Asian woman on an album cover.

Ironically, our band was too Asian to use the word *slant*. USPTO thought people would draw the conclusion that our band's name was a reference to our ethnicity. In other words, anyone who wasn't Asian could register a trademark for slant without it being considered a racial slur. It was startling and deeply frustrating to realize that despite trying to use language to help protect my community from stereotypes and racism, I was being denied the right to trademark my band's name because of my race.

Through this process, I've come to understand that laws are designed to maintain the status quo. But shifts in language and identity politics require that bureaucracies move beyond simple cultural competency and instead navigate inconvenient and unknown waters.

Some may argue that the trademark office's actions were not racist. But racism doesn't look only like white supremacists burning crosses or wearing white hoods. Racist actions don't have to fit a stereotype of what racism is to be racist. Denying a right based on race is the very essence of racism. It is evidence of a racist system. And like all other systems, this is one that is resistant to change.

In my opinion, the role of the government shouldn't include deciding how   20
a group can define itself; that right should belong to the community itself. It's clear in example after example that the dominant group is not only inconsistent but also sometimes completely off base when it comes to understanding the sentiments of people who have been marginalized for centuries.

We're fighting for more than a band name: we're fighting for the right of self-determination for all minorities. Things like this are the subtle indignities that people of color have to face every day: slights that don't seem big enough to make a fuss over, yet continually remind us that challenges to the norm (read: white, homogenous culture) are not welcome. One of the more amusing instances was the trademark office's denial of the Japanese word for luck — *fuku* — as a restaurant name, for fear that it might look like an obscenity.

The USPTO can say it doesn't have enough resources to do research on every application that comes in, or that it has to wait for a massive shift in popular culture over sentiments toward a particular word, phrase, or image. However, this subjective application of the law brings a chilling effect to free expression, especially on the part of individuals who wish to convey irony, neutralize slurs, convey artistic or political ideals, or engage in parody.

And it is subjective indeed: The USPTO has refused "wanker"[2] for use on clothing, but approved it for beer. "Pussy Power" was rejected for entertainment services, but "Pussy Power Revolution" was considered acceptable for clothing. "Madonna" was rejected for wines on the grounds that it would be scandalous, but a different "Madonna" application was then approved. And nearly every racial slur known for Asian Americans has become a registered trademark at some point: jap, Oriental, chink, slope, and, of course, slant.

---

2 **wanker:** A general insult — literally "one who wanks (masturbates)." Of English origin, it is a term common in Britain and other parts of the world. — Eds.

The fact of the matter is that this law has been unfairly targeting minorities since it was drawn up in the 1940s, and overcoming it would be a small but important victory in the greater battle for equality. For anyone who has been marginalized because of race, sexual orientation, gender, age, religion, or anything else, this is especially meaningful, because the law says that our communities should have the right to set the tone on appropriateness, rather than some disconnected government agency that believes it should protect others from uncomfortable or disagreeable ideas.

In April of this year, the U.S. Court of Appeals for the Federal Circuit 25 affirmed the trademark office's decision about our band's name. One week later, in an unprecedented move, the court vacated its ruling and issued a legal order for me to argue the constitutionality of the law so the court could reexamine it. Our case suddenly proved to be useful, especially to a federal judge who routinely has expressed interest in protecting the trademarked name of the Washington Redskins.

Some fear the disruption of this law: after all, if it were to be repealed by my band's trademark case, then there would be almost no legal recourse to have the Redskins' trademark registrations cancelled. Some also worry that my case will serve as a Pandora's box[3] or floodgate for disparaging or offensive trademark registrations. For instance, the law that could cancel Redskins might also be used to cancel the NAACP's[4] registration, since the phrase "colored people" in the organization's name could be considered disparaging by many people. Yes, these things might happen, but we shouldn't let the fear of some offensive trademark registrations trump the rights of marginalized communities.

And if we believe that the trademark office has been protecting minority groups, then we've all been fooled. As it is being applied in our case, this law is discriminatory. It only maintains the norm, and that norm is white homogenous culture, with no recognition of people who are practitioners of change. We live in a country where equality has been defined by white, heterosexual, cisgender men for hundreds of years, and it's time to bring other community groups to the table. We should not be afraid of using the expression of who we are to catalyze change.

Artists don't begin their careers thinking about how to dismantle laws that they aren't even aware of, and I'm certainly not an exception. When I first started the band, the intention was to take on stereotypes about Asian Americans, inject pride into our ethnic heritages, and increase our community's visibility in the entertainment industry.

But what I've come to see is that assumptions can be efficacious. The trademark office assumed that our name was inherently a racial slur and that the Asian American community would feel disparaged by it. When our community loudly expressed otherwise, officials assumed that approving our

---

3 *Pandora's box:* The container opened by the Greek mythological woman Pandora releasing all the evils of humanity into the world. —EDS.

4 *NAACP:* National Association for the Advancement of Colored People, a civil rights organization formed in 1909 in the United States. —EDS.

name would set a precedent that would create more paperwork and open the door for other controversial trademark applications. What if, instead, they treated us as applicants of any other race, as people instead of ideologies? What if our government's laws reflected the capacity for people, entire communities, and words and identities to change?

As it is, our legal system on trademark law feels like a prison created to   30 keep disruptive ideas from coming into the mainstream. Officials may believe they are protecting the general public from harm, but they are actually erecting walls that discourage people from mobilizing for social justice by using language to reappropriate ideas. Just because we don't understand or agree with how someone creates social change doesn't mean we should prevent it. When it comes to social justice, we should ask questions and have meaningful conversations instead of making assumptions.

In the winter of 2012, our band spent the holidays performing for soldiers serving overseas. While one branch of the government was working against our band, another branch, the Department of Defense, called on us to do some outreach on its behalf. This was shortly after news spread about harsh hazing practices used on Asian American military recruits. One encounter on that tour really stood out.

We had just finished playing a concert at a NATO base when the local commander approached me. "That was incredible," he said. "We've had a lot of acts here — big names, too — but I've never seen soldiers from all of the different countries dance together like that."

He continued: "Also, I have to apologize. As the commander of the base, I'm expected to make appearances at these kinds of things. But when I first saw your poster, I didn't know what to make of this 'Oriental' band. However, now I know I should never really judge these things on the surface."

"Thank you so much. It's an honor to be here," I said. "Also, you shouldn't use the word 'Oriental,' because it makes you sound like a racist. But thank you."

That night, fighting stereotypes of Asian Americans didn't come in the   35 form of a lecture or a workshop on the model minority myth or a debate over "Asian privilege." It happened through sincere fellowship powered by Chinatown dance rock. That night, the victory happened simply by showing up and having a meaningful conversation. ■

The Reader's Presence

1. Simon Tam's essay opens with a narrative about his band playing at the Oregon State Penitentiary. In what specific ways does this account anticipate and support his overarching argument challenging the U.S. Patent and Trademark Office's (USPTO) decision to reject his band's application to trademark their name, the Slants? Summarize the series of points Tam makes to support the substance and spirit of his argument. Which points do you find most — and least — convincing? Explain why.

2. List each of the arguments the USPTO presents to support its decision to deny the Slants' request to trademark the name of their band. How do you assess the USPTO's

calling the Slants' application "laudable, but not influential" (paragraph 14). Review the rationale for its decision and comment on the persuasiveness of each point the USPTO makes. Later, Tam declares the ultimate motive of his lawsuit: "We're fighting for more than a band name: we're fighting for the right of self-determination for all minorities. Things like this are the subtle indignities that people of color have to face every day: slights that don't seem big enough to make a fuss over yet continually remind us that challenges to the norm (read white homogenous culture) are not welcome" (paragraph 21). Summarize—and assess—the points Tam makes to support this argument. To what extent do you agree with Tam's declaration that securing the rights of self-determination and free expression are more important than the possible consequences of allowing potentially disparaging or offensive names?

3. **CONNECTIONS:** In "What's Your Name, Girl?" (page 34), Maya Angelou observes: "Every person I know had a hellish horror of being 'called out of his name.' It was a dangerous practice to call a Negro anything that could be loosely construed as insulting because of the centuries of their having been called niggers, jigs, dinges, blackbirds, crows, boots, and spooks" (paragraph 30). In what specific ways is Tam's challenge of the USPTO's decision to deny a trademark for the name of their band—the Slants—similar to and different from Angelou's decrying the racism embedded in the names assigned to blacks in America while denying them the dignity of calling them by their own names?

Sherry Turkle

THE EMPATHY GAP

Technology has become ubiquitous in our world, and its presence modifies our interactions and relationships in ways we don't always recognize. According to sociology and psychology professor **SHERRY TURKLE** (b. 1948), the rise of the Internet and social networks has limited our ability to engage in meaningful conversation. "Two-person conversations that take place with a phone on the table," she says, "leave each person feeling less of a sense of connection and commitment to the other." Technology thrives on divided attention: we can talk to everyone all the time. This digital environment, Turkle explains, deprives us of the intimacy and empathy of genuine conversation.

> **Our digital environment, Turkle explains, deprives us of the intimacy and empathy of genuine conversation.**

Turkle has written frequently on the ways in which humans interact with technology and has researched the subject for more than thirty years. She has written several books, including *The Second Self* (1984), *Life on the Screen* (1995), and *Alone Together* (2011). Her latest book, *Reclaiming Conversation: The Power of Talk in a Digital Age* (2015), was a *New York Times* best-seller. Turkle teaches at the Massachusetts Institute of Technology, where she founded the MIT Initiative on Technology and Self in 2001.

In "The Empathy Gap," Turkle examines the consequences of our digital lives for the practice of psychotherapy, which relies on our ability to form personal connections.

WHEN I FIRST BEGAN STUDYING ONLINE life in the early 1980s, I saw it as a place where people had an opportunity to express aspects of themselves that were typically repressed in their daily life. Back then, they did this in simple online chat rooms and, more elaborately, when they constructed game avatars. In those days, I was something of an enthusiast, trying to alert clinicians—psychoanalysts, psychologists, psychiatrists, social workers, and pediatricians—to the importance of these new digital spaces. In particular, I hoped my work would make psychotherapists more comfortable with technology and make them feel that they had a role to play in its development. In essence, my message to psychotherapists was this: here's a technology that functions as a kind of intimate machine and touches deeply on questions of identity. Watch for it as you do your work. In your practice, when clients talk about their web pages, their desktop designs, their avatars, they'll be talking about matters that reach far beyond the technical. Digital life isn't a realm of culture whose elaboration and interpretation should be left to engineers. We need therapeutic practitioners to understand its deeper dimensions.

Through the mid-'90s, my writings about technology and self were mainly hopeful about the psychological impact of digital culture. Indeed, in 1996, I was on the cover of *Wired* magazine for my work portraying online avatars as part of a new kind of "identity play" that expanded people's sense of themselves. Ironically, that cover story appeared just as I was changing my mind about where we were allowing technology to take us. I had two related concerns: we expected more from technology and less from each other. We were increasingly willing to talk to machines, even about intimate matters. And increasingly, with the rise of mobile devices, we were paying attention to our phones rather than each other. In both cases, there was a flight from face-to-face conversation. In both cases, technology was encouraging us to forget that the essence of conversation is one where human meanings are understood, where empathy is engaged.

These technical proposals were seductive. In my studies of artificial intelligence, I interviewed hundreds of people across generations who, in the course of the 1990s and early 2000s, warmed to the idea of robots as friends, of computer programs as counselors. In this, they were not only willing to take the simulation of understanding as genuine understanding, but the simulation of feeling as feeling itself. Consider a high school senior who told me that a computer program with artificial intelligence would be a better resource than his father for talking about girls and dating because the program would have so much more "information" and "cases" to work with.

What an artificial intelligence *can* know is your schedule, the literal content of your email, your preferences in film, TV, and food. If you wear body-sensing technologies, it can know the degree to which these things emotionally activate you because it may infer this from physiological markers. But it doesn't understand what any of these things *mean* to you, because it's not judging them from the point of view of being human.

Our willingness to talk to machines is a part of a *culture of forgetting*   5
that challenges psychotherapy today. What we're forgetting is what makes people special, what makes conversation authentic, what makes it human, what makes psychotherapy the talking cure.

These are some of the consequences of expecting more from technology than technology can offer. I've also said that in our flight from conversation, we expect less from each other. Here, mobile communication and social media are key actors. Of course, we don't live in a silent world. We talk to each other. And we communicate online almost all the time. But we're always distracted by the worlds on our phones, and it's become more common to go to great lengths to avoid a certain kind of conversation: those that are spontaneous and face-to-face and require our full attention, those in which people go off on a tangent and circle back in unpredictable and self-revealing ways. In other words, what people are fleeing is the kind of conversation that talk therapy tries to promote, the kind in which intimacy flourishes and empathy thrives.

In this cultural environment, what happens in the consulting room? When I talk to therapists, they tell me that clients today find it harder to concentrate on face-to-face conversation. They may not even see its value, feeling more comfortable with the self they can present on their screens. And in the spirit of the robotic moment, they may be comfortable with apps on their phone that, for them, serve at least part of the job that therapy once did. Rather than relating directly to a real-life therapist, they use apps in which you tell your story, and apps that analyze it. They're drawn to apps to calm you down and let you know if you may be guilty of distorting your cognitive field. We now face a generation of clients who may need talk therapy in order to be schooled in the very rudiments of emotionally revealing talk.

While technology seduces with its offer of control, in-person talk offers the chance to directly experience imperfection, empathy, and relationship. And so we find ourselves in a cultural moment in which talk therapy is being marginalized for not being "scientific" enough, for not providing enough outcome studies to legitimate it for insurers and make it seem cost effective. At the same time, it's needed more than ever in a larger culture that has, in important ways, gone silent. Otherwise put, psychotherapists are experts at the kind of talk that digital culture needs most, the kind of talk in which we give each other full attention, the kind of talk that's relational rather than transactional. But in order to take this role, to step up in this way, therapists have to take themselves out of the defensive posture they too often take when it comes to matters technical and scientific.

I speak to therapists in many contexts, as colleagues and also as informants in formal interviews as I pursue my studies. In all these situations,

I find that so many talented clinicians suffer from a crisis of confidence, unsure of the relevance of their profession in a high-tech world that in many ways seems to have passed it by. This demoralization can take many forms. It can be harder to find psychotherapy clients, for instance, as more and more people ask for medication and a "check in" every few months, even as you encourage them to try two or more sessions of psychotherapy a week.

For one psychiatric social worker in a hospital setting, demoralization is   10 this: she works in a clinic that will lose funding if she doesn't produce evidence of effective therapeutic outcomes for her mixture of talk therapy and cognitive behavioral techniques. It's not clear to her that she can produce these papers. For one thing, she admits that she doesn't fully believe in the ways she's measuring "success." She feels she's leaving out something she's giving to her patients that she hasn't known how to capture in an instrument. As she puts it, "My patients feel in a relationship." While she thinks that this fact alone is success, she realizes that it's not easily measurable.

THE EMPATHY GAP

Research shows that when people are together, say for lunch or a cup of coffee, even the presence of a phone on the table (even a phone turned off) does two things. First, it changes what people talk about—it keeps conversation light because the phone is a reminder that at any point, we might be interrupted, and we don't want to be interrupted when we're talking about something important to us. Second, conversation with phones on the table or even phones on the periphery of our vision, interferes with empathic connection. Two-person conversations that take place with a phone on the table leave each person feeling less of a sense of connection and commitment to the other.

Considering an empathy gap underscores the importance of the therapist's role in our digital culture. The basic work of therapy is now the work that's most needed: sitting quietly with a client, giving that person your full attention, creating a space to pay attention to one's own thoughts and to listen to another. Making the point that these things are important is a point that life today doesn't make. Conditioned by the experience of life on the screen, people's expectation is that the world will come to them in a constant, steady stream. Solitude becomes painful. At a stoplight, at a line at a supermarket, you see people turn immediately to their phones. As a culture, our capacity for solitude is challenged by the culture of the continual feed.

The culture of therapy affects our culture as a whole. How we seek help, what we expect help to look like, changes our values in a broader way. Right now, digital culture closes down the questions that talk therapy knows how to open up.

The mores of therapy—the value it places on being with, forming an empathic bond, and the quiet attention necessary to do this—become more central as a cultural corrective. If therapy once allowed patients to develop the capacity to talk about sexuality in a way that was prohibited outside of the consulting room, now there's a new imperative: to experience solitude and an experience of quiet, empathic connection.

Digital connection is a way to keep my job simple and my life tidier. We   15
have to remember why it's important to be the messy, complex, people that we are. We have to support each other in remembering that the kind of conversations that may seem old-fashioned are actually, of our moment, and most necessary and essential. And all the more essential because they can be portrayed as superseded by something faster, cheaper, and more precise. What therapists need to recognize is the reason we need to talk: to forge relationships that are the triumph of messy, breathing human connection over the cold instrumentality of treating each other as apps. ■

The Reader's Presence

1. Sherry Turkle's essay focuses on the distinctions between online and face-to-face communication, and it reads like a psychological case study in both comparison and contrast as well as cause and effect. Recount the many differences she establishes between talking in each setting. What vocabulary does she associate with each context? Identify several examples, and examine the connotations—and the implications—each term carries. How does Turkle define the "empathy gap"? To what extent do you agree with Turkle's assertion that "digital culture closes down the questions that talk therapy knows how to open up" (paragraph 13)? How does her vocabulary characterizing these different forms of conversation support her conclusion?

2. Much of Turkle's essay centers on the important contributions psychotherapy can make to contemporary life and the dangers of increasingly relying on digital culture. In what specific ways is digital culture increasingly incompatible with the traditional values and goals of therapy? For example, what distinctions does she draw between "the simulation of understanding" and "genuine understanding" (paragraph 3) as well as "relational" and "transactional" kinds of talk (paragraph 8)? To what extent could Turkle argue digital culture is damaging personal relationships far beyond someone's relationship with a psychotherapist? For example, how does she define the "empathy gap," and what examples does she provide to support her argument?

3. Create a list of examples Turkle invokes to support her position advocating "face-to-face" conversation. Which do you find convincing? Explain why. What does she mean when she says "our willingness to talk to machines is part of a *culture of forgetting*"? In her view, what "makes people special, what makes conversation authentic" (paragraph 5)? Overall, how convinced are you by Turkle's argument? Explain why. How could you support her argument? Challenge it? Be as specific as possible in responding.

4. **CONNECTIONS:** Compare and contrast Sherry Turkle's assessment of the extent—and the consequences—of the ways technology impacts human interactions with Malcolm Gladwell's points in "Small Change: Why the Revolution Will Not Be Tweeted" (page 386). How is Turkle's "empathy gap" similar to what Gladwell calls the "weak lies" of social media? How are their positions different? In light of their respective positions, what do you believe are the advantages and disadvantages of digital networks and our connections to them?

David Foster Wallace

CONSIDER THE LOBSTER

DAVID FOSTER WALLACE (1962–2008) is probably best known for his 1996 novel, *Infinite Jest*. Widely considered one of the most important works of American fiction in recent memory, *Infinite Jest* made *Time* magazine's list of the 100 greatest novels spanning the period 1926–2006, and firmly established Wallace at the forefront of American letters. Wallace double-majored in English and philosophy at Amherst College and went on to receive an MFA in creative writing at the University of Arizona in 1987. He published his first novel, *The Broom of the System*, in 1987, and, shortly thereafter, moved to Boston, Massachusetts, to work toward a graduate degree in philosophy at Harvard University. He soon abandoned the endeavor, dedicating himself instead to writing. He taught creative writing at Illinois State University from 1992 through 2002, when he moved to Claremont, California, to take a position as the Roy E. Disney Professor of Creative Writing at Pomona College. In addition to *Infinite Jest* and *The Broom of the System*, Wallace published several short story collections, including *Brief Interviews with Hideous Men* (1999), which was adapted for the screen in a 2009 film of the same name. Wallace also published essays and stories in magazines, including the *Paris Review*, *Harper's*, the *Atlantic Monthly*, *Esquire*, and *Gourmet*. When Wallace committed suicide in 2008, he left behind an unfinished novel titled *The Pale King*, which was published posthumously in 2011 and was a finalist for the Pulitzer Prize in fiction in 2012.

> **Widely considered one of the most important works of American fiction in recent memory, *Infinite Jest* made *Time* magazine's list of the 100 greatest novels spanning the period 1926–2006, and firmly established David Foster Wallace at the forefront of American letters.**

Wallace wrote "Consider the Lobster" on assignment from *Gourmet*, a culinary magazine, in 2004.

Note: Extensive personal footnotes are part of Wallace's prose style; unless otherwise specified, all the footnotes are Wallace's.

THE ENORMOUS, pungent, and extremely well-marketed Maine Lobster Festival is held every late July in the state's midcoast region, meaning the western side of Penobscot Bay, the nerve stem of Maine's lobster industry. What's called the midcoast runs from Owl's Head and Thomaston in the south to Belfast in the north. (Actually, it might extend all the way up to Bucksport, but we were never able to get farther north than Belfast on Route 1, whose summer traffic is, as you can imagine, unimaginable.) The region's two main communities are Camden, with its very old money and yachty harbor and five-star restaurants and phenomenal B&Bs, and Rockland, a serious old fishing town that hosts the festival every summer in historic Harbor Park, right along the water.[1]

Tourism and lobster are the midcoast region's two main industries, and they're both warm-weather enterprises, and the Maine Lobster Festival represents less an intersection of the industries than a deliberate collision, joyful and lucrative and loud. The assigned subject of this *Gourmet* article is the 56th Annual MLF, 30 July–3 August 2003, whose official theme this year was "Lighthouses, Laughter, and Lobster." Total paid attendance was over 100,000, due partly to a national CNN spot in June during which a senior editor of *Food & Wine* magazine hailed the MLF as one of the best food-themed galas in the world. 2003 festival highlights: concerts by Lee Ann Womack and Orleans, annual Maine Sea Goddess beauty pageant, Saturday's big parade, Sunday's William G. Atwood Memorial Crate Race, annual Amateur Cooking Competition, carnival rides and midway attractions and food booths, and the MLF's Main Eating Tent, where something over 25,000 pounds of fresh-caught Maine lobster is consumed after preparation in the World's Largest Lobster Cooker near the grounds' north entrance. Also available are lobster rolls, lobster turnovers, lobster sauté, Down East lobster salad, lobster bisque, lobster ravioli, and deep-fried lobster dumplings. Lobster thermidor is obtainable at a sit-down restaurant called the Black Pearl on Harbor Park's northwest wharf. A large all-pine booth sponsored by the Maine Lobster Promotion Council has free pamphlets with recipes, eating tips, and Lobster Fun Facts. The winner of Friday's Amateur Cooking Competition prepares Saffron Lobster Ramekins, the recipe for which is now available for public downloading at www.mainelobsterfestival.com. There are lobster T-shirts and lobster bobblehead dolls and inflatable lobster pool toys and clamp-on lobster hats with big scarlet claws that wobble on springs. Your assigned correspondent saw it all, accompanied by one girlfriend and both his own parents — one of which parents was actually born and raised in Maine, albeit in the extreme northern inland part, which is potato country and a world away from the touristic midcoast.[2]

For practical purposes, everyone knows what a lobster is. As usual, though, there's much more to know than most of us care about — it's all a matter of what your interests are. Taxonomically speaking, a lobster is a marine crustacean of the family Homaridae, characterized by five pairs of jointed legs, the first pair terminating in large pincerish claws used for subduing prey. Like many other species of benthic carnivore, lobsters are both

---

[1] There's a comprehensive native apothegm: "Camden by the sea, Rockland by the smell."

[2] N.B. All personally connected parties have made it clear from the start that they do not want to be talked about in this article.

hunters and scavengers. They have stalked eyes, gills on their legs, and antennae. There are a dozen or so different kinds worldwide, of which the relevant species here is the Maine lobster, *Homarus americanus*. The name "lobster" comes from the Old English *loppestre*, which is thought to be a corrupt form of the Latin word for locust combined with the Old English *loppe*, which meant spider.

Moreover, a crustacean is an aquatic arthropod of the class Crustacea, which comprises crabs, shrimp, barnacles, lobsters, and freshwater crayfish. All this is right there in the encyclopedia. And arthropods are members of the phylum Arthropoda, which phylum covers insects, spiders, crustaceans, and centipedes/millipedes, all of whose main commonality, besides the absence of a centralized brain-spine assembly, is a chitinous exoskeleton composed of segments, to which appendages are articulated in pairs.

The point is that lobsters are basically giant sea insects.[3] Like most   5
arthropods, they date from the Jurassic period, biologically so much older than mammalia that they might as well be from another planet. And they are—particularly in their natural brown-green state, brandishing their claws like weapons and with thick antennae awhip—not nice to look at. And it's true that they are garbagemen of the sea, eaters of dead stuff,[4] although they'll also eat some live shellfish, certain kinds of injured fish, and sometimes one another.

But they are themselves good eating. Or so we think now. Up until sometime in the 1800s, though, lobster was literally low-class food, eaten only by the poor and institutionalized. Even in the harsh penal environment of early America, some colonies had laws against feeding lobsters to inmates more than once a week because it was thought to be cruel and unusual, like making people eat rats. One reason for their low status was how plentiful lobsters were in old New England. "Unbelievable abundance" is how one source describes the situation, including accounts of Plymouth Pilgrims wading out and capturing all they wanted by hand, and of early Boston's seashore being littered with lobsters after hard storms—these latter were treated as a smelly nuisance and ground up for fertilizer. There is also the fact that premodern lobster was cooked dead and then preserved, usually packed in salt or crude hermetic containers. Maine's earliest lobster industry was based around a dozen such seaside canneries in the 1840s, from which lobster was shipped as far away as California, in demand only because it was cheap and high in protein, basically chewable fuel.

Now, of course, lobster is posh, a delicacy, only a step or two down from caviar. The meat is richer and more substantial than most fish, its taste subtle compared to the marine-gaminess of mussels and clams. In the U.S. pop-food imagination, lobster is now the seafood analog to steak, with which it's so often twinned as Surf 'n' Turf on the really expensive part of the chain steakhouse menu.

---

[3] Midcoasters' native term for a lobster is, in fact, "bug," as in "Come around on Sunday and we'll cook up some bugs."

[4] Factoid: Lobster traps are usually baited with dead herring.

In fact, one obvious project of the MLF, and of its omnipresently spon-sorial Maine Lobster Promotion Council, is to counter the idea that lobster is unusually luxe or unhealthy or expensive, suitable only for effete palates or the occasional blow-the-diet treat. It is emphasized over and over in pre-sentations and pamphlets at the festival that lobster meat has fewer calories, less cholesterol, and less saturated fat than chicken.[5] And in the Main Eating Tent, you can get a "quarter" (industry shorthand for a 1¼-pound lobster), a four-ounce cup of melted butter, a bag of chips, and a soft roll w/but-ter-pat for around $12.00, which is only slightly more expensive than supper at McDonald's.

Be apprised, though, that the Maine Lobster Festival's democratization of lobster comes with all the massed inconveniences and aesthetic compromise of real democracy. See, for example, the aforementioned Main Eating Tent, for which there is a constant Disneyland-grade queue, and which turns out to be a square quarter mile of awning-shaded cafeteria lines and rows of long institutional tables at which friend and stranger alike sit cheek by jowl, cracking and chewing and dribbling. It's hot, and the sagged roof traps the steam and the smells, which latter are strong and only partly food-related. It is also loud, and a good percentage of the total noise is masticatory. The suppers come in styrofoam trays, and the soft drinks are iceless and flat, and the coffee is convenience-store coffee in yet more styrofoam, and the utensils are plastic (there are none of the special long skinny forks for pushing out the tail meat, though a few savvy diners bring their own). Nor do they give you near enough napkins considering how messy lobster is to eat, especially when you're squeezed onto benches alongside children of various ages and vastly different levels of fine-motor development — not to mention the people who've somehow smuggled in their own beer in enormous aisle-blocking coolers, or who all of a sudden produce their own plastic tablecloths and spread them over large portions of tables to try to reserve them (the tables) for their own little groups. And so on. Any one example is no more than a petty inconvenience, of course, but the MLF turns out to be full of irksome little downers like this — see for instance the Main Stage's headliner shows, where it turns out that you have to pay $20 extra for a folding chair if you want to sit down; or the North Tent's mad scramble for the Nyquil-cup-sized samples of finalists' entries handed out after the Cooking Competition; or the much-touted Maine Sea Goddess pageant finals, which turn out to be excruciatingly long and to consist mainly of endless thanks and tributes to local sponsors. Let's not even talk about the grossly inadequate Port-A-San facilities or the fact that there's nowhere to wash your hands before or after eating. What the Maine Lobster Festival really is is a midlevel county fair with a culinary hook, and in this respect it's not unlike Tidewater crab festi-vals, Midwest corn festivals, Texas chili festivals, etc., and shares with these venues the core paradox of all teeming commercial demotic events: It's not

---

[5] Of course, the common practice of dipping the lobster meat in melted butter torpedoes all these happy fat-specs, which none of the council's promotional stuff ever mentions, any more than potato industry PR talks about sour cream and bacon bits.

for everyone.[6] Nothing against the euphoric senior editor of *Food & Wine*, but I'd be surprised if she'd ever actually been here in Harbor Park, amid crowds of people slapping canal-zone mosquitoes as they eat deep-fried Twinkies and watch Professor Paddywhack, on six-foot stilts in a raincoat with plastic lobsters protruding from all directions on springs, terrify their children.

Lobster is essentially a summer food. This is because we now prefer our   10
lobsters fresh, which means they have to be recently caught, which for both tactical and economic reasons takes place at depths less than 25 fathoms. Lobsters tend to be hungriest and most active (i.e., most trappable) at summer water temperatures of 45–50 degrees. In the autumn, most Maine lobsters migrate out into deeper water, either for warmth or to avoid the heavy waves that pound New England's coast all winter. Some burrow into the bottom. They might hibernate; nobody's sure. Summer is also lobsters' molting season—specifically early- to mid-July. Chitinous arthropods grow by molting, rather the way people have to buy bigger clothes as they age and gain weight. Since lobsters can live to be over 100, they can also get to be quite large, as in 30 pounds or more—though truly senior lobsters are rare now because New England's waters are so heavily trapped.[7] Anyway, hence the culinary distinction between hard- and soft-shell lobsters, the latter sometimes a.k.a. shedders. A soft-shell lobster is one that has recently molted. In midcoast restaurants, the summer menu often offers both kinds, with shedders being slightly cheaper even though they're easier to dismantle and the meat is allegedly sweeter. The reason for the discount is that a molting lobster uses a layer of seawater for insulation while its new shell is hardening, so there's

---

[6] In truth, there's a great deal to be said about the differences between working-class Rockland and the heavily populist flavor of its festival versus comfortable and elitist Camden with its expensive view and shops given entirely over to $200 sweaters and great rows of Victorian homes converted to upscale B&Bs. And about these differences as two sides of the great coin that is US tourism. Very little of which will be said here, except to amplify the above-mentioned paradox and to reveal your assigned correspondent's own preferences. I confess that I have never understood why so many people's idea of a fun vacation is to don flip-flops and sunglasses and crawl through maddening traffic to loud, hot, crowded tourist venues in order to sample a "local flavor" that is by definition ruined by the presence of tourists. This may (as my festival companions keep pointing out) all be a matter of personality and hardwired taste: the fact that I do not like tourist venues means that I'll never understand their appeal and so am probably not the one to talk about it (the supposed appeal). But, since this FN will almost surely not survive magazine-editing anyway, here goes:

As I see it, it probably really is good for the soul to be a tourist, even if it's only once in a while. Not good for the soul in a refreshing or enlivening way, though, but rather in a grim, steely-eyed, let's-look-honestly-at-the-facts-and-find-some-way-to-deal-with-them way. My personal experience has not been that traveling around the country is broadening or relaxing, or that radical changes in place and context have a salutary effect, but rather that intranational tourism is radically constricting, and humbling in the hardest way—hostile to my fantasy of being a real individual, of living somehow outside and above it all. (Coming up is the part that my companions find especially unhappy and repellent, a sure way to spoil the fun of vacation travel:) To be a mass tourist, for me, is to become a pure late-date American: alien, ignorant, greedy for something you cannot ever have, disappointed in a way you can never admit. It is to spoil, by way of sheer ontology, the very unspoiledness you are there to experience. It is to impose yourself on places that in all non-economic ways would be better, realer, without you. It is, in lines and gridlock and transaction after transaction, to confront a dimension of yourself that is as inescapable as it is painful: As a tourist, you become economically significant but existentially loathsome, an insect on a dead thing.

[7] Datum: In a good year, the US industry produces around 80,000,000 pounds of lobster, and Maine accounts for more than half that total.

slightly less actual meat when you crack open a shedder, plus a redolent gout of water that gets all over everything and can sometimes jet out lemonlike and catch a tablemate right in the eye. If it's winter or you're buying lobster someplace far from New England, on the other hand, you can almost bet that the lobster is a hard-shell, which for obvious reasons travel better.

As an à la carte entrée, lobster can be baked, broiled, steamed, grilled, sautéed, stir-fried, or microwaved. The most common method, though, is boiling. If you're someone who enjoys having lobster at home, this is probably the way you do it, since boiling is so easy. You need a large kettle w/cover, which you fill about half full with water (the standard advice is that you want 2.5 quarts of water per lobster). Seawater is optimal, or you can add two tbsp salt per quart from the tap. It also helps to know how much your lobsters weigh. You get the water boiling, put in the lobsters one at a time, cover the kettle, and bring it back up to a boil. Then you bank the heat and let the kettle simmer — ten minutes for the first pound of lobster, then three minutes for each pound after that. (This is assuming you've got hard-shell lobsters, which, again, if you don't live between Boston and Halifax is probably what you've got. For shedders, you're supposed to subtract three minutes from the total.) The reason the kettle's lobsters turn scarlet is that boiling somehow suppresses every pigment in their chitin but one. If you want an easy test of whether the lobsters are done, you try pulling on one of their antennae — if it comes out of the head with minimal effort, you're ready to eat.

A detail so obvious that most recipes don't even bother to mention it is that each lobster is supposed to be alive when you put it in the kettle. This is part of lobster's modern appeal — it's the freshest food there is. There's no decomposition between harvesting and eating. And not only do lobsters require no cleaning or dressing or plucking, they're relatively easy for vendors to keep alive. They come up alive in the traps, are placed in containers of seawater, and can — so long as the water's aerated and the animals' claws are pegged or banded to keep them from tearing one another up under the stresses of captivity[8] — survive right up until they're boiled. Most of us have been in supermarkets or restaurants that feature tanks of live lobsters, from which you can pick out your supper while it watches you point. And part of the overall spectacle of the Maine Lobster Festival is that you can see actual lobstermen's vessels docking at the wharves along the northeast grounds and unloading fresh-caught product, which is transferred by hand or cart 150 yards to the great clear tanks stacked up around the festival's cooker — which is, as mentioned, billed as the World's Largest Lobster Cooker and can process over 100 lobsters at a time for the Main Eating Tent.

---

[8] N.B. Similar reasoning underlies the practice of what's termed "debeaking" broiler chickens and brood hens in modern factory farms. Maximum commercial efficiency requires that enormous poultry populations be confined in unnaturally close quarters, under which conditions many birds go crazy and peck one another to death. As a purely observational side-note, be apprised that debeaking is usually an automated process and that the chickens receive no anesthetic. It's not clear to me whether most *Gourmet* readers know about debeaking, or about related practices like dehorning cattle in commercial feed lots, cropping swine's tails in factory hog farms to keep psychotically bored neighbors from chewing them off, and so forth. It so happens that your assigned correspondent knew almost nothing about standard meat-industry operations before starting work on this article.

B. Anthony Stewart/Getty Images

A crate of lobsters is loaded onto a platform in preparation for cooking at the Maine Lobster Festival.

So then here is a question that's all but unavoidable at the World's Largest Lobster Cooker, and may arise in kitchens across the U.S.: Is it all right to boil a sentient creature alive just for our gustatory pleasure? A related set of concerns: Is the previous question irksomely PC or sentimental? What does "all right" even mean in this context? Is the whole thing just a matter of personal choice?

As you may or may not know, a certain well-known group called People for the Ethical Treatment of Animals thinks that the morality of lobster-boiling is not just a matter of individual conscience. In fact, one of the very first things we hear about the MLF . . . well, to set the scene: We're coming in by cab from the almost indescribably odd and rustic Knox County Airport[9] very late on the night before the festival opens, sharing the cab with a wealthy political consultant who lives on Vinalhaven Island in the bay half the year

---

[9] The terminal used to be somebody's house, for example, and the lost-luggage-reporting room was clearly once a pantry.

(he's headed for the island ferry in Rockland). The consultant and cabdriver are responding to informal journalistic probes about how people who live in the midcoast region actually view the MLF, as in is the festival just a big-dollar tourist thing or is it something local residents look forward to attending, take genuine civic pride in, etc. The cabdriver (who's in his seventies, one of apparently a whole platoon of retirees the cab company puts on to help with the summer rush, and wears a U.S.-flag lapel pin, and drives in what can only be called a very *deliberate* way) assures us that locals do endorse and enjoy the MLF, although he himself hasn't gone in years, and now come to think of it no one he and his wife know has, either. However, the demilocal consultant's been to recent festivals a couple times (one gets the impression it was at his wife's behest), of which his most vivid impression was that "you have to line up for an ungodly long time to get your lobsters, and meanwhile there are all these ex–flower children coming up and down along the line handing out pamphlets that say the lobsters die in terrible pain and you shouldn't eat them."

And it turns out that the post-hippies of the consultant's recollection were   15
activists from PETA. There were no PETA people in obvious view at the 2003 MLF,[10] but they've been conspicuous at many of the recent festivals. Since at least the mid-1990s, articles in everything from the *Camden Herald* to the *New York Times* have described PETA urging boycotts of the Maine Lobster Festival, often deploying celebrity spokesmen like Mary Tyler Moore for open letters and ads saying stuff like "Lobsters are extraordinarily sensitive" and "To me, eating a lobster is out of the question." More concrete is the oral testimony of Dick, our florid and extremely gregarious rental-car liaison,[11] to the effect that PETA's been around so much in recent years that a kind of brittlely tolerant homeostasis now obtains between the activists and the festival's locals, e.g.: "We had some incidents a couple years ago. One lady took most of her clothes off and painted herself like a lobster, almost got herself arrested. But for the most part they're let alone. [Rapid series of small ambiguous laughs, which with Dick happens a lot.] They do their thing and we do our thing."

---

10 It turned out that one Mr. William R. Rivas-Rivas, a high-ranking PETA official out of the group's Virginia headquarters, was indeed there this year, albeit solo, working the festival's main and side entrances on Saturday, 2 August, handing out pamphlets and adhesive stickers emblazoned with "Being Boiled Hurts," which is the tagline in most of PETA's published material about lobsters. I learned that he'd been there only later, when speaking with Mr. Rivas-Rivas on the phone. I'm not sure how we missed seeing him *in situ* at the festival, and I can't see much to do except apologize for the oversight — although it's also true that Saturday was the day of the big MLF parade through Rockland, which basic journalistic responsibility seemed to require going to (and which, with all due respect, meant that Saturday was maybe not the best day for PETA to work the Harbor Park grounds, especially if it was going to be just one person for one day, since a lot of diehard MLF partisans were off-site watching the parade (which, again with no offense intended, was in truth kind of cheesy and boring, consisting mostly of slow homemade floats and various midcoast people waving at one another, and with an extremely annoying man dressed as Blackbeard ranging up and down the length of the crowd saying "Arrr" over and over and brandishing a plastic sword at people, etc.; plus it rained)).

11 By profession, Dick is actually a car salesman; the midcoast region's National Car Rental franchise operates out of a Chevy dealership in Thomaston.

This whole interchange takes place on Route 1, 30 July, during a four-mile, 50-minute ride from the airport[12] to the dealership to sign car-rental papers. Several irreproducible segues down the road from the PETA anecdotes, Dick—whose son-in-law happens to be a professional lobsterman and one of the Main Eating Tent's regular suppliers—explains what he and his family feel is the crucial mitigating factor in the whole morality-of-boiling-lobsters-alive issue: "There's a part of the brain in people and animals that lets us feel pain, and lobsters' brains don't have this part."

Besides the fact that it's incorrect in about nine different ways, the main reason Dick's statement is interesting is that its thesis is more or less echoed by the festival's own pronouncement on lobsters and pain, which is part of a Test Your Lobster IQ quiz that appears in the 2003 MLF program courtesy of the Maine Lobster Promotion Council:

> The nervous system of a lobster is very simple, and is in fact most similar to the nervous system of the grasshopper. It is decentralized with no brain. There is no cerebral cortex, which in humans is the area of the brain that gives the experience of pain.

Though it sounds more sophisticated, a lot of the neurology in this latter claim is still either false or fuzzy. The human cerebral cortex is the brain-part that deals with higher faculties like reason, metaphysical self-awareness, language, etc. Pain reception is known to be part of a much older and more primitive system of nociceptors and prostaglandins that are managed by the brain stem and thalamus.[13] On the other hand, it is true that the cerebral cortex is involved in what's variously called suffering, distress, or the emotional experience of pain—i.e., experiencing painful stimuli as unpleasant, very unpleasant, unbearable, and so on.

Before we go any further, let's acknowledge that the questions of whether and how different kinds of animals feel pain, and of whether and why it might be justifiable to inflict pain on them in order to eat them, turn out to be extremely complex and difficult. And comparative neuroanatomy is only part of the problem. Since pain is a totally subjective mental experience, we do not have direct access to anyone or anything's pain but our own; and even just the principles by which we can infer that other human beings experience pain and have a legitimate interest in not feeling pain involve hard-core philosophy—metaphysics, epistemology, value theory, ethics. The fact that even the most highly evolved nonhuman mammals can't use language to communicate with us about their subjective mental experience is only the first

---

[12] The short version regarding why we were back at the airport after already arriving the previous night involves lost luggage and a miscommunication about where and what the midcoast's National franchise was—Dick came out personally to the airport and got us, out of no evident motive but kindness. (He also talked nonstop the entire way, with a very distinctive speaking style that can be described only as manically laconic; the truth is that I now know more about this man than I do about some members of my own family.)

[13] To elaborate by way of example: The common experience of accidentally touching a hot stove and yanking your hand back before you're even aware that anything's going on is explained by the fact that many of the processes by which we detect and avoid painful stimuli do not involve the cortex. In the case of the hand and stove, the brain is bypassed altogether; all the important neurochemical action takes place in the spine.

layer of additional complication in trying to extend our reasoning about pain and morality to animals. And everything gets progressively more abstract and convoluted as we move farther and farther out from the higher-type mammals into cattle and swine and dogs and cats and rodents, and then birds and fish, and finally invertebrates like lobsters.

The more important point here, though, is that the whole animal-   20
cruelty-and-eating issue is not just complex, it's also uncomfortable. It is, at any rate, uncomfortable for me, and for just about everyone I know who enjoys a variety of foods and yet does not want to see herself as cruel or unfeeling. As far as I can tell, my own main way of dealing with this conflict has been to avoid thinking about the whole unpleasant thing. I should add that it appears to me unlikely that many readers of *Gourmet* wish to think about it, either, or to be queried about the morality of their eating habits in the pages of a culinary monthly. Since, however, the assigned subject of this article is what it was like to attend the 2003 MLF, and thus to spend several days in the midst of a great mass of Americans all eating lobster, and thus to be more or less impelled to think hard about lobster and the experience of buying and eating lobster, it turns out that there is no honest way to avoid certain moral questions.

There are several reasons for this. For one thing, it's not just that lobsters get boiled alive, it's that you do it yourself—or at least it's done specifically for you, on-site.[14] As mentioned, the World's Largest Lobster Cooker, which is highlighted as an attraction in the festival's program, is right out there on the MLF's north grounds for everyone to see. Try to imagine a Nebraska Beef Festival[15] at which part of the festivities is watching trucks pull up and the live cattle get driven down the ramp and slaughtered right there on the World's Largest Killing Floor or something—there's no way.

The intimacy of the whole thing is maximized at home, which of course is where most lobster gets prepared and eaten (although note already the semiconscious euphemism "prepared," which in the case of lobsters really means killing them right there in our kitchens). The basic scenario is that we come in from the store and make our little preparations like getting the kettle filled and boiling, and then we lift the lobsters out of the bag or whatever

---

[14] Morality-wise, let's concede that this cuts both ways. Lobster-eating is at least not abetted by the system of corporate factory farms that produces most beef, pork, and chicken. Because, if nothing else, of the way they're marketed and packaged for sale, we eat these latter meats without having to consider that they were once conscious, sentient creatures to whom horrible things were done. (N.B. PETA distributes a certain video—the title of which is being omitted as part of the elaborate editorial compromise by which this note appears at all—in which you can see just about everything meat-related you don't want to see or think about. (N.B.[2] Not that PETA's any sort of font of unspun truth. Like many partisans in complex moral disputes, the PETA people are fanatics, and a lot of their rhetoric seems simplistic and self-righteous. Personally, though, I have to say that I found this unnamed video both credible and deeply upsetting.))

[15] Is it significant that "lobster," "fish," and "chicken" are our culture's words for both the animal and the meat, whereas most mammals seem to require euphemisms like "beef" and "pork" that help us separate the meat we eat from the living creature the meat once was? Is this evidence of some kind of deep unease about eating higher animals is endemic enough to show up in English usage, but that the unease diminishes as we move out of the mammalian order? (And is "lamb"/"lamb" the counterexample that sinks the whole theory, or are there special biblico-historical reasons for that equivalence?)

retail container they came home in . . . whereupon some uncomfortable things start to happen. However stuporous the lobster is from the trip home, for instance, it tends to come alarmingly to life when placed in boiling water. If you're tilting it from a container into the steaming kettle, the lobster will sometimes try to cling to the container's sides or even to hook its claws over the kettle's rim like a person trying to keep from going over the edge of a roof. And worse is when the lobster's fully immersed. Even if you cover the kettle and turn away, you can usually hear the cover rattling and clanking as the lobster tries to push it off. Or the creature's claws scraping the sides of the kettle as it thrashes around. The lobster, in other words, behaves very much as you or I would behave if we were plunged into boiling water (with the obvious exception of screaming).[16] A blunter way to say this is that the lobster acts as if it's in terrible pain, causing some cooks to leave the kitchen altogether and to take one of those little lightweight plastic oven-timers with them into another room and wait until the whole process is over.

There happen to be two main criteria that most ethicists agree on for determining whether a living creature has the capacity to suffer and so has genuine interests that it may or may not be our moral duty to consider.[17] One is how much of the neurological hardware required for pain-experience the animal comes equipped with—nociceptors, prostaglandins, neuronal opioid receptors, etc. The other criterion is whether the animal demonstrates behavior associated with pain. And it takes a lot of intellectual gymnastics and behaviorist hairsplitting not to see struggling, thrashing, and lid-clattering as just such pain-behavior. According to marine zoologists, it usually takes lobsters between 35 and 45 seconds to die in boiling water. (No source I could find talks about how long it takes them to die in superheated steam; one rather hopes it's faster.)

There are, of course, other ways to kill your lobster on-site and so achieve maximum freshness. Some cooks' practice is to drive a sharp heavy knife point-first into a spot just above the midpoint between the lobster's eyestalks (more or less where the Third Eye is in human foreheads). This is alleged either to kill the lobster instantly or to render it insensate, and is said at least to eliminate some of the cowardice involved in throwing a creature into

[16] There's a relevant populist myth about the high-pitched whistling sound that sometimes issues from a pot of boiling lobster. The sound is really vented steam from the layer of seawater between the lobster's flesh and its carapace (this is why shedders whistle more than hard-shells), but the pop version has it that the sound is the lobster's rabbit-like death scream. Lobsters communicate via pheromones in their urine and don't have anything close to the vocal equipment for screaming, but the myth's very persistent—which might, once again, point to a low-level cultural unease about the boiling thing.

[17] "Interests" basically means strong and legitimate preferences, which obviously require some degree of consciousness, responsiveness to stimuli, etc. See, for instance, the utilitarian philosopher Peter Singer [page 615], whose 1974 *Animal Liberation* is more or less the bible of the modern animal-rights movement:

> It would be nonsense to say that it was not in the interests of a stone to be kicked along the road by a schoolboy. A stone does not have interests because it cannot suffer. Nothing that we can do to it could possibly make any difference to its welfare. A mouse, on the other hand, does have an interest in not being kicked along the road, because it will suffer if it is.

boiling water and then fleeing the room. As far as I can tell from talking to proponents of the knife-in-the-head method, the idea is that it's more violent but ultimately more merciful, plus that a willingness to exert personal agency and accept responsibility for stabbing the lobster's head honors the lobster somehow and entitles one to eat it (there's often a vague sort of Native American spirituality-of-the-hunt flavor to pro-knife arguments). But the problem with the knife method is basic biology: Lobsters' nervous systems operate off not one but several ganglia, a.k.a. nerve bundles, which are sort of wired in series and distributed all along the lobster's underside, from stem to stern. And disabling only the frontal ganglion does not normally result in quick death or unconsciousness.

Another alternative is to put the lobster in cold saltwater and then very   25
slowly bring it up to a full boil. Cooks who advocate this method are going mostly on the analogy to a frog, which can supposedly be kept from jumping out of a boiling pot by heating the water incrementally. In order to save a lot of research-summarizing, I'll simply assure you that the analogy between frogs and lobsters turns out not to hold—plus, if the kettle's water isn't aerated seawater, the immersed lobster suffers from slow suffocation, although usually not decisive enough suffocation to keep it from still thrashing and clattering when the water gets hot enough to kill it. In fact, lobsters boiled incrementally often display a whole bonus set of gruesome, convulsionlike reactions that you don't see in regular boiling.

Ultimately, the only certain virtues of the home-lobotomy and slow-heating methods are comparative, because there are even worse/crueler ways people prepare lobster. Time-thrifty cooks sometimes microwave them alive (usually after poking several extra vent-holes in the carapace, which is a precaution most shellfish-microwavers learn about the hard way). Live dismemberment, on the other hand, is big in Europe—some chefs cut the lobster in half before cooking; others like to tear off the claws and tail and toss only these parts in the pot.

And there's more unhappy news respecting suffering-criterion number one. Lobsters don't have much in the way of eyesight or hearing, but they do have an exquisite tactile sense, one facilitated by hundreds of thousands of tiny hairs that protrude through their carapace. "Thus it is," in the words of T. M. Prudden's industry classic *About Lobster*, "that although encased in what seems a solid, impenetrable armor, the lobster can receive stimuli and impressions from without as readily as if it possessed a soft and delicate skin." And lobsters do have nociceptors,[18] as well as invertebrate versions of the prostaglandins and major neurotransmitters via which our own brains register pain.

Lobsters do not, on the other hand, appear to have the equipment for making or absorbing natural opioids like endorphins and enkephalins, which are what more advanced nervous systems use to try to handle intense pain. From this fact, though, one could conclude either that lobsters are maybe even

---

[18] This is the neurological term for special pain-receptors that are "sensitive to potentially damaging extremes of temperature, to mechanical forces, and to chemical substances which are released when body tissues are damaged."

more vulnerable to pain, since they lack mammalian nervous systems' built-in analgesia, or, instead, that the absence of natural opioids implies an absence of the really intense pain-sensations that natural opioids are designed to mitigate. I for one can detect a marked upswing in mood as I contemplate this latter possibility. It could be that their lack of endorphin/enkephalin hardware means that lobsters' raw subjective experience of pain is so radically different from mammals' that it may not even deserve the term "pain." Perhaps lobsters are more like those frontal-lobotomy patients one reads about who report experiencing pain in a totally different way than you and I. These patients evidently do feel physical pain, neurologically speaking, but don't dislike it—though neither do they like it; it's more that they feel it but don't feel anything *about* it—the point being that the pain is not distressing to them or something they want to get away from. Maybe lobsters, who are also without frontal lobes, are detached from the neurological-registration-of-injury-or-hazard we call pain in just the same way. There is, after all, a difference between (1) pain as a purely neurological event, and (2) actual suffering, which seems crucially to involve an emotional component, an awareness of pain as unpleasant, as something to fear/dislike/want to avoid.

Still, after all the abstract intellection, there remain the facts of the frantically clanking lid, the pathetic clinging to the edge of the pot. Standing at the stove, it is hard to deny in any meaningful way that this is a living creature experiencing pain and wishing to avoid/escape the painful experience. To my lay mind, the lobster's behavior in the kettle appears to be the expression of a preference; and it may well be that an ability to form preferences is the decisive criterion for real suffering.[19] The logic of this (preference → suffering) relation may be easiest to see in the negative case. If you cut certain kinds of worms in half, the halves will often keep crawling around and going about their vermiform business as if nothing had happened. When we assert, based on their post-op behavior, that these worms appear not to be suffering, what we're really saying is that there's no sign the worms know anything bad has happened or would *prefer* not to have gotten cut in half.

Lobsters, though, are known to exhibit preferences. Experiments have   30 shown that they can detect changes of only a degree or two in water temperature; one reason for their complex migratory cycles (which can often cover 100-plus miles a year) is to pursue the temperatures they like best.[20] And, as

---

[19] "Preference" is maybe roughly synonymous with "interests," but it is a better term for our purposes because it's less abstractly philosophical—"preference" seems more personal, and it's the whole idea of a living creature's personal experience that's at issue.

[20] Of course, the most common sort of counterargument here would begin by objecting that "like best" is really just a metaphor, and a misleadingly anthropomorphic one at that. The counter-arguer would posit that the lobster seeks to maintain a certain optimal ambient temperature out of nothing but unconscious instinct (with a similar explanation for the low-light affinities about to be mentioned in the main text). The thrust of such a counterargument will be that the lobster's thrashings and clankings in the kettle express not unpreferred pain but involuntary reflexes, like your leg shooting out when the doctor hits your knee. Be advised that there are professional scientists, including many researchers who use animals in experiments, who hold to the view that nonhuman creatures have no real feelings at all, merely "behaviors." Be further advised that this view has a long history that goes all the way back to Descartes, although its modern support comes mostly from behaviorist psychology.

mentioned, they're bottom-dwellers and do not like bright light—if a tank of food-lobsters is out in the sunlight or a store's fluorescence, the lobsters will always congregate in whatever part is darkest. Fairly solitary in the ocean, they also clearly dislike the crowding that's part of their captivity in tanks, since (as also mentioned) one reason why lobsters' claws are banded on capture is to keep them from attacking one another under the stress of close-quarter storage.

In any event, at the MLF, standing by the bubbling tanks outside the World's Largest Lobster Cooker, watching the fresh-caught lobsters pile over one another, wave their hobbled claws impotently, huddle in the rear corners, or scrabble frantically back from the glass as you approach, it is difficult not to sense that they're unhappy, or frightened, even if it's some rudimentary version of these feelings . . . and, again, why does rudimentariness even enter into it? Why is a primitive, inarticulate form of suffering less urgent or uncomfortable for the person who's helping to inflict it by paying for the food it results in? I'm not trying to give you a PETA-like screed here—at least I don't think so. I'm trying, rather, to work out and articulate some of the troubling questions that arise amid all the laughter and saltation and community pride of the Maine Lobster Festival. The truth is that if you, the festival attendee, permit yourself to think that lobsters can suffer and would rather not, the MLF begins to take on the aspect of something like a Roman circus or medieval torture-fest.

Does that comparison seem a bit much? If so, exactly why? Or what about this one: Is it possible that future generations will regard our own present agribusiness and eating practices in much the same way we now view Nero's[21] entertainments or Mengele's[22] experiments? My own initial reaction is that such a comparison is hysterical, extreme—and yet the reason it seems extreme to me appears to be that I believe animals are less morally important than human beings;[23] and when it comes to defending such a belief, even to myself, I have to acknowledge that (a) I have an obvious selfish interest in this belief, since I like to eat certain kinds of animals and want to be able to keep doing it, and (b) I haven't succeeded in working out any sort of personal ethical system in which the belief is truly defensible instead of just selfishly convenient.

---

20 (*continued*)

To these what-looks-like-pain-is-really-just-reflexes counterarguments, however, there happen to be all sorts of scientific and pro–animal rights counter-counterarguments. And then further attempted rebuttals and redirects, and so on. Suffice it to say that both the scientific and the philosophical arguments on either side of the animal-suffering issue are involved, abstruse, technical, often informed by self-interest or ideology, and in the end so totally inconclusive that as a practical matter, in the kitchen or restaurant, it all still seems to come down to individual conscience, going with (no pun) your gut.

21 **Nero** (37–68): First-century Roman emperor noted for his cruelty.—EDS.

22 **Mengele:** Dr. Mengele, the infamous Nazi concentration camp physician (1911–1979) who inspected new prisoners to select those fit for labor and those who would be exterminated. He also was responsible for performing medical experiments on prisoners.—EDS.

23 Meaning *a lot* less important, apparently, since the moral comparison here is not the value of one human's life vs. the value of one animal's life, but rather the value of one animal's life vs. the value of one human's taste for a particular kind of protein. Even the most diehard carniphile will acknowledge that it's possible to live and eat well without consuming animals.

Given this article's venue and my own lack of culinary sophistication, I'm curious about whether the reader can identify with any of these reactions and acknowledgments and discomforts. I'm also concerned not to come off as shrill or preachy when what I really am is more like confused. For those *Gourmet* readers who enjoy well-prepared and -presented meals involving beef, veal, lamb, pork, chicken, lobster, etc.: Do you think much about the (possible) moral status and (probable) suffering of the animals involved? If you do, what ethical convictions have you worked out that permit you not just to eat but to savor and enjoy flesh-based viands (since of course refined enjoyment, rather than mere ingestion, is the whole point of gastronomy)? If, on the other hand, you'll have no truck with confusions or convictions and regard stuff like the previous paragraph as just so much fatuous navel-gazing, what makes it feel truly okay, inside, to just dismiss the whole thing out of hand? That is, is your refusal to think about any of this the product of actual thought, or is it just that you don't want to think about it? And if the latter, then why not? Do you ever think, even idly, about the possible reasons for your reluctance to think about it? I am not trying to bait anyone here—I'm genuinely curious. After all, isn't being extra aware and attentive and thoughtful about one's food and its overall context part of what distinguishes a real gourmet? Or is all the gourmet's extra attention and sensibility just supposed to be sensuous? Is it really all just a matter of taste and presentation?

These last few queries, though, while sincere, obviously involve much larger and more abstract questions about the connections (if any) between aesthetics and morality —about what the adjective in a phrase like "The Magazine of Good Living" is really supposed to mean—and these questions lead straightaway into such deep and treacherous waters that it's probably best to stop the public discussion right here. There are limits to what even interested persons can ask of each other. ●

The Reader's Presence

1. What is the occasion behind "Consider the Lobster"? Why did Wallace write it? How would you describe the audience he is writing for? What relation does he establish with that audience? What is Wallace's overall attitude toward the event that he was assigned to write about?

2. Wallace refers to "Consider the Lobster" as an "article." How does it differ from the magazine articles you may typically read? Note the title: "Consider" is often a term used by essayists. What does the word *consider* suggest to you? It's common in essays for the essayist to examine different sides of an issue and, instead of coming up with a definite conclusion, offer various ways that we might think of, or "consider," that issue. What features of the selection resemble a magazine article? What features appear essayistic?

3. **CONNECTIONS:** "Consider the Lobster" is a well-known, highly complex essay that attempts to engage its reader in a difficult ethical argument. You might want to compare Wallace's essay to another challenging ethical argument found in this section, Peter Singer's "The Singer Solution to World Poverty" (page 615). Singer identifies

himself as a utilitarian philosopher, someone "who judges whether acts are right or wrong by their consequences." Do you think Wallace shares this philosophy? Can you cite evidence from Wallace's essay that either supports Singer's ethical views or that refutes them? How do you think Singer would assess Wallace's argument from an ethical standpoint?

The Writer at Work

Another Version of "Consider the Lobster"

Suzy Allman /The New York Times

When David Foster Wallace submitted "Consider the Lobster" to *Gourmet*, which calls itself "The Magazine of Good Living," the piece was edited by the magazine before it appeared in its August 2004 issue. After it was selected for the *Best American Essays 2005*, Wallace asked if he could make some changes before it was published in that volume. Basically, he wanted to restore some of his original remarks that the magazine had revised. Then, when he included the essay in his own collection, *Consider the Lobster and Other Essays* (2005), he made even further revisions. It is that final text that we have included in this book.

Most of Wallace's revisions occur in the conclusion of the essay. The following passage is taken from the first appearance of the essay in *Gourmet* magazine and represents the essay's final four paragraphs. As you compare the concluding paragraphs as they appeared in *Gourmet* to those Wallace preferred and used in his book (pages 662–63), what do you find significant about the differences? What kind of changes had *Gourmet* made? Why do you think Wallace wanted to change what *Gourmet* had done? Note the substitution of "Aztec sacrifices" for "Mengele's experiments" (for more on Mengele see Elie Wiesel's "Eight Simple, Short Words" on page 264). Which is the better example in your opinion? Why do you think Wallace preferred to address his readers as "you" in his version and not as "they" as appears in paragraph 3 of the *Gourmet* version? Why do you think the magazine preferred to drop the direct address to readers in this context?

From *Gourmet* magazine:

[31] ❝I'm not trying to give you a PETA-like screed here—at least I don't think so. I'm trying, rather, to work out and articulate some of the troubling questions that arise amid all the laughter and saltation and community pride of the Maine Lobster Festival. The truth is that if you, the Festival attendee, permit yourself to think that lobsters can suffer and would rather not, the MLF can begin to take on aspects of something like a Roman circus or medieval torture-fest.

[32] Does that comparison seem a bit much? If so, exactly why? Or what about this one: Is it not possible that future generations will regard our own present agribusiness and eating practices in much the same way we now view Nero's entertainments or Aztec sacrifices? My own immediate reaction is that such a comparison is hysterical, extreme—and

yet the reason it seems extreme to me appears to be that I believe animals are less morally important than human beings; and when it comes to defending such a belief, even to myself, I have to acknowledge that (a) I have an obvious selfish interest in this belief, since I like to eat certain kinds of animals and want to be able to keep doing it, and (b) I have not succeeded in working out any sort of personal ethical system in which the belief is truly defensible instead of just selfishly convenient.

[33] Given this article's venue and my own lack of culinary sophistication, I'm curious about whether the reader can identify with any of these reactions and acknowledgments and discomforts. I am also concerned not to come off as shrill or preachy when what I really am is confused. Given the (possible) moral status and (very possible) physical suffering of the animals involved, what ethical convictions do gourmets evolve that allow them not just to eat but to savor and enjoy flesh-based viands (since of course refined *enjoyment*, rather than just ingestion, is the whole point of gastronomy)? And for those gourmets who'll have no truck with convictions or rationales and who regard stuff like the previous paragraph as just so much pointless navel-gazing, what makes it feel okay, inside, to dismiss the whole issue out of hand? That is, is their refusal to think about any of this the product of actual thought, or is it just that they don't want to think about it? Do they ever think about their reluctance to think about it? After all, isn't being extra aware and attentive and thoughtful about one's food and its overall context part of what distinguishes a real gourmet? Or is all the gourmet's extra attention and sensibility just supposed to be aesthetic, gustatory?

[34] These last couple queries, though, while sincere, obviously involve much larger and more abstract questions about the connections (if any) between aesthetics and morality, and these questions lead straightaway into such deep and treacherous waters that it's probably best to stop the public discussion right here. There are limits to what even interested persons can ask of each other.**

John Edgar Wideman

FATHERALONG*

Asa Messen Professor and professor of Africana studies and Literary Arts at Brown University, **JOHN EDGAR WIDEMAN** (b. 1941) was the first author to twice win the International PEN/Faulkner Award for Fiction. After receiving his BA in English in 1963, he won a Rhodes scholarship to study philosophy at Oxford University's New College. He returned to the

* The word I heard as a child when the church sang "Farther Along."

United States in 1966, spent a year as a Kent Fellow at the famous University of Iowa Writer's Workshop, and published his first novel, *A Glance Away*, in 1967. He has written many novels since then, including *The Lynchers* (1973), *Hiding Place* (1981), *Philadelphia Fire* (1990), *Two Cities* (1998), and *Fanon* (2008), to name but a few. He is also the author of a memoir, *Brothers and Keepers* (1984), as well as several other nonfiction books and collections of short stories. *Conversations with John Edgar Wideman*, a series of nineteen interviews spanning three decades, was pub-

> **John Edgar Wideman was the first author to twice win the International PEN/Faulkner Award for Fiction.**

lished by the University Press of Mississippi in 1998. He's won the American Book Award for Fiction, the Lannan Literary Fellowship for fiction, and a MacArthur Fellowship. "Fatheralong" was published in *Harper's* in 2009. The book Wideman published by the same title in 1994 was a finalist for the National Book Award for nonfiction. In 2016, Wideman further expanded part of this essay and published *Writing to Save a Life: The Louis Till File*. Wideman has written widely on African American issues and culture, and his articles on Malcolm X, Spike Lee, Denzel Washington, Michael Jordan, Emmett Till, Thelonius Monk, and women's professional basketball have appeared in the *New Yorker*, *Vogue*, *Esquire*, *Emerge*, and the *New York Times Magazine*. His daughter, Jamila, is a professional basketball player.

LOUIS TILL, THE FATHER OF EMMETT TILL, the fourteen-year-old Chicago boy murdered in Mississippi in 1955, one year after the Supreme Court's school desegregation decision, is the first father I think about when I am asked to comment on the alleged failure of black males to assume properly the responsibilities of fatherhood. I also think about Freud, about the global crisis demanding a metamorphosis of family that's not new, not black. President Barack Obama, who addressed such issues earlier and eloquently in his *Dreams from My Father* (1995), is clearly the catalyst of the present discussions as he works to apply his personal insights and experiences to a national dilemma. I'm moved by his honest explorations of fatherhood, his witness. The world is a troubled, dangerous place, at best. Unfairly dangerous for young Americans in free fall, growing up too fast or not growing at all, deprived of the love, guidance, positive example, the material, intellectual, and moral support of fathers negotiating the perils with them.

Louis Till's Non-Battle Casualty Report lists his rank as PVT, his serial number as 36392273, lists the Date of Casualty as July 2, his Reporting Theatre as MTO, the Mediterranean Theatre of Operations, lists his Arm or Service as TC, the Transportation Command, a non-combat unit to which nearly every colored soldier in the segregated U.S. Army was assigned, lists the Place of Casualty as Italy, and leaves blank, except for an asterisk, the space in which Type of Casualty should be listed. Mrs. Mamie Till's name (misspelled "Mammie") appears on the Battle Casualty Report, but it does not mention Till's son, Emmett.

Emmett Till

Bettmann/Getty Images

The first time Mamie Till knew her husband had been hanged in Italy by the United States Army was in the fall of 1955, not long after their son Emmett was murdered, about a dozen years after she'd seen Louis Till last in Chicago. The telegram she had received from the Army on July 13, 1945, composed of selected facts from the Non-Battle Casualty Report, informed her that her husband, Private Louis Till, had died of willful misconduct, but omitted "sol died in non-battle status" and "judicial asphixiation," words typed into a confidential footnote below the official report. Although assisted by a lawyer, Mrs. Till's attempt to investigate the circumstances surrounding the death of her husband and father of her only child had been stymied by the government's terminal unresponsiveness, the very same government that ordered its colored soldiers to serve in what amounted to a separate, second-class army of conscripted laborers.

The government that at its highest levels chose to break its own rules and violate the rights of Private Louis Till by sending his confidential service record, which included a transcript of his court martial (CM288642), to lawyers defending the kidnappers and killers of his son, Emmett. Driven by their desire to repair the public image of a state that was being drubbed nationwide by press coverage of Emmett Till's murder, the Mississippi arch-segregationist Senators James Eastland and John Stennis are likely the ones who obtained and leaked Louis Till's papers, as only officials with their rank and clout could demand and receive, from the Army adjutant general, a soldier's classified service record. A Colonel Ralph K. Johnson, TJAG (The Judge Advocate General) on October 14, 1955, did the dirty work of signing off on the release and penciling out the word confidential stamped on the cover and pages of the Record of Trial by General Courts Martial, dated February 17, 1945.

In November 1955, approximately six weeks after a trial that found World 5 War II veterans—J. W. Milam and his brother-in-law Roy Bryant—not guilty of murdering Emmett Till, a trial that the Cleveland *Post and Call* derided ("Mississippi Jungle Law Frees Slayers of Child") and the Greenwood, Mississippi, *Morning Star* complimented ("Fair Trial Was Credit to Mississippi"), the state of Mississippi, compelled by the testimony of a sheriff during the trial that Milam and Bryant admitted to him they had taken Emmett Till from his great-uncle Moses Wright's home, sought indictments against the two men for kidnapping. Parties unknown leaked to the press that

Emmett Till's father, Mamie Till's husband, Louis, far from being the martyred war hero portrayed in Northern papers during the trial, had been hanged by the U.S. Army for committing rape and murder.

This revelation of the crimes of the father doomed any chance that jurors in Sumner, Mississippi, would indict the killers of Louis Till's son for any wrongdoing whatever. Instead of what measure of comfort she might have felt if the court had punished her son's murderers, Mamie Bradley Till found herself watching in dismay as Emmett Till's already dead and brutalized body was tarred, feathered, and lynched again for the father's sins, her fourteen-year-old boy stigmatized, scorned as rotten fruit from a rotten tree.

The novelist Chester Himes, expressing the despair shared by many of his fellow citizens, published a letter in the *New York Post* on September 25, 1955, in which he wrote, "The real horror comes when your dead brain must face the fact that we as a nation don't want it to stop. If we wanted to, we would. So let us all share the guilt, those in New York as well as those in Sumner, Mississippi."

As a father, Louis Till didn't have much time to spend with his son. Emmett Till was born in July of 1941 (a month after I was born), and Louis Till (like my father) went off to war in a segregated army in 1942, returning to Chicago only once, one AWOL night before the Army came and knocked on Mamie's door in the morning and hauled him back. A ring Louis Till purchased in Casablanca and had engraved with his initials and the date May 25, 1943, was included among the personal effects Mamie Till received from the Army after she was notified of his death. This silver ring, cached in Emmett Till's jewelry box or occasionally worn on his finger, padded by tape until his finger grew thick enough the last year of his life to keep it in place, may have been the most intimate link between father and son, an irony, since the ring also served to identify Emmett Till's battered, bloated, disfigured body when it was pulled from the Tallahatchie River.

What kind of father did Emmett Till imagine when he wore the silver ring? Looking down at the ring encircling his own dark finger, did Louis Till ever think about a son bearing his name, *Till*, wearing the ring one day?

While his sentence of death by hanging was receiving its mandatory   10
review by The Judge Advocate General's Division, Louis Till was confined in the Disciplinary Training Center, a United States military prison in Metato, near Pisa. The poet Ezra Pound, facing a capital sentence himself, on charges of treasonous radio broadcasts, was Till's fellow prisoner, the only civilian in a population of 3,600 mostly colored inmates. The Pisan *Cantos*, written during Pound's internment in the DTC, imagine Louis Till as *Outis*, Greek for "no one," "nobody," the wanderer of the Odyssey, as Zeus the lusty ram, Till's sign, the Chinese ideogram "M4," "a man upon whom the sun has gone down" (Canto LXXIV: 170–178, edited by Richard Sieburth).

If Louis Till had been around to school Emmett about the perils of the South, about how white men treat black boys down south and up north, would Emmett have returned to Chicago safely on the *City of New Orleans* train from his trip to visit relatives in Money, Mississippi, started up public school in the fall, earned good grades, maybe even have become successful and rich, eluding the fate of his father? Or does his father's fate draw Emmett like a fluttering moth to its flame, Emmett flying backward and forward at once, like the African sankofa bird flies, because part of the father's fate is not to be around to advise and supervise and support the son, the fate of father and son to be divided always? A cycle of predictable missings and absence eternally renewed. A flicker of wings igniting, quickly extinguished, then darkness.

Race is myth. When we stop talking about race, stop believing in race, it will disappear. Except for its career historically and in people's memories as the antithesis of human freedom, the embodiment of inequality and injustice that remained far too long a toxic, unresolved paradox in nations proclaiming themselves free. In a raceless society color wouldn't disappear. Difference wouldn't disappear. Africa wouldn't disappear. In post-race America "white" people would disappear. That is, no group could assume as birthright and identity a privileged, supernaturally ordained superiority at the top of a hierarchy of other groups, a supremacy that bestows upon their particular kind the right perpetually to rule and regulate the lives of all other kinds. This idea, this belief in "whiteness," whether the belief is expressed in terms of color, ethnicity, nationality, gender, tribe, etc., constitutes the founding principle of race, its appeal and its discontents.

To dismiss race as myth is not to underestimate its power. Race, like religion, is immune to critiques of science and logic because it rests on belief. And people need beliefs. Although science has discredited the biological underpinnings of the notion of race, faith rushes in to seal the cracks, paper over glaring omissions in arrested explanations of human difference offered by racial ideology. Louis Till's color, the color of his son, Emmett, the color of Richard Wright's fictional character Bigger Thomas, Colin Powell's color, are not problems until the myth of race and the racialized perspective it authorizes turn color into an indictment, into instant proof of innocence or guilty-as-charged. We should understand by now that race can mean anything, everything, or nothing, depending upon whom we ask.

The continuing existence of race in the United States indicates conspiracy and cover-up. An attempt to make more palatable to ourselves, and anyone watching, the not-so-secret dirty secret shared by all Americans that our country, in spite of public professions to the contrary, entertains a deeply internalized, segregated vision of itself. We look at ourselves and believe we see White Americans or Black Americans. We perceive our problems as Black or White problems, The urgent task of redressing the shameful neglect of American children gets postponed by hand-wringing and finger-pointing at feckless black fathers and the damage they're inflicting upon their black offspring. Or sidetracked just as effectively by blaming society and exempting blacks because race tells us blacks are permanent victims, not agents of change. The truth of too many black boys in prison, too many black babies dying, too many hungry black youngsters being raised in dire poverty, too many terrible black schools—these truths misrepresented by discourses perpetuating the myth of separate races don't spur us to action but become an occasion for shedding crocodile tears, washing our hands of personal as well as collective responsibility. More than half a century ago James Baldwin,[1] outed this kind of hiding from the consequences of racialized thinking as *willed innocence*. At this late date, displays of surprise or ignorance about how bad things are for our children suggest dishonesty, signify complicity, conscious or unconscious, with the cover-up.

Louis Till was born fatherless in Madrid, Missouri. One could argue that   15
the concept of race abiding today in America is a profound orphaning of all black children. Argue that any attempt to understand black fathers and to interpret their responsibilities, successes, and failures should begin right there, with a consideration of the fact that myths of race isolate children, place them at risk, disinherit and repudiate. Start by listening a moment to the roaring silence in which Louis Till is buried, the silence neither his voice nor his son's voice can break, the dark, impervious silence in which words — *good, bad, responsible, black, white* — vanish. ●

The Reader's Presence

1. Comment on Wideman's decision to frame his essay with the story of Louis Till's hanging while in military service in Italy during World War II and the murder of his son, Emmett, "the fourteen-year-old Chicago boy murdered in Mississippi in 1955, one year after the Supreme Court's school desegregation decision" (paragraph 1). In what specific ways does Wideman's account of their deaths — and the reports on each — enable him to build an argument about the role of race in American culture? Demonstrate how Wideman builds his argument step-by-step toward his concluding assertion: "One could argue that the concept of race abiding today in America is a profound orphaning of all black children" (paragraph 15).

2. Wideman explains in an epigraph to his essay that the title, "Fatheralong," is "[t]he word I heard as a child when the church sang 'Farther Along.'" In the light of reading Wideman's essay, what literal and figurative meanings do you think Wideman associates with the word *Fatheralong*? In what specific ways can this word serve as a painfully ironic commentary on the state of race relations in contemporary American society? Support your response by pointing to — and then analyzing — specific passages. What evidence does Wideman present to support his argument that "[r]ace is myth" (paragraph 12)? What distinctions does Wideman draw between "belief" and "faith" in the context of race relations in the United States (paragraph 13)?

3. **CONNECTIONS:** Near the end of his essay, Wideman invokes James Baldwin's phrase *"willed innocence"* to challenge the "truths misrepresented by discourses perpetuating the myth of separate races" as "an occasion for shedding crocodile tears, washing our hands of personal as well as collective responsibility" (paragraph 14). Compare and contrast Wideman's and Baldwin's attitudes toward — and suggestions for improving — race relations in the United States. In what specific ways is Wideman's essay similar to — and different from — Kwame Anthony Appiah's view of racial concepts in his "Race in the Modern World" (page 291)?

1 See Baldwin's "Notes of a Native Son" (page 40). —EDS.

Wendy Willis

BOXED IN

For those with mixed ancestry, forms and surveys requiring us to identify with a specific race or ethnic group can present a particular quandary. How do we accurately represent heritage without appropriating other cultures? This is the question poet **WENDY WILLIS** attempts to answer as she reflects on her identity as a white woman with Native American ancestors. "If I just check 'White' and call it good," she writes, "I feel like a liar willing to leave a whole branch of my family behind for the sake of simplicity and safety."

> Willis examines the experience of "passing" as white and the privilege and discomfort it presents.

A former public defender, Willis is the founder and director of Oregon's Kitchen Table, a program at Portland State University that encourages and facilitates statewide civic engagement. She is also the executive director of the national nonprofit organization Kitchen Table Democracy and a faculty member of the Attic Institute of Arts and Letters. In 2012, she published her first book of poems, *Blood Sisters of the Republic*.

WE HAVE BECOME A NATION OF inquiry. Every time we turn around, we are being asked our opinion about breakfast cereal or the governor's race or the mood of the country. We send each other surveys to set meeting times and to extend birthday party invitations. But then those queries often turn toward us. The purveyors of all those forms say they want to "get to know us." They say they want to know "who is in the room." So we gamely comply. Of course, the forms include the basic fill-in-the blanks—address and phone number, name and preferred salutation.

But there are also the true, honest-to-goodness forced-choice questions. The ones where we actually have to choose from among a finite set of options. I do pretty well with gender and marital status and age, though I know that is not true for everyone. I'm not even shy about answering questions about my family income. But we are also usually asked to check a box to identify ourselves by race or "ethnic origin." And that's where my confidence starts to break down. That's where my hand wavers and my heart races a bit.

It shouldn't be that hard. The simple story is that I am a middle-aged white lady, and in most instances that's how I identify myself. But that is not the whole story. In fact, my grandfather and his family were Cherokees who stopped in Arkansas and then pulled up stakes and moved again when

Oregon looked a little more promising than northern Arkansas through the smudge of the Dust Bowl. Eventually my grandfather met my German-Norwegian grandmother on Main Street in Springfield. She worked at the grocery store. He worked at the bakery. They married, he never returned to Arkansas, and he died in his fifties, when I was not quite three years old.

Now, forty-five years later, I still haven't sorted out how to capture that story within the confines of a single—or even a double—check mark. I tell it to my friends and loved ones in pretty much the way I relayed it here. But the forms aren't asking for a story; they're asking for an outright choice. And they're asking for a choice for mostly good reasons—to make sure that people of color are visible and accounted for in our institutions and our thinking, and to make sure we are cognizant of who's benefiting from society and who isn't.

Most of the time, I check "White, non-Hispanic." But not always. On   5
forms that seem somehow less official, I occasionally choose "Mixed Race" or both "White" and "Native American." I am not sure why I waffle or why I sometimes choose one or the other. I suppose it is partially because identity is dynamic, but more than that, it is because I struggle over the right thing to do. I'm not used to that feeling. At this stage of life, I have a pretty good idea of what the right thing to do is in most circumstances. But this case is different. I really don't know what is right. Or to put it more accurately, I feel like both choices are wrong. I feel a sense of prickly discomfort and guilt either way. If I check "Mixed Race" or "Native American" in addition to "White," I worry that I am being an appropriator or a poseur. As one friend put it, "everyone wants to be an Indian until they have to deal with the realities." And I don't want to be that person—the one that appropriates but doesn't give back. The one that takes on the mantle of suffering without actually experiencing any of the suffering. The one that takes on legacies of power and pride that are not hers, legacies that she has not earned.

For me, like for many mixed race Americans, it is easy enough to "pass" as simply white, and the uncomplicated story often seems like the preferable one, the one less fraught with moral and political risk. After all, I've had all the privileges of being a white, educated, middle-class woman, and most of the time I think that's where I should stay. I think of Elizabeth Warren[1] and Johnny Depp[2] and others who have been publicly castigated for calling themselves Indian. I don't want to feel like that kind of pretender or subject myself to that type of ridicule, even if it's only in my own mind. On the other hand, if I just check "White" and call it good, I feel like a liar willing to leave a whole branch of my family behind for the sake of simplicity and safety. I feel like I am letting the assimilationists win.

Because the fact is, this is just how the founders and authors of the capital-A, capital-S "American Story" wanted it, and not just that nasty Andrew Jackson[3]

---

1 *Elizabeth Warren* (b. 1949): A Democratic Senator from Massachusetts.—EDS.

2 *Johnny Depp* (b. 1963): An American actor, producer, and musician.—EDS.

3 *Andrew Jackson* (1767–1845): An American soldier and statesman who served as the seventh president of the United States from 1829–1837.—EDS.

either. Thomas Jefferson, who both admired Native culture and set wheels in motion to obliterate it, wrote to the U.S. Indian Agent Benjamin Hawkins:

> In truth, the ultimate point of rest & happiness for them is to let our settlements and theirs meet and blend together, to intermix, and become one people. Incorporating themselves with us as citizens of the U.S., this is what the natural progress of things will of course bring on, and it will be better to promote than to retard it. Surely it will be better for them to be identified with us, and preserved in the occupation of their lands, than be exposed to the many casualties which may endanger them while a separate people. I have little doubt but that your reflections must have led you to view the various ways in which their history may terminate, and to see that this is the one most for their happiness.

Teddy Roosevelt summarized it this way: "But all of the Indians who had attained to an even low grade of industrial and social efficiency have remained in the land, and have for the most part simply been assimilated with the intruders, the assimilation marking on the whole a very considerable rise in their conditions."

And Henry Pratt, the founder of the notorious federal Indian boarding schools, put it even more bluntly when he advocated that the government "kill the Indian and save the man" and then proceeded to aggressively pursue what he called "assimilation through education."

So here I am, living in the twenty-first-century West, in exactly the position that Jefferson and Jackson and Roosevelt and Pratt designed for me: assimilated and white and anchoring down their vision of civilization in the far corner of the American frontier. To continue calling myself white without footnote or protest makes me feel complicit in imperialism and like a pawn of their genocidal impulses. 10

I recognize that my version of this dilemma is a small one in a long line of uncomfortable — and often unjust — problems created by these check boxes. On the 1790 Census form, the only racial categories included were "Free White Males; Free White Females; All Other Free Persons; Slaves." In 1910, they were "White; Black; Mulatto; Chinese; Japanese; Indian; Other." The Census Bureau essentially created a new race in 1980 by separating out "Hispanics." And Native Hawaiian wasn't included as an option on the Census form until 2000, which was also the first year that individuals were allowed to identify as belonging to more than one race. Since the time of the founding, Americans have struggled to find themselves in the categories they have been presented with. But in this particular iteration, it is not that the categories are not there for me; it's that I feel like a fraud no matter what I choose.

When it gets down to putting pen to paper and filling in the box with my own hand, questions of identity have other, less visible complexities. Yes, they present issues of race. And race and all that goes with it have deep political and social consequences. Race is the source of the gravest injustices Americans have perpetrated upon one another. So those questions are fraught from their inception.

But the questions also raise issues of family loyalty and gratitude and just plain good manners. In twenty-first-century America, we are rarely asked to think beyond the current moment and its short-term gains and losses. We are rarely asked to acknowledge our past or take account of our future. We are a nation that values the here and now, the hot story of the moment. So when we are asked to identify ourselves by racial and ethnic origin, it is one of the very few times when we are asked, "Who are your people? Where did they come from? Who do you bring with you?" In that context, when I check the box "White" and nothing else, I am bringing treasured people along with me — my German-Norwegian grandmother and my great-great-grandfather who was a "ship boy" between Germany and New York. I am bringing along sons and daughters of the American Revolution. And I am glad to have them there beside me.

But if I leave it at that, I abandon a whole bunch of other ancestors. I abandon my great-great-grandmother who lived on a dirt farm near the Arkansas-Missouri border, and my great-uncle, whom we remember because of the one photo we have of him with his rifle and his "pup dog," as he wrote on the back. I deny my legendary great-grandfather who had a naughty streak and a taste for whiskey. And I leave behind my grandfather, who I remember for his sweet-smelling pipe and gravelly voice. When I think about all of them, it's not about passing or blood quantum[4] or federal recognition. It is about my connection to real people. It is about being honest about who I love and honor. And to deny those dear ones to the likes of an Internet provider or census taker or employer feels disloyal and ungrateful. It's like bragging about the accomplishments of one of my children and pretending the other one doesn't exist. It makes me feel like I should be struck by lightning.

I also think that the urgency of the question of who comes along with me   15 across generations and who is left behind is amplified by middle age and its nagging shadow of mortality. As I fill out some of the last school forms I will ever be faced with, I can't help but wonder what boxes my daughters and their children and the children after that will check. I wonder whether they will choose the simple boxes they inherited from their father, the ones that flow from England and Ireland and Germany. I wonder if I will get left behind because I make things too complicated or — worse — because I chose to make things simple.

All that said, though, I know this dilemma is a privilege: I live in a cloak of whiteness. Anytime I want, I can shelve my moral hand-wringing, check the "White" box, and never have to think or talk about race and its power dynamics and its ugly legacy unless I want to, and if I do, it can be on my own terms. This ability partially answers the question about what box I should check.

But it doesn't answer it entirely. There is a kind of polite, middle-class timidity in checking "White" in order not to offend, in trying to stay far from the line where anyone could possibly criticize me for being a poseur or an appropriator. There is privilege, yes, in taking the path of least resistance. But there is also cowardice and complicity. I want to come to this question with more fierceness, with more outrage and courage. I am reminded of and chastened by James

---

4 **blood quantum:** a measurement of an individual's Native American ancestry. —EDS.

Dickey's[5] magnificent poem "For the Last Wolverine." The entire poem embodies the snarl and wildness of an imagined wolverine before the species becomes entirely extinct. In Dickey's poem, the wolverine eats an "elk's horned heart" and mates with the last eagle in the branches of a tree. Here is where the poem ends:

> Your unnoticed going will mean:
> How much the timid poem needs
>
> The mindless explosion of your rage,
>
> The glutton's internal fire   the elk's
> Heart in the belly, sprouting wings,
>
> The pact of the "blind swallowing
> Thing," with himself, to eat
> The world, and not to be driven off it
> Until it is gone, even if it takes
>
> Forever. I take you as you are
> And make of you what I will,
> Skunk-bear, carcajoy, bloodthirsty
> Non-survivor.
>
>   *Lord, let me die but not die*
> Out.

In the face of this invitation to "eat / The world, and not to be driven off it," I am ashamed of my own "timid poem," of my own quiet dithering over which box to check on the survey about cereal preferences. Despite the best efforts of Andrew Jackson and his cronies past and present, Native cultures are alive and well in America. They have thrived in the face of tremendous adversity and violence.

But in my own lineage, the thread has grown thin. My grandparents are gone, and I fear their legacy is passing into milk-white obscurity. I am embarrassed by the placidity of my response. I certainly do not want to pretend that I carry the lived experience of Native peoples who are facing down fracking and depletion of fisheries and centuries of struggle to regain traditional lands. I can't speak to those injustices, but I do carry a different lived experience—one that is nameless and amorphous and without a box. If I were a braver woman and less timorous in the face of what my Cowlitz[6]-French friend calls the "internalized fear of ridicule" or the "Johnny Depp syndrome," I might approach those boxes more like the wolverine. I might spit on the form and scrawl across it: "I know you have to ask these questions. Go ahead. And what is my answer? You have turned me into a house cat with your Indian Removal Act and blood quantum measurements and deep concerns for my happiness that come tied up with a bow of obliteration. I am three generations removed from knowing what month the tart-sweet berries turn red or where best to hunt the fattest turkey. I am declawed and weak and trembling. So here's the answer: I cannot answer your questions. I have no idea what I am. Move along. Oh Lord, let me die. But not die out." ■

---

5 **James Dickey** (1923–1997): An American poet who served as the U.S. Poet Laureate (1966–68). His work often deals with nature and the American South. Although considered a leading modern poet, he is perhaps best known for his novel that became a major film, *Deliverance* (1970).—EDS.

6 **Cowlitz:** An indigenous people of the Pacific Northwest.—EDS.

The Reader's Presence

1. The title of Willis's essay, "Boxed In," refers to the questions in forms and surveys which ask us to identify our race by checking boxes. Willis observes, however, that her answer often changes, and she occasionally selects more than one option. What causes her to feel "boxed in" by these decisions? To what extent—and how—does she resolve these tensions about self-identity? What does the metaphor suggest about the way we define race and ethnicity? Support each point you make with detailed references to Willis's essay and additional identified sources.

2. Consider Willis's memories of her Native American ancestors. What does she mean when she writes, "When I think about all of them, it's not about passing or blood quantum or federal recognition" (paragraph 14)? As her efforts to come to terms with her mixed identity move her closer to clarity and resolution, Willis observes: "There is privilege, yes, in taking the path of least resistance. But there is also cowardice and complicity. I want to come to this question with more fierceness, with more outrage and courage" (paragraph 17). At this point, Willis reminds herself and "is chastened by" the final few stanzas of James Dickey's poem "For the Last Wolverine." Explain what impact citing Dicky's poem has on Willis. How does Dickey's invitation to "eat / The world, and not to be driven off it" enable Willis to appreciate better her "own quiet dithering over which box to check on the survey about cereal preferences" (paragraph 18)?

3. **CONNECTIONS:** Compare and contrast the inflexibility of racial identity in "Boxed In" with the fluidity of identity, especially gender, described by Amanda Hess in "Multiple Choice" (page 397). In what specific ways does each author trade on the title of her essay to support and underscore the points she makes? Make a list of points you think prevent us from "thinking outside the box" about race.

Howard Zinn

STORIES HOLLYWOOD NEVER TELLS

HOWARD ZINN (1922–2010) was professor emeritus of political science at Boston University and is known both for his active involvement in the civil rights and peace movements and for his scholarship. He published scores of books that reflected the issues of their times yet remain in print, demonstrating their continuing relevance. A sampling includes *The Southern Mystique* (1964); *Disobedience and Democracy: Nine Fallacies on Law and Order* (1968); *A People's History of the United States: 1492–Present* (1980), which has sold more than two million copies; *Declarations of Independence: Cross-Examining American Ideology* (1990); *Three Strikes: Miners, Musicians, Salesgirls, and the Fighting Spirit of Labor's Last*

Century (2001); and *Artists in Times of War* (2003). The essay "Stories Hollywood Never Tells," adapted from *Artists in Times of War*, was published in the *Sun* in 2004.

Zinn also wrote plays, a musical, and an autobiography, *You Can't Be Neutral on a Moving Train* (1994).

Throughout his career, Zinn argued that perseverance in the face of opposition is essential: "I am totally confident not that the world will get better, but that we should not give up the game before all the cards have been played. The metaphor is deliberate; life is a gamble. Not to play is to foreclose any chance of winning. To play, to act, is to create at least a possibility of changing the world."

> "I am totally confident not that the world will get better, but that we should not give up the game before all the cards have been played."

HOWEVER HATEFUL they may be sometimes, I have always loved the movies. When I began reading and studying history, I kept coming across incidents and events that led me to think, *Wow, what a movie this would make.* I would look to see if a movie had been made about it, but I'd never find one. It took me a while to realize that Hollywood isn't going to make movies like the ones I imagined. Hollywood isn't going to make movies that are class-conscious, or antiwar, or conscious of the need for racial equality or gender equality.

I wondered about this. It seemed to me that the people in Hollywood didn't all get together in a room and decide, "We're going to do just this kind of film and not the other kind of film." Yet it's not just an oversight or an accident, either. Leon Trotsky once used an expression to describe events that are not accidents, and are not planned deliberately, but are something in between. He called this the "natural selection of accidents," in which, if there's a certain structure to a situation, then these "accidents" will inevitably happen, whether anyone plans them or not. It seems that the structure of Hollywood is such that it will not produce the kinds of films that I imagined. It's a structure where money and profit are absolutely the first consideration: before art, before aesthetics, before human values.

When you consider the films about war that have come out of Hollywood — and there have been hundreds and hundreds, maybe even thousands — they almost always glorify military heroism. We need to think about telling the story of war from a different perspective.

Let's take one of our most popular wars to begin with: the Revolutionary War. How can you speak against the Revolutionary War, right? But to tell the story of the American Revolution, not from the standpoint of the schoolbooks, but from the standpoint of war as a complex phenomenon intertwined with moral issues, we must acknowledge not just that Americans were oppressed by the English, but that some Americans were oppressed by other Americans. For instance, American Indians did not rush to celebrate the victory of the colonists over England, because for them it meant that the line that the British had drawn to limit westward expansion in the Proclamation of 1763 would now be obliterated. The colonists would be free to move west into Indian lands.

John Adams, one of the Founding Fathers and a revolutionary leader, estimated that one-third of the colonists supported the American Revolution, one-third were opposed, and one-third were neutral. It would be interesting to tell the story of the American Revolution from the viewpoint of an ordinary workingman who hears the Declaration of Independence read to him from a balcony in Boston, promising freedom and equality and so on, and immediately is told that rich men can get out of service by paying several hundred dollars. This man then joins the army, despite his misgivings, despite his own feelings of being oppressed—not just by the British, but by the leaders of the colonial world—because he is promised some land. But as the war progresses and he sees the mutilations and the killing, he becomes increasingly disaffected. There's no place in society where class divisions are more clear-cut than in the military, and he sees that the officers are living in splendor while the ordinary enlisted men don't have any clothes or shoes, aren't being paid, and are being fed slop. So he joins the mutineers.

In the Revolutionary War, there were two mutinies against Washington's army: the mutiny of the Pennsylvania Line, and the mutiny of the New Jersey Line. Let's say our workingman joins the Pennsylvania Line, and they march on the Continental Congress, but eventually are surrounded by Washington's army, and several of their former comrades are forced to shoot several of the mutineers. Then this soldier, embittered by what he's seen, gets out of the army and gets some land in western Massachusetts. After the war is over, he becomes part of Shays's Rebellion, in which a group of small farmers rebel against the rich men who control the legislature in Boston and who are imposing heavy taxes on them, taking away their land and farms. The farmers, many of them Revolutionary War veterans, surround the courthouses and refuse to let the auctioneer go in to auction off their farms. The militia is called out to suppress them, and the militia also goes over to their side. Finally an army is raised by the moneyed class in Boston to suppress Shays's Rebellion.

I have never seen Hollywood tell this kind of story. If you know of a film that has been made about it, I wish you'd tell me so that we could have a celebration of that rare event.

Wars are more complicated than the simple good-versus-evil scenario presented to us in our history books and our culture. Wars are not simply conflicts of one people against another; wars always involve class differences within each side, and victory is very often not shared by everybody, but only among a few. The people who fight the wars are not the people who benefit from the wars.

I think somebody should make a new movie about the Mexican War. I haven't seen one that tells how the Mexican War started, or how the president of the United States deceived the American people. I know it's surprising to hear that a president would willfully deceive the people of the

United States, but this was one of those rare cases. President James Polk told Americans that Mexican troops had fired at our troops on U.S. soil. Really the fighting broke out on disputed soil that both Mexico and the U.S. had claimed. The war had been planned in advance by the Polk administration, because it coveted this beautiful territory of the Southwest.

It would be interesting to tell that story from the viewpoint of an ordinary   10
soldier, who sees the mayhem and the bloodshed as the army moves into Mexico and destroys town after town. More and more U.S. soldiers grow disaffected from the war, and as they make their final march toward Mexico City, General Scott wakes up one morning to discover that half his army has deserted.

It would be interesting, too, to tell the story from the point of view of one of the Massachusetts volunteers who comes back at the end of the war and is invited to a victory celebration. When the commander of the Massachusetts volunteers gets up to speak, he is booed off the platform by the surviving half of his men, who resent what happened to their comrades in the war and who wonder what they were fighting for. I should tell you: this really happened.

The film could also include a scene after the war in which the U.S. Army is moving to suppress a rebellion in Santa Fe, because mostly Mexicans still live there. The army marches through the streets of Santa Fe, and all the townspeople go into their houses and close the shutters. The army is met by total silence, an expression of how the population feels about this great American victory.

Another little story about the Mexican War is the tale of the deserters. Many of those who volunteered to fight in the Mexican War did so for the same reason that people volunteer for the military today: they were desperately poor and hoped that their fortunes would improve as a result of enlisting. During the Mexican War, some of these volunteers were recent Irish immigrants. When these immigrant soldiers saw what was being done to the people of Mexico, a number of them deserted and went over to the Mexican side. They formed their own battalion, which they called St. Patrick's Battalion, or the San Patricio Battalion, and they fought for the Mexicans.

It's not easy to make the Spanish-American War look like a noble enterprise—though of course Hollywood can do anything. The war has gotten a certain amount of attention, because of the heroism of Theodore Roosevelt and his Rough Riders, but not a lot. In the history textbooks, the Spanish-American War is called "a splendid little war." It lasted three months. We fought it to free the Cubans, because we're always going to war to free somebody. We expelled the Spaniards from Cuba, but we didn't expel ourselves, and the United States in effect took over Cuba after the war. One grievance we have against Fidel Castro is that he ended U.S. control of Cuba. We're certainly not against him simply because he's a dictator. We've never had anything against dictators in general.

I remember learning in school that, as a result of the Spanish-American   15
War, we somehow took over the Philippines, but I never knew the details. When you look into it, you'll find that the Spanish-American War lasted three

months; the Philippine War lasted for years and was a brutal, bloody suppression of the Filipino movement for independence. In many ways, it was a precursor of the Vietnam War, in terms of the atrocities committed by the U.S. Army. Now, that's a story that has never been told.

Black American soldiers in the Philippines soon began to identify more with the Filipinos than with their fellow white Americans. While these black soldiers were fighting to suppress the Filipinos, they also were hearing from relatives about the lynchings and race riots in their hometowns. They were hearing about black people being killed in large numbers — and here they were, fighting against a nonwhite people on behalf of the United States government. A number of black soldiers deserted and went over to fight with the Filipinos.

In 1906, when the Philippine War was supposedly over — but really the U.S. Army was still suppressing pockets of rebellion — there was a massacre. That's the only way to describe it. The Moros are inhabitants of a southern island in the Philippines. The army swooped down and annihilated a Moro village of six hundred men, women, and children — all of whom were unarmed. Every last one of them was killed. Mark Twain wrote angrily about this. He was especially angry about the fact that President Theodore Roosevelt sent a letter of congratulations to the military commander who had ordered this atrocity, saying it was a great military victory. Have you ever seen a movie in which Theodore Roosevelt was presented as a racist? As an imperialist? As a supporter of massacres? And there he is, up on Mount Rushmore. I've had the thought: *A hammer, a chisel.* But no, it wouldn't do.

War needs to be presented on film in such a way as to encourage the population simply to say no to war. We need a film about those heroic Americans who protested World War I. When you look at them, you see socialists, pacifists, and just ordinary people who saw the stupidity of entering a war that was taking the lives of ten million people in Europe. You see Emma Goldman, the feminist and anarchist, who went to prison for opposing the draft and the war. You see Helen Keller. Every film about Helen Keller concentrates on the fact that she was disabled. I've never seen a film in which Helen Keller is presented as what she was: a radical, a socialist, an antiwar agitator. You also see Kate Richards O'Hare, a socialist who was put in jail for opposing World War I. There is a story from her time in prison that would make a great scene in a movie: The prisoners are stifling for lack of air, and O'Hare takes a book that she's been reading, reaches through the bars, and hurls the book through a skylight to let the air in. All the prisoners applaud and cheer.

I have to acknowledge that there have been a few antiwar films made about World War I. *All Quiet on the Western Front* is an extraordinary film. I recently wrote an article comparing it to *Saving Private Ryan*. Despite the mayhem, *Saving Private Ryan* was essentially a glorification of war, whereas *All Quiet on the Western Front* expresses a diamond-clear antiwar sentiment.

What about the many films devoted to World War II, the "good war"?   20
When Studs Terkel did his oral history of World War II, he called it *The "Good War,"* with quotation marks around *Good War*. In that war, we fought against a terrible evil — fascism — but our own atrocities multiplied as the war went

on, culminating in the bombings of Hiroshima and Nagasaki. I have not seen a Hollywood film about the bombing of Hiroshima. The closest we've come to a movie that deals with our bombing of civilian populations was the film version of Kurt Vonnegut's book *Slaughterhouse-Five*, about the bombing of Dresden, Germany, and that was a rarity.

Films about the Civil War tend to focus on the famous battles, like Gettysburg, Fredericksburg, and Bull Run. The Civil War is, again, one of our "good wars"—the slaves were freed because of it—but it is not that simple. There is the class element of who was and who was not drafted, who paid substitutes, who made huge amounts of money off the war. And then there is what happened to the Indians. In the midst of the Civil War, while the armies were fighting in the South, another part of the Union Army was out west, destroying Indian settlements and taking over Indian land. In 1864, not long after the Emancipation Proclamation, the U.S. Army was in Colorado attacking an Indian village, killing hundreds of men, women, and children at Sand Creek, in one of the worst Indian massacres in American history. This massacre occurred during the war to end slavery. In the years of the Civil War, more land was taken from the Indians than in any other comparable period in history.

There's a lot of historical work to be done, a lot of films that need to be made. There are so many class struggles in the U.S. that could be dealt with in movies. We've seen movies that deal with working-class people, but it's always some individual who rises up out of his or her situation and "makes it" in society. Stories of Americans who organize and get together to oppose the powers that hold them down have been very rare.

The American political system and the revered and celebrated Constitution of the United States do not grant any economic rights to the American people. We very often forget that the Constitution gives political rights but not economic rights. If you are not wealthy, then your political rights are limited, even though they are guaranteed on paper in the Constitution. The freedom of speech is granted there, but how much free speech you have depends on how much money and what access to resources you have. The Declaration of Independence talks about the right to life, liberty, and the pursuit of happiness. But how can you have life, liberty, and the pursuit of happiness if you don't have food, housing, and healthcare?

Working people throughout history have had to organize, struggle, go on strike, declare boycotts, and face the police and the army. They have had to do it themselves, against the opposition of government, in order to win the eight-hour workday and other slight improvements to their working conditions. A great film remains to be made about the Haymarket Affair of 1886, which was part of the struggle for the eight-hour workday. The Haymarket Affair culminated in the execution of four anarchists who were charged with planting a bomb, though in the end nobody ever found out who really had planted it.

The great railroad strike of 1894 tied up the railway system of the United States, and all the power of the army and the courts had to be brought against the striking workers. Eugene Debs, who organized the railroad workers, has never been the central figure in a movie. He was sent to prison for opposing

25

Engraving depicting the 1886 Haymarket Riot.

World War I, and he made such an impression on his fellow prisoners that, when he was released, the warden let all the inmates out into the yard, and they applauded as Debs was granted his freedom.

I've met someone who is actually writing a script about the Lawrence textile strike of 1912, a magnificent episode in American history, because the striking workers won. It was a multicultural strike. A working population that spoke twelve different languages got together and defied the textile companies and the police, who were sent to the railroad station to prevent the children of the workers from leaving town. Police literally attacked the women and children at the station, because the company wanted to starve out the strikers, and that would be less likely to happen if their children were safe. But the strikers held out, and with the help of the Industrial Workers of the World, they finally won.

Then there's the Ludlow Massacre, which took place during the Colorado coal strike of 1913–1914, one of the most bitter, bloody, dramatic strikes in American history. The workers were up against the Rockefeller interests. (It's not easy to make an unflattering film about the Rockefellers.) One of the strike's leaders was Mother Jones, an eighty-three-year-old woman who had previously organized textile workers in West Virginia and Pennsylvania. That's another story that should be told. There were kids working in the textile mills at the age of eleven and twelve. Mother Jones led these children on a march from Pennsylvania to Oyster Bay, New York, where President Theodore Roosevelt was on summer vacation. They stood there outside the resort with signs that said, WE WANT TIME TO PLAY. Has there ever been a film made about that?

We've had films on Christopher Columbus, but I don't know of any film that shows Columbus as what he was: a man ruled by the capitalist ethic. Columbus and the Spaniards were killing people for gold. The Catholic priest Bartolomé de Las Casas was an eyewitness. He exposed what was going on, and a remarkable debate took place before the Royal Commission of Spain in 1650. The debate was between Las Casas and Sepulveda, another priest, who argued that the Indians were not human and therefore you could do anything you wanted to them.

There's also the story of the Trail of Tears—the expulsion of the Cherokees from the Southeast. Andrew Jackson, one of our national heroes, signed the order to expel them. That was ethnic cleansing on a large scale: the march across the continent, the U.S. Army driving the Indians from their homeland to a little space in Oklahoma that was then called "Indian Territory." When oil was later discovered there, the Indian population was once again evicted. Of the sixteen thousand people who marched westward, four thousand died on the march, while the U.S. Army pushed them, and the U.S. president extolled what happened.

Of course someone should finally tell the story of black people in the   30
United States from a black person's point of view. We've had a number of

Immigrant women striking in Lawrence, Massachusetts, 1912.

Lawrence History Center

films about the civil-rights movement from white points of view. *The Long Walk Home* (1991) tells the story of the Montgomery bus boycott from Sissy Spacek's point of view. *Mississippi Burning* (1988) is about the murder of three civil-rights workers in Mississippi in 1964. The FBI agents are the heroes of the film, but every person who was in Mississippi in 1964 — my wife and I were both there at the time — knew that the FBI was the enemy. The FBI was watching people being beaten and not doing anything about it. The FBI was silent and absent when people needed protection against murderers. In this Hollywood film, they become heroes. We need the story of the civil-rights movement told from the viewpoint of black people.

Of course, many good movies and wonderful documentaries have been made. Michael Moore's film *Roger and Me*, which has been seen by tens of millions of people, is a remarkable success story. So the possibilities do exist to practice a kind of guerrilla warfare and make films outside of the Hollywood establishment.

If such films are made — about war, about class conflict, about the history of governmental lies, about broken treaties and official violence — if those stories reach the public, we might produce a new generation. As a teacher, I'm not interested in just reproducing class after class of graduates who will get out, become successful, and take their obedient places in the slots that society has prepared for them. What we must do — whether we teach or write or make films — is educate a new generation to do this very modest thing: change the world. ▇

The Reader's Presence

1. Explain what Zinn means by what Leon Trotsky called the "natural selection of accidents" (paragraph 2) preventing true depictions of war, class, and race from appearing in films. Do you agree that Hollywood's structure works against such depictions? Why or why not?

2. Reading the essay, who did you imagine Zinn's audience to be? How sympathetic to his argument would you expect them to be? What evidence can you find for your answers?

3. **VISUAL PRESENCE:** Zinn's essay calls attention to several little-known instances of protest and rebellion throughout American history. In what specific ways do the images of the 1886 Haymarket Riot (page 682) and the 1912 strike of immigrant women in Lawrence, Massachusetts (page 683) illustrate the points that Zinn makes in his argument? Which of these two images do you find more compelling? Explain why.

4. **CONNECTIONS:** Zinn says, "Stories of Americans who organize and get together to oppose the powers that hold them down have been very rare" in Hollywood (paragraph 22), but he presents examples to indicate such stories have appeared again and again throughout American history. Compare and contrast the points Zinn makes about race in American culture with those that John Edgar Wideman discusses in his essay "Fatheralong" (page 665). What "American values" would Zinn and Wideman share? Point to specific passages in each essay to validate your response.

ACKNOWLEDGMENTS *(continued from page iv)*

Text Credits

Meher Ahmad. "My Homeland Security Journey." First published in the *Progressive,* May 2012. Reprinted by permission of the publisher.

Maya Angelou. "What's Your Name, Girl?" From *I Know Why the Caged Bird Sings* by Maya Angelou. Copyright © 1969 and renewed 1997 by Maya Angelou. Used by permission of Random House, an imprint and division of Penguin Random House LLC. All rights reserved. Any third party use of this material, outside of this publication, is prohibited. Interested third parties must apply directly to Penguin Random House LLC for permission.

Kwame Anthony Appiah. "Race in the Modern World." Republished with permission of the Council on Foreign Relations from *Foreign Affairs,* March 1, 2015. Copyright © 2015. Permission conveyed through Copyright Clearance Center, Inc.

James Baldwin. "If Black English Isn't a Language, Then Tell Me, What Is?" Originally published in the *New York Times,* July 29, 1979. Copyright © 1979 by James Baldwin. Collected in *James Baldwin Essays,* published by Library of America. Used by arrangement with the James Baldwin Estate. "Notes of a Native Son." From *Notes of a Native Son.* Copyright © 1955, renewed 1983 by James Baldwin. Reprinted by permission of Beacon Press, Boston.

Michael Bérubé. "Analyze, Don't Summarize." First published in the *Chronicle of Higher Education,* October 1, 2004. Copyright © 2004 by Michael Bérubé. Reprinted by permission of the author.

Eula Biss. "Sentimental Medicine." Reproduced from the January issue of *Harper's Magazine* by special permission. Copyright © 2013 Harper's Magazine. All rights reserved.

Charles Bowden. "Our Wall." First published in *National Geographic* magazine, May 2007. Reprinted by permission of National Geographic Creative.

David Brooks. "People Like Us." From the *Atlantic Monthly,* September 2003. Reprinted by permission of the author.

Lauren Carter. "Isn't Watermelon Delicious?" Originally published in *The Bridge,* vol. 2, Spring 2005. Reprinted by permission of the author.

Raymond Carver. "My Father's Life." Copyright © 1984 by Raymond Carver. Used by permission of the Wylie Agency LLC.

Amy Chua. Excerpt from *Battle Hymn of the Tiger Mother* by Amy Chua. Copyright © 2011 by Amy Chua. Used by permission of Penguin Press, an imprint of Penguin Publishing Group, a division of Penguin Random House LLC. All rights reserved. Any third party use of this material, outside of this publication, is prohibited. Interested third parties must apply directly to Penguin Random House LLC for permission.

Ta-Nehisi Coates. Excerpt from *Between the World and Me* by Ta-Nehisi Coates. Copyright © 2015 by Ta-Nehisi Coates. Used by permission of Spiegel & Grau, an imprint of Random House, a division of Penguin Random House LLC. All rights reserved. Any third party use of this material, outside of this publication, is prohibited. Interested third parties must apply directly to Penguin Random House LLC for permission.

Judith Ortiz Cofer. "Silent Dancing." From *Silent Dancing.* Copyright © 1991 Arte Público Press–University of Houston. Reprinted by permission of the publisher.

Alys Culhane. "Interview with Lauren Slater." From *Fourth Genre: Explorations in Nonfiction* 7.1 (2005). Reproduced with the permission of Michigan State University Press in the format Republish in a book via Copyright Clearance Center.

Amy Cunningham. "Why Women Smile." First published in *Lear's* (1993). Reprinted by permission of the author.

Edwidge Danticat. "Message to My Daughters." From Jesmyn Ward, ed., *The Fire This Time* (Scribner, 2016), pp. 205–15. Copyright © 2016 by Edwidge Danticat. Reprinted by permission.

James Dickey. "For the Last Wolverine" (excerpted), from *The Whole Motion: Collected Poems 1945–1992* by James Dickey. Copyright © 1992 by James Dickey. Published by Wesleyan University Press. Used by permission.

Joan Didion. "The Santa Ana." Excerpted from "The Los Angeles Notebook" in *Slouching Towards Bethlehem* by Joan Didion. Copyright © 1966, 1968, renewed 1996 by Joan Didion. Reprinted by permission of Farrar, Straus and Giroux, LLC. "Why I Write." Copyright © 1976 by Joan

Didion. Originally published in the *New York Times Book Review*. Reprinted by permission of the author.

Brian Doyle. "Dawn and Mary" from *The Sun*, August 2013; "His Last Game" from *Notre Dame Magazine*, Autumn 2012; and "A Note on Mascots." Reprinted by permission of the author. "On the Pleasures of Craft and Writing and Reading" from a personal interview. Reprinted by permission of the author.

Andre Dubus III. "The Land of No: Love in Class-Riven America." From the March 1, 2012, issue of the *New Republic*. All rights reserved. Used by permission and protected by the Copyright Laws of the United States. The printing, copying, redistribution, or retransmission of this Content without express written permission is prohibited. Excerpt from "Writing and Publishing a Memoir: What in the Hell Have I Done?" From *River Teeth*, Fall 2012. Copyright © 2012. Reprinted by permission of the author.

Lars Eighner. "On Dumpster Diving." From *Travels with Lizbeth*. Copyright © 1993 by Lars Eighner. Reprinted by permission of St. Martin's Press. All rights reserved. "On the Challenges of Writing While Homeless." Excerpted from pp. ix–x in the introduction to *Travels with Lizbeth*. Copyright © 1993 by Lars Eighner. Reprinted by permission of St. Martin's Press. All rights reserved.

Anne Fadiman. "Under Water." From *At Large and at Small: Familiar Essays* by Anne Fadiman. Copyright © 2007 by Anne Fadiman. Reprinted by permission of Farrar, Straus and Giroux, LLC. Excerpts from the Introduction by Anne Fadiman to *The Best American Essays, 2003*, edited by Robert Atwan and Anne Fadiman. Copyright © 2003 by Anne Fadiman. Reprinted by permission of the author.

Megan Garber. "Barbie's Hips Don't Lie." Copyright © 2016 The Atlantic Media Co., as first published in the *Atlantic Magazine*, January 28, 2016. All rights reserved. Distributed by Tribune Content Agency, LLC.

Henry Louis Gates Jr. "In the Kitchen." From *Colored People: A Memoir* by Henry Louis Gates Jr. Copyright © 1994 by Henry Louis Gates Jr. Used by permission of Alfred A. Knopf, an imprint of the Knopf Doubleday Publishing Group, a division of Penguin Random House LLC. All rights reserved. Any third party use of this material, outside of this publication, is prohibited. Interested third parties must apply directly to Penguin Random House LLC for permission.

John Taylor Gatto. "Against School." From *Harper's*, September 2003. Reprinted by permission of the author.

Roxane Gay. "The Careless Language of Sexual Violence." First published in the *Rumpus*, March 10, 2011. Copyright © 2011 by Roxane Gay. Reprinted by permission of the author.

Malcolm Gladwell. "Small Change: Why the Revolution Will Not Be Tweeted." From the *New Yorker*, October 4, 2010. Reprinted by permission of the author.

Michiko Hachiya. "Pikadon." From *Hiroshima Diary: The Journal of a Japanese Physician, August 6–September 30, 1945* by Michiko Hachiya, trans. and ed. by Warner Wells, M.D. Copyright © 1955 by the University of North Carolina Press, renewed 1983 by Warner Wells. Foreword by John W. Dower © 1995 by the University of North Carolina Press. Used by permission of the publisher. www.uncpress.org

Silas Hansen, "What Real Men Do," *The Normal School*, Fall 2016. Copyright © 2016. Reprinted by permission of the author.

Amanda Hess. "Multiple Choice." From the *New York Times Magazine*, April 3, 2016. Copyright © 2016 by the New York Times. All rights reserved. Used by permission and protected by the Copyright Laws of the United States. The printing, copying, redistribution, or retransmission of this Content without express written permission is prohibited.

Christopher Hitchens. "Believe Me, It's Torture." Originally appeared in *Vanity Fair*, August 2008. Reprinted with the kind permission of the Estate of Christopher Hitchens. All rights reserved.

Edward Hoagland. "On Stuttering." Originally published as "The Football Game in My Head" in *U.S. News & World Report*, April 2, 2001. Reprinted by permission of the author. "What an Essay Is." From "To the Point: Truths Only Essays Can Tell" by Edward Hoagland. Copyright © 1993 by Edward Hoagland. Originally published in *Harper's*. Republished by permission of the author.

Langston Hughes. "How to Be a Bad Writer (In Ten Easy Lessons)." From *The Langston Hughes Reader*. Copyright © 1958 by Langston Hughes. Copyright renewed 1986 by George Houston

Index of Authors and Titles